DIGITAL
ELECTRONICS

P. Tang

A PRACTICAL APPROACH

DIGITAL ELECTRONICS

A PRACTICAL APPROACH

Second Edition

WILLIAM KLEITZ

Tompkins Cortland Community College

Prentice Hall, Englewood Cliffs, New Jersey 07632

Library of Congress Cataloging-in-Publication Data

Kleitz,William
    Digital electronics: a practical Approach/William Kleitz
    2nd ed.
      Includes bibliographical references.
    ISBN 0-13-211657-X
    1. Digital electronics   I. Title
TK86.D5K55   1990   89-22808
621,381--dc20   CIP

Editorial production supervision and interior design: Marcia Krefitz/Lillian Glennon
Cover design: Photo Plus Art
Cover photograph: ©Ken Cooper, The Image Bank
Manufacturing buyer: Dave Dickey

If your diskette is defective or damaged in transit, return it directly to Prentice Hall at the address below for a no-charge replacement within 90 days of the date of purchase. Mail the defective diskette together with your name and address.
    Prentice Hall
    Attention: Ryan Colby
    College Operations
    Englewood Cliffs, NJ 07632

©1990, 1987 by Prentice-Hall, Inc.
A Division of Simon & Schuster
Englewood Cliffs, New Jersey 07632

LIMITS OF LIABILITY AND DISCLAIMER OF WARRANTY:
The author and publisher of this book have used their best efforts in preparing this book and software. These efforts include the development, research, and testing of the theories and programs to determine their effectiveness. The author and publisher make no warranty of any kind, expressed or implied, with regard to these programs or the documentation contained in this book. The author and publisher shall not be liable in any event for incidental or consequential damages in connection with or arising out of, the furnishing, performance, or use of these programs.

Printed in the United States of America

10 9 8 7 6 5 4 3 2

ISBN 0-13-211657-X

Prentice-Hall International (UK) Limited, *London*
Prentice-Hall of Australia Pty. Limited, *Sydney*
Prentice-Hall Canada Inc., *Toronto*
Prentice-Hall Hispanoamericana, S.A., *Mexico*
Prentice-Hall of India Private Limited, *New Delhi*
Prentice-Hall of Japan, Inc, *Tokyo*
Simon & Schuster Asia Pte. Ltd., *Singapore*
Editora Prentice-Hall do Brasil, Ltda., *Rio de Janeiro*

To my wife, *Leeann*,
for typing the manuscript and providing encouragement and understanding
throughout the preparation of this text;
and to my daughters, *Shirelle* and *Hayley*.

Contents

Contents

Preface

TO THE INSTRUCTOR

It is time to reevaluate the way that digital electronics is taught. At first, digital electronics was a theoretical science, but now it is a down-to-earth, workable technology that can be taught using a practical approach.

Digital Electronics: A Practical Approach, 2/E, places emphasis on analytical reasoning and basic digital design using the standard integrated circuits that are used in industry today. Throughout the text actual ICs are used, and reference is made to the appropriate manufacturers' data sheets. Because of this approach, the student becomes proficient at using the terminology and timing diagrams that are the standard in manufacturers' data manuals and industrial settings.

A strong effort was made to make the text easy to read and understand so that motivated students can teach themselves topics that require extra work without the constant attention of the instructor. Several digital system design applications and troubleshooting exercises are included. Also, there are ample illustrations, examples, and review questions to help students reach a point where they can reason out the end of chapter problems on their own. After all, that is the main goal of this book—to help students think and reason on their own.

This book can be used for a one- or two-semester course in digital electronics and is intended for students of technology, computer science, or engineering programs. Although not mandatory, it is helpful if the student using this text has an understanding of, or is concurrently enrolled in, a basic electricity course. A laboratory component to provide hands-on reenforcement of the material presented in this book can be very helpful. Laboratory exercises can be developed by building, testing, debugging, and analyzing the operation of any of the examples or system design applications that are provided within the text.

CHAPTER ORGANIZATION

Basically the text can be divided into two halves: Chapters 1–8 cover basic digital logic and combinational logic, and Chapters 9–16 cover sequential logic and digital systems. *Chapters 1 and 2* provide the procedures for converting between the various number systems and introduce the student to the electronic signals and switches used in digital circuitry. *Chapters 3 and 4* cover the basic logic gates and introduces the student to timing analysis and troubleshooting techniques. *Chapter 5* shows how several of the basic gates can be connected together to form combinational logic. Boolean algebra, DeMorgan's theorem and Karnaugh mapping are used to reduce the logic to its simplest form. *Chapters 6, 7 and 8* discuss combinational logic used to provide more advanced functions like parity checking, arithmetic operations and code converting.

The second half of this book begins with a discussion of the operating characteristics and specifications of the TTL and CMOS logic families (*Chapter 9*). *Chapter 10* introduces flip flops and the concept of sequential timing analysis. *Chapter 11* makes the reader aware of the practical limitations of digital ICs and some common circuits that are used in later chapters to facilitate the use of medium-scale ICs. *Chapters 12 and 13* expose the student to the operation and use of several common medium-scale ICs used to implement counter and shift register systems. *Chapter 14* deals with oscillator and timing circuits built with digital ICs and with the 555 timer IC. *Chapter 15* teaches the theory behind analog and digital conversion schemes and the practical implementation of ADC and DAC IC converters. *Chapter 16* covers memory and microprocessor bus concepts and then uses memory ICs and programmable logic to implement several system designs. The book concludes with several Appendices used to supplement the chapter material.

If time constraints only allow for a single-semester course, then the following sections should be covered to provide a coherent overview in Digital Electronics:

Sections 1.1–1.5, 1.8–1.12
Sections 2.1–2.2
Sections 3.1–3.3, 3.5–3.6
Sections 4.1–4.3, 4.5–4.6
Sections 5.1–5.4
Sections 6.1–6.2
Sections 9.1–9.2
Sections 10.1–10.8
Sections 12.1–12.6
Sections 13.1–13.6
Sections 15.1, 15.5, 15.6, 15.10
Sections 16.1, 16.2, 16.4

Also, if the course is intended for nonelectrical technology students, then the following sections could be omitted to eliminate any basic electricity requirements:

Sections 2.6–2.8
Sections 9.1–9.3, 9.8
Sections 11.3–11.6
Sections 14.2–14.4
Sections 15.2–15.4, 15.12

UNIQUE LEARNING TOOLS

Special features included in this textbook to enhance the learning and comprehension process are:

- Performance-based *objectives* at the beginning of each chapter outline the goals to be achieved.
- Over 200 *examples* are worked out step-by-step to clarify problems that are normally stumbling blocks.
- A *two-color format* provides a visual organization to the various parts of each section.
- *Troubleshooting applications* and problems are used throughout the text to teach testing and debugging procedures.
- Chapter-end *review questions* summarize each chapter and are answered to see that each learning objective is met.
- Over 660 *problems* and *questions* are provided to enhance problem-solving skills. A complete range of problems, from straight-forward to very challenging, is included.
- A *glossary* at the end of each chapter serves as a summary of the terminology just presented.
- Over 1000 detailed *illustrations* give visual explanations and serve as the basis for all discussions.
- Reference to *manufacturers' data sheets* throughout the book provides a valuable experience with ''real world'' problem solving.
- A *supplementary index of ICs* provides a quick way to locate a particular IC by number.
- *Timing waveforms* are used throughout the text to illustrate the timing analysis techniques used in industry and give a graphical picture of the sequential operations of digital ICs.

EXTENSIVE SUPPLEMENTS PACKAGE

An extensive package of supplementary material is available to aid in the teaching and learning process.

- An *Instructor's Resource Manual*, authored by William Kleitz, contains solutions to all problems, 29 class-tested quizzes with solutions, and a list of suggested lab experiments and equipment.
- An *Experiments Manual*, authored by Michael Wiesner (Heald Technical College), provides hands-on laboratory experience to reenforce the material presented in the textbook.
- An *Instructor's Manual*, authored by Michael Wiesner, provides the data results for each experiment, and the answers to all lab experiment questions.
- An *Instructor's Test Item File*, authored by Les Taylor (DeVry Institute of Technology), contains over 1000 additional multiple-choice questions that can be used to develop weekly quizzes, tests, or final exams. Available in manual or disk form (IBM or Apple compatible).
- A *Student Study Guide*, authored by David Bechtel (DeVry Institute of Technology), contains an overview of each chapter and several additional review questions.

- An *Interactive Software Disk*, authored by Scott Musser and technically checked by Kevin Light, provides over 500 additional review questions. (The IBM compatible disk is included free with each textbook.)
- An *Instructor's Transparency Masters Manual*, authored by William Kleitz, contains enlarged versions of over 100 of the most commonly referred to illustrations from the textbook.

CHANGES IN THE SECOND EDITION

The first edition was developed from an accumulation of seven years worth of class notes. Having taught from the first edition for the past three years has given me the opportunity to review several suggestions from my students and other faculty regarding such things as: ways to improve a circuit diagram, clarifying an explanation, and redesigning an application to make it easier to duplicate in lab.

Over 120 schools have adopted the first edition. To write the second edition, I have taken advantage of the comments from these schools as well as my own experience and market research to develop an even more practical and easier-to-learn-from textbook.

Besides rewriting several of the examples and applications based on my classroom experience, the following material has been added:

- over 260 chapter-end review questions
- a two-color format
- a new section on digital representation of analog quantities
- a new section on analog transducers and signal conditioning circuitry
- a new section on octal buffers, latches, and transceivers
- an updated and expanded discussion of programmable logic devices (PAL and PLA)

TO THE STUDENT

Digital electronics is the foundation of computers and microprocessor-based systems found in automobiles, industrial control systems and home entertainment systems. You are beginning your study of digital electronics at a good time. Technological advances made in the past twenty years have provided us with integrated circuits that can perform complex tasks with a minimum amount of abstract theory and complicated circuitry. Before you are through with this book, you'll be developing exciting designs that you've always wondered about, but now can experience first hand.

The study of digital electronics also provides the prerequisite background required for your future studies in microprocessors and microcomputer interfacing. It also provides the job skills to become a computer service technician, production test technician, digital design technician or a multitude of other jobs related to computer and microprocessor-based systems.

This book is written as a learning tool, not just as a reference. The concept and theory of each topic is presented first. Then, an explanation of its operation is given. That is followed by several worked-out examples and in some cases, a system design application. The review questions at the end of each chapter will force you to dig back into the reading to see that you have met the learning objectives given at the beginning of the chapter. The problems at the end of each chapter will require more analytical reasoning, but the procedures for their solutions were already given to you in the examples. One good way to prepare for homework problems and tests is to cover up the solutions to the examples and try to work them out yourself.

If you get stuck, you've got the answer and an explanation for the answer right there.

I also suggest that you take advantage of your interactive disk and study guide. The more practice you get, the easier the course will be. I wish you the best of luck in your studies and future employment.

William Kleitz

Acknowledgments

Thanks are due to Peter J. Holsberg, Mercer County Community College, David J. Leitch, DeVry Institute of Technology, and John L. Keown, Southern Technical Institute, who reviewed the manuscript and provided several valuable suggestions. I am grateful to Russell Hunt, Simco Company, and Kevin White, Bob Dean Corporation, for their technical assistance, and to Signetics Corporation, Intel Corporation, Texas Instruments, Inc., and Hewlett-Packard Company for providing data sheets and photographs used in this book. Also, thank you to Kevin Light at Electronics Consulting Service for technically checking the intricate software disk.

Also, thanks to my students of the past ten years, who have helped me to develop better teaching strategies and have provided suggestions for clarifying several of the explanations contained in this book, and to Alice Barr of Prentice-Hall for her support and enthusiasm during this project.

1

Number Systems and Codes

OBJECTIVES

Upon completion of this chapter, you should be able to:

- Determine the weighting factor for each digit position in the decimal, binary, octal, and hexadecimal numbering systems.
- Convert any number in one of the four number sytems (decimal, binary, octal, or hexadecimal) to its equivalent value in any of the remaining three numbering systems.
- Describe the format, and use of, binary-coded-decimal (BCD) numbers.
- Determine the ASCII code for any alphanumeric data by using the ASCII code translated table.

INTRODUCTION

Digital circuitry is the foundation of digital computers and many automated control systems. In a modern home, digital circuitry controls the appliances, alarm systems, and heating systems. Under the control of digital circuitry and microprocessors, newer automobiles have added safety features, are more energy efficient, and are easier to diagnose and correct when malfunctions arise.

Other uses of digital circuitry include the areas of automated machine control, energy monitoring and control, inventory management, medical electronics, and music. For example, the numerically controlled (NC) milling machine can be programmed by a production engineer to mill a piece of stock material to prespecified dimensions with very accurate repeatability, within 0.01% accuracy. Another use is energy monitoring and control. With the high cost of energy it is very important for large industrial and commercial users to monitor the energy flows within their buildings. Effective control of heating, ventilating, and air-conditioning can reduce energy bills significantly. More and more grocery stores are using the universal product code (UPC) to check out and total the sale of grocery orders as well as control inventory and replenish stock automatically. The area of medical electronics uses digital thermometers, life-support systems, and monitors. We have also seen more use of digital electronics in the reproduction of music. Digital reproduction is less susceptible to electrostatic noise and therefore can reproduce music with greater fidelity.

Digital electronics evolved from the principle that transistor circuitry could easily be fabricated and designed to output one of two voltage levels based on the levels placed at its inputs. The two distinct levels (usually +5 volts and 0 volts) are "HIGH" and "LOW" and can be represented by 1 and 0.

The binary numbering system is made up of only 1s and 0s and is therefore used extensively in digital electronics. Other numbering systems and codes covered in this chapter represent groups of binary digits and therefore are also widely used.

1-1 DIGITAL REPRESENTATIONS OF ANALOG QUANTITIES

Most naturally-occurring physical quantities in our world are *analog* in nature. An analog signal is a continuously variable electrical or physical quantity. Think about a mercury-filled tube thermometer; as the temperature rises, the mercury expands in analog fashion, and makes a smooth, continuous motion relative to a scale measured in degrees. A baseball player swings a bat in an analog motion. The velocity and force with which a musician strikes a piano key is analog in nature. Even the resulting vibration of the piano string is an analog, sinusoidal vibration.

So why do we need to use digital representations in a world that is naturally analog? The answer is that if we want an electronic machine to interpret, communicate, and store analog information, it is much easier for the machine to handle if we first convert the information to a digital format. A digital value is represented by a combination of ON and OFF voltage levels that are written as a string of 1's and 0's.

For example, an analog thermometer that registers 72 degrees can be represented in a digital circuit as a series of ON and OFF voltage levels. (We'll learn later that the number 72 converted to digital levels is 0100 1000.) The convenient feature of using ON/OFF voltage levels is that the circuitry used to generate, manipulate, and store them is very simple. Instead of dealing with the infinite span and intervals of analog voltage levels, all we need to use is ON or OFF voltages (usually +5 volts = ON and 0 volts = OFF).

A good example of the use of a digital representation of an analog quantity is the audio recording of music. Compact Disks (CD's) and Digital Audio Tapes (DAT's) are becoming common-place and are proving to be superior means of recording and playing back music. Musical instruments and the human voice produce analog signals, and the human ear naturally responds to analog signals. So, where does the digital format fit in? Although the process requires what appears to be extra work, the recording industries convert analog signals to a digital format and then store the information on a CD or DAT. The CD or DAT player then converts the digital levels back to their corresponding analog signals before playing them back for the human ear.

To accurately represent a complex musical signal as a digital string, several samples of an analog signal must be taken, as shown in Figure 1–1.

The first conversion illustrated is at a point on the rising portion of the analog signal. At that point, the analog voltage is 2 volts. Two volts is represented as the digital string 0000 0010. The next conversion is taken as the analog signal is still rising, and the third is taken at its highest level. This process will continue throughout the entire piece of music to be recorded. To play the music back, the process is reversed. Digital-to-analog conversions are made to recreate the original analog signal. If a high enough number of samples are taken of the original analog signal, an almost exact reproduction of the original music can be made.

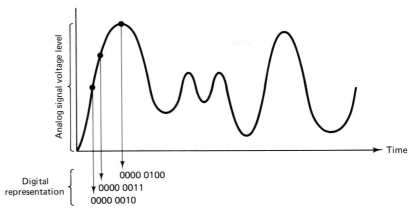

Figure 1–1 Digital representations of three data points on an analog waveform.

It certainly is extra work, but digital recordings have virtually eliminated problems such as record wear and the magnetic tape hiss associated with earlier methods of audio recording. These problems have been eradicated because when imperfections are introduced to a digital signal, the slight variation in the digital level does not change an ON level to an OFF level. Whereas, a slight change in an analog level is easily picked up by the human ear.

1–2 DIGITAL VERSUS ANALOG

Digital systems operate on discrete digits that represent numbers, letters, or symbols. They deal strictly with ON and OFF states, which we can represent by 0's and 1's. *Analog* systems measure and respond to continuously varying electrical or physical magnitudes. Analog devices are integrated electronically into systems to continuously monitor and control such quantities as temperature, pressure, velocity, and position, and to provide automated control based on the levels of those quantities. Figure 1–2 shows some examples of digital and analog quantities.

Figure 1–2 Analog versus digital: (a) analog waveform; (b) digital waveform; (c) analog watch; (d) digital watch.

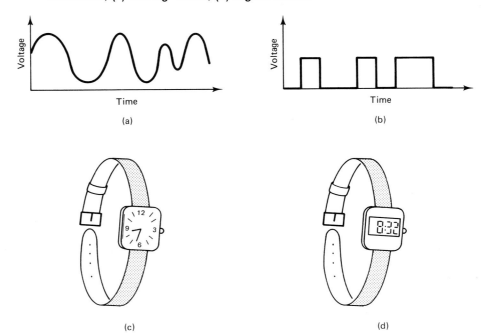

1–3 DECIMAL NUMBERING SYSTEM (BASE 10)

In the decimal numbering system, each position will contain 10 different possible digits. These digits are 0, 1, 2, 3, 4, 5, 6, 7, 8, and 9. Each position in a multidigit number will have a weighting factor based on a power of 10.

EXAMPLE 1–1

In a four-digit decimal number the least significant position (rightmost) will have a weighting factor of 10^0; the most significant position (leftmost) will have a weighting factor of 10^3:

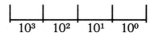

$$10^3 \quad 10^2 \quad 10^1 \quad 10^0$$

where $10^3 = 1000$
            $10^2 = 100$
            $10^1 = 10$
            $10^0 = 1$

To evaluate the decimal number 4623, the digit in each position is multiplied by the appropriate weighting factor:

$$
\begin{array}{cccc}
4 & 6 & 2 & 3
\end{array}
$$

$$
\begin{aligned}
3 \times 10^0 &= 3 \\
2 \times 10^1 &= 20 \\
6 \times 10^2 &= 600 \\
4 \times 10^3 &= +4000 \\
\hline
& 4623 \quad \textit{answer}
\end{aligned}
$$

Example 1–1 illustrates the procedure used to convert from some number system to its decimal (base 10) equivalent. (In that example we converted a base 10 number to a base 10 answer.) Now let's look at base 2 (binary), base 8 (octal), and base 16 (hexadecimal).

1–4 BINARY NUMBERING SYSTEM (BASE 2)

Digital electronics use the binary numbering system because it uses only the digits 0 and 1, which can be represented simply in a digital system by two distinct voltage levels, such as $+5\text{ V} = 1$ and $0\text{ V} = 0$.

The weighting factors for binary positions will be the powers of 2 shown in Table 1–1.

TABLE 1–1

Powers-of-2 Binary Weighting Factors

$$2^7 \quad 2^6 \quad 2^5 \quad 2^4 \quad 2^3 \quad 2^2 \quad 2^1 \quad 2^0$$

$$
\begin{aligned}
2^0 &= 1 \\
2^1 &= 2 \\
2^2 &= 4 \\
2^3 &= 8 \\
2^4 &= 16 \\
2^5 &= 32 \\
2^6 &= 64 \\
2^7 &= 128
\end{aligned}
$$

EXAMPLE 1–2

Convert the binary number 01010110_2 to decimal. (Notice the subscript 2 used to indicate that 01010110 is a base 2 number.)

Solution: Multiply each binary digit by the appropriate weighting factor and total the results.

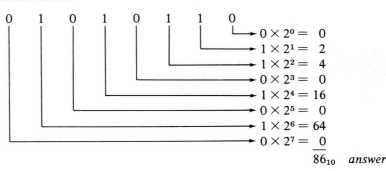

$$
\begin{aligned}
0 \times 2^0 &= 0 \\
1 \times 2^1 &= 2 \\
1 \times 2^2 &= 4 \\
0 \times 2^3 &= 0 \\
1 \times 2^4 &= 16 \\
0 \times 2^5 &= 0 \\
1 \times 2^6 &= 64 \\
0 \times 2^7 &= \underline{0} \\
&\ \ 86_{10} \quad \textit{answer}
\end{aligned}
$$

1–5 DECIMAL-TO-BINARY CONVERSION

The conversion from binary to decimal is usually performed by the digital computer for ease of interpretation by the person reading the number. On the other hand, when a person enters a decimal number into a digital computer, that number must be converted to binary before it can be operated on. Let's look at decimal-to-binary conversion.

EXAMPLE 1–3

Convert 133_{10} to binary.

Solution: Referring to Table 1–1, we can see that the largest power of 2 that will fit into 133 is 2^7 ($2^7 = 128$). But that will still leave the value 5 ($133 - 128 = 5$) to be accounted for. Five can be taken care of by 2^2 and 2^0 ($2^2 = 4$, $2^0 = 1$). So the process looks like this:

$$
\begin{array}{r}
133 \\
-128 \to 2^7 \\
\hline
5 \\
-\ \ 4 \to 2^2 \\
\hline
1 \\
-\ \ 1 \to 2^0 \\
\hline
0
\end{array}
\qquad
\begin{array}{|c|c|c|c|c|c|c|c|}
\hline
1 & 0 & 0 & 0 & 0 & 1 & 0 & 1 \\
\hline
2^7 & 2^6 & 2^5 & 2^4 & 2^3 & 2^2 & 2^1 & 2^0 \\
\end{array}
$$

Answer: 10000101_2.

Note: The powers of 2 that fit into the number 133 were first determined. Then all other positions were filled with zeros.

EXAMPLE 1–4

Convert 122_{10} to binary.

Solution:

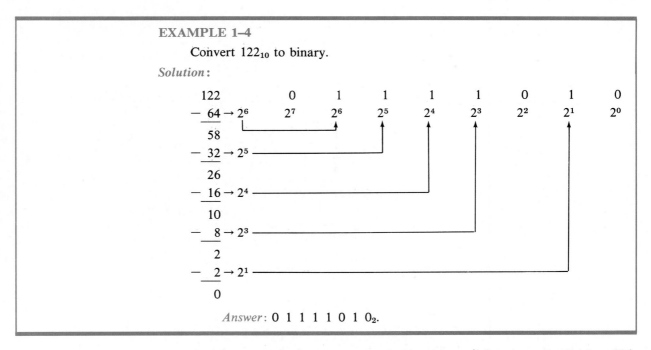

Answer: 0 1 1 1 1 0 1 0₂.

Another method of converting decimal to binary is by *successive division*. This is done by repeated division by the number of the base to which you are converting. For example, to convert 122_{10} to base 2, use the following procedure:

$$122 \div 2 = 61 \quad \text{with a remainder of} \quad 0 \quad \text{(LSB)}$$
$$61 \div 2 = 30 \quad \text{with a remainder of} \quad 1$$
$$30 \div 2 = 15 \quad \text{with a remainder of} \quad 0$$
$$15 \div 2 = 7 \quad \text{with a remainder of} \quad 1$$
$$7 \div 2 = 3 \quad \text{with a remainder of} \quad 1$$
$$3 \div 2 = 1 \quad \text{with a remainder of} \quad 1$$
$$1 \div 2 = 0 \quad \text{with a remainder of} \quad 1 \quad \text{(MSB)}$$

The first remainder, 0, is the *least significant bit* (LSB) of the answer; the last remainder, 1, is the *most significant bit* (MSB) of the answer; therefore, the answer is

$$1\ 1\ 1\ 1\ 0\ 1\ 0_2$$

However, since most computers or digital systems deal with groups of 4, 8, 16, or 32 *bits* (binary digits), we should keep all our answers in that form. Adding a leading zero to the number 1 1 1 1 0 1 0₂ will not change its numeric value; therefore, the 8-bit answer is

$$1\ 1\ 1\ 1\ 0\ 1\ 0_2 = 0\ 1\ 1\ 1\ 1\ 0\ 1\ 0_2$$

EXAMPLE 1–5

Convert 152_{10} to binary using successive division.

Solution:

$$152 \div 2 = 76 \quad \text{remainder} \quad 0 \quad \text{(LSB)}$$
$$76 \div 2 = 38 \quad \text{remainder} \quad 0$$
$$38 \div 2 = 19 \quad \text{remainder} \quad 0$$
$$19 \div 2 = 9 \quad \text{remainder} \quad 1$$
$$9 \div 2 = 4 \quad \text{remainder} \quad 1$$

$$4 \div 2 = 2 \quad \text{remainder} \quad 0$$
$$2 \div 2 = 1 \quad \text{remainder} \quad 0$$
$$1 \div 2 = 0 \quad \text{remainder} \quad 1 \quad \text{(MSB)}$$

Answer: $1\ 0\ 0\ 1\ 1\ 0\ 0\ 0_2$.

1-6 OCTAL NUMBERING SYSTEM (BASE 8)

The octal numbering system is a method of grouping binary numbers in groups of three. The eight allowable digits are 0, 1, 2, 3, 4, 5, 6, and 7.

The octal numbering system is used by manufacturers of computers that utilize 3-bit codes to indicate instructions or operations to be performed. By using the octal representation instead of binary, the user can simplify the task of entering or reading computer instructions and thus save time.

In Table 1-2 we see that when the octal number exceeds 7, the least significant octal position resets to zero, while the next most significant position increases by 1.

TABLE 1-2

Octal Numbering System

Decimal	Binary	Octal
0	000	0
1	001	1
2	010	2
3	011	3
4	100	4
5	101	5
6	110	6
7	111	7
8	1000	10
9	1001	11
10	1010	12

1-7 OCTAL CONVERSIONS

Converting from *binary to octal* is simply a matter of grouping the binary positions in groups of three (starting at the least significant position) and writing down the octal equivalent.

EXAMPLE 1-6

Convert $0\ 1\ 1\ 1\ 0\ 1_2$ to octal.

Solution:

$$0\ 1\ 1 \quad 1\ 0\ 1$$
$$\underbrace{} \quad \underbrace{}$$
$$3 \quad\quad 5 \quad\quad = 35_8 \quad answer$$

EXAMPLE 1-7

Convert $1\ 0\ 1\ 1\ 1\ 0\ 0\ 1_2$ to octal.

Solution:

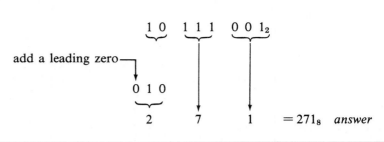

$$= 271_8 \quad answer$$

To convert *octal to binary*, you reverse the process.

EXAMPLE 1–8

Convert 6 2 4$_8$ to binary.

Solution:

$$
\begin{array}{ccc}
6 & 2 & 4 \\
110 & 010 & 100
\end{array}
\quad = 1\,1\,0\,0\,1\,0\,1\,0\,0_2 \quad answer
$$

To convert from *octal to decimal*, follow a process similar to that in Section 1–3 (multiply by weighting factors).

EXAMPLE 1–9

Convert 3 2 6$_8$ to decimal.

Solution:

$$
\begin{array}{ccc}
3 & 2 & 6
\end{array}
$$

$$6 \times 8^0 = 6 \times 1 = 6$$
$$2 \times 8^1 = 2 \times 8 = 16$$
$$3 \times 8^2 = 3 \times 64 = \underline{192}$$
$$214_{10} \quad answer$$

To convert from *decimal to octal* the succesive-division procedure can be used.

EXAMPLE 1–10

Convert 4 8 6$_{10}$ to octal.

Solution:

$$
\left.
\begin{array}{l}
486 \div 8 = 60 \quad \text{remainder} \quad 6 \\
60 \div 8 = 7 \quad \text{remainder} \quad 4 \\
7 \div 8 = 0 \quad \text{remainder} \quad 7
\end{array}
\right\} 746_8
$$

$$486_{10} = 746_8 \quad answer$$

Check:

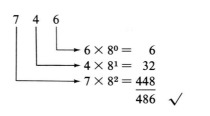

$$6 \times 8^0 = 6$$
$$4 \times 8^1 = 32$$
$$7 \times 8^2 = \underline{448}$$
$$486 \; \checkmark$$

1–8 HEXADECIMAL NUMBERING SYSTEM (BASE 16)

The hexadecimal numbering system, like the octal system, is a method of grouping bits to simplify entering and reading instructions or data present in digital computer systems. Hexadecimal uses 4-bit groupings; therefore, instructions or data used in 8-, 16-, or 32-bit computer systems can be represented as a two-, four-, or eight-digit hexadecimal code instead of as a long string of binary digits (see Table 1–3).

Hexadecimal (hex) uses 16 different digits and is a method of grouping binary numbers in groups of four. The 16 allowable hex digits are 0, 1, 2, 3, 4, 5, 6, 7, 8, 9, A, B, C, D, E, and F.

TABLE 1–3

Hexadecimal Numbering System

Decimal	Binary	Hexadecimal
0	0000 0000	0 0
1	0000 0001	0 1
2	0000 0010	0 2
3	0000 0011	0 3
4	0000 0100	0 4
5	0000 0101	0 5
6	0000 0110	0 6
7	0000 0111	0 7
8	0000 1000	0 8
9	0000 1001	0 9
10	0000 1010	0 A
11	0000 1011	0 B
12	0000 1100	0 C
13	0000 1101	0 D
14	0000 1110	0 E
15	0000 1111	0 F
16	0001 0000	1 0
17	0001 0001	1 1
18	0001 0010	1 2
19	0001 0011	1 3
20	0001 0100	1 4

1–9 HEXADECIMAL CONVERSIONS

To convert from binary to hexadecimal, group the binary number in groups of four (starting in the least significant position) and write down the equivalent hex digit.

EXAMPLE 1–11

Convert $0\ 1\ 1\ 0\ 1\ 1\ 0\ 1_2$ to hex.

Solution:

$$\underbrace{0\ 1\ 1\ 0}_{6}\quad \underbrace{1\ 1\ 0\ 1_2}_{D}\quad = 6D_{16}\quad answer$$

To convert *hexadecimal to binary*, use the reverse process.

EXAMPLE 1–12

Convert $A9_{16}$ to binary.

Solution:

$$\begin{matrix} A & 9 \\ 1\ 0\ 1\ 0 & 1\ 0\ 0\ 1 \end{matrix} = 1\ 0\ 1\ 0\ 1\ 0\ 0\ 1_2\quad answer$$

To convert *hexadecimal to decimal*, use a process similar to that in Section 1–3.

EXAMPLE 1–13

Convert $2\ A\ 6_{16}$ to decimal.

Solution:

$$
\begin{aligned}
&2\quad A\quad 6 \\
&\quad\quad\longrightarrow 6 \times 16^0 = 6 \times 1 = 6 \\
&\quad\longrightarrow A \times 16^1 = 10 \times 16 = 160 \\
&\longrightarrow 2 \times 16^2 = 2 \times 256 = \underline{512} \\
&\hspace{9em} 678_{10}\quad answer
\end{aligned}
$$

To convert from *decimal to hexadecimal*, use successive division.

EXAMPLE 1–14

Convert 151_{10} to hex.

Solution:

$$
\begin{aligned}
151 \div 16 &= 9 \quad \text{remainder}\quad 7 \quad \text{(LSD)} \\
9 \div 16 &= 0 \quad \text{remainder}\quad 9 \quad \text{(MSD)} \\
151_{10} &= 97_{16}\quad answer
\end{aligned}
$$

Check:

$$
\begin{aligned}
&97_{16} \\
&\quad\longrightarrow 7 \times 16^0 = 7 \\
&\longrightarrow 9 \times 16^1 = \underline{144} \\
&\hspace{6em} 151 \quad \checkmark
\end{aligned}
$$

EXAMPLE 1–15

Convert 498_{10} to hex.

Solution:

$$498 \div 16 = 31 \quad \text{remainder} \quad 2 \qquad \text{(LSD)}$$
$$31 \div 16 = 1 \quad \text{remainder} \quad 15 \quad (= F)$$
$$1 \div 16 = 0 \quad \text{remainder} \quad 1 \qquad \text{(MSD)}$$
$$498_{10} = 1 \ F \ 2_{16}$$

Check:

$$1 \ F \ 2_{16} \qquad 2 \times 16^0 = 2 \times 1 = 2$$
$$F \times 16^1 = 15 \times 16 = 240$$
$$1 \times 16^2 = 1 \times 256 = \underline{256}$$
$$498 \quad \checkmark$$

1–10 BINARY-CODED-DECIMAL SYSTEM

The binary-coded-decimal system is used to represent each of the 10 decimal digits as a 4-bit binary code. This code is useful for outputting to displays that are always numeric (0 to 9), such as those found in digital clocks or digital voltmeters.

To form a BCD number, simply convert each decimal digit to its 4-bit binary code.

EXAMPLE 1–16

Convert $4 \ 9 \ 6_{10}$ to BCD.

Solution:

$$
\begin{array}{ccc}
4 & 9 & 6 \\
\overbrace{0100} & \overbrace{1001} & \overbrace{0110} = 0100 \ 1001 \ 0110_{BCD} \quad answer
\end{array}
$$

To convert BCD to decimal, just reverse the process.

EXAMPLE 1–17

Convert $0111 \ 0101 \ 1000_{BCD}$ to decimal.

Solution:

$$
\begin{array}{ccc}
0111 & 0101 & 1000 \\
\underbrace{} & \underbrace{} & \underbrace{} \\
7 & 5 & 8 = 758_{10} \quad answer
\end{array}
$$

EXAMPLE 1–18

Convert 0110 0100 1011$_{BCD}$ to decimal.

Solution:

$$0110 \quad 0100 \quad 1011$$
$$6 \qquad\quad 4 \qquad\quad *$$

* This conversion is impossible because 1011 is not a valid binary-coded decimal. It is not in the range 0 to 9.

1–11 COMPARISON OF NUMBERING SYSTEMS

Table 1–4 shows a comparison of the five number systems commonly used in digital electronics and computer systems.

TABLE 1–4

Comparison of Numbering Systems

Decimal	Binary	Octal	Hexadecimal	BCD
0	0000 0000	0 0	0 0	0000 0000
1	0000 0001	0 1	0 1	0000 0001
2	0000 0010	0 2	0 2	0000 0010
3	0000 0011	0 3	0 3	0000 0011
4	0000 0100	0 4	0 4	0000 0100
5	0000 0101	0 5	0 5	0000 0101
6	0000 0110	0 6	0 6	0000 0110
7	0000 0111	0 7	0 7	0000 0111
8	0000 1000	1 0	0 8	0000 1000
9	0000 1001	1 1	0 9	0000 1001
10	0000 1010	1 2	0 A	0001 0000
11	0000 1011	1 3	0 B	0001 0001
12	0000 1100	1 4	0 C	0001 0010
13	0000 1101	1 5	0 D	0001 0011
14	0000 1110	1 6	0 E	0001 0100
15	0000 1111	1 7	0 F	0001 0101
16	0001 0000	2 0	1 0	0001 0110
17	0001 0001	2 1	1 1	0001 0111
18	0001 0010	2 2	1 2	0001 1000
19	0001 0011	2 3	1 3	0001 1001
20	0001 0100	2 4	1 4	0010 0000

1–12 THE ASCII CODE

To get information into and out of a computer we need more than just numeric representations; we also have to take care of all the letters and symbols used in day-to-day processing. Information such as names, addresses, and item descriptions must be input and output in a readable format. But remember that a digital system can deal only with 1's and 0's. Therefore, we need a special code to represent all alphanumeric data (letters, symbols, and numbers).

Most industry has settled on an input/output (I/O) code called the American Standard Code for Information Interchange (ASCII). The ASCII code uses 7 bits to represent all the alphanumeric data used in computer I/O. Seven bits will yield 128 different code combinations, as listed in Table 1–5.

TABLE 1–5

American Standard Code for Information Interchange

LSB \ MSB	000	001	010	011	100	101	110	111
0000	NUL	DLE	SP	0	@	P	`	p
0001	SOH	DC₁	!	1	A	Q	a	q
0010	STX	DC₂	"	2	B	R	b	r
0011	ETX	DC₃	#	3	C	S	c	s
0100	EOT	DC₄	$	4	D	T	d	t
0101	ENQ	NAK	%	5	E	U	e	u
0110	ACK	SYN	&	6	F	V	f	v
0111	BEL	ETB	'	7	G	W	g	w
1000	BS	CAN	(	8	H	X	h	x
1001	HT	EM	)	9	I	Y	i	y
1010	LF	SUB	*	:	J	Z	j	z
1011	VT	ESC	+	;	K	[	k	{
1100	FF	FS	,	<	L	\	l	|
1101	CR	GS	–	=	M	]	m	}
1110	SO	RS	.	>	N	↑	n	~
1111	SI	US	/	?	O	—	o	DEL

Definitions of control abbreviations:

ACK	Acknowledge	FF	Form feed
BEL	Bell	FS	Form separator
BS	Backspace	GS	Group separator
CAN	Cancel	HT	Horizontal tab
CR	Carriage return	LF	Line feed
DC₁–DC₄	Direct control	NAK	Negative acknowledge
DEL	Delete idle	NUL	Null
DLE	Data link escape	RS	Record separator
EM	End of medium	SI	Shift in
ENQ	Enquiry	SO	Shift out
EOT	End of transmission	SOH	Start of heading
ESC	Escape	STX	Start text
ETB	End of transmission block	SUB	Substitute
ETX	End text	SYN	Synchronous idle
		US	Unit separator
		VT	Vertical tab

Each time a key is depressed on an ASCII keyboard, that key is converted into its ASCII code and processed by the computer. Then before outputting the computer contents to a display terminal or printer, all information is put into the ASCII format.

To use the table, place the 4-bit group in the least significant positions and the 3-bit group in the most-significant positions.

EXAMPLE 1–19

100 0111 is the code for G.

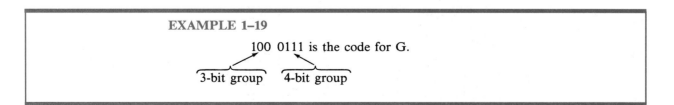

3-bit group 4-bit group

EXAMPLE 1–20

Using Table 1–5, determine the ASCII code for the lowercase letter p.

Solution: 1110000.

EXAMPLE 1–21

If the part number 651-M is stored in ASCII in a computer memory, list the binary contents of those memory locations.

Solution:

$$6 = 011\ 0110$$
$$5 = 011\ 0101$$
$$1 = 011\ 0001$$
$$\text{-} = 010\ 1101$$
$$M = 100\ 1101$$

Since most computer memory locations are formed by groups of 8 bits, let's add a zero to the leftmost position to fill each 8-bit memory location. (The leftmost position is sometimes filled by a parity bit, which is discussed in Chapter 6.)

Therefore, the serial number, if strung out in five memory locations, would look like

0011 0110   0011 0101   0011 0001   0010 1101   0100 1101

If you look at those memory locations in hexadecimal, they will read

36   35   31   2D   4D

GLOSSARY

Analog: A system that deals with continuous varying physical quantities such as voltage, temperature, pressure, or velocity. Most quantities in nature occur in analog, yielding an infinite number of different levels.

ASCII Code: American Standard Code for Information Interchange. ASCII is a 7-bit code used in digital systems to represent all letters, symbols, and numbers to be input or output to the outside world.

BCD: Binary-coded decimal. A 4-bit code used to represent the 10 decimal digits, 0 to 9.

Binary: The base 2 numbering system. Binary numbers are made up of 1's and 0's, each position being equal to a different power of 2 (2^3, 2^2, 2^1, 2^0, etc.).

Bit: A single binary digit. The binary number 1101 is a 4-bit number.

Decimal: The base-10 numbering system. The 10 decimal digits are 0, 1, 2, 3, 4, 5, 6, 7, 8, and 9. Each decimal position is a different power of 10 (10^3, 10^2, 10^1, 10^0, etc.)

Digital: A system that deals with discrete digits or quantities. Digital electronics deals exclusively with 1's and 0's, or ONs and OFFs. Digital codes (such as ASCII) are then used to convert the 1's and 0's to a meaningful number, letter, or symbol for some output display.

Hexadecimal: The base 16 numbering system. The 16 hexadecimal digits are 0, 1, 2, 3, 4, 5, 6, 7, 8, 9, A, B, C, D, E, and F. Each hexadecimal position is worth a different power of 16 (16^3, 16^2, 16^1, 16^0, etc.).

Least significant bit (LSB): The bit having the least significance in a binary string. The LSB will be in the position of the lowest power of 2 within the binary number.

Most significant bit (MSB): The bit having the most significance in a binary string. The MSB will be in the position of the highest power of 2 within the binary number.

Octal: The base 8 numbering system. The eight octal numbers are 0, 1, 2, 3, 4, 5, 6, and 7. Each octal position is worth a different power of 8 (8^3, 8^2, 8^1, 8^0, etc.).

REVIEW QUESTIONS

Sections 1–1 and 1–2
1–1. List three examples of *analog* quantities. *Temperature, pressure, velocity*

1–2. Why do computer systems deal with *digital* quantities instead of *analog* quantities? *are easy for computer to store and interpret.*

Sections 1–3 through 1–9
1–3. Why is the binary numbering system commonly used in digital electronics? *0 . 1*

1–4. How are the weighting factors determined for each binary position in a base 2 number? *by 2^i*

– 1–5. The only digits allowed in the octal numbering system are 0–8 (true or <u>false</u>)?

1–6. Why is hexadecimal used instead of the octal numbering system when working with 8-bit and 16-bit digital computers? *4 bits grouping.*

1–7. The *successive division* method can be used whenever converting from base 10 to any other base numbering system (<u>true</u> or false)?

Sections 1–10 through 1–12
1–8. How does BCD differ from the base 2 binary numbering system? *4 bit grouping*

1–9. Why is ASCII code required by digital computer systems? *to get alphanumeric data in and out of computer.*

PROBLEMS

1–1. Convert the following binary numbers to decimal.
    (a) 0110   (b) 1011   (c) 1001   (d) 0111   (e) 1100
    (f) 01001011   (g) 00110111   (h) 10110101   (i) 10100111   (j) 01110110

1–2. Convert the following decimal numbers to 8-bit binary.
    (a) 186_{10} (b) 214_{10} (c) 27_{10} (d) 251_{10} (e) 146_{10}

1–3. Convert the following binary numbers to octal.
    (a) 011001   (b) 11101   (c) 1011100   (d) 01011001   (e) 1101101

1–4. Convert the following octal numbers to binary.
    (a) 46_8 (b) 74_8 (c) 61_8 (d) 32_8 (e) 57_8

1–5. Convert the following octal numbers to decimal.
    (a) 27_8 (b) 37_8 (c) 14_8 (d) 72_8 (e) 51_8

1–6. Convert the following decimal numbers to octal.
    (a) 126_{10} (b) 49_{10} (c) 87_{10} (d) 94_{10} (e) 108_{10}

1–7. Convert the following binary numbers to hexadecimal.
    (a) 1011 1001   (b) 1101 1100   (c) 0111 0100
    (d) 1111 1011   (e) 1100 0110

1–8. Convert the following hexadecimal numbers to binary.
    (a) $C5_{16}$ (b) FA_{16} (c) $D6_{16}$ (d) $A94_{16}$ (e) 62_{16}

1–9. Convert the following hexadecimal numbers to decimal.
    (a) 86_{16} (b) $F4_{16}$ (c) 92_{16} (d) AB_{16} (e) $3C5_{16}$

1–10. Convert the following decimal numbers to hexadecimal.
    (a) 127_{10} (b) 68_{10} (c) 107_{10} (d) 61_{10} (e) 29_{10}

1–11. Convert the following BCD numbers to decimal.
    (a) 10011000_{BCD} (b) 01101001_{BCD} (c) 01110100_{BCD}
    (d) 00110110_{BCD} (e) 10000001_{BCD}

1–12. Convert the following decimal numbers to BCD.
    (a) 87_{10} (b) 142_{10} (c) 94_{10} (d) 61_{10} (e) 44_{10}

1–13. Use Table 1–5 to convert the following letters, symbols, and numbers to ASCII.
    (a) %   (b) $14   (c) N − 6   (d) CPU   (e) Pg

1–14. Insert a zero in the MSB of your answers to Problem 1–13 and list your answers in hexadecimal.

2

Digital Electronic Signals and Switches

OBJECTIVES

Upon completion of this chapter, you should be able to:

- Describe the parameters associated with digital voltage-versus-time waveforms.
- Convert between frequency and period for a periodic clock waveform.
- Sketch the timing waveform for any binary string in either the serial or parallel representation.
- Discuss the application of manual switches and electromechanical relays in electric circuits.
- Explain the basic characteristics of diodes and transistors when they are forward biased and reverse biased.
- Calculate the output voltage in an electric circuit containing diodes or transistors operating as digital switches.
- Perform input/output timing analysis in electric circuits containing electromechanical relays or transistors.
- Explain the operation of a common-emitter transistor circuit used as a digital inverter switch.

INTRODUCTION

As mentioned in Chapter 1, digital electronics deals with 1's and 0's. These logic states will typically be represented by a high and a low voltage level (usually 1 = 5 V and 0 = 0 V).

In this chapter we see how these logic states can be represented by means of a timing diagram and how electronic switches are used to generate meaningful digital signals.

2–1 DIGITAL SIGNALS

A digital signal is made up of a series of 1's and 0's that represent numbers, letters, symbols, or control signals. Figure 2–1 shows the timing diagram of a typical digital signal. Timing diagrams are used to show the HIGH and LOW (1 and 0) levels of a digital signal as it changes relative to time. In other words, it is a plot of *voltage versus time*. Figure 2–1 is a timing diagram showing the bit configuration 1 0 1 0 as it would appear on an oscilloscope. Notice in Figure 2–1 that the LSB comes first in time. In this case, the LSB is transmitted first. The MSB could have been transmitted first as long as the system on the receiving end knows which method is used.

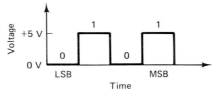

Figure 2–1 Typical digital signal.

2–2 CLOCK WAVEFORM TIMING

Most digital signals require precise timing. Special clock and timing circuits are used to produce clock waveforms to trigger the digital signals at precise intervals (timing circuit design is covered in Chapter 14).

Figure 2–2 shows a typical *periodic clock waveform* as it would appear on an oscilloscope displaying voltage versus time. The term *periodic* means that the waveform is repetitive, at a specific time interval, with each successive pulse identical to the previous one.

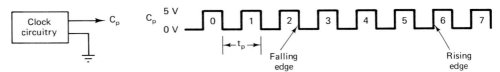

Figure 2–2 Periodic clock waveform as seen on an oscilloscope displaying voltage versus time.

Figure 2–2 shows eight clock pulses, which we will label 0, 1, 2, 3, 4, 5, 6, and 7. The *period* of the clock waveform is defined as the length of time from the falling edge of one pulse to the falling edge of the next pulse (or rising edge to rising edge) and is abbreviated t_p in Figure 2–2. The *frequency* of the clock waveform is defined as the reciprocal of the clock period. Written as a formula,

$$f = \frac{1}{t_p} \quad \text{and} \quad t_p = \frac{1}{f}$$

The basic unit for frequency is hertz and the basic unit for period is seconds.

EXAMPLE 2–1

What is the frequency of a clock waveform whose period is 2 microseconds (μs)?

Solution:

$$f = \frac{1}{t_p} = \frac{1}{2 \ \mu s} = 0.5 \text{ megahertz (0.5 MHz)}$$

Hint: To review scientific notation, see Table 2–1.

TABLE 2–1

Common Scientific Prefixes

Prefix	Abbreviation	Power of 10
giga	G	10^9
mega	M	10^6
kilo	k	10^3
milli	m	10^{-3}
micro	μ	10^{-6}
nano	n	10^{-9}
pico	p	10^{-12}

EXAMPLE 2–2

If the frequency of a waveform is 4.17 MHz, what is its period?

Solution:

$$t_p = \frac{1}{f} = \frac{1}{4.17 \text{ MHz}} = 0.240 \ \mu s$$

2–3 SERIAL REPRESENTATION

Binary information to be transmitted from one location to another will be in a format called *Serial* or in another format called *Parallel*. The serial format uses a single electrical conductor (and a ground) for the data to travel on. The serial format is inexpensive because it requires only a single line, but slow because each bit transmitted exists for one clock period. Let's use Figure 2–3 to illustrate the serial representation of the binary number 0 1 1 0 1 1 0 0. The serial representation (S_o) is shown with respect to some clock waveform (C_p) and its LSB is drawn first. Each bit from the original binary number occupies a separate clock period with the change from one bit to the next occurring at each *falling* edge of C_p.

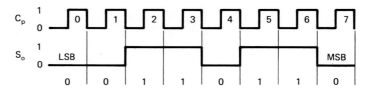

Figure 2–3 Serial representation of a binary number.

2–4 PARALLEL REPRESENTATION

The parallel format uses a separate electrical conductor for each bit to be transmitted (and a ground). For example, if the digital system is using 8-bit numbers, eight lines are required. This tends to be expensive, but the entire 8-bit number can be transmitted in one clock period, making it very fast. Figure 2–4 illustrates the same binary number, 0 1 1 0 1 1 0 0, this time in the parallel representation.

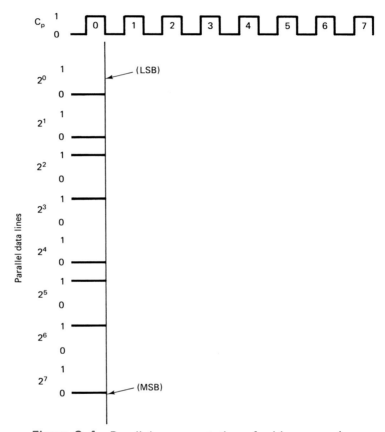

Figure 2–4   Parallel representation of a binary number.

Notice that if the clock period were 2 μs, it would take 2 μs $\times$ 8 periods = 16 μs to transmit the number in serial and only 2 μs $\times$ 1 period = 2 μs to transmit the same 8-bit number in parallel. Thus you can see that when speed is important, the parallel representation is preferred over the serial representation.

The following examples further illustrate the use of serial and parallel representations.

EXAMPLE 2–3

Sketch the serial and parallel representation of the 4-bit number 0 1 1 1. If the clock frequency is 5 MHz, find the time to transmit using each method.

Solution: Figure 2–5 shows the representation of the 4-bit number 0 1 1 1.

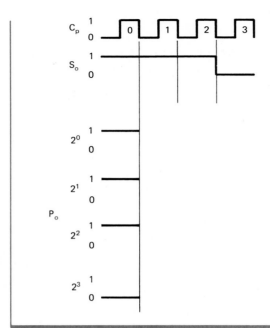

$$t_p = \frac{1}{f} = \frac{1}{5 \text{ MHz}} = 0.2 \ \mu s$$

$$t_{\text{serial}} = 4 \times 0.2 \ \mu s = 0.8 \ \mu s$$

$$t_{\text{parallel}} = 1 \times 0.2 \ \mu s = 0.2 \ \mu s$$

Figure 2–5

EXAMPLE 2–4

Sketch the serial and parallel representation (least significant digit first) of the hexadecimal number 4A. (Assume a 4-bit parallel system and a clock frequency of 4 kHz.) Also, what is the state (1 or 0) of the serial line 1.2 ms into the transmission?

Solution: $4A_{16} = 0 \ 1 \ 0 \ 0 \ 1 \ 0 \ 1 \ 0_2$.

$$t_p = \frac{1}{f} = \frac{1}{4 \text{ kHz}} = 0.25 \text{ ms}$$

Therefore, the increment of time at each falling edge increases by 0.25 ms. Since each period is 0.25 ms, 1.2 ms will occur within the 0 period of the number 4, which, on the S_o line, is a *0 state* (see Figure 2–6).

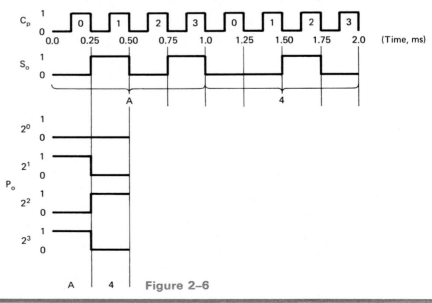

Figure 2–6

2–5 SWITCHES IN ELECTRONIC CIRCUITS

The transitions between 0 and 1 digital levels are caused by switching from one voltage level to another (usually 0 V to +5 V). One way that switching is accomplished is to make and break a connection between two electrical conductors by way of a manual switch or an electromechanical relay. Another way to switch digital levels is by use of semiconductor devices such as diodes and transistors.

Manual switches and relays have almost *ideal* ON and OFF resistances in that when their contacts are closed (ON) the resistance (measured by an ohmmeter) is 0 ohms (Ω) and when their contacts are open (OFF), the resistance is infinite. Figure 2–7 shows the manual switch. When used in a digital circuit, a single-pole, double-throw manual switch can produce 0 and 1 states at some output terminal, as shown in Figures 2–8 and 2–9, by moving the switch (SW) to the up or down position.

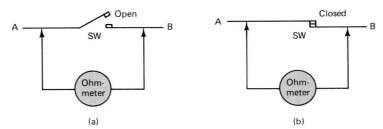

(a)   (b)

Figure 2–7 Manual switch: (a) switch open, $R = \infty$ ohms; (b) switch closed, $R = 0$ ohms.

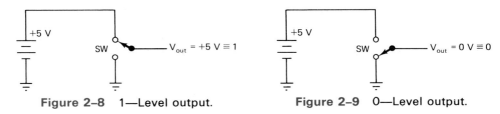

Figure 2–8 1—Level output.   **Figure 2–9** 0—Level output.

2–6 A RELAY AS A SWITCH

An electromechanical relay has contacts like a manual switch, but it is controlled by external voltage instead of being operated manually. Figure 2–10 shows the physical layout of an electromechanical relay. In Figure 2–10a the magnetic coil is energized by placing a voltage at terminals C_1–C_2; this will cause the lower contact to bend downward, opening the contact between X_1 and X_2. This relay is called *normally closed* (NC) because, at rest, the contacts are touching, or closed. In Figure 2–10b, when the coil is energized, the upper contact will be attracted downward, making a connection between X_1 and X_2. This is called a *normally open* (NO) relay.

A relay provides total isolation between the triggering source applied to C_1–C_2 and the output at X_1–X_2. That total isolation is important in many digital applications and it is a feature that certain semiconductor switches (such as transistors, diodes, and integrated circuits) cannot provide. Also, the contacts are normally rated for currents much higher than the current rating of semiconductor switches.

There are several disadvantages, however, of using a relay in electronic circuits. To energize the relay coil, the triggering device must supply several milliamperes, whereas a semiconductor requires only a few microamperes to operate. A relay is

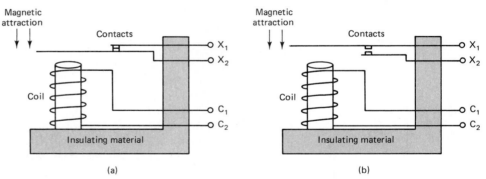

Figure 2–10 Physical representation of an electromechanical relay: (a) normally closed (NC) relay; (b) normally open (NO) relay.

also much slower than a semiconductor. It will take several milliseconds to switch compared to microseconds (or nanoseconds) for a semiconductor switch.

In Figure 2–11 a relay is used as a shorting switch in an electric circuit. The +5 V source is used to energize the coil and the +12 V source is supplying the external electric circuit. When the switch (SW) in Figure 2–11a is closed, the relay coil will become energized, causing the relay contacts to open, which will make V_{out} change from 0 V to 6 V with respect to ground. The voltage-divider equation is used to calculate V_{out}:

$$V_{out} = \frac{12\ V \times 5\ k\Omega}{5\ k\Omega + 5\ k\Omega} = 6\ V$$

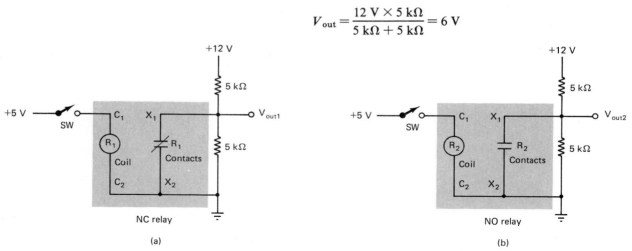

Figure 2–11 Symbolic representation of an electromechanical relay: (a) NC relay used in a circuit; (b) NO relay used in a circuit.

When the switch in Figure 2–11b is closed, the relay coil energizes, causing the relay contacts to close, changing V_{out2} from 6 V to 0 V.

Now, let's go a step further and replace the 5-V battery and switch with a clock oscillator, and use a timing diagram to analyze the results. In Figure 2–12 the relay is triggered by the clock waveform, C_p. The diode D_1 is placed across the relay coil to protect it from arcing each time the coil is deenergized. Timing diagrams are very useful for comparing one waveform to another as the waveform changes states (1 or 0) relative to time. The timing diagram in Figure 2–13 shows that when the clock goes HIGH (1), the relay is energized, causing V_{out3} to go LOW (0). When C_p goes LOW (0), the relay is deenergized, causing V_{out3} to go to +5 V (using the voltage-divider equation, $V_{out} = (10\ V \times 5\ k\Omega)/(5\ k\Omega + 5\ k\Omega) = 5\ V$).

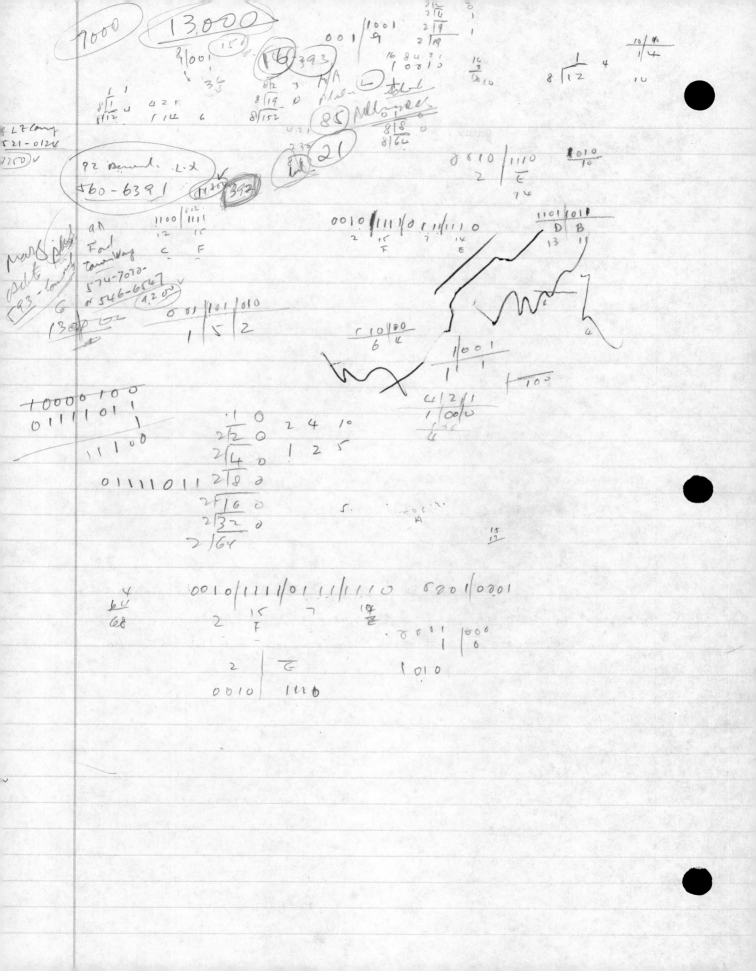

(Philip)

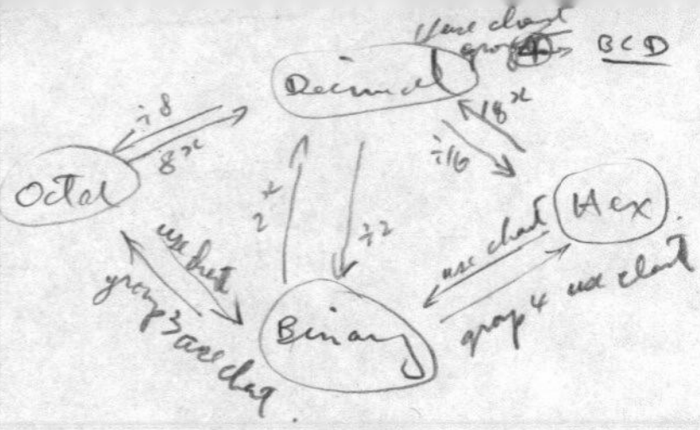

$8x\ 8^2|8^1|8^0$

16|‾ ‾ ‾

2^9	2^8	2^7	2^6	2^5	2^4	2^3	2^2	2^1	2^0
512	256	128	64	32	16	8	4	2	1

8^8	8^7	8^6	8^5	8^4	8^3	8^2	8^1	8^0
				32768	4096	512	64	8	1

16^8	16^7	16^6	16^5	16^4	16^3	16^2	16^1	16^0
				65536	4096	256	16	1

1 6

(2). Transmit 11 bit in serially $\frac{11}{9600} = 1.15$ (8 bit in parallel $= \frac{1}{350} = 2.86$ ws., frequency $= \frac{1}{T\,period}$ and $t_P = \frac{1}{f}$

diode = Anode is more + than cathode = closed switch,

digital Timing - Volt vs Time, CMOS-less power,

IC = (transistor, diodes, resistors), Logic State A 1 or 0 digital level, serial - LSD go first →, Totem-pole. 1 on or saturated 1 off a cut

(3) 3 input and gate 8 diff. (2^3) ($4\ 2^4 = 16$), or gate - high. and gate to disable d signal - low, or gate used to enable a digital signal = digital signal is

logic probe to test high or low, logic pulser to test digital pulse, truth table - illustrate all possible combination of digital input levels

(4) = NAND. $X = \overline{AB}$ Johnson shift counter 8 separate repetitive waveforms,

$X = \overline{A+B}$

(5). POS $= X(A+\overline{B}+C)(B+A)(\overline{A}+C)$, SOP $X = (ABC + \overline{B}D\overline{E} + \overline{A}D)$ Universal Gate = NOR and NAND - because any other can b formed from them

Associative Law (+) $= B + (D + E) = D + (B + E)$, commutative (×) $= CAB = BCA$, distributive $= (B+C)(A+D) = BA + BD + CA + CD$.

(6) Excl or (00 = 0, 01 = 1, 10 = 1, 11 = 0) $X = A \oplus B = \overline{A}B + A\overline{B}$, ($X = AB + \overline{A}\overline{B}$) Excl-Nor is complement of excl-OR, Excl Nor $X = \overline{A \oplus B} = AB + \overline{A}\overline{B}$, Exc-OR provide High output for only high - not for

Excl Nor provide High output for both input high., Ex-OR & Ex Nor in both TTL and CMOS)

$X = \overline{A}B(B+C) + AB(\overline{B}+C)$, odd parity make all 5 bit odd (0101 1), even parity make all 5 bits even (0111 1, 0000 0), Transmission - transfer of digital

$A(B+C) = AB + AC$, $A(A+B) = A$, $A(\overline{A}+B) = AB$, $\overline{A}(A+B) = \overline{A}B$,

$(A+B)(C+D) = AC + AD + BC + BD$, $(A+B)(A+C) = A + BC$, $(A+B)(\overline{A}+C) = \overline{A}B + AC$,

$A + AB = A$, $A + \overline{A}B = A + B$, $\overline{A} + AB = \overline{A} + B$,

$A \cdot 0 = 0$, $A \cdot 1 = A$, $A \cdot A = A$, $A \cdot \overline{A} = 0$, $\overline{A \cdot B} = \overline{A} + \overline{B}$, $A + 0 = A$, $A + 1 = 1$, $A + A = A$, $A + \overline{A} = 1$, $\overline{A} + \overline{B} = \overline{A \cdot B}$

Gate — and = all (AB), or = any (A+B), (Buf), = Not (0), = Not (1), Driver, NAND $X = \overline{AB}$

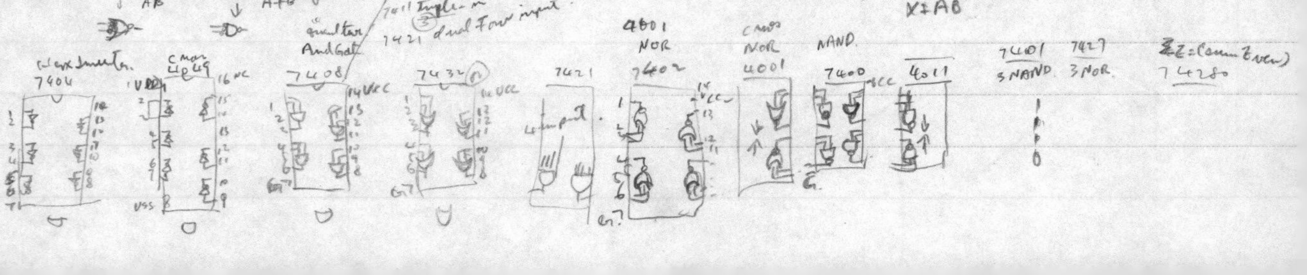

- Decoder may be TO one of more
- Encoder - of many and too many not
- Multiplexer - one of many to the one out
- Demux - one of one or many

D/C = PW / Period × 100%

(8) Out to binary, encoder, binary into Octal device (decoder) encoder convert character a Nor, a code). BCD to decimal (decoder) demultiplexer is used to data distribution (one out of several ones) decode the several codes in Nor) multiplex can select one of several input

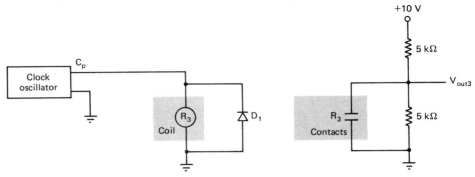

Figure 2–12   Relay used in a digital circuit.

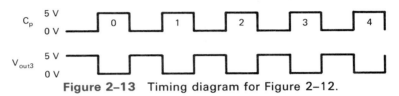

Figure 2–13   Timing diagram for Figure 2–12.

The following examples illustrate electronic switching and help prepare you for more complex timing analysis in subsequent chapters.

EXAMPLE 2–5

Draw a timing diagram for the circuit shown in Figure 2–14, given the C_p waveform.

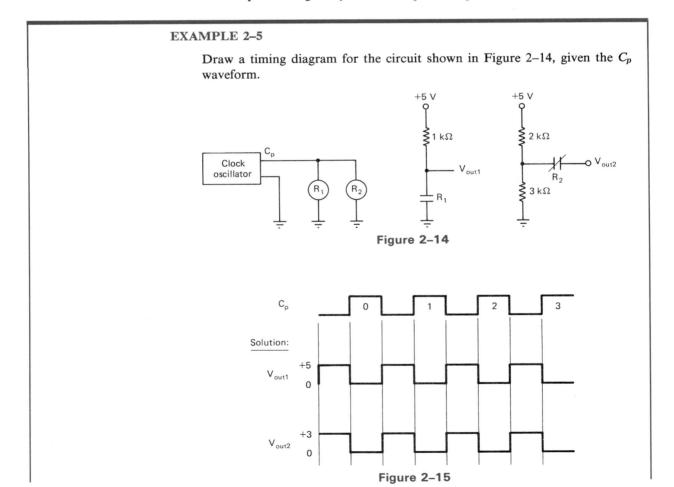

Figure 2–14

Figure 2–15

Explanation: V_{out1}: When C_p is LOW, the R_1 coil is deenergized, the R_1 contacts are open, $I_{1k\Omega} = 0$ A, $V_{drop\ 1\ k\Omega} = I \times R = 0$ V, and $V_{out1} = 5$ V $- 0_{Vdrop} = 5$ V. When C_p is HIGH, the R_1 coil is energized, the R_1 contacts are closed, and $V_{out1} = 0$ V.

V_{out2}: When C_p is LOW, the R_2 coil is deenergized, the R_2 contacts are closed (normally closed), and

$$V_{out2} = \frac{5 \text{ V} \times 3 \text{ k}\Omega}{2 \text{ k}\Omega + 3 \text{ k}\Omega} = 3 \text{ V}$$

When C_p is HIGH, the R_2 coil is energized, the R_2 contacts are open, and $V_{out2} = 0$ V.

EXAMPLE 2–6

Draw a timing diagram for the circuit shown in Figure 2–16 given C_{p1} and C_{p2}.

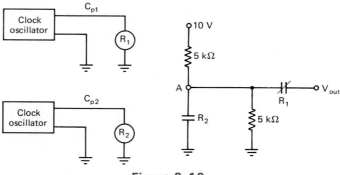

Figure 2–16

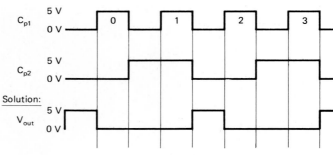

Figure 2–17

Explanation: When the R_2 contacts are closed (R_2 is energized) the voltage at point A is 0 V, making V_{out} equal 0 V. Also, when the R_1 contacts are open (R_1 is energized), $V_{out} = 0$ V. Both the R_1 and R_2 coils must be deenergized to get an output of 5 V ($V_{out} = (10 \text{ V} \times 5 \text{ k}\Omega)/(5 \text{ k}\Omega + 5 \text{ k}\Omega) = 5$ V). Therefore, $V_{out} = 5$ V only when *both* C_{p1} and C_{p2} are LOW.

2–7 A DIODE AS A SWITCH

Manual switches and electromechanical relays have limited application in today's digital electronic circuits. Most digital systems are based on semiconductor technology, which uses diodes and transistors. In Chapter 9 we discuss in detail the formation of digital circuits using transistors and diodes. Most electronics students should also take a separate course in electronic devices to cover the in-depth theory of operation of diodes and transistors. However, without getting into a lot of detail, let's look at how a diode and a transistor can operate as a simple ON/OFF switch.

A diode is a semiconductor device that allows current to flow in one direction but not the other. Figure 2–18 shows a diode in both the conducting and nonconducting states. The term *forward biased* refers to a diode whose anode voltage is *more positive* than its cathode, thus allowing current flow in the direction of the arrow. A reverse-biased diode will not allow current flow because its anode voltage is *equal to*, or is *more negative* than, its cathode. A diode is analogous to a check valve in a water system (see Figure 2–19).

A diode is not a perfect short in the forward-biased condition, however. The voltage-versus-current curve shown in Figure 2–20 shows the characteristics of a diode. Notice in the figure that for the reverse-biased condition, as V_{rev} becomes more negative, there is still practically zero current flow.

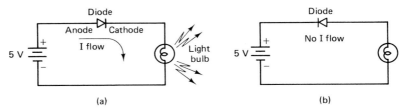

Figure 2–18   Diode in a series circuit: (a) forward biased; (b) reverse biased.

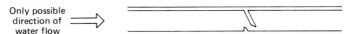

Figure 2–19   Water system check valve.

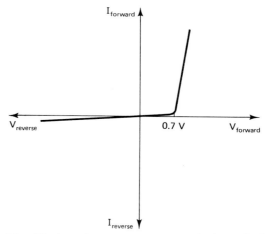

Figure 2–20   Diode voltage versus current characteristic curve.

In the forward-biased condition, as V_{forw} becomes more positive, no current flows until a 0.7-V "cut-in voltage" is reached.[1] After that point, the voltage across the diode (V_{forw}) will remain at approximately 0.7 V and I_{forw} will flow, limited only by the external resistance of the circuit and the 0.7-V internal voltage drop.

---

[1] 0.7 V is the typical cut-in voltage of a silicon diode, while 0.3 V is typical for a germanium diode. However, we will use the silicon diode because it is most commonly used in industrial applications.

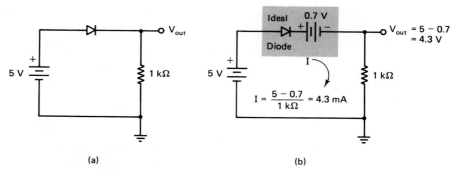

(a)   (b)

Figure 2–21 Forward-biased diode in an electric circuit: (a) original circuit; (b) equivalent circuit showing the diode voltage drop and $V_{out} = 5 - 0.7 = 4.3$ V.

What this means is that current will flow only if the anode is more positive than the cathode, and under those conditions the diode acts like a short circuit except for the 0.7 V across it's terminals. This fact is better illustrated in Figure 2–21.

The following examples and the problems at the end of the chapter demonstrate the effect that diodes have on electric circuits.

EXAMPLE 2–7

Determine if the diodes shown in Figure 2–22 are forward biased or reverse biased.

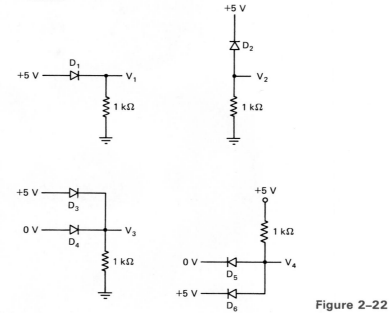

Figure 2–22

Solution:

D_1 is forward biased.

D_2 is reverse biased.

D_3 is forward biased.

D_4 is reverse biased.

D_5 is forward biased.

D_6 is reverse biased.

EXAMPLE 2–8

Determine V_1, V_2, V_3, and V_4 (with respect to ground) for the circuits in Example 2–7.

Solution: V_1: D_1 is forward biased, dropping 0.7 V across its terminals. Therefore, $V_1 = 4.3$ V (5.0 − 0.7).

V_2: D_2 is reverse biased. No current will flow through the 1-kΩ resistor, so $V_2 = 0$ V.

V_3: Since D_4 is reverse biased (open), it has no effect on the circuit. D_3 is forward biased, dropping 0.7 V, making $V_3 = 4.3$ V.

V_4: D_6 is reverse biased (open), so it has no effect on the circuit. D_5 is forward biased, so it has +0.7 V on its anode side, which is +0.7 V above the 0-V ground level, making $V_4 = +0.7$ V.

2–8   A TRANSISTOR AS A SWITCH

The transistor is a very commonly used switch in digital electronic circuits. It is a three-terminal semiconductor component that allows an input signal at one of its terminals to cause the other two terminals to become a short or an open circuit. The transistor is most commonly made of silicon that has been altered into N-type material and P-type material.

Three distinct regions make up a transistor: *emitter*, *base*, and *collector*. They can be a combination of N-P-N-type material or P-N-P-type material bonded together as a three-terminal device. Figure 2–23 shows the physical layout and symbol for an *NPN* transistor. (In a *PNP* transistor, the emitter arrow points the other way.)

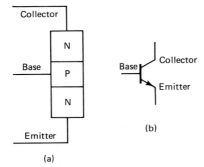

Figure 2–23 *NPN* transistor: (a) physical layout; (b) symbol.

In an electronic circuit, the input signal (1 or 0) is usually applied to the base of the transistor, which causes the collector–emitter junction to become a short or an open circuit. The rules of transistor switching are as follows:

1. In an *NPN* transistor, applying a positive voltage from base to emitter will cause the collector-to-emitter junction to short (this is called "turning the transistor ON"). Applying a negative voltage or 0 V from base to emitter will cause the collector-to-emitter junction to open (this is called "turning the transistor OFF").

2. In a *PNP*[2] transistor, applying a negative voltage from base to emitter will turn it ON. Applying a positive voltage or 0 V from base to emitter turns it OFF.

[2] *PNP* transistor circuits are analyzed in the same way as *NPN* circuits except that all voltage and current polarities are reversed. *NPN* circuits are much more common in industry and will be used most often in this book.

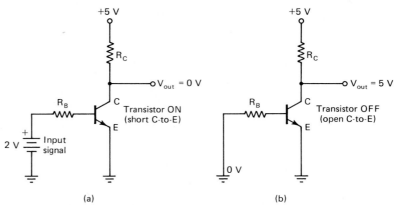

Figure 2–24   *NPN* transistor switch: (a) transistor ON; (b) transistor OFF.

Figure 2–24 shows how an *NPN* transistor functions as a switch in an electronic circuit.

In Figure 2–24 resistors R_B and R_C are used to limit the base current and the collector current. In Figure 2–24a the transistor is turned ON because the base is more positive than the emitter (input signal = +2 V). This causes the collector-to-emitter junction to short, placing ground potential at V_{out} ($V_{out} = 0$ V).

In Figure 2–24b the input signal is removed, making the base-to-emitter junction 0 V, turning the transistor OFF. With the transistor OFF there is no current through R_C, so $V_{out} = 5$ V $- (0$ A $\times R_C) = 5$ V.

Digital input signals are usually brought in at the base of the transistor and the output is taken off the collector or emitter. The following examples use timing analysis to compare the input and output waveforms.

EXAMPLE 2–9

Sketch the waveforms at the collector and emitter of the circuit shown in Figure 2–25, given the input signal C_p.

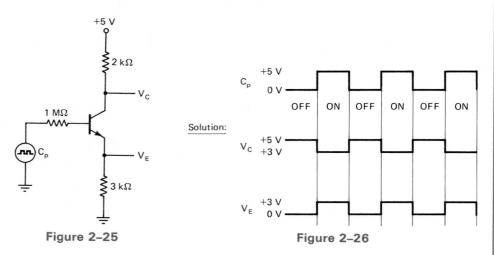

Figure 2–25   **Figure 2–26**

Explanation: When $C_p = 0$ V the transistor is OFF and the equivalent circuit is as shown in Figure 2–27a.

$$I_C = 0 \text{ A}$$
$$I_E = 0 \text{ A}$$

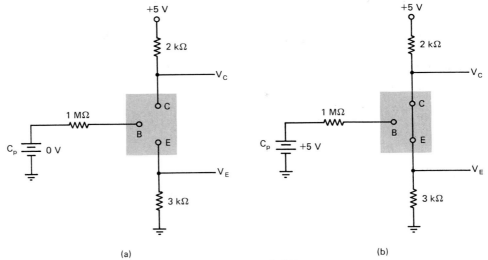

(a)   (b)

Figure 2–27

Therefore,

$$V_C = 5 \text{ V} - (0 \text{ A} \times 2 \text{ k}\Omega) = 5 \text{ V}$$
$$V_E = 0 \text{ A} \times 3 \text{ k}\Omega = 0 \text{ V}$$

When $C_p = +5$ V the transistor is ON and the equivalent circuit is as shown in Figure 2–27b.

$$I_C = I_E = \frac{5 \text{ V}}{2 \text{ k}\Omega + 3 \text{ k}\Omega} = 1 \text{ mA}$$

$$V_C = \frac{5 \text{ V} \times 3 \text{ k}\Omega}{3 \text{ k}\Omega + 2 \text{ k}\Omega} = 3 \text{ V}$$

$$V_E = \frac{5 \text{ V} \times 3 \text{ k}\Omega}{3 \text{ k}\Omega + 2 \text{ k}\Omega} = 3 \text{ V}$$

EXAMPLE 2–10

Sketch the waveform at V_{out} in the circuit shown in Figure 2–28, given the input signal C_p.

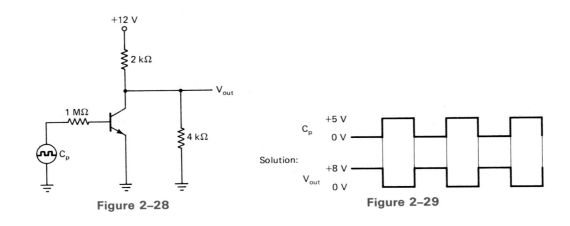

Figure 2–28

Solution:

Figure 2–29

Explanation: When $C_p = 0$ V the transistor is OFF and the equivalent circuit is as shown in Figure 2–30a. From the voltage-divider equation,

$$V_{out} = \frac{12 \text{ V} \times 4 \text{ k}\Omega}{4 \text{ k}\Omega + 2 \text{ k}\Omega} = 8 \text{ V}$$

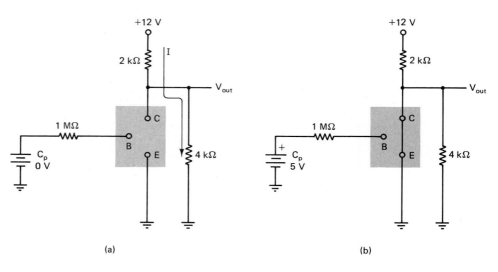

(a)   (b)

Figure 2–30

Next, when $C_p = +5$ V the transistor is ON and the equivalent circuit is as shown in Figure 2–30b. Now the collector is shorted to ground, making $V_{out} = 0$ V.

2–9 THE TTL INTEGRATED CIRCUIT

Transistor-transistor logic (TTL) is one of the most widely used integrated-circuit technologies. TTL integrated circuits use a combination of several transistors, diodes, and resistors integrated together in a single package.

One basic function of a TTL integrated circuit is as a complementing switch or *inverter*. The inverter is used to take a digital level at its input and complement it to the opposite state at its output (1 becomes 0, 0 becomes 1). Figure 2–31 shows how a common-emitter-connected transistor switch can be used to perform the same function.

When V_{in} equals 1 (+5 V) the transistor is turned on (called *saturated*) and V_{out} equals 0 (0 V). When V_{in} equals 0 (0 V) the transistor is turned off (called *cutoff*) and V_{out} equals 1 (approximately 5 V), assuming that R_L is much greater than R_C ($R_L \gg R_C$).

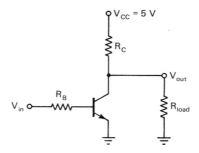

Figure 2–31 Common-emitter transistor circuit operating as an inverter.

EXAMPLE 2–11

Let's assume that $R_C = 1\ k\Omega$, $R_L = 10\ k\Omega$, and $V_{in} = 0$ in Figure 2–31. V_{out} will equal 4.55 V:

$$\frac{5\ V \times 10\ k\Omega}{1\ k\Omega + 10\ k\Omega} = 4.55\ V$$

But if R_L decreases to 1 kΩ by adding more loads in parallel with it, V_{out} will drop to 2.5 V:

$$\frac{5\ V \times 1\ k\Omega}{1\ k\Omega + 1\ k\Omega} = 2.5\ V$$

We can see from Example 2–11 that the 1-level output of that inverter is very dependent on the size of the load resistor (R_L), which can typically vary by a factor of 10. So right away you might say: "Let's keep R_C very small so that R_L is always much greater than R_C" ($R_L \gg R_C$). Well, that's fine for the case when the transistor is cut off ($V_{out} = 1$), but when the transistor is saturated ($V_{out} = 0$) the transistor collector current will be excessive if R_C is very small ($I_C = 5\ V/R_C$; see Figure 2–32).

Therefore, it seems that when the transistor is cut off ($V_{out} = 1$) we want R_C to be small to ensure that V_{out} is close to 5 V, but when the transistor is saturated, we want R_C to be large to avoid excessive collector current.

This idea of needing a variable R_C resistance is accommodated by the TTL integrated circuit (Figure 2–33). It uses another transistor (Q_4) in place of R_C to act like a varying resistance. Q_4 is cut off (acts like a high R_C) when the output transistor (Q_3) is saturated, and then Q_4 is saturated (acts like a low R_C) when Q_3 is cut off. (In other words, "when one transistor is "ON," the other one is "OFF") This combination of Q_3 and Q_4 is referred to as the *totem-pole* arrangement.

Transistor Q_1 is the input transistor used to drive Q_2, which is used to control Q_3 and Q_4. Diode D_1 is used to protect Q_1 from negative voltages that might inadvertently be placed at the input. D_2 is used to ensure that when Q_3 is saturated, Q_4 will be cut off totally.

TTL is a very popular family of integrated circuits. It is much more widely

Figure 2–32 Common-emitter calculations.

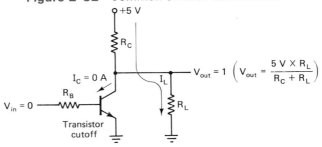

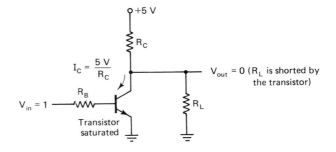

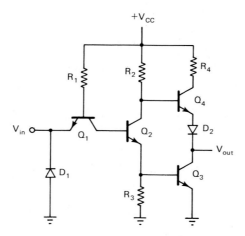

Figure 2–33   Schematic of a TTL circuit.

used than RTL (resistor-transistor logic) or DTL (diode-transistor logic) circuits, which were the forerunners of TTL. Details on the operation and specifications of TTL ICs are given in Chapter 9.

A single TTL integrated-circuit (IC) package such as 7404 has six complete logic circuits fabricated into a single silicon chip, each logic circuit being the equivalent of Figure 2–33. The 7404 has 14 metallic pins connected to the outside of a plastic case containing the silicon chip. The 14 pins, arranged seven on a side, are aligned on 14 holes of a printed-circuit board, where they will then be soldered. The 7404 is called a 14-pin DIP (dual-in-line package) and costs less than 25 cents. Figure 2–34 shows a sketch of a 14-pin DIP IC. In subsequent chapters we will see how to use ICs in actual digital circuitry.

The pin configuration of the 7404 is shown in Figure 2–35. The power supply connections to the IC are made to pin 14 (+5 V) and pin 7 (ground), which supplies power to all six logic circuits. In the case of the 7404, the logic circuits are called *inverters*. The symbol for each inverter is a triangle with a circle at the output. The circle is used to indicate the inversion function.

2–10   THE CMOS INTEGRATED CIRCUIT

Another common integrated-circuit technology used in digital logic is the CMOS (complementary metal-oxide-semiconductor). CMOS uses a complementary pair of metal-oxide-semiconductor field-effect transistors (MOSFETs) instead of the bipolar transistors used in TTL chips. (Complete coverage of TTL and CMOS is given in Chapter 9.)

Figure 2–34   A 7404 TTL IC chip.

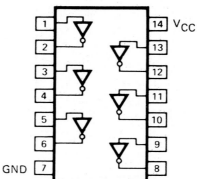

Figure 2–35   A 7404 hex inverter pin configuration.

The major advantage of using CMOS is its low power consumption. Because of that, it is commonly used in battery-powered devices such as hand-held calculators and digital thermometers. The disadvantage of using CMOS is that generally its switching speed is slower than TTL and it is susceptible to burnout due to electrostatic charges if not handled properly. Figure 2–36 shows the pin configuration for a 4049 CMOS hex inverter.

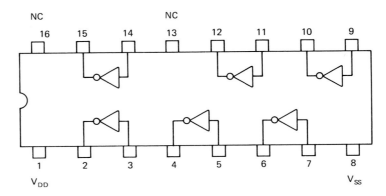

Figure 2–36 A 4049 CMOS hex inverter pin configuration.

GLOSSARY

Bias: The voltage necessary to cause a semiconductor device to conduct or cut off current flow. A device can be forward biased or reverse biased, depending on what action is desired.

Chip: The term given to an integrated circuit. It comes from the fact that each integrated circuit comes from a single "chip" of silicon crystal.

CMOS: Complementary-metal-oxide semiconductor. A family of integrated circuits used to perform logic functions in digital circuits. The CMOS is noted for its low power consumption but sometimes slow speed.

Cutoff: A term used in transistor switching which signifies that the collector-to-emitter junction is turned off, or is not allowing current flow.

Diode: A semiconductor device used to allow current flow in one direction but not the other. As an electronic switch, it acts like a short in the forward-biased condition and like an open in the reverse-biased condition.

DIP: Dual-in-line package. The most common pin layout for integrated circuits. The pins are aligned in two straight lines, one on each side of the IC.

Energized relay coil: By applying a voltage to the relay coil, a magnetic force is induced within it; this is used to attract the relay contacts away from their resting positions.

Frequency: A measure of the number of cycles or pulses occurring each second. Its unit is the hertz and it is the reciprocal of the period.

Hex inverter: An integrated circuit containing six inverters on a single DIP package.

Integrated circuit: The fabrication of several semiconductor and electronic devices (transistors, diodes, and resistors) onto a single piece of silicon crystal. Integrated circuits are increasingly being used to perform the functions that used to require several hundred discrete semiconductors.

Inverter: A logic function that changes its input into the opposite logic state at its output (0 to 1 and 1 to 0).

Logic state: A 1 or 0 digital level.

Oscilloscope: An electronic measuring device used in design and troubleshooting to display a picture of waveform magnitude (y-axis) versus time (x-axis).

Parallel: A digital signal representation that uses several lines or channels to transmit binary information. The parallel lines allow for the transmission of an entire 4-bit (or more) number with each clock pulse.

Period: The measurement of time from the beginning of one periodic cycle or clock pulse to the beginning of the next. Its unit is the second, and it is the reciprocal of frequency.

Relay: An electric device containing an electromagnetic coil and normally open or normally closed contacts. It is useful because by supplying a small triggering current to its coil, the contacts will open or close, switching a higher current on or off.

Saturation: A term used in transistor switching which signifies that the collector-to-emitter junction is turned on, or conducting current heavily.

Serial: A digital signal representation that uses one line or channel to transmit binary information. The binary logic states are transmitted one bit at a time with the LSB first.

Timing diagram: A diagram used to display the precise relationship between two or more digital waveforms as they vary relative to time.

Totem-pole: The term used to describe the output stage of most TTL integrated circuits. The totem-pole stage consists of one transistor in series with another, configured in such a way that when one transistor is saturated, the other is cut off.

Transistor: A semiconductor device that can be used as an electronic switch in digital circuitry. By applying an appropriate voltage at the base, the collector-to-emitter junction will act like an open or a shorted switch.

TTL: Transistor-transistor logic. The most common integrated circuit used in digital electronics today. A large family of different TTL ICs is used to perform all the logic functions necessary in a complete digital system.

REVIEW QUESTIONS

Sections 2–1 and 2–2

2–1.   What are the labels on the X-axis and Y-axis of a digital signal measured on an oscilloscope?

2–2.   What is the relationship between clock frequency and clock period?

Sections 2–3 and 2–4

2–3.   What advantage does parallel have over serial in the transmission of digital signals?

2–4.   Which system requires more electrical conductors and circuitry: serial or parallel?

Sections 2–5 and 2–6

2–5.   Describe the operation of a relay coil and relay contacts.

2–6.   How does a normally open relay differ from a normally closed relay?

Section 2–7

2–7.   To forward-bias a diode, the anode is made more _____ (positive, negative) than the cathode.

2–8.   A forward-biased diode has how many volts across its terminals?

Section 2–8

2–9.   Name the three pins on a transistor.

2–10. To "turn ON" an NPN transistor, a _____ (positive, negative) voltage is applied to the base.

2–11. When a transistor is "turned ON" its collector-to-emitter becomes a _____ (short, open).

Section 2–9

2–12. In a common-emitter transistor circuit, when V_{out} is 0, R_c should be _____ (small, large), and when V_{out} is 1, R_c should be _____ (small, large).

2–13. Which transistor in the schematic of a TTL circuit serves as a variable R_c resistance?

PROBLEMS

2–1. Determine the period of a clock waveform whose frequency is:
   (a) 2 MHz   (b) 500 KHz   (c) 4.27 MHz   (d) 17 MHz
   Determine the frequency of a clock waveform whose period is:
   (e) 2 μs   (f) 100 μs   (g) 0.75 ms   (h) 1.5 μs

2–2. Sketch the serial and parallel representations (similar to Figure 2–6) of the following numbers and calculate how long they will take. (Clock frequency = 2 MHz.)
   (a) $45B_{16}$ (b) $A3C_{16}$

2–3. How long will it take to transmit the number 33_{10} in serial if the clock frequency is 3.7 MHz? (Transmit the number as an 8-bit binary number.)

2–4. How long will it take to transmit the three ASCII-coded characters $14 in 8-bit parallel if the clock frequency is 8 MHz?

2–5. Draw the timing diagram for the circuits of Figure P2–5.

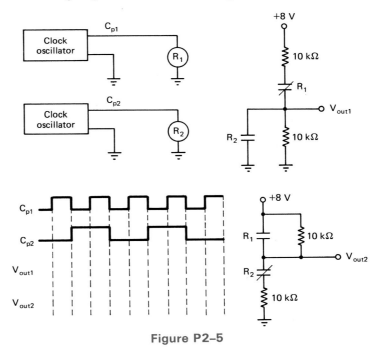

Figure P2–5

2–6. Determine if the diodes in Figure P2–6 are reverse or forward biased.

2–7. Determine V_1, V_2, V_3, V_4, V_5, V_6, and V_7 in the circuits of Figure P2–6.

2–8. In Figure P2–6, if the cathode of any one of the diodes D_8, D_9, or D_{10} is connected to 0 V instead of +5 V, what happens to V_6?

2–9. In Figure P2–6, if the anode of any of the diodes D_{11}, D_{12}, or D_{13} is connected to +5 V instead of 0 V, what happens to V_7?

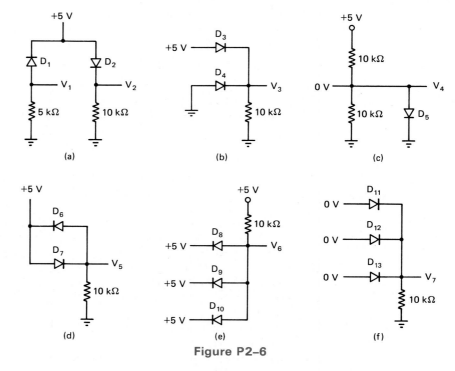

Figure P2–6

2–10. Find V_{out1} and V_{out2} for the circuits of Figure P2–10.

2–11. Sketch the waveforms at V_C and V_E in the circuit of Figure 2–25 using $R_C = 6$ kΩ and $R_E = 4$ kΩ.

2–12. To use a common-emitter transistor circuit as an inverter, the input signal is connected to the (base, collector, or emitter) and the output signal is taken from the (base, collector, or emitter).

2–13. Determine V_{out} for the common-emitter transistor inverter circuit of Figure 2–31 using $V_{in} = 0$ V, $R_B = 1$ MΩ, $R_C = 330$ Ω and $R_{load} = 1$ MΩ.

2–14. If the load resistor (R_{load}) used in problem 2–13 is changed to 470 Ω, describe what happens to V_{out}.

2–15. In the circuit of Figure 2–31 with $V_{in} = 0$ V, V_{out} will be almost 5 V as long as R_{load} is much greater than R_C. Why not make R_C real small to ensure that the circuit will work for all values of R_{load}?

2–16. In Figure 2–31 if $R_C = 100$ Ω, find the collector current when $V_{in} = +5$ V.

2–17. Describe how the totem-pole output arrangement in a TTL circuit overcomes the problems faced when using the older common-emitter transistor inverter circuit.

Figure P2–10

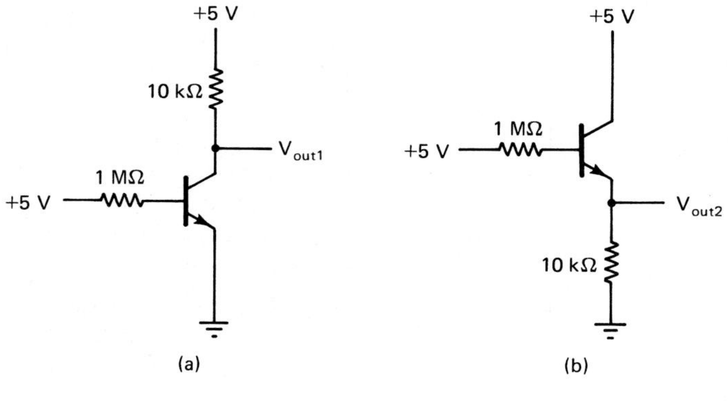

3

Basic Logic Gates

OBJECTIVES

Upon completion of this chapter, you should be able to:

- Describe the operation and use of AND gates and OR gates.
- Construct truth tables for two-, three-, and four-input AND and OR gates.
- Draw timing diagrams for AND and OR gates.
- Describe the operation, using timing analysis, of an ENABLE function.
- Sketch the external connections to integrated-circuit chips to implement AND and OR logic circuits.
- Explain how to use a logic pulser and a logic probe to troubleshoot digital integrated circuits.

INTRODUCTION

Logic gates are the basic building blocks for forming digital electronic circuitry. A logic gate has one output terminal and one or more input terminals. Its output will be HIGH (1) or LOW (0) depending on the digital level(s) at the input terminal(s). Through the use of logic gates we can design digital systems that will evaluate digital input levels and produce a specific output response based on that particular logic circuit design. The seven logic gates are AND, OR, NAND, NOR, INVERTER, exclusive-OR, and exclusive-NOR. The AND and OR are discussed in this chapter.

3–1 THE AND GATE

Let's start by looking at the two-input AND gate shown in Figure 3–1. The operation of the AND gate is simple and is defined as follows: *The output, X, will be HIGH if input A AND input B are* both *HIGH*. In other words, if *A* = 1 *AND B* = 1, then *X* = 1. If either *A* or *B* or both are LOW, the output will be LOW.

Figure 3–1 Two-input AND gate.

The best way to illustrate how the output level of a gate responds to all the possible input-level combinations is with a *truth table*. Table 3–1 is a truth table for a two-input AND gate. On the left side of the truth table, all possible input-level combinations are listed, and on the right side the resultant output is listed.

TABLE 3–1

Truth Table for a Two-
Input AND Gate

Inputs		Output
A	*B*	*X*
0	0	0
0	1	0
1	0	0
1	1	1

From the truth table we can see that the output at *X* is HIGH *only* when *both A* AND *B* are HIGH. If this AND gate is a TTL integrated circuit, HIGH means +5 V and LOW means 0 V (i.e., 1 is defined as +5 V and 0 is defined as 0 V).

One example of how an AND gate might be used is in a bank burglary alarm system. The output of the AND gate would go HIGH to turn on the alarm if the alarm activation key is in the ON position *AND* the front door is opened. This setup is illustrated in Figure 3–2.

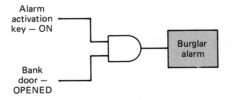

Figure 3–2 AND gate used to activate a burglar alarm.

Another way to illustrate the operation of an AND gate is by use of a series electric circuit. In Figure 3–3, using manual and transistor switches, the output at *X* will be HIGH if *both* switches *A AND B* are HIGH (1).

Figure 3–3 also shows what is known as the *Boolean Equation* for the AND function, *X = A* and *B*, which can be thought of as *X equals 1 if A AND B both equal 1*. The Boolean equation for the AND function can more simply be written as $X = A \cdot B$ or just $X = AB$. *Boolean equations* will be used throughout the rest of the book to depict algebraically the operation of a logic gate or combination of logic gates.

AND gates can have more than two inputs. Figure 3–4 shows a four-input and an eight-input AND gate. The truth table for an AND gate with four inputs is

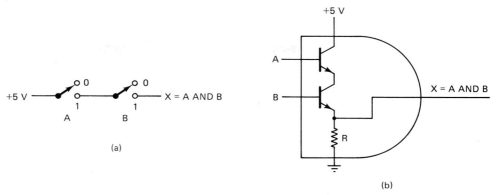

Figure 3-3 Electrical analogy of an AND gate: (a) using manual switches; (b) using transistor switches.

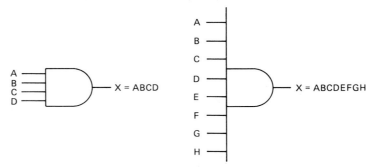

Figure 3-4 Multiple-input AND gate symbols.

shown in Table 3-2. To determine the total number of different combinations to be listed in the truth table, use the equation

$$\text{number of combinations} = 2^N \qquad \text{where } N = \text{number of inputs} \qquad (3\text{-}1)$$

Therefore, in the case of a four-input AND gate, the number of possible input combinations is $2^4 = 16$.

TABLE 3-2

Truth Table for a Four-Input AND Gate

A	B	C	D	X
0	0	0	0	0
0	0	0	1	0
0	0	1	0	0
0	0	1	1	0
0	1	0	0	0
0	1	0	1	0
0	1	1	0	0
0	1	1	1	0
1	0	0	0	0
1	0	0	1	0
1	0	1	0	0
1	0	1	1	0
1	1	0	0	0
1	1	0	1	0
1	1	1	0	0
1	1	1	1	1

When building the truth table, be sure to list all 16 *different* combinations of input levels. One easy way to ensure that you do not miss a combination or duplicate a combination is to list the inputs in the order of a binary counter (0000, 0001, 0010, . . . , 1111). Also notice in Table 3–2 that the *A* column lists eight 0's, then eight 1's; the *B* column lists four 0's, four 1's, four 0's, four 1's; the *C* column lists two 0's, two 1's, two 0's, two 1's, etc.; and the *D* column lists one 0, one 1, one 0, one 1, etc.

3–2   THE OR GATE

The OR gate also has two or more inputs and a single output. The symbol for a two-input OR gate is shown in Figure 3–5. The operation of the two-input OR gate is defined as follows: *The output at X will be HIGH whenever input A OR input B is HIGH or both are HIGH.* As a Boolean equation this can be written $X = A + B$. Notice the use of the $+$ symbol to represent the OR function.

Figure 3–5   Two-input OR gate.

The truth table for a two-input OR gate is shown in Table 3–3.

TABLE 3–3

Truth Table for a Two-Input OR Gate

Inputs		Output
A	B	X
0	0	0
0	1	1
1	0	1
1	1	1

From the truth table you can see that *X* is 1 whenever *A OR B* is 1 or if *both A* and *B* are 1. Using manual or transistor switches in an electric circuit as shown in Figure 3–6, we can observe the electrical analogy to an OR gate. From the figure we see that the output at *X* will be 1 if *A or B*, or *both*, are HIGH (1).

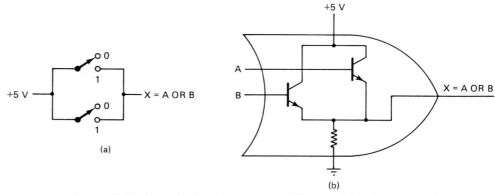

Figure 3–6   Electrical analogy of an OR gate: (a) using manual switches; (b) using transistor switches.

OR gates can also have more than two inputs. Figure 3–7 shows a three-input OR gate and Figure 3–8 shows an eight-input OR gate. The truth table for the three-input OR gate will have eight entries ($2^3 = 8$) and the eight-input OR gate will have 256 entries ($2^8 = 256$).

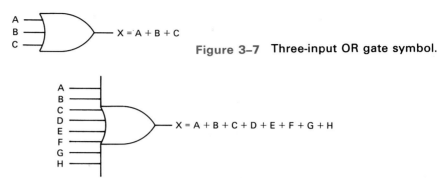

$$X = A + B + C$$

Figure 3–7 Three-input OR gate symbol.

$$X = A + B + C + D + E + F + G + H$$

Figure 3–8 Eight-input OR gate symbol.

Let's build a truth table for the three-input OR gate.

TABLE 3–4

Truth Table for a Three-Input OR Gate

A	B	C	X
0	0	0	0
0	0	1	1
0	1	0	1
0	1	1	1
1	0	0	1
1	0	1	1
1	1	0	1
1	1	1	1

The truth table of Table 3–4 is built by first using Equation 3–1 to determine that there will be eight entries, then listing the eight combinations of inputs in the order of a binary counter (000 to 111), then filling in the output column (X) by realizing that X will always be HIGH as long as at least one of the inputs is HIGH. When you look at the completed truth table you can see that the only time the output is LOW is when *all* the inputs are LOW.

3–3 TIMING ANALYSIS

Another useful means of analyzing the output response of a gate to varying input-level changes is by means of a *timing diagram*. A timing diagram, as described in Chapter 2, is used to illustrate graphically how the output levels change in response to input-level changes.

The timing diagram in Figure 3–9 shows the two input waveforms (A and B) that are applied to a two-input AND gate, and the X output that will result from the AND operation. (For TTL and most CMOS logic gates, 1 = +5 V, 0 = 0 V.) As you can see, timing analysis is very useful for visually illustrating the level at the output for varying input-level changes.

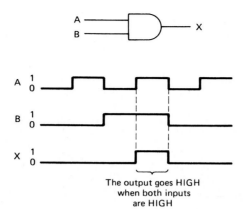

Figure 3–9   Timing analysis of an AND gate.

Timing waveforms are observed on an *oscilloscope* or a *logic analyzer*. A dual-trace oscilloscope is capable of displaying *two* voltage-versus-time waveforms on the same *x*-axis. That is ideal for comparing the relationship of one waveform relative to another. The other timing analysis tool is the logic analyzer. It can, among other things, display 8 or 16 voltage-versus-time waveforms on the same *x*-axis. It can also display the levels of the digital signals in a *state table*, which lists the binary levels of all the waveforms, at predefined intervals, in binary, hexadecimal, or octal. Timing analysis of 8 or 16 channels concurrently is very important when analyzing advanced digital and microprocessor systems, where the interrelationship of several digital signals is critical for proper circuit operation.

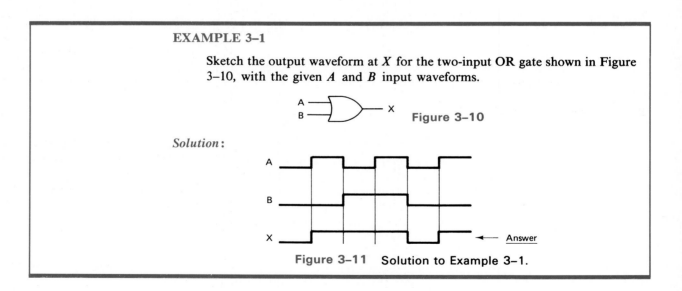

EXAMPLE 3–1

Sketch the output waveform at *X* for the two-input **OR** gate shown in Figure 3–10, with the given *A* and *B* input waveforms.

Figure 3–10

Solution:

Figure 3–11   Solution to Example 3–1.

EXAMPLE 3–2

Sketch the output waveform at *X* for the three-input **AND** gate shown in Figure 3–12, with the given *A*, *B*, and *C* input waveforms.

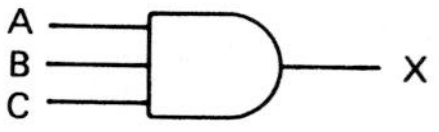

Figure 3–12

Solution:

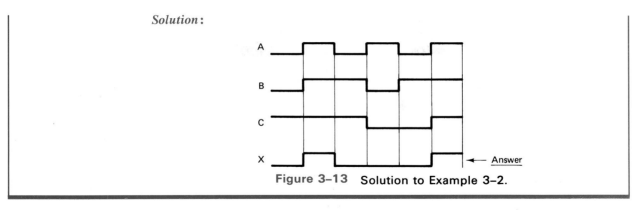

Figure 3-13 Solution to Example 3-2.

EXAMPLE 3-3

The input waveform at *A* and the output waveform at *X* are given for the AND gate in Figure 3-14. Sketch the input waveform that is required at *B* to produce the output at *X*.

Figure 3-14

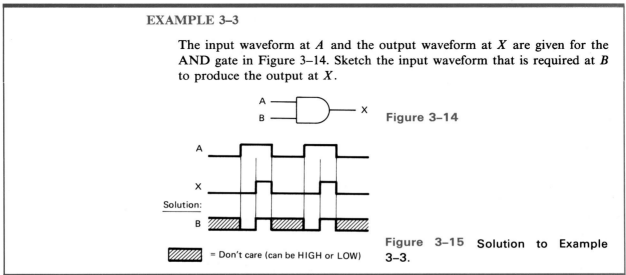

= Don't care (can be HIGH or LOW)

Figure 3-15 Solution to Example 3-3.

3-4 ENABLE AND DISABLE FUNCTIONS

AND and OR gates can be used to *enable* or *disable* a waveform from being transmitted from one point to another. For example, let's say that you wanted a 1-MHz clock oscillator to transmit only four pulses to some receiving device. You would want to *enable* four clock pulses to be transmitted, then *disable* the transmission from then on.

The clock frequency of 1 MHz converts to 1 μs $\left(\dfrac{1}{1 \text{ MHz}}\right)$ for each clock period. Therefore, to transmit four clock pulses we have to provide an *enable* signal for 4 μs. Figure 3-16 shows the circuit and waveforms to *enable* four clock pulses. In order for the HIGH clock pulses to get through the AND gate to point *X*, the second input to the AND gate (enable signal input) must be HIGH; otherwise, the output of the AND gate will be LOW. Therefore, when the enable signal is HIGH for 4 μs, four clock pulses will pass through the AND gate. When the enable signal goes LOW, the AND gate *disables* any further clock pulses from reaching the receiving device.

An OR gate can also be used to disable a function. The difference is that the enable signal input is made HIGH to disable, and the output of the OR gate goes HIGH when it is disabled, as shown in Figure 3-17.

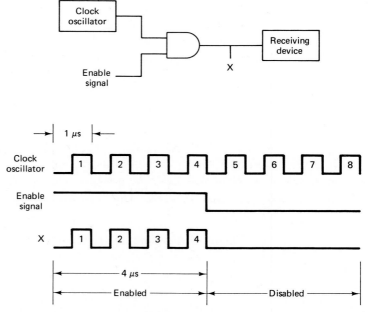

Figure 3–16   Using an AND gate to enable/disable a clock oscillator.

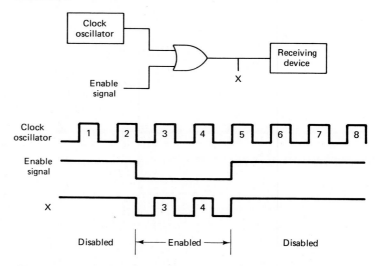

Figure 3–17   Using an OR gate to enable/disable a clock oscillator.

3–5   USING INTEGRATED-CIRCUIT LOGIC GATES

AND and OR gates are available as integrated circuits (ICs). The IC pin layout, logic gate type, and technical specifications are all contained in the logic data manual supplied by the manufacturer of the IC. For example, referring to a TTL or a CMOS logic data manual, we can see that there are several AND and OR gate ICs. To list just a few:

1. The 7408 (74HC08) is a quad two-input AND gate.
2. The 7411 (74HC11) is a triple three-input AND gate.

3. The 7421 (74HC21) is a dual four-input AND gate.
4. The 7432 (74HC32) is a quad two-input OR gate.

In each case, the HC stands for "high-speed CMOS." For example, the 7408 is a TTL AND gate and the 74HC08 is the equivalent CMOS AND gate. The terms *quad* (four), *triple* (three), and *dual* (two) refer to the number of separate gates on a single IC.

Let's look in more detail at one of these ICs, the 7408 (Figure 3–18). The 7408 is a 14-pin dual-in-line package (DIP) IC. The power supply connections are made to pins 7 and 14. Four separate AND gates are available for use. Let's make the external connections to the IC to form a clock oscillator enable circuit similar to Figure 3–16.

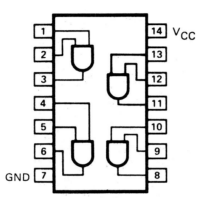

Figure 3–18   The 7408 quad two-input AND gate IC pin configuration.

In Figure 3–19 the first AND gate in the IC was used and the other three are ignored. The IC is powered by connecting pin 14 to the positive power supply and pin 7 to ground. The other connections are made by following the original design from Figure 3–16. The clock oscillator signal passes on to the receiving device when the switch is in the *enable* (1) position, and it stops when in the *disable* (0) position.

The pin configurations for some other logic gates are shown in Figure 3–20.

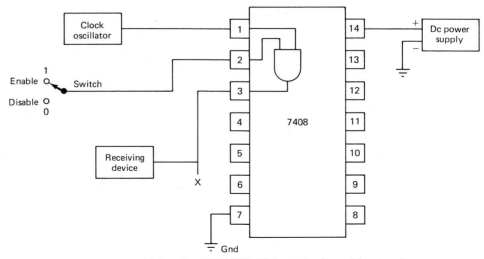

Figure 3–19   Using the 7408 TTL IC in a clock enable circuit.

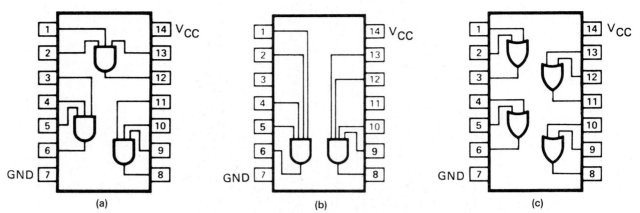

Figure 3–20 Pin configurations for other popular TTL and CMOS AND and OR gate ICs: (a) 7411(74HC11); (b) 7421(74HC21); (c) 7432(74HC32).

3–6 *INTRODUCTION TO TROUBLESHOOTING TECHNIQUES*

Like any other electronic device, integrated circuits and digital electronic circuits can go bad. *Troubleshooting* is the term given to the procedure used to find the *fault* or *trouble* in the circuits.

To be a good troubleshooter you must first *understand the theory and operation* of the circuit, devices, and ICs that are suspected to be bad. If you understand how a particular IC is *supposed* to operate, it is a simple task to put the IC through a test or to exercise its functions to see if it operates as you expect.

There are two simple tools that we will start with to test the ICs and digital circuits. They are the logic pulser and logic probe (Figure 3–21). The *logic probe*

Figure 3–21 Logic pulser and logic probe. (Courtesy of Hewlett-Packard Company.)

has a metal tip that is placed on the IC pin, printed-circuit-board trace, or device lead that you want to test. It also has an indicator lamp that glows, telling you the digital level at that point. If the level is HIGH (1), the lamp glows brightly. If the level is LOW (0), the lamp goes out. If the level is floating (open circuit, neither HIGH nor LOW), the lamp is dimly lit. Table 3–5 summarizes the states of the logic probe.

TABLE 3–5

Logic Probe States

Logic level	Indicator lamp
HIGH (1)	On
LOW (0)	Off
Float	Dim

The *logic pulser* is used to provide digital pulses to a circuit being tested. By applying a pulse to a circuit and simultaneously observing a logic probe, you can tell if the pulse signal is getting through the IC or device as you would expect. As you become more and more experienced at troubleshooting, you will find that most IC and device faults are due to an open or short at the input or output terminals. The following troubleshooting examples will illustrate some basic troubleshooting techniques using the logic probe and pulser.

EXAMPLE 3–4

The integrated-circuit AND gate in Figure 3–22 is suspected of having a fault and you want to test it. What procedure should you follow?

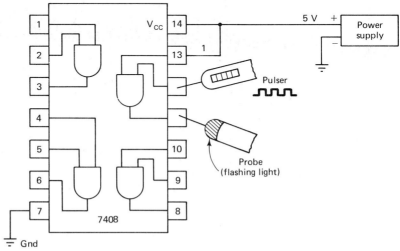

Figure 3–22 Connections for troubleshooting one gate of a quad AND IC.

Solution: First you apply power to V_{cc} (pin 14) and Gnd (pin 7). Next you want to check each AND gate with the pulser/probe. Since it takes a HIGH (1) on *both* inputs to an AND gate to make the output go HIGH, if we put a HIGH (+5 V) on one input and pulse the other, we would expect to get pulses at the output of the gate. Figure 3–22 shows the connections to test one of the gates of a quad AND IC. When the pulser is put on pin 12, the light in the end of the probe flashes at the same speed as the pulser, indicating that the AND gate is passing the pulses through the gate (similar in operation to the clock enable circuit of Figure 3–16).

The next check is to reverse the connections to pins 12 and 13 and check the probe. If the probe still flashes, that gate is okay. Proceed to the other three gates and follow the same procedure. When one of the gate outputs does not flash, you have found the fault.

As mentioned earlier, *the key to troubleshooting an IC is understanding how the IC works*.

EXAMPLE 3–5

Sketch the connections for troubleshooting the first gate of a 7421 dual AND gate.

Solution: The connections are shown in Figure 3–23. The probe should be flashing if the gate is good. Check each of the four inputs with the pulser by keeping three inputs high and pulsing the fourth while you look at the probe. In any case, if the probe does not flash, you have found a bad gate.

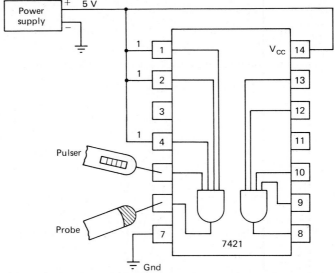

Figure 3–23 Connections for troubleshooting one gate of a 7421 dual four-input AND gate.

EXAMPLE 3–6

Sketch the connections for troubleshooting the first gate of a 7432 quad OR gate.

Solution: The connections are shown in Figure 3–24. The probe should be flashing if the gate is good. Notice that the second input to the OR gate being checked is connected to a LOW (0) instead of a HIGH. The reason for this is that the output would *always* be HIGH if one input was connected HIGH. Since one input is connected LOW instead, the output will flash together with the pulses from the logic pulser if the gate is good.

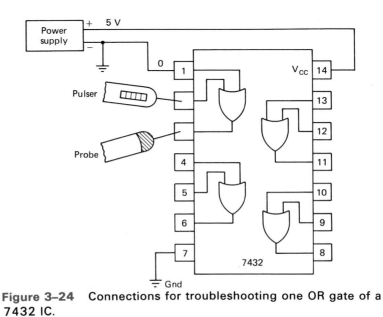

Figure 3–24   Connections for troubleshooting one OR gate of a 7432 IC.

GLOSSARY

Boolean equation: An algebraic expression that illustrates the functional operation of a logic gate or combination of logic gates.

Disable: To disallow or deactivate a function or circuit.

Enable: To allow or activate a function or circuit.

Fault: The problem in a nonfunctioning electrical circuit. It is usually due to an open circuit, short circuit, or defective component.

Float: A logic level in a digital circuit which is neither HIGH nor LOW. It acts like an open circuit to anything connected to it.

Gate: The basic building block of digital electronics. The basic logic gate has one or more inputs and one output and is used to perform one of the following logic functions: AND, OR, NOR, NAND, INVERT, exclusive-OR, or exclusive-NOR.

Logic probe: An electronic tool used in the troubleshooting procedure to indicate a HIGH, LOW, or float level at a particular point in a circuit.

Logic pulser: An electronic tool used in the troubleshooting procedure to inject a pulse or pulses into a particular point in a circuit.

Troubleshooting: The work that is done to find the problem in a faulty electrical circuit.

Truth table: A tabular listing that is used to illustrate all the possible combinations of digital input levels to a gate and the output that will result.

REVIEW QUESTIONS

Sections 3–1 and 3–2
3–1. All inputs to an AND gate must be HIGH for it to output a HIGH (true or false)?
3–2. What is the purpose of a truth table? *output to input.*
3–3. What is the purpose of a Boolean Equation? *depict algebra*
3–4. What input conditions must be satisfied for the output of an OR gate to be LOW?

Sections 3–3 and 3–4
3–5. Describe the purpose of a *timing diagram*.
3–6. Under what circumstances would diagonal ''don't care'' hash marks be used in a timing diagram?
3–7. A _____ (HIGH, LOW) level is required at the input to an AND gate to *enable* the signal at the other input to pass to the output.

Sections 3–5 and 3–6
3–8. Which pins on the 7408 AND IC are used for power supply connections, and what voltage levels are placed on those pins? *Pin 14 Power   Pin 7 GND.*
3–9. How is a *logic probe* used to troubleshoot digital ICs?
3–10. How is a *logic pulser* used to troubleshoot digital ICs?

PROBLEMS

3–1. Build the truth table for a three-input AND gate.
3–2. Build the truth table for a four-input AND gate.
3–3. If we were to build a truth table for an eight-input AND gate, how many different combinations of inputs would we have?
3–4. Describe, in words, the operation of an AND gate.
3–5. Describe, in words, the operation of an OR gate.
3–6. Write the Boolean equation for:
    (a) A three-input AND gate
    (b) A four-input AND gate
    (c) A three-input OR gate

3-7. Sketch the output waveform at X for the two-input AND gates shown in Figure P3-7.

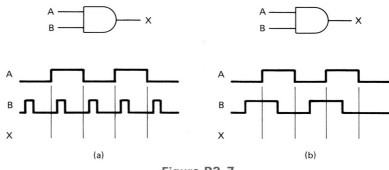

Figure P3-7

3-8. Sketch the output waveform at X for the two-input OR gates shown in Figure P3-8.

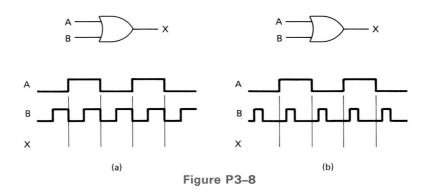

Figure P3-8

3-9. Sketch the output waveform at X for the three-input AND gates shown in Figure P3-9.

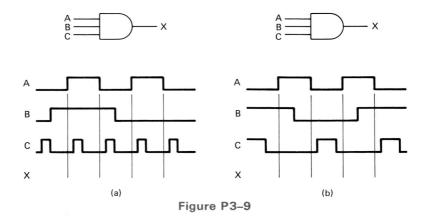

Figure P3-9

3-10. The input waveform at A is given for the two-input AND gates shown in Figure P3-10. Sketch the input waveform at B that will produce the output at X.

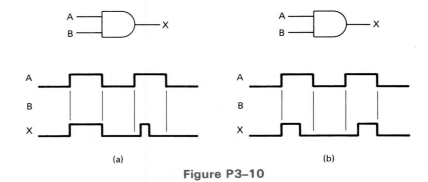

Figure P3–10

3–11. Repeat Problem 3–10 for the two-input OR gates shown in Figure P3–11.

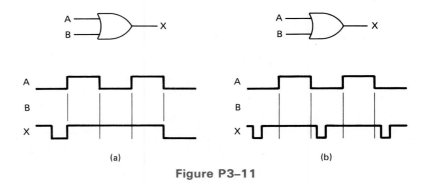

Figure P3–11

3–12. Using Figure P3–12, sketch the waveform for the *enable signal* that will allow pulses 2, 3 and 6, 7 to get through to the receiving device.

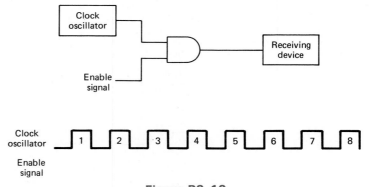

Figure P3–12

3–13. Repeat Problem 3–12, but this time sketch the waveform that will allow only the even pulses (2, 4, 6, 8) to get through.

3–14. How many separate OR gates are contained within the 7432 TTL IC?

3–15. Sketch the actual pin connections to a 7432 quad two-input OR TTL IC to implement the circuit of Figure 3–17.

3–16. How many inputs are there on each AND gate of a 7421 TTL IC?

3–17. The 7421 IC is a 14-pin dual-in-line package (DIP). How many of the pins are *not* used for anything?

Troubleshooting

3–18. What are the three logic levels that can be indicated by a logic probe?

3–19. What is the function of the logic pulser?

3–20. When troubleshooting an OR gate such as the 7432, when the pulser is applied to one input, should the other input be connected HIGH or LOW? Why?

3–21. When troubleshooting an AND gate such as the 7408, when the pulser is connected to one input, should the other input be connected HIGH or LOW? Why?

3–22. The clock enable circuit shown in Figure P3–22 is not working. The enable switch is up in the "enable" position. A logic probe is placed on the following pins and gets the following results. Find the cause of the problem.

Probe on pin:	Indicator lamp
1	Flashing
2	On
3	Off
7	Off
14	On

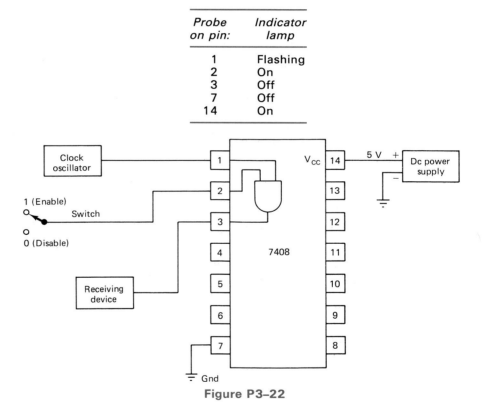

Figure P3–22

3–23. Repeat Problem 3–22 for the following troubleshooting results.

Probe on pin:	Indicator lamp
1	Flashing
2	Off
3	Off
7	Off
14	On

3–24. Repeat Problem 3–22 for the following troubleshooting results.

Probe on pin:	Indicator lamp
1	Flashing
2	On
3	Off
7	Dim
14	On

4 Inverting Logic Gates

OBJECTIVES

Upon completion of this chapter, you should be able to:

- Describe the operation and use of inverter, NAND, and NOR gates.
- Construct truth tables for two-, three-, and four-input NAND and NOR gates.
- Draw timing diagrams for inverter, NAND, and NOR gates.
- Use the outputs of a Johnson shift counter to generate specialized waveforms utilizing various combinations of the five basic gates.
- Develop a comparision of the Boolean equations and truth tables for the five basic gates.

INTRODUCTION

Inverting logic gates are used like the basic AND and OR logic gates except that the inverting gates have *complemented* (inverted) outputs. Basically, there are three inverting logic gates: the *inverter*, the *NAND* (NOT-AND), and the *NOR* (NOT-OR). These gates are explained in this chapter and later combined with AND and OR gates to form the combinational logic used to provide the functional operations of complete digital systems.

4–1 THE INVERTER

The inverter is used to complement or invert a digital signal. It has a single input and a single output. If a HIGH level (1) comes in, it produces a LOW level (0)

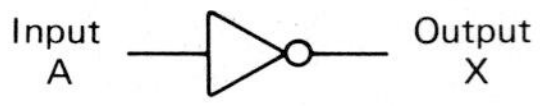

Input A $\longrightarrow\!\!\!\triangleright\!\!\circ\longrightarrow$ Output X

Input A	Output X
0	1
1	0

Figure 4–1   Inverter symbol and truth table.

output. If a LOW level (0) comes in, it produces a HIGH level (1) output. The symbol and truth table for the inverter gate are shown in Figure 4–1.

The operation of the inverter is very simple and can be illustrated further by studying the timing diagram of Figure 4–2. The timing diagram graphically shows us the operation of the inverter. When the input is HIGH, the output is LOW, and when the input is LOW, the output is HIGH. The output waveform is therefore the exact complement of the input.

A $\longrightarrow\!\!\!\triangleright\!\!\circ\longrightarrow$ $X = \overline{A}$

Input A

Output X

Figure 4–2   Timing analysis of an inverter gate.

The Boolean equation for an inverter is written $X = \overline{A}$ ($X = $ NOT A). The *bar* over the A is an inversion bar, used to signify the *complement*.

4–2   THE NAND GATE

The operation of the NAND gate is the same as the AND gate except that its output is inverted. You can think of NAND gate as an AND gate with an inverter at its output. The symbol for a NAND gate is made from an AND gate with a small circle (bubble) or triangle at its output, as shown in Figure 4–3.

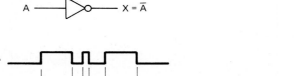

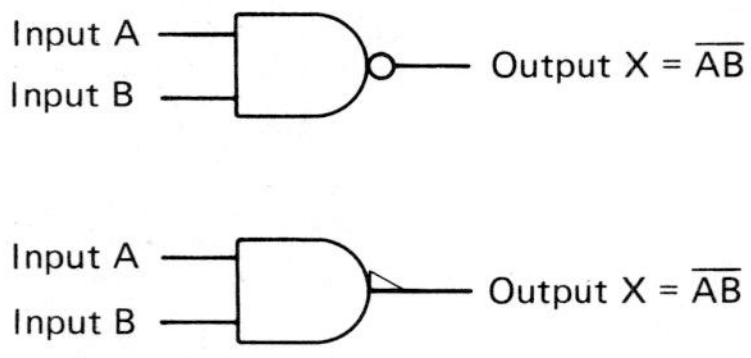

Input A
Input B   Output $X = \overline{AB}$

Input A
Input B   Output $X = \overline{AB}$

Figure 4–3   Symbols for a NAND gate.

In digital circuit diagrams, you will find the small circle or triangle used whenever complementary action (inversion) is to be indicated. (The circle is more commonly used, however, and will be used most often in this text.) The circle or triangle at the output acts just like an inverter, so a NAND gate can be drawn symbolically as an AND gate with an inverter connected to its output, as shown in Figure 4–4.

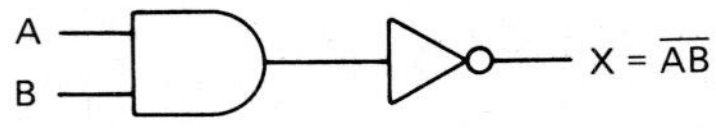

A
B $X = \overline{AB}$

Figure 4–4   AND–INVERT equivalent of a NAND gate.

The Boolean equation for the NAND gate is written $X = \overline{AB}$. The inversion bar is drawn over the (A and B) meaning that the output of the NAND is the complement of (A and B) [NOT (A and B)]. Since we are inverting the output, the truth table outputs in Table 4–1 will be the complement of the AND gate truth table outputs. The easy way to construct the truth table is to think of how an AND gate would respond to the inputs, then invert your answer. From Table 4–1 we can see that the output is LOW when *both* inputs *A and B* are HIGH (just the opposite of an AND gate). Also, the output is HIGH whenever either input is LOW.

TABLE 4–1

Two-Input
NAND Gate
Truth Table

A	B	X
0	0	1
0	1	1
1	0	1
1	1	0

NAND gates can also have more than two inputs. Figure 4–5 shows three-input and eight-input NAND gate symbols. The truth table for a three-input NAND gate (Table 4–2) shows that the output is always HIGH unless *all* inputs go HIGH.

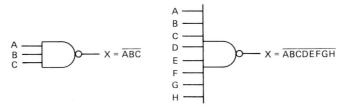

Figure 4–5   Symbols for three-input and eight-input NAND gates.

TABLE 4–2

Truth Table for
a Three-Input
NAND Gate

A	B	C	X
0	0	0	1
0	0	1	1
0	1	0	1
0	1	1	1
1	0	0	1
1	0	1	1
1	1	0	1
1	1	1	0

Timing analysis can also be used to illustrate the operation of NAND gates. The following examples will contribute to your understanding.

EXAMPLE 4–1

Sketch the output waveform at X for the NAND gate shown in Figure 4–6, with the given input waveforms.

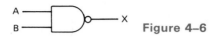

Figure 4–6

Solution:

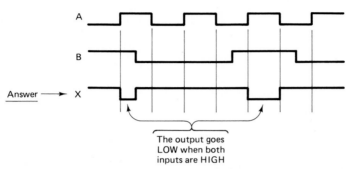

The output goes
LOW when both
inputs are HIGH

Figure 4–7   Timing analysis of a NAND gate.

EXAMPLE 4–2

Sketch the output waveform at X for the NAND gate shown in Figure 4–8, with the given input waveforms at A, B, and Control.

Figure 4–8

Solution:

In Figure 4–9 the Control input waveform is used to *enable/disable* the NAND gate. When it is LOW, the output is stuck HIGH. When it goes HIGH, the output will respond LOW when A and B go HIGH.

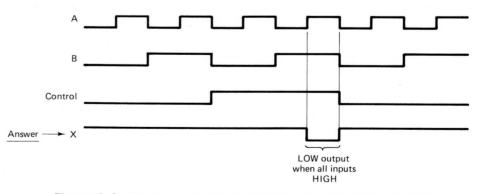

LOW output
when all inputs
HIGH

Figure 4–9   Timing analysis of a NAND gate with a "Control" input.

4–3   THE NOR GATE

The operation of the NOR gate is the same as that of the OR gate except that its output is inverted. You can think of a NOR gate as an OR gate with an inverter at its output. The symbols for a NOR gate and its equivalent OR–INVERT symbol are shown in Figure 4–10.

A —⌐\
B —⌐   )o— X = $\overline{A + B}$

A —⌐\
B —⌐   )⊳— X = $\overline{A + B}$

A —⌐\
B —⌐   )— ⊳o— X = $\overline{A + B}$

Figure 4–10   NOR gate symbols and its OR–INVERT equivalent.

The Boolean equation for the NOR function is $X = \overline{A + B}$. The equation is stated "X equals *not* (A or B)." In other words, X is LOW if A or B is HIGH. The truth table for a NOR gate is given in Table 4–3. Notice that the output column is the complement of the OR gate truth table output column.

TABLE 4–3

Truth Table
for a NOR Gate

A	B	$X = \overline{A + B}$
0	0	1
0	1	0
1	0	0
1	1	0

Now let's study some timing analysis examples to get a better grasp of NOR gate operation.

EXAMPLE 4–3

Sketch the output waveform at X for the NOR gate shown in Figure 4–11, with the given input waveforms.

A —⌐\
B —⌐   )o— X = $\overline{A + B}$ **Figure 4–11**

Solution:

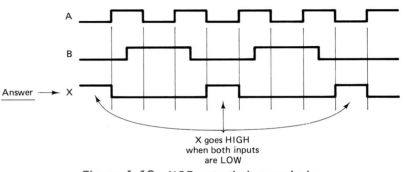

X goes HIGH
when both inputs
are LOW

Figure 4–12   NOR gate timing analysis.

EXAMPLE 4–4

Sketch the output waveform at X for the NOR gate shown in Figure 4–13 with the given input waveforms.

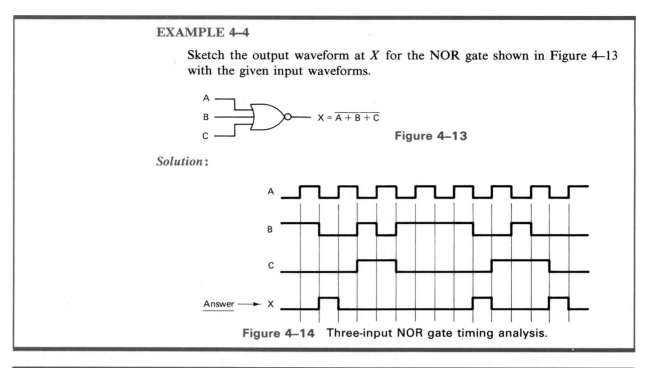

Figure 4–13

Solution:

Figure 4–14   Three-input NOR gate timing analysis.

EXAMPLE 4–5

Sketch the waveform at the B input of the gate shown in Figure 4–15 that will produce the output waveform shown for X.

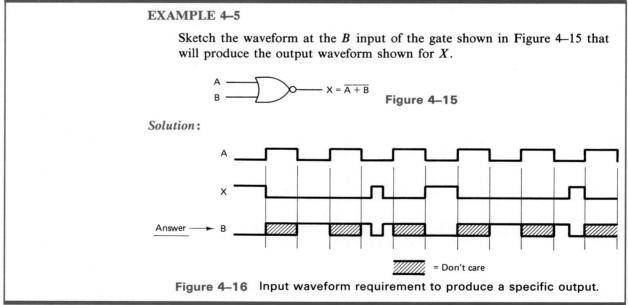

Figure 4–15

Solution:

= Don't care

Figure 4–16   Input waveform requirement to produce a specific output.

4–4   *LOGIC GATE WAVEFORM GENERATION*

Using the basic gates, a clock oscillator, and a repetitive waveform generator circuit, we can create specialized waveforms to be used in digital control and sequencing circuits. A popular general-purpose repetitive waveform generator is the Johnson shift counter, whose operation is explained in detail in Chapter 13. For now, all we need is the output waveforms from it so that we may use them to create our own, specialized waveforms.

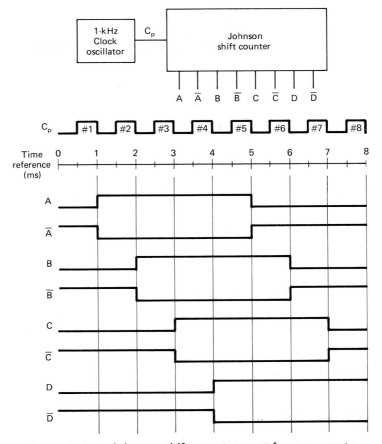

Figure 4–17 Johnson shift counter waveform generator.

The Johnson shift counter that we will use outputs eight separate repetitive waveforms: A, B, C, D and their complements, $\overline{A}$, $\overline{B}$, $\overline{C}$, $\overline{D}$. The input to the Johnson shift counter is a clock oscillator (C_p). Figure 4–17 shows a Johnson shift counter with its input and output waveforms.

The clock oscillator produces the C_p waveform, which is input to the Johnson shift counter. The shift counter uses C_p and internal circuitry to generate the eight repetitive output waveforms shown.

Now, if one of those waveforms is exactly what you want, you are all set. But let's say we need a waveform that is HIGH for 3 ms, from 2 until 5 on the millisecond time reference scale. Looking at Figure 4–17, we can see that that waveform is not available.

Using some logic gates, however, will enable us to get any waveform that we desire. In this case, if we feed the A and B waveforms into an AND gate, we will get our HIGH level from 2 to 5 as shown in Figure 4–18.

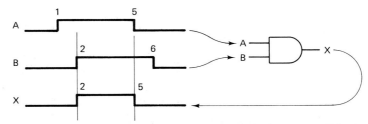

Figure 4–18 Generating a 3-ms HIGH pulse using an AND gate and a Johnson shift counter.

Working through the following examples will help you understand logic gate operation and waveform generation.

EXAMPLE 4–6

Which Johnson counter outputs will you connect to an AND gate to get a 1-ms HIGH-level output from 4 ms to 5 ms?

Solution: Referring to Figure 4–17, we see that the two waveforms which are *both* HIGH from 4 to 5 ms are A and D; therefore, the circuit of Figure 4–19 will give us the required output.

Figure 4–19 Solution to Example 4–6.

EXAMPLE 4–7

Which Johnson counter outputs must be connected to a three-input AND gate to enable just the C_p 4 pulse to be output?

Solution: Referring to Figure 4–17, we see that the C and $\overline{D}$ waveforms are both HIGH only during the C_p 4 *period*. To get just the C_p 4 *pulse*, you must provide C_p as the third input. Now when you look at all three input waveforms, you will see that they are all HIGH only during the C_p 4 *pulse* (see Figure 4–20).

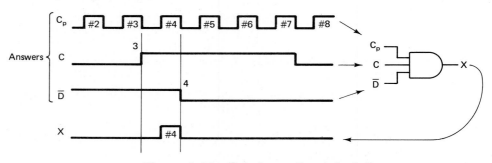

Figure 4–20 Solution to Example 4–7.

EXAMPLE 4–8

Sketch the output waveform that will result from inputting A, $\overline{B}$, and $\overline{C}$ into the three-input OR gate shown in Figure 4–21.

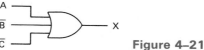

Figure 4–21

Solution: The output of an OR gate is always HIGH unless *all* inputs are LOW. Therefore, the output is always HIGH except between 5 and 6, as shown in Figure 4–22.

Figure 4–22 Solution to Example 4–8.

EXAMPLE 4-9

Sketch the output waveform that will result from inputting C_p, $\overline{B}$, and C into the NAND gate shown in Figure 4-23.

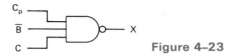

Figure 4-23

Solution: From reviewing the truth table of a NAND gate we determine that the output is always HIGH unless *all* inputs are HIGH. Therefore, the output will always be HIGH except during pulse 7, as shown in Figure 4-24.

Figure 4-24 Solution to Example 4-9.

EXAMPLE 4-10

Sketch the output waveforms that will result from inputting A, B, and D into the NOR gate shown in Figure 4-25.

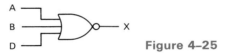

Figure 4-25

Solution: Reviewing the truth table for a NOR gate, we determine that the output is always LOW except when ALL inputs are LOW. Therefore, the output will always be LOW except from 0 to 1, as shown in Figure 4-26.

Figure 4-26 Solution to Example 4-10.

EXAMPLE 4-11

Sketch the output waveforms for the gates shown in Figure 4-27. The inputs are connected to the Johnson shift counter of Figure 4-17.

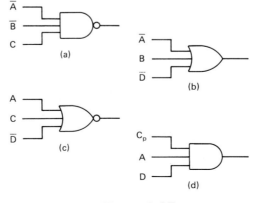

Figure 4-27

Solution: The output waveforms are shown in Figure 4–28.

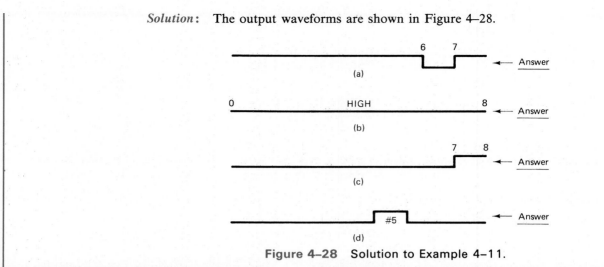

Figure 4–28   Solution to Example 4–11.

EXAMPLE 4–12

Determine which shift counter waveforms from Figure 4–17 will produce the output waveforms shown in Figure 4–29.

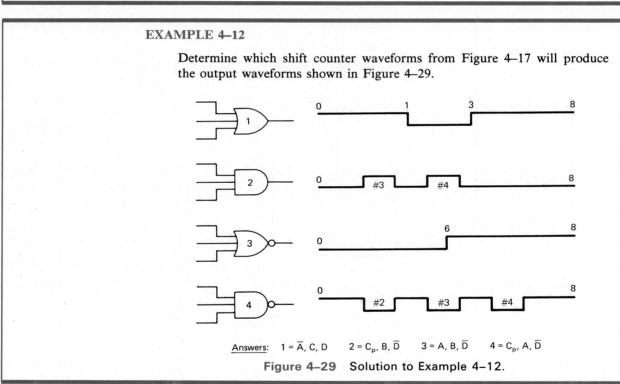

Answers: $1 = \overline{A}, C, D$ $2 = C_p, B, \overline{D}$ $3 = A, B, \overline{D}$ $4 = C_p, A, \overline{D}$

Figure 4–29   Solution to Example 4–12.

EXAMPLE 4–13

By using combinations of gates, we can obtain more specialized waveforms. Sketch the output waveforms for the circuit shown in Figure 4–30.

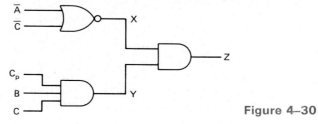

Figure 4–30

Solution: The output waveforms are shown in Figure 4–31.

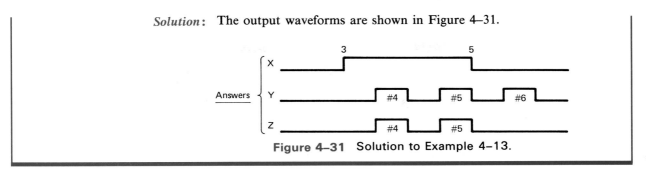

Figure 4–31 Solution to Example 4–13.

EXAMPLE 4–14

Sketch the output waveforms for the circuit shown in Figure 4–32.

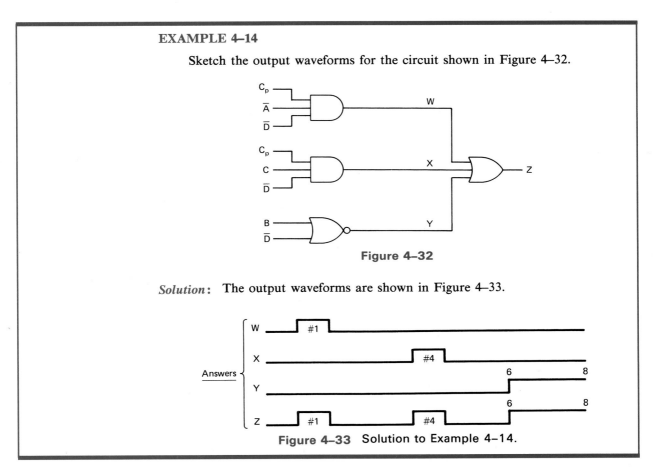

Figure 4–32

Solution: The output waveforms are shown in Figure 4–33.

Figure 4–33 Solution to Example 4–14.

4–5 USING INTEGRATED-CIRCUIT LOGIC GATES

All the logic gates are available in various configurations in the TTL and CMOS families. To list just a few: The 7404 TTL and the 4049 CMOS are hex (six) inverter ICs, the 7400 TTL and the 4011 CMOS are quad (four) two-input NAND ICs, and the 7402 TTL and the 4001 CMOS are quad two-input NOR ICs. Other popular NAND and NORs are available in three-input, four-input, and eight-input configurations. Consult a TTL or CMOS data manual for availability and pin configuration of those ICs. The pin configurations for the hex inverter, the quad NOR, and the quad NAND are given in Figures 4–34 and 4–35. (High-speed CMOS 74HC04, 74HC00, and 74HC02 have the same pin configuration as the TTL ICs.)

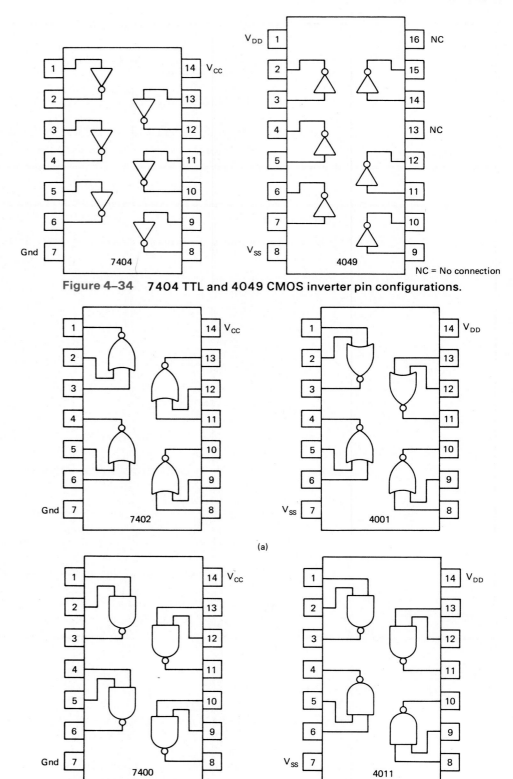

Figure 4–34   7404 TTL and 4049 CMOS inverter pin configurations.

(a)

(b)

Figure 4–35   (a) 7402 TTL NOR and 4001 CMOS NOR pin configurations; (b) 7400 TTL NAND and 4011 CMOS NAND pin configurations.

EXAMPLE 4–15

Draw the external connections to a 4011 CMOS IC to form the circuit shown in Figure 4–36.

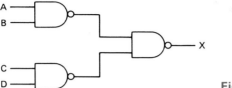

Figure 4–36

Solution: Referring to Figure 4–37, notice that V_{DD} is connected to the +5 V supply and V_{SS} to ground. According to the CMOS data manual, V_{DD} can be any positive voltage from +3 to +15 V with respect to V_{SS} (usually ground).

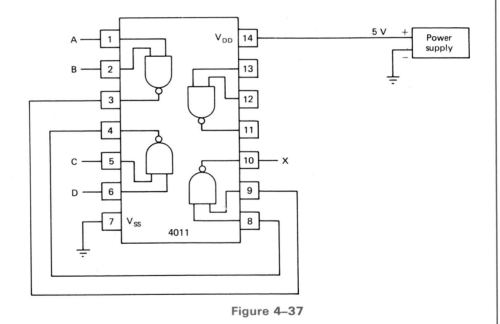

Figure 4–37

4–6 SUMMARY OF LOGIC GATE OPERATION

By now you should have a thorough understanding of the basic logic gates: inverter, AND, OR, NAND, and NOR. In Chapter 5 we will be combining several gates together to form complex logic functions. Since the basic logic gates are the building blocks for larger-scale integrated circuits and digital systems, it is very important that the operation of these gates is second nature to you.

A summary of the basic logic gates is given in Figure 4–38. You should memorize those logic symbols, Boolean equations, and truth tables. Also, a table of the most common integrated-circuit gates in the TTL and CMOS families is given in Table 4–4. You will need to refer to a TTL or CMOS data book for the pin layout and specifications.

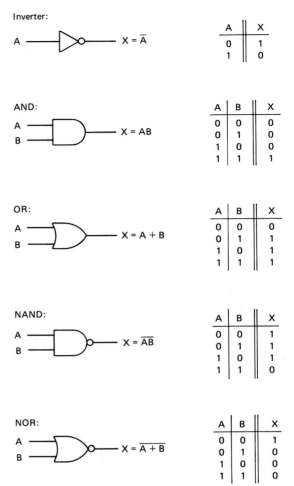

Figure 4–38 Summary of logic gates, Boolean equations, and truth tables.

TABLE 4–4

Common IC Gates in the TTL and CMOS Families

Gate name	Number of inputs per gate	Number of gates per chip	Part number		
			Standard TTL	Standard CMOS	High-speed CMOS
Inverter	1	6	7404	4069	74HC04
AND	2	4	7408	4081	74HC08
	3	3	7411	4073	74HC11
	4	2	7421	4082	—
OR	2	4	7432	4071	74HC32
	3	3	—	4075	74HC4075
	4	2	—	4072	—
NAND	2	4	7400	4011	74HC00
	3	3	7410	4013	74HC10
	4	2	7420	4012	74HC20
	8	1	7430	4068	—
	12	1	74134	—	—
	13	1	74133	—	—
NOR	2	4	7402	4001	74HC02
	3	3	7427	4025	74HC27
	4	2	7425	4002	74HC4002
	5	2	74260	—	—
	8	1	—	4078	—

GLOSSARY

Complement: A change to the opposite digital state. A 1 becomes a 0, a 0 becomes a 1.

Hex: When dealing with integrated circuits, this term specifies that there are *six* gates on a single IC package.

Inversion: A change to the opposite digital state.

Inversion bar: A line over variables in a Boolean equation signifying that the digital state of the variables is to be complemented. For example, the output of a two-input NAND gate is written $X = \overline{AB}$.

Johnson shift counter: A digital circuit that produces several repetitive digital waveforms useful for specialized waveform generation.

NOT: When reading a Boolean equation, the word "NOT" is used to signify an inversion bar. For example, the equation $X = \overline{AB}$ would read "X equals NOT AB."

Quad: When dealing with integrated circuits, this term specifies that there are *four* gates on a single IC package.

Repetitive waveform: A waveform that repeats itself after each cycle.

Waveform generation: The production of specialized digital waveforms.

REVIEW QUESTIONS

Sections 4–1 through 4–3

4–1. What is the purpose of an inverter in a digital circuit?

4–2. How does a NAND gate differ from an AND gate?

4–3. The output of a NAND gate is always HIGH unless *all* inputs are made _____ (HIGH, LOW).

4–4. Write the Boolean Equation for a three-input NOR gate.

Sections 4–4 through 4–6

4–5. What is the function of the Johnson shift counter in this chapter?

4–6. What are the part numbers of a TTL inverter IC and A CMOS NOR IC?

4–7. What type of logic gate is contained within the 7410 IC?, the 74HC27 IC?

PROBLEMS

4–1. For Figure P4–1, write the Boolean equation at X. If $A = 1$, what is X?

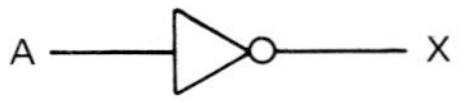

Figure P4–1

4–2. For Figure P4–2, write the Boolean equation at X and Z. If $A = 0$, what is X? What is Z?

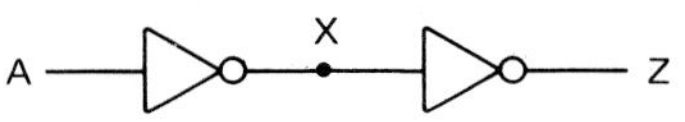

Figure P4–2

4–3. Using Figure P4–2, sketch the output waveform at X and   if the timing waveform shown in Figure P4–3 is input at A.

Figure P4–3

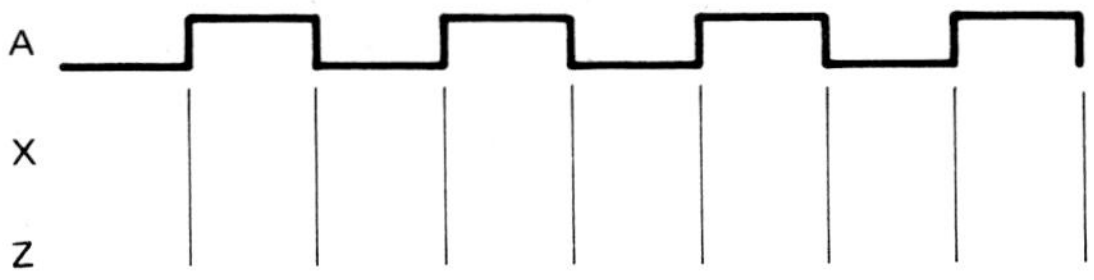

4–4. For Figure P4–4, write the Boolean equation at X and Y.

Figure P4–4

4–5. Build a truth table for each gate in Figure P4–4.

4–6. Using Figure P4–4, sketch the output waveforms for X and Y given the input waveforms shown in Figure P4–6.

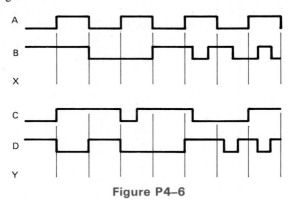

Figure P4–6

4–7. Using Figure P4–7, sketch the waveforms at X and Y with the switches in the down (0) position. Repeat with the switches in the up (1) position.

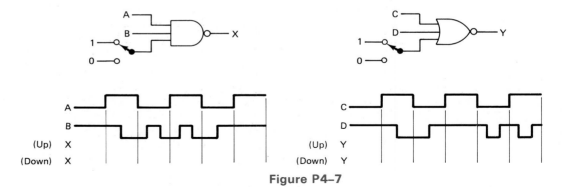

Figure P4–7

4–8. In words, what effect does the switch have on each circuit in Figure P4–7?

4–9. For Figure P4–9, write the Boolean equation at X and Y.

Figure P4–9

4–10. Make a truth table for the first NOR gate in Figure P4–9.

4–11. Refering to Figure P4–9, sketch the output at X and Y given the input waveforms in Figure P4–11.

Figure P4–11

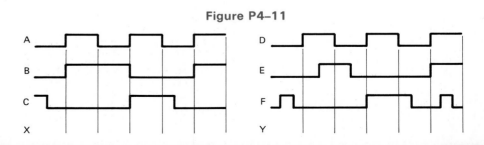

4–12. The Johnson shift counter outputs shown in Figure 4–17 are connected to the inputs of the logic gates shown in Figure P4–12. Sketch and label the output waveform at U, V, W, X, Y, and Z.

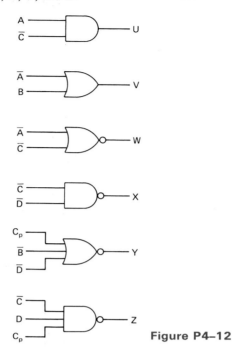

Figure P4–12

4–13. Repeat Problem 4–12 for the gates shown in Figure P4–13.

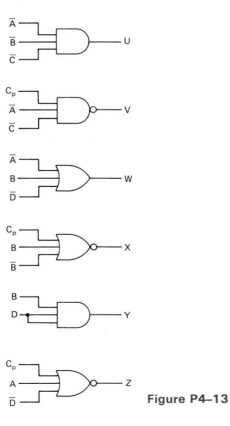

Figure P4–13

4–14. Using the Johnson shift counter outputs from Figure 4–17, label the inputs to the logic gates shown in Figure P4–14 so that they will produce the indicted output.

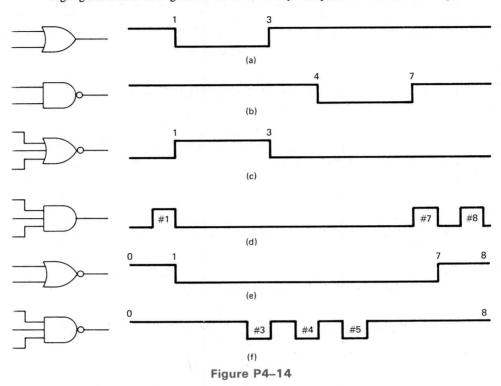

Figure P4–14

4–15. Determine which lines from the Johnson shift counter are required at the inputs of the circuits shown in Figure P4–15 to produce the waveforms at U, V, W, and X.

4–16. The waveforms at U, V, W, and X are given in Figure P4–15. Sketch the waveforms at Y and Z.

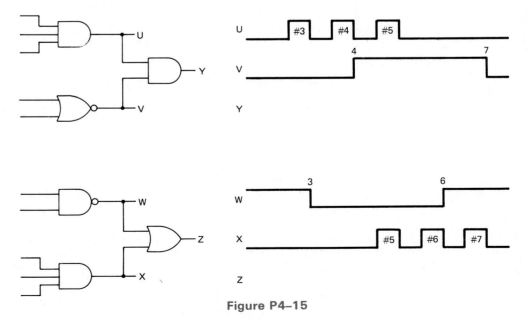

Figure P4–15

4–17. Make the external connections to a 7404 inverter IC and a 7402 NOR IC to implement the function $X = \overline{\overline{A} + B}$.

Troubleshooting

4–18. When troubleshooting a NOR gate like the 7402, with the logic pulser applied to one input, should the other input be held HIGH or LOW? Why?

4–19. When troubleshooting a NAND gate like the 7400, with the logic pulser applied to one input, should the other input be held HIGH or LOW? Why?

4–20. The following data table was built by putting a logic probe on every pin of the hex inverter shown in Figure P4–20. Are there any problems with the chip? If so, which gate(s) are bad?

Pin	Logic level
1	HIGH
2	LOW
3	LOW
4	LOW
5	LOW
6	HIGH
7	LOW
8	HIGH
9	LOW
10	LOW
11	LOW
12	LOW
13	HIGH
14	HIGH

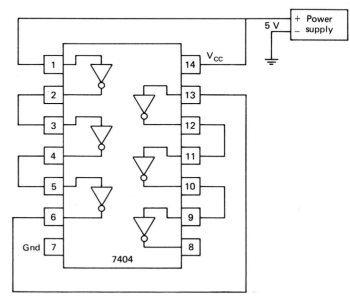

Figure P4–20

4–21. The logic probe in Figure P4–21 is always OFF (0) whether the switch is in the up position or the down position. Is the problem with the inverter, the NOR, or is there no problem?

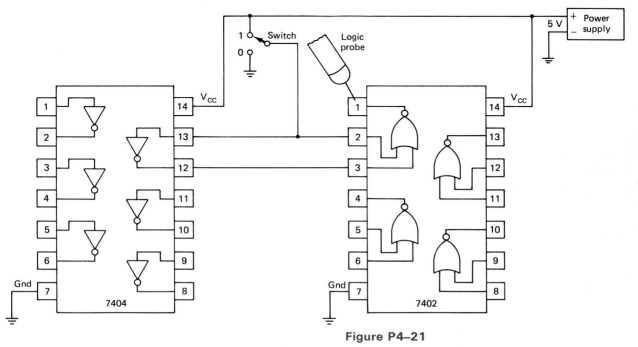

Figure P4–21

4–22. Another circuit constructed the same way as Figure P4–21 causes the logic probe to come on when the switch is in the down (0) position. Further testing with the probe shows that pins 2 and 3 of the NOR IC are both LOW. Is anything wrong? If so, where is the fault?

4–23. Your company has purchased several of the 7430 eight-input NANDS shown in Figure P4–23. List the steps that you would follow to determine if they are all good ICs.

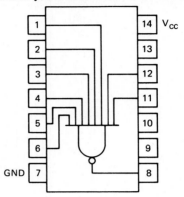

4–24. The following data table was built by putting a logic probe on every pin of the 7427 NOR IC shown in Figure P4–24 while it was connected in a digital circuit. Which gates, if any, are bad, and why?

Pin	Logic level
1	LOW
2	LOW
3	LOW
4	LOW
5	LOW
6	HIGH
7	LOW
8	Flashing
9	HIGH
10	LOW
11	Flashing
12	HIGH
13	HIGH
14	HIGH

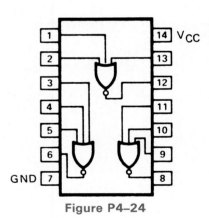

Figure P4–24

5

Boolean Algebra and Reduction Techniques

OBJECTIVES

Upon completion of this chapter, you should be able to:

- Write Boolean equations for combinational logic applications.
- Utilize Boolean algebra laws and rules for simplifying combinational logic circuits.
- Apply DeMorgan's theorem to complex Boolean equations to arrive at simplified equivalent equations.
- Design single-gate logic circuits by utilizing the universal capability of NAND and NOR gates.
- Troubleshoot combinational logic circuits.
- Implement sum-of-products expressions utilizing AND–OR–INVERT gates.
- Utilize the Karnaugh mapping procedure to systematically reduce complex Boolean equations to their simplest form.
- Describe the steps involved in solving a complete system design application.

INTRODUCTION

Generally you will find that the simple gate functions AND, OR, NAND, NOR, and INVERT by themselves are not enough to implement the complex requirements of digital systems. The basic gates will be used as the building blocks for the more complex logic that is implemented by using combinations of gates called *combinational logic*.

5-1 COMBINATIONAL LOGIC

Combinational logic employs the use of two or more of the basic logic gates to form a more useful, complex function. For example, let's design the logic for an automobile warning buzzer using combinational logic. The criterion for the activation of the warning buzzer is as follows: The buzzer will activate if the headlights are on *and* and driver's door is opened, *or* if the key is in the ignition *and* the door is opened.

The logic function for the automobile warning buzzer is illustrated symbolically in Figure 5–1. The figure illustrates a "combination" of logic functions that can be written as a Boolean equation in the form

$$B = K \text{ and } D \quad \text{or} \quad H \text{ and } D$$

also written as

$$B = KD + HD$$

That equation can be stated: *B* is HIGH if *K and D* are HIGH, *or* if *H and D* are HIGH.

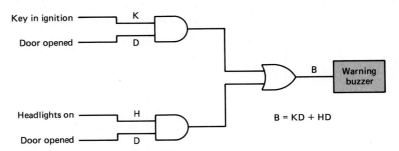

Figure 5–1   Combinational logic requirements for an automobile warning buzzer.

When you think about the operation of the warning buzzer, you may realize that it is activated whenever the door is opened *and* either the key is in the ignition *or* the headlights are on. If you can realize that, you have just performed your first *Boolean reduction* using Boolean algebra. (The systematic reduction of logic circuits is performed using Boolean algebra, named after the nineteenth-century mathematician George Boole.)

The new Boolean equation becomes $B = D$ and (K or H), also written as $B = D(K + H)$. (Notice the use of parentheses. Without them, the equation would imply that the buzzer activates if the door is opened with the key in the ignition or any time the headlights are on, which is invalid. $B \neq DK + H$.) The new equation represents the same logic operation but is a simplified implementation because it requires only two logic gates, as shown in Figure 5–2.

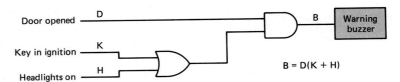

Figure 5–2   Reduced logic circuit for the automobile buzzer.

EXAMPLE 5–1

Write the Boolean logic equation and draw the logic circuit that represent the following function: A bank burglar alarm (A) is to activate if it is after banking hours (H) *and* the front door (F) is opened, *or* if it is after banking hours (H) and the vault door is opened (V).

Solution: $A = HF + HV$. The logic circuit is shown in Figure 5–3.

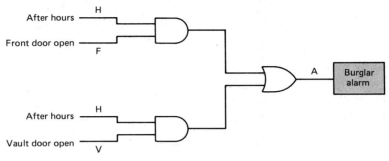

Figure 5–3 Solution to Example 5–1.

EXAMPLE 5–2

Using common reasoning, reduce the logic function described in Example 5–1 to a simpler form.

Solution: The alarm is activated if it is after banking hours *and* the front door is opened *or* the vault door is opened (see Figure 5–4). The simplified equation is written as

$$A = H(F + V) \qquad \text{(notice the use of parentheses)}$$

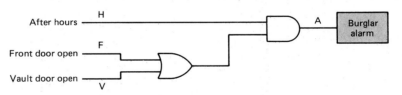

Figure 5–4 Solution to Example 5–2.

EXAMPLE 5–3

Draw the logic circuit that could be used to implement the following Boolean equation:

$$X = AB + C(M + N)$$

Solution: The logic circuit is shown in Figure 5–5.

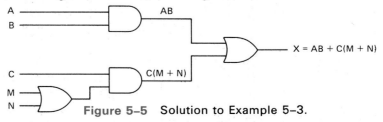

Figure 5–5 Solution to Example 5–3.

EXAMPLE 5–4

Write the Boolean equation for the logic circuit shown in Figure 5–6.

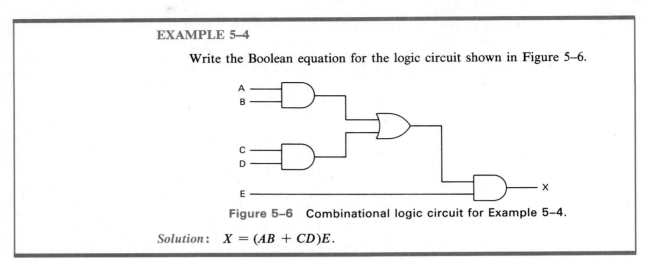

Figure 5–6   Combinational logic circuit for Example 5–4.

Solution: $X = (AB + CD)E$.

5–2   BOOLEAN ALGEBRA LAWS AND RULES

Boolean algebra uses many of the same laws as those of ordinary algebra. The OR function ($X = A + B$) is *Boolean addition* and the AND function ($X = AB$) is *Boolean multiplication*. The following three laws are the same for Boolean algebra as they are for ordinary algebra:

1. *The commutative law of addition*: $A + B = B + A$, *and multiplication*: $AB = BA$. This means that the order of ORing or ANDing does not matter.
2. *The associative law of addition*: $A + (B + C) = (A + B) + C$, *and multiplication*: $A(BC) = (AB)C$. This means that the grouping of several variables ORed or ANDed together does not matter.
3. *The distributive law*: $A(B + C) = AB + AC$, *and*, $(A + B)(C + D) = AC + AD + BC + BD$. This shows the method for expanding an equation containing ORs and ANDs.

Those three laws hold true for any number of variables. For example, the associative law can be applied to $X = A + BC + D$ to form the equivalent equation, $X = BC + A + D$.

You may wonder when you will need to use one of the laws. Later in this chapter you will see that by using these laws to rearrange Boolean equations, you will be able to change some combinational logic circuits to simpler equivalent circuits using fewer gates. You can gain a better understanding of the application of these laws by studying Figures 5–7 to 5–12.

Figure 5–7   Using the commutative law of addition to rearrange an OR gate.

Figure 5–8   Using the commutative law of multiplication to rearrange an AND gate.

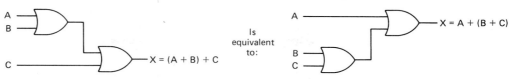

Figure 5-9 Using the associative law of addition to rearrange the grouping of OR gates.

Figure 5-10 Using the associative law of multiplication to rearrange the grouping of AND gates.

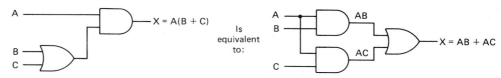

Figure 5-11 Using the distributive law to form an equivalent circuit.

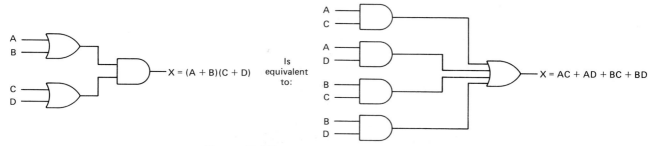

Figure 5-12 Using the distributive law to form an equivalent circuit.

Besides the three basic laws, there are several rules concerning Boolean algebra. The rules of Boolean algebra allow us to combine or eliminate certain variables in the equation to form simpler equivalent circuits.

The following example illustrates the use of the first Boolean rule, which states: Anything ANDed with a 0 will always output a 0.

EXAMPLE 5-5

A bank burglar alarm (B) will activate if it is after banking hours (A) and someone opens the front door (D). The logic level of the variable A is 1 after banking hours and 0 during banking hours. Also, the logic level of the variable D is 1 if the door sensing switch is opened and 0 if the door sensing switch is closed. The Boolean equation is therefore $B = AD$. The logic circuit to implement this function is shown in Figure 5-13a.

Figure 5-13 (a) Logic circuit for a simple burglar alarm; (b) disabling the burglar alarm by making $D = 0$.

> Later, a burglar comes along and puts tape on the door sensing switch, holding it closed so that it always puts out a 0 logic level. Now the Boolean equation ($B = AD$) becomes $B = A \cdot 0$ because the door sensing switch is always 0. The alarm will never sound in this condition because one input to the AND gate is always 0. The burglar must have studied the Boolean rules and realized that anything ANDed with a 0 will output a 0, as shown in Figure 5–13b.

Example 5–5 helped illustrate the reasoning for Boolean rule 1. The other nine rules can be derived using common sense and knowing basic gate operation.

Rule 1:   Anything ANDed with a 0 is equal to 0 ($A \cdot 0 = 0$).

Rule 2:   Anything ANDed with a 1 is equal to itself ($A \cdot 1 = A$). From Figure 5–14 we can see that with one input tied to a 1, if the A input is 0, the X output is 0; if A is 1, X is 1; therefore, X is equal to whatever the logic level of A is ($X = A$).

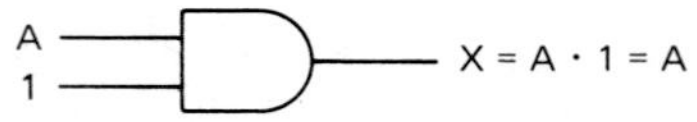

Figure 5–14   Logic circuit illustrating Rule 2.

Rule 3:   Anything ORed with a 0 is equal to itself ($A + 0 = A$). In Figure 5–15, since one input is always 0, if $A = 1$, $X = 1$, and if $A = 0$, $X = 0$; therefore, X is equal to whatever the logic level of A is ($X = A$).

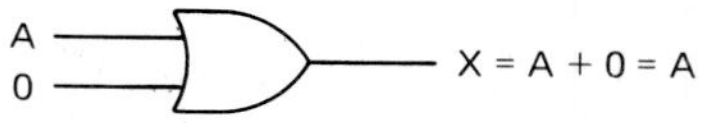

Figure 5–15   Logic circuit illustrating Rule 3.

Rule 4:   Anything ORed with a 1 is equal to 1 ($A + 1 = 1$). In Figure 5–16, since one input to the OR gate is always 1, the output will always be 1, no matter what A is ($X = 1$).

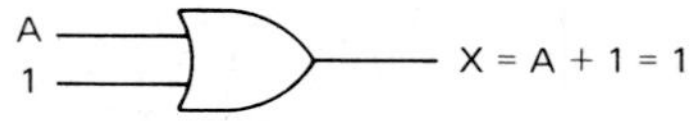

Figure 5–16   Logic circuit illustrating Rule 4.

Rule 5:   Anything ANDed with itself is equal to itself ($A \cdot A = A$). In Figure 5–17, since both inputs to the AND gate are A, if $A = 1$, 1 and 1 equals 1, and if $A = 0$, 0 and 0 equals 0. Therefore, X will be equal to whatever the logic level of A is ($X = A$).

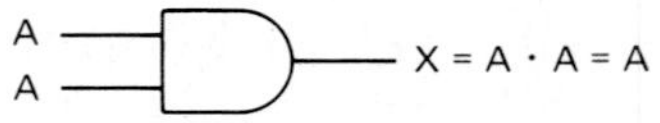

Figure 5–17   Logic circuit illustrating Rule 5.

Rule 6:   Anything ORed with itself is equal to itself ($A + A = A$). In Figure 5–18, since both inputs to the OR gate are A, if $A = 1$, 1 or 1 equals 1, and if $A = 0$, 0 or 0 equals 0. Therefore, X will be equal to whatever the logic level of A is ($X = A$).

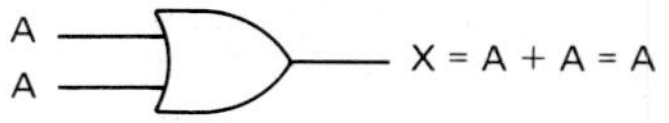

Figure 5–18   Logic circuit illustrating Rule 6.

Rule 7:   Anything ANDed with its own complement equals 0. In Figure 5–19, since the inputs are complements of each other, one of them will always be 0. With a zero at the input, the output will always be 0 ($X = 0$).

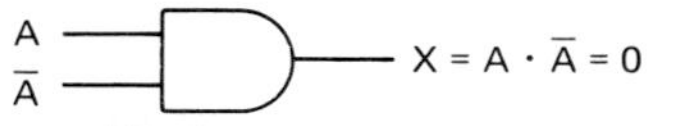

$$A \quad \rightarrow\!\!\supset\!\!- \quad X = A \cdot \overline{A} = 0$$

Figure 5–19 Logic circuit illustrating Rule 7.

Rule 8: Anything ORed with its own complement equals 1. In Figure 5–20, since the inputs are complements of each other, one of them will always be 1. With a 1 at the input, the output will always be 1 ($X = 1$).

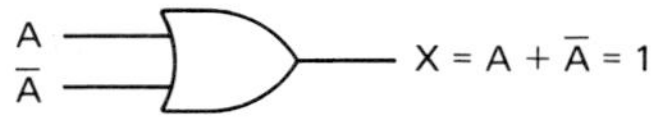

$$\overline{A} \quad \rightarrow\!\!\!\supset\!\!\!- \quad X = A + \overline{A} = 1$$

Figure 5–20 Logic circuit illustrating Rule 8.

Rule 9: A variable that is complemented twice will return to its original logic level. As shown in Figure 5–21, when a variable is complemented once, it changes to the opposite logic level. When it is complemented a second time, it changes back to its original logic level ($\overline{\overline{A}} = A$).

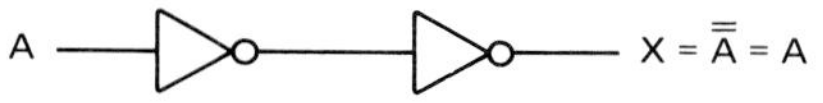

$$A \quad \rightarrow\!\!\triangleright\!\!\circ\!\!- \rightarrow\!\!\triangleright\!\!\circ\!\!- \quad X = \overline{\overline{A}} = A$$

Figure 5–21 Logic circuit illustrating Rule 9.

Rule 10: $A + \overline{A}B = A + B$ and $\overline{A} + AB = \overline{A} + B$. This rule differs from the others because it involves two variables. It is useful because when an equation is in this form, one variable in the second term can be eliminated. Proof of this rule is performed very simply by using a Karnaugh map, which will be done in Section 5–7.

Table 5–1 summarizes the laws and rules that relate to Boolean algebra. By using them, we can reduce complicated combinational logic circuits to their simplest form, as we will see in the next sections.

TABLE 5–1

Boolean Laws and Rules for the Reduction of Combinational Logic Circuits

Laws	
1	$A + B = B + A$
	$AB = BA$
2	$A + (B + C) = (A + B) + C$
	$A(BC) = (AB)C$
3	$A(B + C) = AB + AC$
	$(A + B)(C + D) = AC + AD + BC + BD$
Rules	
1	$A \cdot 0 = 0$
2	$A \cdot 1 = A$
3	$A + 0 = A$
4	$A + 1 = 1$
5	$A \cdot A = A$
6	$A + A = A$
7	$A \cdot \overline{A} = 0$
8	$A + \overline{A} = 1$
9	$\overline{\overline{A}} = A$
10	$A + \overline{A}B = A + B$
	$\overline{A} + AB = \overline{A} + B$

5–3 SIMPLIFICATION OF COMBINATIONAL LOGIC CIRCUITS USING BOOLEAN ALGEBRA

Quite often in the design and development of digital systems, a designer will start with simple logic gate requirements but add more and more complex gating, making the final design a complex combination of several gates, some having the same inputs.

At that point the designer must step back and review the combinational logic circuit that has been developed and see if there are ways of reducing the number of gates without changing the function of the circuit. If an equivalent circuit can be formed with fewer gates, the cost of the circuit is reduced and its reliability is improved. This process is called the *reduction* or *simplification of combinational logic circuits* and is performed by using the laws and rules of Boolean algebra presented in the preceding section.

The following examples illustrate the use of Boolean algebra and present some techniques for the simplification of logic circuits.

EXAMPLE 5–6

The logic circuit shown in Figure 5–22 is used to turn on a warning buzzer at X based on the input conditions at A, B, and C. A simplified equivalent circuit that will perform the same function can be formed by using Boolean algebra. Write the equation of the circuit in Figure 5–22, simplify the equation, and draw the logic circuit of the simplified equation.

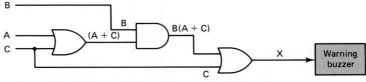

Figure 5–22   Logic circuit for Example 5–6.

Solution: The Boolean equation for X is

$$X = B(A + C) + C$$

To simplify, first apply Law 3 $[B(A + C) = BA + BC]$:

$$X = BA + BC + C$$

Next, factor a C from terms 2 and 3:

$$X = BA + C(B + 1)$$

Apply Rule 4 $(B + 1 = 1)$:

$$X = BA + C \cdot 1$$

Apply Rule 2 $(C \cdot 1 = C)$:

$$X = BA + C$$

Apply Law 1 $(BA + AB)$:

$$X = AB + C \leftarrow \text{simplified equation}$$

The logic circuit of the simplified equation is shown in Figure 5–23.

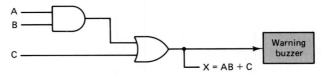

Figure 5–23   Simplified logic circuit for Example 5–6.

EXAMPLE 5–7

Repeat Example 5–6 for the logic circuit shown in Figure 5–24.

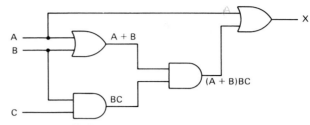

Figure 5–24   Logic circuit for Example 5–7.

Solution: The Boolean equation for X is

$$X = (A + B)BC + A$$

To simplify, first apply Law 3 $[(A + B)BC = ABC + BBC]$:

$$X = ABC + BBC + A$$

Apply Rule 5 ($B \cdot B = B$):

$$X = ABC + BC + A$$

Factor a BC from terms 1 and 2:

$$X = BC(A + 1) + A$$

Apply Rule 4 ($A + 1 = 1$):

$$X = BC \cdot 1 + A$$

Apply Rule 2 ($BC \cdot 1 = BC$):

$$X = BC + A \leftarrow \text{simplified equation}$$

The logic circuit for the simplified equation is shown in Figure 5–25.

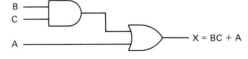

$X = BC + A$ Figure 5–25   Simplified logic circuit for Example 5–7.

EXAMPLE 5–8

Repeat Example 5–6 for the logic circuit shown in Figure 5–26.

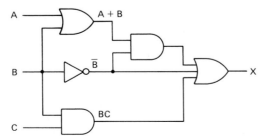

Figure 5–26   Logic circuit for Example 5–8.

Solution: The Boolean equation for X is

$$X = (A + B)\bar{B} + \bar{B} + BC$$

To simplify, first apply Law 3 $[(A + B)\bar{B} = A\bar{B} + B\bar{B}]$:

$$X = A\bar{B} + B\bar{B} + \bar{B} + BC$$

Apply Rule 7 ($B\bar{B} = 0$):

$$X = A\bar{B} + 0 + \bar{B} + BC$$

Apply Rule 3 ($A\bar{B} + 0 = A\bar{B}$):

$$X = A\bar{B} + \bar{B} + BC$$

Factor a $\bar{B}$ from terms 1 and 2:

$$X = \bar{B}(A + 1) + BC$$

Apply Rule 4 ($A + 1 = 1$):

$$X = \bar{B} \cdot 1 + BC$$

Apply Rule 2 ($\bar{B} \cdot 1 = \bar{B}$):

$$X = \bar{B} + BC$$

Apply Rule 10 ($\bar{B} + BC = \bar{B} + C$):

$$X = \bar{B} + C \leftarrow \text{simplified equation}$$

The logic circuit of the simplified equation is shown in Figure 5–27.

Figure 5–27 Simplified logic circuit for Example 5–8.

EXAMPLE 5–9

Repeat Example 5–6 for the logic circuit shown in Figure 5–28.

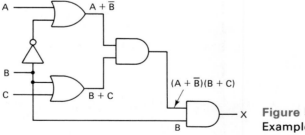

Figure 5–28 Logic circuit for Example 5–9.

Solution: The Boolean equation for X is

$$X = [(A + \bar{B})(B + C)]B$$

To simplify, first apply Law 3:

$$X = (AB + AC + \bar{B}B + \bar{B}C)B$$

The $\bar{B}B$ term can be eliminated using Rule 7, then Rule 3:

$$X = (AB + AC + \bar{B}C)B$$

Apply Law 3 again:

$$X = ABB + ACB + \overline{B}CB$$

Apply Law 1:

$$X = ABB + ABC + \overline{B}BC$$

Apply Rule 5 and Rule 7:

$$X = AB + ABC + 0 \cdot C$$

Apply Rule 1:

$$X = AB + ABC$$

Factor an AB from both terms:

$$X = AB(1 + C)$$

Apply Rule 4, then Rule 2:

$$X = AB \leftarrow \text{simplified equation}$$

The logic circuit of the simplified equation is shown in Figure 5–29.

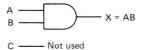

Figure 5–29 Simplified logic circuit for Example 5–9.

5–4 DeMORGAN'S THEOREM

You may have noticed that we did not use NANDs or NORs in any of the logic circuits in Section 5–3. In order to simplify circuits containing NANDs and NORs, we need to use a theorem developed by the mathematician DeMorgan. This theorem allows us to convert an expression having an inversion bar over two or more variables into an expression having inversion bars over single variables only. That allows us to use the rules presented in the preceding section for the simplification of the equation.

In the form of an equation, DeMorgan's theorem is stated as follows:

$$\overline{A \cdot B} = \overline{A} + \overline{B}$$
$$\overline{A + B} = \overline{A} \cdot \overline{B}$$

Also, for three or more variables,

$$\overline{A \cdot B \cdot C} = \overline{A} + \overline{B} + \overline{C}$$
$$\overline{A + B + C} = \overline{A} \cdot \overline{B} \cdot \overline{C}$$

Basically, to use the theorem, you break the bar over the variables and either change the AND to an OR or change the OR to an AND.

To prove to ourselves that this works, let's apply the theorem to a NAND gate and then compare the truth table of the equivalent circuit to that of the original NAND gate. As you can see in Figure 5–30, to use DeMorgan's theorem on a NAND gate, first break the bar over the $A \cdot B$, then change the AND symbol to an OR. The new equation becomes $X = \overline{A} + \overline{B}$. Notice that inversion bubbles are used on the OR gate instead of using inverters. By observing the truth tables of the two

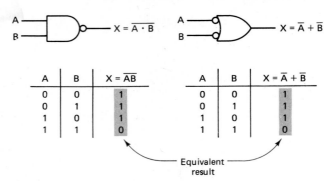

Figure 5–30 DeMorgan's theorem applied to a NAND gate produces two identical truth tables.

equations, we can see that the result in the X column is the same for both, which proves that they provide an equivalent output result.

Also, by looking at the two circuits we can say that "an AND gate with its output inverted is equivalent to an OR gate with its inputs inverted." Therefore, the OR gate with inverted inputs is sometimes used as an alternative symbol for a NAND gate.

By applying DeMorgan's theorem to a NOR gate, we will also produce two identical truth tables, as shown in Figure 5–31a. Therefore, we can also think of an OR gate with its output inverted as being equivalent to an AND gate with its inputs inverted. The inverted input AND gate symbol is also sometimes used as an alternative to the NOR gate symbol.

When you write the equation for an AND gate with its inputs inverted, be careful to keep the inversion bar over each individual variable (not both) because $\overline{A \cdot B}$ is not equal to $\overline{A} \cdot \overline{B}$. (Prove that to yourself by building a truth table for both. Also, $\overline{A + B}$ is not equal to $\overline{A} + \overline{B}$.)

The question always arises: Why would a designer ever use an *inverted-input-OR-gate* symbol instead of a NAND? Or, why use an *inverted-input-AND-gate* symbol instead of a NOR? In complex logic diagrams you will see both the inverted-input and the inverted-output symbols being used. The designer will use whichever symbol makes more sense for the particular application.

For example, referring to Figure 5–30, let's say you need a HIGH output level whenever either A or B is LOW. It makes sense to think of that function as an OR gate with inverted A and B inputs, but you could save two inverters by just using a NAND gate.

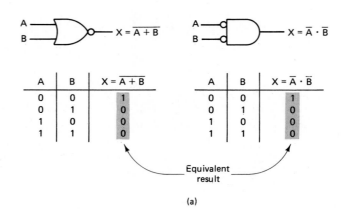

(a)

Figure 5–31 (a) DeMorgan's theorem applied to a NOR gate produces two identical truth tables;

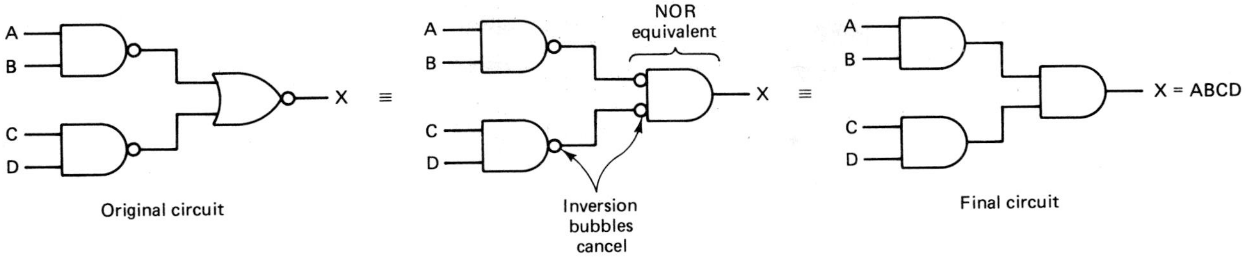

Figure 5–31 *(Continued)* (b) using the alternative NOR symbol eases circuit simplification; (c) summary of alternative gate symbols.

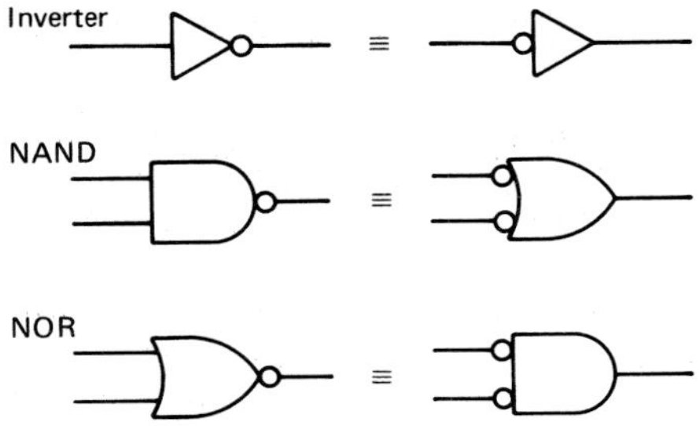

Also, referring to Figure 5–31a, let's say you need a HIGH output whenever both *A* and *B* are LOW. You would probably use the *inverted-input-AND gate* for your logic diagram because it makes sense logically, but you would use a NOR gate to actually implement the circuit because you could eliminate the inverters.

The alternative methods of drawing NANDs and NORs are also useful for the simplification of logic circuits. Take, for example, the circuit of Figure 5–31b. By changing the NOR gate to an *inverted-input-AND gate*, the inversion bubbles cancel and the equation becomes simply $X = ABCD$. Figure 5–31c summarizes the alternative representations for the inverter, NAND, and NOR gates.

The following examples illustrate the application of DeMorgan's theorem for the simplification of logic circuits.

EXAMPLE 5–10

Write the Boolean equation for the circuit shown in Figure 5–32. Use DeMorgan's theorem, then Boolean algebra rules to simplify the equation. Draw the simplified circuit.

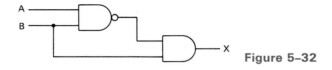

Figure 5–32

Solution: The Boolean equation at *X* is

$$X = \overline{AB} \cdot B$$

Applying DeMorgan's theorem produces

$$X = (\overline{A} + \overline{B}) \cdot B$$

(Notice the use of parentheses to maintain proper grouping.) Using Boolean algebra rules produces

$$\begin{aligned} X &= \bar{A}B + \bar{B}B \\ &= \bar{A}B + O \\ &= \bar{A}B \leftarrow \text{simplified equation} \end{aligned}$$

The simplified circuit is shown in Figure 5–33.

A
B
X = $\bar{A}$B
OR
A
B
X = $\bar{A}$B

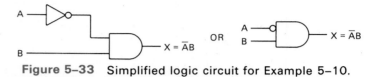

Figure 5–33 Simplified logic circuit for Example 5–10.

EXAMPLE 5–11

Repeat Example 5–10 for the circuit shown in Figure 5–34.

A
B
C
X

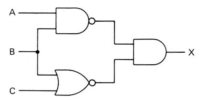

Figure 5–34

Solution: The Boolean equation at X is

$$X = \overline{AB} \cdot \overline{B + C}$$

Applying De Morgan's theorem produces

$$X = (\bar{A} + \bar{B}) \cdot \bar{B}\bar{C}$$

(Notice the use of parentheses to maintain proper grouping.) Using Boolean algebra rules produces

$$\begin{aligned} X &= \bar{A}\bar{B}\bar{C} + \bar{B}\bar{B}\bar{C} \\ &= \bar{A}\bar{B}\bar{C} + \bar{B}\bar{C} \\ &= \bar{B}\bar{C}\,(\bar{A} + 1) \\ &= \bar{B}\bar{C} \leftarrow \text{simplified equation} \end{aligned}$$

The simplified circuit is shown in Figure 5–35.

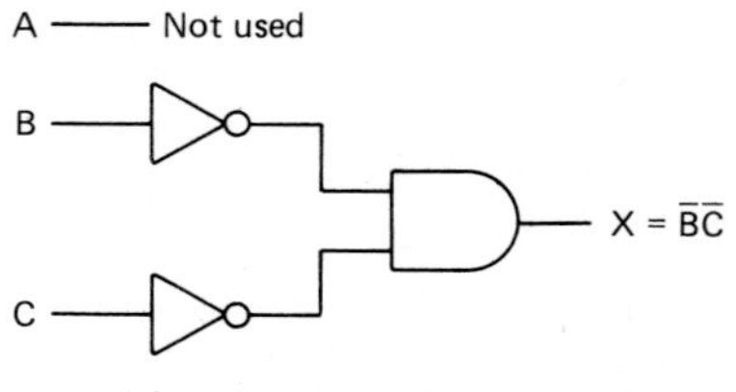

A
Not used
B
C
X = $\bar{B}\bar{C}$

Figure 5–35 Simplified logic circuit for Example 5–11.

Also remember from Figure 5–31a that an AND gate with inverted inputs is equivalent to a NOR gate. Therefore, an equivalent solution to Example 5–11 would be a NOR gate with B and C as inputs as shown in Figure 5–36.

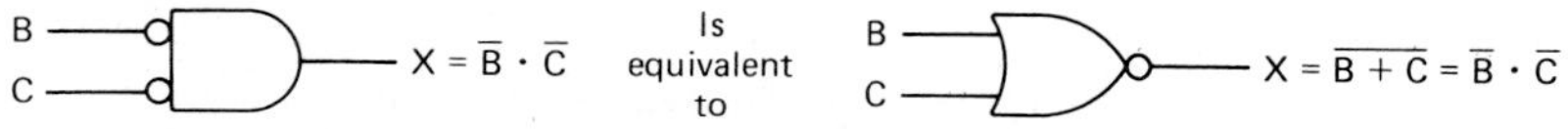

B
C
X = $\bar{B} \cdot \bar{C}$
Is equivalent to
B
C
X = $\overline{B + C} = \bar{B} \cdot \bar{C}$

Figure 5–36 Equivalent solution to Example 5–11.

EXAMPLE 5-12

Repeat Example 5-10 for the circuit shown in Figure 5-37.

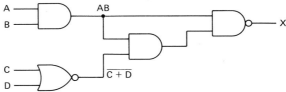

Figure 5-37

Solution:

$$X = \overline{(AB \cdot \overline{C+D}) \cdot AB}$$
$$= \overline{AB \cdot \overline{C+D}} + \overline{AB}$$
$$= \overline{AB} + \overline{\overline{C+D}} + \overline{AB}$$
$$= \overline{A} + \overline{B} + C + D + \overline{A} + \overline{B}$$
$$= \overline{A} + \overline{B} + C + D \leftarrow \text{simplified equation}$$

The simplified circuit is shown in Figure 5-38.

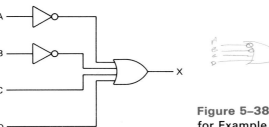

Figure 5-38   Simplified logic circuit for Example 5-12.

EXAMPLE 5-13

Use DeMorgan's theorem and Boolean algebra on the circuit shown in Figure 5-39 to develop an equivalent circuit that has inversion bars covering only single variables.

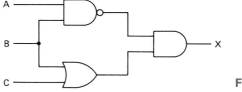

Figure 5-39

Solution: The Boolean equation at X is

$$X = \overline{AB} \cdot (B + C)$$

Applying DeMorgan's theorem produces

$$X = (\overline{A} + \overline{B}) \cdot (B + C)$$

(Notice the use of parentheses to maintain proper grouping). Using Boolean algebra rules produces

$$X = \overline{A}B + \overline{A}C + \overline{B}B + \overline{B}C$$
$$= \overline{A}B + \overline{A}C + \overline{B}C \leftarrow \text{final equation (sum-of-products form)}$$

The equivalent circuit is shown in Figure 5–40.

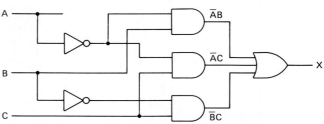

Figure 5–40   Logic circuit equivalent for Example 5–13.

Notice that the final equation actually produces a circuit that is more complicated than the original. In fact, if a technician were to build a circuit, he or she would choose the original because it is simpler and has fewer gates. However, the final equation is in a form called the *sum of products*. That form of the equation was achieved by using Boolean algebra and is very useful for building truth tables and Karnaugh maps, which are covered in Section 5–8.

EXAMPLE 5–14

Prove, using DeMorgan's theorem and Boolean algebra, that the two circuits shown in Figure 5–41 are equivalent.

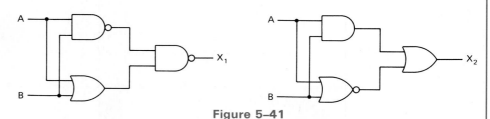

Figure 5–41

Solution: They can be proven to be equivalent if their simplified equations match.

$$X_1 = \overline{\overline{AB} \cdot (A + B)} \qquad\qquad X_2 = AB + \overline{A + B}$$
$$= \overline{\overline{AB}} + \overline{A + B} \qquad\qquad\qquad = AB + \overline{A}\,\overline{B}$$
$$= AB + \overline{A}\,\overline{B} \longleftarrow \text{Equivalent}$$

EXAMPLE 5–15

Draw the logic circuit for the following equation, simplify the equation, and construct a truth table for the simplifed equation.

$$X = \overline{A \cdot \overline{B}} + \overline{A \cdot (\overline{A} + C)}$$

Solution: To draw the circuit, we have to reverse our thinking from the previous examples. When we study the equation we see that we need two NANDS feeding into an OR gate, as shown in Figure 5–42a. Then we have to provide the inputs to the NAND gates as shown in Figure 5–42b. Next, we will use DeMorgan's theorem and Boolean algebra to simplify the equation:

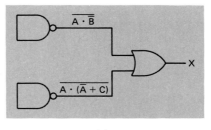

(a)

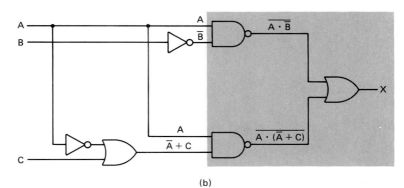

(b)

Figure 5–42 (a) Partial solution to Example 5–15; (b) logic circuit of the equation for Example 5–15.

$$X = \overline{\overline{A} \cdot \overline{\overline{B}}} + \overline{A \cdot (\overline{A} + C)}$$
$$= (\overline{A} + \overline{\overline{B}}) + (\overline{A} + \overline{\overline{A} + C})$$
$$= \overline{A} + B + \overline{A} + \overline{\overline{A}} \cdot \overline{C}$$
$$= \overline{A} + \overline{A} + A\overline{C} + B$$
$$= \overline{A} + A\overline{C} + B$$

Apply Rule 10:

$$X = \overline{A} + \overline{C} + B \leftarrow \text{simplified equation}$$

Now, to construct a truth table (Table 5–2), we need three input columns (*A*, *B*, *C*), eight entries ($2^3 = 8$), and fill in a 1 for *X* when *A* = 0 or *C* = 0 or *B* = 1.

TABLE 5–2

Truth Table for Example 5–15

A	B	C	$X = \overline{A} + \overline{C} + B$
0	0	0	1
0	0	1	1
0	1	0	1
0	1	1	1
1	0	0	1
1	0	1	0
1	1	0	1
1	1	1	1

EXAMPLE 5–16

Repeat Example 5–15 for the following equation:

$$X = \overline{A\overline{B} \cdot (A + C)} + \overline{A}B \cdot \overline{\overline{A} + \overline{B} + \overline{C}}$$

Solution: The required logic circuit is shown in Figure 5–43. Boolean equation simplification:

$$X = \overline{A\overline{B} \cdot (A + C)} + \overline{A}B \cdot \overline{\overline{A} + \overline{B} + \overline{\overline{C}}}$$
$$= \overline{A\overline{B}} + \overline{A + C} + \overline{A}B \cdot (\overline{\overline{A}} \cdot \overline{\overline{B}} \cdot \overline{\overline{C}})$$
$$= (\overline{A} + \overline{\overline{B}}) + \overline{A} \cdot \overline{C} + \overline{A}ABBC$$
$$= \overline{A} + B + \overline{A}\overline{C} + \overline{A}BC$$
$$= \overline{A}(1 + \overline{C}) + B + \overline{A}BC$$
$$= \overline{A} + B + \overline{A}BC$$
$$= \overline{A} + B(1 + \overline{A}C)$$
$$= \overline{A} + B \leftarrow \text{simplified equation}$$

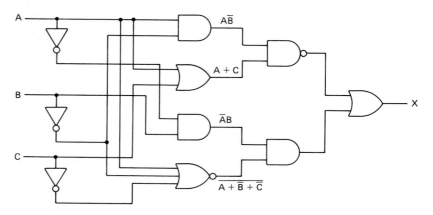

Figure 5–43 Logic circuit for the equation of Example 5–16.

TABLE 5–3

Truth Table for Example 5–16

A	B	C	$X = \overline{A} + B$
0	0	0	1
0	0	1	1
0	1	0	1
0	1	1	1
1	0	0	0
1	0	1	0
1	1	0	1
1	1	1	1

Three columns are used in the truth table (Table 5–3) because the original equation contained three variables (A, B, C). C is considered a "don't care," however, because it does not appear in the final equation and it does not matter whether it is 1 or 0.

From the simplified equation ($X = \overline{A} + B$) we can determine that $X = 1$ when A is 0 or when B is 1, and fill in the truth table accordingly.

EXAMPLE 5–17

Complete the truth table and timing diagram for the following simplified Boolean equation:

$$X = AB + B\overline{C} + \overline{A}\,\overline{B}C$$

Solution: The required truth table and timing diagram are shown in Figure 5–44. To fill in the truth table for X, we first put a 1 for X when $A = 1$, $B = 1$. Then $X = 1$ for $B = 1$, $C = 0$; then $X = 1$ for $A = 0$, $B = 0$, $C = 1$. All other entries for X are 0.

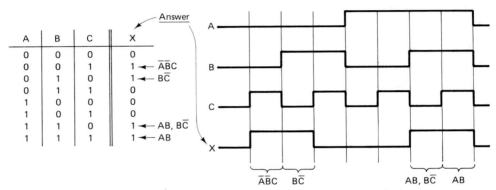

Figure 5–44 Truth table and timing diagram depicting the logic levels at X for all combinations of inputs.

The timing diagram performs the same function as the truth table except that it is a more graphic illustration of the HIGH and LOW logic levels of X as the A, B, C inputs change over time. The logic levels at X are filled in the same way as they were for the truth table.

EXAMPLE 5–18

Repeat Example 5–17 for the following simplified equation:

$$X = A\overline{B}\,\overline{C} + \overline{A}\,\overline{B}C + ABC$$

Solution: The required truth table and timing diagram are shown in Figure 5–45.

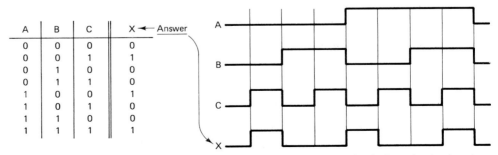

Figure 5–45 Truth table and timing diagram depicting the logic levels at X for all combinations of inputs.

Bubble Pushing

Another trick that can be used, based on DeMorgan's theorem, is called *bubble pushing* and is illustrated in Figure 5–46. As you can see, to form the equivalent logic circuit, you must:

1. Change the logic gate (AND to OR or OR to AND).
2. Add bubbles to the inputs and outputs where there were none, and remove the original bubbles.

Prove to yourself that this method works by comparing to its equivalent the truth table of each original circuit.

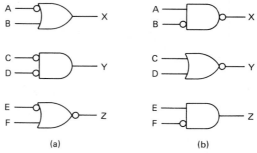

(a)   (b)

Figure 5–46   (a) Original logic circuits; (b) equivalent logic circuits.

5–5 *THE UNIVERSAL CAPABILITY OF NAND AND NOR GATES*

NAND and NOR gates are sometimes referred to as *universal gates*. This is because by utilizing a combination of NANDs, all the other logic gates (inverter, AND, OR, NOR) can be formed. Also, by utilizing a combination of NORs, all the other logic gates (inverter, AND, OR NAND) can be formed.

This is a useful principle because quite often you may have extra NANDs available but actually need some other logic function. For example, let's say that you designed a circuit that required a NAND, an AND, and an inverter. You would probably purchase a 7400 quad NAND TTL IC. This chip has four NANDs in a single package. One of the NANDs will be used directly in your circuit. The AND requirement could actually be fulfilled by connecting the third and forth NANDs on the chip to form an AND. The inverter can be formed from the second NAND on the chip. How do we convert a NAND into an inverter and two NANDS into an AND? Let's see.

An inverter can be formed from a NAND simply by connecting both NAND inputs together as shown in Figure 5–47. Both inputs to the NAND will therefore be connected to A. The equation at X will be $X = \overline{A \cdot A} = \overline{A}$, which is the inverter function.

The next task is to form an AND from two NANDs. Do you have any ideas? What is the difference between a NAND and an AND? If we invert the output of a NAND, it will act like an AND, as shown in Figure 5–48.

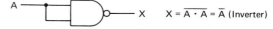

$$X = \overline{A \cdot A} = \overline{A} \text{ (Inverter)}$$

Figure 5–47   Forming an inverter from a NAND.

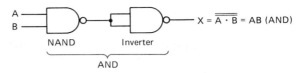

$$X = \overline{\overline{A \cdot B}} = AB \text{ (AND)}$$

Figure 5–48 Forming an AND from two NANDs.

Now back to the original problem; we wanted to form a circuit requiring a NAND, an AND, and an inverter using a single 7400 quad NAND TTL IC. Let's make the external connections to the 7400 IC to form the circuit of Figure 5–49, which contains a NAND, an AND, and an inverter.

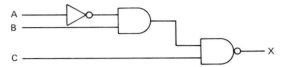

Figure 5–49 Logic circuit to be implemented using only NANDs.

First, let's redraw the logic circuit using only NANDs. Now, using the configuration shown in Figure 5–50, we can make the actual connections to the 7400 IC, as shown in Figure 5–51.

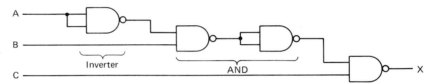

Figure 5–50 Equivalent logic circuit using only NANDs.

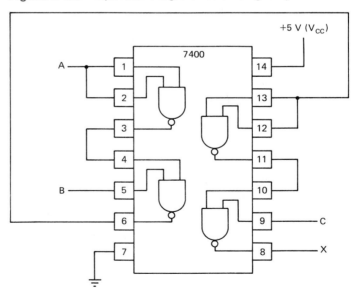

Figure 5–51 External connections to a 7400 TTL IC to form the circuit of Figure 5–50.

Besides forming inverters and ANDs from NANDs, we can form ORs and NORs from NANDs. Remember from DeMorgan's theorem that an AND with an inverted output (NAND) is equivalent to an OR with inverted inputs. Therefore, if we invert the inputs to a NAND, we should find that it is equivalent to an OR, as shown in Figure 5–52.

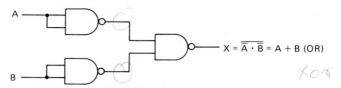

$$X = \overline{\overline{A} \cdot \overline{B}} = A + B \text{ (OR)}$$

Figure 5–52   Forming an OR from three NANDs.

Now, to form a NOR from NANDs, all we need to do is invert the output of Figure 5–52, as shown in Figure 5–53.

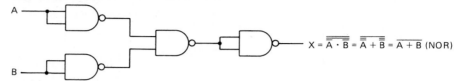

$$X = \overline{\overline{\overline{A} \cdot \overline{B}}} = \overline{\overline{\overline{A} + \overline{\overline{B}}}} = \overline{A + B} \text{ (NOR)}$$

Figure 5–53   Forming a NOR from four NANDs.

The procedure for converting NOR gates into an inverter, OR, AND, or NAND is similar to the conversions just discussed for NAND gates. For example, to form an inverter from a NOR gate, just connect the inputs as shown in Figure 5–54.

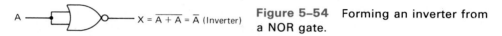

$X = \overline{A + A} = \overline{A}$ (Inverter)

Figure 5–54   Forming an inverter from a NOR gate.

Take some time now to try to convert NORs to an OR, NORs to an AND, and NORs to a NAND. Prove to yourself that your solution is correct by using DeMorgan's theorem and Boolean algebra.

EXAMPLE 5–19

Make the external connections to a 4001 CMOS NOR IC to implement the function $X = \overline{A} + B$.

Solution: We will need an inverter and an OR gate to provide the function for X. An inverter can be made from a NOR by connecting the inputs together and an OR can be made by inverting the output of a NOR as shown in Figure 5–55.

The pin configuration for the 4001 CMOS quad NOR can be found in a CMOS data book. Figure 5–56 shows the pin configuration and external connections to implement $X = \overline{A} + B$.

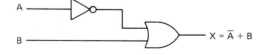

$X = \overline{A} + B$

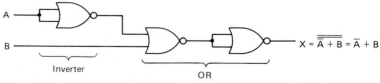

$X = \overline{\overline{\overline{A} + B}} = \overline{A} + B$

Inverter   OR

Figure 5–55   Implementing the function $X = \overline{A} + B$ using only NOR gates.

EXAMPLE 5–20: (Troubleshooting)

You have connected the circuit of Figure 5–56 and want to test it. Since the Boolean equation is $X = \overline{A} + B$, you desire first to try $A = 0$, $B = 1$ and expect to get a 1 output at X, *but you don't*. V_{DD} is set to +5 V and V_{SS} is connected to ground. Using a logic probe, you record the results shown in Table 5–4 at each pin. Determine the trouble with the circuit.

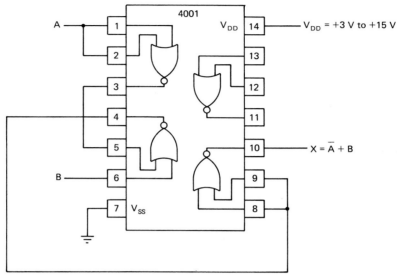

Figure 5–56 External connections to a 4001 CMOS IC to implement the circuit of Figure 5–55.

TABLE 5–4

Logic Probe Operation[a]

Probe on pin:	Indicator lamp
1	Off
2	Off
3	On
4	Off
5	On
6	On
7	Off
8	Dim
9	Off
10	Off
11	On
12	Dim
13	Dim
14	On

[a] Lamp off, 0; lamp on, 1; lamp dim, float.

Solution: Since $A = 0$, pins 1 and 2 should both be 0, which they are. Pin 3 is a 1 because 0–0 into a NOR will produce a 1 output. Pin 6 is 1 because it is connected to the 1 at B. Pin 5 matches pin 3, as it is supposed to. Pin 4 sends a 0 to pins 8 and 9, but pin 8 is floating (not 0 or 1). That's it! The connection to pin 8 must be broken.

To be sure that the circuit operates properly, the problem at pin 8 should be corrected and all four combinations of inputs at A and B should be tested.

EXAMPLE 5–21

(a) Write the simplified equation that will produce the output waveform at X given the inputs at A, B, and C shown in Figure 5–57.
(b) Draw the logic circuit for that equation.
(c) Redraw the logic circuit using only NAND gates.

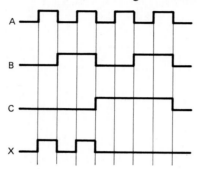

Figure 5–57

Solution: (a) The first HIGH pulse at X is produced for $A = 1$, $B = 0$, $C = 0(A\overline{B}\,\overline{C})$. The second HIGH pulse at X happens when $A = 1$, $B = 1$, $C = 0(AB\overline{C})$. Therefore, X is 1 for $A\overline{B}\,\overline{C}$ or $AB\overline{C}$.

$$X = A\overline{B}\,\overline{C} + AB\overline{C}$$

Simplifying yields

$$X = A\overline{C}(\overline{B} + B)$$
$$= A\overline{C}(1)$$
$$= A\overline{C} \leftarrow \text{simplified equation}$$

(b) The logic circuit is shown in Figure 5–58a.
(c) Redrawing the same circuit using only NANDs produces the circuit shown in Figure 5–58b.

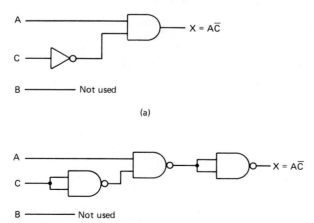

Figure 5–58 (a) Logic circuit that yields the waveform at X; (b) circuit of part (a) redrawn using only NANDS.

5-6 AND–OR–INVERT GATES FOR IMPLEMENTING SUM–OF–PRODUCTS EXPRESSIONS

Most Boolean reductions result in an equation in one of two forms:

1. *Product-of-sums* (POS) expression
2. *Sum-of-products* (SOP) expression

The POS expression usually takes the form of two or more ORed variables within parentheses ANDed with two or more other variables within parentheses. Examples of POS expressions:

$$X = (A + \bar{B}) \cdot (B + C)$$
$$X = (B + \bar{C} + \bar{D}) \cdot (BC + \bar{E})$$
$$X = (A + \bar{C}) \cdot (\bar{B} + E) \cdot (C + B)$$

The SOP expression usually takes the form of two or more variables ANDed together ORed with two or more other variables ANDed together. Examples of SOP expressions:

$$X = A\bar{B} + AC + \bar{A}BC$$
$$X = AC\bar{D} + \bar{C}D + B$$
$$X = BC\bar{D} + A\bar{B}DE + CD$$

The SOP expression is used most often because it lends itself nicely to the development of truth tables and timing diagrams. SOP circuits can also be constructed easily using a special combinational logic gate called the *AND–OR–INVERT* gate.

For example, let's work with the equation

$$X = \overline{A\bar{B} + \bar{C}D}$$

Using DeMorgan's theorem yields

$$X = \overline{A\bar{B}} \cdot \overline{\bar{C}D}$$

Using DeMorgan's theorem again puts it into a POS format:

$$X = (\bar{A} + B) \cdot (C + \bar{D}) \leftarrow \text{POS}$$

Using the distributive law produces an equation in the SOP format:

$$X = \bar{A}C + \bar{A}\bar{D} + BC + B\bar{D} \leftarrow \text{SOP}$$

Now, let's fill in a truth table for X (Table 5–5). Using the *SOP* expression, we will put a 1 at X for $A = 0$, $C = 1$; and for $A = 0$, $D = 0$; and for $B = 1$, $C = 1$; and for $B = 1$, $D = 0$. That wasn't hard, was it?

However, if we were to use the POS expression, it would be more difficult to visualize. We would put a 1 at X for $A = 0$ or $B = 1$ whenever $C = 1$ or $D = 0$. Confusing? Yes, it is much more difficult to deal intuitively with POS expressions.

Drawing the logic circuit for the POS expression involves using OR gates feeding into an AND gate, as shown in Figure 5–59. Drawing the logic circuit for the SOP expression involves using AND gates feeding into an OR gate, as shown in Figure 5–60. The logic circuit for the SOP expression used more gates for this particular example, but the SOP form *is* easier to deal with and besides, there is an IC gate specifically made to simplify the implementation of SOP circuits.

That gate is the *AND–OR–INVERT* (AOI). AOIs are available in several different configurations within the TTL or CMOS families. Skim through your TTL and CMOS data books to identify some of the available AOIs. One AOI that is particularly well suited for implementing the logic of Figure 5–60 is the 74LS54 TTL IC. The pin configuration and logic symbol for the 74LS54 are shown in Figure 5–61.

TABLE 5–5

Truth Table
Completed Using
the SOP Expression

A	B	C	D	X
0	0	0	0	1
0	0	0	1	0
0	0	1	0	1
0	0	1	1	1
0	1	0	0	1
0	1	0	1	0
0	1	1	0	1
0	1	1	1	1
1	0	0	0	0
1	0	0	1	0
1	0	1	0	0
1	0	1	1	0
1	1	0	0	1
1	1	0	1	0
1	1	1	0	1
1	1	1	1	1

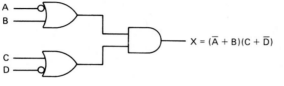

$$X = (\overline{A} + B)(C + \overline{D})$$

Figure 5–59   Logic circuit for the POS expression.

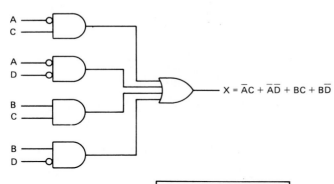

$$X = \overline{A}C + \overline{A}\,\overline{D} + BC + B\overline{D}$$

Figure 5–60   Logic circuit for the SOP expression.

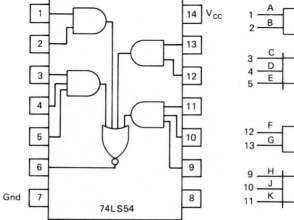

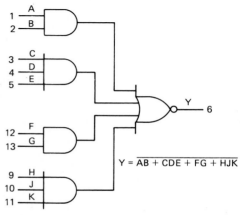

$$Y = \overline{AB + CDE + FG + HJK}$$

Figure 5–61   Pin configuration and logic symbol for the 74LS54 AOI gate.

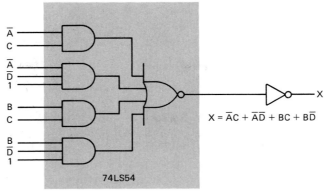

$X = \overline{A}C + \overline{A}\overline{D} + BC + B\overline{D}$

Figure 5–62 Using an AOI IC to implement an SOP equation.

Notice that the output at Y is inverted, so we have to place an inverter after Y. Also, two of the AND gates have *three* inputs instead of just the two-input gates that we need, so we just connect the unused third input to a 1. Figure 5–62 shows the required connections to the AOI to implement the SOP logic circuit of Figure 5–60.

EXAMPLE 5–22

Simplify the circuit shown in Figure 5–63 down to its SOP form, then draw the logic circuit of the simplified form using a 74LS54 AOI gate.

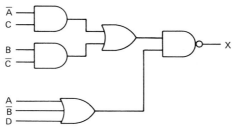

Figure 5–63 Original circuit for Example 5–22.

Solution:

$$X = \overline{(\overline{AC} + B\overline{C}) \cdot (A + \overline{B} + D)}$$
$$= \overline{\overline{AC} + B\overline{C}} + \overline{A + \overline{B} + D}$$
$$= \overline{\overline{AC}} \cdot \overline{B\overline{C}} + \overline{A}B\overline{D}$$
$$= (A + \overline{C})(\overline{B} + C) + \overline{A}B\overline{D}$$
$$= A\overline{B} + AC + \overline{B}\,\overline{C} + \overline{C}C + \overline{A}B\overline{D}$$
$$= A\overline{B} + AC + \overline{B}\,\overline{C} + \overline{A}B\overline{D} \leftarrow (\text{SOP})$$

The simplified circuit is shown in Figure 5–64.

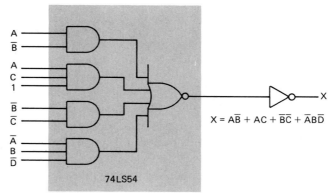

$X = A\overline{B} + AC + \overline{B}\,\overline{C} + \overline{A}B\overline{D}$

Figure 5–64 Using an AOI IC to implement the simplified SOP equation for Example 5–22.

101

5–7 KARNAUGH MAPPING

We learned in previous sections that by using Boolean algebra and DeMorgan's theorem, we can minimize the number of gates that are required to implement a particular logic function. This is very important for the reduction of circuit cost, physical size, and gate failures. You may have found some of the steps in the Boolean reduction process to require ingenuity on your part, and a lot of practice.

Karnaugh mapping, named for its originator, is another method of simplifying logic circuits. It still requires that you reduce the equation to an SOP form, but from there you follow a *systematic approach* which will always produce the simplest configuration possible for the logic circuit.

A Karnaugh map (K-map) is similar to a truth table in that it graphically shows the output level of a Boolean equation for each of the possible input variable combinations. Each output level is placed in a separate *cell* of the K-map. K-maps can be used to simplify equations having two, three, four, five, or six different input variables. Solving five- and six-variable K-maps is extremely cumbersome and can be more practically solved using advanced computer techniques. In this book we will solve two-, three-, and four-variable K-maps.

Determining the number of cells in a K-map is the same as finding the number of combinations or entries in a truth table. A two-variable map will require $2^2 = 4$ cells. A three-variable map will require $2^3 = 8$ cells. A four-variable map will require $2^4 = 16$ cells. The three different K-maps are shown in Figure 5–65.

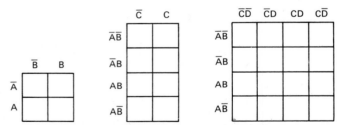

Figure 5–65 Two-variable, three-variable, and four-variable Karnaugh maps.

Each cell within the K-map corresponds to a particular combination of the input variables. For example, in the two-variable K-map, the upper-left cell corresponds to $\overline{A}\,\overline{B}$, the lower-left cell is $A\overline{B}$, the upper-right cell is $\overline{A}B$, and the lower-right cell is AB.

Also notice that when moving from one cell to an adjacent cell, only one variable changes. For example, look at the three-variable K-map. The upper-left cell is $\overline{A}\,\overline{B}\,\overline{C}$, the adjacent cell just below it is $\overline{A}B\overline{C}$. In that case the $\overline{A}\,\overline{C}$ remained the same and only the $\overline{B}$ changed to B. The same holds true for each adjacent cell.

To use the K-map reduction procedure, you must perform the following steps:

1. Transform the Boolean equation to be reduced into an SOP expression.
2. Fill in the appropriate cells of the K-map.
3. Encircle adjacent cells in groups of two, four, or eight. (The more adjacent cells encircled, the simpler the final equation.)
4. Find each term of the final SOP equation by determining which variables remain constant within each circle.

Now, let's consider the equation

$$X = \overline{A}(\overline{B}C + \overline{B}\,\overline{C}) + \overline{A}B\overline{C}$$

First, transform the equation to an SOP expression:

$$X = \overline{A}\,\overline{B}C + \overline{A}\,\overline{B}\,\overline{C} + \overline{A}B\overline{C}$$

The terms of that SOP expression can be put into a truth table, then transferred to a K-map, as shown in Figure 5–66. Working with the K-map, we will now encircle adjacent 1's in groups of two, four, or eight. We end up with two circles of two cells each, as shown in Figure 5–67. The first circle surrounds the two 1's at the top of the K-map and the second circle surrounds the two 1's in the left column of the K-map.

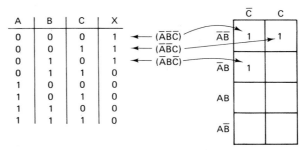

Figure 5–66 Truth table and Karnaugh map of $X = \overline{A}\,\overline{B}\,\overline{C} + \overline{A}\,\overline{B}C + \overline{A}B\overline{C}$.

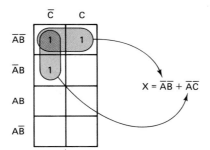

Figure 5–67 Encircling adjacent cells in a Karnaugh map.

Once the circles have been drawn encompassing all the 1's in the map, the final simplified equation is obtained by determining *which variables remain the same within each circle*. Well, the first circle (across the top) encompasses $\overline{A}\,\overline{B}\,\overline{C}$ and $\overline{A}\,\overline{B}C$. The variables that remain the same within the circle are $\overline{A}\,\overline{B}$. Therefore, $\overline{A}\,\overline{B}$ becomes one of the terms in the final SOP equation. The second circle (left column) encompasses $\overline{A}\,\overline{B}\,\overline{C}$ and $\overline{A}B\overline{C}$. The variables that remain the same within that circle are $\overline{A}\,\overline{C}$. Therefore, the second term in the final equation is $\overline{A}\,\overline{C}$.

Since the final equation is always written in the SOP format, the answer is $X = \overline{A}\,\overline{B} + \overline{A}\,\overline{C}$. Actually, the original equation was simple enough that we could have reduced it using standard Boolean algebra. Let's do it just to check our answer:

$$\begin{aligned}
X &= \overline{A}\,\overline{B}C + \overline{A}\,\overline{B}\,\overline{C} + \overline{A}B\overline{C} \\
&= \overline{A}\,\overline{B}(C + \overline{C}) + \overline{A}B\overline{C} \\
&= \overline{A}\,\overline{B} + \overline{A}B\overline{C} \\
&= \overline{A}(\overline{B} + B\overline{C}) \\
&= \overline{A}(\overline{B} + \overline{C}) \\
&= \overline{A}\,\overline{B} + \overline{A}\,\overline{C} \quad \checkmark
\end{aligned}$$

There are several other points to watch out for when applying the Karnaugh mapping technique. The following examples will be used to illustrate several important points in filling in the map, determining adjacencies, and obtaining the final equation. Work through these examples carefully so that you do not miss any special techniques.

EXAMPLE 5–23

Simplify the following SOP equation using the Karnaugh mapping technique:

$$X = \overline{A}B + \overline{A}\,\overline{B}\overline{C} + AB\overline{C} + A\overline{B}\,\overline{C}$$

Solution:

1. Construct an eight-cell K-map (Figure 5–68) and fill in a 1 in each cell that corresponds to a term in the original equation. (Notice that $\overline{A}B$ has no C variable in it. Therefore, $\overline{A}B$ is satisfied whether C is HIGH or LOW, so $\overline{A}B$ will fill in two cells; $\overline{A}BC + \overline{A}B\overline{C}$.)
2. Encircle adjacent cells in the largest group of two or four or eight.
3. Identify the variables that remain the same within each circle and write the final simplified SOP equation by ORing them together.

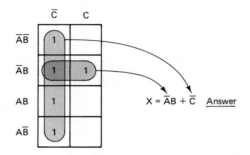

X = $\overline{A}B + \overline{C}$ Answer

Figure 5–68   Karnaugh map and final equation for Example 5–23.

EXAMPLE 5–24

Simplify the following equation using the Karnaugh mapping procedure:

$$X = \overline{A}B\overline{C}D + A\overline{B}CD + \overline{A}\,\overline{B}CD + AB\overline{C}D + ABC\overline{D} + ABCD$$

Solution: Since there are four different variables in the equation, we need a 16-cell map ($2^4 = 16$), as shown in Figure 5–69.

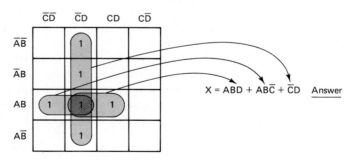

X = ABD + AB$\overline{C}$ + $\overline{C}$D   Answer

Figure 5–69   Solution to Example 5–24.

EXAMPLE 5–25

Simplify the following equation using the Karnaugh mapping procedure:

$$X = B\overline{C}\overline{D} + \overline{A}B\overline{C}D + AB\overline{C}D + \overline{A}BCD + ABCD$$

Solution: Notice in Figure 5–70 that the $B\overline{C}\overline{D}$ term in the original equation fills in *two* cells: $AB\overline{C}\overline{D} + \overline{A}B\overline{C}\overline{D}$. Also notice in Figure 5–70 that we could have encircled four cells, then two cells, but that would not have given us the simplest final equation. By encircling four cells, then four cells, we will be sure to get the simplest final equation. (Always encircle the largest number of cells possible, even if some of the cells have already been encircled in another group.)

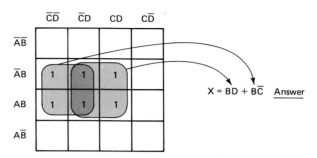

Figure 5–70 Solution to Example 5–25.

EXAMPLE 5–26

Simplify the following equation using the Karnaugh mapping procedure:

$$X = \overline{A}\,\overline{B}\,\overline{C} + A\overline{C}\overline{D} + A\overline{B} + ABC\overline{D} + \overline{A}\,\overline{B}C$$

Solution: Notice in Figure 5–71 a new technique called *wraparound* is introduced. You have to think of the K-map as a continuous cylinder in the horizontal direction, like the label on a soup can. This makes the left row of cells adjacent to the right row of cells. Also, in the vertical direction, a continuous cylinder like a soup can lying on its side makes the top row of cells adjacent to the bottom row of cells. In Figure 5–71, for example, the four top cells are adjacent to the four bottom cells, to combine as eight cells having the variable $\overline{B}$ in common.

Another circle of four is formed by the wraparound adjacencies of the lower-left and lower-right pairs combining to have $A\overline{D}$ in common. The final equation becomes $X = \overline{B} + A\overline{D}$. Compare that simple equation with the original equation that had five terms in it.

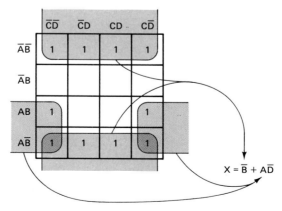

Figure 5–71 Solution to Example 5–26 illustrating the wraparound feature.

EXAMPLE 5–27

Simplify the following equation using the Karnaugh mapping procedure:

$$X = \overline{B}(CD + \overline{C}) + C\overline{D}(\overline{A + B} + AB)$$

Solution:　Before filling in the K-map, an SOP expression must be formed:

$$X = \overline{B}CD + \overline{B}\,\overline{C} + C\overline{D}(\overline{A}\,\overline{B} + AB)$$
$$= \overline{B}CD + \overline{B}\,\overline{C} + \overline{A}\,\overline{B}C\overline{D} + ABC\overline{D}$$

The group of four 1's can be encircled to form $\overline{A}\,\overline{B}$ as shown in Figure 5–72. Another group of four can be encircled using wraparound to form $\overline{B}\,\overline{C}$. That leaves two 1's that are not combined with any others. The unattached 1 in the bottom row can be combined within a group of four, as shown, to form $\overline{B}D$.

The last 1 is not adjacent to any other, so it must be encircled by itself to form $ABC\overline{D}$. The final simplified equation is

$$X = \overline{A}\,\overline{B} + \overline{B}\,\overline{C} + \overline{B}D + ABC\overline{D}$$

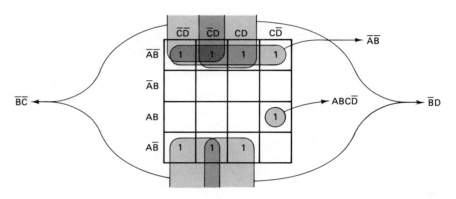

Figure 5–72　Solution to Example 5–27.

EXAMPLE 5–28

Simplify the following equation using the Karnaugh mapping procedure:

$$X = \overline{A}\,\overline{D} + A\overline{B}\,\overline{D} + \overline{A}\,\overline{C}D + \overline{A}CD$$

Solution:　First, the group of eight cells can be encircled as shown in Figure 5–73. $\overline{A}$ is the only variable present in each cell within the circle, so that the circle of eight simply reduces to $\overline{A}$. (Notice that larger circles will reduce to fewer variables in the final equation.)

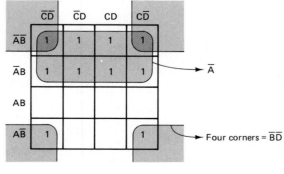

Four corners = $\overline{B}\,\overline{D}$

Figure 5–73　Solution to Example 5–28.

Also, all four corners are adjacent to each other because the K-map can be wrapped around in both the vertical *and* horizontal directions. Encircling the four corners results in $\overline{B}\overline{D}$. The final equation is

$$X = \overline{A} + \overline{B}\overline{D}$$

EXAMPLE 5–29

Simplify the following equation using the Karnaugh mapping procedure:

$$X = \overline{A}\overline{B}\overline{D} + A\overline{C}\overline{D} + \overline{A}B\overline{C} + ABC\overline{D} + A\overline{B}C\overline{D}$$

Solution: Encircling the four corners forms $\overline{B}\overline{D}$, as shown in Figure 5–74. The other group of four forms $B\overline{C}$. You may be tempted to encircle the $\overline{C}\overline{D}$ group of four as shown by the dotted line, but that would be *redundant* because each of those 1's is already contained within an existing circle. Therefore, the final equation is

$$X = \overline{B}\overline{D} + B\overline{C}$$

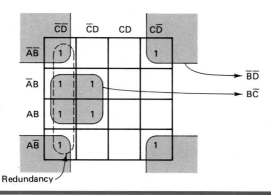

Figure 5–74 Solution to Example 5–29.

5–8 SYSTEM DESIGN APPLICATIONS

Let's summarize the entire chapter now by working through two complete design problems. The following examples illustrate practical applications of a K-map to ensure that when we implement the circuit using an AOI we will have the simplest possible solution.

NOTE: The construction of digital circuits with higher complexity than those of these examples will be more practically suited for implementation using what is called *semicustom logic ICs*, which are discussed in Chapter 16.

SYSTEM DESIGN 5–1

Design a circuit that can be built using an AOI and inverters that will output a HIGH (1) whenever the 4-bit hexadecimal input is an odd number from 0 to 9.

Solution: First, build a truth table (Table 5–6) to identify which hex codes from 0 to 9 produce odd numbers. (Use the variable A to represent the 2^0 hex input, B for 2^1, C for 2^2, and D for 2^3.) Next, reduce that equation into its simplest form by using a Karnaugh map, as shown in Figure 5–75a. Finally, using an AOI with inverters, the circuit can be constructed, as shown in Figure 5–75b.

TABLE 5–6

Hex Truth Table Used
to Determine the Equation
for Odd Numbers[a] from 0 to 9

D	C	B	A	DEC	
0	0	0	0	0	
0	0	0	1	1	$\leftarrow A\overline{B}\,\overline{C}\overline{D}$
0	0	1	0	2	
0	0	1	1	3	$\leftarrow AB\overline{C}\overline{D}$
0	1	0	0	4	
0	1	0	1	5	$\leftarrow A\overline{B}C\overline{D}$
0	1	1	0	6	
0	1	1	1	7	$\leftarrow ABC\overline{D}$
1	0	0	0	8	
1	0	0	1	9	$\leftarrow A\overline{B}\,\overline{C}D$

[a] Odd number $= A\overline{B}\,\overline{C}\overline{D} + AB\overline{C}\overline{D} + A\overline{B}C\overline{D} + ABC\overline{D} + A\overline{B}\,\overline{C}D$.

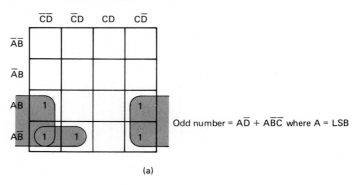

Odd number $= A\overline{D} + A\overline{B}\,\overline{C}$ where A = LSB

(a)

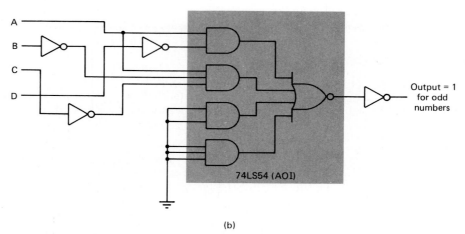

74LS54 (AOI)

Output = 1
for odd
numbers

(b)

Figure 5–75 (a) Simplified equation derived from a Karnaugh map; (b) implementation of the "odd-number decoder" using an AOI.

SYSTEM DESIGN 5–2

A chemical plant needs an alarm system developed to warn of critical conditions in one of its chemical tanks. The tank has four HIGH/LOW (1/0) switches, monitoring temperature (T), pressure (P), fluid level (L), and weight

(*W*). Design a system that will activate an alarm when any of the following conditions arise:

1. A high fluid level with a high temperature and a high pressure
2. A low fluid level with a high temperature and a high weight
3. A low fluid level with a low temperature and a high pressure
4. A low fluid level with a low weight and a high temperature

Solution: First, write in Boolean equation form, the conditions that will activate the alarm:

$$\text{alarm} = LTP + \overline{L}TW + \overline{L}\,\overline{T}P + \overline{L}\,\overline{W}T$$

Next, factor the equation into its simplest form by using a Karnaugh map, as shown in Figure 5–76a. Finally, using an AOI with inverters, the circuit can be constructed, as shown in Figure 5–76b.

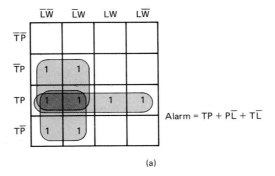

Alarm = TP + P$\overline{L}$ + T$\overline{L}$

(a)

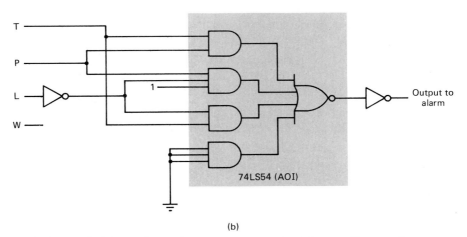

74LS54 (AOI)

(b)

Figure 5–76 (a) Simplified equation derived from a Karnaugh map; (b) implementation of the "chemical tank alarm" using an AOI.

GLOSSARY

Adjacent cell: Cells within a Karnaugh map are considered adjacent if they border each other on one side or the top or bottom of the cell.

AND-OR-INVERT gate: (AOI) An integrated circuit containing combinational logic consisting of several AND gates feeding into an OR gate, then an inverter. It is used to implement logic equations that are in the SOP format.

Boolean reduction: An algebraic technique that follows specific rules in order to convert a Boolean equation into a simpler form.

Cell: Each box within a Karnaugh map is a cell. Each cell corresponds to a particular combination of input variable logic levels.

Combinational logic: Logic circuits formed by combining several of the basic logic gates together to form a more complex function.

DeMorgan's theorem: A Boolean law used for equation reduction that allows the user to convert an equation having an inversion bar over several variables into an equivalent equation having inversion bars over single variables only.

Don't care: A variable appearing in a truth table or timing waveform that will have no effect on the final output regardless of the logic level of the variable. Therefore, don't-care variables can be ignored.

Equivalent circuit: A simplified version of a logic circuit that can be used to perform the exact logic function of the original complex circuit.

Inversion bubbles: An alternative to drawing the triangular inversion symbol. The bubble (or circle) can appear at the input or output of a logic gate.

Karnaugh map: A two-dimensional table of Boolean output levels used as a tool to perform a systematic reduction of complex logic circuits into simplified equivalent circuits.

Product-of-sums (POS) form: A Boolean equation in the form of a group of ORed variables ANDed with another group of ORed variables [e.g., $X = (A + \overline{B} + C)(B + D)(\overline{A} + \overline{C})$].

Redundancy: Once all filled-in cells in a Karnaugh map are contained within a circle, the final simplified equation can be written. Drawing another circle around a different group of cells is redundant.

Sum-of-products (SOP) form: A Boolean equation in the form of a group of ANDed variables ORed with another group of ANDed variables (e.g., $X = ABC + \overline{B}DE + \overline{A}\,\overline{D}$).

Universal gates: The NOR and NAND logic gates are sometimes called universal gates because any of the other logic gates can be formed from them.

Wraparound: The left and right cells and the top and bottom cells of a Karnaugh map are actually adjacent to each other by means of the wraparound feature.

REVIEW QUESTIONS

Sections 5–1 through 5–3

  5–1. How many gates are required to implement the following Boolean equations?
      (a) $X = (A + B)C$ 2
      (b) $Y = AC + BC$ 3
      (c) $Z = (ABC + CD)E$ 4

  5–2. Which Boolean law is used to transform each of the following equations?
      (a) $B + (D + E) = D + (B + E)$ Asso Law +
      (b) $CAB = BCA$ Commut (commutple) ×
      (c) $(B + C)(A + D) = BA + BD + CA + CD$ dist

5–3. The output of an AND gate with one of its inputs connected to 1 will always output a level equal to the level at the other input (true or false)?

5–4. The output of an OR gate with one of its inputs connected to 1 will always output a level equal to the level at the other input (true or false)?

5–5. If one input to an OR gate is connected to 0, the output will always be 0 regardless of the level on the other input (true or false)?

Section 5–4

5–6. Why is DeMorgan's theorem important in the simplification of Boolean equations?

5–7. Using DeMorgan's theorem you can prove that a NOR gate is equivalent to an _____(OR, AND) gate with inverted inputs.

5–8. Using the ''bubble-pushing'' technique, an AND gate with one of its inputs inverted is equivalent to a _____ (NAND, NOR) gate with its other input inverted.

Section 5–5

5–9. Why are NAND gates and NOR gates sometimes referred to as *universal* gates?

5–10. Why would a designer want to form an AND gate from two NAND gates?

5–11. How many inverters could be formed using a 7400 quad NAND IC?

Sections 5–6 through 5–8

5–12. Which form of Boolean equation is better suited for completing truth tables and timing diagrams, SOP or POS?

5–13. AOI ICs are used to implement _____ (SOP, POS) expressions.

5–14. The equation X = AB + BCD + DE has only three product terms. If a 74LS54 AOI IC is used to implement the equation, what must be done with the three inputs to the unused fourth AND gate?

5–15. The number of cells in a Karnaugh map is equal to the number of entries in a corresponding truth table (true or false)?

5–16. The order in which you label the rows and columns of a Karnaugh map does not matter as long as every combination of variables is used (true or false)?

5–17. Adjacent cells in a Karnaugh map are encircled in groups of 2, 4, 6 or 8 (true or false)?

5–18. Which method of encircling eight adjacent cells in a Karnaugh map produces the simplest equation: two groups of four, or one group of eight?

PROBLEMS

5–1. Write the Boolean equation for each of the logic circuits shown in Figure P5–1.

Figure P5–1

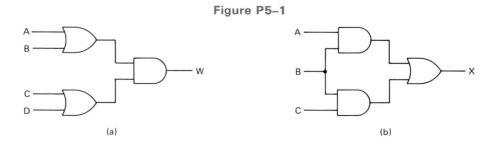

(a)   (b)

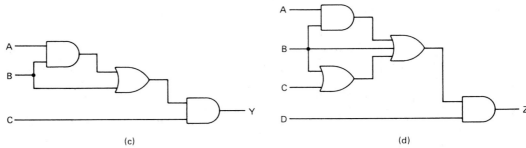

(c)   (d)

Figure P5–1 (*Continued*)

5–2. Draw the logic circuit that would be used to implement the following Boolean equations.
  (a) $M = (AB) + (C + D)$
  (b) $N = (A + B + C)D$
  (c) $P = (AC + BC)(A + C)$
  (d) $Q = (A + B)BCD$
  (e) $R = BC + D + AD$
  (f) $S = B(A + C) + AC + D$

5–3. Construct a truth table for each of the equations given in Problem 5–2.

5–4. Write the Boolean equation, then complete the timing diagram at W, X, Y, and Z for the logic circuits shown in Figure P5–4.

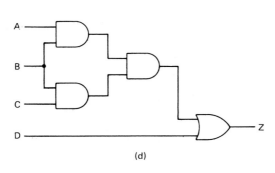

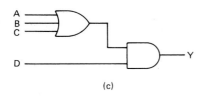

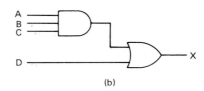

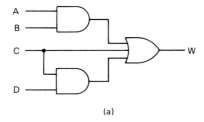

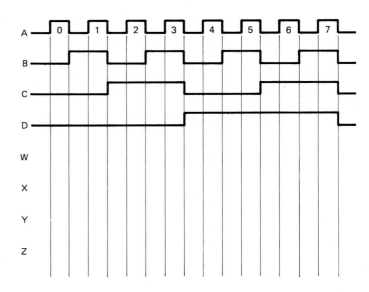

(a)

(b)

(c)

(d)

Figure P5–4

5–5. State the Boolean law that makes each of the equivalent circuits shown in Figure P5–5 valid.

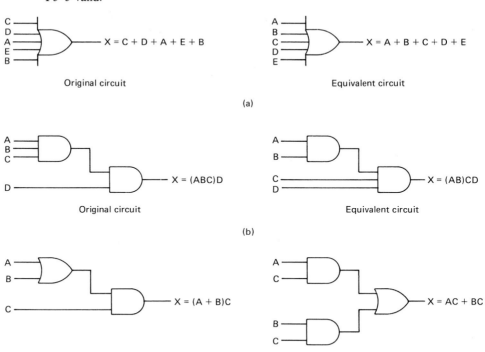

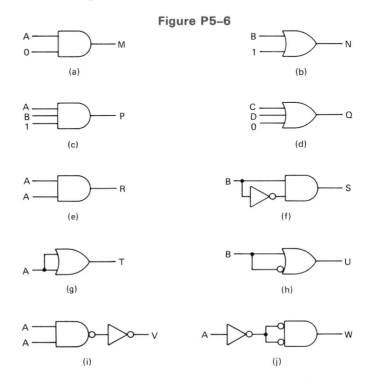

Figure P5–5

5–6. Using the 10 Boolean rules presented in Table 5–1, determine the outputs of the logic circuits shown in Figure P5–6.

Figure P5–6

5–7. Write the Boolean equation for the circuits of Figure P5–7. Simplify the equations and draw the simplified logic circuit.

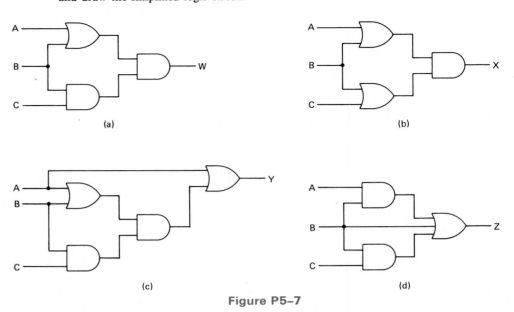

Figure P5–7

5–8. Repeat Problem 5–7 for the circuits shown in Figure P5–8.

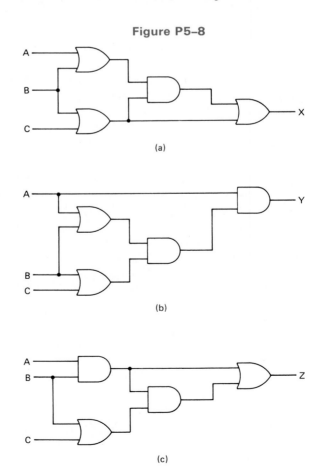

Figure P5–8

5–9. Draw the logic circuit for the following equations. Simplify the equations and draw the simplified logic circuit.

(a) $V = AC + ACD + CD$

(b) $W = (BCD + C)CD$

(c) $X = (B + D)(A + C) + ABD$

(d) $Y = AB + BC + ABC$

(e) $Z = ABC + CD + CDE$

5–10. Construct a truth table for each of the simplified equations of Problem 5–9.

5–11. The pin layouts for a 74HCT08 CMOS AND gate and a 74HCT32 CMOS OR gate are given in Figure P5–11. Make the external connections to the chips to implement the following logic equation. (Simplify the logic equation first.)

$$X = (A + B)(D + C) + ABD$$

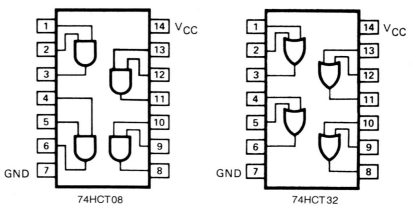

Figure P5–11

5–12. Repeat Problem 5–11 for the following equation:

$$Y = AB(C + BD) + BD$$

5–13. Write a sentence describing how DeMorgan's theorem is applied in the simplification of a logic equation.

5–14. (a) DeMorgan's theorem can be used to prove that an OR gate with inverted inputs is equivalent to what type of gate?

(b) An AND gate with inverted inputs is equivalent to what type of gate?

5–15. Which two circuits in Figure P5–15 produce equivalent output equations?

Figure P5–15

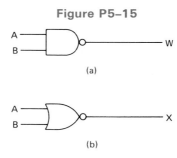

(a)

(b)

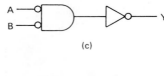

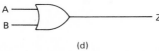

Figure P5–15 (*Continued*)

5–16. Use DeMorgan's theorem to prove that a NOR gate with inverted inputs is equivalent to an AND gate.

5–17. Draw the logic circuit for the following equations. Apply DeMorgan's theorem and Boolean algebra rules to reduce them to equations having inversion bars over single variables only. Draw the simplified circuit.
  (a) $W = \overline{\overline{AB} + \overline{A}} + C$
  (b) $X = A\overline{B} + \overline{C + \overline{B}C}$
  (c) $Y = \overline{(\overline{AB}) + C} + B\overline{C}$
  (d) $Z = \overline{AB + (\overline{A} + C)}$

5–18. Write the Boolean equation for the circuits of Figure P5–18. Use DeMorgan's theorem and Boolean algebra rules to simplify the equation. Draw the simplified circuit.

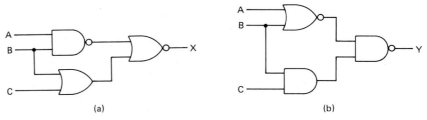

Figure P5–18

5–19. Repeat Problem 5–17 for the following equations.
  (a) $W = \overline{\overline{AB} + CD} + AC\overline{\overline{D}}$
  (b) $X = \overline{\overline{\overline{A} + B} \cdot BC} + \overline{B}C$
  (c) $Y = \overline{AB\overline{C} + D} + \overline{A\overline{B} + B\overline{C}}$
  (d) $Z = \overline{(C + D)\overline{A\overline{C}D}(\overline{A}C + \overline{D})}$

5–20. Repeat Problem 5–18 for the circuits of Figure P5–20.

Figure P5–20

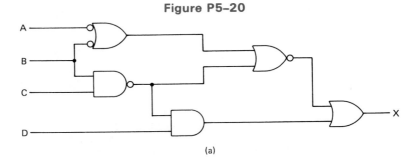

(a)

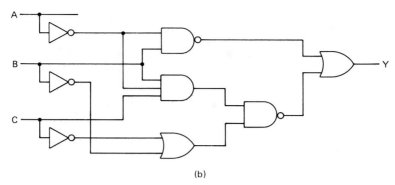

(b)

Figure P5–20 (Continued)

5–21. Draw a logic circuit that will put out a 1 (HIGH) if A and B are both 1, while either C or D is 1.

5–22. Draw a logic circuit that will put out a 0 if A or B is 0.

5–23. Draw a logic circuit that will put out a LOW if A or B is HIGH while C or D is LOW.

5–24. Draw a logic circuit that will put out a HIGH if only one of the inputs A, B, or C is LOW.

5–25. Complete a truth table for the following simplified Boolean equations.
   (a) $W = A\overline{B}\,\overline{C} + \overline{B}C + \overline{A}B$
   (b) $X = \overline{A}\,\overline{B} + A\overline{B}C + B\overline{C}$
   (c) $Y = \overline{C}D + \overline{A}\,\overline{B}\,\overline{C}\,\overline{D} + BCD + \overline{A}C\overline{D}$
   (d) $Z = \overline{A}C + C\overline{D} + \overline{B}\,\overline{C} + \overline{A}BC\overline{D}$

5–26. Complete the timing diagram in Figure P5–26 for the following simplified Boolean equations.
   (a) $X = \overline{A}\,\overline{B}\,\overline{C} + ABC + A\overline{C}$
   (b) $Y = \overline{B} + \overline{A}B\overline{C} + AC$
   (c) $Z = B\overline{C} + A\overline{B} + \overline{A}BC$

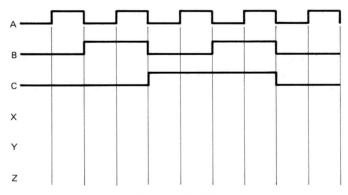

Figure P5–26

5–27. Draw the connections required to convert:
   (a) A NAND gate into an inverter
   (b) A NOR gate into an inverter

5–28. Draw the connections required to construct:
  (a)   An OR gate from two NOR gates
  (b)   An AND gate from two NAND gates
  (c)   An AND gate from several NOR gates
  (d)   A NOR gate from several NAND gates

5–29. Redraw the logic circuits of Figure P5–29 to their equivalents *using only* NOR gates.

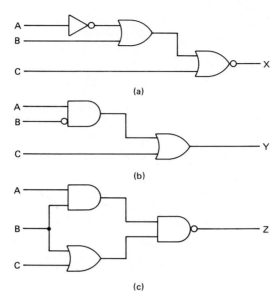

(a)

(b)

(c)   **Figure P5–29**

5–30. Convert the circuits of Figure P5–30 to their equivalents *using only* NAND gates. Next, make the external connections to a 7400 quad NAND to implement the new circuit. (Each new equivalent circuit is limited to *four* NAND gates.)

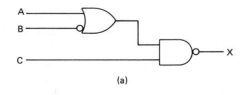

(a)

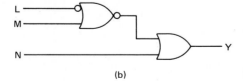

(b)   **Figure P5–30**

5–31. Identify each of the following Boolean equations as a product-of-sums (POS) expression or sum-of-products (SOP) expression, or both.
  (a) $U = A\bar{B}C + BC + \bar{A}C$
  (b) $V = (A + C)(\bar{B} + \bar{C})$
  (c) $W = A\bar{C}(\bar{B} + C)$
  (d) $X = AB + \bar{C} + BD$
  (e) $Y = (A\bar{B} + D)(A + \bar{C}D)$
  (f) $Z = (A + \bar{B})(BC + A) + \bar{A}B + CD$

5–32. Simplify the circuit of Figure P5–32 down to its SOP form, then draw the logic circuit of the simplified form, implemented using a 74LS54 AOI gate.

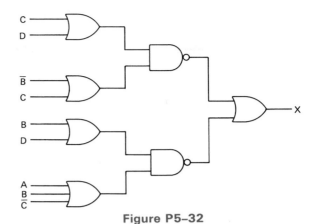

Figure P5–32

5–33. Using a Karnaugh map, reduce the following equations to a minimum sum-of-products form.
  (a) $X = AB\overline{C} + \overline{A}B + \overline{A}\,\overline{B}$
  (b) $Y = BC + \overline{A}\,\overline{B}C + B\overline{C}$
  (c) $Z = ABC + A\overline{B}\,\overline{C} + \overline{A}\,\overline{B}C + AB\overline{C}$

5–34. Using a Karnaugh map, reduce the following equations to a minimum sum-of-products form.
  (a) $W = \overline{B}(C\overline{D} + \overline{A}D) + \overline{B}\,\overline{C}(A + \overline{A}\,\overline{D})$
  (b) $X = \overline{A}\,\overline{B}\,\overline{D} + B(\overline{C}\,\overline{D} + ACD) + A\overline{B}\,\overline{D}$
  (c) $Y = A(C\overline{D} + \overline{C}\overline{D}) + A\overline{B}D + \overline{A}\,\overline{B}C\overline{D}$
  (d) $Z = \overline{B}CD + B\overline{C}D + \overline{C}\,\overline{D} + CD(B + \overline{A}\,\overline{B})$

5–35. Use a Karnaugh map to simplify the circuits in Figure P5–35.

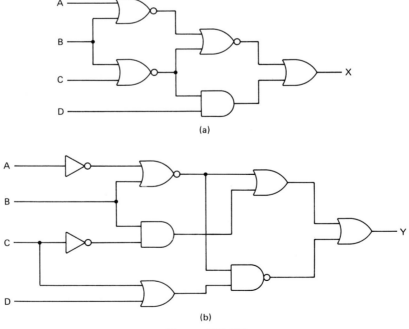

(a)

(b)

Figure P5–35

Design

5–36. Seven-segment displays are commonly used in calculators to display each of the decimal digits. Each segment of a digit is controlled separately and when all seven of the segments are on, the number ⯊ is displayed. The upper-right segment of the display comes on when displaying the numbers 0, 1, 2, 3, 4, 7, 8, and 9. (The numerical designation for each of the digits 0 to 9 is shown in Figure P5–36.) Design a circuit that puts out a HIGH (1) whenever a 4-bit BCD code translates to a number that uses the upper-right segment. Implement your design with an AOI and inverters.

Figure P5–36

5–37. Repeat Problem 5–36 for the lower-left segment of a seven-segment display (0, 2, 6, 8).

Troubleshooting

5–38. The logic circuit of Figure P5–38a is implemented by making connections to the 7400 as shown in Figure P5–38b. The circuit is not working properly. The problem is in the IC connections or in the IC itself. The data table in Figure P5–38c is completed by using a logic probe at each pin. Identify the problem.

Figure P5–38

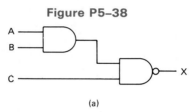

(a)

Test conditions:
A = 1
B = 1
C = 1
X should equal 0

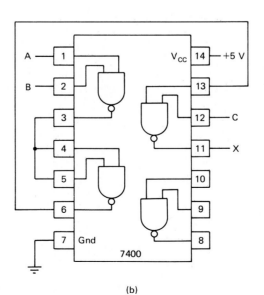

(b)

Probe on pin:	Indicator lamp
1	On
2	On
3	Off
4	Off
5	Off
6	Off
7	Off
8	On
9	Dim
10	Dim
11	On
12	On
13	Off
14	On

(c)

5–39. Repeat Problem 5–38 for the circuit shown in Figure P5–39.

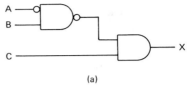

(a)

Test conditions:
A = 0
B = 1
C = 1
X should equal 0

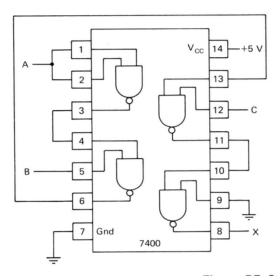

(b)   **Figure P5–39**

Probe on pin:	Indicator lamp
1	Off
2	Off
3	On
4	On
5	On
6	Off
7	Off
8	On
9	Off
10	On
11	On
12	On
13	Off
14	On

(c)

6

Exclusive-OR
and Exclusive-NOR Gates

OBJECTIVES

Upon completion of this chapter, you should be able to:

- Describe the operation and use of exclusive-OR and exclusive-NOR gates.
- Construct truth tables and draw timing diagrams for exclusive-OR and exclusive-NOR gates.
- Simplify combinational logic circuits containing exclusive-OR and exclusive-NOR gates.
- Design odd and even-parity generator and checker systems.
- Explain the operation of a binary comparator and a controlled inverter.

INTRODUCTION

We have seen in the previous chapters that by using various combinations of the basic gates, we can form most any logic function that we need. Quite often a particular combination of logic gates provide a function that is especially useful for a wide variety of tasks. The AOI discussed in Chapter 5 is one such circuit. In this chapter we learn about, and design, systems using two new combinational logic gates: the exclusive-OR and the exclusive-NOR.

6–1 THE EXCLUSIVE-OR GATE

Remember, the OR gate provides a HIGH output if one input or the other input is HIGH, *or if both inputs are HIGH*. The *exclusive-OR*, on the other hand, provides a HIGH output if one input or the other input is HIGH *but not both*. This point

TABLE 6–1

Truth Tables for an OR Gate
Versus an Exclusive-OR Gate

A	B	X	A	B	X
0	0	0	0	0	0
0	1	1	0	1	1
1	0	1	1	0	1
1	1	1	1	1	0
(OR)			(Exclusive-OR)		

is made more clear by comparing the truth tables for an OR gate versus an exclusive-OR gate, as shown in Table 6–1.

The Boolean equation for the Ex-OR function is written $X = \overline{A}B + A\overline{B}$ and can be constructed using the combinational logic shown in Figure 6–1. By experimenting and using Boolean reduction, we can find several other combinations of the basic gates that provide the Ex-OR function. For example, the combination of AND, OR, and NAND gates shown in Figure 6–2 will reduce to the "one-or-the-other-but-not-both" (Ex-OR) function.

The exclusive-OR gate is common enough to deserve its own logic symbol and equation, shown in Figure 6–3. (Note the shorthand method of writing the Boolean equation is to use a plus sign with a circle around it.)

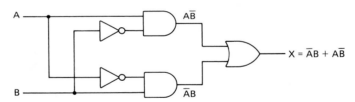

Figure 6–1   Logic circuit for providing the exclusive-OR function.

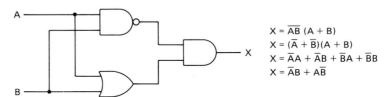

Figure 6–2   Exclusive-OR built with an AND–OR–NAND combination.

$X = \overline{AB} (A + B)$
$X = (\overline{A} + \overline{B})(A + B)$
$X = \overline{A}A + \overline{A}B + \overline{B}A + \overline{B}B$
$X = \overline{A}B + A\overline{B}$

$X = A \oplus B = \overline{A}B + A\overline{B}$ Figure 6–3   Logic symbol and equation for the exclusive-OR.

6–2   THE EXCLUSIVE-NOR GATE

The exclusive-NOR is the complement of the exclusive-OR. A comparison of the truth tables in Table 6–2 illustrates that point.

The truth table for the Ex-NOR shows a HIGH output for both inputs LOW or both inputs HIGH. The Ex-NOR is sometimes called the "equality gate" because both inputs must be equal to get a HIGH output. The basic logic circuit and symbol for the Ex-NOR is shown in Figure 6–4.

TABLE 6–2

Truth Tables of the Exclusive-
NOR Versus the Exclusive-OR

A	B	X	A	B	X
0	0	1	0	0	0
0	1	0	0	1	1
1	0	0	1	0	1
1	1	1	1	1	0

Exclusive-NOR   Exclusive-OR

$$X = AB + \overline{A}\overline{B} \qquad X = \overline{A}B + A\overline{B}$$

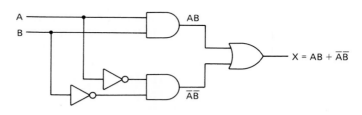

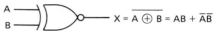

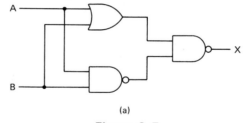

Figure 6–4   Exclusive-NOR logic circuit and logic symbol.

Summary

The exclusive-OR and exclusive-NOR gates are two-input logic gates that provide a very important commonly used function that we will see in upcoming examples. Basically, the operation of the gates is as follows:

> The exclusive-OR gate provides a HIGH output for one or the other inputs HIGH, but not both ($X = \overline{A}B + A\overline{B}$).

> The exclusive-NOR gate provides a HIGH output for both inputs HIGH or both inputs LOW ($X = AB + \overline{A}\overline{B}$).

Also, the Ex-OR and Ex-NOR gates are available in both TTL and CMOS integrated-circuit packages. For example, the 7486 is a TTL quad Ex-OR and the 4077 is a CMOS quad Ex-NOR.

EXAMPLE 6–1

Determine for each of the circuits shown in Figure 6–5 if their output provides the Ex-OR function, the Ex-NOR function, or neither.

(a)

Figure 6–5

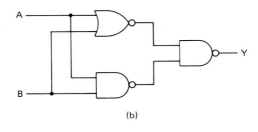

(b)

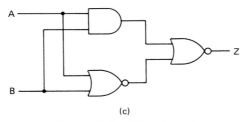

(c)

Figure 6-5 (*Continued*)

Solution:

(a) $X = \overline{(A+B)\overline{AB}}$

$= \overline{A+B} + \overline{\overline{AB}}$

$= \overline{A}\,\overline{B} + AB \leftarrow \text{Ex-NOR}$

(b) $Y = \overline{\overline{A+B}\,\overline{AB}}$

$= \overline{\overline{A+B}} + \overline{\overline{AB}}$

$= A + B + AB$

$= A + B(1+A)$

$= A + B \leftarrow \text{neither (OR function)}$

(c) $Z = \overline{AB + \overline{A+B}}$

$= \overline{AB}\,\overline{\overline{A+B}}$

$= (\overline{A}+\overline{B})(A+B)$

$= \overline{A}B + \overline{A}A + \overline{B}A + \overline{B}B$

$= \overline{A}B + A\overline{B} \leftarrow \text{Ex-OR}$

EXAMPLE 6-2

Write the Boolean equation for the circuit shown in Figure 6-6, and simplify.

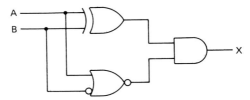

Figure 6-6

Solution:

$$X = (\overline{A}B + A\overline{B})\overline{\overline{A}+\overline{B}}$$
$$= (\overline{A}B + A\overline{B})A\overline{\overline{B}}$$
$$= \overline{A}B\overline{A}B + A\overline{B}\overline{A}B$$
$$= \overline{A}B$$

EXAMPLE 6–3

Write the Boolean equation for the circuit shown in Figure 6–7, and simplify.

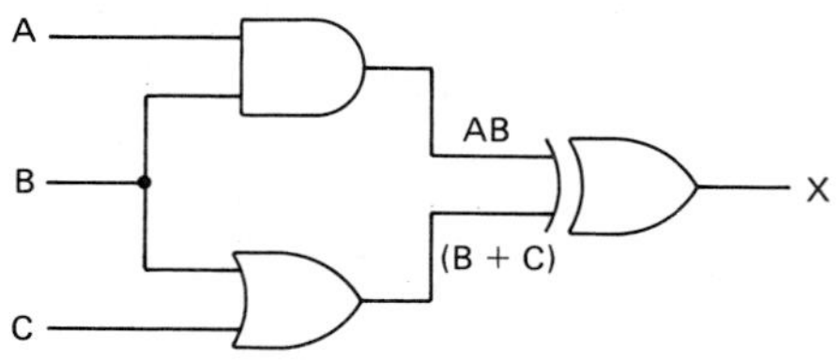

Figure 6–7

Solution:

$$X = \overline{AB}(B + C) + AB\overline{(B + C)}$$
$$= (\overline{A} + \overline{B})(B + C) + AB\overline{B}\overline{C}$$
$$= \overline{A}B + \overline{A}C + \overline{B}B + \overline{B}C$$
$$= \overline{A}B + \overline{A}C + \overline{B}C$$

6–3 PARITY GENERATOR/CHECKER

Now let's look at some digital systems that use the Ex-OR and Ex-NOR gates. We start by studying the parity generator.

In the transmission of binary information from one digital device to another digital device, it is possible for external electrical noise or other disturbances to cause an error in the digital signal. For example, if a 4-bit digital system is transmitting a BCD 5 (0101), electrical noise present on the line during the transmission of the LSB may change a 1 to a 0. If so, the receiving device on the other end of the transmission line would receive a BCD 4 (0100), which is wrong. If a parity system is used, that error would be recognized and the receiving device would signal an "error condition" or ask the transmitting device to retransmit.

Parity systems are defined as either *odd parity* or *even parity*. The parity system adds an extra bit to the digital information being transmitted. A 4-bit system will require a fifth bit, an 8-bit system will require a ninth bit, and so on.

In a 4-bit system such as BCD or hexadecimal, the fifth bit is the parity bit and will be a 1 or 0, depending on what the other 4 bits are. In an *odd-parity* system, the parity bit that is added must make the *sum of all 5 bits odd*. In an *even-parity* system, the parity bit makes the *sum of all 5 bits even*.

The parity generator is the circuit that creates the parity bit. On the receiving end, a parity checker determines if the 5-bit result is of the right parity. The type of system (odd or even) must be agreed on beforehand so that the parity checker knows what to look for (this is called *protocol*). Also, the parity bit can be placed next to the MSB *or* LSB as long as the device on the receiving end knows which bit is parity and which bits are data.

Let's look at the example of transmitting the BCD number 5 (0101) in an odd-parity system.

As shown in Figure 6–8, the transmitting device puts a 0101 on the BCD lines. The parity generator puts a 1 on the parity-bit line, making the sum of the bits odd (0 + 1 + 0 + 1 + 1 = 3). The parity checker at the receiving end checks to see that the 5 bits are odd, and if so, assumes that the BCD information is valid.

If, however, the data in the LSB were changed due to electrical noise somewhere in the transmission cable, the parity checker would detect that an even-parity number was received, and signal an error condition.

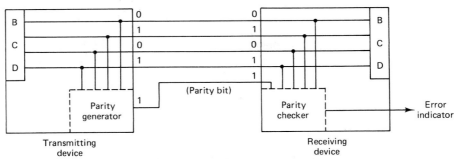

Figure 6–8 Odd-parity generator/checker system.

This scheme detects only errors that occur to 1 bit. If 2 bits were changed, the parity checker would think everything is okay. However, the likelihood of 2 bits being affected is highly unusual. An error occurring to even 1 bit is unusual.

EXAMPLE 6–4

Add a parity bit next to the LSB of the following hexadecimal codes to form even parity: 0111, 1101, 1010, 1111, 1000, 0000.

Solution:

$$01111$$
$$11011$$
$$10100$$
$$11110$$
$$10001$$
$$00000$$

⤒——parity bit

The parity generator and checker can be constructed from exclusive-OR gates. Figure 6–9 shows the connections to form a 4-bit even and a 4-bit odd-parity generator. The odd-parity generator has the BCD number 5 (0101) at its inputs. If you follow the logic through with those bits, you will see that the parity bit will be a 1, just as we want. Try some different 4-bit numbers at the inputs to both the even- and odd-parity generators to prove to yourself that they work properly. Computer systems generally transmit 8 or 16 bits of parallel data at a time. An 8-bit even-parity generator can be constructed by adding more gates, as shown in Figure 6–10.

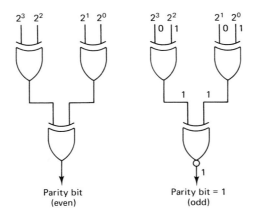

Parity bit (even)

Parity bit = 1 (odd)

Figure 6–9 Even- and odd-parity generators.

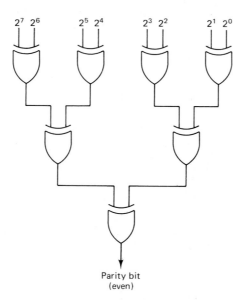

Figure 6–10   Eight-bit even-parity generator.

Parity bit (even)

A parity checker is constructed in the same way as the parity generator except that in a 4-bit system, there must be five inputs (including the parity bit) and the output is used as the error indicator (1 = error condition). Figure 6–11 shows a 5-bit even-parity checker. The BCD 6 with even parity is input. Follow the logic through the diagram to prove to yourself that the output will be 0, meaning "no error."

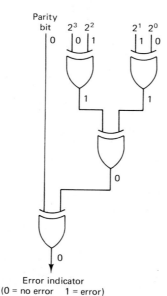

Error indicator
(0 = no error   1 = error)

Figure 6–11   Five-bit even-parity checker.

Integrated-Circuit Parity Generator/Checker

You may have guessed by now that parity generator and checker circuits are available in single integrated-circuit packages. One popular 9-bit parity generator/checker is the 74280 TTL IC (or 74HC280 CMOS IC). The logic symbol and function for the 74280 are given in Figure 6–12.

The 74280 has nine inputs. If used as a parity checker, the first eight inputs would be the data input and the ninth would be the parity-bit input. If your system is looking for even parity, the sum of the nine inputs should be even, which will produce a HIGH at the Σ_E output and a LOW at the Σ_0 output.

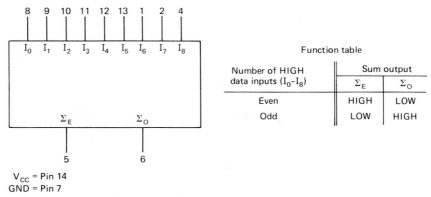

| Number of HIGH | Sum output | |
data inputs (I_0–I_8)	Σ_E	Σ_O
Even	HIGH	LOW
Odd	LOW	HIGH

Function table

V_{CC} = Pin 14
GND = Pin 7

Figure 6–12 Logic symbol and function table for the 74280 9-bit parity generator/checker.

6–4 SYSTEM DESIGN APPLICATIONS

SYSTEM DESIGN 6–1: Parity Error Detection System

Using 74280s, design a complete parity generator/checking system. It is to be used in an 8-bit even-parity computer configuration.

Solution:

Parity generator: Since the 74280 has nine inputs, we will have to connect the unused ninth input (I_8) to ground (0) so that it will not affect our result. The 8-bit input data will be connected to I_0 to I_7.

Now, the generator sums bits I_0 to I_7 and puts out a LOW on Σ_O and a HIGH on Σ_E if the sum is even. Therefore, the parity bit generated should be taken from the Σ_O output because we want the sum of all 9 bits sent to the receiving device to be even.

Parity Checker: The checker will receive all 9 bits and check if their sum is even. If their sum *is* even, the Σ_E line goes HIGH. We will use the Σ_O output because it will be LOW for "no error," HIGH for "error." The complete circuit design is shown in Figure 6–13.

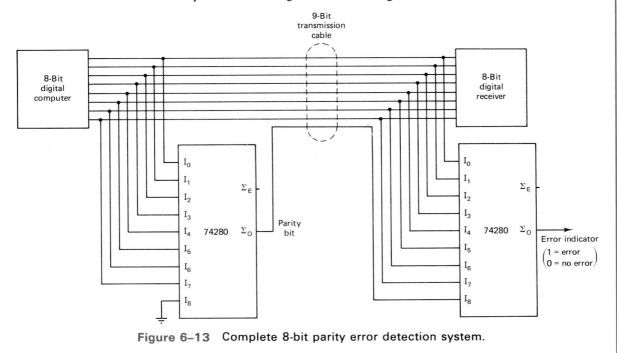

Figure 6–13 Complete 8-bit parity error detection system.

129

SYSTEM DESIGN 6–2: Parallel Binary Comparator

Design a system that compares the 4-bit binary string A to the 4-bit binary string B. If the strings are exactly equal, provide a HIGH-level output to drive a warning buzzer.

Solution: Using four exclusive-NOR gates, we can compare string A to string B, bit by bit. Remember, if both inputs to an exclusive-NOR are the same (0–0 or 1–1), it outputs a 1. If all four Ex-NOR gates are outputting a 1, the 4 bits of string A must match the 4 bits of string B. The complete circuit design is shown in Figure 6–14.

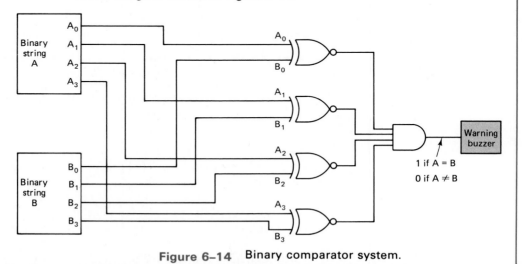

Figure 6–14 Binary comparator system.

SYSTEM DESIGN 6–3: Controlled Inverter

Often in binary arithmetic circuits we need to have a device that complements an entire binary string when told to do so by some control signal. Design an 8-bit controlled inverter (complementing) circuit. The circuit will receive a control signal that, if HIGH, will cause the circuit to complement the 8-bit string, and if LOW, will not.

Solution: The circuit shown in Figure 6–15 can be used to provide the complementing function. If the control signal (C) is HIGH, each of the input data

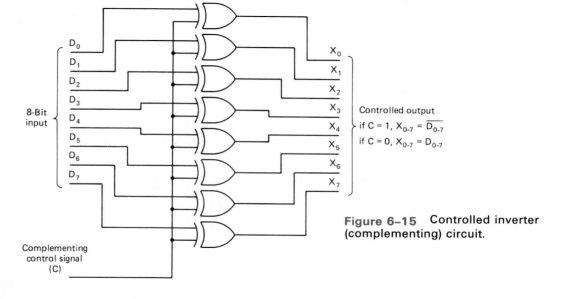

Figure 6–15 Controlled inverter (complementing) circuit.

bits will be complemented at the output. If the control signal is LOW, the data bits will pass through to the output uncomplemented. Two 7486 quad exclusive-OR ICs could be used to implement this design.

GLOSSARY

Binary string: Two or more binary bits used collectively to form a meaningful binary representation.

Comparator: A device or system that identifies an equality between two quantities.

Controlled inverter: A digital circuit capable of complementing a binary string of bits based on an external control signal.

Electrical noise: Unwanted electrical irregularities that can cause a change in a digital logic level.

Error indicator: A visual display or digital signal that is used to signify that an error has occurred within a digital system.

Exclusive-NOR: A gate that produces a HIGH output for both inputs HIGH, or both inputs LOW.

Exclusive-OR: A gate that produces a HIGH output for one or the other inputs HIGH, but not both.

Function table: A chart that illustrates the input/output operating characteristics of an integrated circuit.

Parity: An error detection scheme used to detect a change in the value of a bit.

Transmission: The transfer of digital signals from one location to another.

REVIEW QUESTIONS

Sections 6–1 and 6–2

6–1.   The exclusive-OR gate is the complement (or inverse) of the OR gate (true or false)?

6–2.   The exclusive-OR gate is the complement of the exclusive-NOR gate (true or false)?

6–3.   Write the Boolean equation for an exclusive-NOR gate. $\leftarrow AB + \bar{A}\bar{B}$

Sections 6–3 and 6–4

6–4.   An *odd* parity generator produces a 1 if the sum of its inputs is odd (true or false)?

6–5.   In an 8-bit parallel transmission system, if one or two of the bits were changed due to electrical noise, the parity checker will detect the error (true or false)?

6–6.   Which output of the 74280 parity generator is used as the parity bit in an *odd* system? Σ_E (sum Even)

PROBLEMS

6–1.   Describe, in words, the operation of an exclusive-OR gate; an exclusive-NOR gate.

6–2.   Describe, in words, the difference between:
   (a)   An exclusive-OR and an OR gate
   (b)   An exclusive-NOR and an AND gate

6–3.   Complete the timing diagram in Figure P6–3 for the exclusive-OR and the exclusive-NOR.

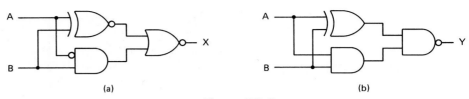

(a)   (b)

Figure P6–3

6–4. Write the Boolean equations for the circuits in Figure P6–4, parts (a) through (d). Simplify the equations and determine if they function as an Ex-OR, Ex-NOR, or neither.

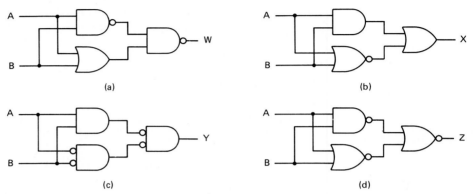

(a)   (b)

(c)   (d)

Figure P6–4

6–5. Design an exclusive-OR gate constructed from all NOR gates.

6–6. Design an exclusive-NOR gate constructed from all NAND gates.

6–7. Write the Boolean equations for the circuits of Figure P6–7. Reduce the equations to their simplest form.

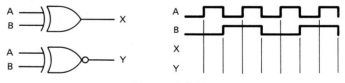

Figure P6–7

6–8. Repeat Problem 6–7 for the circuits of Figure P6–8.

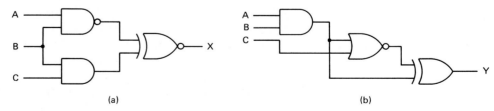

(a)   (b)

Figure P6–8

6–9. Convert the following hexadecimal numbers to their 8-bit binary code. Add a parity bit next to the LSB to form odd parity.

A7   4C   79   F3   00   FF

6–10. The pin configuration of the 74HC86 CMOS quad exclusive-OR IC is given in Figure P6–10. Make the external connections to the IC to form a 4-bit even-parity generator.

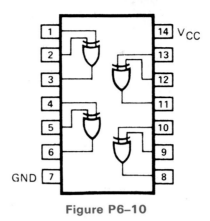

Figure P6–10

6–11. Repeat Problem 6–10 for a 5-bit even-parity checker. Use the pin configuration shown in Figure P6–11.

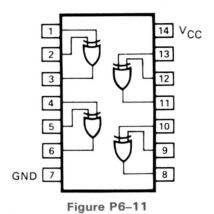

Figure P6–11

Design

6–12. Figure P6–12 shows another design used to form a 4-bit parity generator. Determine if the circuit will function as an odd- or an even-parity generator.

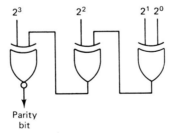

Figure P6–12

6–13. Referring to Figure 6–13, design and sketch a 4-bit odd-parity error detection system. Use two 74280 ICs and a five-line transmission cable between the sending and receiving devices.

6–14. Design a binary comparator system similar to Figure 6–14 using exclusive-ORs instead of exclusive-NORs.

6–15. If the exclusive ORs in Figure 6–15 are replaced by exclusive NORs, will the circuit still function as a controlled inverter? If so, should C be HIGH or LOW to complement?

7

Arithmetic Circuits

OBJECTIVES

Upon completion of this chapter, you should be able to:

- Perform the four binary arithmetic functions: addition, subtraction, multiplication, and division.
- Convert positive and negative numbers to signed two's-complement notation.
- Perform two's-complement, hexadecimal, and BCD arithmetic.
- Explain the design and operation of a half-adder and a full-adder circuit.
- Utilize full-adder ICs to implement arithmetic circuits.
- Explain the operation of a two's-complement adder/subtractor circuit and a BCD adder circuit.
- Explain the function of an arithmetic/logic unit (ALU).

INTRODUCTION

An important function of digital systems and computers is the execution of arithmetic operations. In this chapter we will see that there is no magic in taking the sum of two numbers electronically. Instead, there is a basic set of logic-circuit building blocks, and the arithmetic operations follow a step-by-step procedure to arrive at the correct answer. All the "electronic arithmetic" will be performed using digital input and output levels with basic combinational logic circuits or medium-scale-integration (MSI) chips.

7–1 BINARY ARITHMETIC

Before studying the actual digital electronic requirements for arithmetic circuits, let's look at the procedures for performing the four basic arithmetic functions: addition, subtraction, multiplication, and division.

Addition

The procedure for adding numbers in binary is similar to adding in decimal except that the binary sum is made up of only 1's and 0's. When the binary sum exceeds 1 you must carry a 1 to the next-more-significant column, as in regular decimal addition.

The four possible combinations of adding two binary numbers can be stated as follows:

$$0 + 0 = 0 \quad \text{carry } 0$$
$$0 + 1 = 1 \quad \text{carry } 0$$
$$1 + 0 = 1 \quad \text{carry } 0$$
$$1 + 1 = 0 \quad \text{carry } 1$$

The general form of binary addition in the least significant column can be written

$$A_0 + B_0 = \Sigma_0 + C_{\text{out}}$$

The sum output is given by the *summation* symbol (Σ) and the carry output is given by C_{out}. The truth table in Table 7–1 shows the four possible conditions when adding two binary digits.

TABLE 7–1

Truth Table for Addition
of Two Binary Digits
in the Least Significant Column

A_0	B_0	Σ_0	C_{out}
0	0	0	0
0	1	1	0
1	0	1	0
1	1	0	1

If a carry *is* produced, it must be added to the next-more-significant column as a carry-in (C_{in}). Figure 7–1 shows that operation and truth table. In the truth table, the C_{in} term comes from the value of C_{out} from the previous addition. Now, with three possible inputs there are eight combinations of outputs ($2^3 = 8$). Review the truth table to be sure that you understand how each sum and carry were determined.

Now let's perform some binary additions. We represent all binary numbers in groups of 8 or 16 because that is the standard used for arithmetic in most digital computers today.

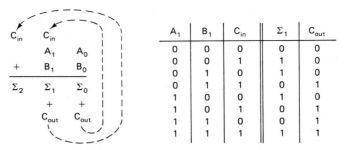

A_1	B_1	C_in	Σ_1	C_out
0	0	0	0	0
0	0	1	1	0
0	1	0	1	0
0	1	1	0	1
1	0	0	1	0
1	0	1	0	1
1	1	0	0	1
1	1	1	1	1

Figure 7–1 Addition in the more significant columns requires including C_{in} with $A_1 + B_1$.

EXAMPLE 7–1

Perform the following decimal additions. Convert the original decimal numbers to binary and add them. Compare answers. **(a)** 5 + 2; **(b)** 8 + 3; **(c)** 18 + 2; **(d)** 147 + 75; **(e)** 31 + 7.

Solution:

	Decimal	*Binary*
(a)	5 + 2 ⎯⎯ 7	0000 0101 + 0000 0010 ⎯⎯⎯⎯⎯⎯ 0000 0111 $= 7_{10}$
(b)	8 + 3 ⎯⎯ 11	0000 1000 + 0000 0011 ⎯⎯⎯⎯⎯⎯ 0000 1011 $= 11_{10}$
(c)	18 + 2 ⎯⎯ 20	0001 0010 + 0000 0010 ⎯⎯⎯⎯⎯⎯ 0001 0100 $= 20_{10}$
(d)	147 + 75 ⎯⎯ 222	1001 0011 + 0100 1011 ⎯⎯⎯⎯⎯⎯ 1101 1110 $= 222_{10}$
(e)	31 + 7 ⎯⎯ 38	0001 1111 + 0000 0111 ⎯⎯⎯⎯⎯⎯ 0010 0110 $= 38_{10}$

Subtraction

The four possible combinations of subtracting two binary numbers can be stated as follows:

$$0 - 0 = 0 \quad \text{borrow } 0$$

$$0 - 1 = 1 \quad \text{borrow } 1$$

$$1 - 0 = 1 \quad \text{borrow } 0$$

$$1 - 1 = 0 \quad \text{borrow } 0$$

The general form of binary subtraction in the least significant column can be written

$$A_0 - B_0 = R_0 + B_{out}$$

The difference, or *remainder*, from the subtraction is R_0 and if a *borrow* is required, B_{out} will be 1. The truth table in Table 7–2 shows the four possible conditions when subtracting two binary digits.

TABLE 7–2

Truth Table for Subtraction
of Two Binary Digits
in the Least Significant Column

A_0	B_0	R_0	B_{out}
0	0	0	0
0	1	1	1
1	0	1	0
1	1	0	0

If a borrow *is* required, the A_0 must borrow from A_1 in the next-more-significant column. When A_0 borrows from its left, A_0 will increase by 2 (just as in decimal subtraction, where the number increases by 10). For example, let's subtract $2 - 1$ ($10_2 - 01_2$).

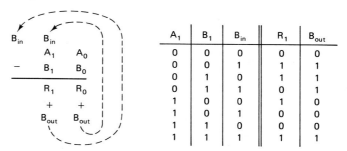

Since A_0 was 0, it borrowed 1 from A_1. A_1 becomes a 0 and A_0 becomes 2 (2_{10} or 10_2). Now the subtraction can take place: in the LS column $2 - 1 = 1$, and in the MS column $0 - 0 = 0$.

As you can see, the second column and all more significant columns first have to determine if A was borrowed from before subtracting $A - B$. Therefore, they have three input conditions, for a total of eight different possible combinations, as illustrated in Figure 7–2.

A_1	B_1	B_{in}	R_1	B_{out}
0	0	0	0	0
0	0	1	1	1
0	1	0	1	1
0	1	1	0	1
1	0	0	1	0
1	0	1	0	0
1	1	0	0	0
1	1	1	1	1

Figure 7–2 Subtraction in the more significant columns.

The outputs in the truth table in Figure 7–2 are a little more complicated to figure out. To help you along, let's look at the subtraction: 4 minus 1 ($0100_2 - 0001_2$).

$$
\begin{array}{rl}
4_{10} & \quad A_3A_2A_1A_0 \\
-\,1_{10} & \quad -\,B_3B_2B_1B_0 \\
\hline
3_{10} & \quad R_3R_2R_1R_0
\end{array}
$$

To subtract $0100 - 0001$, A_0 must borrow from A_1, but A_1 is 0. Therefore, A_1 must first borrow from A_2, making A_2 a 0. Now A_1 is a 2. A_0 borrows from A_1, making A_1 a 1 and A_0 a 2. Now we can subtract to get 0011 (3_{10}). Actually, the process is very similar to the process you learned many years ago for regular decimal subtraction. Work through each entry in the truth table (Figure 7–2) to determine how it was derived.

Fortunately, as we will see in Section 7–2, digital computers use a much easier method for subtracting binary numbers, called two's complement. We do, however, need to know the standard method for subtracting binary numbers. Work through the following example to better familarize yourself with the binary subtraction procedure.

EXAMPLE 7–2

Perform the following decimal subtractions. Convert the original decimal numbers to binary and subtract them. Compare answers. **(a)** $27 - 10$; **(b)** $9 - 4$; **(c)** $172 - 42$; **(d)** $154 - 54$; **(e)** $192 - 3$.

Solution:

	Decimal	*Binary*
(a)	27	0001 1011
	− 10	− 0000 1010
	17	0001 0001 = 17_{10} ✓
(b)	9	0000 1001
	− 4	− 0000 0100
	5	0000 0101 = 5_{10} ✓
(c)	172	1010 1100
	− 42	− 0010 1010
	130	1000 0010 = 130_{10} ✓
(d)	154	1001 1010
	− 54	− 0011 0110
	100	0110 0100 = 100_{10} ✓
(e)	192	1100 0000
	− 3	− 0000 0011
	189	1011 1101 = 189_{10} ✓

Multiplication

Binary multiplication is like decimal multiplication except you deal only with 1's and 0's. Figure 7–3 illustrates the procedure for multiplying 13×11.

	Decimal	*Binary*
	13	0000 1101 (multiplicand)
	× 11	× 0000 1011 (multiplier)
	13	0000 1101
	13	00001 101
	143	000000 00
		0000110 1
		0001000 1111 (product)

8-bit answer = 1000 1111 = 143_{10} ✓

Figure 7–3 Binary multiplication procedure.

The procedure for the multiplication in Figure 7–3 is as follows:

1. Multiply the 2^0 bit of the multiplier times the multiplicand.
2. Multiply the 2^1 bit of the multiplier times the multiplicand. Shift the result one position to the left before writing it down.
3. Repeat step 2 for the 2^2 bit of the multiplier. Since the 2^2 bit is a 0, the result will be 0.
4. Repeat step 2 for the 2^3 bit of the multiplier.
5. Repeating step 2 for the four leading 0's in the multiplier will have no effect on the answer, so don't bother.
6. Take the sum of the four partial products to get the final product of 143_{10}. (Written as an 8-bit number, the product is $1000\ 1111_2$.)

EXAMPLE 7–3

Perform the following decimal multiplications. Convert the original decimal numbers to binary and multiply them. Compare answers. **(a)** 5×3; **(b)** 45×3; **(c)** 15×15; **(d)** 23×9.

Solution:

	Decimal	*Binary*

(a)
$$\begin{array}{r} 5 \\ \times\ 3 \\ \hline 15 \end{array} \qquad \begin{array}{r} 0000\ 0101 \\ \times\ 0000\ 0011 \\ \hline 0000\ 0101 \\ +\ 00000\ 101 \\ \hline 00000\ 1111 = 0000\ 1111 = 15_{10}\ ✓ \end{array}$$

(b)
$$\begin{array}{r} 45 \\ \times\ 3 \\ \hline 135 \end{array} \qquad \begin{array}{r} 0010\ 1101 \\ \times\ 0000\ 0011 \\ \hline 0010\ 1101 \\ +\ 00101\ 101 \\ \hline 01000\ 0111 = 1000\ 0111 = 135_{10}\ ✓ \end{array}$$

(c)
$$\begin{array}{r} 15 \\ \times\ 15 \\ \hline 75 \\ +\ 15 \\ \hline 225 \end{array} \qquad \begin{array}{r} 0000\ 1111 \\ \times\ 0000\ 1111 \\ \hline 0000\ 1111 \\ 00001\ 111 \\ 000011\ 11 \\ +\ 0000111\ 1 \\ \hline 0001110\ 0001 = 1110\ 0001 = 225_{10}\ ✓ \end{array}$$

(d)
$$\begin{array}{r} 23 \\ \times\ 9 \\ \hline 207 \end{array} \qquad \begin{array}{r} 0001\ 0111 \\ \times\ 0000\ 1001 \\ \hline 0001\ 0111 \\ 00000\ 000 \\ 000000\ 00 \\ 0001011\ 1 \\ \hline 0001100\ 1111 = 1100\ 1111 = 207_{10}\ ✓ \end{array}$$

Division

Binary division uses the same procedure as decimal division. Example 7–4 illustrates this procedure.

EXAMPLE 7–4

Perform the following decimal divisions. Convert the original decimal numbers to binary and divide them. Compare answers. **(a)** $9 \div 3$; **(b)** $35 \div 5$; **(c)** $135 \div 15$; **(d)** $221 \div 17$.

Solution:

	Decimal	*Binary*

(a)
$$
\begin{array}{r}
3 \\
3\overline{\smash{\big)}\ 9} \\
-9 \\
\hline
0
\end{array}
\qquad
\begin{array}{r}
11 = 3_{10}\ \checkmark \\
0000\ 0011\overline{\smash{\big)}0000\ 1001} \\
-\underline{11} \\
11 \\
-\underline{11} \\
0
\end{array}
$$

(b)
$$
\begin{array}{r}
7 \\
5\overline{\smash{\big)}\ 35} \\
-35 \\
\hline
0
\end{array}
\qquad
\begin{array}{r}
111 = 7_{10}\ \checkmark \\
0000\ 0101\overline{\smash{\big)}0010\ 0011} \\
-\underline{1\ 01} \\
111 \\
-\underline{101} \\
101 \\
-\underline{101} \\
0
\end{array}
$$

(c)
$$
\begin{array}{r}
9 \\
15\overline{\smash{\big)}\ 135} \\
-135 \\
\hline
0
\end{array}
\qquad
\begin{array}{r}
1001 = 9_{10}\ \checkmark \\
0000\ 1111\overline{\smash{\big)}1000\ 0111} \\
-\underline{111\ 1} \\
1111 \\
-\underline{1111} \\
0
\end{array}
$$

(d)
$$
\begin{array}{r}
13 \\
17\overline{\smash{\big)}\ 221} \\
-17 \\
\hline
51 \\
51 \\
\hline
0
\end{array}
\qquad
\begin{array}{r}
1101 = 13_{10}\ \checkmark \\
0001\ 0001\overline{\smash{\big)}1101\ 1101} \\
-\underline{1000\ 1} \\
101\ 01 \\
-\underline{100\ 01} \\
1\ 0001 \\
-\underline{1\ 0001} \\
0
\end{array}
$$

7–2 TWO'S-COMPLEMENT REPRESENTATION

The most widely used method of representing binary numbers and performing arithmetic in computer systems is by using the *two's-complement* method. Using that method, both positive and negative numbers can be represented using the same format, and binary subtraction is greatly simplified.

All along we have been representing binary numbers in groups of eight for a reason. Most computer systems are based on 8-bit or 16-bit numbers. In an 8-bit system, the total number of different combinations of bits is 256 (2^8); in a 16-bit system the number is 65,536 (2^{16}).

To be able to represent both positive *and* negative numbers the two's-complement format uses the most significant bit (MSB) of the 8- or 16-bit number to signify whether the number is positive or negative. The MSB is therefore called the *sign*

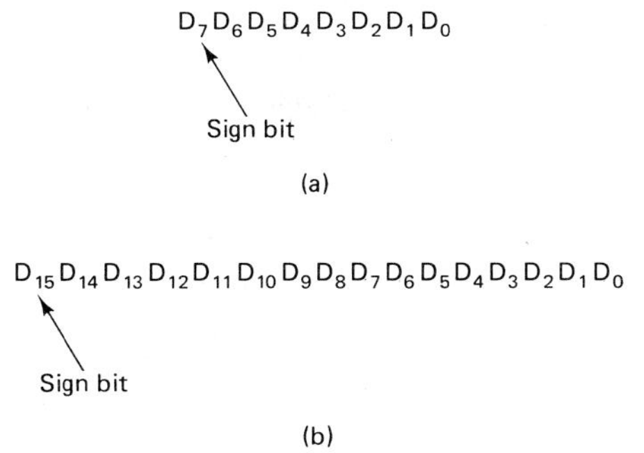

$$D_7 D_6 D_5 D_4 D_3 D_2 D_1 D_0$$

Sign bit

(a)

$$D_{15} D_{14} D_{13} D_{12} D_{11} D_{10} D_9 D_8 D_7 D_6 D_5 D_4 D_3 D_2 D_1 D_0$$

Sign bit

(b)

Figure 7–4 Two's-complement numbers: (a) 8-bit number; (b) 16-bit number.

bit and is defined as 0 for positive numbers and 1 for negative numbers. *Signed two's-complement* numbers are shown in Figure 7–4.

The *range of positive numbers* in an 8-bit system is 0000 0000 to 0111 1111 (0 to 127). The *range of negative numbers* is 1111 1111 to 1000 0000 (−1 to −128). In general, the maximum positive number is equal to $2^{N-1} - 1$ and the maximum negative number is -2^{N-1}, where N is the number of bits in the number, including the sign bit (e.g., for an 8-bit positive number, $2^{8-1} - 1 = 127$).

A table of two's-complement numbers can be developed by starting with some positive number and continuously subtracting 1. Table 7–3 shows the signed two's-complement numbers from +7 to −8.

TABLE 7–3

Signed Two's-Complement
Numbers +7 Through −8

Decimal	Two's complement
+7	0000 0111
+6	0000 0110
+5	0000 0101
+4	0000 0100
+3	0000 0011
+2	0000 0010
+1	0000 0001
0	0000 0000
−1	1111 1111
−2	1111 1110
−3	1111 1101
−4	1111 1100
−5	1111 1011
−6	1111 1010
−7	1111 1001
−8	1111 1000

Converting a decimal number to two's complement, and vice versa, is simple and can be done easily using logic gates, as we will see later in this chapter. For now, let's deal with 8-bit numbers; however, the procedure for 16-bit numbers is exactly the same.

Steps for Decimal to Two's-Complement Conversion

1. If the decimal number is positive, the two's-complement number is the regular binary equivalent of the decimal number (e.g., +18 = 0001 0010).

2. If the decimal number is negative, the two's-complement number is found by:
   (a) Complementing each bit in the binary equivalent of the decimal number (this is called the *one's complement*).
   (b) Adding 1 to the one's-complement number to get the magnitude bits. (The sign bit will always end up being 1.)

Steps for Two's-Complement to Decimal Conversion

1. If the two's-complement number is positive (sign bit = 0), do a regular binary-to-decimal conversion.
2. If the two's-complement number is negative (sign bit = 1), the decimal sign will be − and the decimal number is found by:
   (a) Complementing the entire two's-complement number, bit by bit.
   (b) Adding 1 to arrive at the regular binary equivalent.
   (c) Doing a regular binary-to-decimal conversion to get the decimal numeric value.

The following examples illustrate the conversion process.

EXAMPLE 7–5

Convert $+35_{10}$ to two's complement.

Solution:

Regular binary $= 0010\ 0011$
Two's complement $= 0010\ 0011$ *answer*

EXAMPLE 7–6

Convert -35_{10} to two's complement.

Solution:

Regular binary $= 0010\ 0011$
One's complement $= 1101\ 1100$
Add 1 $+1$
Two's complement $= 1101\ 1101$ *answer*

EXAMPLE 7–7

Convert 1101 1101 two's complement back to decimal.

Solution: The sign bit is 1, so the decimal result will be negative.

Two's complement $= 1101\ 1101$
Complement $= 0010\ 0010$
Add 1 $=\quad\quad +1$
Regular binary $= 0010\ 0011$
Decimal equivalent $= -35$ *answer*

EXAMPLE 7–8

Convert -98_{10} to two's complement.

Solution:

$$
\begin{aligned}
\text{Regular binary} &= 0110\ 0010 \\
\text{One's complement} &= 1001\ 1101 \\
\text{Add 1} &= \qquad +1 \\
\text{Two's complement} &= 1001\ 1110 \quad answer
\end{aligned}
$$

EXAMPLE 7–9

Convert 1011 0010 two's complement to decimal.

Solution: The sign bit is 1, so the decimal result will be negative.

$$
\begin{aligned}
\text{Two's complement} &= 1011\ 0010 \\
\text{Complement} &= 0100\ 1101 \\
\text{Add 1} &= \qquad +1 \\
\text{Regular binary} &= 0100\ 1110 \\
\text{Decimal equivalent} &= -78 \quad answer
\end{aligned}
$$

7–3 TWO'S-COMPLEMENT ARITHMETIC

All four of the basic arithmetic functions involving positive *and* negative numbers can be dealt with very simply using two's-complement arithmetic. Subtraction is done by *adding* the two two's-complement numbers. Thus the same digital circuitry can be used for additions *and* subtractions and there is no need always to subtract the smaller number from the larger number. We must be careful, however, not to exceed the *maximum range* of the two's-complement number: $+127$ to -128 for 8-bit systems, $+32,767$ to $-32,768$ for 16-bit systems ($+2^{N-1} - 1$ to -2^{N-1}).

When *adding* numbers in the two's-complement form, simply perform a regular binary addition to get the result. When *subtracting* numbers in the two's-complement form, convert the number being subtracted to a *negative* two's-complement number and perform a regular binary addition [e.g., $5 - 3 = 5 + (-3)$]. The result will be a two's-complement number, and if the result is negative, the sign bit will be 1.

Work through the following examples to familiarize yourself with the addition and subtraction procedure.

EXAMPLE 7–10

Add $19 + 27$ using 8-bit two's-complement arithmetic.

Solution:

$$
\begin{aligned}
19 &= 0001\ 0011 \\
27 &= 0001\ 1011 \\
\hline
\text{Sum} &= 0010\ 1110 = 46_{10}
\end{aligned}
$$

EXAMPLE 7–11

Perform the following subtractions using 8-bit two's-complement arithmetic: **(a)** $18 - 7$; **(b)** $21 - 13$; **(c)** $118 - 54$; **(d)** $59 - 96$.

Solution:

(a) $18 - 7$ is the same as $18 + (-7)$, so just add 18 to negative 7.

$$+18 = 0001\ 0010$$
$$-\ 7 = \underline{1111\ 1001}$$
$$\text{Sum} = 0000\ 1011 = 11_{10}$$

Note: The carry-out of the MSB is ignored. (It will always occur for positive sums.) The 8-bit answer is 0000 1011.

(b)
$$+21 = 0001\ 0101$$
$$-13 = \underline{1111\ 0011}$$
$$\text{Sum} = 0000\ 1000 = 8_{10}$$

(c)
$$+118 = 0111\ 0110$$
$$-\ 54 = \underline{1100\ 1010}$$
$$\text{Sum} = 0100\ 0000 = 64_{10}$$

(d)
$$+59 = 0011\ 1011$$
$$-96 = \underline{1010\ 0000}$$
$$\text{Sum} = 1101\ 1011 = -37_{10}$$

7–4 HEXADECIMAL ARITHMETIC

Hexadecimal representation, as discussed in Chapter 1, is a method of representing groups of 4 bits as a single digit. Hexadecimal notation has been widely adopted by manufacturers of computers and microprocessors because it simplifies the documentation and use of their equipment. Eight- and 16-bit computer system data, program instructions, and addresses use hexadecimal to make them easier to interpret and work with than their binary equivalents.

Hexadecimal Addition

Remember, hexadecimal is a base 16 numbering system, meaning that it has 16 different digits (as shown in Table 7–4). Adding $3 + 6$ in hex equals 9, and $5 + 7$ equals C. But adding $9 + 8$ in hex equals a sum greater than F, which will create a carry. The sum of $9 + 8$ is 17_{10}, which is 1 larger than 16 making the answer 11_{16}.

TABLE 7–4

Hexadecimal Digits with Their Equivalent Binary and Decimal Values

Hexadecimal	Binary	Decimal
0	0000	0
1	0001	1
2	0010	2
3	0011	3
4	0100	4
5	0101	5
6	0110	6

TABLE 7–4 (*Continued*)

Hexadecimal	Binary	Decmial
7	0111	7
8	1000	8
9	1001	9
A	1010	10
B	1011	11
C	1100	12
D	1101	13
E	1110	14
F	1111	15

The procedure for adding hex digits is as follows:

1. Add the two hex digits by working with their decimal equivalents.
2. If the decimal sum is less than 16, write down the hex equivalent.
3. If the decimal sum is 16 or more, subtract 16, write down the hex result in that column and carry 1 to the next-more-significant column.

Work through the following examples to familiarize yourself with this procedure.

EXAMPLE 7–12

Add $9 + C$ in hex.

Solution: C is equivalent to decimal 12.

$$12 + 9 = 21$$

Since 21 is greater than 16, then (1) subtract $21 - 16 = 5$, and (2) carry 1 to the next-more-significant column. Therefore

$$9 + C = 15_{16}$$

EXAMPLE 7–13

Add $4F + 2D$ in hex.

Solution:

$$
\begin{array}{r}
4\ F \\
+\ 2\ D \\
\hline
7\ C
\end{array}
$$

Explanation: $F + D = 15 + 13 = 28$, which is 12 with a carry ($28 - 16 = 12$). 12 is written down as C. $4 + 2 + \text{carry} = 7$.

EXAMPLE 7–14

Add $A\,7\,C\,5 + 2\,D\,A\,8$ in hex.

Solution:

$$
\begin{array}{r}
A\ 7\ C\ 5 \\
+\ 2\ D\ A\ 8 \\
\hline
D\ 5\ 6\ D
\end{array}
$$

Explanation: $5 + 8 = 13$, which is a D. $C + A = 22$, which is a 6 with a carry. $7 + D + \text{carry} = 21$, which is a 5 with a carry. $A + 2 + \text{carry} = 13$, which is a D.

Alternative Method. An alternative method of hexadecimal addition, which you might find more straightforward, is to convert the hex numbers to binary and perform a regular binary addition. The binary sum is then converted back to hex. For example:

$$
\begin{array}{r}
4\ F \\
+\ 2\ D
\end{array}
\Rightarrow
\begin{array}{r}
0100\ 1111_2 \\
+\ 0010\ 1101_2 \\
\hline
0111\ 1100_2 = 7\ C_{16}\ \checkmark
\end{array}
$$

Hexadecimal Subtraction

Subtraction of hexadecimal numbers is similar to decimal subtraction except that when you borrow 1 from the left, the borrower increases in value by 16. Consider the hexadecimal subtraction $24 - 0C$.

$$
\begin{array}{r}
24 \\
-\ 0C \\
\hline
18
\end{array}
$$

Explanation: We cannot subtract C from 4, so the 4 borrows 1 from the 2. That changes the 2 to a 1 and the 4 increases in value to 20 $(4 + 16 = 20)$. Now, $20 - C = 20 - 12 = 8$, and $1 - 0 = 1$. Therefore,

$$24 - 0C = 18$$

The next two examples illustrate hexadecimal subtraction.

EXAMPLE 7–15

Subtract $D7 - A8$ in hex.

Solution:

$$
\begin{array}{r}
D\ 7 \\
-\ A\ 8 \\
\hline
2\ F
\end{array}
$$

Explanation: 7 borrows from the D, which increases its value to 23 $(7 + 16 = 23)$. $23 - 8 = 15$, which is an F. D becomes a C, and $C - A = 12 - 10 = 2$.

EXAMPLE 7–16

Subtract $A\ 0\ 5\ C - 2\ 4\ C\ A$ in hex.

Solution:

$$
\begin{array}{r}
A\ 0\ 5\ C \\
-\ 2\ 4\ C\ A \\
\hline
7\ B\ 9\ 2
\end{array}
$$

Explanation: $C - A = 12 - 10 = 2$. 5 borrows from the 0, which borrows from the A $(5 + 16 = 21)$, $21 - C = 21 - 12 = 9$. The 0 borrowed from the A, but it was also borrowed from, so it is now a 15, $15 - 4 = 11$, which is a B. The A was borrowed from, so it is now a 9, $9 - 2 = 7$.

7–5 BCD ARITHMETIC

If human beings had 16 fingers and toes, we probably would have adopted hexadecimal as our primary numbering system instead of decimal, and dealing with microprocessor-generated numbers would have been so much easier. (Just think how much better we could play a piano, too!) But unfortunately, we normally deal in base 10, decimal numbers. Digital electronics naturally works in binary, and we have to group four binary digits together to get enough combinations to represent the 10 different decimal digits. That 4-bit code is called *binary-coded-decimal* (BCD).

So what we have is a 4-bit code that is used to represent the decimal digits that we need when reading a display on calculators or computer output. The problem arises when we try to add or subtract these BCD numbers. For example, digital circuitry would naturally like to add the BCD numbers 1000 + 0011 to get 1011, but 1011 is an invalid BCD result. (In Chapter 1 we described the range of valid BCD numbers as 0000 to 1001.) Therefore, when adding BCD numbers, we have to build extra circuitry to check the result to be certain that each group of 4 bits is a valid BCD number.

BCD Addition

Addition is the most important operation because subtraction, multiplication, and division can all be done by a series of additions or two's-complement additions.

Procedure for BCD addition:

1. Add the BCD numbers as regular true binary numbers.
2. If the sum is 9 (1001) or less, it is a valid BCD answer; leave it as is.
3. If the sum is greater than 9 or if there is a carry out of the MSB, it is an invalid BCD number; do step 4.
4. If it is invalid, add 6 (0110) to the result to make it valid. Any carry out of the MSB is added to the next-more-significant BCD number.
5. Repeat steps 1 to 4 for each group of BCD bits.

Use the procedure outlined above for the following example.

EXAMPLE 7–17

Convert the following decimal numbers to BCD and add them. Convert the result back to decimal to check your answer. **(a)** 8 + 7; **(b)** 9 + 9; **(c)** 52 + 63; **(d)** 78 + 69.

Solution:

(a)
$$
\begin{aligned}
8 &= 1000 \\
+7 &= \underline{0111} \\
\text{Sum} &= 1111 \quad \text{(invalid)} \\
\text{Add } 6 &= \underline{0110} \\
1\;\; &0101 = 0001\;\;0101_{\text{BCD}} = 15_{10} \;\checkmark
\end{aligned}
$$

(b)
$$
\begin{aligned}
9 &= \;\;1001 \\
+9 &= \;\;\underline{1001} \\
\text{Sum} &= 1\;\;0010 \quad \text{(invalid because of carry)} \\
&\quad \searrow \text{cy} \\
\text{Add } 6 &= \;\;\;\underline{0110} \\
1\;\; &1000 = 0001\;\;1000_{\text{BCD}} = 18_{10} \;\checkmark
\end{aligned}
$$

(c) $52 =$ 0101   0010
        $+ 63 =$ 0110   0011
        Sum $=$ 1011   0101 ——invalid
        Add 6 $=$ 0110
            1   0001   0101 $= 0001\ 0001\ 0101 = 115_{10}$ ✓

(d) $78 =$ 0111   1000
        $+ 69 =$ 0110   1001
        Sum $=$ 1110   0001   (both groups of 4
                        cy   BCD bits are invalid)
        Add 6 $=$ 0110
                1110   0111
        Add 6 $=$ 0110
            1   0100   0111 $= 0001\ 0100\ 0111 = 147_{10}$ ✓

When one of the numbers being added is negative (such as in subtraction), the procedure is much more difficult, but basically it follows a complement-then-add procedure which will not be covered in this book, but is similar to that introduced in Section 7–3.

Now that we understand the more common arithmetic operations that take place within digital equipment, we are ready for the remainder of the chapter, which explains the actual circuitry used to perform those operations.

7–6   ARITHMETIC CIRCUITS

All the arithmetic operations and procedures covered in the previous sections can be implemented using adders formed from the basic logic gates. For a large number of digits we can use medium-scale-integrated (MSI) circuits, which actually have several adders within a single integrated package.

The Basic Adder Circuit

By reviewing the truth table in Figure 7–5, we can determine the input conditions that produce each combination of sum and carry output bits. Figure 7–5 shows the addition of two 2-bit numbers. This could easily be expanded to cover 4-bit, 8-bit, or 16-bit addition. Notice that addition in the least-significant-bit column requires analyzing only two inputs (A_0 plus B_0) to determine the output sum (Σ_0) and carry (C_{out}). But any more significant columns (2^1 column and up) require the inclusion of a third input, which is the carry (C_{in}) from the column to its right. For example, the carry-out (C_{out}) of the 2^0 column becomes the carry-in (C_{in}) to the 2^1 column. Figure 7–5c shows the inclusion of a third input for the truth table of the more significant column additions.

Half-Adder

Designing logic circuits to automatically implement the desired outputs for those truth tables is simple. Look at the LSB truth table; for what input conditions are the Σ_0 bit HIGH? The answer is: *A or B* HIGH, but *not both* (exclusive-OR function). For what input condition is the C_{out} bit high? The answer is: *A and B* high (AND function). Therefore, the circuit design to perform addition in the LSB column can be implemented using an exclusive-OR and an AND gate. That circuit is called a *half-adder* and is shown in Figure 7–6. If the exclusive-OR function in Figure 7–6

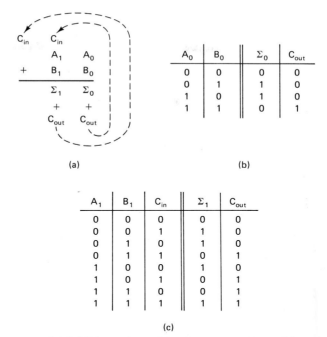

(a)   (b)

A_1	B_1	C_{in}	Σ_1	C_{out}
0	0	0	0	0
0	0	1	1	0
0	1	0	1	0
0	1	1	0	1
1	0	0	1	0
1	0	1	0	1
1	1	0	0	1
1	1	1	1	1

(c)

Figure 7–5 (a) Addition of two 2-bit binary numbers; (b) truth table for the LSB addition; (c) truth table for the more significant column.

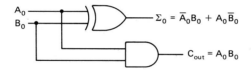

Figure 7–6 Half-adder circuit for addition in the LSB column.

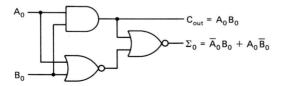

Figure 7–7 Alternate half-adder circuit built from an AND–NOR–NOR configuration.

is implemented using an AND–NOR–NOR configuration, we can tap off the AND gate for the carry, as shown in Figure 7–7.

Full-Adder

As you can see in Figure 7–5, addition in the 2^1 (or higher) column requires three inputs to produce the sum (Σ_1) and carry (C_{out}) outputs. Look at the truth table (Figure 7–5c); for what input conditions are the sum output (Σ_1) HIGH? The answer is: The Σ_1 bit is HIGH whenever the three inputs (A_1, B_1, C_{in}) are *odd*. From Chapter 6 you may remember that an even-parity generator produces a HIGH output whenever the sum of the inputs is odd. Therefore, we can use an even-parity generator to generate our Σ_1 output bit, as shown in Figure 7–8.

Figure 7–8 The sum (Σ_1) function of the full-adder is generated from an even-parity generator.

How about the carry-out (C_{out}) bit? What input conditions produce a HIGH at C_{out}? The answer is: C_{out} is HIGH whenever any two of the inputs are HIGH. Therefore, we can take care of C_{out} with three ANDs and an OR, as shown in Figure 7–9.

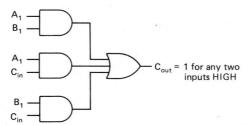

Figure 7–9   Carry-out (C_{out}) function of the full-adder.

The two parts of the full-adder circuit shown in Figures 7–8 and 7–9 can be combined to form the complete *full-adder* circuit shown in Figure 7–10. In the figure the Σ_1 function is produced using the same logic as that in Figure 7–8. The C_{out} function comes from $A_1 B_1$ or $C_{in} (A_1 \bar{B}_1 + \bar{A}_1 B_1)$. Prove to yourself that the Boolean equation at C_{out} will produce the necessary result. Also, the following example will help you better understand the operation of the full-adder.

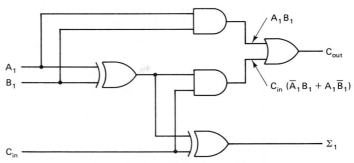

Figure 7–10   Logic diagram of a full-adder.

EXAMPLE 7–18

Apply the following input bits to the full-adder of Figure 7–10 to verify its operation ($A_1 = 0$, $B_1 = 1$, $C_{in} = 1$).

Solution: The full-adder operation is shown in Figure 7–11.

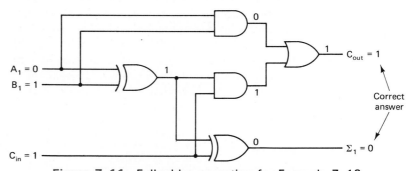

Figure 7–11   Full-adder operation for Example 7–18.

Block Diagrams

Now that we know the construction of half-adder and full-adder circuits, we can simplify their representation by just drawing a box with the input and output lines shown in Figure 7–12. When drawing multibit adders, a block diagram is used to represent the addition in each column. For example, in the case of a 4-bit adder, the 2^0 column needs only a half-adder because there will be no carry-in. Each of the more significant columns will require a full-adder, as shown in Figure 7–13.

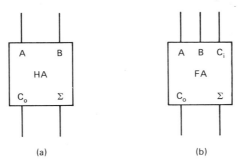

(a) (b)

Figure 7–12 Block diagrams of (a) half-adder; (b) full-adder.

Notice in Figure 7–13 that the LSB half-adder has no carry-in. The carry-out (C_o) of the LSB becomes the carry-in (C_i) to the next full-adder to its left. The carry-out (C_o) of the MSB full-adder is actually the highest-order sum output (Σ_4).

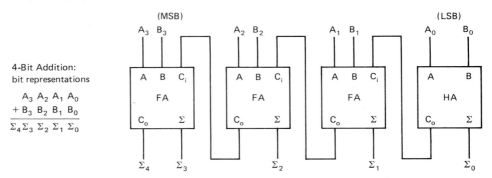

4-Bit Addition:
bit representations

$$A_3\ A_2\ A_1\ A_0$$
$$+ B_3\ B_2\ B_1\ B_0$$
$$\overline{\Sigma_4 \Sigma_3\ \Sigma_2\ \Sigma_1\ \Sigma_0}$$

Figure 7–13 Block diagram of a 4-bit binary adder.

7–7 FOUR-BIT FULL-ADDER ICs

There are medium-scale-integration (MSI) ICs available with four full-adders in a single package. Table 7–5 lists the most popular adder ICs. Each of the adders in the table contain four full-adders, and all are functionally equivalent; however, their pin layouts differ (refer to your data manual for the pin layouts). They each will add two 4-bit binary words plus one incoming carry. The binary sum appears on the sum outputs (Σ_1 to Σ_4) and the outgoing carry.

TABLE 7–5

MSI Adder ICs

Device	Family	Description
7483	TTL	4-Bit binary full-adder, fast carry
74HC283	CMOS	4-Bit binary full-adder, fast carry
4008	CMOS	4-Bit binary full-adder, fast carry

Figure 7–14 shows the functional diagram, the logic diagram, and the logic symbol for the 7483. In the figure the least significant binary inputs (2^0) come into the A_1B_1 terminals and the most significant (2^3) come into the A_4B_4 terminals. (Be careful, because depending on which manufacturer's data manual you are using, the inputs may be labeled A_1B_1 to A_4B_4 *or* A_0B_0 to A_3B_3). The carry-out (C_o) from each full-adder is *internally* connected to the carry-in of the next full-adder. The carry-out of the last full-adder is brought out to a terminal to be used as the Sum$_5$ (Σ_5) output, or to be used as a carry-in (C_{in}) to the next full-adder IC if more than 4 bits are to be added (as in Example 7–19).

Something else that we have not seen before is the *fast-look-ahead carry* (see Figure 7–14a). This is very important for speeding up the arithmetic process. For example, if we were adding two 8-bit numbers using two 7483s, the fast-look-ahead carry evaluates the four low-order inputs (A_1B_1 to A_4B_4) to determine if they are going to produce a carry-out of the fourth full-adder to be passed on to the next-higher-order adder IC (see Example 7–19). In this way the addition of the high-order bits (2^4 to 2^7) can take place concurrently with the low order (2^0 to 2^3) addition *without having to wait* for the carries to propagate, or "ripple" through FA$_1$-to-FA$_2$-to-FA$_3$-to-FA$_4$ to become available to the high-order addition. A discussion of the connections for the addition of two 8-bit numbers using two 7483s is presented in the following example.

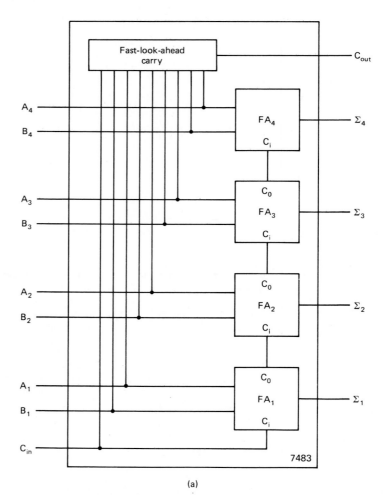

(a)

Figure 7–14 The 7483 4-bit full-adder: (a) functional diagram;

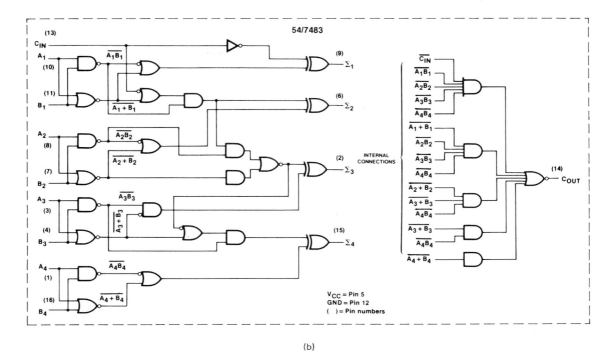

(b)

(c)

Figure 7–14 (*Continued*)   (b) logic diagram; (c) logic symbol. [(b) Courtesy of Signetics Corporation.]

EXAMPLE 7–19

Show the external connections to two 4-bit adder ICs to form an 8-bit adder capable of performing the following addition:

$$\begin{array}{r} A_7A_6A_5A_4A_3A_2A_1A_0 \\ + B_7B_6B_5B_4B_3B_2B_1B_0 \\ \hline \Sigma_8\Sigma_7\Sigma_6\Sigma_5\Sigma_4\Sigma_3\Sigma_2\Sigma_1\Sigma_0 \end{array}$$

Solution: We can choose any of the IC adders listed in Table 7–5 for our design. Let's choose the 74HC283, which is the high-speed CMOS version of the 4-bit adder (it has the same logic symbol as the 7483). As you can see in Figure 7–15, the two 8-bit numbers are brought into the A_1B_1-to-A_4B_4 inputs of each chip and the sum output comes out of the Σ_4-to-Σ_1 outputs of each chip.

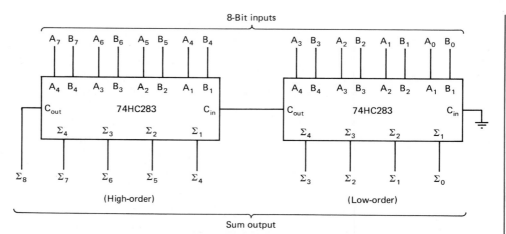

Figure 7–15 Eight-bit binary adder using two 74HC283 ICs.

The C_{in} of the least significant addition ($A_0 + B_0$) is grounded (0) because there is no carry-in (it acts like a half-adder) and if it were left floating, the IC would not know whether to assume a 1 state or 0 state.

The carry-out (C_{out}) from the addition of $A_3 + B_3$ must be connected to the carry-in (C_{in}) of the $A_4 + B_4$ addition, as shown. The fast-look-ahead-carry circuit ensures that the carry-out (C_{out}) signal from the low-order addition is provided to the carry-in (C_{in}) of the high-order addition within a very short period of time so that the $A_4 + B_4$ addition can take place without having to wait for all the internal carries to propagate through all four of the low-order additions first. (The actual time requirements for the sum and carry outputs are discussed in Chapter 9 when we look at IC specifications.)

7–8 SYSTEM DESIGN APPLICATIONS

Each of the arithmetic operations discussed in Sections 7–1 through 7–5 can be performed by using circuits built from integrated-circuit adders and logic gates. First, we will design a circuit to perform two's-complement arithmetic, and next we will design a BCD adder.

Two's-Complement Adder/Subtractor Circuit

A quick review of Section 7–3 reminds us that positive two's-complement numbers are exactly the same as regular true binary numbers and can be added using regular binary addition. Also, subtraction in two's-complement arithmetic is performed by converting the number to be subtracted to a *negative* number in the two's-complement form and then using regular binary addition. Therefore, once our numbers are in two's-complement form, we can use a binary adder to get the answer whether we are adding *or* subtracting.

For example, to subtract 18 minus 9, we would first convert 9 to a negative two's-complement number by complementing each bit, then adding 1. We would then add $18 + (-9)$:

$$
\begin{array}{r}
\text{two's complement of } 18 = 0001\ 0010 \\
+ \text{ two's complement of } -9 = \underline{1111\ 0111} \\
\text{sum} = \underline{0000\ 1001} = +9_{10} \quad \textit{answer}
\end{array}
$$

So it looks like all we need for a combination adder/subtractor circuit is an input switch or signal to signify addition or subtraction so that we will know whether to form a positive or a negative two's complement of the second number. Then we will just use a binary adder to get the final result.

To form negative two's complement, we can use the controlled inverter circuit presented in Chapter 6 (Figure 6-15) and add 1 to its output. Figure 7-16 shows the complete circuit used to implement a two's-complement adder/subtractor using two 4008 CMOS adders. The 4008s are CMOS 4-bit binary adders. The 8-bit number on the A inputs (A_7 to A_0) is brought directly into the adders. The other 8-bit binary number comes in on the B_7 to B_0 lines. If the B number is to be subtracted, the complementing switch will be in the up (1) position, causing each bit in the B number to be complemented (one's complement). At the same time, the low-order C_{in} receives a 1, which has the effect of adding a 1 to the already complemented B number, making it a negative two's-complement number.

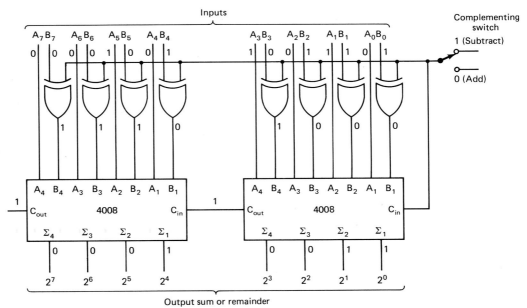

Figure 7-16   Eight-bit two's-complement adder/subtractor illustrating the subtraction $42 - 23 = 19$.

Now the 4008s perform a regular binary addition. If the complementing switch is up, the number on the B inputs will be subtracted from the number on the A inputs. If it is down, the sum is taken. As discussed in Section 7-3, the C_{out} of the MSB is ignored. The result can range from 0111 1111 (+127) to 1000 0000 (−128).

EXAMPLE 7-20

Prove that the subtraction $42-23$ produces the correct answer at the outputs by labeling the input and output lines on Figure 7-16.

Solution: $42-23$ should equal 19 (0001 0011). Convert the decimal input numbers to regular binary and label Figure 7-16 (42 = 0010 1010, 23 = 0001 0111). The B input number is complemented, the LSB C_{in} is 1, and the final answer is 0001 0011, which proves that the circuit works for that number.

Try adding and subtracting some other numbers to better familiarize yourself with the operation of the circuit of Figure 7-16.

BCD Adder Circuit

BCD adders can also be formed using the integrated circuit 4-bit binary adders. The problem, as you may remember from Section 7–5, is that when any group-of-four BCD sum exceeds 9, or when there is a carry-out, the number is invalid and must be corrected by adding 6 to the invalid answer to get the correct BCD answer. (The valid range of BCD numbers is 0000 to 1001.)

For example, adding $0111_{BCD} + 0110_{BCD}$ (7 + 6) gives us an invalid result.

$$
\begin{array}{r}
0111 \\
+0110 \\
\hline
1101 \quad \text{invalid} \\
+0110 \quad \text{add 6 to correct} \\
\hline
1\llap{\diagdown}\;0011 \\
\end{array}
$$

carry to next BCD digit

The corrected answer is $0001\ 0011_{BCD}$, which equals 13.

Checking for a sum greater than 9 or a carry-out can be done easily using logic gates. Then, when an invalid sum occurs, it can be corrected by adding 6 (0110) via the connections shown in Figure 7–17. The upper 7483 performs a basic 4-bit addition. If its sum is greater than 9, the Σ_4 (2^3) output *and* either the Σ_3 or Σ_2 ($2^2\ 2^1$) output must be HIGH. A sum greater than 9 *or* a carry-out produces a HIGH out of the OR gate, placing a HIGH-HIGH at the A_3 and A_2 inputs of the correction adder, which has the effect of adding a 6 to the original addition. If there is no carry and the original sum is not greater than 9, the correction adder adds 0000.

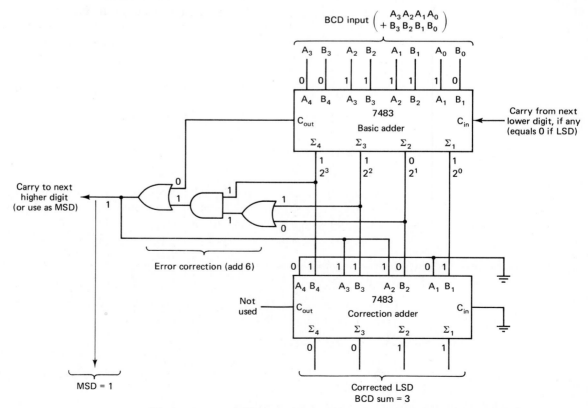

Figure 7–17   BCD adder illustrating the addition $6 + 7 = 13$ (0110 + 0111 = 0001 0011 BCD).

EXAMPLE 7–21

Prove that the BCD addition 0111 + 0110 (7 + 6) produces the correct answer at the outputs by labeling the input and output lines on Figure 7–17.

Solution: The sum out of the basic adder is 13 (1101). Since the 2^3 bit and the 2^2 bit are both HIGH, the error correction OR gate puts out a HIGH, which is added to the next more significant BCD digit and also puts a HIGH-HIGH at A_3, A_2 of the correction adder, which adds 6. The correct answer has a 3 for the least significant digit (LSD) and a 1 in the next more significant digit, for the correct answer of 13.

Familiarize yourself with the operation of Figure 7–17 by testing the addition of several other BCD numbers.

7–9 ARITHMETIC/LOGIC UNITS

Arithmetic/logic units (ALUs) are available in large-scale integrated-circuit packages (LSI). Typically, an ALU is a multipurpose device, capable of providing several different arithmetic and logic operations. The specific operation to be performed is chosen by the user by placing a specific binary code on the mode select inputs.

The ALU that we learn to use in this section is the 74181 (TTL) or 74HC181 (CMOS). The 74181 is a 4-bit ALU which provides 16 arithmetic plus 16 logic operations. Its logic symbol and function table are given in Figure 7–18. The mode control input (M) is used to set the mode of operation as either *logic* ($M = H$) *or arithmetic* ($M = L$). When M is HIGH, all internal carries are disabled, and the device performs *logic operations* on the individual bits (A_0 to A_3, B_0 to B_3), as indicated in the function table.

When M is LOW, the internal carries are enabled and the device performs *arithmetic operations* on the two 4-bit binary inputs. Ripple carry is provided at $\overline{C_{N+4}}$ and fast-look-ahead carry is provided at G and P for high-speed arithmetic operations. The carry-in and carry-out terminals are each active-LOW (as signified by the bubble), which means that a 0 signifies a carry.

Once the mode control (M) is set, you have 16 choices within either the logic or arithmetic categories. The specific function you want is selected by applying the appropriate binary code to the function select inputs (S_3 to S_0).

For example, with $M = H$ and $S_3S_2S_1S_0 = LLLL$, the F outputs will be equal to the complement of A (see the function table). That means that $F_0 = \overline{A}_0$, $F_1 = \overline{A}_1$, $F_2 = \overline{A}_2$, and $F_3 = \overline{A}_3$. Another example is with $M = H$, $S_3S_2S_1S_0 = HHHL$; the F outputs will be equal to $A + B$ (A *or* B). That means that $F_0 = A_0 + B_0$, $F_1 = A_1 + B_1$, $F_2 = A_2 + B_2$, $F_3 = A_3 + B_3$.

From the function table we can see that other logic operations—AND, NAND, NOR, Ex-OR, Ex-NOR, and several others—are available.

The function table in Figure 7–18b also shows the result of the 16 different *arithmetic operations* available when $M = L$. Note that the results listed are with carry-in ($\overline{C_N}$) equal to H (no carry). For $\overline{C_N} = L$, just add 1 to all results. All results produced by the device are in two's-complement notation. Also, in the function table, note that the $+$ sign means *logical-OR* and the word "PLUS" means *arithmetic-SUM*.

For example, to subtract B from A ($A_3A_2A_1A_0 - B_3B_2B_1B_0$), set $M = L$ and $S_3S_2S_1S_0 = LHHL$. The result at the F outputs will be the two's complement

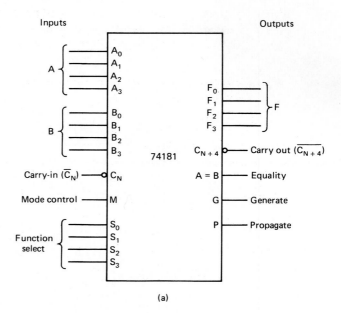

Selection				M = H Logic functions	M = L Arithmetic operations
S_3	S_2	S_1	S_0		$\overline{C}_n = H$ (no carry)
L	L	L	L	$F = \overline{A}$	$F = A$
L	L	L	H	$F = \overline{A + B}$	$F = A + B$
L	L	H	L	$F = \overline{A}B$	$F = A + \overline{B}$
L	L	H	H	$F = 0$	$F = $ minus 1 (2's comp.)
L	H	L	L	$F = \overline{AB}$	$F = A$ plus $A\overline{B}$
L	H	L	H	$F = \overline{B}$	$F = (A + B)$ plus $A\overline{B}$
L	H	H	L	$F = A \oplus B$	$F = A$ minus B minus 1
L	H	H	H	$F = A\overline{B}$	$F = A\overline{B}$ minus 1
H	L	L	L	$F = \overline{A} + B$	$F = A$ plus AB
H	L	L	H	$F = \overline{A \oplus B}$	$F = A$ plus B
H	L	H	L	$F = B$	$F = (A + \overline{B})$ plus AB
H	L	H	H	$F = AB$	$F = AB$ minus 1
H	H	L	L	$F = 1$	$F = A$ plus A*
H	H	L	H	$F = A + \overline{B}$	$F = (A + B)$ plus A
H	H	H	L	$F = A + B$	$F = (A + \overline{B})$ plus A
H	H	H	H	$F = A$	$F = A$ minus 1

*Each bit is shifted to the next-more-significant position.

(b)

Figure 7–18 The 74181 ALU: (a) logic symbol; (b) function table.

of A minus B minus 1; therefore, to get just A minus B, we need to add 1. (This can be done automatically by setting $\overline{C_N} = 0$.) Also, as discussed earlier with two's-complement subtraction, a carry-out (borrow) is generated ($\overline{C_{N+4}} = 0$) when the result is positive or zero. Just ignore it.

Read through the function table to see the other 15 arithmetic operations that are available.

EXAMPLE 7–22

Show the external connections to a 74181 to form a 4-bit subtractor. Label the input and output pins with the binary states that occur when subtracting $13 - 7$ ($A = 13$, $B = 7$).

Solution: The 4-bit subtractor is shown in Figure 7–19. The ALU is set in the subtract mode by setting $M = 0$ and $S_3 S_2 S_1 S_0 = 0110$ ($LHHL$). 13 (1101) is input at A and 7 (0111) is input at B.

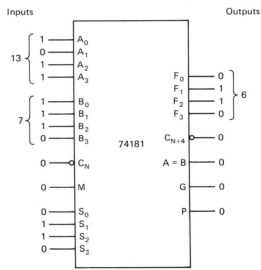

Figure 7–19 Four-bit binary subtractor using the 74181 ALU to subtract $13 - 7$.

By setting $\overline{C_N} = 0$, the output at F_0, F_1, F_2, F_3 will be A minus B instead of A minus B minus 1 as shown in the function table (Figure 7–18b). The result of the subtraction is a positive 6 (0110) with a carry-out ($\overline{C_{N+4}} = 0$). (As before, with two's-complement subtraction, there is a carry-out for any positive or zero answer, which is ignored.)

GLOSSARY

ALU: Arithmetic/logic unit. A multifunction integrated-circuit device used to perform a variety of user-selectable arithmetic and logic operations.

Binary word: A group, or string, of binary bits. In a 4-bit system a word is 4 bits long. In an 8-bit system a word is 8 bits long, and so on.

Block diagram: A simplified functional representation of a circuit or system drawn in a box format.

Borrow: When subtracting numbers, if the number being subtracted from is not large enough, it must "borrow," or take an amount from, the next-more-significant digit.

Carry-in: An amount from a less-significant-digit addition that is applied to the current addition.

Carry-out: When adding numbers, when the sum is greater than the amount allowed in that position, part of the sum must be applied to the next-more-significant position.

Fast-look-ahead carry: When cascading several full-adders end to end, the carry-out of the last full-adder cannot be determined until each of the previous full-adder additions is completed. The internal carry must "ripple" or "propagate" through each of the lower-order adders before reaching the last full-adder. A fast-look-ahead-carry system is used to speed up the process in a multibit system by reading all the input bits simultaneously to determine ahead of time if a carry-out of the last full-adder is going to occur.

Full-adder: An adder circuit having three inputs, used to add two binary digits plus a carry. It produces their sum and carry as outputs.

Function select: On an ALU these pins are used to select the actual arithmetic or logic operation to be performed.

Half-adder: An adder circuit used in the LS position when adding two binary digits with no carry-in to consider. It produces their sum and carry as outputs.

High order: In numbering systems, the high-order positions are those representing the larger magnitudes.

Low order: In numbering systems, the low-order positions are those representing the smaller magnitudes.

Mode control: On an ALU, this pin is used to select either the arithmetic or the logic mode of operation.

MSI: (Medium-scale integration). An IC chip containing combinational logic that is packed more dense than a basic logic gate IC (small-scale integration, SSI), but not as dense as a microprocessor IC (large-scale integration, LSI).

One's complement: A binary number that is a direct (true) complement, bit by bit of some other number.

Product: The result of the multiplication of numbers.

Remainder: The result of the subtraction of numbers.

Ripple carry: *See* Fast-look-ahead carry.

Sign bit: The leftmost, or MSB, in a two's-complement number used to signify the sign of the number (1 = negative, 0 = positive).

Sum: The result of the addition of numbers.

Two's complement: A binary numbering representation that simplifies arithmetic in digital systems.

REVIEW QUESTIONS

Section 7–1

7–1. Binary addition in the least significant column deals with how many inputs and how many outputs?

7–2. In binary subtraction, the borrow-out of the least-significant column becomes the borrow-in of the next-more-significant column (true or false)?

7–3. Binary multiplication and division is performed by a series of additions and subtractions (true or false)?

Sections 7–2 and 7–3

7–4. Which bit in an 8-bit two's-complement number is used as the sign bit?

7–5. Are the following two's-complement numbers positive or negative?
   (a) 1010 0011
   (b) 0010 1101
   (c) 1000 0000

Sections 7–4 and 7–5

7–6. Which of the following decimal numbers cannot be converted to 8-bit two's-complement notation:
   (a) 89
   (b) 135
   (c) −107
   (d) −144

7–7. The procedure for subtracting numbers in two's-complement notation is exactly the same as for adding numbers (true or false)?

Sections 7–4 and 7–5

7–8. Why is hexadecimal arithmetic commonly used when working with 8-, 16- and 32-bit computer systems?

7–9. What procedure is used to correct the result of a BCD addition if the sum is greater than 9?

Sections 7–6 and 7–7

7–10. Name the inputs and outputs of a half-adder.

7–11. Why are the input requirements of a full-adder different than those of a half-adder?

7–12. The sum output (Σ) of a full-adder is 1 if the sum of its three inputs is _____ (odd, even).

7–13. What input conditions to a full-adder produce a 1 at the carry-out (C_o)?

7–14. All of the adders in the 7483 4-bit adder are full-adders. What is done with the carry-in (C_{in}) to make the first adder act like a half-adder?

7–15. What is the purpose of the "fast-look-ahead carry" in the 7483 IC?

Sections 7–8 and 7–9

7–16. The complementing switch in Figure 7–16 is placed in the "1" position to subtract B from A. Explain how this position converts the binary number on the B-inputs into a signed two's-complement number. *Xor gate inverts.*

7–17. What is the purpose of the AND and OR gates in the BCD adder circuit of Figure 7–17? *Check the sum greater than 9 and correct.*

7–18. What is the purpose of the *mode control* input to the 74181 arithmetic/logic unit?

7–19. If M = H and S_3, S_2, S_1, S_0 = L, L, H, H on the 74181, then F_3, F_2, F_1, F_0 will be set to L, L, L, L (true or false)?

7–20. The arithmetic operations of the 74181 include both F = A + B and F = A plus B. How are the two designations different? *+ means logic or plus means Arith/sum*

PROBLEMS

7–1. Perform the following decimal additions, convert the original decimal numbers to binary, and add them. Compare answers.

(a)	6	(b)	8	(c)	22	(d)	29
	+3		+7		+6		+37

(e)	134	(f)	254	(g)	208	(h)	196
	+ 66		+ 36		+127		+156

7–2. Repeat Problem 7–1 for the following subtractions.

(a)	15	(b)	22	(c)	84	(d)	66
	− 4		−11		−36		−31

(e)	126	(f)	113	(g)	109	(h)	111
	− 64		− 88		− 60		−104

7–3. Repeat Problem 7–1 for the following multiplications.

(a)	7	(b)	6	(c)	12	(d)	39
	×3		×7		× 5		× 7

(e)	63	(f)	127	(g)	31	(h)	255
	×125		× 15		×13		×127

7–4. Repeat Problem 7–1 for the following divisions.

(a) $4/\overline{12}$ (b) $3/\overline{15}$ (c) $12/\overline{48}$ (d) $5/\overline{25}$

(e) $5/\overline{125}$ (f) $14/\overline{294}$ (g) $15/\overline{195}$ (h) $12/\overline{228}$

7–5. Produce a table of 8-bit two's-complement numbers from +15 to −15.

7–6. Convert the following decimal numbers to 8-bit two's complement notation.

(a) 7   (b) −7   (c) 14   (d) 36   (e) −36
(f) 66   (g) −48   (h) 112   (i) −112   (j) −125

7–7. Convert the following two's-complement numbers to decimal.
  (a) 0001 0110   (b) 0000 1111
  (c) 0101 1100   (d) 1000 0110
  (e) 1110 1110   (f) 1000 0001
  (g) 0111 1111   (h) 1111 1111

7–8. What is the maximum positive-to-negative range of a two's-complement number in:
  (a) An 8-bit system?
  (b) A 16-bit system?

7–9. Convert the following decimal numbers to two's-complement form and perform the operation indicated.
  (a)   5   (b)   12   (c)   32   (d)   32
          +7   − 6   +18   −18

  (e)   −28   (f)   125   (g)   36   (h)   −36
         +38   − 66   −48   −48

7–10. Build a table similar to Table 7–4 for hex digits 0C to 22.

7–11. Add the following hexadecimal numbers.
  (a)   A   (b)   7   (c)   0B   (d)   23
          +4   +6   +16   +A7

  (e)   8A   (f)   A7   (g)   A049   (h)   0FFF
         +82   +BB   +0AFC   +9001

7–12. Subtract the following hexadecimal numbers.
  (a)   A   (b)   8   (c)   1B   (d)   A7
          −4   −2   −06   −18

  (e)   2A   (f)   A7   (g)   4A2D   (h)   8BB0
         −07   −1D   −1A2F   −4AC8

7–13. Which of the following bit strings cannot be valid BCD numbers?
  (a) 0111 1001
  (b) 0101 1010
  (c) 1110 0010
  (d) 0100 1000
  (e) 1011 0110
  (f) 0100 1001

7–14. Convert the following decimal numbers to BCD and add them. Convert the result back to decimal to check your answer.
  (a)   8   (b)   12   (c)   43   (d)   47
         + 3   +16   +72   +38

  (e)   12   (f)   36   (g)   99   (h)   80
         +89   +22   +11   +23

7–15. Under what circumstances would you use a half-adder instead of a full-adder?

7–16. Reconstruct the half-adder circuit of Figure 7–7 using only NOR gates.

7–17. The circuit in Figure P7–17 is an attempt to build a half-adder. Will the C_{out} and Σ_0 function properly? (Hint: Write the Boolean equation at C_{out} and Σ_0.)

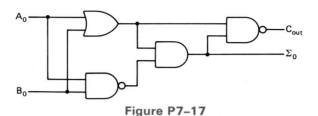

Figure P7–17

7–18. Draw the block diagram of a 4-bit full-adder using *four full-adders*.

7–19. In Figure 7–15, the C_{in} to the first adder is grounded; explain why. Also, why isn't the C_{in} to the second adder grounded?

7–20. Design and draw a 6-bit binary adder similar to Figure 7–15 using two 7483 4-bit adders.

7–21. The 7483 has a fast-look-ahead carry. Explain why that is beneficial in some adder designs.

7–22. Design and draw a 16-bit binary adder using four 4008 CMOS 4-bit adders.

7–23. What changes would have to be made to the adder/subtractor circuit of Figure 7–16 if exclusive-NORs are to be used instead of exclusive-ORs?

Troubleshooting

7–24. Figure P7–24 is a 4-bit two's-complement adder/subtractor. We are attempting to subtract $9 - 3$ ($1001 - 0011$) but keep getting the wrong answer of 10 (1010). Each test node in the circuit is labeled with the logic state observed using a logic probe. Find the two faults in the circuit.

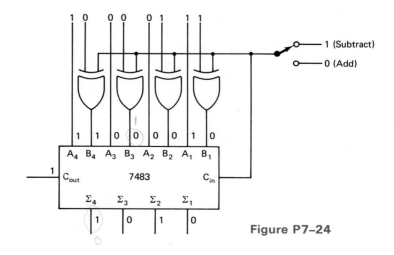

Figure P7–24

7-25. Figure P7-25 is supposed to be set up as a one-digit hexadecimal adder. To test it the values C and 2 (1100 + 0010) are input to the A and B inputs. The answer should be C + 2 = E (1110), but it is not! The figure is labeled with the states observed with a logic probe. Find the problem(s)!

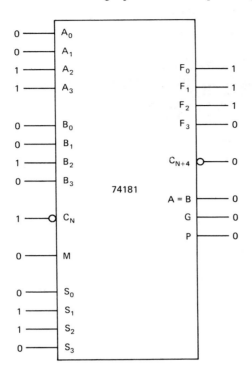

Figure P7-25

8 Code Converters, Multiplexers, and Demultiplexers

OBJECTIVES

Upon completion of this chapter, you should be able to:

- Utilize an integrated-circuit magnitude comparator to perform binary comparisons.
- Describe the function of a decoder and an encoder.
- Design the internal circuitry for encoding and decoding.
- Utilize manufacturers' data sheets to determine the operation of IC decoder and encoder chips.
- Explain the procedure involved in binary, BCD, and Gray code converting.
- Explain the operation of code converter circuits built from SSI and MSI ICs.
- Describe the function and uses of multiplexers and demultiplexers.
- Design circuits that employ multiplexer and demultiplexer ICs.

INTRODUCTION

Information, or data, that is used by digital devices comes in many formats. The mechanisms for conversion, transfer, and selection of data are handled by combinational logic ICs.

In this chapter we first take a general approach to the understanding of data-handling circuits, then deal with the specific operation and application of practical data-handling MSI chips. The MSI chips covered include comparators, decoders, encoders, code converters, multiplexers, and demultiplexers.

166

8–1 COMPARATORS

Quite often in the evaluation of digital information it is important to compare two binary strings (or binary words) to determine if they are exactly equal. This comparison process is performed by a digital *comparator*.

The basic comparator will evaluate two binary strings bit by bit and output a 1 if they are exactly equal. An exclusive-NOR gate is the easiest way to compare the equality of 2 bits. If both bits are equal (0–0 or 1–1), the Ex-NOR puts out a 1.

To compare more than just 2 bits, we need additional Ex-NORs, and the output of all of them must be 1. For example, to design a comparator to evaluate two 4-bit numbers, we need four Ex-NORs. To determine total equality, connect all four outputs into an AND gate. That way, if all four outputs are 1's, the AND gate puts out a 1. Figure 8–1 shows a comparator circuit built from exclusive-NORs and an AND gate.

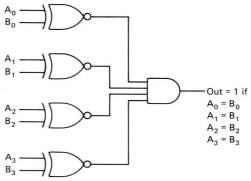

Figure 8–1   Binary comparator for comparing two 4-bit binary strings.

Studying Figure 8–1, you should realize that if A_0–B_0 equals 1–1 or 0–0, the top Ex-NOR will output a 1. The same holds true for the second, third, and fourth ex-NOR gates. If all of them output a 1, the AND gate outputs a 1, indicating equality.

EXAMPLE 8–1

Referring to Figure 8–1, determine if the following pairs of input binary numbers will output a 1.

(a) $A_3A_2A_1A_0 = 1\ 0\ 1\ 1$
     $B_3B_2B_1B_0 = 1\ 0\ 1\ 1$
(b) $A_3A_2A_1A_0 = 0\ 1\ 1\ 0$
     $B_3B_2B_1B_0 = 0\ 1\ 1\ 1$

Solution: (a) When the A and B numbers are applied to the inputs, each of the four Ex-NORs will output 1's, so the output of the AND gate will be 1 (equality).

(b) For this case, the first three Ex-NORs will output 1's, but the last Ex-NOR will output a 0 because its inputs are not equal. The AND gate will output a 0 (inequality).

Integrated-circuit *magnitude comparators* are available in both the TTL and CMOS families. A magnitude comparator not only determines if A equals B, but also if A is *greater than* B or A is *less than* B.

The 7485 is a TTL 4-bit magnitude comparator. The pin configuration and logic symbol for the 7485 are given in Figure 8–2. The 7485 can be used just like the basic comparator of Figure 8–1 by using the A inputs, B inputs, and the equality output ($A = B$). The 7485 has the additional feature of telling you which number is larger if the equality is not met. The $A > B$ output is 1 if A is larger than B, and the $A < B$ output is 1 if B is larger than A.

The expansion inputs $I_A < B$, $I_A = B$, and $I_A > B$ are used for expansion to a system capable of comparisons greater than 4 bits. For example, to set up a circuit capable of comparing two *8-bit words*, two 7485s are required. The $A > B$, $A = B$, $A < B$ outputs of the low order (least significant) comparator are connected to the expansion inputs of the high-order comparator. That way the comparators act together, comparing two entire 8-bit words, outputting the result from the high-order

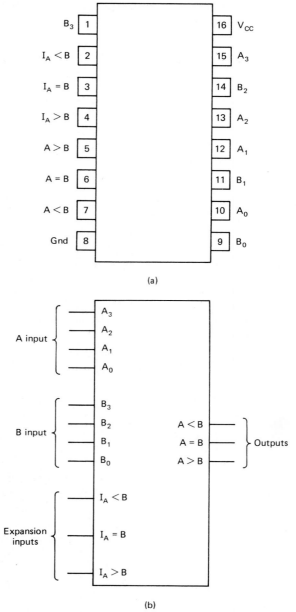

(a)

(b)

Figure 8–2 The 7485 4-bit magnitude comparator: (a) pin configuration; (b) logic symbol.

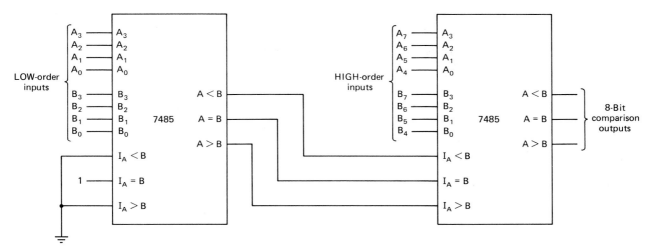

Figure 8-3 Magnitude comparison of two 8-bit binary strings (or binary words).

comparator outputs. For proper operation, the expansion inputs to the low-order comparator should be tied as follows: $I_A > B = $ LOW, $I_A = B = $ HIGH, and $I_A < B = $ LOW. Expansion to greater than 8 bits using multiple 7485s is also possible. Figure 8-3 shows the connections for magnitude comparison of two 8-bit binary strings. If the high-order A-inputs are equal to the high-order B-inputs then the expansion inputs are used as a "tie-breaker."

8-2 DECODING

Decoding is the process of converting some code (such as binary, BCD, or hex) into some recognizable number or character. Take, for example, a system that reads a 4-bit BCD code and converts it to its appropriate decimal number by turning on a decimal indicating lamp. Figure 8-4 illustrates such a system. This decoder is made up of a combination of logic gates that produce a HIGH at one of the 10 outputs, based on the levels at the four inputs.

Figure 8-4 A BCD decoder selects the correct decimal indicating lamp based on the BCD input.

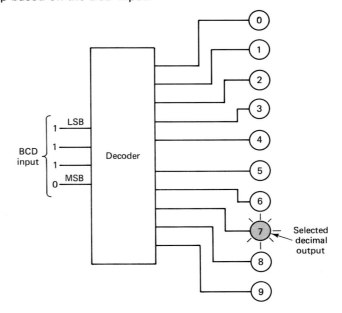

In this section we learn how to use decoder ICs by first looking at the combinational logic that makes them work, and then by selecting the actual decoder IC and making the appropriate pin connections.

3-Bit Binary-to-Octal Decoding

To design a decoder, it is useful first to make a truth table of all possible input/output combinations. An octal decoder must provide eight outputs, one for each of the eight different combinations of inputs, as shown in Table 8–1.

TABLE 8–1

Truth Tables for an Octal Decoder
(a) Active-HIGH outputs

Input			Output							
2^2	2^1	2^0	*0*	*1*	*2*	*3*	*4*	*5*	*6*	*7*
0	0	0	1	0	0	0	0	0	0	0
0	0	1	0	1	0	0	0	0	0	0
0	1	0	0	0	1	0	0	0	0	0
0	1	1	0	0	0	1	0	0	0	0
1	0	0	0	0	0	0	1	0	0	0
1	0	1	0	0	0	0	0	1	0	0
1	1	0	0	0	0	0	0	0	1	0
1	1	1	0	0	0	0	0	0	0	1

(b) Active-LOW outputs

Input			Output							
2^2	2^1	2^0	*0*	*1*	*2*	*3*	*4*	*5*	*6*	*7*
0	0	0	0	1	1	1	1	1	1	1
0	0	1	1	0	1	1	1	1	1	1
0	1	0	1	1	0	1	1	1	1	1
0	1	1	1	1	1	0	1	1	1	1
1	0	0	1	1	1	1	0	1	1	1
1	0	1	1	1	1	1	1	0	1	1
1	1	0	1	1	1	1	1	1	0	1
1	1	1	1	1	1	1	1	1	1	0

Before the design is made, we must decide if we want an *active-HIGH-level* output or an *active-LOW-level* output to indicate the value selected. For example, the *active-HIGH* truth table in Table 8–1a shows us that for an input of 011 (3), output 3 will be HIGH while all other outputs are LOW. The *active-LOW* truth table is just the opposite (output 3 is LOW, all other outputs are HIGH).

Therefore, we have to know whether the indicating lamp (or other receiving device) requires a HIGH level to activate, or a LOW level. We will learn in Chapter 9 that most devices used in digital electronics are designed to activate from a LOW-level signal, so most decoder designs use *active-LOW* outputs, as shown in Table 8–1b. The combinational logic requirements to produce a LOW at output 3 for an input of 011 is shown in Figure 8–5.

To design the complete octal decoder, we need a separate NAND gate for each of the eight outputs. The input connections for each of the NAND gates can be determined by referring to Table 8–1b. For example, the NAND gate 5 inputs will be connected to the $2^2 - \overline{2^1} - 2^0$ input lines, NAND gate 6 will be connected

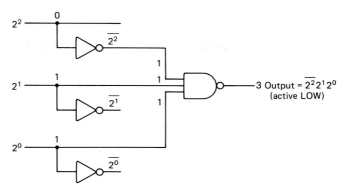

Figure 8–5 Logic requirements to produce a LOW at output 3 for a 0 1 1 input.

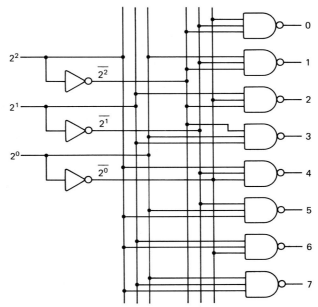

Figure 8–6 Complete circuit for an active-LOW output octal (1-of-8) decoder.

to the $2^2 - 2^1 - \overline{2^0}$ input lines, and so on. The complete circuit is shown in Figure 8–6. Each of the NAND gates in Figure 8–6 is wired so that its output will go LOW when the correct combination of input levels are present at their input. BCD and hexadecimal decoders can be designed in a similar manner.

The octal decoder is sometimes referred to as a *1-of-8 decoder* because, based on the input code, one of the eight outputs will be active. It is also known as a *3-line-to-8-line decoder* because it has three input lines and eight output lines.

Integrated-circuit decoder chips provide basic decoding as well as several other useful functions. Manufacturers' data books list several decoders and give function tables illustrating the input/output operation and special functions. Rather than designing decoders using combinational logic, it is much more important to be able to use a data book to find the decoder that you need and to determine the proper pin connections and operating procedure to perform a specific decoding task. Table 8–2 lists some of the more popular TTL decoder ICs. (Equivalent CMOS ICs are also available.)

TABLE 8–2

Decoder ICs

Device number	Function
74138	1-of-8 octal decoder (3 line-to-8 line)
7442	1-of-10 BCD decoder (4 line-to-10 line)
74154	1-of-16 hex decoder (4 line-to-16 line)
7447	BCD-to-seven segment decoder (covered in Chapter 12)

Octal Decoder IC

The 74138 is an octal decoder capable of decoding the eight possible octal codes into eight separate active-LOW outputs, just like our combinational logic design. It also has three enable inputs for additional flexibility. Figure 8–7 shows information presented in a data book for the 74138.

Just by looking at the logic symbol (Figure 8–7b) and function table (Figure 8–7d) we can figure out the complete operation of the chip. First of all, the inversion bubbles on the decoded outputs indicate active-LOW operation. The three inputs $\overline{E_1}$, $\overline{E_2}$, and E_3 are used to *enable* the chip. The function table shows that the chip is disabled (all outputs HIGH) *unless* $\overline{E_1}$ = LOW *and* $\overline{E_2}$ = LOW *and* E_3 = HIGH. The enables are useful for go/no-go operation of the chip based on some external control signal.

When the chip is *disabled*, the ×'s in the binary input columns A_0, A_1, and A_2 indicate *don't-care* levels, meaning the outputs will all be HIGH no matter what level A_0, A_1, and A_2 are. When the chip is *enabled*, the binary inputs A_0, A_1, and A_2 are used to select which output goes LOW. In this case, A_0 is the least significant bit (LSB) input. Be aware that some manufacturers label the inputs A, B, C instead of A_0, A_1, A_2 and assume that A is the LSB.

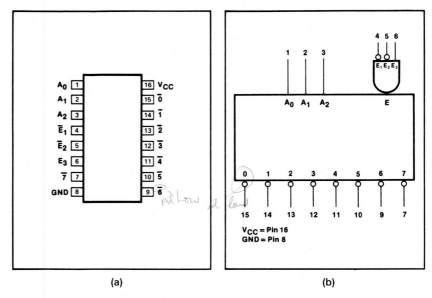

(a)   (b)

Figure 8–7   The 74138 octal decoder: (a) pin configuration; (b) logic symbol;

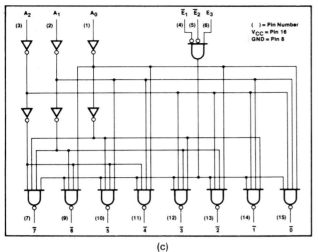

	INPUTS					OUTPUTS							
$\overline{E}_1$	$\overline{E}_2$	E_3	A_0	A_1	A_2	$\overline{0}$	$\overline{1}$	$\overline{2}$	$\overline{3}$	$\overline{4}$	$\overline{5}$	$\overline{6}$	$\overline{7}$
H	X	X	X	X	X	H	H	H	H	H	H	H	H
X	H	X	X	X	X	H	H	H	H	H	H	H	H
X	X	L	X	X	X	H	H	H	H	H	H	H	H
L	L	H	L	L	L	L	H	H	H	H	H	H	H
L	L	H	H	L	L	H	L	H	H	H	H	H	H
L	L	H	L	H	L	H	H	L	H	H	H	H	H
L	L	H	H	H	L	H	H	H	L	H	H	H	H
L	L	H	L	L	H	H	H	H	H	L	H	H	H
L	L	H	H	L	H	H	H	H	H	H	L	H	H
L	L	H	L	H	H	H	H	H	H	H	H	L	H
L	L	H	H	H	H	H	H	H	H	H	H	H	L

NOTES
H = HIGH voltage level
L = LOW voltage level
X = Don't care

(d)

(c)

Figure 8-7 (*Continued*) (c) logic diagram; (d) function table. (Courtesy of Signetics Corporation.)

The logic diagram in Figure 8-7(c) shows the actual internal combinational logic required to perform the decoding. The extra inverters on the inputs are required to prevent excessive loading of the driving source(s). Those internal inverters supply the driving current to the eight NAND gates instead of the driving source(s) having to do it. (Gate loading is discussed in Chapter 9.) The three enable inputs ($\overline{E}_1$, $\overline{E}_2$, E_3) are connected to an AND gate which can disable all the output NANDs by sending them a LOW input level if $\overline{E}_1$, $\overline{E}_2$, E_3 is not 001.

EXAMPLE 8-2

Sketch the output waveforms of the 74138 in Figure 8-8. Figure 8-9 shows the input waveforms to the 74138.

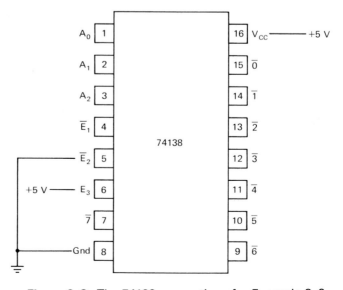

Figure 8-8 The 74138 connections for Example 8-2.

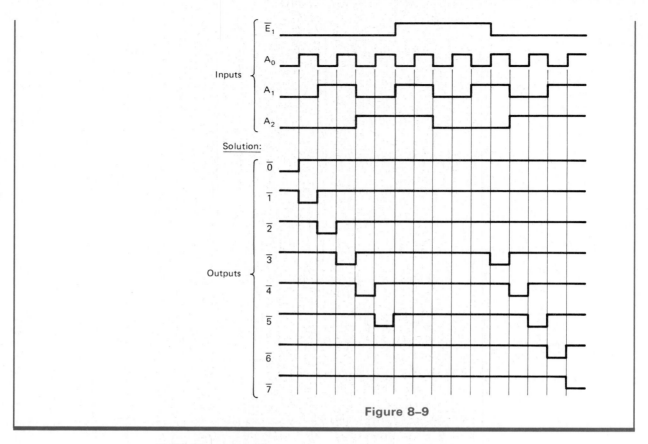

Figure 8–9

BCD Decoder IC

The 7442 is a BCD-to-decimal (1-of-10) decoder. It has four pins for the BCD input bits (0000 to 1001) and has 10 active-LOW outputs for the decoded decimal numbers. Figure 8–10 gives the operational information for the 7442 from a manufacturer's data book.

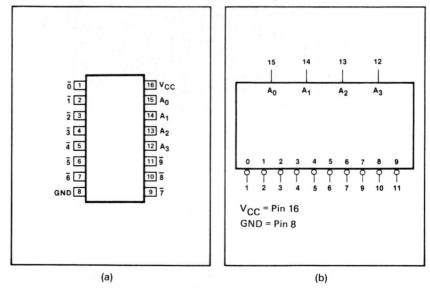

(a)   (b)

Figure 8–10   The 7442 BCD-to-DEC decoder: (a) pin configuration; (b) logic symbol;

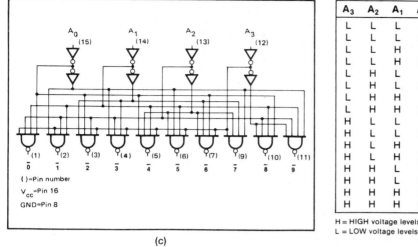

A₃	A₂	A₁	A₀	$\bar{0}$	$\bar{1}$	$\bar{2}$	$\bar{3}$	$\bar{4}$	$\bar{5}$	$\bar{6}$	$\bar{7}$	$\bar{8}$	$\bar{9}$
L	L	L	L	L	H	H	H	H	H	H	H	H	H
L	L	L	H	H	L	H	H	H	H	H	H	H	H
L	L	H	L	H	H	L	H	H	H	H	H	H	H
L	L	H	H	H	H	H	L	H	H	H	H	H	H
L	H	L	L	H	H	H	H	L	H	H	H	H	H
L	H	L	H	H	H	H	H	H	L	H	H	H	H
L	H	H	L	H	H	H	H	H	H	L	H	H	H
L	H	H	H	H	H	H	H	H	H	H	L	H	H
H	L	L	L	H	H	H	H	H	H	H	H	L	H
H	L	L	H	H	H	H	H	H	H	H	H	H	L
H	L	H	L	H	H	H	H	H	H	H	H	H	H
H	L	H	H	H	H	H	H	H	H	H	H	H	H
H	H	L	L	H	H	H	H	H	H	H	H	H	H
H	H	L	H	H	H	H	H	H	H	H	H	H	H
H	H	H	L	H	H	H	H	H	H	H	H	H	H
H	H	H	H	H	H	H	H	H	H	H	H	H	H

H = HIGH voltage levels
L = LOW voltage levels

(c)   (d)

Figure 8–10 (*Continued*)   (c) logic diagram; (d) function table. (Courtesy of Signetics Corporation.)

Hexadecimal 1-of-16 Decoder IC

The 74154 is a 1-of-16 decoder. It accepts a 4-bit binary input (0000 to 1111), decodes it, and provides an active-LOW output to one of the 16 output pins. It also has a two-input active-LOW enable gate for disabling the outputs. If either enable input ($\overline{E_0}$ or $\overline{E_1}$) is made HIGH, the outputs are forced HIGH regardless of the A_0 to A_3 inputs. The operational information for the 74154 is given in Figure 8–11.

The logic diagram in Figure 8–11(c) shows the actual combinational logic circuit that is used to provide the decoding. The inverted-input AND gate is used in the circuit to disable all output NAND gates if either $\overline{E_0}$ or $\overline{E_1}$ is made HIGH. Follow the logic levels through the circuit for several combinations of inputs to A_0 through A_3 to prove its operation.

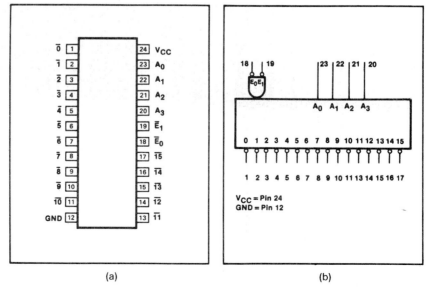

(a)   (b)

Figure 8–11   The 74154 1-of-16 decoder: (a) pin configuration; (b) logic symbol;

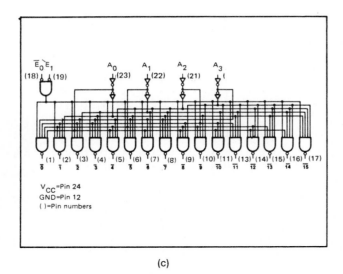

V_{CC} = Pin 24
GND = Pin 12
( ) = Pin numbers

(c)

INPUTS						OUTPUTS															
$\overline{E}_0$	$\overline{E}_1$	A_3	A_2	A_1	A_0	$\bar 0$	$\bar 1$	$\bar 2$	$\bar 3$	$\bar 4$	$\bar 5$	$\bar 6$	$\bar 7$	$\bar 8$	$\bar 9$	$\overline{10}$	$\overline{11}$	$\overline{12}$	$\overline{13}$	$\overline{14}$	$\overline{15}$
L	H	X	X	X	X	H	H	H	H	H	H	H	H	H	H	H	H	H	H	H	H
H	L	X	X	X	X	H	H	H	H	H	H	H	H	H	H	H	H	H	H	H	H
H	H	X	X	X	X	H	H	H	H	H	H	H	H	H	H	H	H	H	H	H	H
L	L	L	L	L	L	L	H	H	H	H	H	H	H	H	H	H	H	H	H	H	H
L	L	L	L	L	H	H	L	H	H	H	H	H	H	H	H	H	H	H	H	H	H
L	L	L	L	H	L	H	H	L	H	H	H	H	H	H	H	H	H	H	H	H	H
L	L	L	L	H	H	H	H	H	L	H	H	H	H	H	H	H	H	H	H	H	H
L	L	L	H	L	L	H	H	H	H	L	H	H	H	H	H	H	H	H	H	H	H
L	L	L	H	L	H	H	H	H	H	H	L	H	H	H	H	H	H	H	H	H	H
L	L	L	H	H	L	H	H	H	H	H	H	L	H	H	H	H	H	H	H	H	H
L	L	L	H	H	H	H	H	H	H	H	H	H	L	H	H	H	H	H	H	H	H
L	L	H	L	L	L	H	H	H	H	H	H	H	H	L	H	H	H	H	H	H	H
L	L	H	L	L	H	H	H	H	H	H	H	H	H	H	L	H	H	H	H	H	H
L	L	H	L	H	L	H	H	H	H	H	H	H	H	H	H	L	H	H	H	H	H
L	L	H	L	H	H	H	H	H	H	H	H	H	H	H	H	H	L	H	H	H	H
L	L	H	H	L	L	H	H	H	H	H	H	H	H	H	H	H	H	L	H	H	H
L	L	H	H	L	H	H	H	H	H	H	H	H	H	H	H	H	H	H	L	H	H
L	L	H	H	H	L	H	H	H	H	H	H	H	H	H	H	H	H	H	H	L	H
L	L	H	H	H	H	H	H	H	H	H	H	H	H	H	H	H	H	H	H	H	L

H = HIGH voltage level
L = LOW voltage level
X = Don't care

(d)

Figure 8–11 (*Continued*) (c) logic diagram; (d) function table. (Courtesy of Signetics Corporation.)

8–3 ENCODING

Encoding is the opposite process from decoding. Encoding is used to generate a coded output (such as BCD or binary) from a numeric input such as decimal or octal. For example, Figure 8–12 shows a typical block diagram for a decimal-to-BCD encoder and an octal-to-binary encoder.

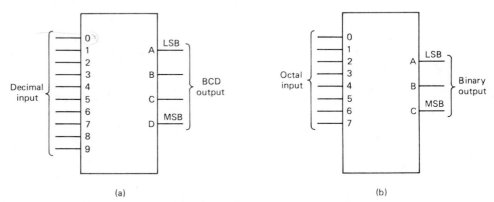

(a)

(b)

Figure 8–12 Typical block diagrams for encoders: (a) decimal-to-BCD encoder; (b) octal-to-binary encoder.

The design of encoders using combinational logic can be done by reviewing the truth table (see Table 8–3) for the operation to determine the relationship each output has with the inputs.

For example, by studying Table 8–3 for a decimal-to-BCD encoder, we can see that the A output (2^0) is HIGH for all odd-decimal input numbers (1, 3, 5, 7, 9). The B output (2^1) is HIGH for decimal inputs 2, 3, 6, and 7. The C output (2^2) is HIGH for decimal inputs 4, 5, 6, and 7, and the D output (2^3) is HIGH for decimal inputs 8 and 9.

TABLE 8-3

Decimal-to-BCD Encoder Truth Table

Decimal input	BCD output			
	D	C	B	A
0	0	0	0	0
1	0	0	0	1
2	0	0	1	0
3	0	0	1	1
4	0	1	0	0
5	0	1	0	1
6	0	1	1	0
7	0	1	1	1
8	1	0	0	0
9	1	0	0	1

Now, from what we have just observed, it seems that we can design a decimal-to-BCD encoder with just four OR gates; the A-output OR gate goes HIGH for any odd-decimal input, the B-output goes HIGH for 2 *or* 3 *or* 6 *or* 7, and so on for the C output and D output. The complete design of a basic decimal-to-BCD encoder is given in Figure 8-13. The design for an octal-to-binary encoder uses the same procedure, but, of course, these encoders are available in integrated-circuit form: the 74147 decimal-to-BCD and the 74148 octal-to-binary.

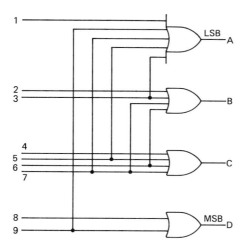

Figure 8-13   Basic decimal-to-BCD encoder.

The 74147 Decimal-to-BCD Encoder

The 74147 operates similarly to our basic design from Figure 8-13 except for two major differences.

1. The inputs *and* outputs are all active-LOW (see the bubbles on the logic symbol, Figure 8-14a).
2. The 74147 is a *priority* encoder. That means that if more than one decimal number is input, the highest numeric input has *priority* and will be encoded to the output (see the function table, Figure 8-14b). For example, looking at the second line in the function table, if $\overline{I}_9$ is LOW (decimal 9), all other inputs are "don't care" (could be HIGH *or* LOW), and the BCD output will be 0110 (active-LOW BCD-9).

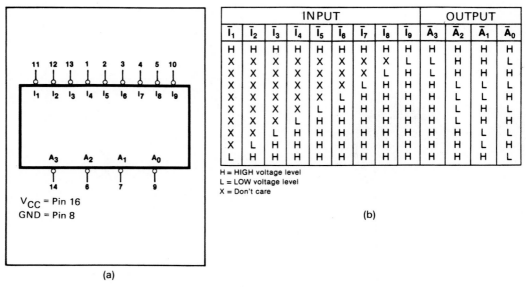

INPUT									OUTPUT			
$\overline{I_1}$	$\overline{I_2}$	$\overline{I_3}$	$\overline{I_4}$	$\overline{I_5}$	$\overline{I_6}$	$\overline{I_7}$	$\overline{I_8}$	$\overline{I_9}$	$\overline{A_3}$	$\overline{A_2}$	$\overline{A_1}$	$\overline{A_0}$
H	H	H	H	H	H	H	H	H	H	H	H	H
X	X	X	X	X	X	X	X	L	L	H	H	L
X	X	X	X	X	X	X	L	H	L	H	H	H
X	X	X	X	X	X	L	H	H	H	L	L	L
X	X	X	X	X	L	H	H	H	H	L	L	H
X	X	X	X	L	H	H	H	H	H	L	H	L
X	X	X	L	H	H	H	H	H	H	L	H	H
X	X	L	H	H	H	H	H	H	H	H	L	L
X	L	H	H	H	H	H	H	H	H	H	L	H
L	H	H	H	H	H	H	H	H	H	H	H	L

H = HIGH voltage level
L = LOW voltage level
X = Don't care

(b)

Figure 8–14 The 74147 decimal-to-BCD (10-line-to-4-line) encoder: (a) logic symbol; (b) function table.

EXAMPLE 8–3

For simplicity, the 74147 IC shown in Figure 8–15 is set up for encoding just three of its inputs (7, 8, and 9). Using the function table from Figure 8–14b, sketch the outputs at $\overline{A_0}$, $\overline{A_1}$, $\overline{A_2}$, and $\overline{A_3}$ as the $\overline{I_7}$, $\overline{I_8}$, and $\overline{I_9}$ inputs are switching as shown in Figure 8–16.

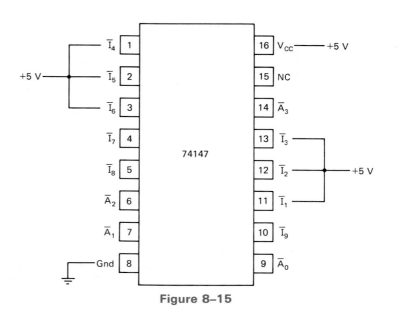

Figure 8–15

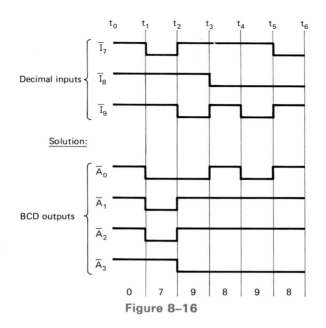

Figure 8–16

The $\overline{I_1}$ to $\overline{I_6}$ inputs are all tied HIGH and will have no effect on the output.

$t_0–t_1$: Dec inputs are all HIGH, BCD outputs represent a 0.

$t_1–t_2$: $\overline{I_7}$ is LOW; BCD outputs represent a 7.

$t_2–t_3$: $\overline{I_9}$ is LOW; BCD outputs represent a 9.

$t_3–t_4$: $\overline{I_8}$ is LOW; BCD outputs represent an 8.

$t_4–t_5$: $\overline{I_8}$ *and* $\overline{I_9}$ are LOW; $\overline{I_9}$ has priority; BCD outputs represent a 9.

$t_5–t_6$: $\overline{I_7}$ *and* $\overline{I_8}$ are LOW: $\overline{I_8}$ has priority; BCD outputs represent an 8.

The 74148 Octal-to-Binary Encoder

The 74148 encoder accepts data from eight active-LOW inputs and provides a binary representation on three active-LOW outputs. It is also a *priority* encoder, so that when two or more inputs are active simultaneously, the input with the highest priority is represented on the output, with input line $\overline{I_7}$ having the highest priority.

The logic symbol and function table in Figure 8–17 gives us some other information as well.

The 74148 can be expanded to any number of inputs by using several 74148s and their $\overline{EI}$, $\overline{EO}$, and $\overline{GS}$ pins. These special pins are defined as follows:

$\overline{EI}$ (active-LOW enable input). A HIGH on this input will force all outputs ($\overline{I_0}$ to $\overline{I_7}$, $\overline{EO}$, $\overline{GS}$) to their inactive (HIGH) state.

$\overline{EO}$ (active-LOW enable output). This output pin goes LOW when all inputs ($\overline{I_0}$ to $\overline{I_7}$) are inactive (HIGH) and $\overline{EI}$ is LOW.

$\overline{GS}$ (active-LOW group signal output). This output pin goes LOW whenever any of the inputs ($\overline{I_0}$ to $\overline{I_7}$) are active (LOW) and $\overline{EI}$ is LOW.

The following example illustrates the use of these pins.

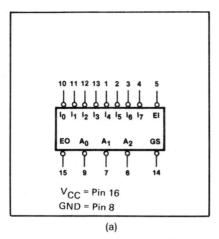

(a)

INPUTS									OUTPUTS				
$\overline{EI}$	$\overline{I_0}$	$\overline{I_1}$	$\overline{I_2}$	$\overline{I_3}$	$\overline{I_4}$	$\overline{I_5}$	$\overline{I_6}$	$\overline{I_7}$	$\overline{GS}$	$\overline{A_0}$	$\overline{A_1}$	$\overline{A_2}$	$\overline{EO}$
H	X	X	X	X	X	X	X	X	H	H	H	H	H
L	H	H	H	H	H	H	H	H	H	H	H	H	L
L	X	X	X	X	X	X	X	L	L	L	L	L	H
L	X	X	X	X	X	X	L	H	L	H	L	L	H
L	X	X	X	X	X	L	H	H	L	L	H	L	H
L	X	X	X	X	L	H	H	H	L	H	H	L	H
L	X	X	X	L	H	H	H	H	L	L	L	H	H
L	X	X	L	H	H	H	H	H	L	H	L	H	H
L	X	L	H	H	H	H	H	H	L	L	H	H	H
L	L	H	H	H	H	H	H	H	L	H	H	H	H

H = HIGH voltage level
L = LOW voltage level
X = Don't care

(b)

Figure 8–17 The 74148 octal-to-binary (8-line-to-3-line) encoder: (a) logic symbol; (b) function table. (Courtesy of Signetics Corporation.)

EXAMPLE 8–4

Sketch the output waveforms for the 74148 connected as shown in Figure 8–18. The input waveforms to $\overline{I_6}$, $\overline{I_7}$, and $\overline{EI}$ are given in Figure 8–19. (Inputs $\overline{I_0}$ to $\overline{I_5}$ are tied HIGH for simplicity.)

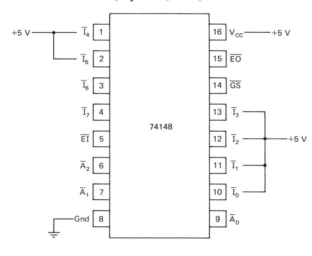

Figure 8–18 The 74148 connections for Example 8–4.

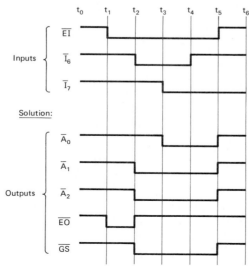

Figure 8–19

t_0–t_1: All outputs are forced HIGH by the HIGH on $\overline{EI}$.

t_1–t_2: $\overline{EI}$ is LOW to enable the inputs, but $\overline{I_0}$ to $\overline{I_7}$ are all HIGH (inactive) so $\overline{EO}$ goes LOW.

t_2–t_3: $\overline{GS}$ goes LOW because one of the inputs ($\overline{I_6}$) is active; the active-LOW binary output is equal to 6.

t_3–t_4: $\overline{I_7}$ *and* $\overline{I_6}$ are LOW; $\overline{I_7}$ has priority; output = 7.

t_4–t_5: $\overline{I_7}$ is LOW; output = 7.

t_5–t_6: All outputs are forced HIGH by the HIGH on $\overline{EI}$.

8–4 CODE CONVERTERS

Quite often it is important to convert a coded number into another form that is more usable by a computer or digital system. The prime example of this is with binary-coded decimal (BCD). We have seen that BCD is very important for visual display communication between a computer and human beings. But BCD is very difficult to deal with arithmetically. Algorithms, or procedures, have been developed for conversion of BCD to binary by computer programs (*software*) so that the computer will be able to perform all arithmetic operations in binary.

Another way to convert BCD to binary, the *hardware* approach, is with MSI integrated circuits. Additional circuitry is involved, but it is much faster to convert using hardware rather than software. We look at both methods of conversion of BCD to binary.

BCD-to-Binary Conversion

If you were going to convert BCD to binary using software program statements, you would first have to develop a procedure, or algorithm, for the conversion. Take, for example, the number 26 in BCD.

$$\underbrace{0010}_{2}\ \underbrace{0110}_{6}$$

If you simply apply regular binary weighting to each bit, you would come up with 38 ($2^1 + 2^2 + 2^5 = 38$). You must realize that the second group of BCD positions have a new progression of powers of 2 but with a weighting factor of 10, as shown in Figure 8–20. Now, if we go back and apply the proper weighting factors to 26 in BCD, we should get the correct binary equivalent.

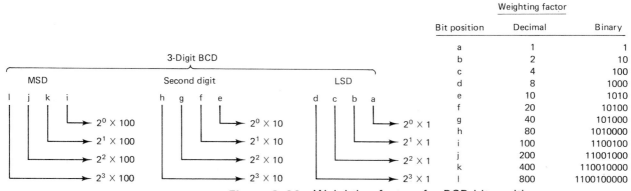

Bit position	Weighting factor Decimal	Binary
a	1	1
b	2	10
c	4	100
d	8	1000
e	10	1010
f	20	10100
g	40	101000
h	80	1010000
i	100	1100100
j	200	11001000
k	400	110010000
l	800	1100100000

Figure 8–20 Weighting factors for BCD bit positions.

EXAMPLE 8–5

Using the weighting factors given in Figure 8–20, convert the BCD equivalent of 26_{10} to binary.

Solution:

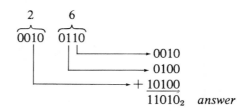

$$
\begin{array}{ll}
& 0010 \\
& 0100 \\
+ & \underline{10100} \\
& 11010_2 \quad \textit{answer}
\end{array}
$$

Check: $11010_2 = 26_{10}$ ✓

EXAMPLE 8–6

Convert the BCD equivalent of 348 to binary.

Solution:

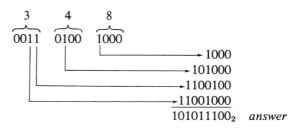

$$
\begin{array}{l}
1000 \\
101000 \\
1100100 \\
\underline{11001000} \\
101011100_2 \quad \textit{answer}
\end{array}
$$

Check: $101011100_2 = 348_{10}$ ✓

Conversion of BCD to Binary Using the 74184

Examples 8–5 and 8–6 illustrate one procedure of conversion that can be used as an algorithm for a computer program (software). The hardware approach using the 74184 IC is another way to accomplish BCD-to-binary conversion.

The logic symbol in Figure 8–21 shows eight active-HIGH binary outputs. Y_1 to Y_5 are outputs for regular BCD-to-binary conversion. Y_6 to Y_8 are used for a special BCD code called nine's complement and ten's complement.

The active-HIGH BCD bits are input on A through E. The $\overline{G}$ is an active-LOW enable input. When $\overline{G}$ is HIGH, all outputs are forced HIGH.

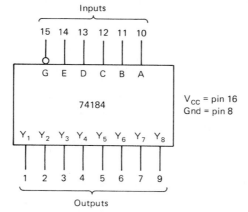

Figure 8–21   Logic symbol for the 74184 BCD-to-binary converter.

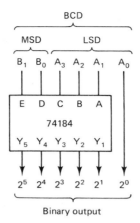

Figure 8–22 Six-bit BCD-to-binary converter.

Figure 8–22 shows the connections to form a 6-bit BCD converter. Since the LSB of the BCD input is always equal to the LSB of the binary output, the connection is made straight from input to output. The other BCD bits are connected to the A to E inputs. They will have the weighting of: $A = 2$, $B = 4$, $C = 8$, $D = 10$, and $E = 20$. Since only 2 bits are available for the MSD BCD input, the largest BCD digit in that position will be 3 (11). More useful setups, providing for the input of two or three complete BCD digits, are shown in Figure 8–23a and b.

Figure 8–23 BCD-to-binary conversions using the 74184 and binary-to-BCD conversions using the 74185: (a) BCD-to-binary converter for two BCD decades; (b) BCD-to-binary converter for three BCD decades.

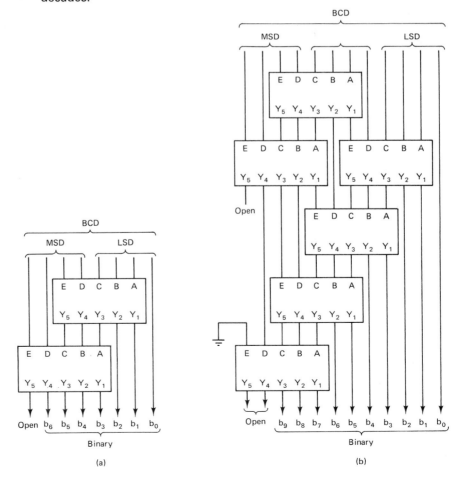

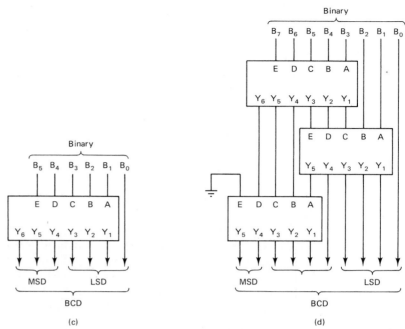

Figure 8–23 (*Continued*)   (c) 6-bit binary-to-BCD converter; (d) 8-bit binary-to-BCD converter. (Courtesy of Texas Instruments, Inc.)

A companion chip, the 74185, is used to work the opposite way, binary to BCD. Figure 8–23c and d show the 74185 used to perform binary-to-BCD conversions.

EXAMPLE 8–7

Show how the BCD code of the number 65 will be converted by the circuit of Figure 8–23a by placing 1's and 0's at the inputs and outputs.

Solution: The BCD-to-binary conversion is shown in Figure 8–24. The upper 74184 is used to convert the least significant 6 bits, which are 100101. Using the proper binary weighting, 100101 becomes 011001.

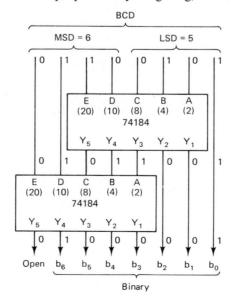

Figure 8–24 Solution to Example 8–7.

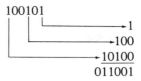

The lower 74184 is used to convert the 2 most significant bits plus 4 bits from the upper 74184, which are 010110. Using proper binary weighting, 010110 becomes 010000.

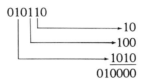

The final binary result is 01000001, which checks out to be equal to 65_{10}.

Gray Code

The Gray code is another useful code used in digital systems. It is used primarily for indicating the angular position of a shaft on rotating machinery such as automated lathes and drill presses. This code is like binary in that it can have as many bits as necessary, and the more bits, the more possible combinations of output codes (number of combinations $= 2^N$). A 4-bit gray code, for example, will have $2^4 = 16$ different representations, giving a resolution of one out of 16 possible angular positions at 22.5 degrees each ($360/16 = 22.5$).

The difference between the Gray code and the regular binary code is illustrated in Table 8-4. Notice in the table that the Gray code varies by only 1 bit from one entry to the next and from the last entry (15) back to the beginning (0). Now, if each Gray code represented a different position on a rotating wheel, as the wheel turns, the code read from one position to the next would vary by only 1 bit (see Figure 8-25).

TABLE 8-4

Four-Bit Gray Code

Decimal	Binary	Gray
0	0000	0000
1	0001	0001
2	0010	0011
3	0011	0010
4	0100	0110
5	0101	0111
6	0110	0101
7	0111	0100
8	1000	1100
9	1001	1101
10	1010	1111
11	1011	1110
12	1100	1010
13	1101	1011
14	1110	1001
15	1111	1000

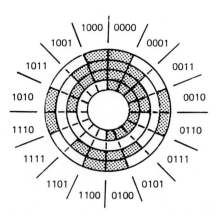

Figure 8–25 Gray code wheel.

If the same wheel were labeled in *binary*, as the wheel turned from 7 to 8, the code would change from 0111 to 1000. If the digital machine happened to be reading the shaft position just as the code was changing, it might see 0111 or 1000, but since all 4 bits are changing (0 to 1 or 1 to 0) the code that it reads may be anything from 0000 to 1111. Therefore, the potential for an error using the regular binary system is great.

With the Gray code wheel, on the other hand, when the position changes from 7 to 8, the code changes from 0100 to 1100. The MSB is the only bit that changes, so if a read is taken right on the border between the two numbers, either a 0100 is read or a 1100 is read (no problem!).

Gray Code Conversions

The determination of the Gray code equivalents and the conversions between Gray code and binary code are done very simply with exclusive-OR gates, as shown in Figures 8–26 and 8–27.

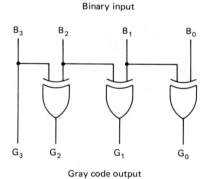

Figure 8–26 Binary-to-Gray code converter.

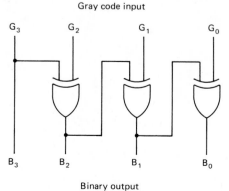

Figure 8–27 Gray code-to-binary converter.

EXAMPLE 8–8

Test the operation of the binary-to-Gray code converter of Figure 8–26 by labeling the inputs and outputs with the conversion of binary 0110 to Gray code.

Solution: The operation of the converter is shown in Figure 8–28.

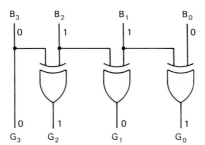

Figure 8–28

EXAMPLE 8–9

Repeat Example 8–8 for the Gray code-to-binary converter of Figure 8–27 by converting a Gray code 0011 to binary.

Solution: The operation of the converter is shown in Figure 8–29.

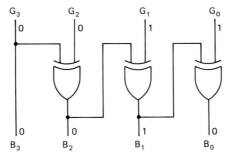

Figure 8–29

8–5 MULTIPLEXERS

A multiplexer is a device capable of funneling several data lines into a single line for transmission to another point. The multiplexer will have two or more digital input signals connected to its input. Control signals will also be input to tell which data-input line to select for transmission (data selection). Figure 8–30 illustrates the function of a multiplexer.

The multiplexer is also known as a *data selector*. Figure 8–30 shows that the *data select control inputs* (S_1, S_0) are responsible for determining which data input (D_0 to D_3) is selected to be transmitted to the data-output line (Y). The S_1, S_0 inputs will be a binary code that corresponds to the data-input line that you want to select. If $S_1 = 0$, $S_0 = 0$, then D_0 is selected; if $S_1 = 0$, $S_0 = 1$, then D_1 is selected; and so on. Table 8–5 lists the codes for input data selection.

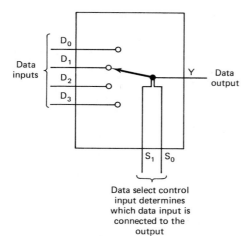

Figure 8–30   Functional diagram of a four-line multiplexer.

TABLE 8–5

Data Select Input Codes
for Figure 8–30

Data select control inputs		Data input selected
S_1	S_0	
0	0	D_0
0	1	D_1
1	0	D_2
1	1	D_3

A sample four-line multiplexer built from SSI logic gates is shown in Figure 8–31. The control inputs (S_1, S_0) take care of enabling the correct AND gate to pass just one of the data inputs through to the output. In Figure 8–31, 1's and 0's were placed on the diagram to show the levels that occur when selecting data input, D_1. Notice that AND gate 1 will be enabled, passing D_1 to the output, while all other AND gates are disabled.

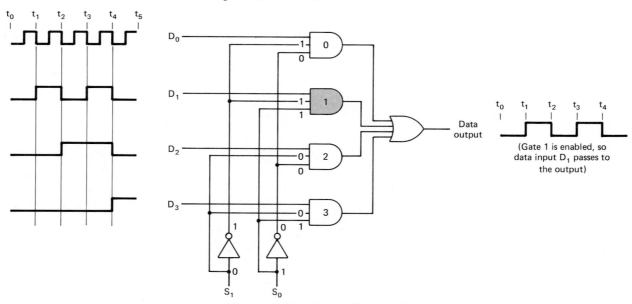

Figure 8–31   Logic diagram for a four-line multiplexer.

TABLE 8–6

TTL and CMOS Multiplexers

Function	Device	Logic family
Quad two-input	74157	TTL
	74HC157	H-CMOS
	4019	CMOS
Dual eight-input	74153	TTL
	74HC153	H-CMOS
	4539	CMOS
Eight-input	74151	TTL
	74HC151	H-CMOS
	4512	CMOS
16-input	74150	TTL

Two-input, four-input, eight-input, and 16-input multiplexers are readily available in MSI packages. Table 8–6 lists some popular TTL and CMOS multiplexers. (H-CMOS, high-speed CMOS, will be compared with the other logic families, in detail in Chapter 9.)

The logic symbol and logic diagram for the 74151 are given in Figure 8–32. Since the 74151 has eight lines to select from (I_0 to I_7), it requires three data select

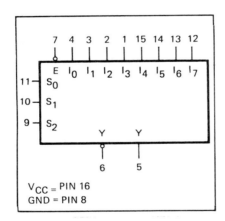

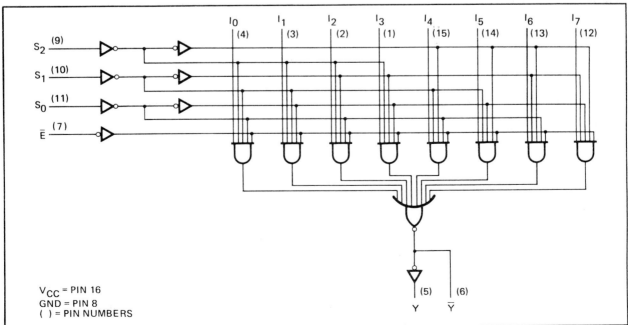

(b)   (a)

Figure 8–32 The 74151 eight-line multiplexer: (a) logic symbol; (b) logic diagram. (Courtesy of Signetics Corporation.)

inputs—S_2, S_1, S_0—to determine which input to choose ($2^3 = 8$). True (Y) and complemented ($\overline{Y}$) outputs are provided. The active-LOW enable input ($\overline{E}$) disables all inputs when it is HIGH and forces Y LOW regardless of all other inputs.

EXAMPLE 8–10

Sketch the output waveforms at Y for the 74151 shown in Figure 8–33. For this example, the eight input lines (I_0 to I_7) are each connected to a constant level and the data select lines (S_0 to S_2) and input enable ($\overline{E}$) are given as input waveforms.

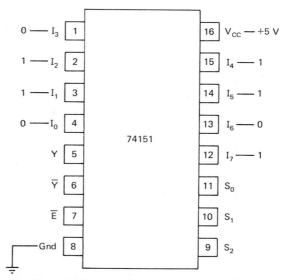

Figure 8–33   The 74151 multiplexer pin connections for Example 8–10.

See Figure 8–34. From t_0 to t_8 the waveforms at S_0, S_1, S_2 form a binary counter from 000 to 111. Therefore, the output at Y will be selected from I_0, then I_1, then I_2, and so on, up to I_7. From t_8 to t_9 the S_0, S_1, S_2 inputs are back to 000, so I_0 will be selected for output. From t_9 to t_{11} the $\overline{E}$ enable line goes HIGH, disabling all inputs and forcing Y LOW.

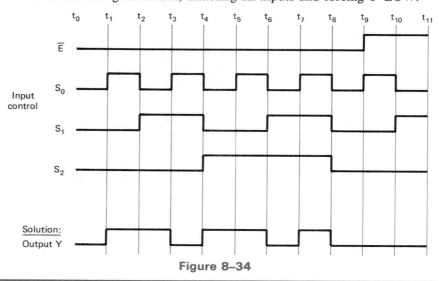

Figure 8–34

EXAMPLE 8-11

Using two 74151s, design a 16-line multiplexer controlled by four data select control inputs.

Solution: The multiplexer is shown in Figure 8–35. Since there are 16 data input lines, we must use four data select inputs ($2^4 = 16$). (A is the LSB data select line and D is the MSB.)

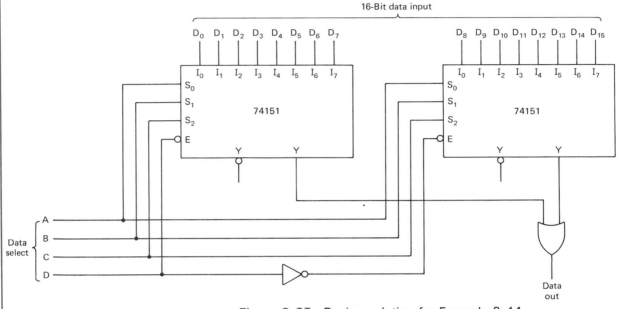

Figure 8–35 Design solution for Example 8–11.

When the data select is in the range 0000 to 0111, the D line is 0, which enables the low-order (left) multiplexer selecting the D_0 to D_7 inputs and disables the high-order (right) multiplexer.

When the data select inputs are in the range 1000 to 1111, the D line is 1, which disables the low-order multiplexer and enables the high-order multiplexer, allowing D_8 to D_{15} to be selected. Since the Y output of a disabled multiplexer is 0, an OR gate is used to combine the two outputs, allowing the output from the enabled multiplexer to pass through.

Providing Combination Logic Functions with a Multiplexer

Multiplexers have many other uses besides being a data selector. Another important role of a multiplexer is for implementing combinational logic circuits. One multiplexer can take the place of several SSI logic gates, as shown in the following example.

EXAMPLE 8-12

Use a multiplexer to implement the function

$$X = \overline{A}\,\overline{B}\,\overline{C}D + A\overline{B}\,\overline{C}D + AB\overline{C}\,\overline{D} + \overline{A}BC + \overline{A}\,\overline{B}C$$

Solution: The equation is in the sum-of-products form. Each term in the equation, when fulfilled, will make $X = 1$. For example, when $A = 0$, $B = 0$, $C =$

0, $D = 1$ ($\overline{A}\,\overline{B}\,\overline{C}D$), X will receive a 1. Also if $A = 1$, $B = 0$, $C = 0$, $D = 1$ ($A\overline{B}\,\overline{C}D$), X will receive a 1, and so on.

If the A, B, C, D variables are used as the data input selectors of a 16-line multiplexer (four input variables can have 16 possible combinations) and the appropriate digital levels are placed at the multiplexer data inputs, we will be able to implement the function for X. We will use the 74150 16-line multiplexer. A 1 must be placed at each data input that satisfies any term in the Boolean equation. The truth table and the 74150 connections to implement the function are given in Figure 8–36.

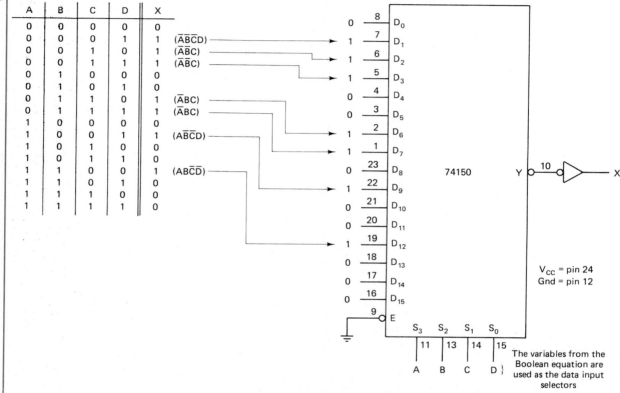

Figure 8–36 Truth table and solution for the implementation of the Boolean equation $X = \overline{A}\,\overline{B}\,\overline{C}D + A\overline{B}\,\overline{C}D + AB\overline{C}\,\overline{D} + \overline{A}BC + \overline{A}\,\overline{B}C$ using a 16-line multiplexer.

The logic symbol for the 74150 is similar to the 74151 except that it has 16 input data lines, four data select lines, and only the complemented output. To test the operation of the operation of the circuit, let's try some entries from the truth table to see that X is valid. For example, if $A = 0$, $B = 0$, $C = 0$, $D = 1$ ($\overline{A}\,\overline{B}\,\overline{C}D$), the multiplexer will select D_1, which is 1. It gets inverted twice before reaching X, so X receives a 1, which is correct. Work through the rest of them yourself and you will see that the Boolean function is fulfilled.

8–6 DEMULTIPLEXERS

Demultiplexing is the opposite procedure from multiplexing. We can think of a demultiplexer as a *data distributor*. It takes a single input data value and routes it to one of several outputs, as illustrated in Figure 8–37.

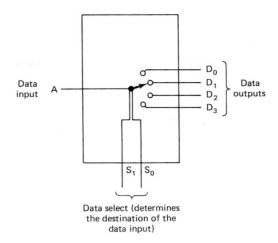

Figure 8-37 Functional diagram of a four-line demultiplexer.

Integrated-circuit demultiplexers come in several configurations of inputs/outputs. The two that we discuss in this section are the 74139 dual four-line demultiplexer and the 74154 16-line demultiplexer.

The logic diagram and logic symbol for the 74139 are given in Figure 8–38. Notice that the 74139 is divided into two equal sections. By looking at the logic diagram, you will see that the schematic is the same as that of a 2-line-to-4-line decoder. Decoders and demultiplexers are the same, except with a decoder you hold the $\overline{E}$ enable line LOW and enter a code at the A_0A_1 inputs. As a demultiplexer, the A_0A_1 inputs are used to select the destination of input data. The input data are brought in via the $\overline{E}$ line. The 74138 3-line-to-8-line decoder that we covered earlier in this chapter can also function as an eight-line demultiplexer.

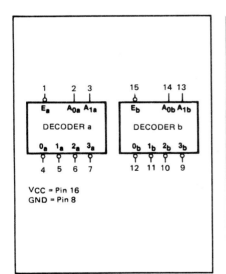

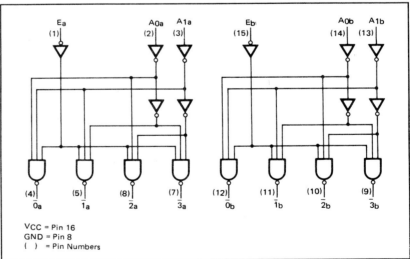

Figure 8-38 The 74139 dual four-line demultiplexer: (a) logic symbol; (b) logic diagram. (Courtesy of Signetics Corporation.)

To use the 74139 as a demultiplexer to route some input data signal to, let's say; the $\overline{2a}$ output, the connections shown in Figure 8–39 would be made. In the figure the destination $\overline{2a}$ is selected by making $A_{1a} = 1$, $A_{0a} = 0$. The input signal is brought into the enable line ($\overline{E_a}$). When $\overline{E_a}$ goes LOW, the selected output line goes LOW; when $\overline{E_a}$ goes HIGH, the selected output line goes HIGH. (All nonselected lines remain HIGH continuously.)

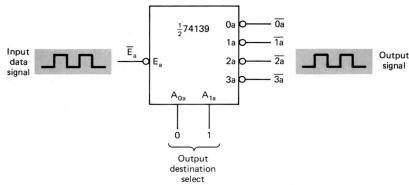

Figure 8–39 Connections to route an input data signal to the $\overline{2_a}$ output of a 74139 demultiplexer.

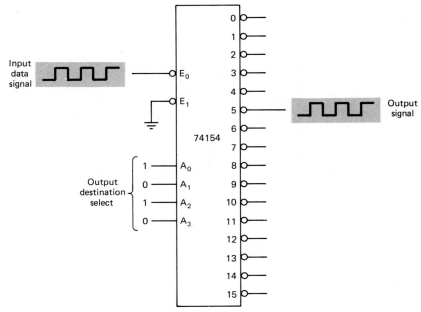

Figure 8–40 The 74154 demultiplexer connections to route an input signal to the $\overline{5}$ output.

The 74154 was used earlier in the chapter as a 4-line-to-16-line hexadecimal decoder. It can also be used as a 16-line demultiplexer. Figure 8–40 shows how it can be connected to route an input data signal to the $\overline{5}$ output.

Analog Multiplexer/Demultiplexer

Several analog multiplexers/demultiplexers are available in the CMOS family. The 4051, 4052, and 4053 are combination multiplexer *and* demultiplexer CMOS ICs. They can function in either configuration because their inputs and outputs are *bidirectional*, meaning that the flow can go in either direction. Also, they are *analog*, meaning that they can input and output levels other than just 1 and 0. The input/output levels can be any analog voltage between the positive and negative supply levels.

The functional diagram for the 4051 eight-channel multiplexer/demultiplexer is given in Figure 8–41. The eight square boxes in the functional diagram represent the bidirectional I/O lines. Used as a multiplexer, the analog levels will come in on the Y_0 to Y_7 lines, and the decoder will select which of these inputs are outputted

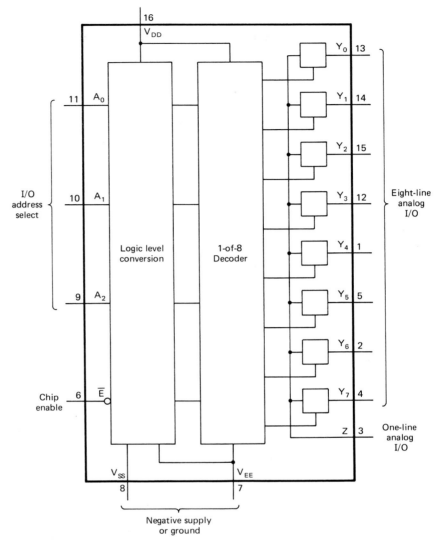

Figure 8-41 The 4051 CMOS analog multiplexer/demultiplexer. (Courtesy of Signetics Corporation.)

to the Z line. As a demultiplexer, the connections are reversed, with the input coming into the Z line and the output going out on one of the Y_0 to Y_7 lines.

8-7 SYSTEM DESIGN APPLICATIONS

Analog Multiplexer Application

The 4051 is very versatile. One use is in the design of multitrace oscilloscope displays for displaying as many as eight traces on the same display screen. To do that, each input signal to be displayed must be superimposed on (added to) a different voltage level so that each trace will be at a different level on the display screen.

The 4051 can be set up to sequentially output eight different voltage levels repeatedly if connected as shown in Figure 8-42. The resistor voltage-divider network in Figure 8-42 is set up to drop 0.5 V across each 100-Ω resistor. That will put 0.5 V at Y_0, 1.0 V at Y_1, and so on. The binary counter outputs a binary progression

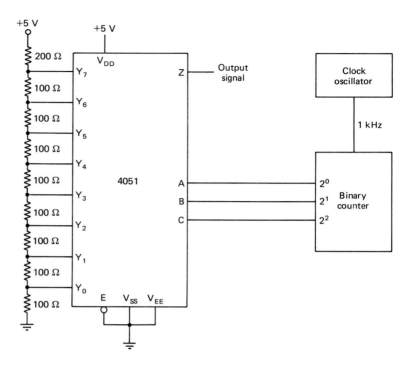

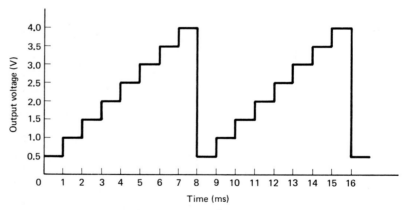

Figure 8–42   The 4051 analog multiplexer used as a staircase generator.

from 000 up to 111, which causes each of the Y_0 to Y_7 inputs to be selected for Z out, one at a time, in order. The result is the staircase waveform shown in Figure 8–42, which can superimpose a different voltage level on each of eight separate digital input signals that are brought in via the 74151 eight-line *digital* multiplexer (not shown) driven by the same binary counter.

Multiplexed Display Application

Figure 8–43 shows a common method of using multiplexing to reduce the cost of producing a multidigit display in a digital system or computer.

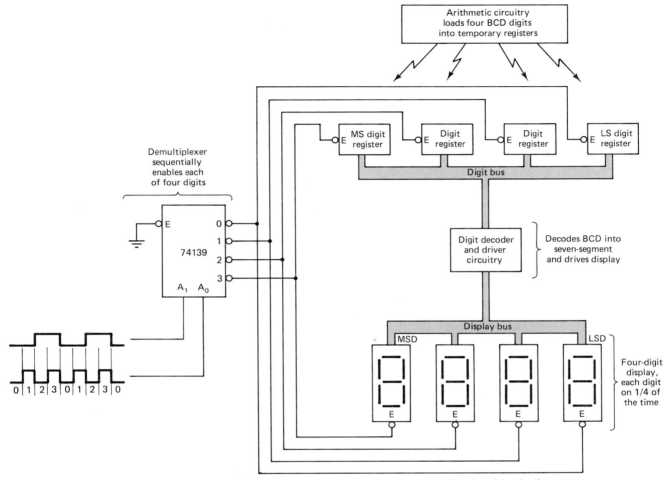

Figure 8–43 Multiplexed four-digit-display block diagram.

Theory of Operation

Multiplexing multidigit displays reduces circuit cost and failure rate by *sharing* common ICs, components, and conductors. The seven-segment digit displays, decoders, and drivers will be covered in detail in Chapter 12. For now, we need to know that a decoding process must take place to convert the BCD digit information to a recognizable digit display.

The digit bus and display bus are each just a common set of conductors *shared by* the digit storage registers and display segments. The four digit registers are therefore multiplexed into a single digit bus, and the display bus is demultiplexed into the four digit displays.

The 74139 four-line demultiplexer takes care of sequentially accessing each of the four digits. It first outputs a LOW on the $\overline{0}$ line. This enables the LS digit register *and* the LS digit display. The LS BCD information travels down the digit bus to the decoder/driver, which *decodes* the BCD into the special seven-segment code used by the LS digit display, and *drives* the LS digit display.

Next, the second digit register and display are enabled, then the third, then the fourth. This process continues repeatedly, each digit being on one-fourth of the time. The circulation is set up fast enough (1 kHz or more) that it appears that all four digits are on at the same time. The external arithmetic circuitry is free to change the display at any time simply by reloading the temporary digit registers.

GLOSSARY

Bidirectional: A device capable of functioning in either of two directions, thus being able to reverse its input/output functions.

Bus: A common set of conductors shared by several devices or ICs.

Comparator: A device used to compare the magnitude or size of two binary bit strings or words.

Decoder: A device that converts a digital code such as hex or octal into a single output representing its numeric value.

Don't care ($\times$): A variable that is signified in a function table as a don't care, or $\times$, can take on either value, HIGH *or* LOW, without having any effect on the output.

Encoder: A device that converts a weighted numeric input line to an equivalent digital code, such as hex or octal.

Gray code: A binary coding system used primarily in rotating machinery to indicate a shaft position. Each successive binary string within the code changes by only 1 bit.

Hardware/software: Sometimes, solutions to digital applications can be done using hardware *or* software. The *software* approach uses computer program statements to solve the application, whereas the *hardware* approach uses digital electronic devices and ICs.

Priority: When more than one input to a device is active and only one can be acted on, the one with the highest "priority" will be acted on.

Superimpose: Combining two waveforms together such that the result is the sum of their levels at each point in time.

Weighting factor: The digit within a numeric string of data is worth more or less depending on which position it is in. A weighting factor is applied to determine its worth.

REVIEW QUESTIONS

Section 8–1

8–1. More than one output of the 7485 comparator can be simultaneously HIGH (true or false)?

8–2. If all inputs to a 7485 comparator are LOW except for the $I_A < B$ input, what will the output be?

Section 8–2

8–3. A BCD-to-decimal decoder has how many inputs and how many outputs?

8–4. An octal decoder with active-LOW outputs will output seven LOWs and one HIGH for each combination of inputs (true or false)?

8–5. A hexadecimal decoder is sometimes called a 4-line-to-10 line decoder (true or false)?

8–6. Only one of the three *enable* inputs must be satisfied to enable the 74138 decoder IC (true or false)?

8–7. The 7442 BCD decoder has active-_____ (LOW, HIGH) inputs and active-_____ (LOW, HIGH) outputs.

Section 8–3

8–8. How does an encoder differ from a decoder.

8–9. If more than one input to a *priority* encoder is active, which input will be encoded?

8–10. (a) If all inputs to a 74147 encoder are HIGH, what will the $A_3 - A_0$ outputs be?

    (b) Repeat (a) for all inputs being LOW.

8–11. What are the five outputs of the 74148? Are they active-LOW or active-HIGH?

Section 8–4

8–12. What is the binary weighting factor of the MSB of a two-digit (8-bit) BCD number?

8–13. How many 74184 ICs are required to convert a 3-digit BCD number to binary?

8–14. Why is gray code used for indicating the shaft position of rotating machinery rather than regular binary code?

Sections 8–5 and 8–6

8–15. Why is a *multiplexer* sometimes called a "data selector."

8–16. Why is a *demultiplexer* sometimes called a "data distributor"?

8–17. What is the function of the S_0, S_1, and S_2 pins on the 74151 multiplexer?

8–18. What is the function of the A_0, A_1, A_2, and A_3 pins on the 74154 demultiplexer?

PROBLEMS

8–1. Design a binary comparator circuit using exclusive-ORs and a NOR gate that will compare two 8-bit binary strings.

8–2. Label all the lines in your design for Problem 8–1 with digital levels that will occur when comparing $A = 1101\ 1001$ and $B = 1101\ 1001$.

8–3. Label the digital levels on all the lines in Figure 8–3 that would occur when comparing the two 8-bit strings $A = 1011\ 0101$ and $B = 1100\ 0011$.

8–4. Write a two-sentence description of the function of a decoder.

8–5. Construct a truth table similar to Table 8–1 for an active-LOW output BCD (1-of-10) decoder.

8–6. What state must the inputs $\overline{E_1}$, $\overline{E_2}$, E_3 be in in order to *enable* the 74138 decoder?

8–7. What does the $\times$ signify in the function table for the 74138?

8–8. Describe the difference between active-LOW outputs and active-HIGH outputs.

8–9. Sketch the output waveforms ($\overline{0}$ to $\overline{7}$) given the inputs shown in Figure P8–9b to the 74138 of Figure P8–9a.

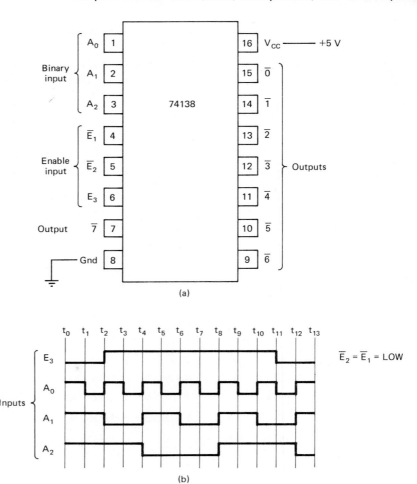

(a)

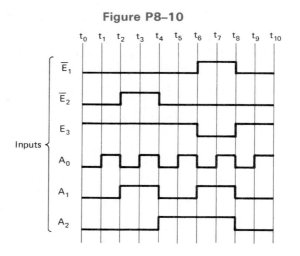

(b)

Figure P8–9

8–10. Repeat Problem 8–9 for the input waveforms shown in Figure P8–10.

8-11. What state does the outputs of a 7442 BCD decoder go to when an invalid BCD number (10 to 15) is input to A_0 to A_3?

8-12. Design a circuit, based on a 74154 4-line-to-16-line decoder, that will output a HIGH whenever the 4-bit binary input is greater than 12. (When the binary input is less than or equal to 12, it will output a LOW.)

8-13. With the 74147 priority encoder, if two different decimal numbers are input at the same time, which will be encoded?

8-14. A 74147 is connected with $\bar{I}_1 = \bar{I}_2 = \bar{I}_3 =$ LOW and $\bar{I}_4 = \bar{I}_5 = \bar{I}_6 = \bar{I}_7 = \bar{I}_8 = \bar{I}_9 =$ HIGH. Determine $\bar{A}_0$, $\bar{A}_1$, $\bar{A}_2$, and $\bar{A}_3$.

8-15. Sketch the output waveforms ($\bar{A}_0$, $\bar{A}_1$, $\bar{A}_2$, $\overline{EO}$, $\overline{GS}$) given the inputs shown in Figure P8–15b to the 74148 of Figure P8–15a.

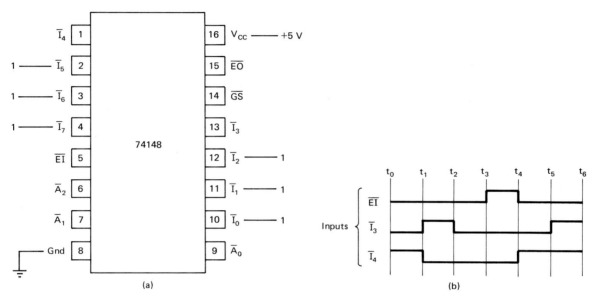

Figure P8–15

8-16. Repeat Problem 8–15 for the waveforms shown in Figure P8–16.

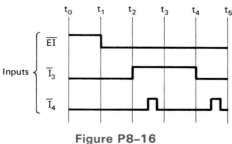

Figure P8–16

8-17. Two 74148s are connected together in Figure P8–17 to form an active-LOW input, active-LOW output hexadecimal (16-line-to-4-line) priority encoder. Show the logic levels on each line in Figure P8–17 for encoding an input hexadecimal C (12) to an output binary 1100 (active-LOW 0011).

8-18. Repeat Problem 8–17 for encoding an input hexadecimal 6 to an output binary six (active-LOW 1001).

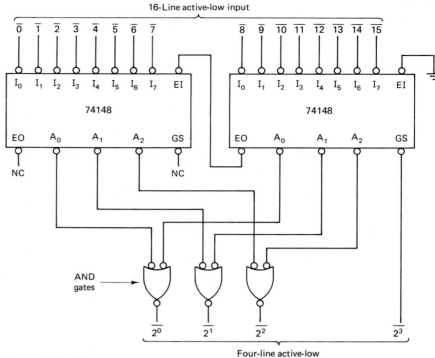

Figure P8–17

8–19. Using the weighting factors given in Figure 8–20, convert the following decimal numbers to BCD, then to binary.

    (a) 32

    (b) 46

    (c) 55

    (d) 68

8–20. Figure P8–20 is a two-digit BCD-to-binary converter. Show how the number 49 ($0100\ 1001_{BCD}$) will be converted to binary by placing 1's and 0's at the inputs and outputs.

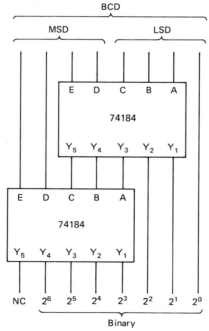

Figure P8–20

8–21. Repeat Problem 8–20 for the number 73.

8–22. Convert the following Gray codes to binary using the circuit of Figure 8–27.

    (a) 1100   **(c)** 1110

    (b) 0101   **(d)** 0111

8–23. Convert the following binary numbers to Gray code using the circuit of Figure 8–26.
- **(a)** 1010
- **(b)** 1111
- **(c)** 0011
- **(d)** 0001

8–24. The connectors shown in Figure P8–24 are made to the 74151 eight-line multiplexer. Determine Y and $\overline{Y}$.

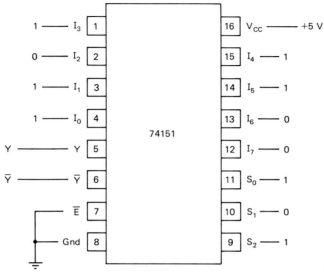

Figure P8–24

8–25. Using a technique similar to that presented in Figure 8–35, *design* a 32-bit multiplexer using four 74151s.

8–26. *Design* a circuit that will output a LOW whenever a month has 31 days. The month number (1 to 12) will be input as a 4-bit binary number (January = 0001, etc.). (*Hint*: Use a 74150.)

Troubleshooting

8–27. *Design* an 8-bit demultiplexer using one 74139.

8–28. *Design* a 16-bit demultiplexer using two 74138s.

8–29. There is a malfunction in a digital system that contains several multiplexer and demultiplexer ICs. A reading was taken at each pin with a logic probe and the results were recorded in Table 8–7. Which IC, or ICs, are not working correctly?

TABLE 8–7

IC Logic States for Troubleshooting Problem 8–29

74150		74151		74139		74154	
Pin	Level	Pin	Level	Pin	Level	Pin	Level
1	0	1	1	1	0	1	1
2	1	2	0	2	1	2	1
3	1	3	0	3	0	3	1
4	0	4	1	4	0	4	1
5	1	5	1	5	1	5	1
6	0	6	0	6	1	6	1
7	1	7	0	7	1	7	1
8	1	8	0	8	0	8	1
9	0	9	0	9	0	9	1
10	0	10	0	10	0	10	1
11	0	11	0	11	1	11	1
12	0	12	0	12	0	12	0
13	1	13	1	13	1	13	1
14	1	14	0	14	0	14	1
15	1	15	0	15	1	15	1
16	0	16	1	16	1	16	1
17	1					17	1
18	0					18	1
19	1					19	0
20	1					20	0
21	1					21	0
22	0					22	1
23	1					23	1
24	1					24	1

9 Logic Families and Their Characteristics

OBJECTIVES

Upon completion of this chapter, you should be able to:

- Analyze the internal circuitry of a TTL gate for both the HIGH and LOW output states.
- Determine IC input and output voltage and current ratings from the manufacturer's data manual.
- Explain gate loading, fan-out, noise margin, and time parameters.
- Design wired-output circuits using open-collector TTL gates.
- Discuss the differences and proper use of the various subfamilies within both the TTL and CMOS lines of ICs.
- Describe the reasoning and various techniques for interfacing between the TTL, CMOS, and ECL families of ICs.

INTRODUCTION

Integrated-circuit logic gates (small-scale integration, SSI), combinational logic circuits, (medium-scale integration, MSI), and microprocessor systems (large-scale-integration and very-large scale integration, LSI and VLSI) are readily available from several manufacturers through distributors and electronic parts suppliers. Basically, there are three commonly used families of digital IC logic: TTL (transistor-transistor logic), CMOS (complementary metal-oxide semiconductor), and ECL (emitter-coupled logic). Within each family there are several subfamilies (or series) of logic types available with different ratings for speed, power consumption, temperature range, voltage levels, and current levels.

Fortunately, the different manufacturers of digital logic ICs have standardized a numbering scheme so that basic part numbers will be the same regardless of the manufacturer. The prefix of the part number, however, will differ because it is the manufacturer's abbreviation. For example, a typical TTL part number might be S74F08N. The 7408 is the basic number used by all manufacturers for a quad *AND* gate. The F stands for the *FAST* TTL sub-family and the S prefix is the manufacturer's code for Signetics. National Semiconductor uses the prefix DM, and Texas Instruments uses the prefix SN. The N suffix at the end of the part number is used to specify the package type. N is used for the plastic dual-in-line (DIP), W is used for the ceramic flatpack, and D is used for the surface-mounted SO plastic package. The best source of information on the available package styles and their dimensions is given in the manufacturers' data manuals. Most data manuals will list the 7408 as 5408/7408. The 54XX series is the military version, which has less stringent power supply requirements and an extended temperature range of -55 to $+125°C$, whereas the 74XX is the commercial version with a temperature range of 0 to $+70°C$ and strict power supply requirements.

For the purposes of this text, reference is usually made to the 74XX commercial version and the manufacturer's prefix code and package-style suffix code are ignored. The XX is used in this book to fill the space normally occupied by the actual part number. For example, the part number for an inverter in the 74XX series is 7404.

9-1 THE TTL FAMILY

The standard 74XX TTL IC family has evolved through several stages since the late 1960s. Along the way, improvements have been made to reduce the internal time delays and power consumption. At the same time, each manufacturer has been introducing chips with new functions and applications.

The fundamental operation of a TTL chip can be explained by studying the internal circuitry of the basic two-input 7400 NAND gate shown in Figure 9-1. The diodes D_1 and D_2 are negative clamping diodes used to protect the inputs from

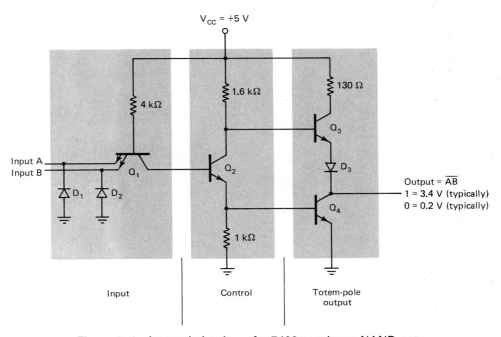

Figure 9-1 Internal circuitry of a 7400 two-input NAND gate.

any short-term negative input voltages. The input transistor, Q_1, acts like an AND gate and is usually fabricated with a *multiemitter* transistor which characterizes TTL technology. (To produce two-, three-, four-, and eight-input NAND gates, the manufacturer uses two-, three-, four-, and eight-emitter transistors.) Q_2 provides control and current boosting to the totem-pole output stage.

The reasoning for the totem-pole setup was discussed in Chapter 2. Basically, when the output is HIGH (1), Q_4 is OFF (open) and Q_3 is ON (short). When the output is LOW (0), Q_4 is ON and Q_3 is OFF. Since one, or the other, transistor is always OFF, the current flow from V_{CC} to ground in that section of the circuit is minimized.

To study the operation of the circuit in more detail, let's first review some basic electronics. An *NPN* transistor is basically two diodes; a P to N from base to emitter and another P to N from base to collector, as shown in Figure 9–2. The base-to-emitter diode is forward biased by applying a positive voltage on the base with respect to the emitter. A forward-biased base-to-emitter diode will have 0.7 V across it and will cause the collector-to-emitter diode to become almost a short circuit with approximately 0.3 V across it.

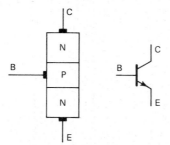

Figure 9–2 *NPN* transistor.

Now, referring to Figure 9–3, we can see the circuit conditions for the 0 output state and 1 output state. In Figure 9–3a ($A = 0$, $B = 0$, output $= 1$), with $A = 0$ or $B = 0$ or both equal to 0, the base-to-emitter diode of Q_1 is forward biased, saturating (turning on) Q_1, placing 0.3 V with respect to ground at the base of Q_2. 0.3 V is not enough to turn Q_2 on, so no current flows through Q_2, but instead, a small current flows through the 1.6 kΩ to the base of Q_3, turning Q_3 on. The HIGH-level output voltage is typically 3.4 V, which is the 4.8 V at the base of Q_3 minus the 0.7-V diode drop at the base-to-emitter diode of Q_3 and the 0.7-V drop across D_3.

In Figure 9–3b ($A = 1$, $B = 1$, output $= 0$), with $A = 1$ *and* $B = 1$, the base-to-emitter diode of Q_1 is reverse biased, *but* the base-to-collector diode of Q_1 is forward biased. Current will flow down through the base to collector of Q_1, turning Q_2 on with a positive base voltage and turning Q_4 on with a positive base voltage. The output voltage will be approximately 0.3 V. Q_3 is kept off because there is not enough voltage between the base of Q_3 (1.0 V) to the cathode of D_3 (0.3 V) to overcome the two 0.7-V diode drops required to allow current flow.

9–2 TTL VOLTAGE AND CURRENT RATINGS

Basically, we like to think of TTL circuits as operating at 0-V and 5-V levels, but as you can see in Figure 9–3, that just is not true. As we draw more and more current out of the HIGH-level output, the output voltage drops lower and lower until finally it will not be recognized as a HIGH level anymore by the other TTL gates that it is feeding.

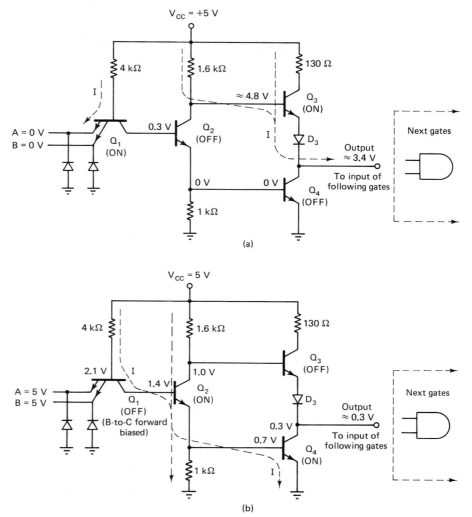

Figure 9–3 Equivalent circuits for a TTL NAND in the (a) HIGH and (b) LOW output states.

Input/Output Current and Fan-Out

The *fan-out* of a subfamily is defined as the number of gates of the same subfamily that can be connected to a single output without exceeding the current ratings of the gate. (A typical fan-out for most TTL subfamilies is 10.) Figure 9–4 shows an example of fan-out with 10 gates driven from a single gate.

To determine fan-out, you must know how much input current a gate load draws (I_I) and how much output current the driving gate can supply (I_O). In Figure 9–4 the single 7400 is the driving gate, supplying current to 10 other gate loads. The output current capability for the HIGH condition is abbreviated I_{OH} and is called a *source* current. I_{OH} for the 7400 is −400 μA maximum. (The minus sign signifies current *leaving* the gate.)

The input current requirement for the HIGH condition is abbreviated I_{IH} and for the 74XX sub-family is equal to 40 μA maximum. To find the fan-out, divide the source current (−400 μA) by the input requirements for a gate (40 μA). The fan-out is 400 μA/40 μA = 10.

For the LOW condition, the maximum output current for the 74XX subfamily

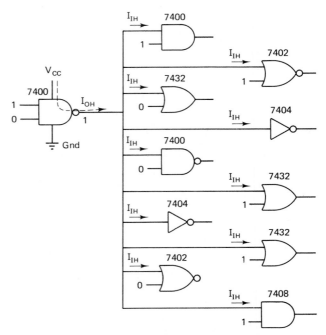

Figure 9–4 Ten gates driven from a single source.

is 16 mA and the input requirements for each 74XX gate is −1.6 mA maximum, also for a fan-out of 10. The fan-out is usually the same for both the HIGH and LOW conditions for the 74XX gates; if not, we use the lower of the two.

Since a LOW output level is close to 0 V, the current will actually flow into the output terminal and sink down to ground. This is called a *sink* current and is illustrated in Figure 9–5. In the figure two gates are connected to the output of gate 1. The total current that gate 1 must sink in this case is 2×1.6 mA = 3.2 mA. Since the maximum current a gate can sink in the LOW condition (I_{OL}) is 16 mA, gate 1 is well within its maximum rating of I_{OL}. (Gate 1 could sink the current from as many as *ten* gate inputs.)

For the HIGH-output condition, the circuitry is the same but the current flow is reversed, as shown in Figure 9–6. In the figure you can see that the 40 μA going into each input is actually a small reverse leakage current flowing against the emitter arrow. In this case, the output of gate 1 is sourcing −80 μA to the inputs of gates 2 and 3. −80μA is well below the maximum allowed HIGH-output current rating of −400 μA.

To summarize input/output current and fan-out:

1. The maximum current that an input to a *standard* (i.e., 74XX) TTL gate will sink or source is

$$I_{IL} = -1.6 \text{ mA}$$
$$I_{IH} = 40 \ \mu\text{A}$$

(The minus sign signifies current *leaving* the gate.)

2. The maximum current that the output of a *standard* TTL gate can sink or source is

$$I_{OL} = 16 \text{ mA}$$
$$I_{OH} = -400 \ \mu\text{A or} -800 \ \mu\text{A}$$

(The *actual* output current depends on the number and type of loads connected.)

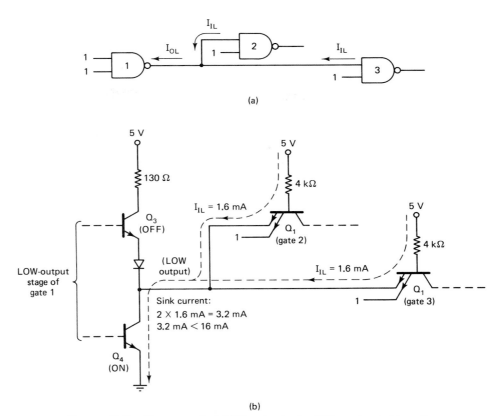

(a)

(b)

Figure 9–5 Totem-pole LOW output of a TTL gate sinking the input currents from two gate inputs: (a) logic gate symbols; (b) logic gate internal circuitry.

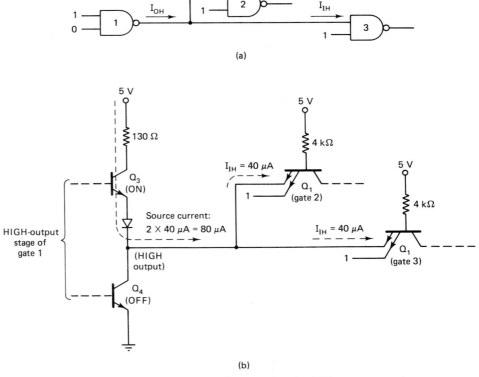

(a)

(b)

Figure 9–6 Totem-pole HIGH output of a TTL gate sourcing current to two gate inputs.

3. The maximum number of gate inputs that can be connected to a *standard TTL* gate output is

$$\text{fan-out} = 10$$

Input/Output Voltages and Noise Margin

We must also concern ourselves with the specifications for the acceptable input and output voltage levels. For the *LOW output condition*, the lower transistor (Q_4) in the totem-pole output stage is saturated (ON) and the upper one (Q_3) is cut off (OFF). V_{out} for the LOW condition (V_{OL}) is the voltage across the saturated Q_4, which has a typical value of 0.2 V and a maximum value of 0.4 V, as specified in the manufacturer's data manual.

For the *HIGH output condition*, the upper transistor (Q_3) is saturated and the lower transistor (Q_4) is cut off. The voltage that reaches the output (V_{OH}) is V_{CC} minus the drop across the 130-Ω resistor, minus the C-E drop, minus the diode drop. Manufacturers' data sheets specify that the HIGH-level output will typically be 3.4 V and they will guarantee that the worst-case minimum value will be 2.4 V. This means that the next gate input must interpret any voltage from 2.4 V up to 5.0 V as a HIGH level. Therefore, we must also consider the *input* voltage-level specifications (V_{IH}, V_{IL}).

Manufacturers will guarantee that any voltage between a minumum of 2.0 V up to 5.0 V will be interpreted as a HIGH (V_{IH}). Also, any voltage from a maximum of 0.8 V down to 0 V will be interpreted as a LOW (V_{IL}).

These values leave us a little margin for error, what is called the *noise margin*. For example, V_{OL} is guaranteed not to exceed 0.4 V and V_{IL} can be as high as 0.8 V to still be interpreted as a LOW. Therefore, we have 0.4 V (0.8 V − 0.4 V) of leeway (noise margin), as illustrated in Figure 9–7.

Table 9–1 is a summary of input/output voltage levels and noise margin for the standard family of TTL ICs.

TABLE 9–1

Standard 74XX Series Voltage Levels

Parameter	Minimum	Typical	Maximum	
V_{OL}		0.2 V	0.4 V	⎫ Noise margin
V_{IL}			0.8 V	⎭ = 0.4 V
V_{OH}	2.4 V	3.4 V		⎫ Noise margin
V_{IH}	2.0 V			⎭ = 0.4 V

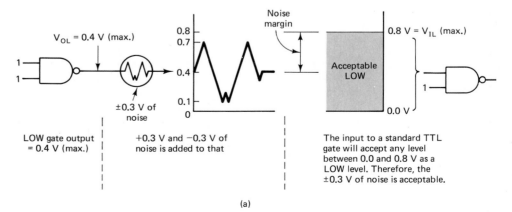

(a)

Figure 9–7   (a) Adding noise to a LOW-level output;

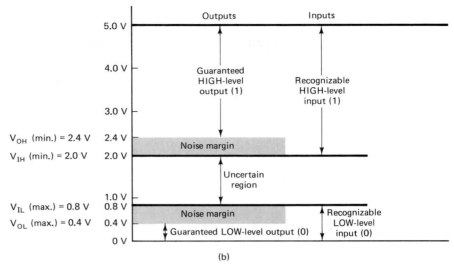

Figure 9-7 (*Continued*) (b) graphical illustration of the input/output voltage levels for the standard 74XX TTL series.

The following examples illustrate the use of the current and voltage ratings for establishing acceptable operating conditions for TTL logic gates.

EXAMPLE 9-1

Find the voltages and currents that are asked for in Figure 9-8 if the gates are all standard (74XX) TTL.

(a) Find V_a and I_a for Figure 9-8a.

(b) Find V_a, V_b, and I_b for Figure 9-8b.

(c) Find V_a, V_b, and I_b for Figure 9-8c.

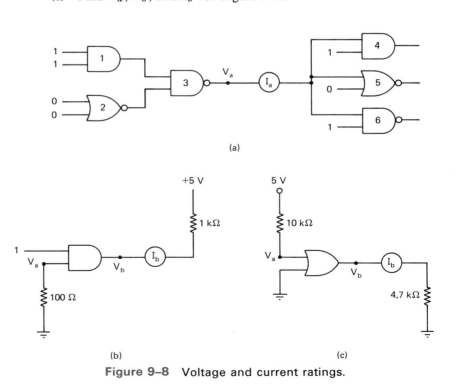

Figure 9-8 Voltage and current ratings.

Solution: **(a)** The input to gate 3 is a 1–1, so the output will be LOW. Using the *typical* value, $V_a = 0.2$ V. Since gate 3 is LOW, it will be sinking current from the three other gates: 4, 5, and 6. The typical value for each I_{IL} is −1.6 mA; therefore, $I_a = -4.8$ mA (−1.6 mA −1.6 mA −1.6 mA).

(b) The 100-Ω resistor to ground will place a LOW level at that input. I_{IL} typically is −1.6 mA, which flows down through the 100-Ω resistor, making $V_a = 0.16$ V (1.6 mA × 100 Ω). The 0.16 V at V_a will be recognized as a LOW level ($V_{IL} = 0.8$ V max.), so the AND gate will output a LOW level; $V_b = 0.2$ V (typ.). The AND gate will sink current from the 1kΩ resistor; $I_b = 4.8$ mA [(5 V − 0.2 V)/1 kΩ]. 4.8 mA is well below the maximum allowed current of 16 mA (I_{OL}), so the AND gate will not burn out.

(c) I_{IH} into the OR gate is 40 μA; therefore, the voltage at $V_a = 4.6$ V [5 V − (10 kΩ × 40 μA)]. The output level of the OR gate will be HIGH (V_{OH}), making $V_b = 3.4$ V and $I_b = 3.4$ V/4.7 kΩ = 723 μA. 723 μA is below the maximum rating of the OR gate ($I_{OH} = -800$ μA max.). Therefore, *the OR gate will not burn out.*

9–3 OTHER TTL CONSIDERATIONS

Pulse-Time Parameters: (Rise Time, Fall Time, and Propagation Delay)

We have been using ideal pulses for the input and output waveforms up until now. Actually, however, the pulse is not perfectly square; it takes time for the digital level to rise from 0 up to 1 and to fall from 1 down to 0.

As shown in Figure 9–9, the *rise time* (t_r) is the length of time it takes for a pulse to rise from its 10% point up to its 90% point. For a 5-V pulse, the 10% point is 0.5 V (10% × 5V) and the 90% point is 4.5 V (90% × 5 V). The *fall time* (t_f) is the length of time it takes to fall from its 90% point to its 10% point.

Not only are input and output waveforms sloped on their rising and falling edges, but there is also a delay time for an input wave to propagate through an IC to the output, called the *propagation delay* (t_{PLH} and t_{PHL}). The propagation delay is due to limitations in transistor switching speeds caused by undesirable internal capacitive stored charges.

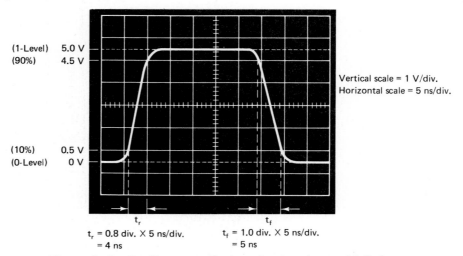

Figure 9–9   Oscilloscope display of pulse rise and fall times.

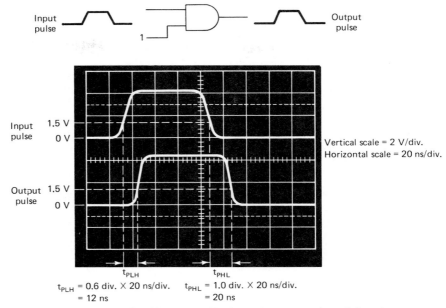

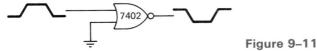

Vertical scale = 2 V/div.
Horizontal scale = 20 ns/div.

t_{PLH} = 0.6 div. × 20 ns/div. t_{PHL} = 1.0 div. × 20 ns/div.
= 12 ns = 20 ns

Figure 9–10 Oscilloscope display of propagation delay times.

Figure 9–10 shows that it takes a certain length of time for an input pulse to reach the output of an IC gate. A specific measurement point (1.5 V for the standard TTL series) is used as a reference. The propagation delay time for the *output* to respond in the LOW-to-HIGH direction is labeled t_{PLH} and in the HIGH-to-LOW direction is labeled t_{PHL}.

EXAMPLE 9–2

The propagation delay times for the 7402 NOR gate shown in Figure 9–11 are listed in a TTL data manual as $t_{PLH} = 22$ ns and $t_{PHL} = 15$ ns. Sketch and label the input and output pulses to a 7402.

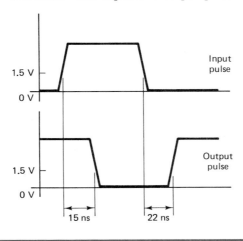

Figure 9–11

Solution: The input and output pulses are shown in Figure 9–12.

1.5 V

0 V

Input
pulse

1.5 V

0 V

Output
pulse

15 ns 22 ns

Figure 9–12 Solution to Example 9–2.

Power Dissipation

Another operating characteristic of integrated circuits that has to be considered is the *power dissipation*. The power dissipated (or consumed) by an IC is equal to the total power supplied to the IC power supply terminals (V_{CC} to Gnd). The current that enters the V_{CC} supply terminal is called I_{CC}. Two values are given for the supply current: I_{CCH} and I_{CCL} for use when the outputs are HIGH or when the outputs are LOW. Since the outputs are usually switching between HIGH and LOW, if we assume a 50% duty cycle (HIGH half of the time, LOW half of the time), then an average I_{CC} can be used and the power dissipation is determined from the formula $P_D = V_{CC} \times I_{CC}$ (av.).

EXAMPLE 9–3

The total supply current for a 7402 NOR IC is given as $I_{CCL} = 14$ mA, $I_{CCH} = 8$ mA. Determine the power dissipation of the IC.

Solution:

$$P_D = V_{CC} \times I_{CC} \text{ (av.)}$$

$$= 5.0 \text{ V} \times \frac{14 \text{ mA} + 8 \text{ mA}}{2} = 55 \text{ mW}$$

Open-Collector Outputs

Instead of using a totem-pole arrangement in the output stage of a TTL gate, another arrangement, called the *open-collector* output, is available. Remember that with the totem-pole output stage, for a LOW output the lower transistor is ON and the upper transistor is OFF, and vice versa for a HIGH output; whereas with the open-collector output, the upper transistor is *removed*, as shown in Figure 9–13. Now the output will be *LOW* when Q_4 is ON and the output will *float* (not HIGH or LOW) when Q_4 is OFF. This means that an open-collector (OC) output can sink current *but it cannot* source current.

To get an OC output to produce a HIGH, an external resistor (called a *pull-up* resistor) must be used, as shown in Figure 9–14. Now when Q_4 is OFF (open) the output is approximately 5 V (HIGH) and when Q_4 is ON (short) the output is approximately 0 V (LOW). The optimum size for a pull-up resistor depends on the

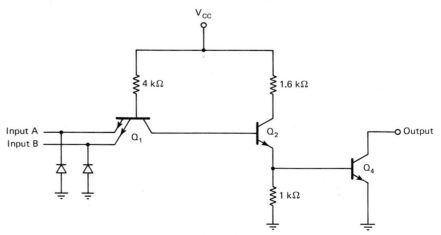

Figure 9–13 TTL NAND with an open-collector output.

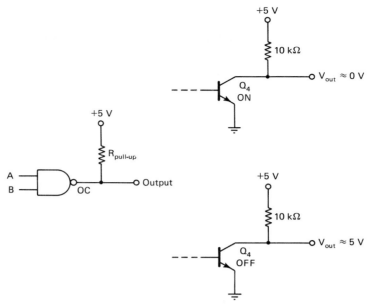

Figure 9–14   Using a pull-up resistor with an open-collector output.

size of the gate load. Usually, a good size for a pull-up resistor is 10 kΩ; 10 kΩ is not too small to allow excessive current flow when Q_4 is ON and it is not too large to cause an excessive voltage drop across itself when Q_4 is OFF.

Wired-Output Operation

The main use of the open-collector gates is whenever the outputs from two or more gates or other devices have to be tied together. Using the regular totem-pole output gates, if a gate having a HIGH output (5 V) is connected to another gate having a LOW output (0 V), you would have a direct short circuit, causing either or both gates to burn out.

   Using open-collector gates, outputs can be connected together without worrying about the 5 V–0 V conflict. When connected together, they form *wired-and* logic, as shown in Figure 9–15. The 7405 IC has six OC inverters in a single package. By tying their outputs together, as shown in Figure 9–15a, we have in effect *ANDed*

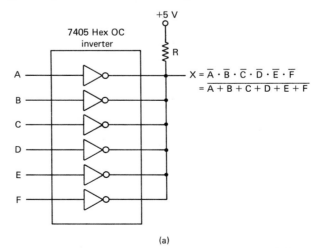

(a)

Figure 9–15   (a) Wired-AND connections to a hex OC inverter to form a six-input NOR gate;

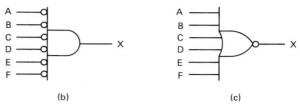

Figure 9–15 (*Continued*)   (b) AND gate representation; (c) alternate NOR gate representation.

all the inverters. The outputs of all six inverters must be floating (all inputs must be LOW) to get a HIGH output. If any of the inverter output transistors (Q_4) turn on, the output will go LOW. The result of this wired-AND connection is the six-input NOR function shown in Figure 9–15c.

EXAMPLE 9–4

Write the Boolean equation at the output of Figure 9–16a.

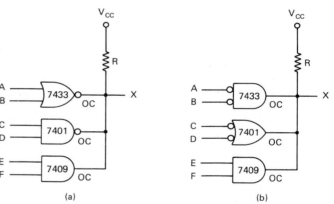

Figure 9–16   Wired-ANDing of open-collector gates for Example 9–4: (a) original circuit; (b) alternative gate representations used for clarity.

Solution: The output of all three gates in either circuit must be floating in order to get a HIGH output at X. Using Figure 9–16b, $X = \overline{A}\,\overline{B} \cdot (\overline{C} + \overline{D}) \cdot EF$.

Disposition of Unused Inputs and Unused Gates

Electrically *open inputs* degrade ac noise immunity as well as the switching speed of a circuit. For example, if two inputs to a three-input NAND gate are being used and the third is allowed to float, unpredictable results will occur if the third input picks up electrical noise from surrounding circuitry.

Unused inputs on AND and NAND gates should be tied HIGH and on OR and NOR gates should be tied to ground. An example of this is a three-input AND gate that is using only two of its inputs. Also, the outputs of *unused gates* on an IC should be forced HIGH to reduce the I_{CC} supply current and thus reduce the power dissipation. To do this, tie AND and OR inputs HIGH, and tie NAND and NOR inputs LOW. An example of this is a quad NOR IC, where only three of the NOR gates are being used.

Power Supply Decoupling

In digital systems, there are heavy current demands on the main power supply. TTL logic tends to create spikes on the main V_{CC} line, especially at the logic-level transition point (LOW to HIGH or HIGH to LOW). At the logic-level transition there is a period of time that the conduction in the upper and lower totem-pole output transistors overlap. That drastically changes the demand for I_{CC} current, which causes sharp high-frequency spikes to occur on the V_{CC} (power supply) line. These spikes cause false switching of other devices connected to the same power supply line and can also induce magnetic fields that radiate electromagnetic interference (EMI).

Decoupling of IC power supply spikes from the main V_{CC} line can be accomplished by placing a 0.01-μF to 0.1-μF capacitor directly across the V_{CC}-to-Gnd pins on each IC in the system. The capacitors will tend to hold the V_{CC} level at each IC constant, thus reducing the amount of EMI radiation that is emitted from the system and reduce the likelihood of false switching.

9–4 IMPROVED TTL SERIES

Integrated-circuit design engineers have constantly been working on the improvement of the standard TTL series. A simple improvement that was made early on was simply reducing all the internal resistor values of the standard TTL series. That increased the power consumption (or dissipation), which was bad, but it reduced the internal $R \times C$ time constants that cause propagation delays. The result was the *74HXX* series, which has almost half the propagation delay time but almost double the power consumption of the standard TTL series. The product of delay time $\times$ power (the speed–power product), which is a figure of merit for IC families, remained approximately the same, however.

Another series, the *74LXX*, was developed using just the opposite approach. The internal resistors were increased, thus reducing the power consumption, but the progagation delay increased, keeping the speed–power product about the same. The 74HXX and 74LXX series have, for the most part, been replaced now by the Schottky TTL and CMOS series of ICs.

Schottky TTL

The major speed limitation of the standard TTL series is due to the capacitive charge in the base region of the transistors. The transistors basically operate at either cutoff or saturation. When the transistor is saturated, charges build up at the base region, and when it comes time to switch to cutoff, the stored charges must be dissipated, which takes time, causing propagation delay.

Schottky logic overcomes the saturation and stored charges problem by placing a Schottky diode across the base-to-collector junction, as shown in Figure 9–17. With the Schottky diode in place, any excess charge on the base is passed on to the collector, and the transistor is held just below saturation. The Schottky diode has a special metal junction that minimizes its own capacitive charge and increases its switching speed. Using Schottky-clamped transistors and decreased resistor values, the propagation delay is reduced by a factor of 4 and the power consumption is only doubled. Therefore, the speed–power product of the 74SXX TTL series is improved to about half that of the 74XX TTL series (the lower, the better).

Low-Power Schottky (LS). By using different integration techniques and increasing the values of the internal resistors, the power dissipation of the Schottky

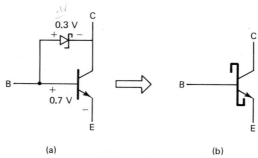

Figure 9–17   Schottky-clamped transistor: (a) Schottky diode reduces stored charges; (b) symbol.

TTL is reduced significantly. The speed–power product of the 74LSXX TTL series is about one-third that of the 74SXX series and about one-fifth that of the 74XX series.

Advanced Low-Power Schottky (ALS). Further improvement on the 74LSXX series reduced the propagation delay time from 9 ns to 4 ns and the power dissipation from 2 mW to 1 mW per gate. The 74ALSXX and 74LS series are rapidly replacing the standard 74XX and 74SXX series because of the speed and power improvements. As with any new technology, they are slightly more expensive and do not yet provide all the functions available from the standard 74XX series.

Fast (F)

It was long clear to TTL IC design engineers that new processing technology was needed to improve the speed of the LS series. A new process of integration, called *oxide isolation* (also used by the ALS series), has reduced the propagation delay in the 74FXX series to below 3 ns. In this process, transistors are isolated from each other, not by a reverse-biased junction, but by an actual channel of oxide. This dramatically reduces the size of the devices, which in turn reduces their associated capacitances and thus reduces propagation delay.

9–5 THE CMOS FAMILY

The CMOS family of integrated circuits uses an entirely different type of transistor as its basic building block. The TTL family uses bipolar transistors (*NPN* and *PNP*). CMOS (complementary metal-oxide semiconductor) uses complementary pairs of transistors (N-type and P-type) called MOSFETs (metal-oxide-semiconductor field-effect transistors). MOSFETs are also used in other families of MOS ICs, including PMOS, NMOS, and VMOS, which are most commonly used for large-scale memories and microprocessors in the LSI and VLSI (large-scale and very-large-scale integration) category. One advantage that MOSFETs have over bipolar transistors is that the input to a MOSFET is electrically isolated from the rest of the MOSFET (see Figure 9–18b), giving it a high input impedance.

The *N*-channel MOSFET is similar to the *NPN* bipolar transistor in that it is two back-to-back *N-P* junctions, and current will not flow down through it until a positive voltage is applied to the base (or gate in the case of the MOSFET). The silicon dioxide (SiO_2) layer between the gate material and the *P*-substrate (base) of the MOSFET prevents any gate current from flowing, which provides a high input impedance and low power consumption.

The MOSFET shown in Figure 9–18b is a normally OFF device because there

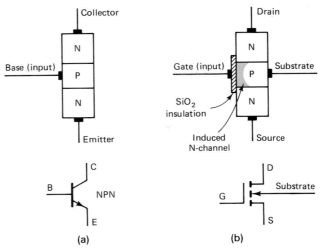

Figure 9–18 Simplified diagrams of bipolar and field effect transistors: (a) *NPN* bipolar transistor used in TTL ICs; (b) *N*-channel MOSFET used in CMOS ICs.

are no negative carries in the *P*-material for current flow to occur. However, conventional current will flow down from drain to source if a positive voltage is applied to the gate with respect to the substrate. That voltage induces an electric field across the SiO$_2$ layer which repels enough of the positive charges in the *P*-material to form a channel of negative charges on the left side of the *P*-material. This allows electrons to flow from source to drain (conventional current flows from drain to source). The channel that is formed is called an *N*-channel because it contains negative carriers.

P-channel MOSFETS are just the opposite, constructed from *P-N-P* materials. The channel is formed by placing a *negative* voltage at the gate with respect to the substrate.

Using an *N*-channel MOSFET with its complement, the *P*-channel MOSFET, a simple complementary-MOS (CMOS) inverter can be formed as shown in Figure 9–19.

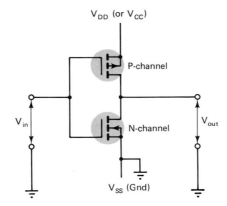

Figure 9–19 CMOS inverter formed from complementary *N*-channel/*P*-channel transistors.

We can think of MOSFETs as ON/OFF switches just as we did for the bipolar transistors. Table 9–2 summarizes the ON/OFF operation of *N*- and *P*-channel MOSFETS.

We can use Table 9–2 to prove that the circuit of Figure 9–19 operates as an inverter. With $V_{in} = 1$, the *N*-channel transistor is ON and the *P*-channel transistor is OFF, so $V_{out} = 0$. With $V_{in} = 0$, the *N*-channel transistor is OFF and the *P*-channel is ON, so $V_{out} = 1$. Therefore, $V_{out} = \overline{V_{in}}$. Notice that this complementary action is very similar to the TTL totem-pole output stage, but much simpler to understand.

TABLE 9–2

Basic MOSFET Switching
Characteristics

Gate level[a]	N-*channel*	P-*channel*
1	ON	OFF
0	OFF	ON

[a] $1 \equiv V_{DD}$ (or V_{CC}); $0 \equiv V_{SS}$ (Gnd).

The other basic logic gates can also be formed using complementary MOSFET transistors. The operation of CMOS NAND and NOR gates can very simply be understood by studying the schematics and data tables presented in Figures 9–20 and 9–21.

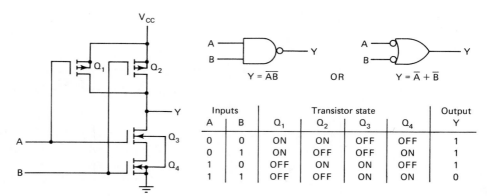

Inputs		Transistor state				Output
A	B	Q_1	Q_2	Q_3	Q_4	Y
0	0	ON	ON	OFF	OFF	1
0	1	ON	OFF	OFF	ON	1
1	0	OFF	ON	ON	OFF	1
1	1	OFF	OFF	ON	ON	0

Figure 9–20   CMOS NAND gate.

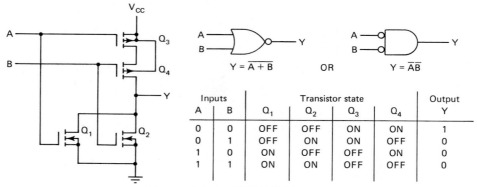

Inputs		Transistor state				Output
A	B	Q_1	Q_2	Q_3	Q_4	Y
0	0	OFF	OFF	ON	ON	1
0	1	OFF	ON	ON	OFF	0
1	0	ON	OFF	OFF	ON	0
1	1	ON	ON	OFF	OFF	0

Figure 9–21   CMOS NOR gate.

Handling MOS Devices

The silicon dioxide layer that isolates the gate from the substrate is so thin that it is very susceptible to burn-through from electrostatic charges. You must be very careful and use the following guidelines when handling MOS devices:

1. Store the integrated circuits in a conductive foam or leave in their original container.
2. Work on a conductive surface (e.g., metal tabletop) that is properly grounded.
3. Ground all test equipment and soldering irons.

4. Connect your wrist to ground with a length of wire and a 1-MΩ series resistor.
5. Do not connect signals to the inputs while the device power supply is off.
6. Connect all unused inputs to V_{DD} or Gnd.
7. Don't wear electrostatic-prone clothing such as wool, silk, or synthetic fibers.
8. Don't remove or insert an IC with the power on.

CMOS Availability

The CMOS family of integrated circuits provides almost all the same functions that are available in the TTL family, plus CMOS has available several "special-purpose" functions not provided by TTL. Like TTL, the CMOS family has evolved into several different subfamilies, or series, each having better performance specifications than the previous one.

4000 Series. The 4000 series (or the improved 4000B) is the original CMOS line. It became popular because it offered very low power consumption and could be used in battery-powered devices. It is much slower than any of the TTL series and has a low level of electrostatic discharge protection. The power supply voltage to the IC can range anywhere from +3 to +15 V with the minimum one-level input equal to $\frac{2}{3}V_{CC}$ and the maximum 0-level input equal to $\frac{1}{3}V_{CC}$.

40H00 Series. This series was designed to be faster than the 4000 series. It did overcome some of the speed limitations but is still much slower than LSTTL.

74C00 Series. This series was developed to be pin compatible with the TTL family, making interchangeability easier. It uses the same numbering scheme as TTL except that it begins with 74C. It has a low-power advantage over the TTL family but is still much slower.

74HC00 and 74HCT00 Series. The 74HC00 (high-speed CMOS) and 74HCT00 (high-speed CMOS, TTL compatible) offer a vast improvement over the original 74C00 series. The HC/HCT series are as speedy as the LSTTL series and still consume less power, depending on the operating frequency. They are pin compatible (the HCT is also input/output voltage level compatible) with the TTL family, yet offer greater noise immunity and greater voltage and temperature operating ranges. Further improvements to the HC/HCT series have led to the Advanced CMOS Logic (ACL) and Fairchild advanced CMOS Technology (FACT) series which have even better operating characteristics.

9–6 EMITTER-COUPLED LOGIC

Another family designed for extremely high-speed applications is emitter-coupled logic (ECL). ECL comes in two series, ECL 10K and ECL 100K. ECL is extremely fast, with propagation delay times as low as 0.8 ns. That speed makes it well suited for large mainframe computer systems that require a high number of operations per second, but are not as concerned about an increase in power dissipation.

The high speed of ECL is achieved by never letting the transistors saturate; in fact, the whole basis for HIGH and LOW levels is determined by which transistor in a differential amplifier is conducting more.

Figure 9–22 shows a simplified diagram of the differential amplifier used in ECL circuits. The HIGH and LOW logic-level voltages (−0.8 V and −1.7 V, respec-

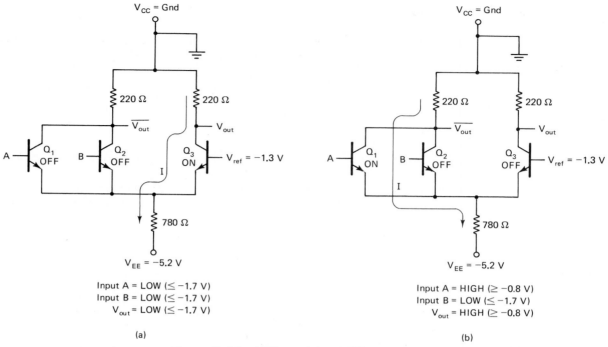

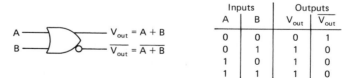

Figure 9–22   Differential amplifier input stage to an ECL OR/NOR gate: (a) LOW output; (b) HIGH output.

tively) are somewhat unusual and cause problems when interfacing to TTL and CMOS logic.

An ECL IC uses a supply voltage of −5.2 V at V_{EE} and 0 V at V_{CC}. The reference voltage on the base of Q_3 is set up by internal circuitry and determines the threshold between HIGH and LOW logic levels. In Figure 9–22a, the base of Q_3 is at a more positive potential with respect to the emitter than Q_1 and Q_2 are. This causes Q_3 to conduct, placing a LOW at V_{out}.

If *either* input A or B is raised to −0.8 V (HIGH), the base of Q_1 or Q_2 will be at a higher potential than the base of Q_3, and Q_3 will stop conducting, making V_{out} HIGH. Figure 9–22b shows what happens when −0.8 V is placed on the A input.

In any case, the transistors never become saturated, so capacitive charges are not built up on the base of the transistors to limit their switching speed. Figure 9–23 shows the logic symbol and truth table for the OR/NOR ECL gate.

Inputs		Outputs	
A	B	V_{out}	$\overline{V_{out}}$
0	0	0	1
0	1	1	0
1	0	1	0
1	1	1	0

A ———⟩ $V_{out} = A + B$

B ———⟩ $\overline{V_{out}} = \overline{A + B}$

Figure 9–23   ECL OR/NOR symbol and truth table.

Developing New Digital Logic Technologies

The quest for logic devices that can operate at even higher frequencies and can be packed more densely in an IC package is a continuing process. Designers have high hopes for other new technologies, such as integrated injection logic (I²L), silicon-on-sapphire (SOS), gallium arsenide (GaAs), and Josephen junction circuits. Eventually, propagation delays will be measured in picoseconds and circuit densities will enable the supercomputer of today to become the desktop computer of tomorrow.

9-7 COMPARING LOGIC FAMILIES

Throughout the years, system designers have been given a wide variety of digital logic to choose from. The main parameters to consider include speed, power dissipation, availability, types of functions, noise immunity, operating frequency, output-drive capability, and interfacing. First and foremost, however, are the basic speed and power concerns. Table 9-3 shows the propagation delay, power dissipation, and speed-power product for the most popular families.

TABLE 9-3

Typical Single-Gate Performance Specifications

Family	Propagation delay (ns)	Power dissipation (mW)	Speed–power product pWs (picowatt-seconds)
74	10	10	100
74S	3	20	60
74LS	9	2	18
74ALS	4	1	4
74F	2.7	4	11
4000B (CMOS)	105	1 at 1 MHz	105
74HC (CMOS)	10	1.5 at 1 MHz	15
100K (ECL)	0.8	40	32

Courtesy of Signetics Corporation

The speed-power product is sort of a figure of merit but does not necessarily tell the ranking within a specific application. For example, to say that the speed-power product of 15 pWs for the 74HC family is better than 32 pWs for the 100K ECL family totally ignores the fact that ECL is a better choice for ultrahigh-speed applications.

Another way to view the speed-power relationships is with the graph shown in Figure 9-24. From the graph you can visually see the wide spectrum of choices

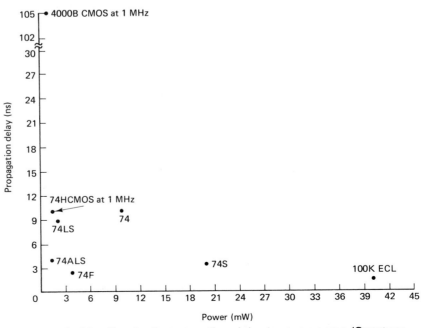

Figure 9-24 Graph of propagation delay versus power. (Courtesy of Signetics Corporation.)

available. 4000B CMOS and 100K ECL are at opposite ends of the spectrum of speed versus power, while 74ALS and 74F seem to offer the best of both worlds.

The operating frequency for CMOS devices is critical for determining the power dissipation. At very low frequencies CMOS devices dissipate almost no power at all, but at higher switching frequencies charging and discharging the gate capacitances draws a heavy current from the power supply (I_{CC}) and thus increases the power dissipation ($P_D = V_{CC} \times I_{CC}$), as shown in Figure 9–25.

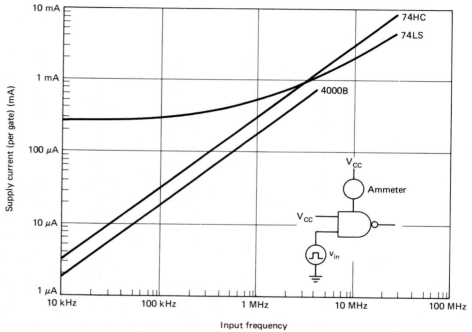

Figure 9–25 Power supply current versus frequency. (Courtesy of Signetics Corporation.)

The graph in Figure 9–25 shows that at high frequencies the power dissipation of 74HC CMOS and 74LS TTL are comparable. At today's microprocessor clock rates, 74HC CMOS ICs actually dissipate more power than 74LS or 74ALS. However, in typical systems, only a fraction of the gates are connected to switch as fast as the clock rate, so significant power savings can be realized by using the 74HC CMOS series.

9–8 INTERFACING LOGIC FAMILIES

Often, the need arises to interface (connect) between the various TTL and CMOS families. You have to make sure that a HIGH out of a TTL gate looks like a HIGH to the input of a CMOS gate, and vice versa. The same holds true for the LOW logic levels. You also have to make sure that the driving gate can sink or source enough current to meet the input current requirements of the gate being driven.

TTL to CMOS

Let's start by looking at the problems that might arise when interfacing a standard 7400 series TTL to a 4000B series CMOS. Figure 9–26 shows the input and output voltage specifications for both, assuming that the 4000B is powered by a 5-V supply.

When the TTL gate is used to drive the CMOS gate, there is no problem for

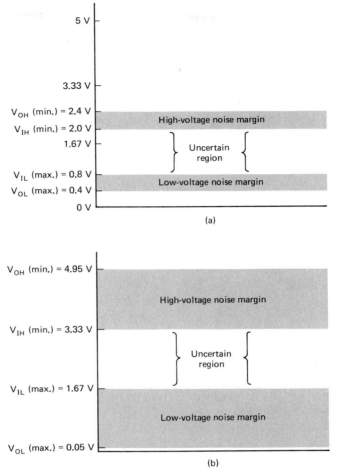

Figure 9–26 Input and output voltage specifications: (a) 7400 series TTL; (b) 4000B series CMOS (5-V supply).

the LOW-level output because the TTL guarantees a maximum LOW-level output of 0.4 V and the CMOS will accept any voltage up to 1.67 V ($\frac{1}{3}V_{CC}$) as a LOW-level input.

But for the HIGH level, the TTL may output as little as 2.4 V as a HIGH. The CMOS expects at least 3.33 V as a HIGH-level input. Therefore, 2.4 V is unacceptable because it falls within the uncertain region. However, a resistor can be connected between the CMOS input to V_{CC} as shown in Figure 9–27 to solve the HIGH-level input problem.

In Figure 9–27, with V_{out1} *LOW*, the 7404 will sink current from the 10-kΩ resistor and the I_{IL} from the 4069B making V_{out2} HIGH. With V_{out1} *HIGH* the

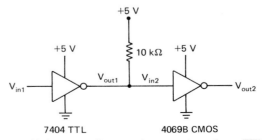

Figure 9–27 Using a pull-up resistor to interface TTL to CMOS.

10-kΩ resistor will "pull" the voltage at V_{in2} up to 5.0 V, causing V_{out2} to go LOW. The 10-kΩ resistor is called a *pull-up resistor* and is used to raise the output of the TTL gate closer to 5 V when it is in a HIGH output state. With V_{out1} HIGH, the voltage at V_{in2} will be almost 5 V because current into the 4069B is so LOW ($\approx$1 μA) that the voltage drop across the 10 kΩ is insignificant, leaving almost 5.0 V at V_{in2} ($V_{in2} = 5$ V $- 1$ μA $\times$ 10 k$\Omega = 4.99$ V).

The other thing to look at when interfacing is the current levels of all gates that are involved. In this case, the 7404 can sink (I_{OL}) 16 mA, which is easy enough for the I_{IL} of the 4069B (1 μA) plus the current from the 10-kΩ resistor (5 V/10 kΩ = 0.5 mA). I_{OH} of the 7404 (-400 μA) is no problem either, because with the pull-up resistor, the 7404 will not have to source current.

CMOS to TTL

When driving TTL from CMOS the voltage levels are no problem because the CMOS will output about 4.95 V for a HIGH and 0.05 V for a LOW, which is easily interpreted by the TTL gate.

But the current levels can be a real concern because 4000B CMOS has severe output current limitations. (The 74C and 74HC series have much better output-current capabilities, however.) Figure 9–28 shows the input/output currents that flow when interfacing CMOS to TTL.

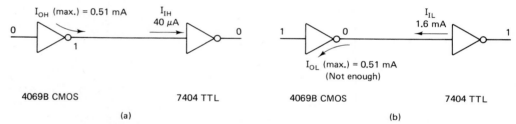

4069B CMOS   7404 TTL   4069B CMOS   7404 TTL

(a)   (b)

Figure 9–28 Current levels when interfacing CMOS to TTL: (a) CMOS I_{OH}; (b) CMOS I_{OL}.

For the HIGH output condition (Figure 9–28a), the 4069B CMOS can source a maximum current of 0.51 mA, which is enough to supply the HIGH-level input current (I_{IH}) to one 7404 inverter. But for the LOW output condition, the 4069B can also sink only 0.51 mA, which is not enough for the 7404 LOW-level input current (I_{IL}).

Most of the 4000B series has the same problem of low-output-drive current capability. To alleviate the problem, two special gates, the 4050 buffer and the 4049 inverting buffer, are specifically designed to provide high output current to solve many interfacing problems. They have drive capabilities of $I_{OL} = 4.0$ mA and $I_{OH} = -0.9$ mA, which is enough to drive two 74XXTTL loads, as shown in Figure 9–29.

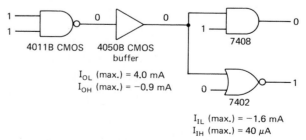

Figure 9–29 Using the 4050B CMOS buffer to supply sink and source current to two standard TTL loads.

If the CMOS buffer was used to drive another TTL series, let's say the 74LS series, we would have to refer to a TTL data book to determine how many loads could be connected without exceeding the output current limits. (The 4050B can actually drive *ten* 74LS loads.) Table 9–4 summarizes the input/output voltage and current specifications of some popular TTL and CMOS series, which enables us to easily determine interface parameters and family characteristics.

TABLE 9–4

Worst-Case Values for Interfacing Considerations[a]

Parameter	4000B CMOS	74HCMOS	74HCTMOS	74TTL	74LSTTL	74ALSTTL
V_{IH} (min.) (V)	3.33	3.5	2.0	2.0	2.0	2.0
V_{IL} (max.) (V)	1.67	1.0	0.8	0.8	0.8	0.8
V_{OH} (min.) (V)	4.95	4.9	4.9	2.4	2.7	2.7
V_{OL} (max.) (V)	0.05	0.1	0.1	0.4	0.4	0.4
I_{IH} (max.) (μA)	1	1	1	40	20	20
I_{IL} (max.) (μA)	-1	-1	-1	-1600	-400	-100
I_{OH} (max.) (mA)	-0.51	-4	-4	-0.4	-0.4	-0.4
I_{OL} (max.) (mA)	0.51	4	4	16	8	4

[a] All values are for $V_{supply} = 5.0$ V.

By reviewing Table 9–4 we can see that the 74HCMOS has relatively low input current requirements compared to the bipolar TTL series. Its HIGH output can source 4 mA, which is 10 times the capability of the TTL series. Also, the noise margin for the 74HCMOS is much wider than any of the TTL series (1.4 V HIGH, 0.9 V LOW).

Because of the low input current requirements, any of the TTL series can drive several of the 74HCMOS loads. An interfacing problem occurs in the voltage level, however. The 74HCMOS logic expects 3.5 V at a minimum for a HIGH-level input. The worst case (which we must always assume could happen) for the HIGH output level of a 74LSTTL is 2.7 V, so we will need to use a pull-up resistor at the 74LSTTL output to ensure an adequate HIGH level for the 74HCMOS input as shown in Figure 9–30.

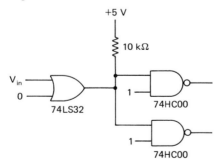

Figure 9–30 Interfacing 74LSTTL to 74HCMOS.

The combinations of interfacing situations are quite extensive (74HCMOS to 74ALSTTL, 74TTL to 74LSTTL, etc.). In each case, reference to a data book must be made to check the worst-case voltage and current parameters, as we will see in upcoming examples. In general, a pull-up resistor is required when interfacing TTL to CMOS to bring the HIGH-level TTL output up to a suitable level for the CMOS input. (The exception to the rule is when using *74HCTMOS*, which is designed for TTL voltage levels.) The disadvantage of using a pull-up resistor is that it takes up valuable room on a printed-circuit board and it dissipates power in the form of heat.

Different series within the TTL family and the TTL-compatible 74HCTMOS series can be interfaced directly. The main concern there is determining how many gate loads can be connected to a single output.

Level Shifting

Another problem arises when you interface families that have different supply voltages. For example, the 4000B series can use anywhere from $+3$ to $+15$ V for a supply and the ECL series uses -5.2 V for a supply.

Well, the problem is solved by using *level-shifter* ICs. The 4049B and 4050B buffer ICs that were introduced earlier are also used for voltage-level shifting. Figure 9–31 shows the connections for interfacing 15-V CMOS to 5-V TTL.

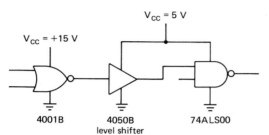

Figure 9–31 Using a level shifter to convert 0 V/15 V logic to 0 V/5 V logic.

The 4050B level-shifting buffer is powered from a 5-V supply and can actually accept 0 V/15 V logic levels at the input, and output the corresponding 0 V/5-V logic levels at the output. For an inverter function, use the 4049B instead of the 4050B.

The reverse conversion, 5-V TTL-to-15-V CMOS is accomplished with the 4504B CMOS level shifter, as shown in Figure 9–32. The 4504B level-shifting buffer requires two power supply inputs: the 5-V V_{CC} supply to enable it to recognize the 0 V/5 V input levels, and the 15-V supply to enable it to provide 0 V/15 V output levels.

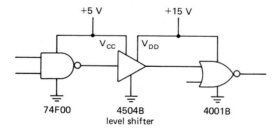

Figure 9–32 Level shifting 0 V/5 V TTL logic to 0 V/15 V CMOS logic.

ECL Interfacing

Interfacing 0 V/5 V logic levels to -5.2 V/0 V ECL circuitry requires another set of level shifters (or translators): the ECL 10125 and the ECL 10124, whose connections are shown in Figure 9–33.

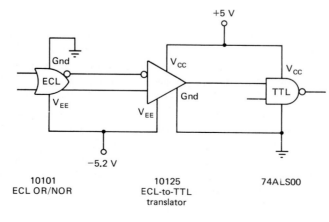

Figure 9–33 Circuit connections for translating between TTL and ECL levels.

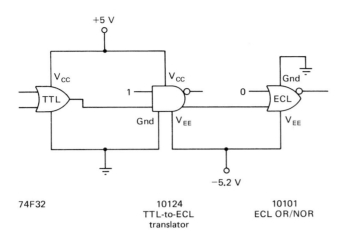

74F32

10124
TTL-to-ECL
translator

10101
ECL OR/NOR

Figure 9–33 (*Continued*)

EXAMPLE 9–5

Determine from Table 9–4 how many 74LSTTL logic gates can be driven by a single 74TTL logic gate.

Solution: The output voltage levels (V_{OL}, V_{OH}) of the 74TTL series are compatible with the input voltage levels (V_{IL}, V_{IH}) of the 74LSTTL series. The voltage noise margin for the LOW level is 0.4 V (2.4 − 2.0) and for the HIGH level is 0.4 V (0.8 − 0.4).

The HIGH-level output current (I_{OH}) for the 74TTL series is −400 μA. Each 74LSTTL gate draws 20 μA of input current for the HIGH level (I_{IH}), so one 74TTL gate can drive 20 74LSTTL loads in the HIGH state (400 μA/20 μA = 20).

For the LOW state, the 74TTL I_{OL} is 16 mA and the 74LSTTL I_{IL} is −400 μA, meaning that for the LOW condition, one 74TTL can drive 40 74LSTTL loads (16 mA/400 μA = 40). Therefore, considering both the LOW and HIGH conditions, a single 74TTL can drive 20 74LSTTL gates.

EXAMPLE 9–6

One 74HCTO4 inverter is to be used to drive one input to each of the following gates: 7400 (NAND), 7402 (NOR), 74LS08 (AND), 74ALS32 (OR). Draw the circuit and label input and output worst-case voltages and currents. Will there be total voltage and current compatibility?

Solution: The circuit is shown in Figure 9–34. Figure 9–34a shows the worst-case HIGH-level values. If you sum all the input currents, the total that the 74HCTO4 must supply is 120 μA (40 μA + 40 μA + 20 μA + 20 μA), which is well below the −4 mA maximum source capability of the 74HCTO4. Also, the 4.9-V output voltage of the 74HCTO4 *is* compatible with the 2.0-V minimum requirement of the TTL inputs, leaving a noise margin of 2.9 V (4.9 V − 2.0 V).

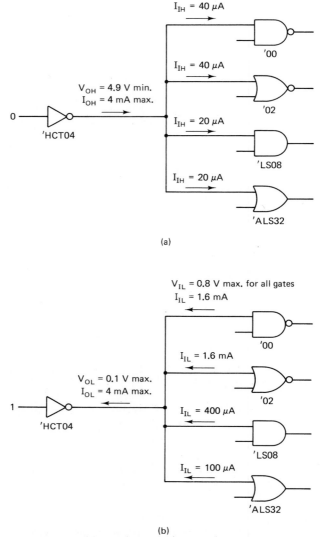

Figure 9–34   Interfacing 74HCTMOS to several different TTL series: (a) HIGH-level values; (b) LOW-level values.

Figure 9–34b shows the worst-case LOW-level values. The sum of all the TTL input currents is 3.7 mA (1.6 mA + 1.6 mA + 400 μA + 100 μA), which is less than the 4 mA maximum sink capability of the 74HCTO4. Also, the 0.1-V output of the 74HCTO4 *is* compatible with the 0.8-V maximum requirement of the TTL inputs, leaving a noise margin of 0.7 V (0.8 V − 0.1 V).

GLOSSARY

Bipolar transistor: Three-layer *N-P-N* or *P-N-P* junction transistor.

Buffer: A device placed between two other devices that provides isolation and current amplification. The input logic level is equal to the output logic level.

CMOS: Complementary metal-oxide semiconductor.

Decoupling: A method of isolating voltage irregularities on the V_{CC} power supply line from an IC V_{CC} input.

Differential amplifier: An amplifier that basically compares two inputs and provides an output signal based on the *difference* between the two input signals.

ECL: Emitter-coupled logic.

EMI: Electromagnetic interference. Undesirable radiated energy from a digital system caused by magnetic fields induced by high-speed switching.

Fall time: The time required for a digital pulse to fall from 90% down to 10% of its maximum voltage level.

Fan-out: The number of logic gate inputs that can be driven from a single gate output of the same subfamily.

Level shifter: A device that provides an interface between two logic families having different power supply voltages.

MOSFET: Metal-oxide-semiconductor field-effect transistor.

Noise margin: The voltage difference between the guaranteed output voltage level and the required input voltage level of a logic gate.   *between min — max*

Open-collector output: A special output stage of the TTL family that has the upper transistor of a totem-pole configuration removed.

Power dissipation: The electrical power (watts) that is consumed by a device and given off (dissipated) in the form of heat.

Propagation delay: The time required for a change in logic level to travel from the input to the output of a logic gate.

Pull-up resistor: A resistor with one end connected to V_{CC} and the other end connected to a point in a logic circuit that needs to be raised to a voltage level closer to V_{CC}.

Rise time: The time required for a digital pulse to rise from 10% up to 90% of its maximum voltage level.

Sink current: Current entering the output or input of a logic gate.

Source current: Current leaving the output or input of a logic gate.

Substrate: The silicon supporting structure or framework of an integrated circuit.

Totem-pole output: The output stage of the TTL family having two opposite-acting transistors, one above the other.

TTL: Transistor-transistor logic.

Wired-AND: The AND function that results from connecting several open-collector outputs together.

REVIEW QUESTIONS

Section 9–1
9–1.   The part number for a basic logic gate varies from manufacturer to manufacturer (true or false)?

9–2. The input signal to a TTL NAND gate travels through three stages of internal circuitry: *input*, *control* and _____ .

9–3. A forward-biased NPN transistor will have approximately _____ volts across its base-emitter junction, and _____ volts across its collector-emitter junction.

Section 9–2

9–4. Why aren't the HIGH/LOW output levels of a TTL gate exactly 5.0 volts and 0 volts?

9–5. Describe what is meant by "fan-out."

9–6. List the names and abbreviations of the four input and output currents of a digital IC.

9–7. Describe the difference between *sink* and *source* output current.

9–8. Determine if the following input voltages will be interpreted as HIGH, LOW, or undetermined logic levels in a standard TTL IC.
   (a) 3.0v
   (b) 2.2v
   (c) 1.0v
   (d) 0.6v

Section 9–3

9–9. The *rise time* is the length of time required for a digital signal to travel from zero volts to its HIGH level (true or false)?

9–10. The letters L and H in the abbreviation t_{PLH} refer to the transition in the _____ (input, output) signal.

9–11. Describe the function of a "pull-up resistor" when it is used with an *open-collector* TTL output.

Sections 9–4 through 9–6

9–12. What effect did the Schottky-clamped transistor have on the operation of the standard TTL IC?

9–13. The earlier 4000 series of CMOS ICs provided what advantage over earlier TTL ICs? What was their disadvantage?

9–14. The high speed of ECL ICs is achieved by fully saturating the ON transistor (true or false)?

Sections 9–7 and 9–8

9–15. Which logic family is faster: 74ALS or 74HC?

9–16. Which logic family has a lower power dissipation: 100K ECL or 74LS?

9–17. What is the function of a "pull-up resistor" when interfacing a TTL IC to a CMOS IC?

9–18. What problem arises when interfacing 4000 series CMOS ICs to standard TTL ICs?

9–19. Which family has more desirable output voltage specifications: 74HCTMOS or 74ALSTTL? Why?

9–20. What IC specifications are used to determine how many gates of one family can be driven from the output of another family?

PROBLEMS

9–1. What is the purpose of diodes D_1 and D_2 in Figure 9–1.

9–2. In Figure 9–1, when input A is connected to ground (0 V), calculate the approximate value of emitter current in Q_1.

9-3. In Figure 9–1, when the output is HIGH, how do you account for the output voltage being only about 3.4 V instead of 5.0 V?

9-4. In Figure 9–1, describe the state (ON or OFF) of Q_3 and Q_4 for:
   (a) Both inputs A and B LOW.
   (b) Both inputs A and B HIGH.

9-5. What does the negative sign in the rating of source current (e.g., $I_{OH} = -400\ \mu A$) signify?

9-6. For TTL outputs, which is higher, the source current or the sink current?

9-7. (a) Find V_a and I_a in the circuits of Figure P9–7 using the following specifications:

$$I_{IL} = -1.6\text{ mA} \qquad I_{IH} = 40\ \mu A \qquad I_{OL} = 16\text{ mA} \qquad I_{OH} = -400\ \mu A$$
$$V_{IL} = 0.8\text{ V max.} \qquad V_{IH} = 2.0\text{ V min} \qquad V_{OL} = 0.2\text{ V typ.} \qquad V_{OH} = 3.4\text{ V typ.}$$

   (b) Repeat part (a) using input/output specifications that you gather from a TTL data book assuming that all gates are 74LSXX series.

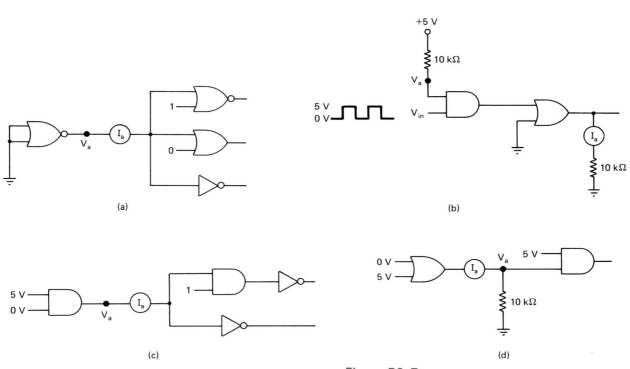

Figure P9–7

9-8. The input and output waveforms to an OR gate are given in Figure P9–8. Determine:
   (a) The period and frequency of V_{in}
   (b) The rise and fall times (t_r, t_f) of V_{in}
   (c) The propagation delay times of (t_{PLH}, t_{PHL}) of the OR gate

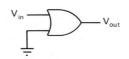

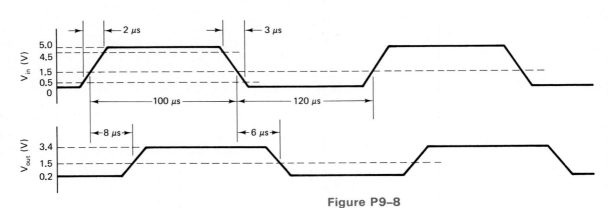

Figure P9–8

9–9. The propagation delay times for a 74LS08 AND gate are t_{PLH} = 15 ns, t_{PHL} = 20 ns and for a 7402 NOR gate are t_{PLH} = 22 ns, t_{PHL} = 15 ns. Sketch V_{out1} and V_{out2} showing the effects of propagation delay. (Assume 0 ns for the rise and fall times.)

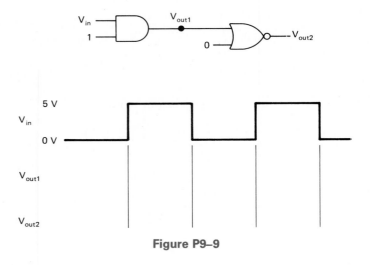

Figure P9–9

9–10. Repeat Problem 9–9 for the circuit of Figure P9–10.

Figure P9–10

9–11. Refer to a TTL data book or the data sheets in Appendix B. Use the total supply current (I_{CCL}, I_{CCH}) to compare the power dissipation of a 7400 versus a 74LS00.

9–12. Refer to a TTL data sheet to compare the typical LOW-level output voltage (V_{OL}) at maximum output current for a 7400 versus a 74LS00.

9–13. (a) Refer to a TTL data sheet to determine the noise margins for the HIGH state and LOW state of both the 7400 and 74LS00.

   (b) Which has better noise margins, the 7400 or 74LS00?

9–14. (a) Refer to a TTL data sheet to determine which can sink more current at its output, the commercial 74LS00 or the military 54LS00.

   (b) Which has a wider range of recommended V_{CC} supply voltage, the 7400 or the 5400?

9–15. Why is a pull-up resistor required at the output of an open-collector gate to achieve a HIGH-level output?

9–16. The wired-AND circuits in Figure P9–16 use all open-collector gates. Write the simplified Boolean equations at X and Y.

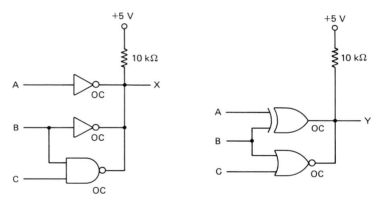

Figure P9–16

9–17. Make a general comparison of both the switching speed and power dissipation of the 7400 TTL series versus the 4000B CMOS series.

9–18. Which type of transistor, bipolar or field-effect, is used in:
   TTL ICs?
   CMOS ICs?

9–19. Why is it important to store MOS ICs in antistatic conductive foam?

9–20. What is the principal reason that ECL ICs reach such high switching speeds?

9–21. Table 9–3 shows that the speed-power product of the 74ALS family is much better than the 100K ECL family. Why, then, are some large mainframe computers based on ECL technology?

9–22. The graph in Figure 9–24 shows the 4000B CMOS family in the opposite corner from the 100K ECL family. What is the significance of this?

9–23. Referring to Figure 9–25, which logic family dissipates less power at low frequencies: 74LS or 74HC?

9–24. (a) Using the data in Table 9–4, draw a graph of input and output specifications similar to Figure 9–26 for the 74HCMOS and the 74ALSTTL IC series.

   (b) From your graphs of the two IC series, compare the HIGH-level and LOW-level noise margins.

   (c) From your graphs, can you see a problem in *directly* interfacing:
      (a) The 74HCMOS to the 74ALSTTL?
      (b) The 74ALSTTL to the 74HCMOS?

9–25. Refer to Table 9–4 to determine which of the following interfacing situations (driving gate-to-gate load) will require a pull-up resistor, and why?
  (a) 74TTL to 74ALSTTL
  (b) 74HCMOS to 74TTL
  (c) 74TTL to 74HCMOS
  (d) 74LSTTL to 74HCTMOS
  (e) 74LSTTL to 4000B CMOS

9–26. Of the interfacing situations given in Problem 9–25, will any of the driving gates have trouble sinking or sourcing current to a single connected gate load?

9–27. From Table 9–4, determine:
  (a) How many 74LSTTL loads can be driven by a single 74HCTMOS gate?
  (b) How many 74HCTMOS loads can be driven by a single 74LSTTL gate?

10

Flip-Flops and Registers

OBJECTIVES

Upon completion of this chapter, you should be able to:

- Explain the internal circuit operation of *S-R* and gated *S-R* flip-flops.
- Compare the operation of *D* latches and *D* flip-flops by using timing diagrams.
- Describe the difference between pulse-triggered and edge-triggered flip-flops.
- Explain the theory of operation of master-slave devices.
- Connect integrated-circuit *J-K* flip-flops as toggle and *D* flip-flops.
- Use timing diagrams to illustrate the synchronous and asynchronous operation of *J-K* flip-flops.

INTRODUCTION

The logic circuits that we have studied in the previous chapters have consisted mainly of logic gates (AND, OR, NAND, NOR, INVERT) and combinational logic. Starting in this chapter, we will be dealing with data storage circuitry that will "latch" on to (remember) a digital state (1 or 0).

This new type of digital circuitry is called *sequential logic* because it is controlled by, and is used for, controlling other circuitry in a specific sequence dictated by a control clock or enable/disable control signals.

The simplest form of data storage is the Set–Reset (*S-R*) flip-flop. These circuits are called *transparent latches* because the outputs respond immediately to changes at the input and the input state will be remembered, or "latched" onto. The latch will sometimes have an "enable input," which is used to control the latch to accept or ignore the *S-R* input states.

More sophisticated flip-flops use a clock as the control input and are used wherever the input and output signals must occur within a particular sequence.

10–1 S-R *FLIP-FLOP*

The *S-R* flip-flop is a data storage circuit that can be constructed using the basic gates covered in previous chapters. Using a cross-coupling scheme with two NOR gates, we can form the flip-flop shown in Figure 10–1.

Let's start our analysis by placing a 1 (HIGH) on the Set and a 0 (LOW) on Reset (Figure 10–1a). This is defined as the Set condition and should make the Q output 1 and $\overline{Q}$ output 0. Well, a HIGH on the Set will make the output of the upper NOR equal 0 ($\overline{Q} = 0$) and that 0 is fed down to the lower NOR, which together with a LOW on the Reset input will cause the lower NOR's output to equal a 1 ($Q = 1$). [Remember, a NOR gate is always 0 output except when *both* inputs are 0 (Chapter 4).]

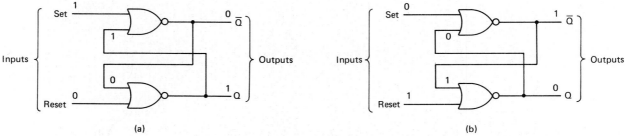

Figure 10–1   Cross-NOR *S-R* flip-flop: (a) Set condition; (b) Reset condition.

Now, when the 1 is removed from the Set input, the flip-flop should "remember" that it is Set (i.e., $Q = 1$, $\overline{Q} = 0$). So with Set = 0, Reset = 0, and $Q = 1$ from previously being Set, let's continue our analysis. The upper NOR has a 0–1 at its inputs, making $\overline{Q} = 0$; while the lower NOR has a 0–0 at its inputs, keeping $Q = 1$. Great—the flip-flop remained Set even after the Set input was returned to 0.

Now we should be able to Reset the flip-flop by making $S = 0$, $R = 1$ (Figure 10–1b). Well, with $R = 1$, the lower NOR will output a 0 ($Q = 0$), placing a 0–0 on the upper NOR, making its output 1 ($Q = 1$); thus the flip-flop "flipped" to its Reset state.

The only other input condition is when both S and R inputs are HIGH. In this case, both NORs will put out a LOW, making Q *and* $\overline{Q}$ equal 0, which is a condition that is not used. (Why would anyone want to Set *and* Reset at the same time, anyway!)

From the previous analysis we can construct the *S-R* flip-flop function table shown in Table 10–1, which will list all input and output conditions.

TABLE 10–1

Function Table for Figure 10–1

S	R	Q	$\overline{Q}$	Comments
0	0	Q	$\overline{Q}$	*Hold* condition (no change)
1	0	1	0	Flip-flop Set
0	1	0	1	Flip-flop Reset
1	1	0	0	Not used

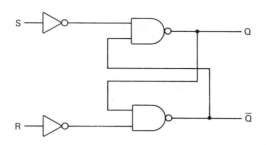

Figure 10–2 Cross-NAND *S-R* flip-flop.

An *S-R* flip-flop can also be made from cross-NAND gates, as shown in Figure 10–2. Prove to yourself that Figure 10–2 will produce the function table shown in Table 10–2. (Start with $S = 1$, $R = 0$ and remember that a NAND is LOW out only when *both* inputs are HIGH.) The symbols used for an *S-R* flip-flop are shown in Figure 10–3. The symbols show that both *true* and *complemented Q*-outputs are available. The second symbol is technically more accurate, but the first symbol is found most often in manufacturers' data manuals and throughout this book.

TABLE 10–2

Function Table for Figure 10–2

S	R	Q	$\overline{Q}$	Comments
0	0	Q	$\overline{Q}$	Hold condition
1	0	1	0	Flip-flop Set
0	1	0	1	Flip-flop Reset
1	1	1	1	Not used

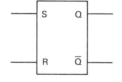 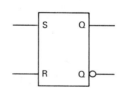

Figure 10–3 Symbol for an *S-R* flip-flop.

Now let's get practical and find an integrated-circuit TTL NOR gate and draw the actual wiring connections to form a cross-NOR like Figure 10–1, so that we may check it in the lab.

The TTL data manual shows a quad NOR gate 7402. Looking at its pin layout in conjunction with Figure 10–1, we can draw the circuit of Figure 10–4. To check

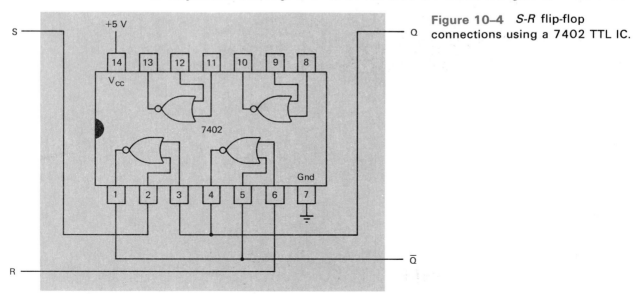

Figure 10–4 *S-R* flip-flop connections using a 7402 TTL IC.

out the operation of Figure 10–4 in the lab, apply 5 V to pin 14 and ground pin 7. Set the flip-flop by placing a HIGH (5 V) to the Set input and a LOW (0 V, ground) to the Reset input. A logic probe attached to the Q output should register a HIGH. When the S-R inputs are returned to the 0-0 state, the Q output should remain "latched" in the 1 state. The Reset function can be checked using the same procedure.

S-R Timing Analysis

By performing a timing analysis on the S-R flip-flop, we can see why it is called "transparent," and also observe the "latching" phenomenon.

EXAMPLE 10–1

The S and R waveforms given in Figure 10–6 are connected to an S-R flip-flop shown in Figure 10–5. Sketch the Q output waveform that will result.

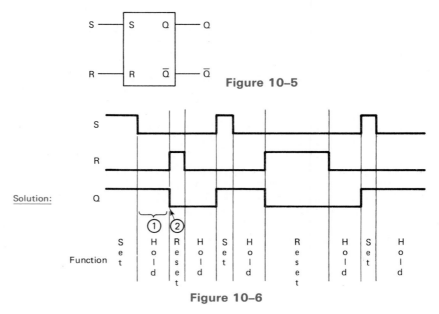

Figure 10–5

Figure 10–6

Note:

1. The flip-flop is "latched" in the Set condition even after the HIGH is removed from the S input.
2. The flip-flop is considered "transparent" because the Q output responds immediately to input changes.

S-R Flip-Flop Application

Let's say that we need a storage register that will "remember" the value of a binary number ($2^3 2^2 2^1 2^0$) which represents the time of the day, at the instant a momentary temperature limit switch goes into a HIGH (1) state. Figure 10–7 could be used to implement such a circuit. Since a 4-bit binary number is to be stored, we need four S-R flip-flops. We will look at their Q outputs with a logic probe to read the stored values.

With the Reset switch in the up position, the R inputs will be zero. With the Temperature Limit switch in the up position, one input to each AND gate is grounded,

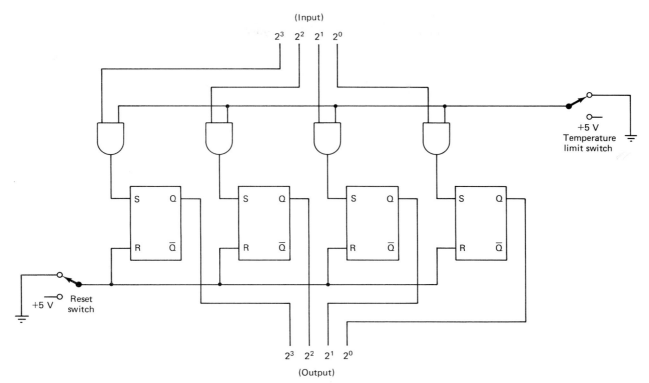

Figure 10–7   *S-R* flip-flop used as a storage register.

keeping the S inputs at zero also. To start the operation, first the Reset switch is momentarily pressed down, placing 5 V (1) on all four R inputs, resetting all flip-flops to 0.

Meanwhile, the binary input number is not allowed to reach the S inputs because there is a 0 at the other input of each AND gate. (Gates used in this method are referred to as *strobe gates* because they let information pass only when they are "enabled").

When the Temperature Limit switch momentarily goes down, 5 V (1) will be placed at each strobe gate, allowing the binary number (1's and 0's) to pass through to the S inputs, setting the appropriate flip-flops.

The binary input number representing the time of the day that the Temperature Switch went down will be stored in the 4-bit register, and could later be read by a logic probe or automatically by a microprocessor system.

10–2 GATED S-R FLIP-FLOP

Simple gate circuits, combinational logic, and transparent *S-R* flip-flops are called *asynchronous* (not synchronous) because the output responds immediately to input changes. *Synchronous* circuits operate sequentially, in step, with a control input. To make an *S-R* flip-flop synchronous, we add a gated input to enable and disable the S and R inputs. Figure 10–8 shows the connections that make the cross-NOR *S-R* flip-flop into a gated *S-R* flip-flop.

The S_x and R_x lines in Figure 10–8 are the original Set and Reset inputs. With the addition of the AND gates, however, the S_x and R_x lines will be kept LOW-LOW (Hold condition) as long as the Gate Enable is LOW. The flip-flop will operate normally while the Gate Enable is HIGH. The function chart (Figure 10–9b) and Example 10–2 illustrate the operation of the gated *S-R* flip-flop.

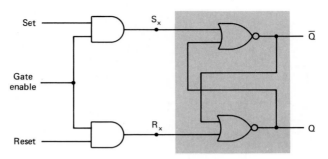

Figure 10-8 Gated *S-R* flip-flop.

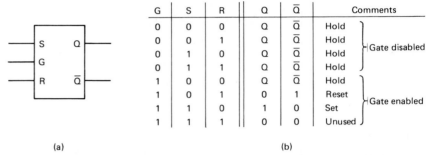

G	S	R	Q	$\overline{Q}$	Comments	
0	0	0	Q	$\overline{Q}$	Hold	
0	0	1	Q	$\overline{Q}$	Hold	
0	1	0	Q	$\overline{Q}$	Hold	Gate disabled
0	1	1	Q	$\overline{Q}$	Hold	
1	0	0	Q	$\overline{Q}$	Hold	
1	0	1	0	1	Reset	Gate enabled
1	1	0	1	0	Set	
1	1	1	0	0	Unused	

(a)   (b)

Figure 10-9 Function table and symbol for the gated *S-R* flip-flop of Figure 10-8.

EXAMPLE 10-2

Feed the following *G*, *S*, and *R* inputs into the gated S-R flip-flop, sketch the output wave at *Q*, and list the flip-flop functions.

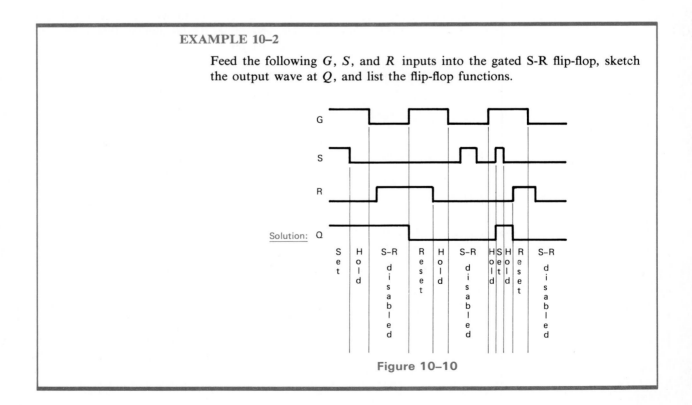

Figure 10-10

EXAMPLE 10–3

Feed the following *G*, *S*, and *R* inputs into the gated *S-R* flip-flop and sketch the output wave at *Q*.

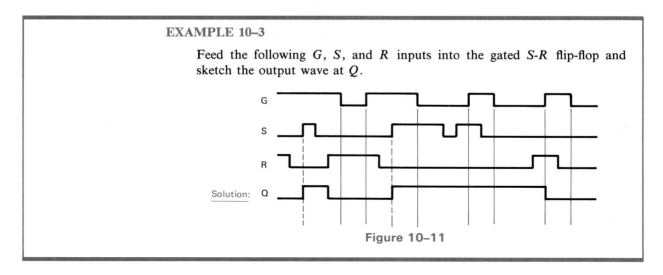

Solution:

Figure 10–11

10–3 GATED D FLIP-FLOP

Another type of flip-flop is the *D* flip-flop (*Data* flip-flop). It can be formed from the gated *S-R* flip-flop by the addition of an inverter.

In Figure 10–12 we can see that *S* and *R* will be complements of each other, and *S* is connected to a single line labeled *D* (Data). The operation is such that *Q* will be the same as *D*, while *G* is HIGH and *Q* will remain "latched" in whatever state it was in before the HIGH-to-LOW transition on *G*.

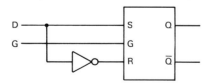

Figure 10–12   Gated *D* flip-flop.

EXAMPLE 10–4

Sketch the output waveform at *Q* for the following inputs at *D* and *G* of a gated *D* flip-flop.

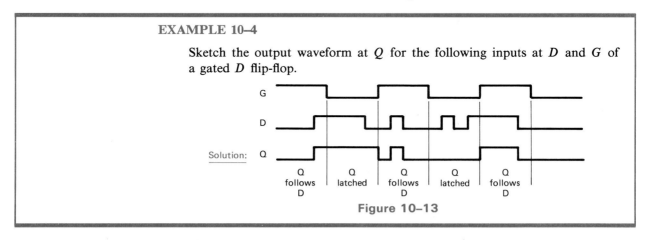

Figure 10–13

10–4 THE INTEGRATED-CIRCUIT D LATCH (7475)

The 7475 is an example of an integrated-circuit *D* latch (also called a *bistable latch*). It contains *four* transparent *D* latches. Its logic symbol and pin configuration are given in Figure 10–14. Latches 0 and 1 share a common Enable (E_{0-1}), and latches 2 and 3 share a common Enable (E_{2-3}).

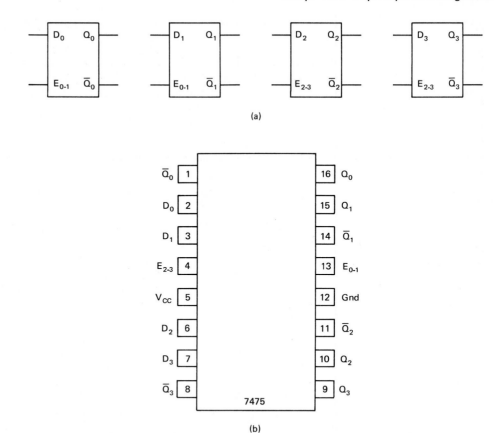

Figure 10–14   The 7475 quad bistable D latch: (a) logic symbol; (b) pin configuration.

From the function table (Table 10–3) we can see that the Q output will follow D (transparent) as long as the enable line (E) is HIGH (called active-HIGH enable). When E goes LOW, the Q output will become "latched" to the value that D was just before the HIGH-to-LOW transition of E.

TABLE 10–3

Function Table for a 7475[a]

Operating Mode	Inputs		Outputs	
	E	D	Q	$\overline{Q}$
Data enabled	H	L	L	H
	H	H	H	L
Data latched	L	×	q	$\overline{q}$

[a] q = State of Q before the HIGH-to-LOW edge of E; X = Don't care.

EXAMPLE 10–5

Sketch the output waveform at Q_0 for the following inputs at D_0 and E_{0-1} for the 7475 D latch shown in Figure 10–15.

Figure 10–15

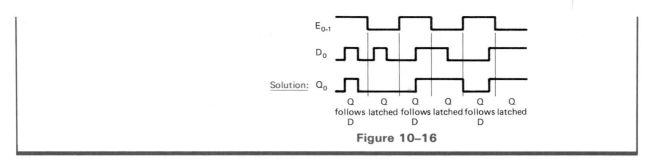

Figure 10–16

10–5 THE INTEGRATED-CIRCUIT D FLIP-FLOP (7474)

The 7474 D flip-flop differs from the 7475 D latch in several ways. Most important, the 7474 is an edge-triggered device. That means that transitions in Q will occur only at the edge of the input trigger pulse. The trigger pulse is usually a clock or timing signal instead of an enable line. In the case of the 7474, the trigger point is at the "positive" edge of C_p (LOW-to-HIGH transition.) The small triangle on the D flip-flop symbol (Figure 10–17a) is used to indicate that it is edge triggered.

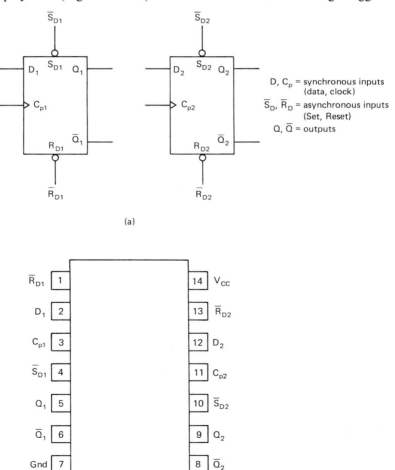

Figure 10–17 The 7474 dual D flip-flop: (a) logic symbol; (b) pin configuration.

The 7474 has two distinct types of inputs: synchronous and asynchronous. The *synchronous inputs* are the D (Data) and C_p (Clock) inputs. The state at the D input will be transferred to Q at the positive edge of the input trigger (LOW-to-HIGH edge of C_p). The *asynchronous inputs* are $\overline{S_D}$ (Set) and $\overline{R_D}$ (Reset), which operate independent of D and C_p. Being asynchronous means that they are *not* in sync with the clock pulse, and the Q outputs will respond *immediately* to input changes at $\overline{S_D}$ and $\overline{R_D}$. The little circle at S_D and R_D means that they are active-LOW inputs, and since the circles act like inverters, the external pin on the IC is labeled as the complement of the internal label.

All of that sounds complicated, but it really is not. Just realize that *a LOW on $\overline{S_D}$ will immediately Set the flip-flop*, and *a LOW on $\overline{R_D}$ will immediately Reset the flip-flop regardless of the states at the synchronous (D, C_p) inputs*.

The function table (Table 10–4) and following examples will help illustrate the operation of the 7474 D flip-flop.

TABLE 10–4

Function Table for a 7474 D Flip-Flop[a]

	Inputs				Outputs	
Operating mode	$\overline{S_D}$	$\overline{R_D}$	C_p	D	Q	$\overline{Q}$
Asynchronous Set	L	H	×	×	H	L
Asynchronous Reset	H	L	×	×	L	H
Not used	L	L	×	×	H	H
Synchronous Set	H	H	↑	h	H	L
Synchronous Reset	H	H	↑	l	L	H

[a] ↑ = Positive edge of clock; H = HIGH; h = HIGH level one setup time prior to positive clock edge; L = LOW; l = LOW level one setup time prior to positive clock edge; × = don't care.

The lowercase h in the D column indicates that in order to do a synchronous Set, the D must be in a HIGH state at least one setup time prior to the positive edge of the clock. The same rules apply for the lowercase l (Reset).

The setup time for this flip-flop is 20 ns, which means that if D is changing while C_p is LOW, that's okay, but D must be held stable (HIGH or LOW) at least 20 ns *before* the LOW-to-HIGH transition of C_p. (We discuss setup time in greater detail in Chapter 11.) Also realize that the only digital level on the D input that is used is the level that is present at the positive edge of C_p.

We have learned a lot of new terms in regard to the 7474 (active-LOW, edge-triggered, asynchronous, etc.). Those terms are important because they apply to almost all of the ICs that are used in the building of sequential circuits.

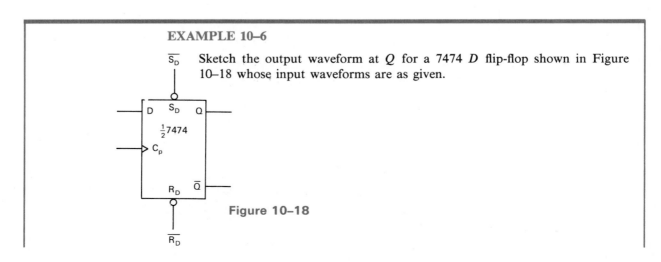

EXAMPLE 10–6

Sketch the output waveform at Q for a 7474 D flip-flop shown in Figure 10–18 whose input waveforms are as given.

Figure 10–18

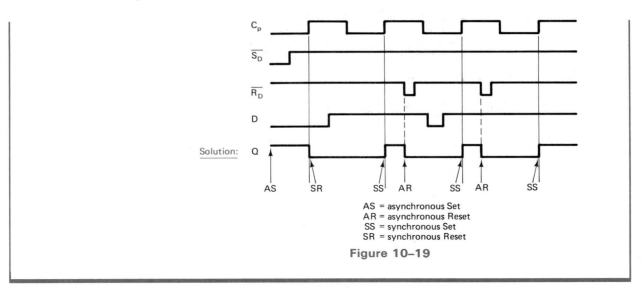

AS = asynchronous Set
AR = asynchronous Reset
SS = synchronous Set
SR = synchronous Reset

Figure 10–19

EXAMPLE 10–7

Sketch the output waveforms at Q for the 7474 D flip-flops shown in Figure 10–20 whose input waveforms are as given.

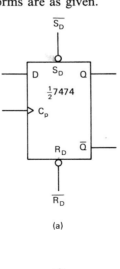

(a)

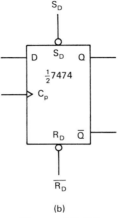

(b)

Figure 10–20

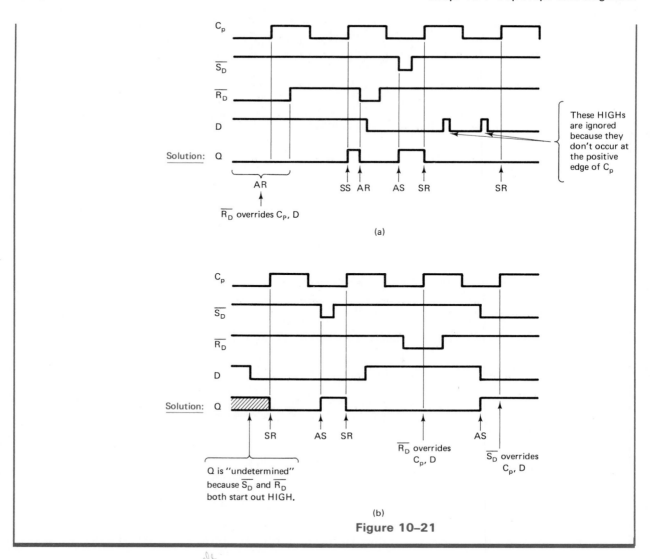

Figure 10–21

10–6 *MASTER-SLAVE* J-K *FLIP-FLOP*

Another type of flip-flop is the *J-K* flip-flop. It differs from the *S-R* flip-flop in that it has one new mode of operation, called *toggle*. Toggle means that Q and $\overline{Q}$ will switch to their *opposite* state at the active clock edge. The synchronous inputs to the *J-K* flip-flop are labeled J, K, and C_p. J acts like the S input to an *S-R* flip-flop and K acts like the R input in an *S-R* flip-flop. The toggle mode is achieved by making *both* J and K HIGH before the active clock edge. Table 10–5 shows the four synchronous operating modes of *J-K* flip-flops.

A number of the older flip-flops (74H71, 7472, 7473, 7476, 7478, 74104, 74105) are of the *master-slave* variety. They consist of two latches: a master latch, which receives data while the input trigger clock is HIGH, and a slave latch that receives data from the master and outputs it when the clock goes LOW. Figure 10–22 shows a simplified equivalent circuit and logic symbol of a master-slave *J-K* flip-flop.

From Figure 10–22 we can see that the master latch will be loaded with the state of the J and K inputs, while AND gates 1 and 2 are enabled by a HIGH C_p (i.e., the *master* is loaded while C_p is HIGH).

When C_p goes LOW, gates 1 and 2 are disabled, but gates 3 and 4 are enabled

TABLE 10–5

Synchronous
Operating Modes
of a J-K Flip-Flop

Operating Mode	J	K
Hold	0	0
Set	1	0
Reset	0	1
Toggle	1	1

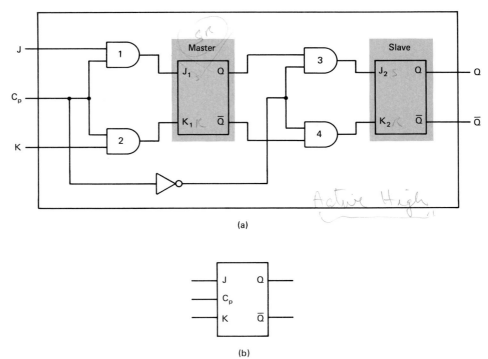

(a)

(b)

Figure 10–22 Positive pulse-triggered master-slave *J-K* flip-flop: (a) equivalent circuit; (b) logic symbol.

by the HIGH from the inverter, allowing the digital state at the master to pass through to the slave latch inputs.

When C_p goes HIGH again, gates 3 and 4 will be disabled, thus keeping the slave latch at its current digital state. Also with C_p HIGH again, the master will be loaded with the digital states of the J and K inputs, and the cycle repeats (see Figure 10–23). Master-slave flip-flops are called *pulse-triggered* or *level-triggered* devices because *input data are read during the entire time that the clock pulse is at a HIGH level*.

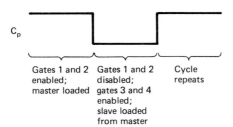

Figure 10–23 Enable/Disable operation of the C_p line of a master-slave flop-flop.

EXAMPLE 10–8

To illustrate the master-slave operation, let's draw the Q output for the master-slave *J-K* flip-flop shown in Figure 10–24. (Assume that Q is initially 0.)

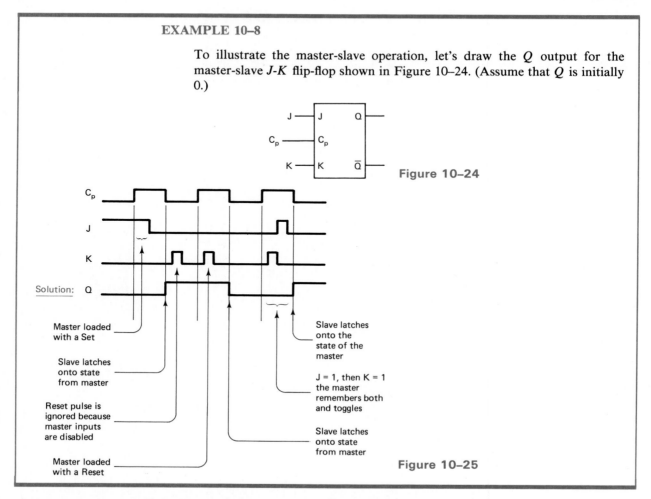

Figure 10–24

Figure 10–25

EXAMPLE 10–9

Sketch the waveform at Q for the master-slave *J-K* flip-flop shown in Figure 10–26. (Assume that Q is initially 0.)

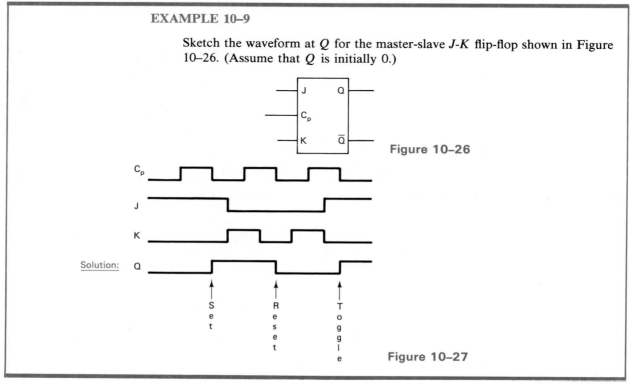

Figure 10–26

Figure 10–27

Occasionally, unwanted pulses or short glitches caused by electrostatic noise appear on J and K while C_p is HIGH. This phenomenon of interpreting unwanted signals on J and K while C_p is HIGH is called *ones catching* and is eliminated by the newer *J-K* flip-flops, which use an edge-triggering technique instead of pulse triggering.

10-7 THE EDGE-TRIGGERED *J-K* FLIP-FLOP

With edge triggering, the flip-flop only accepts data on the J and K inputs that are present at the active clock edge (either the HIGH-to-LOW edge of C_p or the LOW-to-HIGH edge of C_p). This gives the design engineer the ability to accept input data on J and K at a precise instant in time. Transitions of the level on J and K before or after the active clock trigger edge are ignored. The logic symbols for edge-triggered flip-flops use a small triangle at the clock input to signify that it is an edge-triggered device (see Figure 10-28).

Transitions of the Q output for the positive edge-triggered flip-flop shown in Figure 10-28a will occur when the C_p input goes from LOW-to-HIGH (positive edge). Figure 10-28b shows a negative edge-triggered flip-flop. The input clock signal will connect to the IC pin labeled $\overline{C_p}$. The small circle indicates that transitions in the output will occur at the HIGH-to-LOW edge (negative edge) of the $\overline{C_p}$ input.

The function table for a negative edge-triggered J-K flip flop is shown in Figure 10-29.

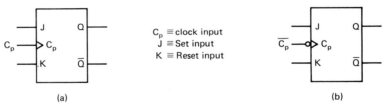

$$C_p \equiv \text{clock input}$$
$$J \equiv \text{Set input}$$
$$K \equiv \text{Reset input}$$

(a)   (b)

Figure 10-28   Symbols for edge-triggered *J-K* flip-flops:
(a) positive edge-triggered; (b) negative edge-triggered.

Operating mode	Inputs			Outputs	
	$\overline{C_p}$	J	K	Q	$\overline{Q}$
Hold	↓	0	0	No change	
Set	↓	1	0	1	0
Reset	↓	0	1	0	1
Toggle	↓	1	1	Opposite state	

↓ ≡ HIGH-to-LOW

$\overline{C_p}$

Negative edge
(HIGH-to-LOW)

Figure 10-29   Function table for a negative edge-triggered *J-K* flip-flop.

The downward arrow in the $\overline{C_p}$ column indicates that the flip-flop is triggered by the HIGH-to-LOW transition (negative edge) of the clock.

EXAMPLE 10-10

To illustrate edge triggering, let's draw the Q output for the negative edge-triggered *J-K* flip-flop shown in Figure 10-30. (Assume that Q is initially 0.)

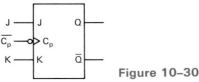

Figure 10-30

Solution:

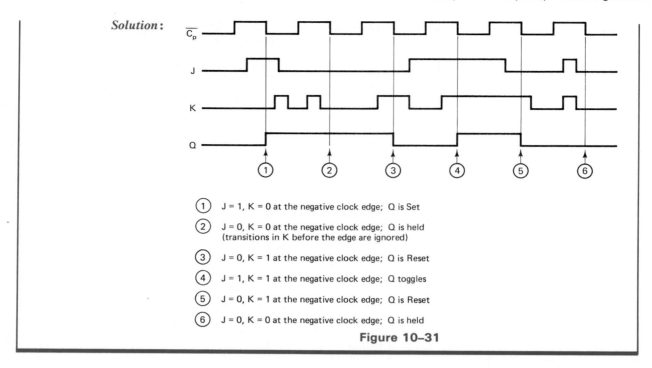

① J = 1, K = 0 at the negative clock edge; Q is Set

② J = 0, K = 0 at the negative clock edge; Q is held
    (transitions in K before the edge are ignored)

③ J = 0, K = 1 at the negative clock edge; Q is Reset

④ J = 1, K = 1 at the negative clock edge; Q toggles

⑤ J = 0, K = 1 at the negative clock edge; Q is Reset

⑥ J = 0, K = 0 at the negative clock edge; Q is held

Figure 10–31

10–8 THE INTEGRATED-CIRCUIT J-K FLIP-FLOP (7476, 74LS76)

Now let's take a look at actual *J-K* flip-flop ICs. The 7476 and 74LS76 are popular *J-K* flip-flops because they are both dual flip-flops (two flip-flops in each IC package) and they have asynchronous inputs ($\overline{R_D}$ and $\overline{S_D}$) as well as synchronous inputs ($\overline{C_p}$, *J*, *K*). The 7476 is a positive pulse-triggered (master-slave) flip-flop, and the 74LS76 is a negative edge-triggered flip-flop, a situation that can trap the unwary technician who attempts to replace the 7476 with the 74LS76!

From Figure 10–32a and Table 10–6 we can see that the asynchronous inputs $\overline{S_D}$ and $\overline{R_D}$ are *active-LOW*. That is, a LOW on $\overline{S_D}$ (Set) will Set the flip-flop ($Q = 1$) and a LOW on $\overline{R_D}$ will Reset the flip-flop ($Q = 0$). Remember, the asynchronous inputs will cause the flip-flop to respond immediately *without* regard to the clock trigger input.

For synchronous operations using *J*, *K*, and $\overline{C_p}$, the asynchronous inputs must be disabled by putting a HIGH level on both $\overline{S_D}$ and $\overline{R_D}$. The *J* and *K* inputs are read one setup time prior to the HIGH-to-LOW edge of the clock ($\overline{C_p}$). One setup time for the 74LS76 is 20 ns. That means that the state of *J* and *K*, 20 ns *before* the negative edge of the clock, is used to determine the synchronous operation to be performed. (Of course, the 7476 master-slave will read the state of *J* and *K* during the entire positive clock pulse.)

Also notice that in the toggle mode ($J = K = 1$), after a negative clock edge, *Q* becomes whatever $\overline{Q}$ was before the clock edge, and vice versa (i.e., if $Q = 1$ before the negative clock edge, then $Q = 0$ after the negative clock edge).

Now let's work through several timing analysis examples to be sure that we fully understand the operation of *J-K* flip-flops.

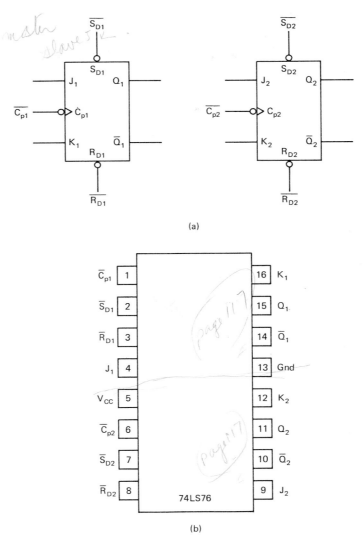

(a)

(b)

Figure 10–32 The 74LS76 negative edge-triggered flip-flop:
(a) logic symbol; (b) pin configuration.

TABLE 10–6

Function Table for the 74LS76[a]

Operating Mode	Inputs					Outputs	
	$\overline{S_D}$	$\overline{R_D}$	$\overline{C_p}$	J	K	Q	$\overline{Q}$
Asynchronous Set	L	H	×	×	×	H	L
Asynchronous Reset	H	L	×	×	×	L	H
Synchronous Hold	H	H	↓	l	l	q	$\overline{q}$
Synchronous Set	H	H	↓	h	l	H	L
Synchronous Reset	H	H	↓	l	h	L	H
Synchronous Toggle	H	H	↓	h	h	$\overline{q}$	q

[a] H = HIGH-voltage steady state; L = LOW-voltage steady state; h = HIGH voltage one
setup time prior to negative clock edge; l = LOW voltage one setup time prior to negative
clock edge; × = don't care; q = state of Q prior to negative clock edge; ↓ = HIGH-to-
LOW (negative) clock edge.

EXAMPLE 10–11

Sketch the Q waveform for the 74LS76 negative edge-triggered J-K flip-flop shown in Figure 10–33, with the given input waveforms.

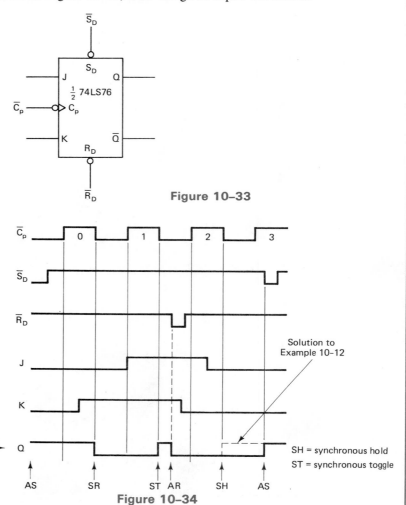

Figure 10–33

Figure 10–34

SH = synchronous hold
ST = synchronous toggle

Note: Q changes only on the negative edge of $\overline{C_p}$ except when asynchronous operations ($\overline{S_D}$, $\overline{R_D}$) are taking place.

EXAMPLE 10–12

How would the Q waveform of Example 10–11 be different if we used a 7476 pulse-triggered master-slave flip-flop instead of the 74LS76?

Solution: During positive pulse 2, J is HIGH for a short time. The master latch within the 7476 will remember that and cause the flip-flop to do a synchronous Set ($Q = 1$) when $\overline{C_p}$ returns LOW. (See Figure 10–34.)

EXAMPLE 10–13

Sketch the Q waveform for a 7476 positive pulse-triggered flip-flop shown in Figure 10–35, with the given input waves.

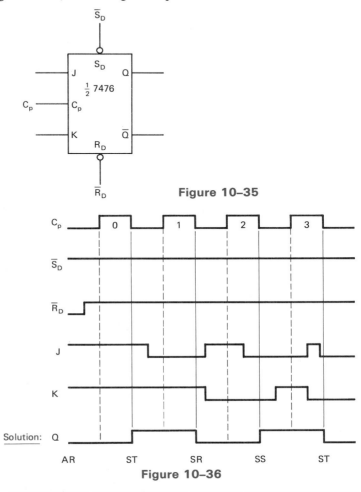

Figure 10–35

Figure 10–36

EXAMPLE 10–14

The 74109 is a positive edge-triggered $J\text{-}\overline{K}$ flip-flop. The logic symbol (Figure 10–37) and input waveforms are given; sketch Q.

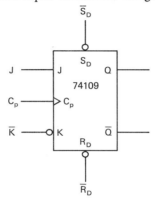

Figure 10–37

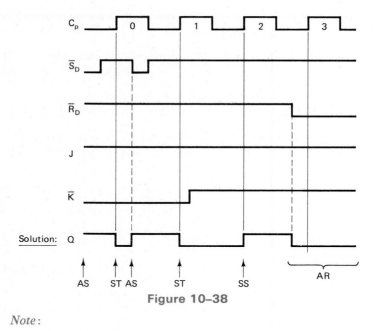

Figure 10–38

Note:

1. *Positive* edge triggering.
2. $\overline{K}$ instead of K; therefore, for a toggle, $J = 1$, $K = 0$.

The *J-K* flip-flop can be used to form other flip-flops by making the appropriate external connections. For example, to form a *D* flip-flop, add an inverter between the *J* and *K* inputs and bring the data into the *J* input as shown in Figure 10–39.

Figure 10–39 will operate as a *D* flip-flop because the data are brought in on the *J* terminal and its complement is at the *K*; so if Data = 1, the flip-flop will be Set after the clock edge; if Data = 0, the flip-flop will be Reset after the clock edge. (*Note:* You lose the toggle mode and hold mode using this configuration.)

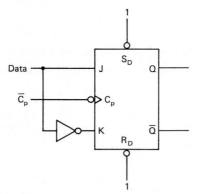

Figure 10–39 *D* flip-flop made from a *J-K* flip-flop.

Also, quite often it is important for a flip-flop to operate in the toggle mode. This can be done simply by connecting both *J* and *K* to 1. This will cause the flip-flop to change states at each active clock edge, as shown in Figure 10–40. Notice that the frequency of the output waveform at *Q* will be one-half the frequency of the input waveform at $\overline{C_p}$.

As we have seen, there is a variety of flip-flops, each with their own operating characteristics. In Chapters 11 through 13, we learn how to use these ICs to perform sequential operations such as counting, data shifting, and sequencing.

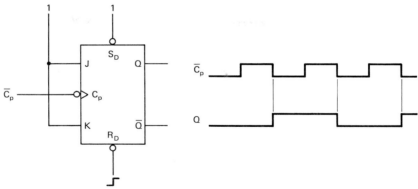

Figure 10–40 *J-K* connected as a toggle flip-flop.

First, let's summarize what we have learned about flip-flops by utilizing four common flip-flops in the same circuit, and supplying input signals and sketching the *Q* outputs of each (Example 10–15).

EXAMPLE 10–15

Sketch the *Q* outputs for each of the flip-flops shown in Figure 10–41.

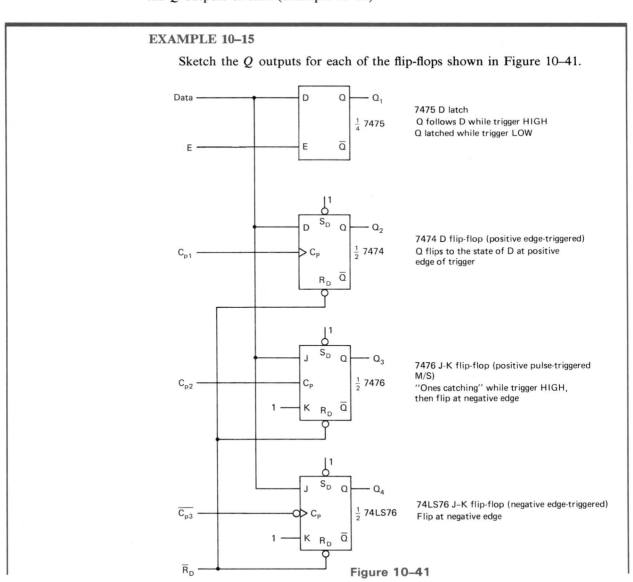

Figure 10–41

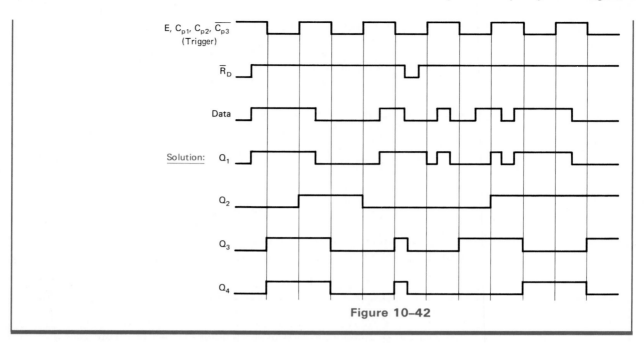

Figure 10–42

GLOSSARY

Active-HIGH: Means that the input to, or the output from, a terminal must be HIGH to be enabled or "active."

Active-LOW: Means that the input to, or the output from, a terminal must be LOW to be enabled or "active."

Asynchronous: (not synchronous). A condition in which the output of a device will switch states instantaneously as the inputs change without regard to an input clock signal.

Clock: A device used to produce a periodic digital signal that repeatedly switches from LOW to HIGH and back at a predetermined rate.

Combinational logic: The use of several of the basic gates (AND, OR, NOR, NAND) together to form more complex logic functions.

Complement: Opposite digital state (i.e., the complement of 0 is 1, and vice versa).

Digital state: The logic levels within a digital circuit (HIGH level = 1 state, and LOW level = 0 state).

Disabled: The condition in which a digital circuit's inputs or outputs are not allowed to accept or transmit digital states.

Edge-triggered: The term given to a digital device that can accept inputs and change outputs only on the positive or negative *edge* of some input control signal or clock.

Enabled: The condition in which a digital circuit's inputs or outputs are allowed to accept or transmit digital states normally.

Flip-flop: A circuit capable of storing a digital 1 or 0 level based on sequential digital levels input to it.

Function Chart: A diagram that illustrates all the possible combinations of input and output states for a given digital IC or device.

Latch: The ability to "hold" onto a particular digital state. A latch circuit will hold the level of a digital pulse even after the input is removed.

Level triggered: *See* Pulse triggered.

Master-slave: A storage device consisting of two sections: the master section, which accepts input data while the clock is HIGH, and the slave section, which receives the data from the master when the clock goes LOW.

Negative edge: The edge on a clock or trigger pulse that is making the transition from HIGH to LOW.

Noise: Any fluctuations in power supply voltages, switching surges, or electrostatic charges will cause irregularities in the HIGH- and LOW-level voltages of a digital signal. These irregularities or fluctuations in voltage levels are called electrical "noise" and can cause false readings of digital levels.

Ones catching: A feature of the master-slave flip-flop that allows the master section to latch on to any 1 level that is felt at the inputs at any time while the input clock pulse is HIGH, then transfer those levels to the slave when the clock goes LOW.

Positive edge: The edge on a clock or trigger pulse that is making the transition from LOW to HIGH.

Pulse triggered: The term given to a digital device that can accept inputs during an entire positive or negative pulse of some input control signal or clock. (Also called "level triggered.")

Reset: A condition that produces a digital LOW (0) state.

Set: A condition that produces a digital HIGH (1) state.

Setup time: The length of time before the active edge of a trigger pulse (control signal) that the inputs of a digital device must be in a stable digital state. [That is, if the setup time of a device is 20 ns, the inputs must be held stable (and will be read) 20 ns before the trigger edge.]

Sequential logic: Digital circuits that involve the use of a sequence of timing pulses in conjunction with storage devices such as flip-flops and latches, and functional ICs such as counters and shift registers.

Storage register: Two or more data storage circuits (such as flip-flops or latches) used in conjunction with each other to hold several bits of information.

Strobe gates: A "control" gate used to enable or disable inputs from reaching a particular digital device.

Synchronous: A condition in which the output of a device will operate only in synchronization (in step with) a specific HIGH or LOW timing pulse or trigger signal.

Toggle: In a flip-flop, a toggle is when Q changes to the level of $\overline{Q}$ and $\overline{Q}$ changes to the level of Q.

Transition: The instant of change in digital state from HIGH to LOW or LOW to HIGH.

Transparent latch: An asynchronous device whose outputs will "hold" onto the most recent digital state of the inputs. The outputs immediately follow the state of the inputs without regard to a trigger input and remain in that state even after the inputs are removed or disabled.

Trigger: The input control signal to a digital device that is used to specify the instant that the device is to accept input or change outputs.

REVIEW QUESTIONS

Section 10–1

10–1. A flip-flop is different from a basic logic gate because it "remembers" the state of the inputs after they are removed (<u>true</u> or false)?

10–2. What levels must be placed on S and R to SET an S-R flip-flop? *S = 1 R = 0*

10–3. What effect does S = 0 and R = 0 have on the output level at Q? *None*

Sections 10–2 and 10–3

10–4. Explain why the S-R flip-flop is called asynchronous and the *gated* S-R flip-flop is called synchronous. *change immediately / sequentially with the control input gate.*

10–5. Changes in S and R while a gate is enabled have no effect on the Q output of a gated S-R flip-flop (true or <u>false</u>)?

10–6. What procedure would you use to RESET the Q output of a gated D flip-flop? *D = 0 G = 1*

Sections 10–4 and 10–5

10–7. The 7475 IC contains how many D latches? *4*

10–8. The Q output of the 7475 D latch follows the level on the D input as long as E is _____ (<u>HIGH</u> or LOW).

10–9. Changes to D are ignored by the 7475 while E is LOW (<u>true</u> or false).

Sections 10–6 and 10–7

10–10. Describe why master-slave flip-flops are called "ones catching." *Latch to High while Clock High and transfer to slave when clock low*

10–11. The *Set* input to a J-K flip-flop is ___*J*___ (J,K) and the *Reset* input is ___*K*___ (J,<u>K</u>).

10–12. The *edge-triggered* J-K flip-flop only looks at the J-K inputs that are present during the active clock edge on C_p (<u>true</u> or false)?

10–13. What effect does the *toggle* operation of a J-K flip-flop have on the Q-output? *switch Q and Q̄ to opposite state.*

Section 10–8

10–14. How do you *asynchronously* Reset the 74LS76 flip-flop? *apply Low on Rd input*

10–15. The synchronous inputs to the 74LS76 override the asynchronous inputs (true or false)?

10–16. To operate a 74LS76 flip-flop synchronously, the $\overline{S_D}$ and $\overline{R_D}$ inputs must be held _____ (<u>HIGH</u>, LOW).

10–17. What is the distinction between upper-case and lower-case letters when used in the function table for the 74LS76 flip-flop? *upper-case – steady state   Lower-case used for levels one setup time to negative clock edge.*

PROBLEMS

10–1. Make the necessary connections to a 7400 quad NAND gate IC to form the cross-NAND *S-R* flip-flop of Figure 10–2. [Remember that an inverter can be formed from a NAND (Chapter 4).]

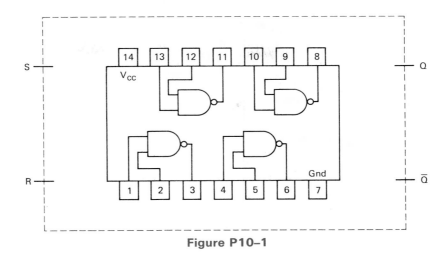

Figure P10–1

10–2. Sketch the Q output waveform for a gated S-R flip-flop (Figure 10–8) given the inputs at S, R, and G shown in Figure P10–2.

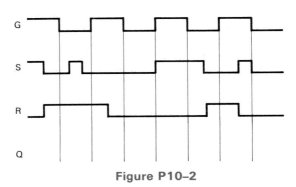

Figure P10–2

10–3. Repeat Problem 10–2 for the input waves shown in Figure P10–3.

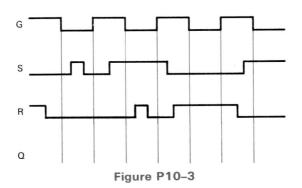

Figure P10–3

10–4. Repeat Problem 10–2 for the input waves shown in Figure P10–4.

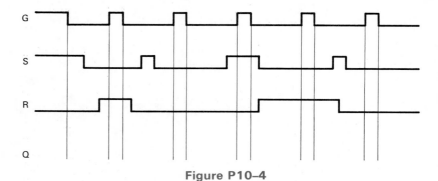

Figure P10–4

10–5. Referring to Figures 10–8 and 10–12, sketch the logic diagram using NORs, ANDs, and inverters that will function as a gated D flip-flop.

10–6. How many integrated-circuit chips will be required to build the gated D flip-flop that you sketched in Problem 10–5?

10–7. Make the necessary connections to a 7402 quad NOR and a 7408 quad AND to form the gated D flip-flop of Problem 10–5.

10–8. Sketch the Q output waveform for the gated D flip-flop of Figure 10–12 given the D and G inputs shown in Figure P10–8.

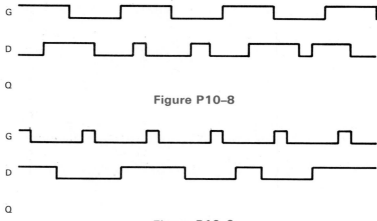

Figure P10–8

Figure P10–9

10–9. Repeat Problem 10–8 for the G and D inputs shown in Figure P10–9.

10–10. The logic symbol for one-fourth of a 7475 transparent D latch is given in Figure P10–10. Sketch the Q output waveform given the inputs at E and D.

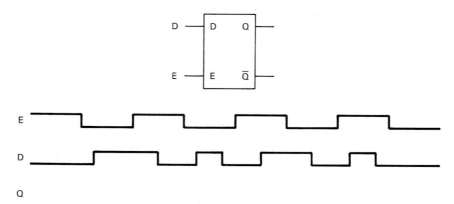

Figure P10–10

10–11. Repeat Problem 10–10 for the waveforms at E and D shown in Figure P10–11.

10–12. Explain why the 7475 is called "transparent" and why it is called a "latch."

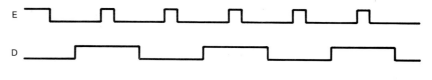

Figure P10–11

10–13. The 7475 is transparent while the E input is _____(LOW or HIGH) and it is latched while E is _____(LOW or HIGH).

10–14 **(a)** What are the asynchronous inputs to the 7474 D flip-flop?
      (b) What are the synchronous inputs to the 7474 D flip-flop?

10–15. The logic symbol for one-half of a 7474 dual D flip-flop is given in Figure P10–15a. Sketch the Q output wave given the inputs at C_p, D, $\overline{S_D}$, and $\overline{R_D}$ shown in Figure P10–15b.

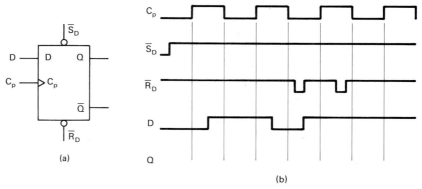

Figure P10–15

10–16. Repeat Problem 10–15 for the input waves shown in Figure P10–16.

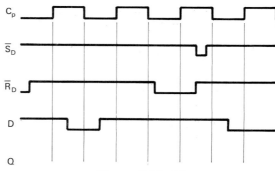

Figure P10–16

10–17. Describe several differences between the 7474 D flip-flop and the 7475 D latch.

10–18. Describe the differences between the asynchronous inputs and the synchronous inputs of the 7474.

10–19. What does the small triangle on the C_p line of the 7474 indicate?

10–20. To disable the asynchronous inputs to the 7474, should they be connected to a **HIGH** or a **LOW**?

10–21. What is the one additional synchronous operating mode that the J-K flip-flop has that the S-R flip-flop did not have?

10–22. What are the asynchronous inputs to the 7476 J-K flip-flop? Are they active-**LOW** or active-**HIGH**?

10–23. The 7476 is called a "pulse-triggered master-slave" flip-flop, while the 74LS76 is called an "edge-triggered" flip-flop. Describe the differences between the two of them.

10–24. The logic symbol and input waveforms for both the 7476 and 74LS76 are given in Figure P10–24. Sketch the waveform at each Q output.

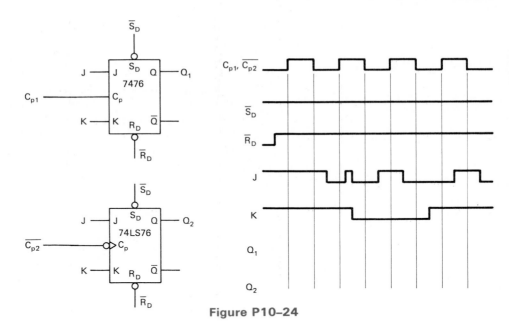

Figure P10–24

10–25. Repeat Problem 10–24 for the input waveforms shown in Figure P10–25.

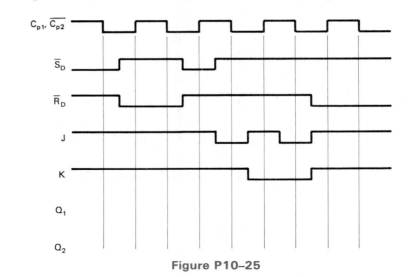

Figure P10–25

10–26. Sketch the output waveform at Q for Figure P10–26.

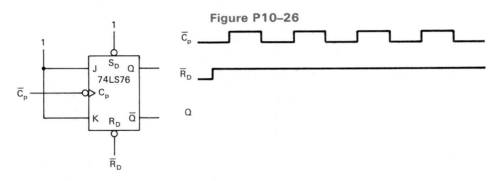

Figure P10–26

10–27. Sketch the output waveform at Q for Figure P10–27.

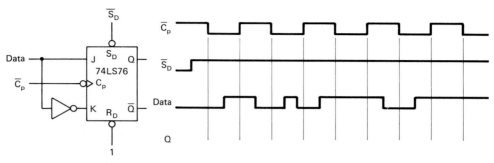

Figure P10–27

10–28. Sketch the output waveform at Q for Figure P10–28.

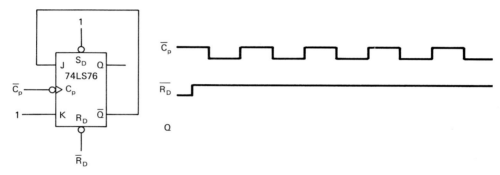

Figure P10–28

10–29. Sketch the output waveform at Q for Figure P10–29.

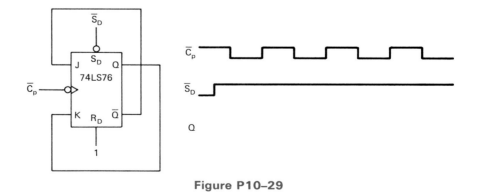

Figure P10–29

10–30. Sketch the output waveform at Q for Figure P10–30.

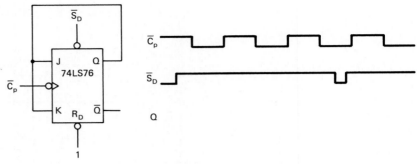

Figure P10–30

11

Practical Considerations for Digital Design

OBJECTIVES

Upon completion of this chapter, you should be able to:

- Describe the causes and effects of a "race" condition on synchronous flip-flop operation.
- Use manufacturers' data sheets to determine IC operating specifications such as setup time, hold time, propagation delay, and input/output voltage and current specifications.
- Perform worst-case analysis on the time-dependent operations of flip-flops and sequential circuitry.
- Design a series RC circuit to provide an automatic power-up reset function.
- Describe the wave-shaping capability and operating characteristics of Schmitt trigger ICs.
- Describe the problems caused by switch bounce and how to eliminate its effects.
- Calculate the optimum size for a pull-up resistor.

INTRODUCTION

Now we have the major building blocks required to form sequential circuits. There are a few practical time and voltage considerations that we have to deal with first, before we connect ICs together to form sequential logic.

For instance, ideally a 74LS76 flip-flop switches on the negative edge of the input clock, but actually it could take the output as long as 30 ns to switch. Thirty nanoseconds (30×10^{-9} s) does not sound like much, but when you cascade several flip-flops end to end or any time you have combinational logic with flip-flops that rely on a high degree of accurate timing, the IC delay times could cause serious design problems.

In this chapter we look at the *actual* operating characteristics of digital ICs as they relate to output delay times, input setup requirements, and input/output voltage and current levels. With a good knowledge of the practical aspects of digital ICs, we then develop the external circuitry needed to deliver the appropriate input voltage levels and also be aware of the output voltage, current, and time limitations.

11–1 FLIP-FLOP TIME PARAMETERS

There are several time parameters listed in IC manufacturers' data manuals that require careful analysis. For example, let's look at Figure 11–1, which uses a 74LS76 flip-flop with the J and $\overline{C_p}$ inputs brought in from some external circuit.

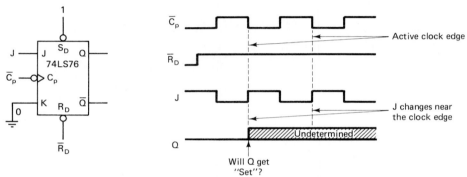

Figure 11–1   A possible "race" condition on a *J-K* flip-flop creates an undetermined result at *Q*.

The waveform shown for J and $\overline{C_p}$ will create a *race condition*. *Race* is the term used when the inputs to a triggerable device (like a flip-flop) are changing at the same time that the active trigger edge of the input clock is making its transition. In the case of Figure 11–1, the J waveform is changing from LOW to HIGH exactly at the negative edge of the clock; so what is J at the negative edge of the clock— LOW or HIGH?

Now when you look at Figure 11–1, you should ask the question "will Q ever get Set?" Remember from Chapter 10 that J must be HIGH at the negative edge of $\overline{C_p}$ in order to set the flip-flop. Actually, J must be HIGH "one *setup time*" prior to the negative edge of the clock.

The *setup time* is the length of time prior to the active clock edge that the flip-flop looks back to determine the levels to use at the inputs. In other words, for Figure 11–1, the flip-flop will look back one setup time prior to the negative clock edge to determine the level at J and K.

The setup time for the 74LS76 is 20 ns, so we must ask, "Were J and K HIGH or LOW 20 ns prior to the negative clock edge?" Well, K is tied to ground, so it was LOW, and depending on when J changed from LOW to HIGH, the flip-flop may have Set ($J = 1$, $K = 0$) or Held ($J = 0$, $K = 0$).

In a data manual, the manufacturer will give you "ac waveforms" which illustrate the measuring points for all the various time parameters. The illustration for setup time will look something like Figure 11–2.

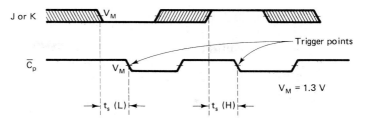

The shaded areas indicate when the input is
permitted to change for predictable output
performance

Figure 11-2 Setup time waveform specifications for a 74LS76.

The active transition (trigger point) of the $\overline{C_p}$ input (clock) occurs when $\overline{C_p}$ goes from above to below the 1.3 V level.

Setup time (LOW), $t_s(L)$, is given as 20 ns. This means that J and K can be changing states 21 ns or more before the active transition of $\overline{C_p}$, but in order to be interpreted as a LOW, they must be 1.3 V *or less* at 20 ns *before* the active transition of $\overline{C_p}$.

Setup time (HIGH), $t_s(H)$, is given as 20 ns also. This means that J and K can be changing states 21 ns or more before the active edge of $\overline{C_p}$, but to be interpreted as a HIGH, they must be 1.3 V *or more* at 20 ns *before* the active transition of $\overline{C_p}$.

Did you follow all of that? If not, go back and read it again! Sometimes, material like this has to be read over and over again, carefully, to be fully understood.

Not only does the input have to be set up some definite time *before* the clock edge, but it also has to be *held* for a definite time after the clock edge. This time is called the *hold time* [$t_h(L)$ and $t_h(H)$].

The hold time for the 74LS76 (and most other flip-flops) is given as 0 ns. This means that the desired levels at J and K must be held 0 ns *after* the active clock edge. In other words, the levels do not have to be held beyond the active clock edge for most flip-flops. In the case of the 74LS76, the desired level for J and K must be present from 20 ns before the negative clock edge to 0 ns after the clock edge.

For example, for a 74LS76 to have a LOW level on J and K, the waveforms in Figure 11-3 illustrate the *minimum* setup and hold times allowed to still have the LOW reliably interpreted as a LOW.

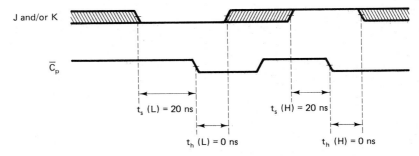

Figure 11-3 Setup and hold parameters for a 74LS76 flip-flop.

Figure 11-3 shows us that J and K are allowed to change states any time greater than 20 ns before the negative clock edge, and since the hold time is zero, they are permitted to change immediately after the negative clock edge.

EXAMPLE 11–1

Follow the rules for setup and hold times, and sketch the waveform at Q for the 74H106 shown in Figure 11–4. [$t_s(L) = 13$ ns, $t_s(H) = 10$ ns, $t_h(L) = t_h(H) = 0$ ns].

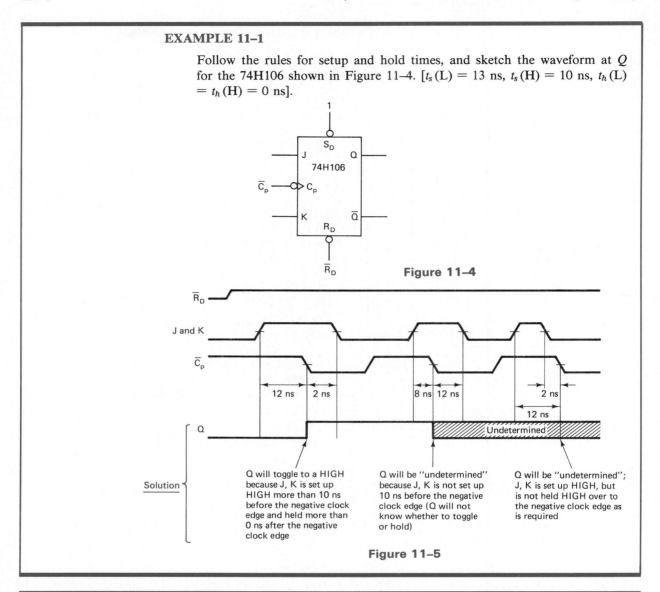

Figure 11–4

Figure 11–5

EXAMPLE 11–2

Sketch the Q output for a 74H106 shown in Figure 11–6, with the given input waveforms [$t_s(L) = 13$ ns, $t_s(H) = 10$ ns, $t_h(L) = t_h(H) = 0$ ns].

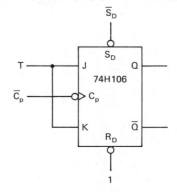

Figure 11–6

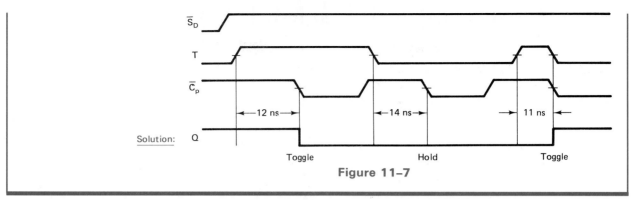

Figure 11–7

Have you noticed in Examples 11–1 and 11–2 that the Q output changes *exactly* on the negative clock edge? Do you really think that it will? It won't! There are electrical charges built up inside any digital logic circuit that won't allow it to change states instantaneously as the inputs change. This delay from input to output is called *propagation delay*. There are propagation delays from the synchronous inputs to the output and also the asynchronous inputs to the output.

For example, there is a propagation delay period from the instant the $\overline{R_D}$ or $\overline{S_D}$ goes LOW until the Q output responds accordingly. The data manual shows a *maximum* propagation delay for $\overline{S_D}$ to Q of 20 ns and $\overline{R_D}$ to Q of 30 ns. Since a LOW on $\overline{S_D}$ causes Q to go *LOW to HIGH*, the propagation delay is abbreviated t_{PLH}. A LOW on $\overline{R_D}$ causes Q to go *HIGH to LOW*; therefore, use t_{PHL} for that propagation delay, as illustrated in Figure 11–8.

The propagation delay from the clock trigger point to the Q output is also called t_{PLH} or t_{PHL}, depending on whether the Q output is going LOW to HIGH or HIGH to LOW. For the 74LS76, clock to output, $t_{PLH} = 20$ ns and $t_{PHL} = 30$ ns. Figure 11–9 illustrates the synchronous propagation delays.

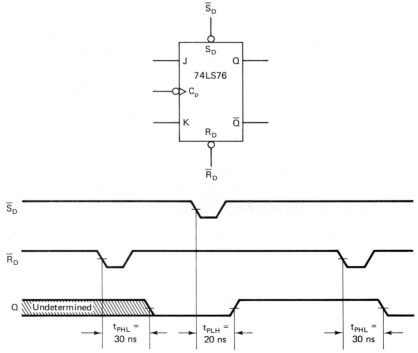

Figure 11–8 Propagation delay for the asynchronous input-to-Q output for a 74LS76.

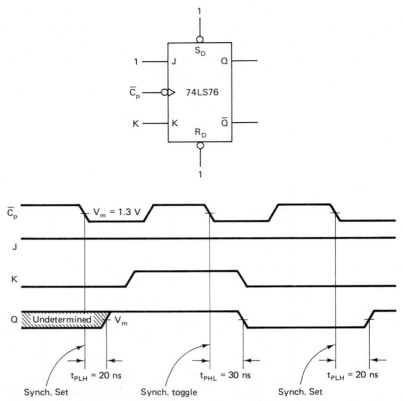

Figure 11–9   Propagation delay for the clock-to-output of the 74LS76.

Besides setup, hold, and propagation delay times, the manufacturer's data manual will also give:

1. Maximum frequency (f_{max}). This is the maximum frequency allowed at the clock input. Any frequency above this limit will yield unpredictable results.

2. Clock pulse width (LOW) [t_w(L)]. This is the minimum width (in nanoseconds) that is allowed at the clock input during the LOW level for reliable operation.

3. Clock pulse width (HIGH) [t_w(H)]. This is the minimum width (in nanoseconds) that is allowed at the clock input during the HIGH level for reliable operation.

4. Set or Reset pulse width (LOW) [t_w(L)]. This is the minimum width (in nanoseconds) of the LOW pulse at the Set ($\overline{S_D}$) or Reset ($\overline{R_D}$) inputs.

Figure 11–10 shows the measurement points for those specifications.

Complete specifications for the 7476/74LS76 flip-flop are given in Figure 11–11. Can you locate all the specifications that we have discussed so far? If you have

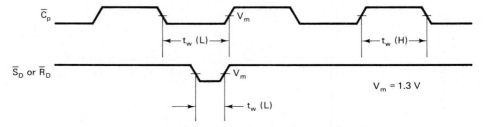

Figure 11–10   Minimum pulse-width specifications.

LOGIC PRODUCTS

FLIP-FLOPS

54/7476, LS76

Dual J-K Flip-Flop

DESCRIPTION

The '76 is a dual J-K flip-flop with individual J, K, Clock, Set and Reset inputs. The 7476 is positive pulse-triggered. JK information is loaded into the master while the Clock is HIGH and transferred to the slave on the HIGH-to-LOW Clock transition. The J and K inputs must be stable while the Clock is HIGH for conventional operation.

The 74LS76 is a negative edge-triggered flip-flop. The J and K inputs must be stable only one setup time prior to the HIGH-to-LOW Clock transition.

The Set ($\overline{S}_D$) and Reset ($\overline{R}_D$) are asynchronous active LOW inputs. When LOW, they override the Clock and Data inputs, forcing the outputs to the steady state levels as shown in the Function Table.

TYPE	TYPICAL f_{MAX}	TYPICAL SUPPLY CURRENT (Total)
7476	20MHz	10mA
74LS76	45MHz	4mA

ORDERING CODE

PACKAGES	COMMERCIAL RANGES $V_{CC} = 5V \pm 5\%$; $T_A = 0°C$ to $+70°C$		MILITARY RANGES $V_{CC} = 5V \pm 10\%$; $T_A = -55°C$ to $+125°C$	
Plastic DIP	N7476N	•	N74LS76N	
Ceramic DIP			S5476F	•	S54LS76F
Flatpack			S5476W	•	S54LS76W

INPUT AND OUTPUT LOADING AND FAN-OUT TABLE

PINS	DESCRIPTION	54/74	54/74LS
$\overline{CP}$	Clock input	2ul	2LSul
$\overline{R}_D$, $\overline{S}_D$	Reset and Set inputs	2ul	2LSul
J, K	Data inputs	1ul	1LSul
Q, $\overline{Q}$	Outputs	10ul	10LSul

NOTE
Where a 54/74 unit load (ul) is understood to be 40μA I_{IH} and −1.6mA I_{IL}, and a 54/74LS unit load (LSul) is 20μA I_{IH} and −0.4mA I_{IL}.

PIN CONFIGURATION

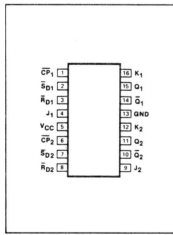

LOGIC SYMBOL

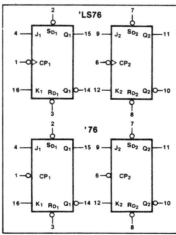

LOGIC SYMBOL (IEEE/IEC)

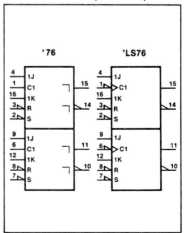

Note: in this figure, the abbreviation for Clock is $\overline{CP}$ instead of $\overline{C_p}$.

Figure 11–11 (Courtesy of Signetics Corporation.)

your own data manual, look at some of the other flip-flops and see how they compare. In the front of the manual you will find a section that describes all the IC specifications and abbreviations used throughout the data manual.

FLIP-FLOPS

54/7476, LS76

LOGIC DIAGRAM

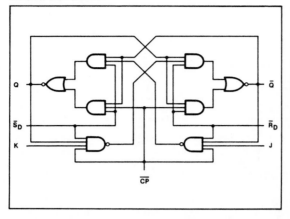

FUNCTION TABLE

OPERATING MODE	INPUTS					OUTPUTS	
	$\bar{S}_D$	$\bar{R}_D$	$\overline{CP}^{(b)}$	J	K	Q	$\bar{Q}$
Asynchronous Set	L	H	X	X	X	H	L
Asynchronous Reset (Clear)	H	L	X	X	X	L	H
Undetermined[a]	L	L	X	X	X	H	H
Toggle	H	H	⊓	h	h	$\bar{q}$	q
Load "0" (Reset)	H	H	⊓	l	h	L	H
Load "1" (Set)	H	H	⊓	h	l	H	L
Hold "no change"	H	H	⊓	l	l	q	$\bar{q}$

H = HIGH voltage level steady state.
h = HIGH voltage level one setup time prior to the HIGH-to-LOW Clock transition.[c]
L = LOW voltage level steady state.
l = LOW voltage level one setup time prior to the HIGH-to-LOW Clock transition.[c]
q = Lower case letters indicate the state of the referenced output prior to the HIGH-to-LOW Clock transition.
X = Don't care.
⊓ = Positive Clock pulse.

NOTES
a. Both outputs will be HIGH while both $\bar{S}_D$ and $\bar{R}_D$ are LOW, but the output states are unpredictable if $\bar{S}_D$ and $\bar{R}_D$ go HIGH simultaneously.
b. The 74LS76 is edge triggered. Data must be stable one setup time prior to the negative edge of the Clock for predictable operation.
c. The J and K inputs of the 7476 must be stable while the Clock is HIGH for conventional operation.

ABSOLUTE MAXIMUM RATINGS (Over operating free-air temperature range unless otherwise noted.)

PARAMETER		54	54LS	74	74LS	UNIT
V_{CC}	Supply voltage	7.0	7.0	7.0	7.0	V
V_{IN}	Input voltage	− 0.5 to + 5.5	− 0.5 to + 7.0	− 0.5 to + 5.5	− 0.5 to + 7.0	V
I_{IN}	Input current	− 30 to + 5	− 30 to + 1	− 30 to + 5	− 30 to + 1	mA
V_{OUT}	Voltage applied to output in HIGH output state	− 0.5 to + V_{CC}	− 0.5 to + V_{CC}	− 0.5 to + V_{CC}	− 0.5 to + V_{CC}	V
T_A	Operating free-air temperature range	− 55 to + 125		0 to 70		°C

RECOMMENDED OPERATING CONDITIONS

PARAMETER			54/74			54/74LS			UNIT
			Min	Nom	Max	Min	Nom	Max	
V_{CC}	Supply voltage	Mil	4.5	5.0	5.5	4.5	5.0	5.5	V
		Com'l	4.75	5.0	5.25	4.75	5.0	5.25	V
V_{IH}	HIGH-level input voltage		2.0			2.0			V
V_{IL}	LOW-level input voltage	Mil			+ 0.8			+ 0.7	V
		Com'l			+ 0.8			+ 0.8	V
I_{IK}	Input clamp current				− 12			− 18	mA
I_{OH}	HIGH-level output current				− 400			− 400	μA
I_{OL}	LOW-level output current	Mil			16			4	mA
		Com'l			16			8	mA
T_A	Operating free-air temperature	Mil	− 55		+ 125	− 55		+ 125	°C
		Com'l	0		70	0		70	°C

Figure 11–11 *(Continued)*

LOGIC DIVISION

FLIP-FLOPS   54/7476, LS76

DC ELECTRICAL CHARACTERISTICS (Over recommended operating free-air temperature range unless otherwise noted.)

PARAMETER		TEST CONDITIONS[1]			54/7476			54/74LS76			UNIT
					Min	Typ[2]	Max	Min	Typ[2]	Max	
V_{OH}	HIGH-level output voltage	V_{CC} = MIN, V_{IH} = MIN, V_{IL} = MAX, I_{OH} = MAX		Mil	2.4	3.4		2.5	3.4		V
				Com'l	2.4	3.4		2.7	3.4		V
V_{OL}	LOW-level output voltage	V_{CC} = MIN, V_{IL} = MAX, V_{IH} = MIN	I_{OL} = MAX	Mil		0.2	0.4		0.25	0.4	V
				Com'l		0.2	0.4		0.35	0.5	V
			I_{OL} = 4mA	74LS					0.25	0.4	V
V_{IK}	Input clamp voltage	V_{CC} = MIN, I_I = I_{IK}					− 1.5			− 1.5	V
I_I	Input current at maximum input voltage	V_{CC} = MAX	V_I = 5.5V				1.0				mA
			V_I = 7.0V	J, K Inputs						0.1	mA
				$\overline{S}_D, \overline{R}_D$ Inputs						0.3	mA
				$\overline{CP}$ Inputs						0.4	mA
I_{IH}	HIGH-level input current	V_{CC} = MAX	V_I = 2.4V	J, K Inputs			40				μA
				$\overline{S}_D, \overline{R}_D$ Inputs			80				μA
				$\overline{CP}$ Inputs			80				μA
			V_I = 2.7V	J, K Inputs						20	μA
				$\overline{S}_D, \overline{R}_D$ Inputs						60	μA
				$\overline{CP}$ Inputs						80	μA
I_{IL}	LOW-level input current[5]	V_{CC} = MAX, V_I = 0.4V		J, K Inputs			− 1.6			− 0.4	mA
				$\overline{S}_D, \overline{R}_D$ Inputs			− 3.2			− 0.8	mA
				$\overline{CP}$ Inputs			− 3.2			− 0.8	mA
I_{OS}	Short-circuit output current[3]	V_{CC} = MAX		Mil	− 20		− 57	− 20		− 100	mA
				Com'l	− 18		− 57	− 20		− 100	mA
I_{CC}	Supply current[4] (total)	V_{CC} = MAX				10	40		4	8	mA

NOTES
1. For conditions shown as MIN or MAX, use the appropriate value specified under recommended operating conditions for the applicable type.
2. All typical values are at V_{CC} = 5V, T_A = 25°C.
3. I_{OS} is tested with V_{OUT} = + 0.5V and V_{CC} = V_{CC} MAX + 0.5V. Not more than one output should be shorted at a time and duration of the short circuit should not exceed one second.
4. With the Clock input grounded and all outputs open, I_{CC} is measured with the Q and $\overline{Q}$ outputs HIGH in turn.
5. $\overline{S}_D$ is tested with $\overline{R}_D$ HIGH, and $\overline{R}_D$ is tested with $\overline{S}_D$ HIGH.

AC CHARACTERISTICS T_A = 25°C, V_{CC} = 5.0V

PARAMETER		TEST CONDITIONS	54/74		54/74LS		UNIT
			C_L = 15pF, R_L = 400Ω		C_L = 15pF, R_L = 2kΩ		
			Min	Max	Min	Max	
f_{MAX}	Maximum Clock frequency	Waveform 3	15		30		MHz
t_{PLH} t_{PHL}	Propagation delay Clock to output	Waveform 1, 'LS76 Waveform 3, '76		25 40		20 30	ns
t_{PLH} t_{PHL}	Propagation delay $\overline{S}_D$ or $\overline{R}_D$ to output	Waveform 2		25 40		20 30	ns

NOTE
Per industry convention, f_{MAX} is the worst case value of the maximum device operating frequency with no constraints on t_r, t_f, pulse width or duty cycle.

Figure 11–11 (*Continued*)

LOGIC DIVISION

FLIP-FLOPS 54/7476, LS76

AC SETUP REQUIREMENTS $T_A = 25\,°C$, $V_{CC} = 5.0V$

	PARAMETER	TEST CONDITIONS	54/74 Min	54/74 Max	54/74LS Min	54/74LS Max	UNIT
$t_W(H)$	Clock pulse width (HIGH)	Waveform 1	20		20		ns
$t_W(L)$	Clock pulse width (LOW)	Waveform 1	47				ns
$t_W(L)$	Reset pulse width (LOW)	Waveform 2	25		25		ns
t_s	Setup time J or K to Clock[c]	Waveform 1	0		20		ns
t_h	Hold time J or K to Clock	Waveform 1	0		0		ns

AC WAVEFORMS

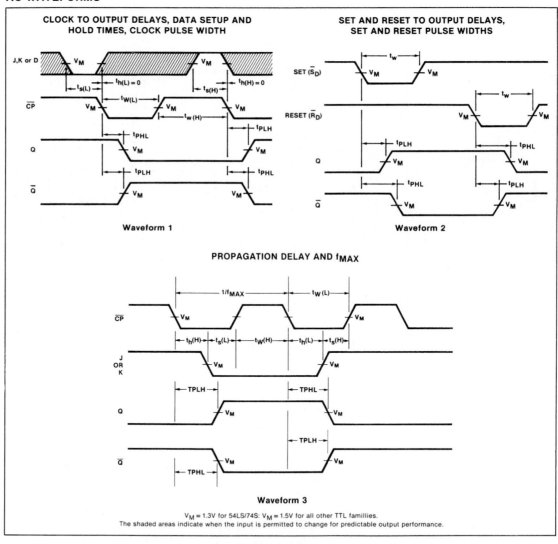

Figure 11–11 (Continued)

Now that we understand most of the operating characteristics of the digital ICs, let's examine why they are so important and what implications they have on our design of digital circuits.

EXAMPLE 11–3

The 74109 is a positive edge-triggered J-$\overline{K}$ flip-flop. If we attach the J input to the clock as shown in Figure 11–12, will the flip-flop's Q output toggle?

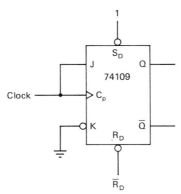

Figure 11–12

Solution: t_s for a 74109 is 10 ns; this means that J must be HIGH and $\overline{K}$ must be LOW 10 ns *before* the positive clock edge. When we draw the waveforms as shown in Figure 11–13, we see that J and C_p are exactly the same. Therefore, since J is not HIGH one setup time prior to the positive clock edge, Q will not toggle.

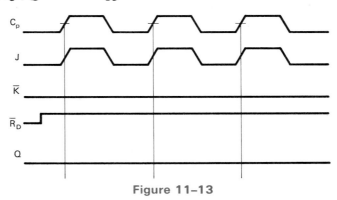

Figure 11–13

To get Example 11–3 to toggle, we have to move C_p to the right by at least 10 ns so that J is HIGH 10 ns *before* the positive edge of C_p. By saying "move it to the right" I mean delay it by at least 10 ns.

One common way to introduce delay is to insert one or more IC gates in the C_p line as shown in Figure 11–14 so that their combined propagation delay is greater than 10 ns.

From the manufacturer's specifications we can see that the propagation delay for a 7432 input to output is $t_{PHL} = 22$ ns max. and $t_{PLH} = 15$ ns max. [typically, the propagation delay will be slightly less than the maximum (worst case) rating].

Now let's redraw the waveforms as shown in Figure 11–15 with the delayed clock to see if the flip-flop will toggle. The 7432 will delay the LOW-to-HIGH edge of the clock by approximately 15 ns, so J *will* be HIGH one setup time prior to the trigger point on C_p; thus Q *will* toggle.

An important point to be made here is that in Figure 11–14 we are relying on the propagation delay of the 7432 to be 15 ns, which according to the manufacturer is the worst case (maximum) for the 7432. What happens if the *actual* propagation

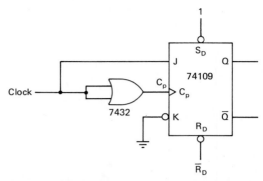

Figure 11–14 Modification of flip-flop in Example 11–3 to allow it to toggle.

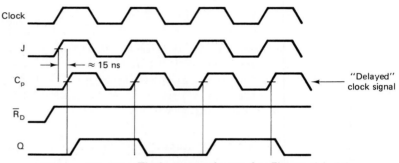

Figure 11–15 Timing waveforms for Figure 11–14.

delay is less than 15 ns, let's say only 8 ns? The clock (C_p) would not be delayed far enough to the right for *J* to be set up in time.

There are special *delay-gate* ICs available that provide exact, predefined delays specifically for the purpose of delaying a particular signal to enable proper time relationships. One such delay gate is shown in Figure 11–16.

To use the delay gate in Figure 11–16 you would connect the signal that you want delayed to the C_p input terminal. You then select the delayed output waveform that suits your needs. The output waveforms are identical to the input except delayed by 5, 10, 15, or 20 ns. Complemented, delayed waveforms are also available at the $\overline{5}$, $\overline{10}$, $\overline{15}$, and $\overline{20}$ outputs. Delay gates with various other delay intervals are also available.

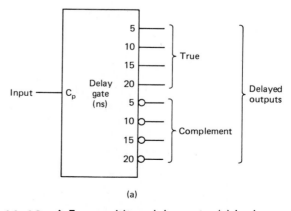

(a)

Figure 11–16 A 5-ns multitap delay gate: (a) logic symbol;

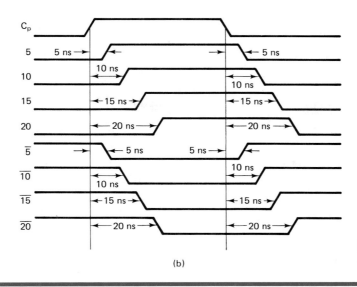

Figure 11–16 (*Continued*)
(b) output waveforms.

(b)

EXAMPLE 11–4

Use the setup, hold, and propagation delay times from a data manual to determine if the 74109 J-$\overline{K}$ flip-flop in the circuit shown in Figure 11–17 will toggle. (Assume that the flip-flop is initially Reset, and remember that for a toggle, $J = 1$, $\overline{K} = 0$.)

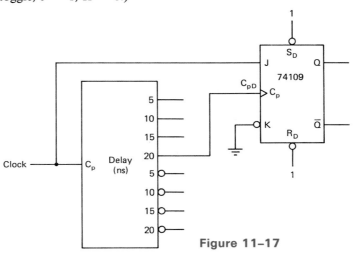

Figure 11–17

Solution: First, draw the waveforms as shown in Figure 11–18. C_{pD}, the delayed clock, makes its LOW-to-HIGH transition and triggers the flip-flop 20 ns *after J* makes its transition. Looking at the waveforms, *J* is HIGH $\geq$ 10 ns *before* the positive edge of C_{pD} and *is* held HIGH $\geq$ 6 ns *after* the positive edge of C_{pD}. Therefore, *the flip-flop will toggle* at each positive edge of C_{pD}.

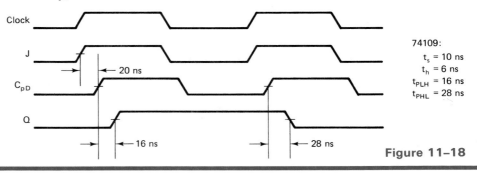

74109:
$t_s = 10$ ns
$t_h = 6$ ns
$t_{PLH} = 16$ ns
$t_{PHL} = 28$ ns

Figure 11–18

EXAMPLE 11–5

Use the specifications from a data manual to determine if the 74LS112 *J-K* flip-flop in the circuit shown in Figure 11–19 will toggle. (Assume that the flip-flop is initially Reset.)

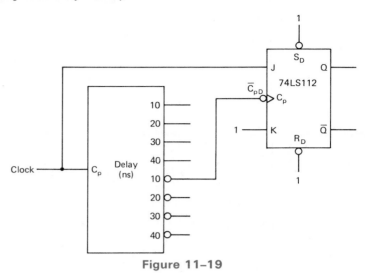

Figure 11–19

Solution: First, draw the waveforms as shown in Figure 11–20. $\overline{C_{pD}}$ is inverted and delayed by 10 ns from the Clock and J waveforms. Each negative edge of $\overline{C_{pD}}$ triggers the flip-flop. Looking at the waveforms, the J input *is not* set up HIGH $\geq$ 20 ns before the negative $\overline{C_{pD}}$ edge and therefore *is not* interpreted as a HIGH. The flip-flop output will be *undetermined* from then on because it cannot distinguish if *J* is a HIGH or a LOW at each negative $\overline{C_{pD}}$ edge.

    To correct the problem, $\overline{C_{pD}}$ should be connected to the $\overline{30}$-ns tap on the delay gate instead of the $\overline{10}$-ns tap. This way, when the flip-flop "looks back" 20 ns from the negative edge of $\overline{C_{pD}}$ it will see a HIGH on *J*, allowing the toggle operation to occur.

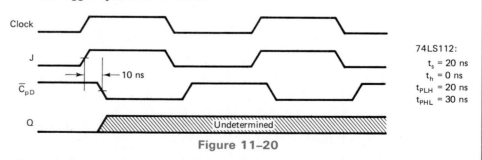

74LS112:

$t_s = 20$ ns
$t_h = 0$ ns
$t_{PLH} = 20$ ns
$t_{PHL} = 30$ ns

Figure 11–20

EXAMPLE 11–6

The repetitive waveforms shown in Figure 11–21b are input to a 7474 D flip-flop shown in Figure 11–21a. Because of poor timing, *Q* never goes HIGH. Add a delay gate to correct the timing problem. (Assume that rise, fall, and propagation delay times are 0 ns.)

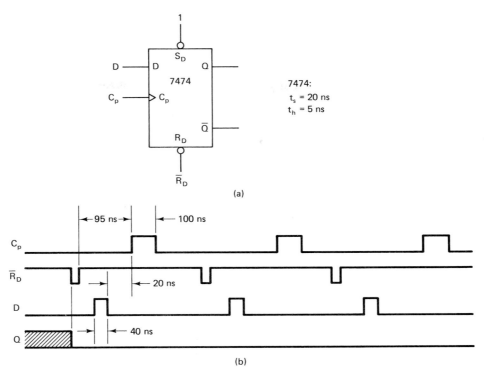

(a)

(b)

Figure 11–21

Solution: Q never goes HIGH because the 40-ns HIGH pulse on D does not occur at the positive edge of C_p. Delaying the D waveform by 30 ns will move D to the right far enough to fulfill the necessary setup and hold times to allow the flip-flop to get Set at every positive edge of C_p as shown in Figure 11–22. (D_D is the delayed D waveform, which has been shifted to the right by 30 ns to correct the timing problem.)

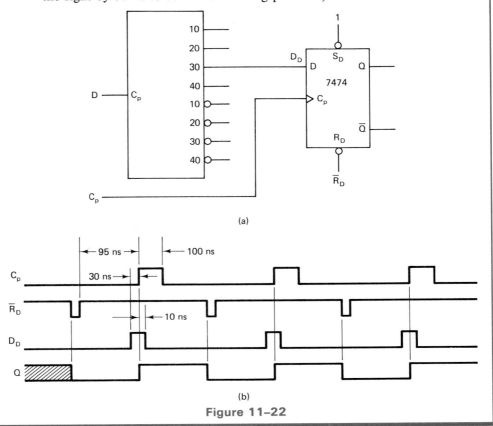

(a)

(b)

Figure 11–22

11–2 AUTOMATIC RESET

Often it is advantageous to automatically Reset (or Set) all resettable (or settable) devices as soon as power is first applied to a digital circuit. In the case of resetting flip-flops, we want a LOW voltage level (0) present at the $\overline{R_D}$ inputs for a short duration immediately following "power-up" but then after a short time (usually a few microseconds), we want the $\overline{R_D}$ line to return to a HIGH (1) level so that the flip-flops can start their synchronous operations.

To implement such an operation, how about using a series RC circuit to charge a capacitor that is initially discharged (0). A short time after the power-up voltage is applied to the RC circuit and the flip-flop's V_{cc}, the capacitor will charge up to a value high enough to be considered a HIGH (1) by the $\overline{R_D}$ input.

Basic electronic theory states that "in a series RC circuit, the capacitor becomes almost fully charged after a time equal to the product $5RC$."

This means that in Figure 11–23a the capacitor (which is initially discharged via the internal resistance of the $\overline{R_D}$ terminal) will begin to charge toward the 5-V level through R as soon as the switch is closed.

Before the capacitor reaches the HIGH-level threshold of the 74LS76 (approximately 2.0 V) the temporary LOW on the $\overline{R_D}$ terminal will cause the flip-flop to Reset. As soon as the capacitor charges to above 2.0 V, the $\overline{R_D}$ terminal will see a HIGH, allowing the flip-flop to perform its normal synchronous operations. The waveforms that will appear on the V_{cc} and $\overline{R_D}$ lines as the power switch is closed and opened are shown in Figure 11–23b.

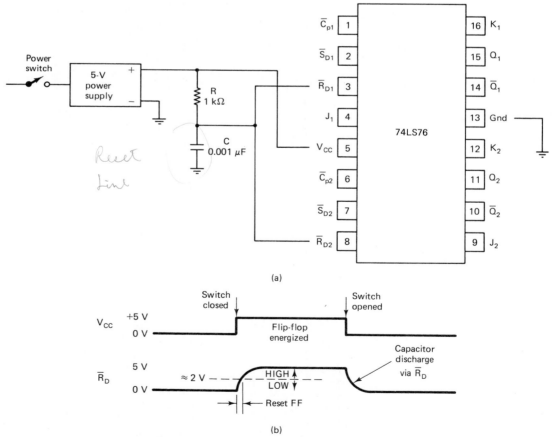

Figure 11–23 Automatic power-up Reset for a J-K flip-flop: (a) circuit connections; (b) waveforms.

This automatic resetting scheme can be used in circuits employing single or multiple resettable ICs. Depending on the device being Reset, the length of time that the Reset line is at a LOW level will be approximately 1 μs.

As you add more and more devices to the Reset line, the time duration of the LOW will decrease because of the additional charging paths supplied by the internal circuitry of the ICs. To increase the time, you can increase the capacitor to 0.01 μF, or to eliminate loading effects and create a sharp edge on the $\overline{R_D}$ line, a 7407 buffer could be inserted in series with the $\overline{R_D}$ input. Remember, there is a minimum allowable width for the LOW Reset pulse (≈ 25 ns for a 74LS76). We utilize the automatic Reset feature several times in Chapter 12 and 13.

11-3 SCHMITT TRIGGER ICs

A Schmitt trigger is a special type of integrated circuit that is used to transform slowly changing waveforms into sharply defined, jitter-free output signals. They are useful for changing clock edges that may have slow rise and fall times into straight vertical edges.

The Schmitt trigger employs a technique called *positive feedback* internally to speed up the level transitions, and also to introduce an effect called *hysteresis*. "Hysteresis" means that the switching threshold on a positive-going input signal is at a higher level than the switching threshold on a negative-going input signal (see Figure 11–24). This is useful for devices that have to ignore small amounts of "jitter" or electrical noise on input signals. Notice in Figure 11–24 that when the positive- and negative-going thresholds are exactly the same, as with standard gates, and a small amount of noise causes the input to "jitter" slightly, the output will switch back and forth several times until the input level is far above the threshold voltage.

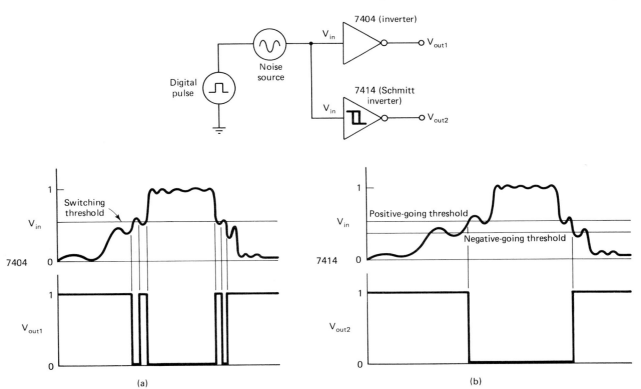

Figure 11–24 Edge-sharpening, jitter-free operation of a Schmitt trigger: (a) regular inverter; (b) Schmitt inverter.

Figure 11–24 illustrates the difference in the output waveforms for a standard 7404 inverter and a 7414 Schmitt trigger inverter. As you can see in Figure 11–24b, the output (V_{out2}) is an inverted, jitter-free pulse. On the other hand, just think if V_{out1} were fed into the $\overline{C_p}$ input of a 74LS76 hooked up as a toggle flip-flop; the flip-flop would toggle three times (three negative edges) instead of once as was intended.

The difference between the positive-going threshold and the negative-going threshold is defined as the hysteresis voltage. For the 7414, the positive-going threshold (V_{T+}) is typically 1.7 V and the negative-going threshold (V_{T-}) is typically 0.9 V, yielding a hysteresis voltage (ΔV_T) of 0.8 V. The small box symbol (⊓) inside the 7414 symbol is used to indicate that it is a Schmitt trigger inverter instead of a regular inverter.

The most important specification for Schmitt trigger devices is illustrated by use of a "transfer function" graph which is a plot of V_{out} versus V_{in}. From the transfer function, we can determine the HIGH- and LOW-level output voltages (typically 3.4 V and 0.2 V, the same as most TTL gates), as well as V_{T+}, V_{T-}, and ΔV_T.

Figure 11–25 shows the transfer function for the 7414. The transfer function graph is produced experimentally by using a variable voltage source at the input to the Schmitt and a voltmeter (VOM) at V_{in} and V_{out} as shown in Figure 11–26.

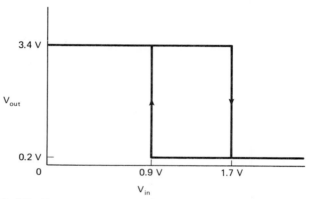

Figure 11–25   Transfer function for a 7414 Schmitt trigger inverter.

As the V_{in} of Figure 11–26 is increased from 0 V up toward 5 V, V_{out} will start out at approximately 3.4 V (1) and switch to 0.2 V (0) when V_{in} exceeds the positive-going threshold ($\approx$ 1.7 V). The output transition from HIGH to LOW is indicated in Figure 11–25 by the downward arrow. As V_{in} is increased up to 5 V, V_{out} remains at 0.2 V (0).

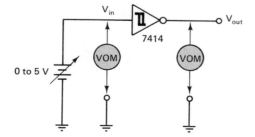

Figure 11–26   Circuit used to experimentally produce a Schmitt trigger transfer function.

As the input voltage is then decreased down toward 0 V, V_{out} will remain LOW until the negative-going threshold is passed ($\approx$ 0.9 V). At that point the output will switch up to 3.4 V (1), as indicated by the upward arrow in Figure 11–25. As V_{in} continues to 0 V, V_{out} remains HIGH at 3.4 V. The hysteresis in this case is 1.7 V − 0.9 V = 0.8 V.

The following four examples illustrate the operation of Schmitt triggers.

EXAMPLE 11-7

Let's use the Schmitt trigger to convert a small signal sine wave (E_s) into a square wave (V_{out}).

Solution: The diode is used to short the negative 4 V from E_s to ground to protect the Schmitt input, as shown in Figure 11-27a. The 1 kΩ-resistor will limit the current through the diode when it is conducting. [$I_{diode} = (4 - 0.7$ V)/1 kΩ = 3.3 mA, which is well within the rating of most silicon diodes.]

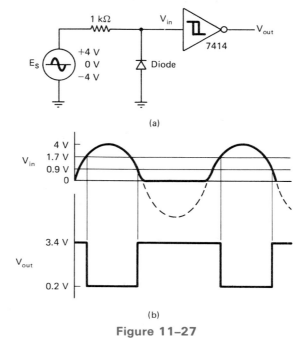

(a)

(b)

Figure 11-27

Also, the HIGH-level input current to the Schmitt (I_{IH}) is only 40 μA, causing a voltage drop of 40 μA $\times$ 1 kΩ = 0.04 V when V_{in} is HIGH. (We can assume that 0.04 V is negligible compared to +4.0 V.)

The input to the Schmitt will therefore be a half-wave signal with a 4.0-V peak. The output will be a square wave, as shown in Figure 11-27b.

EXAMPLE 11-8

The V_{in} waveform to a 74132 Schmitt trigger NAND gate is given in Figure 11-29.

74132

V_{in} ──── V_{out} Figure 11-28

(a) Sketch the V_{out} waveform. (The 74132 has the same voltage specifications as the 7414.)

(b) Determine the duty cycle of the output waveform (the duty cycle is defined as

$$\frac{\text{time HIGH}}{\text{time HIGH} + \text{time LOW}} \times 100\%).$$

Solution: **(a)** The V_{out} waveform is shown in Figure 11–29.

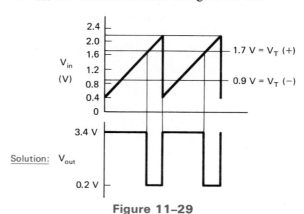

Figure 11–29

(b) V_{out} stays **HIGH** while V_{in} increases from 0.4 V to 1.7 V, for a change of 1.3 V. V_{out} stays **LOW** while V_{in} increases from 1.7 V to 2.2 V, for a change of 0.5 V. Since the input voltage increases linearly with respect to time, the change in V_{in} is proportional to time duration, so

$$\text{duty cycle} = \frac{1.3 \text{ V}}{1.3 \text{ V} + 0.5 \text{ V}} \times 100\% = 72.2\%$$

EXAMPLE 11–9

Sketch V_{out} of a 7414 given the V_{in} waveform shown in Figure 11–31.

Figure 11–30

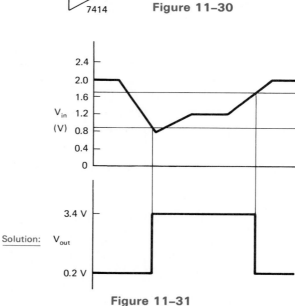

Figure 11–31

EXAMPLE 11–10

Draw and completely label the V_{out} versus V_{in} transfer function for the Schmitt trigger device whose V_{in} and V_{out} waveforms are given in Figure 11–32.

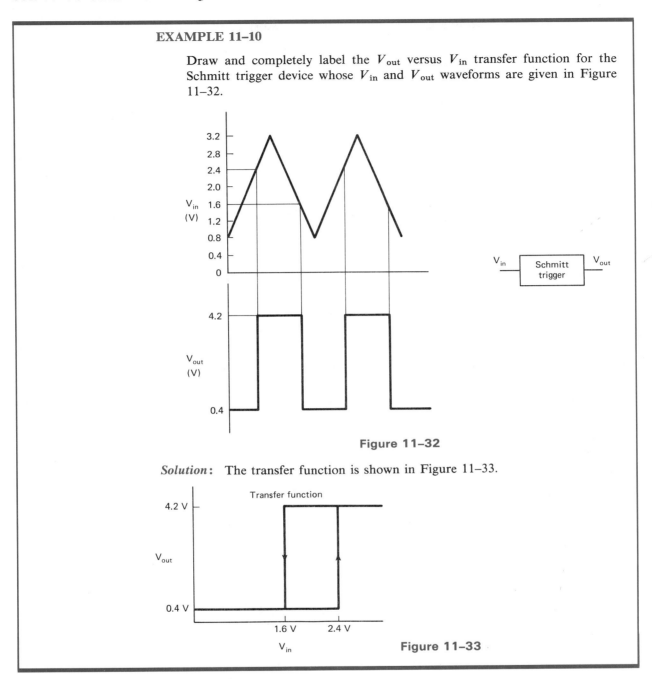

Figure 11–32

Solution: The transfer function is shown in Figure 11–33.

Figure 11–33

11–4 SWITCH DEBOUNCING

Quite often, mechanical switches are used in the design of digital circuits. Unfortunately, however, most switches exhibit a phenomenon called *switch bounce*. Switch bounce is the action that occurs when a mechanical switch is opened or closed. For example, when the contacts of a switch are closed together, the electrical and mechanical connection is first made, but due to a slight springing action of the contacts, they will bounce back open, then close, then open, then close repeatedly until they finally settle down in the closed position. This bouncing action will typically take place for as long as 50 ms.

A typical connection for a single-pole, single-throw switch is shown in Figure 11–34. This is a poor design because if we expect the toggle to operate only once when we close the switch, we will be out of luck because of switch bounce. Why do I say that? Let's look at the waveform at $\overline{C_p}$ to see what actually happens when a switch is closed.

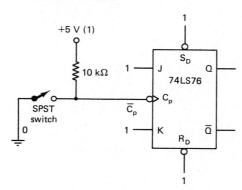

Figure 11–34   Switch used as a clock input to a toggle flip-flop.

Figure 11–35 shows that $\overline{C_p}$ will receive several LOW pulses each time the switch is closed instead of the single pulse that we expect.

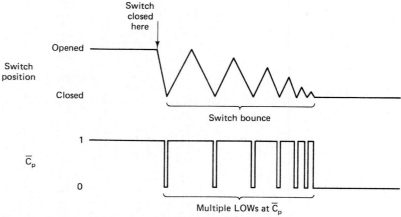

Figure 11–35   Waveform at point $\overline{C_p}$ for Figure 11–34.

(The 10kΩ pull-up resistor in Figure 11–34 is necessary to hold the voltage level at $\overline{C_p}$ up close to +5 V while the switch is open. If the pull-up resistor were not used, the voltage at $\overline{C_p}$ with the switch open would be undetermined; but *with* the 10kΩ, and realizing that the current into the $\overline{C_p}$ terminal is negligible, the level at the $\overline{C_p}$ terminal will be held at approximately +5 V while the switch is open.)

There are several ways to eliminate the effects of switch bounce. If you need to debounce a single-pole, single-throw switch or pushbutton, the Schmitt trigger scheme shown in Figure 11–36 can be used. With the switch open, the capacitor will be charged to +5 V (1), keeping $V_{out} = 0$. When the switch is closed, the capacitor will discharge rapidly to zero via the 100-Ω current-limiting resistor, making V_{out} equal to 1. Then, as the switch bounces, the capacitor will repeatedly try to charge slowly back up to a HIGH, then discharge rapidly to zero. The *RC* charging time constant (10 kΩ × 0.47 μF) is long enough that the capacitor will not get the chance to charge up high enough (above V_{T+}) before the switch bounces back to the closed position. This keeps V_{out} equal to 1.

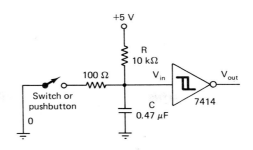

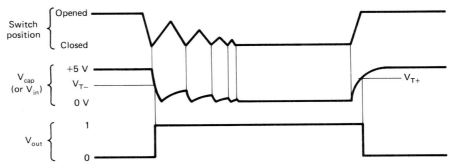

Figure 11-36 Debouncing a single-pole, single-throw switch or pushbutton.

When the switch is reopened, the capacitor is allowed to charge all the way up to +5 V. When it crosses V_{T+}, V_{out} will switch to 0, as shown in Figure 11-36. The result is that by closing the switch or pushbutton once, *you will get only a single pulse at the output even though the switch is bouncing*.

To debounce single-pole, double-throw switches, a different method is required, as illustrated in Figures 11-37 and 11-38. The single-pole, double throw switch shown in Figure 11-37a actually has three positions: (1) position A, (2) in between position A and position B while it is making its transition, and (3) position B. The cross-NAND debouncer works very similar to the cross-NAND *S-R* flip-flop presented in Figure 10-2.

When the switch is in position A, OUT will be Set (1). When the switch is moved to position B, it bounces, causing OUT to Reset, Hold, Reset, Hold, Reset, Hold repeatedly until the switch stops bouncing and settles into position B. From

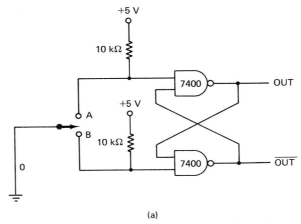

(a)

Figure 11-37 (a) Cross-NAND method of debouncing a single-pole, double-throw switch;

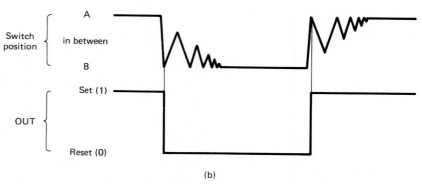

(b)

Figure 11–37 (Continued) (b) waveforms for part (a).

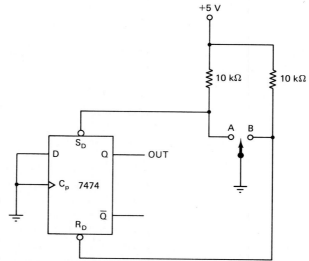

Figure 11–38 *D* flip-flop method of debouncing a single-pole, double-throw switch.

the time the switch first touched position B until it is returned to position A, OUT will be Reset even though the switch is bouncing.

When the switch is returned to position A it will bounce, causing OUT to be Set, Hold, Set, Hold, Set, Hold repeatedly until the switch stops bouncing. In this case, OUT will be Set, and remain Set, from the moment the switch first touched position A, even though the switch is bouncing.

Figure 11–38 shows another way to debounce a single-pole, double-throw switch using a 7474 *D* flip-flop. (Actually, any flip-flop with asynchronous $\overline{S_D}$ and $\overline{R_D}$ inputs can be used.)

The waveforms created from Figure 11–38 will look the same as Figure 11–37b. As the switch is moved to position A but is still bouncing, the flip-flop will Set, Hold, Set, Hold, Set, Hold repeatedly until the switch settles into position A, keeping the flip-flop Set. When it is moved to position B, the flip-flop will Reset, Hold, Reset, Hold, and so on, until it settles down, keeping the flip-flop Reset.

11–5 SIZING PULL-UP RESISTORS

By the way, how do we know what size pull-up resistors to use in circuits like the one in Figure 11–38? Remember, the object of the pull-up resistor is to keep a terminal at a HIGH level when it would normally be at a float (not 1 or 0) level. In Figure

11–38 when the switch is *between* points A and B, current will flow down through the 10-kΩ resistor to $\overline{S_D}$. I_{IH} for $\overline{S_D}$ is 80 μA. This causes a voltage drop of 80 μA × 10 kΩ = 0.8 V, leaving 4.2 V at $\overline{S_D}$, which is well within the HIGH specificiations of the 7474.

You may ask: Why not just make the pull-up resistor real small to minimize the voltage drop across it? Well, when the switch is in position A or B, we have a direct connection to ground. If the resistor is too small, we will have excessive current and high power consumption, when a 10 kΩ or larger resistor will work just fine. So check the I_{IH} and V_{IH} values in a data book and keep within their ratings. Usually, a 10-kΩ pull-up resistor is a good size for most digital circuits.

When you have to come up with a pull-down resistor (to keep a floating terminal LOW) a much smaller resistor is required because I_{IL} is typically much higher than I_{IH}. For example, if I_{IL} = −1.6 mA and a 100-Ω pull-down resistor is used, the voltage across the resistor is 0.160 V, which will be interpretted as a LOW. One concern of using a pull-down resistor is the high power dissipation of the resistor.

EXAMPLE 11–11

Determine the power dissipation of the 10-kΩ pull-up resistors used in Figure 11–37a. Also, determine the HIGH-level voltage at the input to the NAND gates.

Solution: The specs for a 7400 NAND from a TTL data manual are:

I input Low I_{IL} = 1.6 mA max.
I input high I_{IH} = 40 μA max. } You can review these
V_{IL} = 0.8 V max. } terms in Chapter 9.
V_{IH} = 2.0 V min.

When the switch is *between* positions A and B, I_{IH} will flow from the +5 V, through the 10-kΩ resistor, into the NAND. The power dissipation

$$P = I^2 \times R$$
$$= (40 \text{ μA})^2 \times 10 \text{ kΩ}$$
$$= 16 \text{ μW}$$

The high-level input voltage

$$V = V_{cc} - I_{IH} \times R$$
$$= 5 \text{ V} - 40 \text{ μA} \times 10 \text{ kΩ}$$
$$= 4.6 \text{ V}$$

The 4.6-V HIGH-level input voltage is above the 2.0-V V_{IH} limit given in the specs, and 16 μW is negligible for most applications.

When the switch is moved to either A or B, the power dissipation in the resistor is

$$P = \frac{E^2}{R}$$
$$= \frac{5 \text{ V}^2}{10 \text{ kΩ}}$$
$$= 2.5 \text{ mW}$$

The value 2.5 mW is still negligible for most applications. If not, increase the size of the 10-kΩ pull-up resistor and recalculate for the HIGH-level input voltage and power dissipation. As long as you keep the HIGH-level input voltage above the specified limit of 2.0 V, the circuit will operate properly.

11–6 PRACTICAL INPUT AND OUTPUT CONSIDERATIONS

Before designing and building the practical digital circuits in the next few chapters, let's study some circuit designs for (1) a simple 5-V power supply, (2) a clock to drive synchronous trigger inputs, and (3) circuit connections for LED interfacing to the outputs of integrated-circuit chips.

A 5-V Power Supply

For now, we limit our discussion to the TTL family of integrated circuits. From the data manual we can see that TTL requires a constant supply voltage of 5.0 V ± 5%. Also, the total supply current requirement into the V_{cc} terminal ranges from 20 to 100 mA for most TTL ICs.

For the power supply, the 78XX series of integrated-circuit voltage regulators are inexpensive and easy to use. To construct a regulated 5.0-V supply, we use the 7805 (the 05 designates 5 V; a 7808 would designate an 8.0-V supply). The 7805 is a three-terminal device (input, ground, output) capable of supplying 5.0 V ± 0.2% at 1000 mA. Figure 11–39 shows how a 7805 voltage regulator is used in conjunction with an ac-to-dc rectifier circuit.

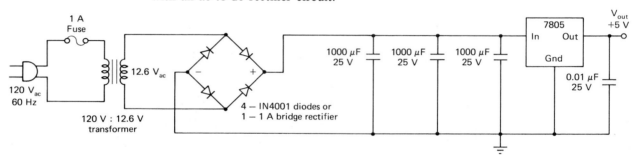

Figure 11–39 Complete 5-V 1-A TTL power supply.

In Figure 11–39 the 12.6 V ac rms is rectified by the diodes (or a four-terminal bridge rectifier) into a full-wave dc of approximately 20 V. The 3000 μF of capacitance is required to hold the dc level into the 7805 at a high, steady level. The 7805 will automatically decrease the 20-V dc input to a solid, ripple-free 5.0 V dc output.

The 0.01-μF capacitor is recommended by TTL manufacturers for "decoupling" the power supply. Tantalum capacitors work best and should be mounted as close as possible to the V_{cc}-to-ground pins on every TTL IC used in your circuit. Their size should be between 0.01 and 0.1 μF with a voltage rating $\geq$ 5 V. The purpose of the capacitor is to eliminate the effects of voltage spikes created from the internal TTL switching and electrostatic noise generated on the power and ground lines.

The 7805 will get very hot when your circuit draws more than 0.5 A. In that case it should be mounted on a heat sink to help dissipate the heat.

A 60-Hz Clock

Figure 11–40 shows a circuit design for a simple 60-Hz TTL-level (0 to 5 V) clock that can be powered from the same transformer used in Figure 11–39 and used to drive the clock inputs to our synchronous ICs. Our electric power industry supplies us with accurate 60-Hz ac voltages. It is a simple task to reduce the voltage to usable levels and still maintain a 60-Hz [60-pulse-per-second (pps)] signal.

From analog electronics courses you may remember that a zener diode will conduct normally in the forward-biased direction, and in the reverse-biased direction it will start conducting when a voltage level equal to its "reverse zener breakdown" rating is reached (4.3 V for the IN749).

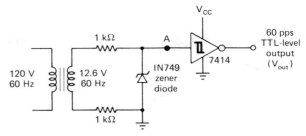

Figure 11-40   Accurate 60-Hz TTL-level clock pulse generator.

The 1-kΩ resistors are required to limit the zener current to reasonable levels. Figure 11-41 shows the waveform that will appear at point A and V_{out} of Figure 11-40. The zener "breaks down" at 4.3 V, which is high enough for a one-level input to the Schmitt trigger but not too high to burn out the chip. The V_{out} waveform will be an accurate 60-pulse-per-second, approximately 50% duty cycle square wave. As we will see in Chapter 12, this frequency can easily be divided down to 1 pulse per second by using toggle flip-flops. One pulse per second is handy because it is slow enough to see on visual displays (like LEDs) and accurate enough to use as a trigger pulse on a digital clock.

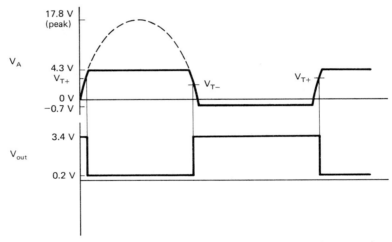

Figure 11-41   Voltage waveform at point A and V_{out} of Figure 11-40.

Driving Light-Emitting Diodes

Light-emitting diodes (LEDs) are good devices to visually display a HIGH (1) or LOW (0) digital state. A typical red LED will drop 1.7 V cathode to anode when forward biased (positive anode-to-cathode voltage) and will illuminate with 10 to 20 mA flowing through it. In the reverse-biased direction (zero or negative anode-to-cathode voltage), the LED will block current flow and not illuminate.

Since it takes 10 to 20 mA to illuminate an LED, we may have trouble driving it with a TTL output. From the TTL data manual, we can determine that most ICs can sink (0-level output) a lot more current than they can source (1-level output). Typically, the maximum sink current, I_{OL}, is 16 mA and the maximum source current, I_{OH}, is only 0.4 mA. Therefore, we better use a LOW level (0) to turn on our LED instead of a HIGH level.

Figure 11-42 shows how we can drive an LED from the output of a TTL circuit (a *J-K* flip-flop in this case). The *J-K* flip-flop is set up in the toggle mode so that Q will flip states once each second.

When Q is LOW (0 V), the LED is forward biased and current will flow

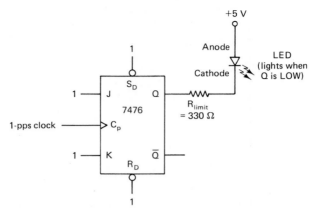

Figure 11–42 Driving an LED.

through the LED and resistor and sink into the Q output. The 330-Ω resistor is required to limit the series current to 10 mA [$I = (5\ \text{V} - 1.7\ \text{V})/330\ \Omega = 10$ mA]. 10 mA into the LOW-level Q output will not burn out the flip-flop. If, however, we were trying to turn the LED on with a HIGH-level output, we would turn the LED around and connect the cathode to ground. But 10 mA would exceed the limit of I_{OH} on the 7476 and burn it out.

GLOSSARY

Active clock edge: A clock edge is the point in time where the waveform is changing from HIGH to LOW (negative edge) or LOW to HIGH (positive edge). The *active* clock edge is the edge (either positive or negative) used to trigger a synchronous device to accept input digital states.

Ac waveforms: Test waveforms that are supplied by IC manufacturers for design engineers to determine timing sequence and measurement points for such quantities as setup, hold, and propagation delay times.

Automatic reset: A scheme used to automatically Set or Reset all storage ICs (usually flip-flops) to a Set or Reset condition when power is first applied to them so that their starting condition can always be determined.

Duty cycle: The ratio of the length of time a periodic wave is "HIGH" versus the total period of the wave.

Float: A condition in which an input or output line in a circuit is neither HIGH nor LOW because it is not directly connected to a high or low voltage level.

Hold time: The length of time *after* the active clock edge that the input data to be recognized (usually, J and K) must be held stable to ensure its recognition.

Hysteresis: In digital Schmitt trigger ICs, hysteresis is the difference in voltage between the positive-going switching threshold and the negative-going switching threshold at the input.

Jitter: A term used in digital electronics to describe a waveform that has some degree of electrical noise on it, causing it to rise and fall slightly between and during level transitions.

Positive feedback: A technique employed by Schmitt triggers that involves taking a small sample of the output of a circuit and feeding it back into the input of the same circuit to increase its switching speed and introduce hysteresis.

Power-up: The term used to describe the initial events or states that occur when power is first applied to an IC or digital system.

Propagation delay: The length of time that it takes for an input level change to pass through an IC and appear as a level change at the output.

Pull-down resistor: A resistor with one end connected to a LOW voltage level and the other end connected to an input or output line so that when that line is in the float condition (not HIGH or LOW), the voltage level on that line will, instead, be "pulled down" to a LOW state.

Pull-up resistor: A resistor with one end connected to a HIGH voltage level, and the other end connected to an input or output line, so that when that line is in a float condition (not HIGH or LOW), the voltage level on that line will instead be "pulled up" to a HIGH state.

Race condition: The condition that occurs when a digital input level (1 or 0) is changing states at the same time as the active clock edge of a synchronous device, making the input level at that time undetermined.

RC circuit: A simple series circuit consisting of a resistor and a capacitor used to provide time delay.

Rectifier: An electronic device used to convert an ac voltage into a dc voltage.

Ripple: A small fluctuation in the output voltage of a power supply which is the result of poor filtering and regulation.

Schmitt trigger: A circuit used in digital electronics to provide ultrafast level transitions and introduce hysteresis for improving jittery or slowly-rising waveforms.

Setup time: The length of time *prior to* the active clock edge that the input data to be recognized (usually, J and K) must be held stable to ensure its recognition.

SPST switch: The abbreviation for single pole, single throw. A SPST switch is used to simply make or break contact in a single electrical line.

Switch bounce: An undesirable characteristic of most switches because they will physically make and break contact several times (bounce) each time they are opened or closed.

Threshold: The exact voltage level at the input to a digital IC that causes it to switch states. In Schmitt trigger ICs, there are two different threshold levels: the positive-going threshold (LOW to HIGH) and the negative-going threshold (HIGH to LOW).

Transfer function: A plot of V_{out} versus V_{in} which is used to graphically determine the operating specifications of a Schmitt trigger.

Voltage regulator: An electronic device or circuit that is used to adjust and control a voltage to remain at a constant level.

Zener breakdown: The voltage across the terminals of a zener diode when it is conducting current in the reverse-biased direction.

REVIEW QUESTIONS

Section 11–1

11–1. A *race* condition occurs when the Q-output of a flip-flop changes at the same time as its clock input (true or false)?

11–2. *Setup time* is the length of time that the clock input must be held stable before its active transition (true or false)?

11–3. Describe what manufacturers mean when they specify a *hold time* of 0 nanoseconds for a flip-flop. *Input level don't have to be held beyond the active clock.*

11–4. The abbreviation t_{PHL} is used to specify the _____ *Propagation delay* of an IC from input-to-output. The letters HL in that abbreviation refer to the _____ (input, output) waveform changing from HIGH-to-LOW.

11–5. Under what circumstances would a digital circuit design require a delay gate? *To enable proper set-up and hold time.*

Sections 11–2 and 11–3

11–6. In an automatic power-up Reset R-C circuit, the voltage across the _____ (resistor, capacitor) provides the initial LOW to the $\overline{R}_D$ inputs.

11–7. The input voltage to a Schmitt trigger IC has to cross two different switching points called the _____ *Pos going threshold* and the _____ *Neg going threshold*. The voltage differential between these two switching points is called the _____ *hysteresis*.

11–8. A Schmitt trigger IC is capable of "cleaning up" a square wave that may have a small amount of noise on it. Briefly explain how it works.

11–9. The transfer function of a Schmitt trigger device graphically shows the relationship between the _____ *input* and _____ *output* voltages.

Sections 11–4 through 11–6 *by spring action, cause false triggering.*

11–10. What is the cause of switch bounce, and why is it harmful in digital circuits?

11–11. What size resistor is better suited for a pull-up resistor; 10KΩ or 100Ω?

11–12. What 78XX-series IC voltage regulator could be used to build an inexpensive 12-volt power supply? *7812*

11–13. The zener diode serves two purposes in the pulse generator design in Figure 11–40. What are those purposes? *cut off neg cycle of sine wave, limit pos to 4.3V*

11–14. Why are LEDs usually connected as active-LOW indicator lights instead of active-HIGH? *because the IC components to can sink more current than they can source.*

PROBLEMS

11–1. Sketch the Q output waveform for a 74LS76 given the input waveforms shown in Figure P11–1 [use $t_s(L) = 20$ ns, $t_s(H) = 20$ ns, $t_h(L) = 0$ ns, $t_h(H) = 0$ ns, $t_{PLH} = 0$ ns, $t_{PHL} = 0$ ns].

Figure P11–1

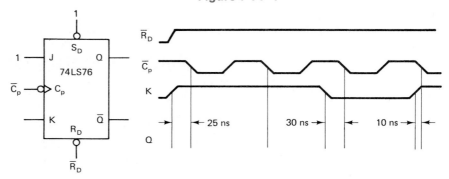

11–2. Repeat Problem 11–1 for the waveforms shown in Figure P11–2.

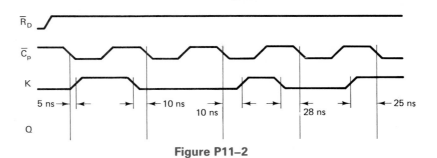

Figure P11–2

11–3. Using actual specifications for a 74LS76, label the propagation delay times on the waveforms shown in Figure P11–3.

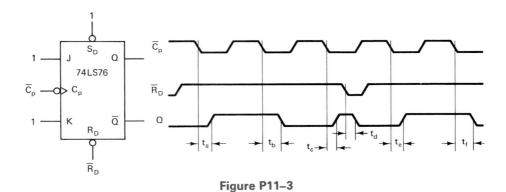

Figure P11–3

11–4. Repeat Problem 11–3 for the waveforms shown in Figure P11–4.

Figure P11–4

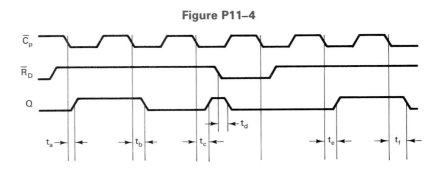

11–5. Describe the problem that may arise when using the 7432 OR gate to delay the clock signal into the flip-flop circuit of Figure 11–14.

11–6. Sketch the output at $\overline{C_{pD}}$ and Q for the flip-flop circuit shown in Figure P11–6. (Ignore propagation delays in the 74LS76.)

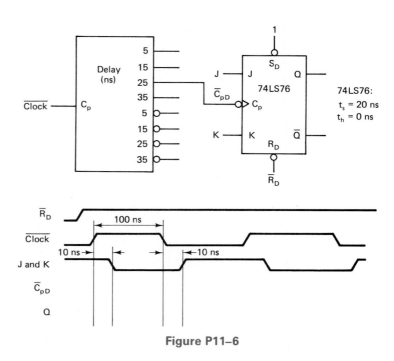

Figure P11–6

11–7. Redraw the waveforms given in Problem 11–6 if the 35-ns delay tap is used instead of the 25-ns tap.

11–8. Sketch the output at D_D and Q for the flip-flop circuit shown in Figure P11–8. (Ignore propagation delays in the 7474.)

11–9. One particular Schmitt trigger inverter has a positive-going threshold of 1.9 V and a negative-going threshold of 0.7 V. Its V_{OH} (typical) is 3.6 V and V_{OL} (typical) is 0.2 V. Sketch the transfer function (V_{out} versus V_{in}) for that Schmitt trigger.

Figure P11–8

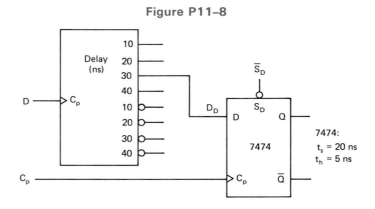

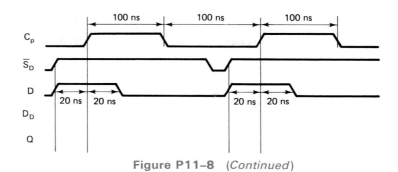

Figure P11–8 (*Continued*)

11–10. If the input waveform (V_{in}) shown in Figure P11–10, is fed into the Schmitt trigger described in Problem 11–9, sketch its output waveform (V_{out}).

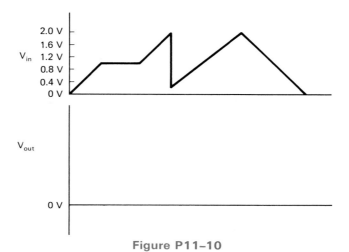

Figure P11–10

11–11. If the wave shown in Figure P11–11, is fed into a 7414 Schmitt trigger inverter, sketch V_{out} and determine the duty cycle of V_{out}.

Figure P11–11

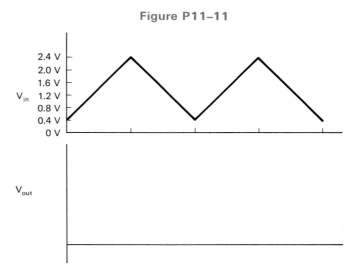

11–12.   If the V_{in} and V_{out} waveforms shown in Figure P11–12 are observed on a Schmitt trigger device, determine its characteristics and sketch the transfer function (V_{out} versus V_{in}).

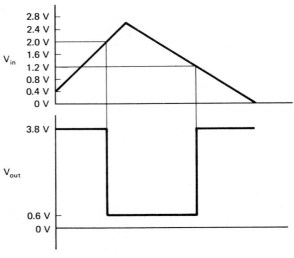

Figure P11-12

12

Counter Circuits and Applications

OBJECTIVES

Upon completion of this chapter, you should be able to:

- Use timing diagrams for the analysis of sequential logic circuits.
- Design any modulus ripple counter and frequency divider using *J-K* flip-flops.
- Describe the difference between ripple counters and synchronous counters.
- Solve various counter design applications using 4-bit counter ICs and external gating.
- Connect seven-segment LEDs and BCD decoders to form multidigit numeric displays.
- Cascade counter ICs to provide for higher counting and frequency division.

INTRODUCTION

Now that we understand the operation of flip-flops and latches, we can apply our knowledge to the design and application of sequential logic circuits. One common application of sequential logic arrives from the need to count events and time the duration of various processes. These applications are called "sequential" because they follow a predetermined sequence of digital states and are triggered by a timing pulse or clock.

To be useful in digital circuitry and microprocessor systems, counters normally count in binary and can be made to stop or recycle to the beginning at any time. In a recycling counter, the number of different binary states defines the modulus (MOD) of the counter. For example, a counter that counts from 0 to 7 is called a

301

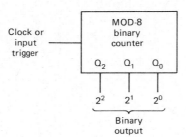

Figure 12–1 Simplified block diagram of a MOD-8 binary counter.

MOD-8 counter. For a counter to count from 0 to 7 it must have three binary outputs and one clock trigger input, as shown in Figure 12–1.

Normally, each binary output will come from the Q output of a flip-flop. Flip-flops are used because they can hold, or remember, a binary state until the next clock or trigger pulse comes along. The count sequence of a 1 to 7 binary counter is shown in Table 12–1 and Figure 12–2.

TABLE 12–1

Binary Count Sequence of a MOD-8
Binary Counter

Q_2	Q_1	Q_0	Count
0	0	0	0
0	0	1	1
0	1	0	2
0	1	1	3
1	0	0	4
1	0	1	5
1	1	0	6
1	1	1	7
0	0	0	0
0	0	1	1
0	1	0	2
0	1	1	3
	Etc.		

eight different binary states

Before studying counter circuits, let's analyze some circuits containing logic gates with flip-flops to get a feeling for the analytical process involved in determining the output waveforms of sequential circuits.

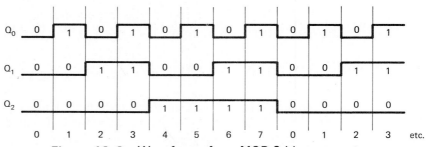

Figure 12–2 Waveforms for a MOD-8 binary counter.

12–1   ANALYSIS OF SEQUENTIAL CIRCUITS

To get our minds thinking in terms of sequential analysis, let's look at the following example that combines regular logic gates with flip-flops and whose operation is dictated by a specific sequence of input waveforms as shown in Example 12–1.

EXAMPLE 12-1

The waveforms shown are applied to the inputs at A and C_p. Sketch the resultant waveform at D, Q, $\overline{Q}$, and X. (The 7474 shown in Figure 12–3 is a positive edge-triggered D flip-flop).

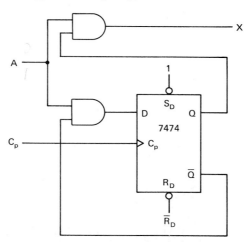

Figure 12-3

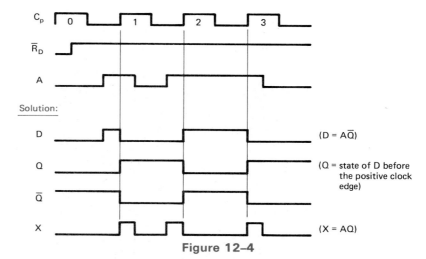

Figure 12-4

1. $Q = 0$, $\overline{Q} = 1$ during the 0 period because of $\overline{R_D}$.

2. D is equal to $A\overline{Q}$; X is equal to AQ (therefore, the level at D and X will change whenever the inputs to the AND gates change regardless of the state of the input clock).

3. At the positive edge of pulse 1, D is HIGH, so Q will go HIGH and $\overline{Q}$ will go LOW and remain there until the positive edge of pulse 2.

4. During period 1, D will equal $A\overline{Q}$ and X will equal AQ as shown.

5. At the positive edge of pulse 2, D is LOW, so the flip-flop will Reset ($Q = 0$; $\overline{Q} = 1$) and remain there until the positive edge of pulse 3.

6. At the positive edge of pulse 3, D is HIGH, so the flip-flop will Set ($Q = 1$; $\overline{Q} = 0$).

EXAMPLE 12–2

Using the same circuit of Example 12–1, sketch the waveforms at D, Q, $\overline{Q}$, and X given the input waves shown below.

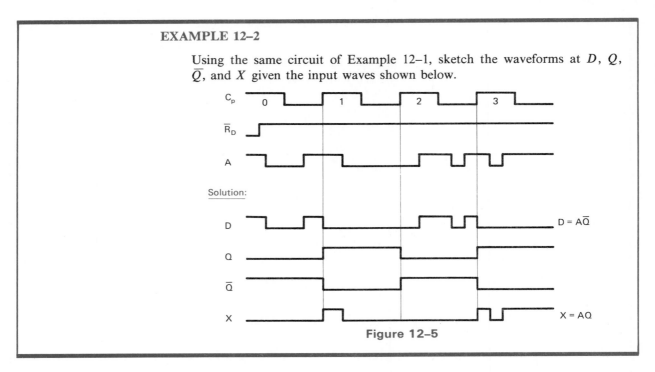

Figure 12–5

The timing analysis in Examples, 12–1 and 12–2 was done by observing the level on D prior to the positive clock edge and realizing that D follows the level of $A\overline{Q}$.

When a J-K flip-flop is used, we have to consider the level at J and K at the active clock edge as well as any asynchronous operations that may be taking place. Examples 12–3 and 12–4 illustrate the timing analysis of sequential circuits utilizing J-K flip-flops.

EXAMPLE 12–3

The following waveforms are applied to the inputs at A and $\overline{C_{p0}}$. Sketch the resultant waveforms at J_1, K_1, Q_0, and Q_1. (Notice that the clock input to the second flip-flop comes from Q_0. Also, $J_1 = AQ_1$, $K_1 = AQ_0$. Remember that the 74LS76 shown in Figure 12–6 is a negative edge-triggered flip-flop.)

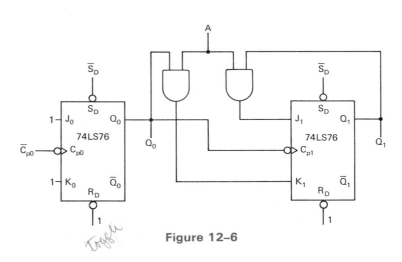

Figure 12–6

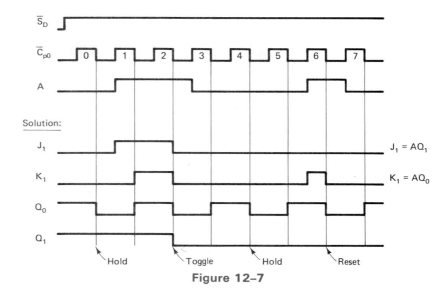

Figure 12-7

1. Since $J_0 = 1$ and $K_0 = 1$, then Q_0 will *toggle* at each negative edge of $\overline{C_{p\,0}}$.

2. The second flip-flop will be triggered at each negative edge of the Q_0 line.

3. The levels at J_1 and K_1 just prior to the negative edge of the Q_0 line will determine the synchronous operation of the second flip-flop.

4. After Q_0 and Q_1 are determined for each period, the new levels for J_1 and K_1 can be determined from $J_1 = AQ_1$ and $K_1 = AQ_0$.

EXAMPLE 12-4

Repeat Example 12-3 for the waveforms shown.

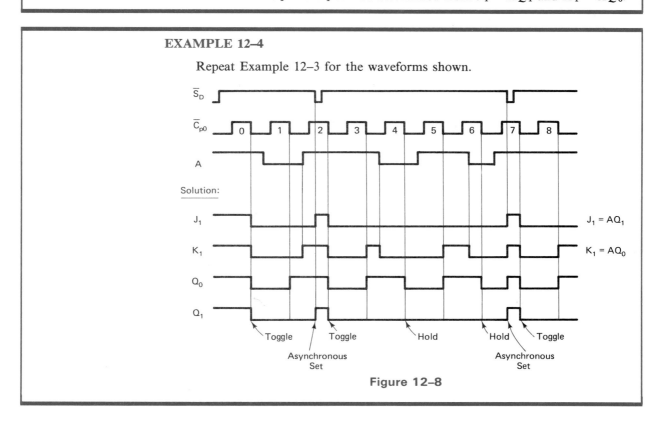

Figure 12-8

12–2 RIPPLE COUNTERS

Flip-flops can be used to form binary counters. The counter output waveforms discussed in the beginning of this chapter (Figure 12–2) could be generated by using three flip-flops cascaded together (cascaded means connecting the Q output of one flip-flop to the clock input of the next). Three flip-flops are needed to form a 3-bit counter (each flip-flop will represent a different power of 2: 2^2, 2^1, 2^0). With three flip-flops we can produce 2^3 different combinations of binary outputs ($2^3 = 8$). The eight different binary outputs from a 3-bit binary counter will be 000, 001, 010, 011, 100, 101, 110, 111.

If we have a 4-bit binary counter, we would count from 0000 up to 1111, which is 16 different binary outputs. As it turns out, we can determine the number of different binary output states (modulus) by using the following formula:

$$modulus = 2^N \qquad \text{where } N = \text{number of flip-flops}$$

To form a 3-bit binary counter, we cascade three *J-K* flip-flops, each operating in the *toggle mode* as shown in Figure 12–9. The clock input used to increment the binary count comes into the $\overline{C_p}$ input of the first flip-flop. Each flip-flop will toggle every time its clock input receives a HIGH-to-LOW edge.

Now, with the knowledge that we have gained by analyzing the sequential circuits in Section 12–1, it should be easy to determine the output waveforms of the 3-bit binary ripple counter of Figure 12–9.

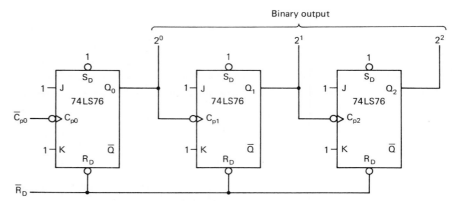

Figure 12–9 Three-bit binary ripple counter.

When we analyze the circuit and waveforms, we see that Q_0 toggles at each negative edge of $\overline{C_{p0}}$, Q_1 toggles at each negative edge of Q_0, and Q_2 toggles at each negative edge of Q_1. The result is that the outputs will "count" from 000 up to 111, then 000 to 111 repeatedly, as shown in Figure 12–10. The term "ripple" is derived from the fact that the input clock trigger is not connected to each flip-flop directly but instead has to propagate down through each flip-flop to reach the next.

For example, look at clock pulse 7. The negative edge of $\overline{C_{p0}}$ causes Q_0 to toggle LOW . . . which causes Q_1 to toggle LOW . . . which causes Q_2 to toggle LOW. There will definitely be a propagation delay between the time that $\overline{C_{p0}}$ goes LOW until Q_2 finally goes LOW. Because of this delay, ripple counters are called *asynchronous counters,* which means that each flip-flop is not triggered at exactly the same time.

Synchronous counters can be formed by driving each flip-flop's clock by the same clock input. Synchronous counters are more complicated, however, and will be covered after we have a thorough understanding of asynchronous ripple counters.

The propagation delay inherent in ripple counters places limitations on the maxi-

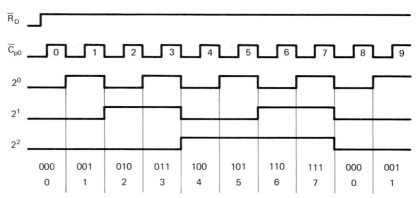

Figure 12–10 Waveforms generated from the 3-bit binary ripple counter.

mum frequency allowed by the input trigger clock. The reason is that if the input clock has an active trigger edge before the previous trigger edge has propagated through all the flip-flops, you will get an erroneous binary output.

Let's look at the 3-bit counter waveforms in more detail, now taking into account the propagation delays of the 74LS76 flip-flops. In reality, the 2^0 waveform will be delayed to the right ("skewed") by the propagation of the first flip-flop. The 2^1 waveform will be skewed to the right from the 2^0 waveform, and the 2^2 waveform will be skewed to the right from the 2^1 waveform. This is an accumulative effect that causes the 2^2 waveform to be skewed to the right of the original $\overline{C_{p0}}$ waveform by three propagation delays. (Remember, however, that the propagation delay for most flip-flops is in the 20-ns range, which will not hurt us until the input clock period is very short, 100 to 200 ns (5 to 10 MHz).) Figure 12–11 illustrates the effect of propagation delay on the output waveform.

From Figure 12–11 we can see that the length of time that it takes to change from binary 011 to 100 (3 to 4) will be

$$t_{PHL1} + t_{PHL2} + t_{PLH3} = 30 \text{ ns} + 30 \text{ ns} + 20 \text{ ns} = 80 \text{ ns}$$

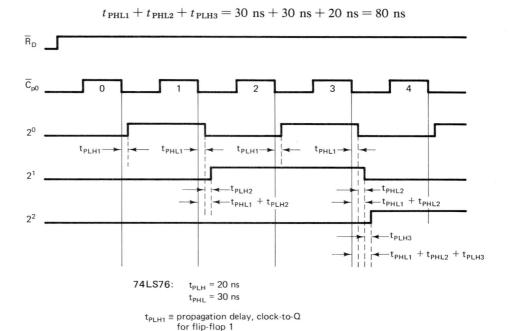

Figure 12–11 Effect of propagation delay on ripple counter outputs.

As we cascade more and more flip-flops to form higher modulus counters, the accumulative effect of the propagation delay becomes more of a problem.

A MOD-16 ripple counter can be built using four ($2^4 = 16$) flip-flops. Figures 12–12 and 12–13 show the circuit design and waveforms for a MOD-16 ripple counter. From the waveforms we can see that the 2^1 line toggles at every negative edge of the 2^0 line, the 2^2 line toggles at every negative edge of the 2^1 line, and so on down through each successive flip-flop. When the count reaches 15 (1111) the next negative edge of $\overline{C_{p0}}$ causes all four flip-flops to toggle and changes the count to 0 (0000).

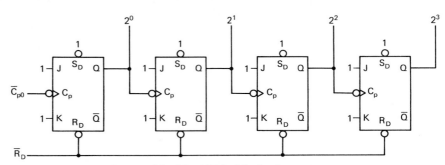

Figure 12–12 MOD-16 ripple counter.

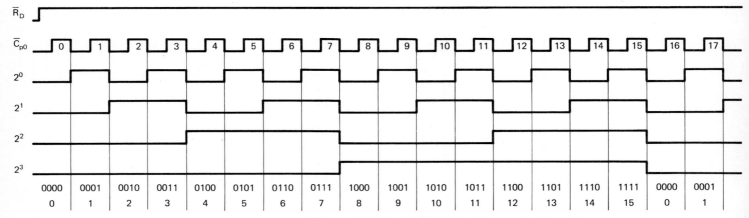

Figure 12–13 MOD-16 ripple counter waveforms.

Down-Counters

On occasion there is a need to count down in binary instead of counting up. To form a down-counter, simply take the binary outputs from the $\overline{Q}$ outputs instead of the Q outputs, as shown in Figure 12–14. The down-counter waveforms are shown in Figure 12–15.

When you compare the waveforms of the up-counter of Figure 12–10 to the down-counter of Figure 12–15, you can see that they are exact complements of each other. That is easy to understand because the binary output is taken from $\overline{Q}$ instead of Q.

12–3   DESIGN OF DIVIDE-BY-N COUNTERS

Counter circuits are also used as frequency dividers to reduce the frequency of periodic waveforms. For example, if we study the waveforms generated by the MOD-8 counter of Figure 12–10, we can see that the frequency of the 2^2 output line is one-eighth

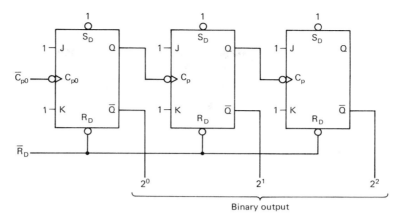

Figure 12–14   MOD-8 ripple down-counter.

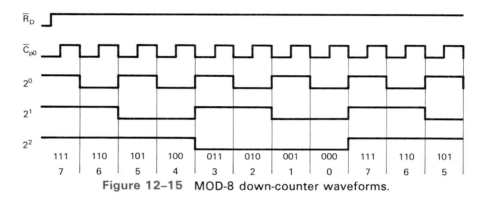

Figure 12–15   MOD-8 down-counter waveforms.

of the frequency of the $\overline{C_{p0}}$ input clock line. This concept is illustrated in the block diagram of Figure 12–16, assuming that the input frequency is 24 kHz. So as it turns out, a MOD-8 counter can be used as a divide-by-8 frequency divider and a MOD-16 can be used as a divide-by-16 frequency divider.

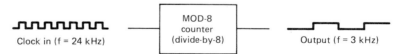

Figure 12–16   Block diagram of a divide-by-8 counter.

What if we need a divide-by-5 (MOD-5) counter? We can modify the MOD-8 counter so that when it reaches the number 5 (101) all flip-flops will be Reset. The new count sequence will be 0–1–2–3–4–0–1–2–3–4–0–etc. To get the counter to Reset at number 5 (binary 101), you will have to monitor the 2^0 and 2^2 lines and when they are both HIGH, put out a LOW Reset pulse to all flip-flops. Figure 12–17 shows a circuit that can do that for us.

As you can see, the inputs to the NAND Gate are connected to the 2^0 and 2^2 lines, so that when the number 5 (101) comes up, the NAND puts out a LOW level to Reset all flip-flops. The waveforms in Figure 12–18 illustrate the operation of the MOD-5 counter of Figure 12–17.

As we can see in Figure 12–18, the number 5 will appear at the outputs for a short duration, just long enough to Reset the flip-flops. The resulting short pulse on the 2^0 line is called a *glitch*. Do you think you could determine how long the glitch is? (Assume that the flip-flop is a 74LS76 and the NAND gate is a 7400.)

Since t_{PHL} of the NAND gate is 15 ns, it takes that long just to drive the $\overline{R_D}$

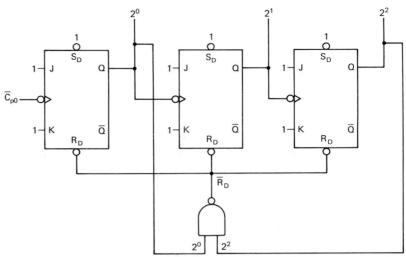

Figure 12–17   Connections to form a divide-by-5 (MOD-5) binary counter.

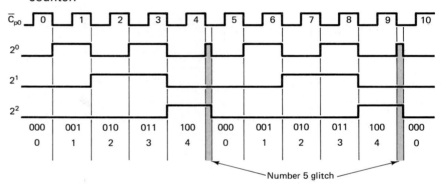

Figure 12–18   Waveforms for the MOD-5 counter.

inputs LOW. But then it also takes 30 ns (t_{PHL}) for the LOW on $\overline{R}_D$ to Reset the Q output to LOW. Therefore, the total length of the glitch is 45 ns. If the input clock period is in the microsecond range, then 45 ns is insignificant, but at extremely high clock frequencies that glitch could give us erroneous results.

Any modulus counter (divide-by-N counter) can be formed by using external gating to Reset at a predetermined number. The following examples illustrate the design of some other divide-by-N counters.

EXAMPLE 12–5

Design a MOD-6 ripple up-counter that can be manually Reset by an external pushbutton.

Solution: The ripple up-counter is shown in Figure 12–19. The count sequence will be 0–1–2–3–4–5. When 6 (binary 110) is reached, the output of the AND gate will go HIGH, causing the NOR gate to put a LOW on the $\overline{R}_D$ line, resetting all flip-flops to zero.

As soon as all outputs return to zero, the AND gate will go back to a LOW output, causing the NOR and $\overline{R}_D$ to return to a HIGH, allowing the counter to count again.

This cycle continues to repeat until the manual Reset pushbutton is pressed. The HIGH from the pushbutton will also cause the counter to Reset. The 100-Ω pull-down resistor will keep the input to the NOR gate LOW

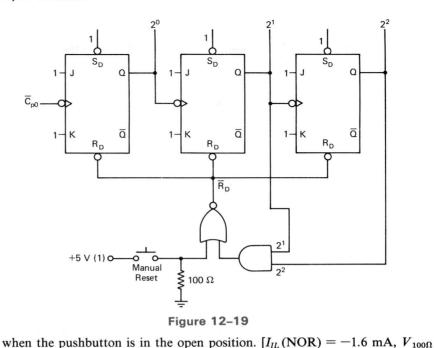

Figure 12–19

when the pushbutton is in the open position. $[I_{IL}(\text{NOR}) = -1.6 \text{ mA}, V_{100\Omega} = 1.6 \text{ mA} \times 100 \ \Omega = 0.160 \text{ V} \equiv \text{LOW}.]$

EXAMPLE 12–6

Design a MOD-10 ripple up-counter with a manual pushbutton Reset.

Solution: The ripple up-counter is shown in Figure 12–20. Four flip-flops are required to give us a possibility of $2^4 = 16$ binary states ($2^3 = 8$ would not be enough). We want to stop the count and automatically Reset when 10 (binary 1010) is reached. This is taken care of by the AND gate feeding into the NOR, making the $\overline{R}_D$ line go LOW when 10 is reached. The count sequence will be 0–1–2–3–4–5–6–7–8–9–0–1–etc., which is a MOD-10 up-counter.

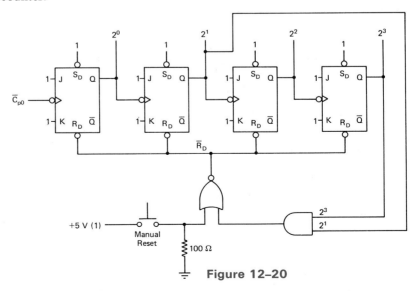

Figure 12–20

EXAMPLE 12–7

Design a MOD-6 down-counter with a manual pushbutton Reset (the count sequence should be 7–6–5–4–3–2–7–6–5–etc.)

Solution: The down-counter is shown in Figure 12–21. First, by pressing the manual Reset pushbutton, all flip-flops will Reset, making the counter outputs, taken from the $\overline{Q}$'s, to be 1 1 1. The count sequence that we want is 7–6–5–4–3–2, then Reset to 7 again when 1 is reached (binary 001). When 1 is reached, that is the first time that 2^1 and 2^2 are both LOW. The NOR gate connected to 2^1 and 2^2 will give a HIGH output when both of its inputs are LOW, causing the $\overline{R_D}$ line to go LOW.

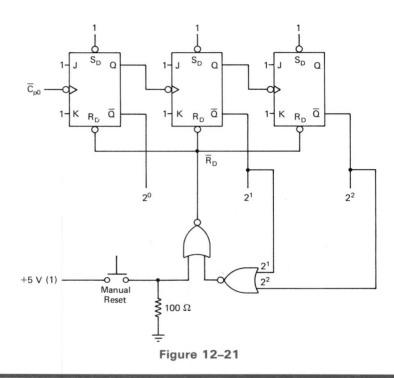

Figure 12–21

EXAMPLE 12–8

Design a MOD-5 up-counter that counts in the sequence 6–7–8–9–10–6–7–8–9–10–6–etc.

Solution: The up-counter is shown in Figure 12–22. By pressing the manual Preset pushbutton, the 2^1 and 2^2 flip-flops get Set while the 2^0 and 2^3 flip-flops get Reset. This will give the number 6 (binary 0110) at the output. In the count mode, when the count reaches 11 (binary 1011) the output of the AND gate goes HIGH, causing the $\overline{\text{Preset}}$ line to go LOW, recycling the count to 6 again.

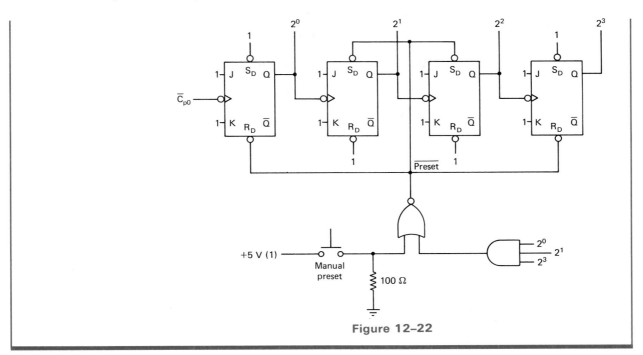

Figure 12–22

EXAMPLE 12–9

Design a down-counter that counts in the sequence 6–5–4–3–2–6–5–4–3–2–6–5–etc.

Solution: The down counter is shown in Figure 12–23. When the $\overline{\text{Preset}}$ line goes LOW, the 2^0 flip-flop is Set and the other two flip-flops are Reset (this gives a 6 at the $\overline{Q}$ *outputs*). As the counter counts down toward zero, the 2^1 and 2^2 will both go LOW at the count of 1 (binary 001) and the $\overline{\text{Preset}}$ line will then go LOW again, starting the cycle over again.

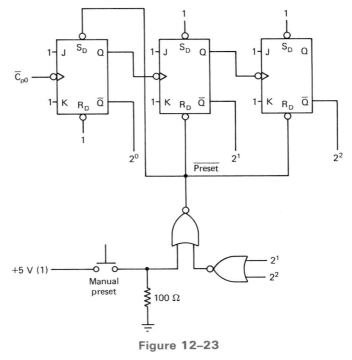

Figure 12–23

EXAMPLE 12–10

Design a counter that counts 0–1–2–3–4–5, then stops and turns on an LED. The process is initiated by pressing a "start" pushbutton.

Solution: The required counter is shown in Figure 12–24. When power is first applied to the circuit ("power-up"), the capacitor will charge up toward 5 V. It starts out at a zero level, however, which causes the 7474 to Reset ($Q_D = 0$). The LOW at Q_D will remain there until the start button is pressed. With a LOW at Q_D the three counter flip-flops are all held in the Reset state (binary 000). The output of the NAND gate is HIGH, so the LED is OFF.

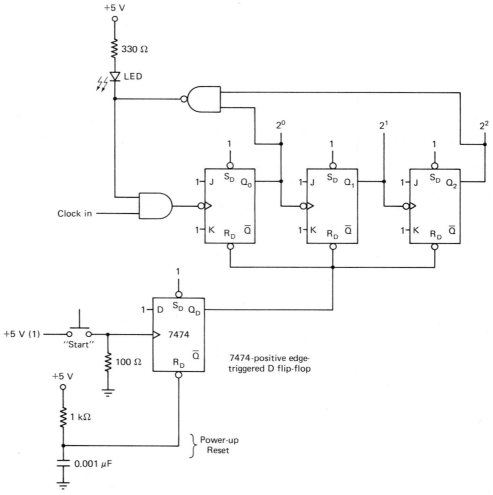

Figure 12–24

When the start button is pressed, Q_D goes HIGH and stays HIGH after the button starts bouncing and is released. With Q_D HIGH the counter begins counting: 0–1–2–3–4–5. When 5 is reached, the output of the NAND gate goes LOW, turning on the LED. The current through the LED will be (5 V − 1.7 V)/330 Ω = 10 mA. The NAND gate can sink a maximum of 16 mA (I_{OL} = 16 mA), so 10 mA will not burn it out.

The **LOW** output of the NAND gate is also fed to the input of the AND gate, which will disable the clock input. Since the clock cannot get through the AND gate to the first flip-flop, the count stays at 5 and the LED stays lit.

If you want to Reset the counter to zero again, you could put a pushbutton in parallel across the capacitor so that when it was pressed, Q_D would go LOW and stay LOW until the "start" button was pressed again.

12–4 RIPPLE COUNTER INTEGRATED CIRCUITS

Four-bit binary ripple counters are available in a single integrated-circuit package. The most popular are the 7490, 7492, and 7493 TTL ICs.

Figure 12–25 shows the internal logic diagram for the 7493 4-bit binary ripple counter. The 7493 has 4 *J-K* flip-flops in a single package. It is divided into two sections: a divide-by-2 and a divide-by-8. The first flip-flop provides the divide-by-2 with its $\overline{C_{p0}}$ input and Q_0 output. The second group of three flip-flops are cascaded to each other and provide the divide-by-8 via the $\overline{C_{p1}}$ input and $Q_1 Q_2 Q_3$ outputs. To get a divide-by-16 you can *externally* connect Q_0 to $\overline{C_{p1}}$ so that all four flip-flops are cascaded end to end as shown in Figure 12–26. Notice that two Master Reset inputs (MR_1, MR_2) are provided to asynchronously Reset all four flip-flops. When MR_1 and MR_2 are both HIGH, all Q's will be Reset to 0. (MR_1 or MR_2 must be held LOW to enable the count mode.)

With the MOD-16 connection, the frequency output at Q_0 is equal to one-half the frequency input at $\overline{C_{p0}}$. Also, $f_{Q1} = \frac{1}{4} f_{\overline{Cp0}}$, $f_{Q2} = \frac{1}{8} f_{\overline{Cp0}}$, and $f_{Q3} = \frac{1}{16} f_{\overline{Cp0}}$.

The 7493 can be used to form any modulus counter less than or equal to MOD-16 by utilizing the MR_1 and MR_2 inputs. For example, to form a MOD-12 counter, simply make the external connections shown in Figure 12–27.

The count sequence of the MOD-12 counter will be 0–1–2–3–4–5–6–7–8–9–10–11–0–1–etc. Each time 12 (1100) tries to appear at the outputs, a HIGH-HIGH is placed on MR_1–MR_2 and the counter resets to zero.

Two other common ripple counter ICs are the 7490 and 7492. They both have four internal flip-flops like the 7493 but through the application of internal gating, they automatically recycle to zero after 9 and 11, respectively.

The 7490 is a 4-bit ripple counter consisting of a divide-by-2 section and a

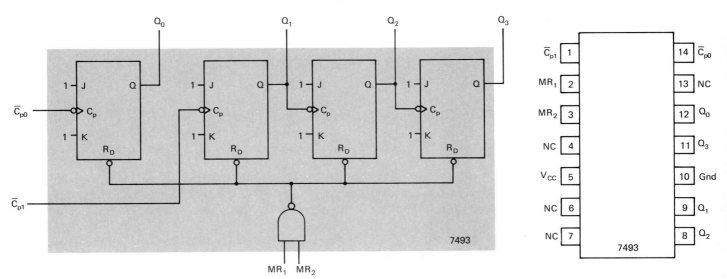

Figure 12–25 Logic diagram and pin configuration for a 7493 4-bit ripple counter IC.

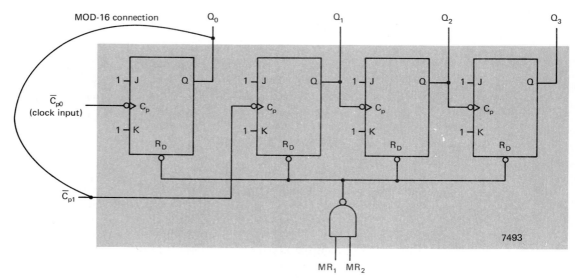

Figure 12–26   A 7493 connected as a MOD-16 ripple counter.

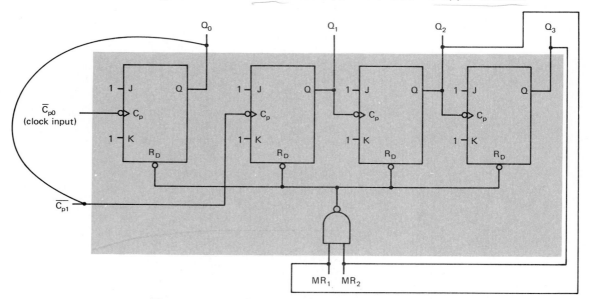

Figure 12–27   External connections to a 7493 to form a MOD-12 counter.

divide-by-5 section (see Figure 12–28). The two sections can be cascaded together to form a divide-by-10 (decade or BCD) counter by connecting Q_0 to $\overline{C_{p1}}$ externally. The 7490 is most commonly used for applications requiring a decimal (0 to 9) display.

Notice in Figure 12–28 that besides having Master Reset inputs (MR_1–MR_2) the 7490 also has Master Set inputs (MS_1–MS_2). When both MS_1 and MS_2 are made HIGH, the clock and MR inputs are overridden and the Q outputs will be asynchronously Set to a 9 (1001). This is a very useful feature because if used, it ensures that *after* the first active clock transition the counter will start counting from 0.

The 7492 is a 4-bit ripple counter consisting of a divide-by-2 section and a divide-by-6 section (see Figure 12–29). The two sections can be cascaded together to form a divide-by-12 (MOD-12) by connecting Q_0 to $\overline{C_{p1}}$ and using $\overline{C_{p0}}$ as the clock input. The 7492 is most commonly used for applications requiring MOD-12 and MOD-6 frequency dividing such as in digital clocks. You can get a divide-by-6

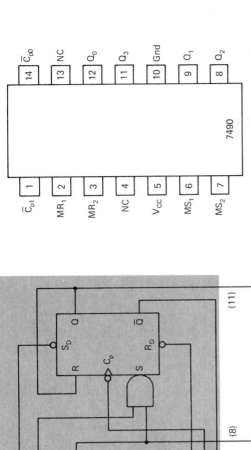

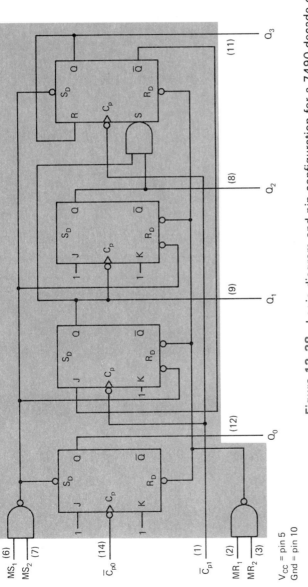

Figure 12–28 Logic diagram and pin configuration for a 7490 decade counter.

( ) = pin numbers
V_{CC} = pin 5
Gnd = pin 10

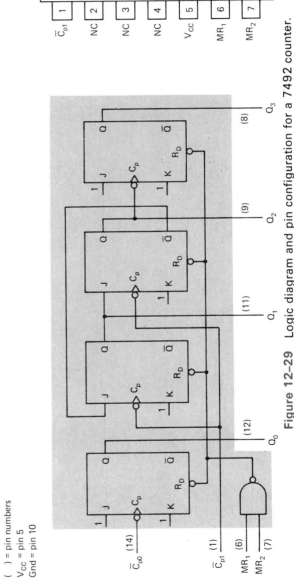

Figure 12–29 Logic diagram and pin configuration for a 7492 counter.

317

frequency divider simply by ignoring the $\overline{C_{p0}}$ input of the first flip-flop and instead, bring the clock input into $\overline{C_{p1}}$, which is the input to the divide-by-6 section. (One peculiarity of the 7492 is that when connected as a MOD-12, it does *not* count sequentially from 0 to 11. Instead, it counts from 0 to 13, skipping 6 and 7, but still functions as a divide-by-12.)

EXAMPLE 12–11

Make the necessary external connections to a 7490 to form a MOD-10 counter.

Solution: The MOD-10 counter is shown in Figure 12–30.

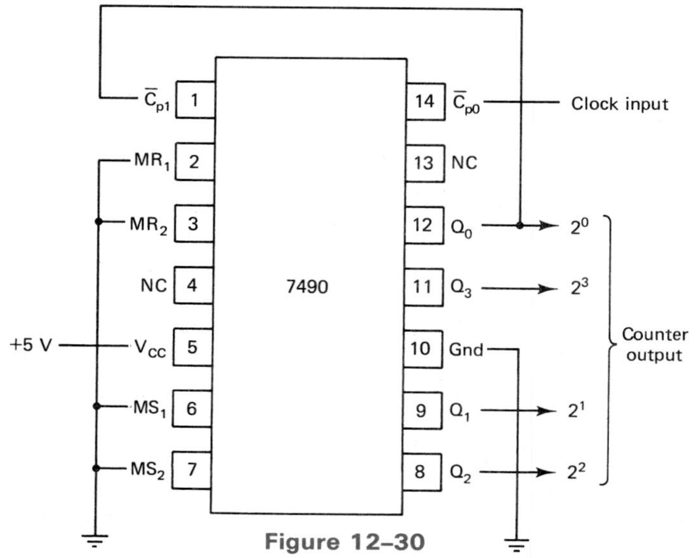

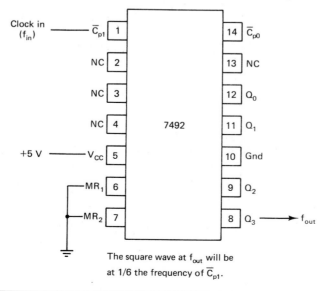

Figure 12–30

EXAMPLE 12–12

Make the necessary external connections to a 7492 to form a divide-by-6 frequency divider ($f_{out} = \frac{1}{6} f_{in}$).

Solution: The frequency divider is shown in Figure 12–31.

The square wave at f_{out} will be at 1/6 the frequency of $\overline{C_{p1}}$.

Figure 12–31

EXAMPLE 12–13

Make the necessary external connections to a 7490 to form a MOD-8 counter (0 to 7). Also, upon initial power-up, Set the counter at 9 so that after the first active input clock edge the output will be 0 and the count sequence will proceed from there.

Solution: The MOD-8 counter is shown in Figure 12–32. The output of the 7414 Schmitt inverter will initially be HIGH when power is first turned on because the capacitor feeding its input is initially discharged to zero. This HIGH on MS_1 and MS_2 will Set the counter to 9. Then, as the capacitor charges up above 1.7 V, the Schmitt will switch to a LOW output, allowing the counter to start its synchronous counting sequence.

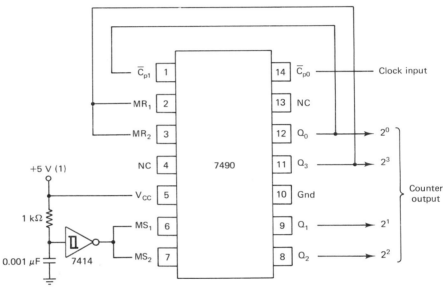

Figure 12–32

Q_0 is connected to $\overline{C_{p1}}$ so that all four flip-flops are cascaded. When the counter reaches 8 (1000), the 2^3 line, which is connected to MR_1 and MR_2, causes the counter to Reset to 0. The counter will continue to count in the sequence 0–1–2–3–4–5–6–7–0–1–2–etc. continuously.

12–5 SYSTEM DESIGN APPLICATIONS

Integrated-circuit counter chips are used in a multitude of applications dealing with timing operations, counting, sequencing, and frequency division. To implement a complete system application, output devices such as LED indicators, seven-segment LED displays, relay drivers, and alarm buzzers must be configured to operate from the counter outputs. The synchronous and asynchronous inputs can be driven by such devices as a clock oscillator, a pushbutton switch, the output from another digital IC, or control signals provided by a microprocessor.

APPLICATION 12–1

For example, let's consider an application that requires a LED indicator to illuminate for 1 s once every 13 s to signal an assembly line worker to perform some manual operation.

Solution: To solve this design problem, we first have to come up with a clock oscillator that produces 1 pulse per second (pps).

The first part of Figure 12–33a, which is used to produce the 60-pps clock, was described in detail in Section 11–6. To divide the 60 pps down

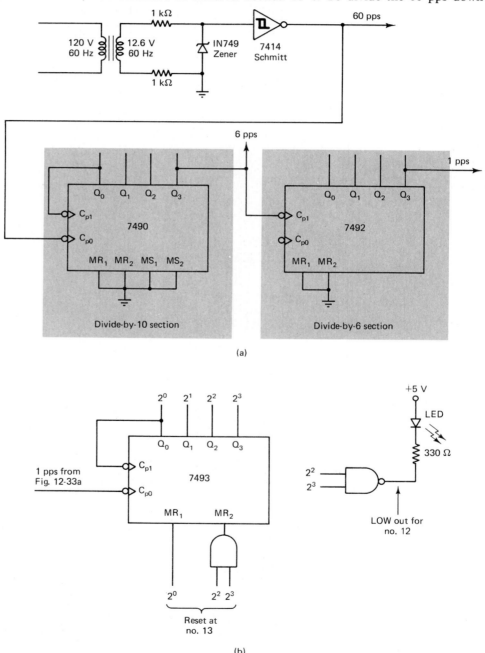

(a)

(b)

Figure 12–33 (a) Circuit used to produce 1 pulse per second; (b) circuit used to illuminate an LED once every 13 s.

to 1 pps, we can cascade a MOD-10 counter with a MOD-6 counter to create a divide-by-60 circuit.

The 7490 connected as a MOD-10 is chosen for the divide-by-10 section. If you study the output waveforms of a MOD-10 counter, you can see that Q_3 will oscillate at a frequency one-tenth of the frequency at $\overline{C_{p0}}$. Then, if we use Q_3 to trigger the input clock of the divide-by-6 section, the overall effect will be a divide-by-60. (The 7492 is used for the divide-by-6 section simply by using $\overline{C_{p1}}$ as the input and taking the 1-pps output from Q_3 as shown in Figure 12–33a.)

The next step in the system design is to use the 1-pps clock to enable a circuit to turn on an LED for 1 s once every 13 s. It sounds like we need a MOD-13 counter (0 to 12) and a gating scheme that turns on a LED when the count is on the number 12. A 7493 can be used for a MOD-13 counter and a NAND gate can be used to sink the current from an LED when the number 12 ($Q_2 = 1$, $Q_3 = 1$) occurs. Figure 12–33b shows the necessary circuit connections.

Notice in Figure 12–33b that a MOD-13 is formed by connecting Q_0 to $\overline{C_{p1}}$ and resetting the counter when the number 13 is reached, resulting in a count of 0 to 12. Also, when the number 12 is reached, the NAND gate's output goes LOW, turning on the LED. [$I_{LED} = (5\ V - 1.7\ V)/330\ \Omega = 10\ mA$].

APPLICATION 12–2

Design a circuit to turn on an LED for 20 ms once every 100 ms. Assume that you have a 50-Hz (50-pps) clock available.

Solution: Since 20 ms is $\frac{1}{5}$ of 100 ms, we should use a MOD-5 counter such as the one available in the 7490 IC. To determine which outputs to use to drive the LED, let's look at the waveforms generated by a 7490 connected as a MOD-5 counter.

Remember that the second section of a 7490 is a MOD-5 counter (0 to 4). If the input frequency is 50 Hz, each count will last for 20 ms ($\frac{1}{50}$ Hz = 20 ms), as shown in Figure 12–34a.

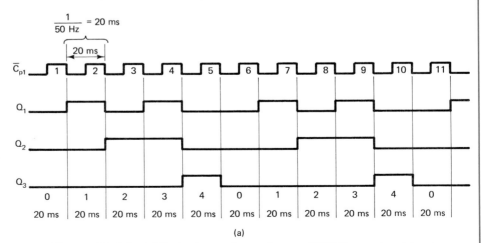

(a)

Figure 12–34 (a) Output waveforms from a MOD-5 counter driven by a 50-Hz input clock;

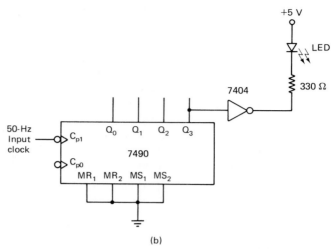

(b)

Figure 12–34 *(Continued)* (b) solution to Application 12–2.

Notice that the Q_3 line goes HIGH for 20 ms once every 100 ms. So if we just invert the Q_3 line and use it to drive the LED, we have the solution to our problem! Figure 12–34b shows the final solution.

APPLICATION 12–3

Design a three-digit-decimal counter that can count from 000 to 999.

Solution: We have already seen that a 7490 is a single-digit-decimal (0 to 9) counter. If we cascade three 7490s together and use the low-order counter to trigger the second digit counter and the second digit counter to trigger the high-order-digit counter, they will count from 000 up to 999. (Keep in mind that the outputs will be binary-coded decimal in groups of 4. In Section 12–6 we will see how we can convert the BCD outputs into actual decimal digits.)

If you review the output waveforms of a 7490 connected as a MOD-10 counter, you can see that at the end of the cycle, when the count changes from 9 (1001) to 0 (0000) the 2^3 output line goes from HIGH to LOW. When cascading counters, you can use that HIGH-to-LOW transition to trigger the input to the next-highest-order counter. That will work out great because we want the next-highest-order decimal digit to increment by 1 each time the lower-order digit has completed its 0-through-9 cycle (i.e., the transition from 009 to 010). The complete circuit diagram for a 000 to 999 BCD counter is shown in Figure 12–35.

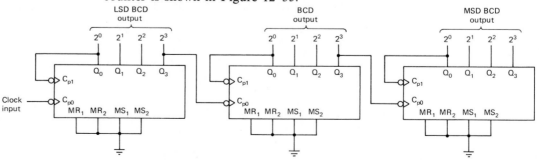

Figure 12–35 Cascading 7490s to form a 000–999 BCD output counter.

APPLICATION 12–4

Design and sketch a block diagram of a digital clock capable of displaying hours, minutes, and seconds.

Solution: First we have to design a 1-pps clock to feed into the least significant digit of the seconds counter. The seconds will be made up of two cascaded counters that count 00 to 59. When the seconds change from 59 to 00, that transition will be used to trigger the minutes digits to increment by 1. The minutes will also be made up of two cascaded counters that count from 00 to 59. When the minutes change from 59 to 00, that transition will be used to trigger the hours digits to increment by 1. Finally, when the hours reach 12, all counters should be Reset to 0. The digital clock will display the time from $00:00:00$ to $11:59:59$.

Figure 12–36 is the final circuit that could be used to implement a digital clock. A 1-pps clock (similar to the one shown in Figure 12–33) is used as the initial clock trigger into the least significant digit (LSD) counter of the seconds display. This counter is a MOD-10 constructed from a 7490 IC. Each second that counter will increment. When it changes from 9 to 0 the HIGH-to-LOW edge on the 2^3 line will serve as a clock pulse into the most-significant-digit (MSD) counter of the seconds display. This counter is a MOD-6 constructed from a 7492 IC.

After 59 s, the 2^2 output of that MOD-6 counter will go HIGH to LOW [once each minute (1 ppm)], triggering the MOD-10 of the minutes section. When the minutes exceed 59, the 2^2 output of that MOD-6 counter will trigger the MOD-10 of the hours section.

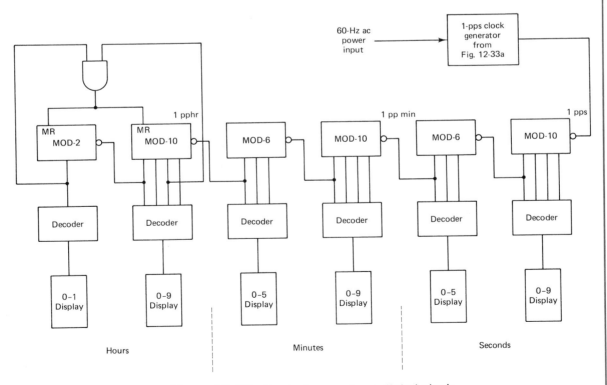

Figure 12–36 Block diagram for a digital clock.

The MOD-2 of the hours section is just a single toggle flip-flop having a 1 or 0 output. The hours section is set up to count from 0 to 11. When 12 is reached, the NAND gate resets both hours counters. The clock display will therefore be 00:00:00 to 11:59:59.

If you want the clock to display 1:00:00 to 12:59:59 instead, you will have to check for a 13 in the hours section instead of 12. When 13 is reached, we will want to Reset the MOD-2 counter and "Preset" the MOD-10 counter to a 1. Presettable counters such as the 74192 are used in a case like this. Presettable counters are covered later in this chapter.

The decoders are required to convert the BCD from the counters into a special code that can be used by the actual display device. Digit displays and decoders are discussed in Section 12–6.

APPLICATION 12–5

Design an egg-timer circuit. The timer will be started when you press a pushbutton. After 3 minutes a 5-V 10-mA dc piezoelectric buzzer will begin buzzing.

Solution: The first thing to take care of is to divide the 1-pps clock previously designed in Figure 12–33a down to a 1-ppm clock. At 1 ppm when the count reaches 3, the buzzer should be enabled and the input clock disabled. An automatic power-up Reset is required on all the counters so that the minute counter will start at zero. A *D* latch can be utilized for the pushbutton starter so that after the pushbutton is released, the latch "remembers" and will keep the counting process going.

The circuit of Figure 12–37 (page 313) can be used to implement this design. When power is first turned on, the automatic Reset circuit will Reset all counter outputs and Reset the 7474 making $\overline{Q} = 1$. With $\overline{Q}$ HIGH, the OR gate will stay HIGH, disabling the clock from getting through to the first 7492.

When the "start" pushbutton is momentarilly depressed, $\overline{Q}$ will go LOW, allowing the 1-pps clock to reach $\overline{C_{p1}}$. The first two counters are connected as a MOD-6 and a MOD-10 to yield a divide-by-60 so that we have 1 ppm available for the last counter, which serves as a minute counter. When the count reaches 3 in the last 7492, the AND gate goes HIGH, disabling the clock input. This causes the 7404 to go LOW, providing sink current for the buzzer to operate. The buzzer is turned off by turning off the main power supply.

12–6 *SEVEN-SEGMENT LED DISPLAY DECODERS*

In Section 12–5 we discussed counter circuits that are used to display decimal (0 to 9) numbers. If a counter is to display a decimal number, the count on each 4-bit counter cannot exceed 9 (1001). In other words, the counters must be outputting binary-coded decimal (BCD). As described in Chapter 2, BCD is a 4-bit binary string used to represent the 10 decimal digits. To be useful, however, the BCD must be decoded by a decoder into a format that can be used to drive a decimal numeric display. The most popular display technique is the seven-segment LED display.

A seven-segment LED display is actually made up of seven separate light-emitting diodes in a single package. The LEDs are oriented so as to form an ⊟ Most seven-segment LEDs have an eighth LED used for a decimal point.

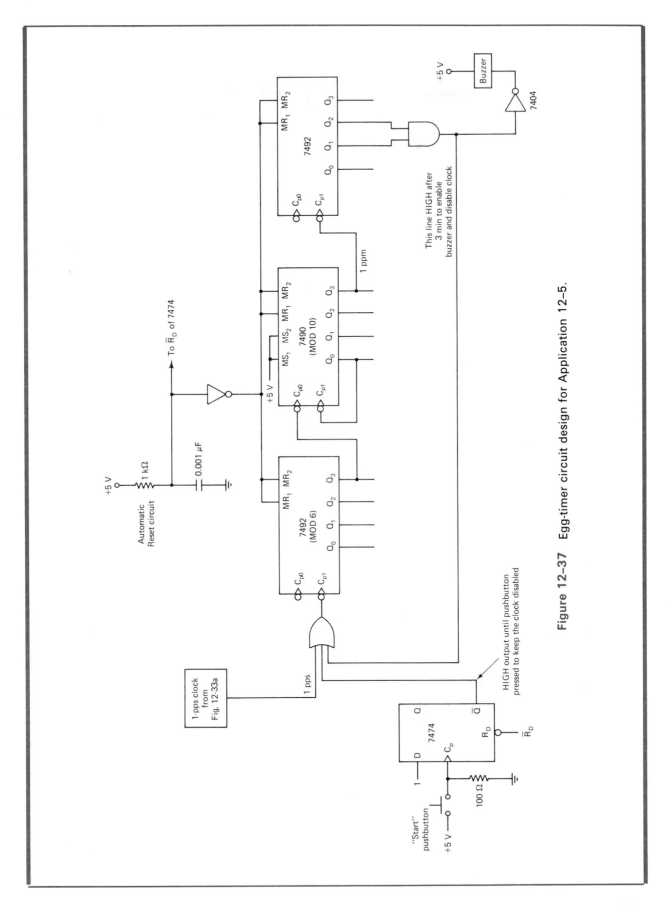

Figure 12-37 Egg-timer circuit design for Application 12-5.

The job of the decoder is to convert the 4-bit BCD code into a "seven-segment code" which will turn on the appropriate LED segments to display the correct decimal digit. For instance, if the BCD is 0111 (7), the decoder must develop a code to turn on the top segment and the two right segments (⌐|).

Common-Anode LED Display

The physical layout of a seven-segment LED display is shown in Figure 12–38. This figure shows that the anode of each LED (segment) is connected to the +5-V supply. Now, to illuminate an LED, its cathode must be grounded through a series-limiting resistor, as shown in Figure 12–39. The value of the limiting resistor can be found by knowing that the voltage drop across an LED is 1.7 V and that it takes approximately 10 mA to illuminate it. Therefore,

$$R_{limit} = \frac{5.0\ V - 1.7\ V}{10\ mA} = 330\ \Omega$$

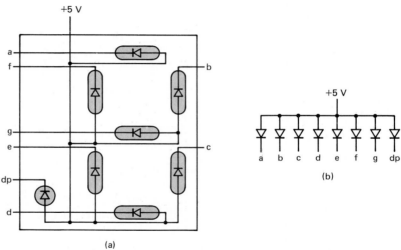

(a)

Figure 12–38   Seven-segment common-anode LED display: (a) physical layout; (b) schematic.

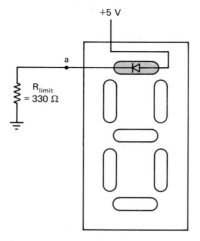

Figure 12–39   Illuminating the *a* segment.

Each segment in the display unit is illuminated in the same way. Figure 12–40 shows the numerical designations for the 10 allowable decimal digits.

Common-anode displays are "active-LOW" (LOW-enable) devices because it

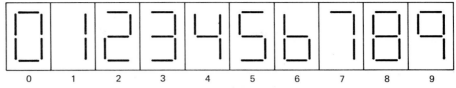

Figure 12–40 Numerical designations for a seven-segment LED.

takes a LOW to turn on (illuminate) a segment. Therefore, the decoder IC used to drive a common-anode LED must have active-LOW outputs.

Common-cathode LEDs and decoders are also available but they are not as popular because they are "active-HIGH" and ICs typically cannot "source" (1 output) as much current as they can "sink" (0 output).

BCD-to-Seven-Segment Decoder/Driver ICs

The 7447 is the most popular common-anode decoder/LED driver. Basically, the 7447 has a 4-bit BCD input and seven individual active-LOW outputs (one for each LED segment). As shown in Figure 12–41, it also has a "lamp test" ($\overline{LT}$) input for testing *all* segments and it also has ripple blanking input and output.

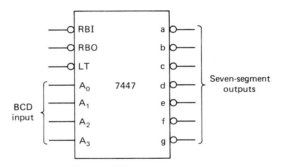

Figure 12–41 Logic symbol for a 7447 decoder.

A very versatile CMOS seven-segment decoder is the 4543, and its high-speed version, the 74HCT4543. The 4543 provides active-HIGH *or* active-LOW outputs and can drive LED displays as well as liquid-crystal displays (LCDs). For the purposes of this chapter, we discuss the 7447 TTL decoder in detail.

To complete the connection between the 7447 and the seven-segment LED, we need seven 330-Ω resistors (eight if the decimal point is included) for current limiting. Dual-in-line-package (DIP) *resistor networks* are available and simplify the wiring process because all seven (or eight) resistors are in a single DIP.

Figure 12–42 shows typical decoder–resistor–DIP–LED connections. An example of how Figure 12–42 works: If a MOD-10 counter's outputs are connected to the BCD input and the count is at six (0110_{BCD}), the following will happen;

1. The decoder will determine that a 0110_{BCD} must send the $\overline{c}$, $\overline{d}$, $\overline{e}$, $\overline{f}$, $\overline{g}$ outputs LOW ($\overline{a}$, $\overline{b}$ will be HIGH for ᑕ).

2. The LOW on those outputs will provide a path for the sink current in the appropriate LED segments via the 330-Ω resistors (the 7447 can sink up to 40 mA at each output).

3. The decimal number ᑕ will be illuminated together with the decimal point if the dp switch is closed.

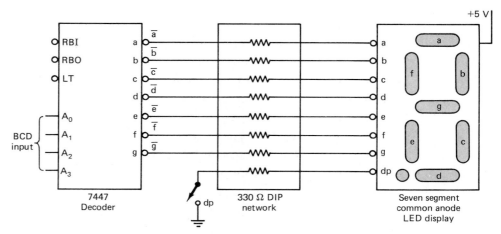

Figure 12–42 Driving a seven-segment LED display.

A complete three-digit decimal display system is shown in Figure 12–43. The three counters in the figure are connected as MOD-10 counters with the input clock oscillator connected to the least significant counter. The three counters are cascaded by connecting the Q_3 output of the first to the $\overline{C_{p\,0}}$ of the next, and so on.

Notice that the decimal point of the LSD is always on, so the counters will therefore count from .0 up to 99.9. If the clock oscillator is set at 10 pps, the LSD will indicate tenths of seconds. Also notice that the ripple blanking inputs and outputs ($\overline{RBI}$ and $\overline{RBO}$) are used in this design. They are active LOW and are used for *leading-zero suppression*. For example, if the display output is at 1.4, would you like it to read 01.4 or 1.4? To suppress the leading zero and make it a blank, ground the $\overline{RBI}$ terminal of the MSD decoder. How about if the output is at .6; would you like it to read 00.6, 0.6, or .6? To suppress the second zero when the MSD is blank, simply connect the $\overline{RBO}$ of the MSD decoder to the $\overline{RBI}$ of the second digit decoder. The way this works is; if the MSD is blank (zero suppressed), the MSD decoder puts a LOW out at $\overline{RBO}$. This LOW is connected to the $\overline{RBI}$ of the second decoder, which forces a blank output (zero suppression) if its BCD input is zero.

The $\overline{RBI}$ and $\overline{RBO}$ can also be used for zero suppression of "trailing" zeros. For example, if you have an eight-digit display, the $\overline{RBI}$s and $\overline{RBO}$s could be used to automatically suppress the number 0046.0910 to be displayed as 46.091.

12–7 SYNCHRONOUS COUNTERS

Remember the problems we discussed with ripple counters due to the accumulated propagation delay of the clock from flip-flop to flip-flop? (See Figure 12–11.) Well, synchronous counters eliminate that problem because all the clock inputs ($\overline{C_p}$'s) are tied to a common clock input line, so each flip-flop will be triggered at the same time (thus any Q output transitions will occur at the same time).

If we want to design a 4-bit synchronous counter, we need four flip-flops, giving us a MOD-16 (2^4) binary counter. Keep in mind that since all the $\overline{C_p}$ inputs receive a trigger at the same time, we must hold certain flip-flops from making output transitions until it is their turn. To design the connection scheme for the synchronous counter, let's first study the output waveforms of a 4-bit binary counter to determine which flip-flops are to be held from toggling, and when.

From the waveforms in Figure 12–44, we can see that the 2^0 output is a continuous toggle off the clock input line. The 2^1 output line toggles on every negative

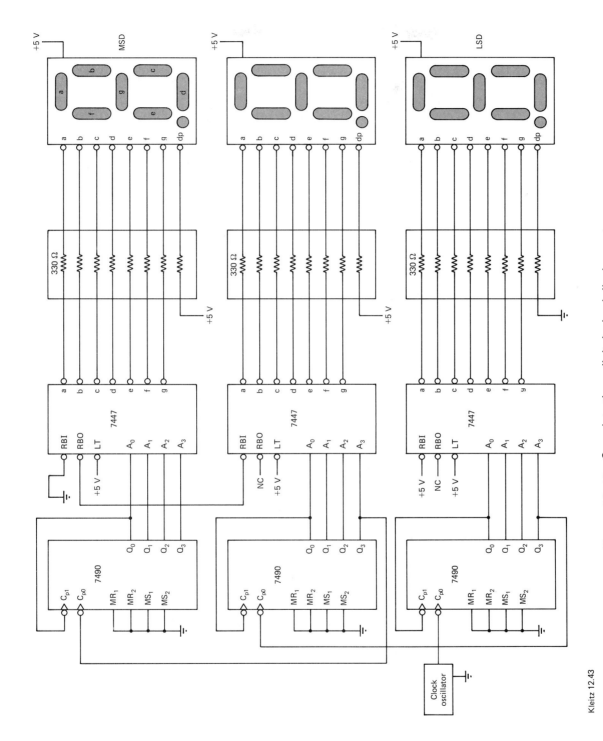

Figure 12–43 Complete three-digit-decimal display system.

Kleitz 12.43

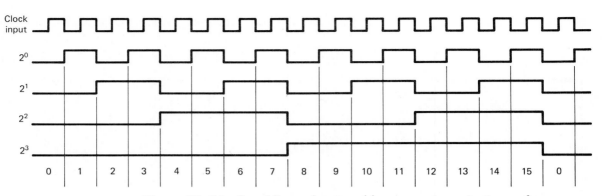

Figure 12–44 Four-bit synchronous binary counter output waveforms.

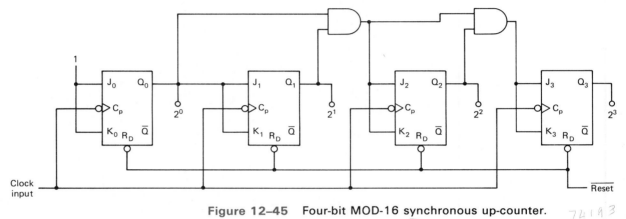

Figure 12–45 Four-bit MOD-16 synchronous up-counter.

edge of the 2^0 line, but since the 2^1's $\overline{C_{p0}}$ input is also connected to the clock input, it must be held from toggling until the 2^0 line is HIGH. This can be done simply by tying the J and K inputs to the 2^0 line as shown in Figure 12–45.

The same logic follows through for the 2^2 and 2^3 output lines. The 2^2 line must be held from toggling until the 2^0 *and* 2^1 lines are both HIGH. Also, the 2^3 line must be held from toggling until the 2^0 *and* 2^1 *and* 2^2 lines are all HIGH.

To keep the appropriate flip-flops in the *hold* condition or *toggle* condition, their J and K inputs are tied together and through use of additional AND gates, as shown in Figure 12–45, the J-K inputs will be both 0 or 1, depending on whether they are to be in the hold or toggle mode.

From Figure 12–45 we can see that the same clock input is driving all four flip-flops. The 2^1 flip-flop will be in the hold mode ($J_1 = K_1 = 0$) until the 2^0 output goes HIGH, which will force J_1-K_1 HIGH, allowing the 2^1 flip-flop to toggle when the next negative clock edge comes in.

Now, observe the output waveforms (Figure 12–44) while you look at the circuit design (Figure 12–45) to determine the operation of the last two flip-flops. From the waveforms we see that the 2^2 output must not be allowed to toggle until 2^0 *and* 2^1 are both HIGH. Well, the first AND gate in Figure 12–45 takes care of that by holding J_2-K_2 LOW. The same method is used to keep the 2^3 output from toggling until the 2^0 *and* 2^1 *and* 2^2 outputs are *all* HIGH.

As you can see, the circuit is more complicated, but the cumulative effect of propagation delays through the flip-flops is not a problem as it was in ripple counters because all output transitions will occur at the same time since all flip-flops are triggered from the same input line. (There *is* a propagation delay through the AND gates, but it will not affect the Q outputs of the flip-flops.)

As with ripple counters, synchronous counters can be used as down-counters by taking the output from the $\overline{Q}$ outputs and can form any modulus count by resetting the count to zero after some predetermined binary number has been reached.

EXAMPLE 12–14

Design a MOD-6 synchronous binary up-counter.

Solution: A MOD-6 counter will count 0–1–2–3–4–5–0–1–etc. To count to 5 we will need three flip-flops and will have to Reset the count to zero when the number 6 (110_2) is reached, as shown in the circuit in Figure 12–46.

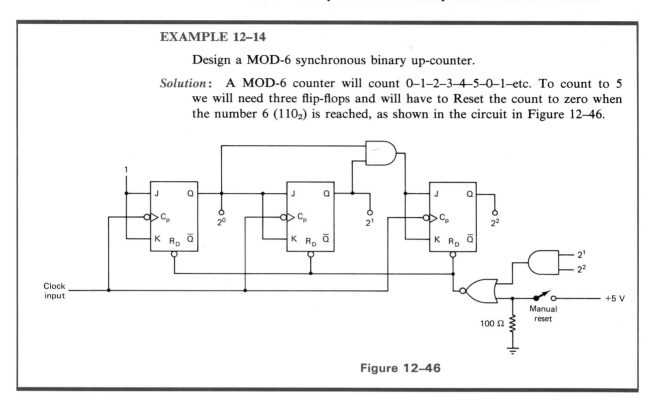

Figure 12–46

System Design Application

Synchronous binary counters have many applications in timing and sequencing of digital systems. The following design will illustrate one of these applications.

APPLICATION 12–6

Let's say that your company needs a system that will count the number of hours of darkness each day. The senior design engineer for your company will be connecting his microprocessor-based system to your counter outputs after you are sure that your system is working correctly. After the counter outputs are read, the microprocessor will issue a LOW Reset pulse to your counter to Reset it to all zeros sometime before sunset.

Solution: You decide to use a synchronous counter but realize that it may be dark outside for as many as 18 hours per day. A 4-bit counter will not count high enough, so first you have to come up with the 5-bit synchronous counter design that is shown in Figure 12–47. That was not hard; you just had to add one more AND gate and a flip-flop to a 4-bit counter.

From analog electronics you remembered that a phototransistor has varying resistance from collector to emitter, depending on how much light strikes it. The phototransistor that you decide to use has a resistance of 10 MΩ when it is in the dark and 10 Ω when it is in the daylight. Your final circuit design is shown in Figure 12–47.

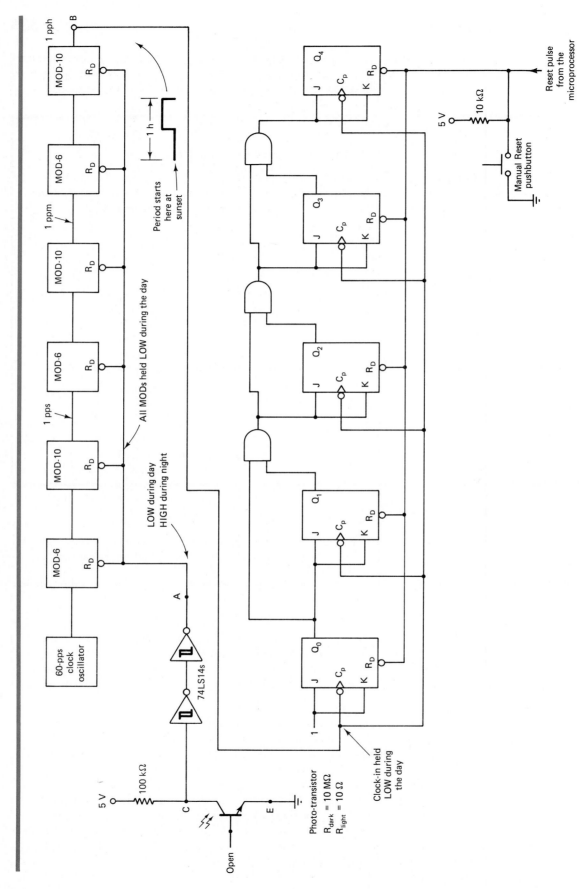

Figure 12–47 System design solution for the "hours of darkness counter."

Explanation: Let's start with the 5-bit synchronous counter. With the addition of the last AND gate and flip-flop, it will be capable of counting from 0 up to 31 (MOD-32). The manual Reset pushbutton, when depressed, will Reset the counter to zero.

The phototransistor collector-to-ground voltage will be almost zero during daylight because the collector-to-emitter resistance acts almost like a short. (Depending on the transistor used, the ON resistance may be as low as 10 Ω). The Schmitt inverters are used to give a "sharp" HIGH-to-LOW and LOW-to-HIGH at sunset and sunrise to eliminate any false clock switching. Schmitt triggers are most commonly available as inverting functions, so two of them are necessary so that a LOW at the collector will come through as a LOW at point A.

The LOW at point A during the daylight will hold all the MOD counters (divide-by-N's) at zero so that at the beginning of sunset the waveform at point B will start out LOW and take one full hour before it goes HIGH to LOW, triggering the first transition at Q. During the nighttime, point B will oscillate at 1 pulse per hour, incrementing the counter once each hour. At sunrise, point A goes LOW, forcing all MODs LOW, disabling the clock. The counter outputs at Q_0 to Q_4 will be read by the microprocessor during the day and then Reset.

12–8 SYNCHRONOUS UP/DOWN-COUNTER ICs

Four-bit synchronous binary counters are available in a single integrated-circuit (IC) package. Two popular synchronous IC counters are the 74192 and 74193. They both have some features that were not available on the ripple counter ICs. They can count *up or down* and can be *preset* to any count that you desire. The 74192 is a BCD decade up/down-counter and the 74193 is a 4-bit binary up/down-counter. The logic symbol used for both counters is shown in Figure 12–48.

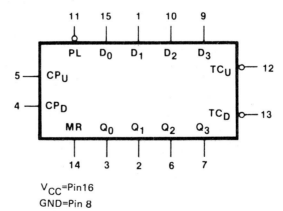

Figure 12–48 Logic symbol for the 74192 and 74193 synchronous counter ICs.

There are two separate clock inputs: C_{pU} for counting up and C_{pD} for counting down. One clock must be held HIGH while counting with the other. The binary output count is taken from Q_0 to Q_3, which are the outputs from four internal *J-K* flip-flops. The Master Reset (*MR*) is an active-HIGH Reset for resetting the Q outputs to zero.

The counter can be preset by placing any binary value on the parallel data inputs (D_0 to D_3) and then driving the Parallel Load ($\overline{PL}$) line LOW. The parallel load operation will change the counter outputs regardless of the conditions of the clock inputs.

The Terminal Count Up ($\overline{TC_U}$) and Terminal Count Down ($\overline{TC_D}$) are normally HIGH. The $\overline{TC_U}$ is used to indicate that the maximum count is reached and the count is about to recycle to zero (carry condition). The $\overline{TC_U}$ line goes LOW for the 74193 when the count reaches 15 *and* the input clock (C_{pU}) goes HIGH to LOW. $\overline{TC_U}$ remains LOW until C_{pU} returns HIGH. This LOW pulse at $\overline{TC_U}$ can be used as a clock input to the next-higher-order stage of a multistage counter.

The $\overline{TC_U}$ output for the 74192 is similar except that it goes LOW at 9 *and* a LOW C_{pU} (see Figure 12–49). The Boolean equations for $\overline{TC_U}$, therefore, are as follows:

$$\text{LOW at } \overline{TC_U} = Q_0 Q_1 Q_2 Q_3 \overline{C_{pU}} \qquad (74193)$$

$$\text{LOW at } \overline{TC_U} = Q_0 Q_3 \overline{C_{pU}} \qquad (74192)$$

The Terminal Count Down ($\overline{TC_D}$) is used to indicate that the minimum count is reached and the count is about to recycle to the maximum (15 or 9) count (borrow condition). Therefore, $\overline{TC_D}$ goes LOW when the down-count reaches zero and the input clock (C_{pD}) goes LOW (see Figure 12–51). The Boolean Equation at $\overline{TC_D}$ is

$$\text{LOW at } \overline{TC_D} = \overline{Q_0}\,\overline{Q_1}\,\overline{Q_2}\,\overline{Q_3}\,\overline{C_{pD}} \qquad (74192 \text{ and } 74193)$$

The function table shown in Table 12–2 can be used to show the four operating modes (Reset, Load, Count Up, and Count Down) of the 74192/74193.

TABLE 12–2

Function Table for the 74192/74193 Synchronous Counter IC[a]

Operating mode	Inputs								Outputs					
	MR	$\overline{PL}$	C_{pU}	C_{pD}	D_0	D_1	D_2	D_3	Q_0	Q_1	Q_2	Q_3	$\overline{TC_U}$	$\overline{TC_D}$
Reset	H	×	×	L	×	×	×	×	L	L	L	L	H	L
	H	×	×	H	×	×	×	×	L	L	L	L	H	H
Parallel Load	L	L	×	L	L	L	L	L	L	L	L	L	H	L
	L	L	×	H	L	L	L	L	L	L	L	L	H	H
	L	L	L	×	H	H	H	H	H	H	H	H	L	H
	L	L	H	×	H	H	H	H	H	H	H	H	H	H
Count Up	L	H	↑	H	×	×	×	×	Count up				H	H
Count Down	L	H	H	↑	×	×	×	×	Count down				H	H

[a] H = HIGH voltage level; L = LOW voltage level; × = don't care; ↑ = LOW-to-HIGH clock transition.

The best way to illustrate how these chips operate is to exercise all its functions and observe the resultant waveforms as shown in the following examples.

EXAMPLE 12–15

Draw the input and output timing waveforms for a 74192 that goes through the following sequence of operation:

1. Reset all outputs to zero.
2. Parallel Load a 7 (0111).
3. Count up five counts.
4. Count down five counts.

Solution: The timing waveforms are shown in Figure 12–49.

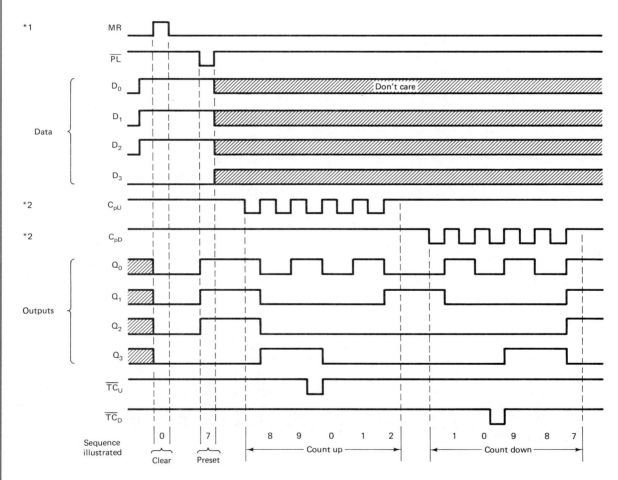

Notes

1. Clear overrides load, data and count inputs.
2. When counting up, count-down input must be HIGH; when counting down, count-up input must be HIGH.

Figure 12–49   Timing waveforms for the 74192 used in Example 12–15.

EXAMPLE 12–16

Draw the output waveforms for the 74193 shown in Figure 12–50, given the waveforms shown in Figure 12–51. (Initially, set $D_0 = 1$, $D_1 = 0$, $D_2 = 1$, $D_3 = 1$ and MR = 0).

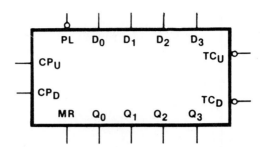

Figure 12–50 Circuit connections for Example 12–16.

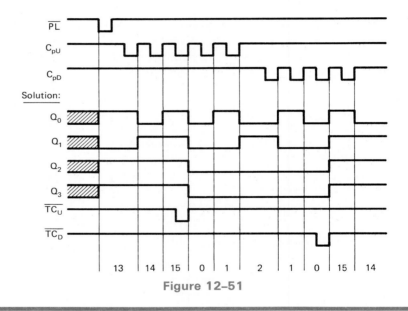

Figure 12–51

EXAMPLE 12–17

Design a decimal counter that will count from 00 to 99 using two 74192 counters and the necessary drive circuitry for the two-digit display. (Display circuitry was explained in Section 12–5.)

Solution: The 74192s can be used to form a multistage counter by connecting the $\overline{TC_U}$ of the first counter to the C_{pU} of the second counter. $\overline{TC_U}$ will go LOW, then HIGH, when the first counter goes from 9 to 0 (carry). That LOW-to-HIGH edge can be used as the clock input to the second stage, as shown in Figure 12–52.

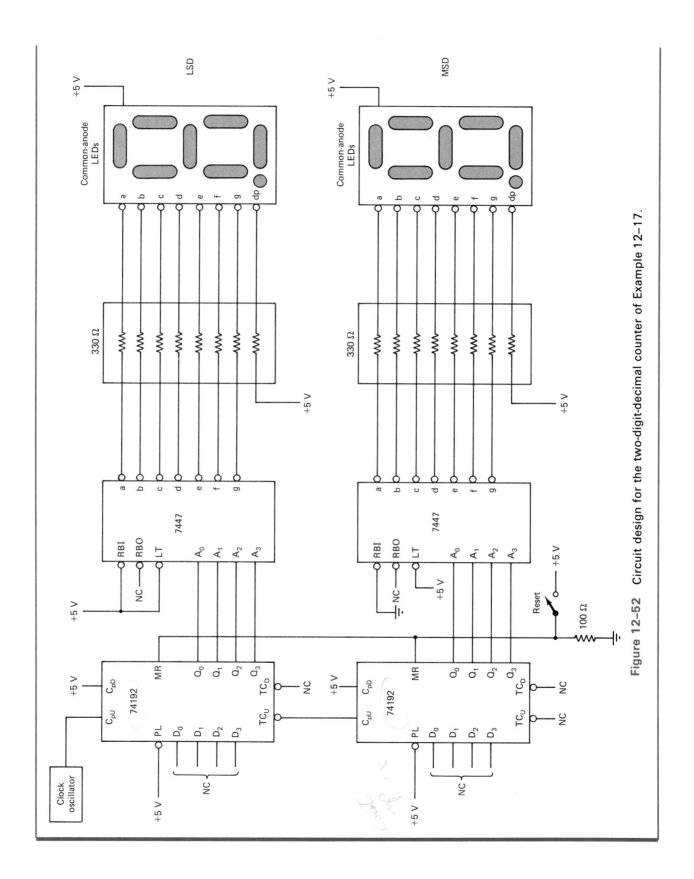

Figure 12-52 Circuit design for the two-digit-decimal counter of Example 12-17.

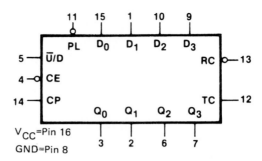

Figure 12–53   Logic symbol for the 74190/74191 synchronous counters.

Another form of synchronous counter is the 74190 and 74191. The 74190 is a BCD counter (0 to 9) and the 74191 is a 4-bit counter (0 to 15). They have some different features and input/output pins as shown in the Figure 12–53.

The 74190/74191 can be preset to any count by using the Parallel Load ($\overline{PL}$) operation. It can count up or down by using the $\overline{U}/D$ input. With $\overline{U}/D = 0$ it will count up, and with $\overline{U}/D = 1$ it will count down. The Count Enable input ($\overline{CE}$) is an active-LOW input used to enable/inhibit the counter. With $\overline{CE} = 0$ the counter is enabled. With $\overline{CE} = 1$ the counter stops and holds the current states of the Q_0 to Q_3 outputs.

The Terminal Count output (TC) is normally LOW, but goes HIGH when the counter reaches zero in the count-down mode and 15 (or 9) in the count-up mode. The ripple clock output ($\overline{RC}$) follows the input clock (C_p) whenever TC is HIGH. In other words, in the count-down mode, when zero is reached, $\overline{RC}$ will go LOW when C_p goes LOW. The $\overline{RC}$ output can be used as a clock input to the next higher stage of a multistage counter just the way that the $\overline{TC}$ outputs of the 74192/74193 were used. In either case, however, the multistage counter will not be truly synchronous because of the small propagation delay from C_p to $\overline{RC}$ of each counter.

For a multistage counter to be truly synchronous, the C_p of each stage must be connected to the *same* clock input line. The 74190/74191 counters enable you to do this by using the TC output to inhibit each successive stage from counting until the previous stage is at its Terminal Count. Figure 12–54 shows how three 74191s can be connected to form a true 12-bit binary synchronous counter.

In Figure 12–54 we can see that each counter stage is driven by the same clock, making it truly synchronous. The second stage is inhibited from counting until the first stage reaches 15. The second stage will then increment by one at the next positive clock edge. Stage 1 will then inhibit stage 2 via the TC-to-$\overline{CE}$ connection while stage 1 is counting up to 15 again. The same operation between stages 2 and 3 also keeps stage 3 from incrementing until stages 1 and 2 both reach 15.

Finally, another type of counter allows you to perform true synchronous counting without using external gates as we had to in Figure 12–54. The 74160/74161/74162/74163 synchronous counter ICs have *two* Count Enable inputs (*CEP* and *CET*) and a Terminal Count output to facilitate high-speed synchronous counting. The logic symbol is given in Figure 12–55. From the logic symbol we can see that this counter is similar to the previous synchronous counters except that it has two active-HIGH Count Enable inputs (*CEP* and *CET*), and an active-HIGH Terminal Count (*TC*) output. (There are other differences between this and other synchronous counters, but I'll leave it up to you to determine those from reading your TTL data manual.)

Both count enables (*CEP* and *CET*) must be HIGH to count. The Terminal Count output (*TC*) will go HIGH when the highest count is reached. *TC* will be forced LOW, however, when *CET* goes LOW even though the highest count may be reached. This is an important feature that enables the multistage counter of Figure 12–56 to operate properly.

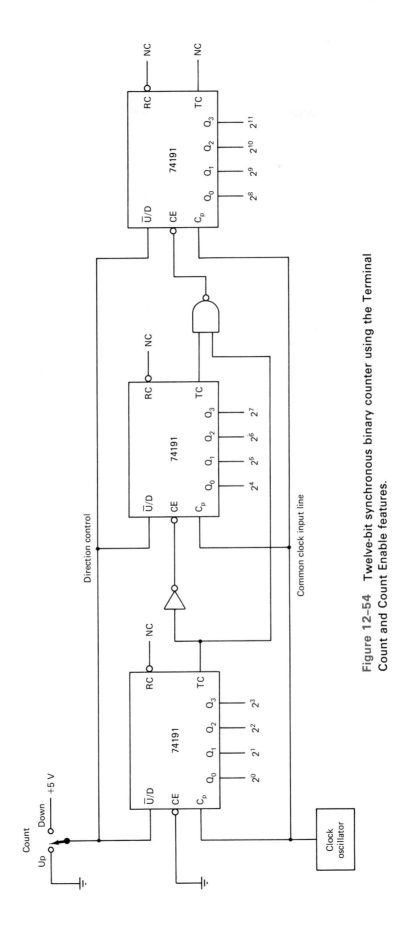

Figure 12–54 Twelve-bit synchronous binary counter using the Terminal Count and Count Enable features.

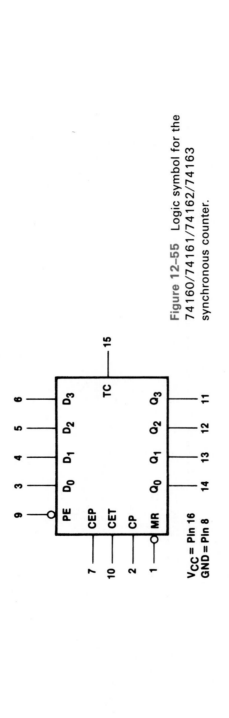

Figure 12-55   Logic symbol for the 74160/74161/74162/74163 synchronous counter.

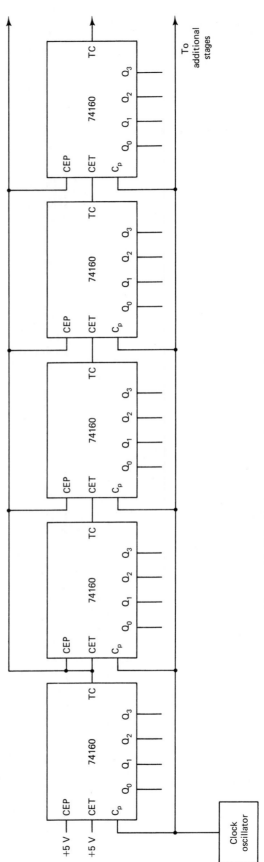

Figure 12-56   High-speed multistage synchronous counter.

12–9 *APPLICATIONS OF SYNCHRONOUS COUNTER ICs*

The following applications will explain some useful design strategy and circuit operation using synchronous counter ICs.

APPLICATION 12–7

Design a counter that will count up 0 to 9, then down 9 to 0, then up 0 to 9 repeatedly using a synchronous counter and various gates.

Solution: Since the count is 0 to 9, a BCD counter will work. Also, we want to go up, then down, then up, and so on, so it would be easy if we had a reversible counter like the 74190 and just toggle the $\overline{U}/D$ terminal each time the Terminal Count is reached. Figure 12–57 could be used to implement this circuit. When power is first applied, the 74190 will be Parallel Loaded with a 5 (0101) and the "direction" line will be 1. (5 is chosen arbitrarily because it is somewhere between the terminal counts 0 and 9.) The counter will count down to 0, at which time *TC* will go HIGH, causing the flip-flop to toggle, changing the "direction" to 0. With the clock oscillator still running the counter will reverse and start counting up. When 9 is reached, *TC* goes HIGH, again changing the "direction" and the cycle repeats.

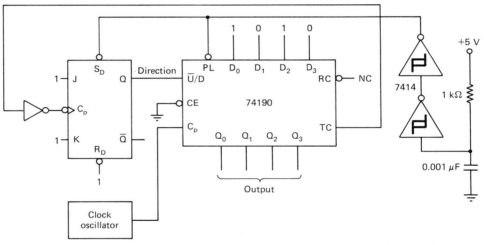

Figure 12–57 Self-reversing BCD counter (solution to Application 12–7).

APPLICATION 12–8

Design and sketch the timing waveforms for a divide-by-9 frequency divider using a 74193 counter.

Solution: We can use the Parallel Load feature of the 74193 to set the counter at some initial value, and then count down to zero. When we reach zero, we will have to Parallel Load the counter to its initial value and count down again, making sure the repetitive cycle repeats once every nine clock periods. Figure 12–58 could be used to implement such a circuit. $\overline{TC_D}$ is fed back into $\overline{PL}$. That means that when the Terminal Count is reached, the LOW out of $\overline{TC_D}$ will enable the Parallel Load, making the outputs equal to the D_0 to D_3 inputs (1001).

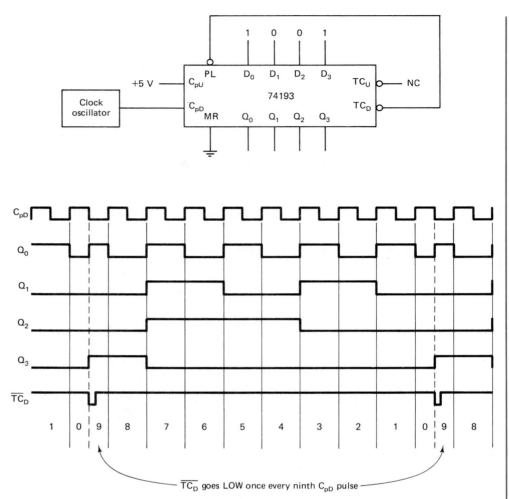

Figure 12–58 Circuit design and timing waveforms for a divide-by-9 frequency divider.

The timing waveforms arbitrarily start at 1 and count down. Notice at zero (Terminal Count) that $\overline{TC_D}$ goes LOW when C_{pD} goes LOW (remember that a LOW at $\overline{TC_D} = \overline{Q_0}\,\overline{Q_1}\,\overline{Q_2}\,\overline{Q_3}\,\overline{C_{pD}}$). As soon as $\overline{TC_D}$ goes LOW, the outputs return to 9, thus causing $\overline{TC_D}$ to go back HIGH again. Therefore, $\overline{TC_D}$ is a narrow pulse just long enough to perform the Parallel Load operation.

The down counting resumes until zero is reached again, which causes the Parallel Load of 9 to occur again. The $\overline{TC_D}$ pulse occurs once every ninth C_{pD} pulse; thus we have a divide-by-9. (A different duty-cycle divide-by-9 can be gotten from the Q_3 or Q_2 outputs.)

APPLICATION 12–9

Design a divide-by-200 using synchronous counters.

Solution: The number 200 exceeds the maximum count of a single 4-bit counter. Two 4-bit counters can be cascaded together to form an 8-bit counter capable of counting 256 states ($2^8 = 256$).

The 74193 is a logical choice for a 4-bit counter. We can cascade two of them together as an 8-bit down-counter. If we preload with the binary equivalent of the number 200 and count down to zero, we can use the borrow output ($\overline{TC_{D\,2}}$) to drive the Parallel Load ($\overline{PL}$) line LOW to recycle back to 200. Figure 12–59 shows the circuit connections to form this 8-bit divide-by-200 counter. The two 74193 counters will start out at some unknown value and start counting down toward zero. The borrow-out ($\overline{TC_{D\,2}}$) line will go LOW when the count reaches zero and $C_{pD\,2}$ is LOW. As soon as $\overline{TC_{D\,2}}$ goes LOW, a Parallel Load of number 200 takes place, making $\overline{TC_{D\,2}}$ go back HIGH again. Therefore, $\overline{TC_{D\,2}}$ is just a short glitch and the number zero will appear at the outputs for just one-half of a clock period and the number 200 will appear the other one-half of the same clock period. The remainder of the numbers will follow a regular counting sequence (199 down to 1), giving us 200 complete clock pulses between the LOW pulses on $\overline{TC_{D\,2}}$. If the short glitch on $\overline{TC_{D\,2}}$ is not wide enough as a divide-by-200 output, it could be widened to produce any duty cycle without affecting the output frequency by using a one-shot multivibrator pulse stretcher. (One shots are discussed in Chapter 14.)

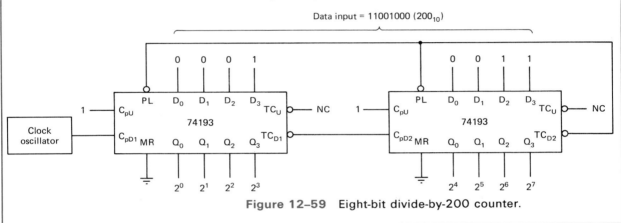

Figure 12–59 Eight-bit divide-by-200 counter.

APPLICATION 12–10

Use a 74163 to form a MOD-7 synchronous up-counter. Sketch the timing waveforms.

Solution: The 74163 has a *synchronous* Reset feature. That is, a LOW level at the Master Reset ($\overline{MR}$) input will Reset all flip-flops (Q_0 to Q_3) at the next positive clock (C_p) edge. Therefore, what we can do is bring the Q_1 and Q_2 (binary 6) lines into a NAND gate to drive the $\overline{MR}$ line LOW when the count is at 6. The next positive C_p edge would normally increase the count to 7 but instead will Reset the count to 0. The result is a count from 0 to 6, which is a MOD-7.

Remember that with previous MOD-N counters we would look for the number that was one greater than the last number to be counted, and when we reached it we would Reset the count to zero because we went beyond the modulus required. That method of resetting after the fact works, but it lets a short-duration glitch (unwanted state) through to the outputs

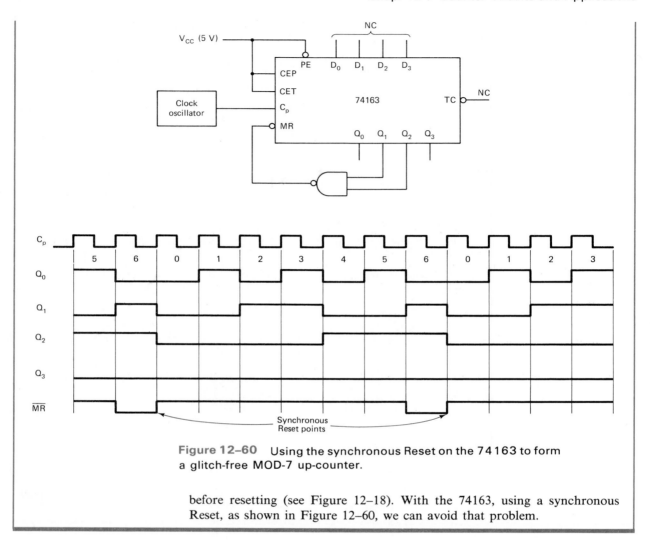

Figure 12–60   Using the synchronous Reset on the 74163 to form a glitch-free MOD-7 up-counter.

before resetting (see Figure 12–18). With the 74163, using a synchronous Reset, as shown in Figure 12–60, we can avoid that problem.

GLOSSARY

Cascade: In multistage systems when the output of one stage is fed directly into the input of the next.

Common-anode LED: A seven-segment LED display whose LED anodes are all connected to a common point and supplied with +5 V. Each LED segment is then turned on by supplying a LOW level (via a limiting resistor) to the appropriate LED cathode.

Divide-by-N: The Q outputs in counter operations will oscillate at a frequency that is at some multiple (N) of the input clock frequency. For example, in a divide-by-8 (MOD-8) counter the output frequency of the highest-order Q (Q_2) is one-eighth the frequency of the input clock.

Glitch: A short-duration-level change in a digital circuit.

Modulus: In a digital counter the modulus is the number of different counter steps.

Oscillate: Change digital states repeatedly (HIGH–LOW–HIGH–LOW–etc.).

Parallel load: A feature on some counters that allows you to load all 4 bits of a counter at the same time, asynchronously.

Phototransistor:A transistor whose collector-to-emitter current and resistance vary, depending on the amount of light shining on its base junction.

Ripple blanking:A feature supplied with display decoders to enable the suppression of leading and trailing zeros.

Ripple counter:(Asynchronous counter) A multibit counter whose clock input trigger is not connected to each flip-flop but instead has to propagate through each flip-flop to reach the input of the next. The fact that the clock has to "ripple" through from stage to stage tends to decrease the maximum operational frequency of the ripple counter.

Sequential:Operations that follow a predetermined sequence of digital states triggered by a timing pulse or clock.

Seven-segment LED:Seven light-emitting diodes fabricated in a single package. By energizing various combinations of LED segments, the 10 decimal digits can be displayed.

Skewed:A "skewed" waveform or pulse is one that is offset to the right or left with respect to the time axis.

Synchronous counter:A multibit counter whose clock input trigger is connected to each flip-flop, so that each flip-flop will operate in step with the same input clock transition.

Terminal count:The highest (or lowest) count in a multibit counting sequence.

Up/down-counter:A counter that is capable of counting up or counting down.

REVIEW QUESTIONS

Sections 12–1 and 12–2

12–1.When analyzing digital circuits containing basic gates combined with sequential logic-like flip-flops, you must remember that gate outputs can change at any time, whereas sequential logic only changes at the active clock edges (true or false)?

12–2.For a binary ripple counter to function properly, all J and K inputs must be tied _____ (HIGH, LOW), and all SD, RD inputs must be tied _____ (HIGH, LOW) to count.

12–3.What effect does propagation delay have on ripple counter outputs?

12–4.How can a ripple up-counter be converted to a down-counter? *by taking output to $\overline{Q}$ point.*

Section 12–3

12–5.A MOD-16 counter can function as a divide-by-16 frequency divider by taking the output from the ___Q^3___ output.

12–6.To convert a 4-bit MOD-16 counter to a MOD-12 counter, the flip-flops must be Reset when the counter reaches the number ___12___ (11, 12, 13).

12–7.Briefly describe the operation of the "Manual Reset" push-button circuitry used in the MOD-N counters in this section.

Section 12–4

12–8.What is the highest modulus of each of the following counter ICs: 7490, 7492, 7493? *MOD 10, – 12, – 16*

12–9.Why does the 7493 counter IC have *two* clock inputs. *one for divide by 2, the other for divide by 8 section*

12–10.What happens to the Q-outputs of the 7490 counter when you put 1s on the MS inputs? *$Q_0 = 1$ $Q_1 = 0$ $Q_2 = 0$ $Q_3 = 1$*

Section 12–5

12–11.How could you form a divide-by-60 using two IC counters?
By cascading a divide-by-10 with a divide by six (6)

12–12. When cascading several counter ICs end-to-end, which Q-output drives the clock input to each successive stage? *the Q will The most significant bit*

Section 12–6

12–13. Seven-segment displays are either common-anode or common-cathode. What does this mean? *all the com-anode or com-cathode are light together*

12–14. List the active segments, by letter, that form the following digits on a seven-segment display: 5, 0. *acd f g , a b c d e f*

12–15. Why are series resistors required when driving a seven-segment LED display? *To limit the current flowing through the LED segment.*

Section 12–7 *don't have the problem of accumulated propagation delay.*

12–16. What advantage do synchronous counters have over ripple counters?

12–17. Because each flip-flop in a synchronous counter is driven by the same clock input, what keeps *all* flip-flops from toggling at each active clock edge? *Tan ic are tied together and control through the use of a and gate .*

Section 12–8

12–18. What is the function of the $\overline{\text{TC}_U}$ and $\overline{\text{TC}_D}$ output pins on the 74193 synchronous counter IC?

12–19. How do you change the 74190 from an up-counter to a down-counter? *u/p = 1*

12–20. The $\overline{\text{CE}}$ input to the 74190 synchronous counter is the *Chip Enable* used to enable/disable the Q-outputs (true or false)?

PROBLEMS

12–1. How are sequential logic circuits different from combinational logic gate circuits?

12–2. The waveforms shown in Figure P12–2 are applied to the inputs at A, $\overline{R_D}$, and C_p. Sketch the resultant waveforms at D, Q, $\overline{Q}$, and X.

Figure P12–2

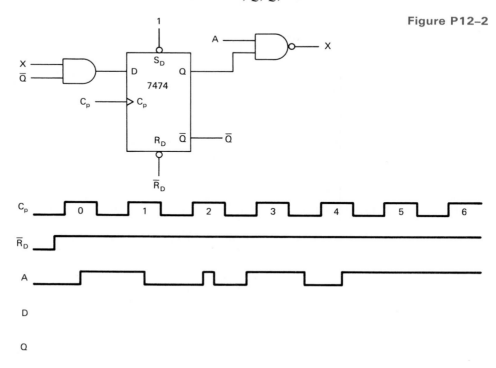

12–3. Repeat Problem 12–2 for the input waveforms shown in Figure P12–3.

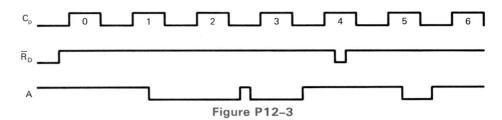

Figure P12–3

12–4. The waveforms shown in Figure P12–4 are applied to the inputs at A, $\overline{C_p}$, and $\overline{R_D}$. Sketch the resultant waveforms at J, K, Q, and $\overline{Q}$.

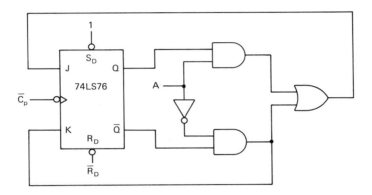

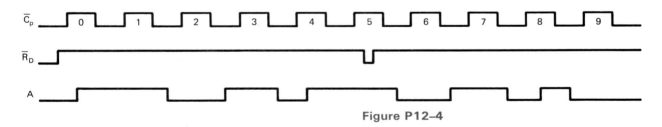

Figure P12–4

12–5. Repeat Problem 12–4 for the input waveforms shown in Figure P12–5.

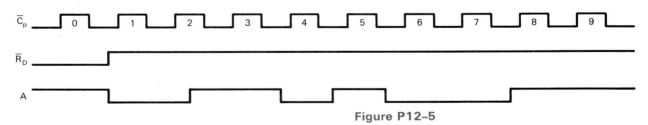

Figure P12–5

12–6. What is the modulus of a counter whose output counts from
    (a)   0 to 7?
    (b)   0 to 18?
    (c)   5 to 0?
    (d)   10 to 0?
    (e)   2 to 15?
    (f)   7 to 3?

12–7. How many *J-K* flip-flops are required to construct the following counters?
   (a) MOD-7
   (b) MOD-8
   (c) MOD-2
   (d) MOD-20
   (e) MOD-33
   (f) MOD-15

12–8. If the input frequency to a 6-bit counter is 10 MHz, what is the frequency at the following output terminals?
   (a) 2^0
   (b) 2^1
   (c) 2^2
   (d) 2^3
   (e) 2^4
   (f) 2^5

12–9. Draw the timing waveforms at $\overline{C_p}$, 2^0, 2^1, and 2^2 for a 3-bit binary up-counter for 10 clock pulses.

12–10. Repeat Problem 12–9 for a binary down-counter.

12–11. What is the highest binary number that can be counted using the following number of flip-flops?
   (a) 2
   (b) 4
   (c) 7
   (d) 1

12–12. In a 5-bit counter the frequency at the following output terminals is what fraction of the input clock frequency?
   (a) 2^0
   (b) 2^1
   (c) 2^2
   (d) 2^3
   (e) 2^4

12–13. How many flip-flops are required to form the following divide-by-*N* frequency dividers?
   (a) Divide-by-4
   (b) Divide-by-15
   (c) Divide-by-12
   (d) Divide-by-18

12–14. Explain why the propagation delay of a flip-flop affects the maximum frequency at which a ripple counter can operate.

12–15. Sketch the $\overline{C_p}$, 2^0, 2^1, and 2^2 output waveforms for the counter shown in Figure P12–15. (Assume that flip-flops are initially Reset).

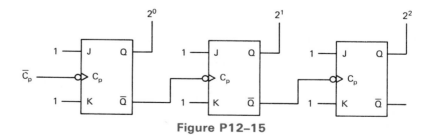

Figure P12–15

12–16. Is the counter of Problem 12–15 an up- or down-counter, and is it a MOD-8 or MOD-16?

12–17. Sketch the connections to a 3-bit ripple up-counter that can be used as a divide-by-6 frequency divider.

12–18.   Design a circuit that will convert a 2 MHz input frequency into a 0.4 MHz output frequency.

12–19.   Design and sketch a MOD-11 ripple up-counter that can be manually Reset by an external pushbutton.

12–20.   Design and sketch a MOD-5 ripple down-counter with a manual Reset pushbutton. (The count sequence should be 7–6–5–4–3–7–6–5–etc.)

12–21.   Repeat Problem 12–20 for a count sequence of 10–9–8–7–6–10–9–8–etc.

12–22.   Design a MOD-4 ripple up-counter that counts in the sequence 10–11–12–13–10–11–12–etc.

12–23.   Describe the major differences between the 7490, 7492, and the 7493 TTL ICs.

12–24.   Assume that you have one 7490 and one 7492. Show the external connections that are required to form a divide-by-24.

12–25.   Repeat Problem 12–24 using two 7492s to form a divide-by-36.

12–26.   Using as many 7492s and 7490s as you need, sketch the external connections required to divide a 60-pps clock down to one pulse per day.

12–27.   Make the necessary external connections to a 7493 to form a MOD-10 counter.

12–28.   Design a ripple counter circuit that will flash an LED ON for 40 ms, OFF for 20 ms (assume that a 100-Hz clock oscillator is available). (*Hint*: Study the output waveforms from a MOD-6 counter.)

12–29.   Design a circuit that will turn on an LED 6 s after you press a momentary pushbutton. (Assume that a 60-pps clock is available.)

12–30.   What modification to the egg-timer circuit of Figure 12–37 could be made to allow you to turn off the buzzer without shutting off the power?

12–31.   Calculate the size of the series current-limiting resistor that could be used in Figure 12–39 to limit the LED current to 15 mA instead of 10 mA.

12–32.   In Figure 12–42, instead of using a resistor dip network, some designers use a single limiting resistor in series with the 5-V supply and connect the 7447 outputs directly to the LED inputs to save money. It works, but the display does not look as good; can you explain why?

12–33.   What advantage does a synchronous counter have over a ripple counter?

12–34.   Sketch the waveforms at $\overline{C_p}$, 2^0, 2^1, and 2^2 for 10 clock pulses for the 3-bit synchronous counter shown in Figure P12–34.

Figure P12–34

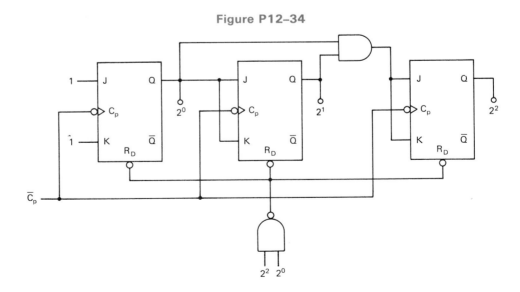

12–35. The duty cycle of a square wave is defined as the time the wave is HIGH, divided by the total time for one period. From the waveforms that you sketched for Problem 12–34, find the duty cycle for the 2^2 output wave.

12–36. Sketch the timing waveforms at $\overline{TC_D}$, $\overline{TC_U}$, Q_0, Q_1, Q_2, and Q_3 for the 74192 counter shown in Figure P12–36.

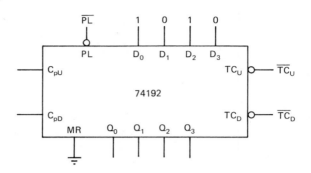

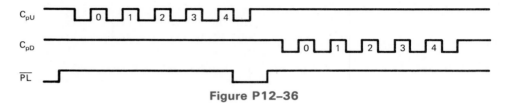

Figure P12–36

12–37. Sketch the timing waveforms at $\overline{RC}$, TC, Q_0, Q_1, Q_2, and Q_3 for the 74191 counter shown in Figure P12–37.

Figure P12–37

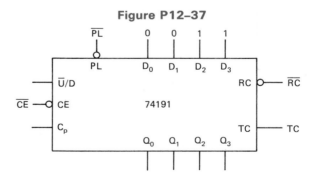

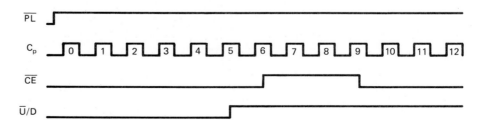

12–38. Make all the necessary pin connections to a 74193 without using external gating to form a divide-by-4 frequency divider. Make it an up-counter and show the waveforms at C_{pU}, $\overline{TC_U}$, Q_0, Q_1, Q_2, and Q_3.

12–39. Using the synchronous Reset feature of the 74163 counter, make the necessary connections to form a glitch-free MOD-12 up-counter.

13

Shift Registers

OBJECTIVES

Upon completion of this chapter, you should be able to:

- Connect *J-K* flip-flops as serial or parallel-in to serial or parallel-out multibit shift registers.
- Draw timing waveforms to illustrate shift register operation.
- Explain the operation and application of ring and Johnson shift counters.
- Make external connections to MSI shift register ICs to perform conversions between serial and parallel data formats.
- Explain the operation and application of three-state output buffers.
- Discuss the operation of circuit design applications that employ shift registers.

INTRODUCTION

Registers are required in digital systems for the temporary storage of a group of bits. Data bits (1's and 0's) traveling through a digital system sometimes have to be temporarily stopped, copied, moved, or even shifted to the right or left one or more positions.

A shift register facilitates this movement and storage of data bits. Most shift registers can handle parallel movement of data bits as well as serial movement, and can also be used to convert from parallel to serial and serial to parallel.

13-1 SHIFT REGISTER BASICS

Let's take a look at a 4-bit shift register contents as it receives 4 bits of parallel data and shifts them to the right four positions into some other digital device. The timing for the shift operations is provided by the input clock and will shift to the right by one position for each input clock pulse, as shown in Figure 13–1.

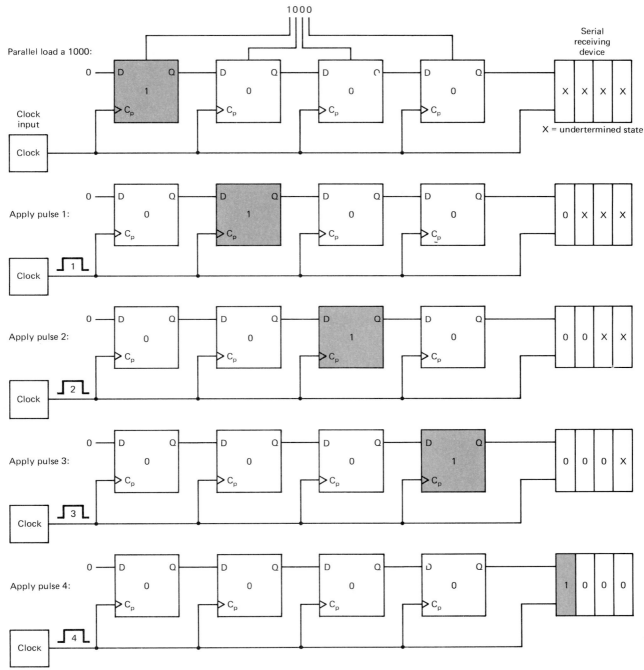

Figure 13-1 Block diagram of a 4-bit shift register used for parallel-to-serial conversion.

In the figure, the group of four boxes are four-D flip-flops comprising the 4-bit shift register. The first step is to parallel load the register with a 1–0–0–0. "Parallel load" means to load all four flip-flops at the same time. This is done by momentarily enabling the appropriate asynchronous Set ($\overline{S_D}$) and Reset ($\overline{R_D}$) inputs.

Next, the first clock pulse causes all bits to shift to the right by one because the input to each flip-flop comes from the Q output of the flip-flop to its left. Each successive pulse causes all data bits to shift one more position to the right.

At the end of the fourth clock pulse, all data bits have been shifted all the way across and now all four original data bits appear, in the correct order, in the serial receiving device. The connections between the fourth flip-flop and the serial receiving device could be a three-conductor serial transmission cable (serial data, clock, and ground).

Figure 13–1 illustrated a parallel-to-serial conversion. Shift registers can also be used for serial-to-parallel, parallel-to-parallel, and serial-to-serial as well as shift-right, shift-left operations as indicated in Figure 13–2. Each of these configurations

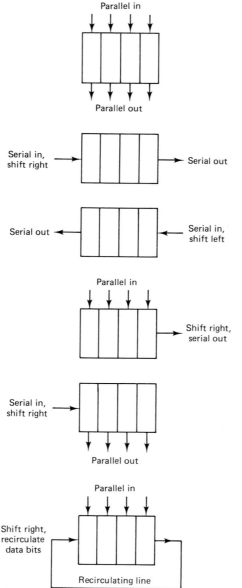

Figure 13–2 Data movement and conversion by shift registers.

and an explanation of the need for a "recirculating line" are explained in upcoming sections.

13–2 *PARALLEL-TO-SERIAL CONVERSION*

Now let's look at the actual circuit connections for a shift register. The data storage elements can be *D* flip-flops, *S-R* flip-flops, or *J-K* flip-flops. We are pretty familiar with *J-K* flip flops, so let's stick with them. Most *J-K*s are negative edge-triggered (like the 74LS76) and will have an active-LOW asynchronous Set ($\overline{S_D}$) and Reset ($\overline{R_D}$).

Figure 13–3 shows the circuit connections for a 4-bit parallel-in, serial-out shift register which is first Reset, then parallel-loaded with an active-LOW 7 (1000), then shifted right four positions.

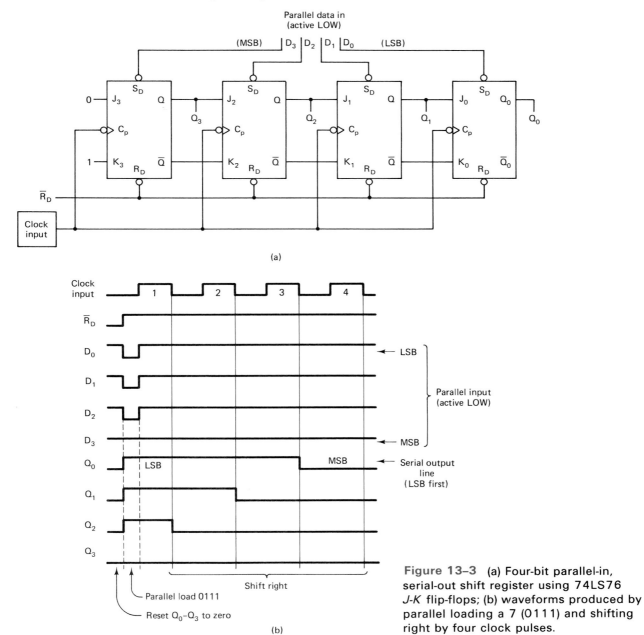

Figure 13–3 (a) Four-bit parallel-in, serial-out shift register using 74LS76 *J-K* flip-flops; (b) waveforms produced by parallel loading a 7 (0111) and shifting right by four clock pulses.

Notice in Figure 13–3a that all $\overline{C_p}$ inputs are fed from a common clock input. Each flip-flop will respond to its *J-K* inputs at every negative clock input edge. Since every *J-K* input is connected to the preceding stage output, then at each negative clock edge, each flip-flop will change to the state of the flip-flop to its left. In other words, all data bits will be shifted one position to the right.

Now, looking at the timing diagram, in the beginning of period 1, $\overline{R_D}$ goes LOW, resetting Q_0 to Q_3 to zero. Next, the parallel data are input (parallel-loaded) via the D_0 to D_3 input lines. (Since the $\overline{S_D}$ inputs are active LOW, the complement of the number to be loaded must be used.)

At the first negative clock edge:

Q_0 takes on the value of Q_1
Q_1 takes on the value of Q_2
Q_2 takes on the value of Q_3
Q_3 is Reset by $J = 0$, $K = 1$

In effect, the bits have all shifted one position to the right. Next, the negative edge of periods 2, 3, and 4 will each shift the bits one more position to the right.

The serial output data comes out of the right-end flip-flop (Q_0). Since the LSB was parallel-loaded into the rightmost flip-flop, the LSB will be shifted out first. The order of the parallel input data bits could have been reversed and the MSB would have come out first. Either case is acceptable. It is up to the designer to know which is first, MSB or LSB, and when to sample (or read) the serial output data line.

13–3 RECIRCULATING REGISTER

Recirculating the rightmost data bits back into the beginning of the register can be accomplished by connecting Q_0 back to J_3 and $\overline{Q_0}$ back to K_3. That way, the original parallel-loaded data bits will never be lost. After every fourth clock pulse, the Q_3 to Q_0 outputs will contain the original 4 data bits. Therefore, with the addition of the recirculating lines to Figure 13–3a the register becomes a parallel-in, serial *and* parallel-out.

13–4 SERIAL-TO-PARALLEL CONVERSION

Serial-in, parallel-out shift registers can also be made up of *J-K* flip-flop storage and a shift-right operation. The idea is to put the serial data in on the serial input line, LSB first (or MSB first, depending on the direction of the shift) and "clock" the shift register four times (for a 4-bit register), stop, then read the parallel data from the Q_0 to Q_3 outputs. Figure 13–4a shows a 4-bit serial-to-parallel shift register converter. The serial data are coming in on the left at D_S. The flip-flops are connected in a shift-right fashion. The inverter at D_S is required to ensure that if $D_S = 1$, then $J = 1$, $K = 0$ and the first flip-flop will Set. Each of the other flip-flops takes on the value of the flip-flop to its left at each negative clock edge.

Each bit of the serial input must be present on the D_S line before the corresponding negative clock edge. After four clock pulses, all 4 serial data bits will be shifted into their appropriate flip-flop. At that time the parallel output data can be read by some other digital device.

If the clock were allowed to continue beyond four pulses, the data bits would continue shifting out of the right end of the register and be lost if you tried to read them again later. That problem is corrected by the *Strobe* line. It is used to Enable-

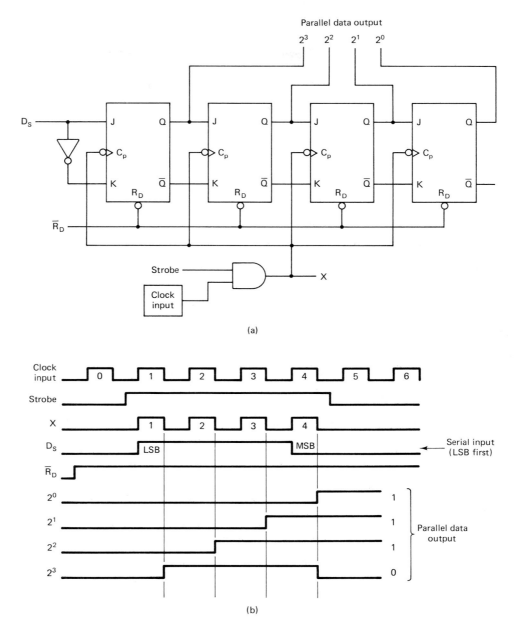

Figure 13–4 (a) Four-bit serial-to-parallel shift register; (b) waveforms produced by a serial-to-parallel conversion of the binary number 0111.

then-Disable the clock at the appropriate time so that the shift-right process will stop. Using a Strobe signal is a popular technique used in digital electronics to Enable or Disable some function during a specific time period.

13–5 RING SHIFT COUNTER AND JOHNSON SHIFT COUNTER

Two common circuits that are used to create sequential control waveforms for digital systems are the ring and Johnson shift counters. They are similar to a synchronous counter because the clock input to each flip-flop is driven by the same clock input. Their outputs do not count in true binary, but instead provide a repetitive sequence

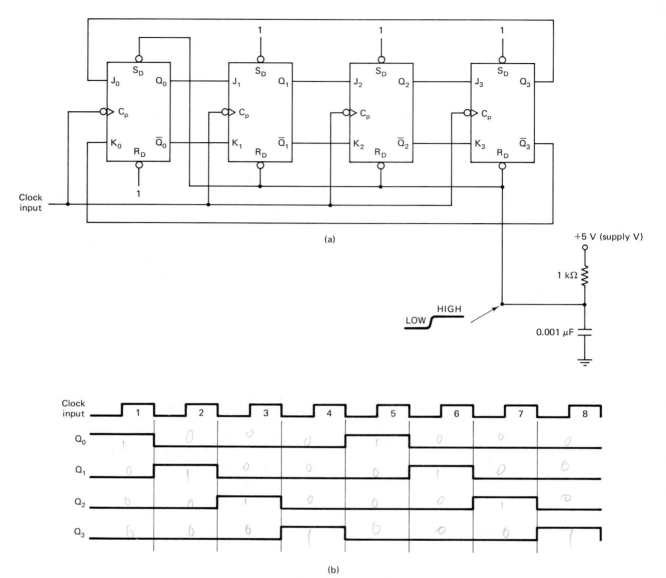

(a)

(b)

Figure 13–5   Ring shift counter: (a) circuit connections; (b) output waveforms.

of digital output levels. These shift counters are used to control a sequence of events in a digital system.

In the case of a 4-bit *ring shift counter*, the output at each flip-flop will be HIGH for one clock period, then LOW for the next three, then repeat, as shown in Figure 13–5b. To form the ring shift counter of Figure 13–5a, the Q-$\overline{Q}$ output of each stage is fed to the J-K input of the next stage and the Q-$\overline{Q}$ output of the last stage is fed back to the J-K input of the first stage. Before applying clock pulses, the shift counter is preset with a 1–0–0–0.

Ring Shift Counter Operation

The RC circuit connected to the power supply will provide a LOW-then-HIGH as soon as the power is turned on, forcing a HIGH–LOW–LOW–LOW at Q_0–Q_1–Q_2–Q_3, which is the necessary preset condition for a ring shift counter. At the first negative clock input edge, Q_0 will go LOW because just before the clock edge J_0

was LOW (from Q_3) and K_0 was HIGH (from $\overline{Q_3}$). At that same clock edge, Q_1 will go HIGH because its *J-K* inputs are connected to Q_0-$\overline{Q_0}$, which were 1–0. The Q_2 and Q_3 flip-flops will remain Reset (LOW) because their *J-K* inputs see a 0–1 from the previous flip-flops.

Now, the ring shift counter is outputting a 0–1–0–0 (period 2). At the negative edge of period 2, the flip-flop outputs will respond to whatever levels are present at their *J-K* inputs, the same as explained in the preceding paragraph. That is, since J_2-K_2 are looking back (connected to) at Q_1-$\overline{Q_1}$ (1–0), then Q_2 will go HIGH. All other flip-flops are looking back at a 0–1, so they will Reset (LOW). This cycle repeats continuously. The system acts like it is continuously "pushing" the initial HIGH level at Q_0 through the four flip-flops.

The *Johnson shift counter* circuit is similar to the ring shift counter except that the output lines of the last flip-flop are crossed (thus an alternative name is "twisted ring counter") before feeding back to the input of the first flip-flop and *all* flip-flops are initially Reset as shown in Figure 13–6.

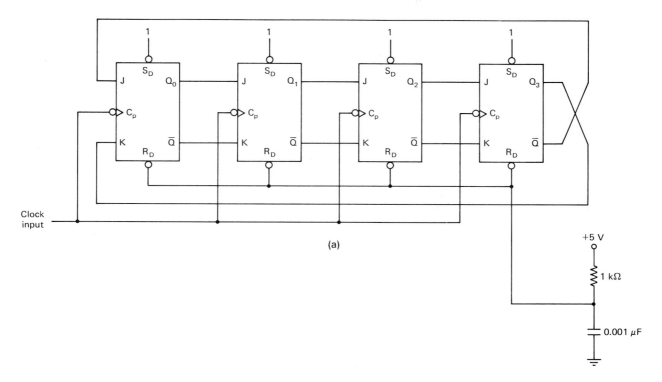

(a)

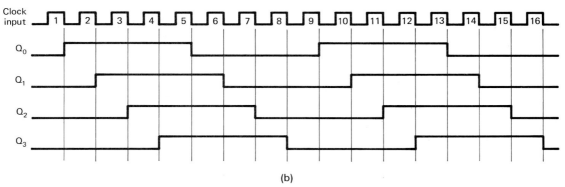

(b)

Figure 13–6 Johnson shift counter: (a) circuit connections; (b) output waveforms.

Johnson Shift Counter Operation

The *RC* circuit provides an automatic Reset to all four flip-flops so the initial outputs will all be Reset (LOW). At the first negative clock edge, the first flip-flop will Set (HIGH) because J_0 is connected to $\overline{Q_3}$ (HIGH) and K_0 is connected to Q_3 (LOW). The Q_1, Q_2, and Q_3 outputs will follow the state of their preceding flip-flop because of their direct connection *J*-to-*Q*. Therefore, during period 2, the output is 1–0–0–0.

At the next negative clock edge, Q_0 remains HIGH because it takes on the *opposite* state of Q_3, Q_1 goes HIGH because it takes on the *same* state as Q_0, Q_2 stays LOW, and Q_3 stays LOW. Now the output is 1–1–0–0.

The sequence continues as shown in Figure 13–6. Notice that during period 5, Q_3 gets Set HIGH. At the end of period 5, Q_0 gets Reset LOW because the outputs of Q_3 are crossed, so Q_0 takes on the opposite state of Q_3.

13–6 SHIFT REGISTER ICs

Four-bit and 8-bit shift registers are commonly available in integrated-circuit packages. Depending on your needs, practically every possible load, shift, and conversion operation is available in a shift register IC.

Let's look at four popular shift register ICs to get familiar with using our data manuals and understanding the terminology and procedure for performing the various operations.

The 74164 8-bit Serial-in, Parallel-Out Shift Register

By looking at the logic symbol and logic diagram for the 74164 (Figure 13–7) we can see that it saves us the task of wiring together eight *D* flip-flops. The 74164 has two serial input lines (D_{Sa} and D_{Sb}), synchronously read in by a positive edge-triggered clock (C_p). The logic diagram (Figure 13–7b) shows both D_S inputs feeding into an AND gate. Therefore, either input can be used as an active-HIGH enable

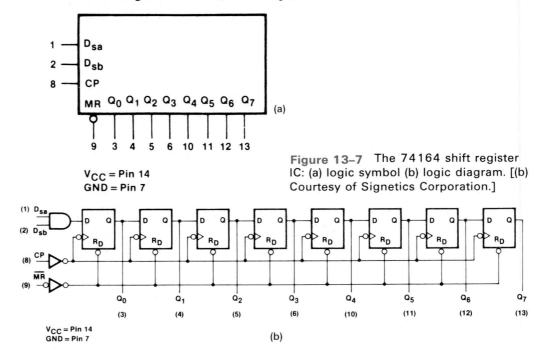

Figure 13–7 The 74164 shift register IC: (a) logic symbol (b) logic diagram. [(b) Courtesy of Signetics Corporation.]

for data entry through the other input. Each positive edge clock pulse will shift the data bits one position to the right. Therefore, the first data bit entered (either LSB or MSB) will end up in the far right D flip-flop (Q_7) after eight clock pulses. The $\overline{MR}$ is an active-LOW Master-Reset that resets all eight flip-flops when pulsed LOW.

EXAMPLE 13–1

Draw the circuit connections and timing waveforms for the serial-to-parallel conversion of the binary number 11010010 using a 74164 shift register.

Solution: The serial-to-parallel conversion circuit and waveforms are shown in Figure 13–8. First, the register is cleared by a LOW on $\overline{MR}$, making $Q_0 - Q_7 = 0$. The Strobe line is required to make sure that we only get eight clock pulses. The serial data are entered on the D_{Sb} line, MSB first. After eight clock pulses, the 8 data bits can be read at the parallel output pins (MSB at Q_7 and LSB at Q_0).

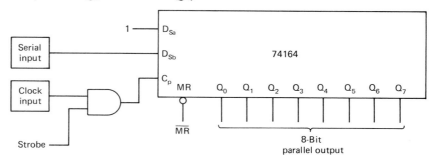

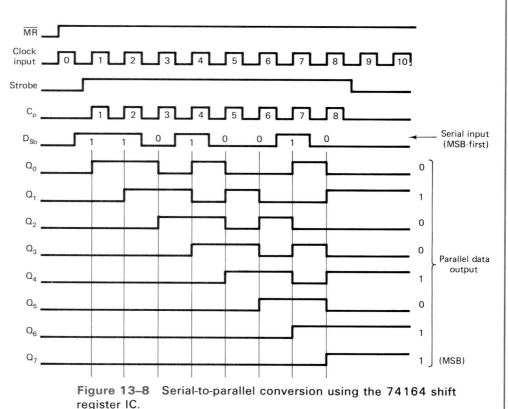

Figure 13–8   Serial-to-parallel conversion using the 74164 shift register IC.

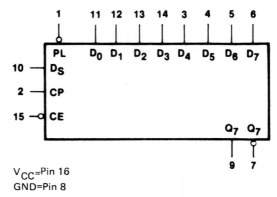

Figure 13-9   Logic symbol for the 74165 8-bit serial or parallel-in, serial-out shift register.

The next IC to consider is the 74165 8-bit serial *or* parallel-in, serial-out shift register. The logic symbol for the 74165 is given in Figure 13–9.

Just by looking at the logic symbol, you should be able to determine the operation of the 74165. The $\overline{PL}$ is an active-LOW terminal for performing a parallel load of the 8 parallel input data bits. The $\overline{CE}$ is an active-LOW clock enable for starting/stopping (shifting/holding) the shift operation by enabling/disabling the clock (same function as the "Strobe" in Example 13–1).

The clock input (C_p) is positive edge triggered, so after each positive edge, the data bits are shifted one position to the right. The serial output (Q_7) and its complement ($\overline{Q_7}$) are available from the rightmost flip-flop's outputs.

Another shift register IC is the 74194 4-bit bidirectional universal shift register. It is called "universal" because it has a wide range of applications, including serial or parallel input; serial or parallel output; shift left or right; hold; and asynchronous Reset. The logic symbol for the 74194 is shown in Figure 13–10.

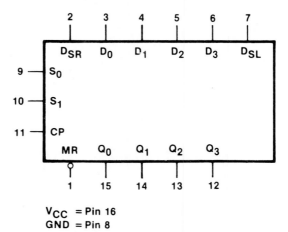

Figure 13–10   Logic symbol for the 74194 universal shift register.

The major differences with the 74194 are that there are separate serial inputs for shifting left or shifting right, and the operating mode is determined by the digital states of the mode control inputs, S_0 and S_1. S_0 and S_1 can be thought of as receiving a 2-bit binary code representing one of four possible operating modes ($2^2 = 4$ combinations). The four operating modes are shown in Table 13–1.

TABLE 13–1

Operating Modes
of the 74194

Operating mode	S_1	S_0
Hold	0	0
Shift Left	1	0
Shift Right	0	1
Parallel Load	1	1

A complete mode select-function table for the 74194 is shown in Table 13–2. Table 13–2 can be used to determine the procedure and expected outcome of the various shift register operations.

TABLE 13–2

Mode Select-Function Table for the 74194[a]

	Inputs							Outputs			
Operating mode	C_p	$\overline{MR}$	S_1	S_0	D_{SR}	D_{SL}	D_n	Q_0	Q_1	Q_2	Q_3
Reset (clear)	×	L	×	×	×	×	×	L	L	L	L
Hold (do nothing)	×	H	l[b]	l[b]	×	×	×	q_0	q_1	q_2	q_3
Shift Left	↑	H	h	l[b]	×	l	×	q_1	q_2	q_3	L
	↑	H	h	l[b]	×	h	×	q_1	q_2	q_3	H
Shift Right	↑	H	l[b]	h	l	×	×	L	q_0	q_1	q_2
	↑	H	l[b]	h	h	×	×	H	q_0	q_1	q_2
Parallel Load	↑	H	h	h	×	×	d_n	d_0	d_1	d_2	d_3

Courtesy of Signetics Corporation

[a] H = HIGH voltage level; h = HIGH voltage level one setup time prior to the LOW-to-HIGH clock transition; L = LOW voltage level; l = LOW voltage level one setup time prior to the LOW-to-HIGH clock transition; d_n (q_n) = lower case letters indicate the state of the referenced input (or output) one setup time prior to the LOW-to-HIGH clock transition; × = don't care; ↑ = LOW-to-HIGH clock transition.
[b] The HIGH-to-LOW transition of the S_0 and S_1 inputs on the 54/74194 should only take place while C_p is HIGH for conventional operation.

From the function table we can see that a LOW input to the Master Reset ($\overline{MR}$) asynchronously resets Q_0 to Q_3 to 0. A parallel load is accomplished by making S_0, S_1 both HIGH and placing the parallel input data on D_0 to D_3. The register will then be parallel loaded synchronously by the first positive clock (C_p) edge. The 4 data bits can then be shifted to the right or left by making S_0–S_1 1–0 or 0–1 and applying an input clock to C_p.

A recirculating shift-right register can be set up by connecting Q_3 back into D_{SR} and applying a clock input (C_p) with $S_1 = 0$, $S_0 = 1$. Also, a recirculating shift-left register can be set up by connecting Q_0 into D_{SL} and applying a clock input (C_p) with $S_1 = 1$, $S_0 = 0$.

The best way to get a "feel" for the operation of the 74194 is to study the timing waveforms for a typical sequence of operations. Figure 13–11 shows the input data, control waveforms, and the output (Q_0 to Q_3) waveforms generated by a clear–load–shift right–shift left–inhibit–clear sequence. Study these waveforms carefully until you thoroughly understand the setup of the mode controls and the reason for each state change in the Q_0 to Q_3 outputs.

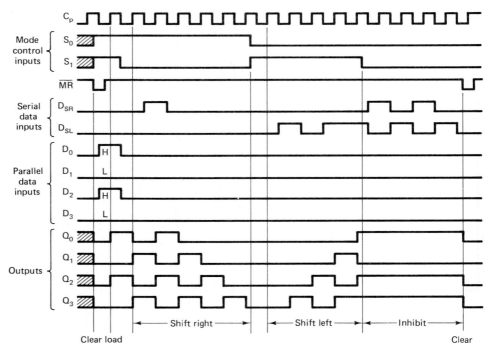

Figure 13–11 Typical clear–load–shift right–shift left–inhibit–clear sequences for a 74194.

EXAMPLE 13–2

Draw the circuit connection and timing waveforms for a recirculating shift-right register. The register should be loaded initially with a hexadecimal D (1101).

Solution: The shift-right register is shown in Figure 13–12. First, the S_0 and S_1 mode controls are set to 1–1 for parallel loading D_0 to D_3. When the first positive clock edge (pulse 0) comes in, the data present on D_0 to D_3 is loaded into Q_0 to Q_3. Next, S_0 and S_1 are made 1–0 to perform shift-right operations. At the positive edge of each successive clock edge, the data are shifted one position to the right (i.e., $Q_0 \rightarrow Q_1$, $Q_1 \rightarrow Q_2$, $Q_2 \rightarrow Q_3$, $Q_3 \rightarrow D_{SR}$, $D_{SR} \rightarrow Q_0$). The recirculating connection from Q_3 back to D_{SR} keeps the data from being lost. After each fourth clock pulse, the circulating data are back in their original position.

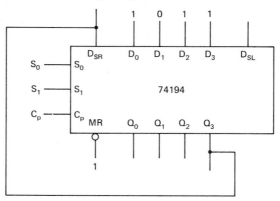

Figure 13–12 Four-bit recirculating shift-right register connections and waveforms using the 74194.

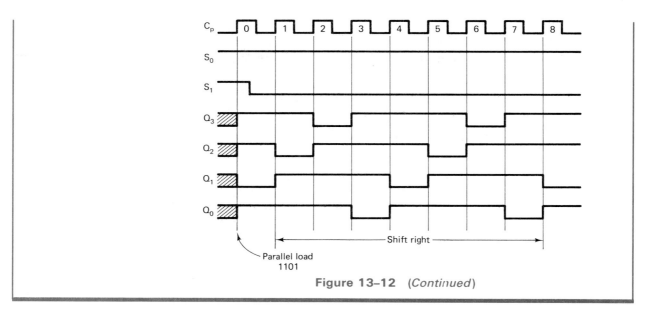

Figure 13-12 (Continued)

Three-State Outputs

Another valuable feature available on some shift registers is a three-state output. The term "three-state" is derived from the fact that the output can have one of three levels: HIGH, LOW, or float. The symbol and function table for a three-state output buffer is shown in Figure 13-13.

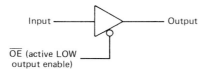

Input	$\overline{OE}$	Output
1	0	1
0	0	0
1	1	Float
0	1	Float

Figure 13-13 Three-state output buffer symbol and function table.

From Figure 13-13 we can see that the circuit acts like a straight buffer (output = input) when $\overline{OE}$ is LOW (active-LOW Output Enable). When the output is disabled ($\overline{OE}$ = HIGH), the output level is placed in the "float" or "high-impedance" state. In the high-impedance state, the output looks like an open circuit to anything else connected to it. In other words, in the float state the output is neither HIGH nor LOW and cannot sink nor source current.

Three-state outputs are necessary when you need to connect more than one register's outputs to the same points. For example, if you have two 4-bit registers, one containing data from device 1, the other containing different data from device 2 and you want to connect both sets of outputs to the same receiving device, one device must be in the float condition while the other's output is enabled, and vice versa. This way, only one set of outputs is connected to the receiving device at a time to avoid a conflict.

To further illustrate the operation of three-state buffers, let's look at a register that has three-state outputs and discuss a system design example that uses two 4-

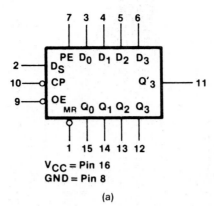

V_CC = Pin 16
GND = Pin 8

(a)

Figure 13-14 The 74395A 4-bit shift register with three-state outputs: (a) logic symbol; (b) logic circuit. [(b) Courtesy of Signetics Corporation.]

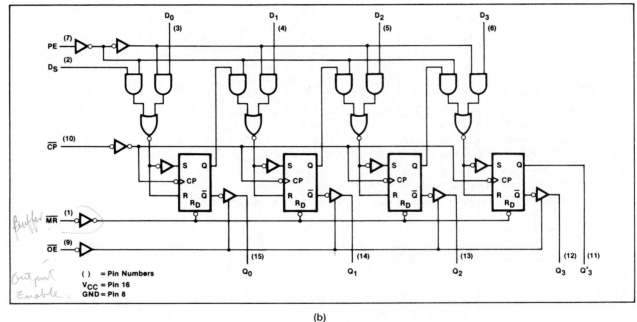

(b)

bit registers to feed a single receiving device. The 74395A is a 4-bit shift (right) register with three-state outputs as shown in Figure 13–14. From the logic circuit diagram (Figure 13–14b) we can see that the Q_0 to Q_3 outputs are "three-stated" and will not be allowed to "pass" data unless a LOW is present at the Output Enable pin ($\overline{OE}$). Also, a non-three-stated output, Q'_3, is made available to enable the user to cascade with another register and shift data bits to the cascaded register whether the regular outputs (Q_0 to Q_3) are enabled or not (i.e., to cascade two 4-bit registers, Q'_3 would be connected to D_S of the second stage).

Otherwise, the chip's operation is similar to previously discussed shift registers. The Parallel Enable (PE) input is active-HIGH for enabling the parallel data input (D_0 to D_3) to be synchronously loaded on the negative clock edge. D_S is the serial data input line for synchronously loading serial data, and $\overline{MR}$ is an active-LOW Master Reset.

EXAMPLE 13–3

Sketch the circuit connections for a two register system that alternately feeds one register, then the other into a 4-bit receiving device. Upon power-up load register 1 with 0111 and register 2 with 1101.

Solution: The two register system is shown in Figure 13–15. Notice that both sets of outputs go to a common point. The three-state outputs allow us to do this by only enabling one set of outputs at a time so that there is no conflict between HIGHs and LOWs. One way to alternately enable one register, then the other is to use a toggle flip-flop and feed the Q output to the upper Output Enable ($\overline{OE}$) and the $\overline{Q}$ to the lower Output Enable as shown in Figure 13–15.

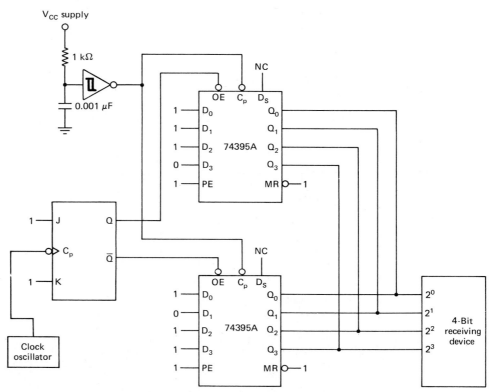

Figure 13–15   Two 4-bit three-state output shift registers feeding a common receiving device.

Also, upon initial power-up we want to parallel-load both 4-bit registers. To do this, the D_0 to D_3 inputs contain the proper bit string to be loaded and the Parallel Enable (PE) is held HIGH. Since the parallel load function is synchronous (needs a clock trigger), we will supply a HIGH-then-LOW pulse to $\overline{C_p}$ via the RC Schmitt circuit.

13–7   SYSTEM DESIGN APPLICATIONS FOR SHIFT REGISTERS

Shift registers have many applications in digital sequencing, storage, and transmission of serial and parallel data. The following designs will illustrate some of these applications.

APPLICATION 13–1

Using a ring shift counter as a sequencing device, design a traffic light controller that goes through the following sequence: green, 20 s; yellow, 10 s; red, 20 s. Also, at night, flash the yellow light on and off continuously.

Solution: By studying the waveforms from Figure 13–5, you will notice that if we add one more flip-flop to that 4-bit ring shift counter and use a clock input of 1 pulse per 10 s, we could tap off the *Q* outputs using OR gates to get a 20–10–20 sequence. Also, we could use a phototransistor to determine night from day. During the night we want to stop the ring shift counter and flash the yellow light. Figure 13–16 shows a 5-bit ring counter that could be used as this traffic light controller. First, let's make sure that the green–yellow–red sequence will work properly during the daytime. During

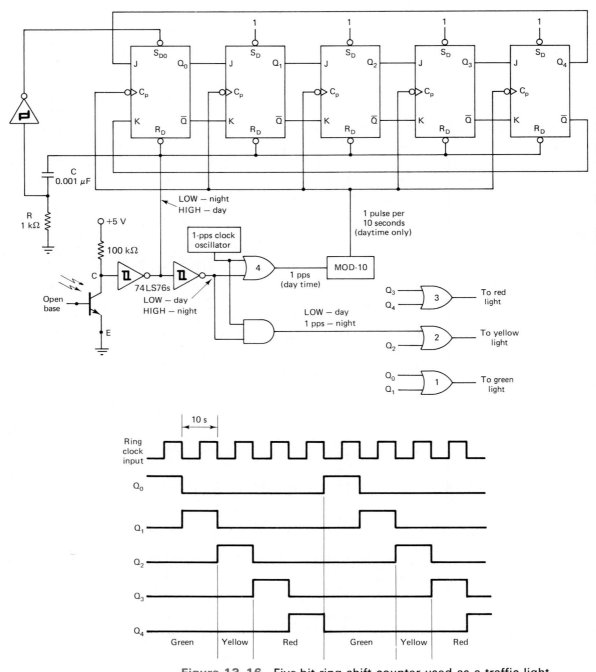

Figure 13–16   Five-bit ring shift counter used as a traffic light controller.

the daytime, outdoor light shines on the phototransistor, making its collector-to-emitter resistance LOW, placing a low voltage at the input to the first Schmitt inverter, causing a LOW input to OR gate 4. The 1-pps clock oscillator will pass through OR gate 4 into the MOD-10, which divides the frequency down to one pulse per 10 s. The output from the MOD-10 is used to drive the clock input to the 5-bit ring shift counter, which will circulate a single HIGH level down through each successive flip-flop for 10 s at each Q output, as shown in the timing waveforms.

OR gates 1, 2, and 3 are connected to the ring counter outputs in such a way that the green light will be on if Q_0 *or* Q_1 are HIGH, which occurs for 20 s. The yellow light will come on next for 10 s due to Q_2 being on, and then the red light will come on for 20 s because either Q_3 *or* Q_4 are HIGH.

At nighttime the phototransistor changes to a high resistance, placing a HIGH at the input to the first Schmitt inverter, which places a HIGH at OR gate 4. This makes its output HIGH, stopping the clock input oscillations to the ring counter.

Also at nighttime, the LOW output from the first Schmitt inverter is connected to the ring counter Resets, holding the Q outputs at 0. The HIGH output from the second Schmitt inverter "enables" the AND gate to pass the 1-pps clock oscillator on to OR gate 2, causing the yellow light to flash.

At sunrise the output from the first Schmitt inverter changes from a LOW to a HIGH, allowing the ring counter to start again. That LOW-to-HIGH transition causes an instantaneous surge of current to flow through the RC circuit. That current will cause a HIGH at the input of the third Schmitt inverter, which places a LOW at $\overline{S_{D_0}}$, setting Q_0 HIGH. When the surge current has passed (a few microseconds), $\overline{S_{D_0}}$ returns to a HIGH and the ring counter will proceed to rotate the HIGH level from Q_0 to Q_1 to Q_2 to Q_3 to Q_4 continuously, all day, as shown in the timing waveforms.

APPLICATION 13–2

Using a Johnson shift counter and various gates, design a digital sequencer that produces a HIGH for 1 s, LOW for 5 s repeatedly, and also a HIGH for 4 s, LOW for 2 s repeatedly, as shown in the two waveforms in Figure 13–17 labeled X and Y.

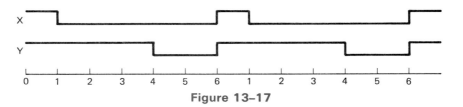

Figure 13–17

Solution: It appears from the waveforms that the cycle of X and Y repeats every 6 s. If we use a 3-bit Johnson shift counter, driven by a 1-pps input clock, we should be able to tap off the Q outputs and get the required digital sequence at X and Y, as shown in Figure 13–18. The 3-bit Johnson shift counter will produce the waveforms shown at the Q outputs of Figure 13–18. Using both the Q and $\overline{Q}$ outputs for inputs to an AND and OR gate, we can produce the required waveforms for X and Y. By ANDing the waveforms at $\overline{Q_0}$ and $\overline{Q_2}$ together we will get a HIGH from 0 to 1 (both $\overline{Q_0}$ and $\overline{Q_2}$ are HIGH) and then a LOW from 1 to 6, then repeat. The waveform

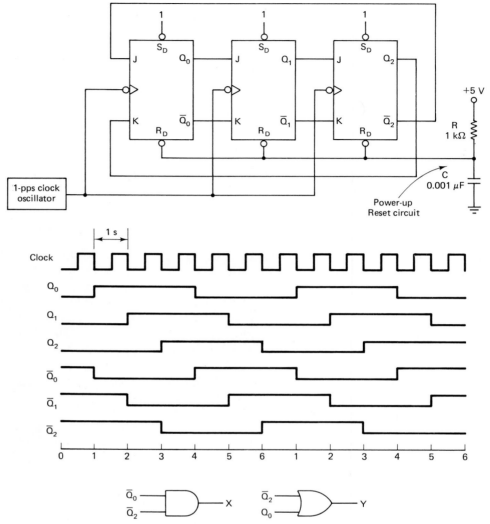

Figure 13–18   Johnson counter used as a digital sequencer.

for Y is achieved by ORing $\overline{Q_2}$ with Q_0 (i.e., one or the other is HIGH from 0 to 4 and both are LOW from 4 to 6).

As you can see, we can get almost any sequence of waveforms from a Johnson shift counter with external gating. (You might remember back in Chapter 4 how we used the Johnson shift counter to create specialized waveforms.)

APPLICATION 13–3

Design a 16-bit serial-to-parallel converter.

Solution: First we have to look through a TTL data manual to see what is available. The 74164 is an 8-bit serial-in, parallel-out shift register. Let's cascade two of them together to form a 16-bit register. Figure 13–19 shows that the Q_7 output is fed into the serial input of the second 8-bit register. That way, as the data bits are shifted through the register, when they reach Q_7 the next shift will pass the data into Q_0 of the second register (via D_{Sa}),

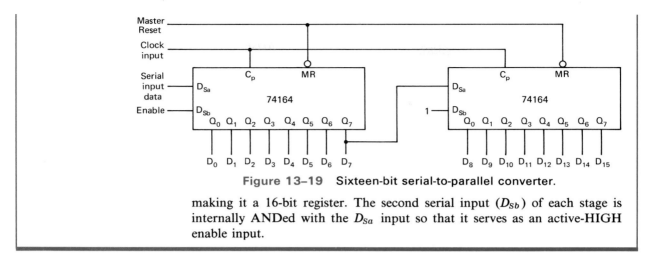

Figure 13–19 Sixteen-bit serial-to-parallel converter.

making it a 16-bit register. The second serial input (D_{Sb}) of each stage is internally ANDed with the D_{Sa} input so that it serves as an active-HIGH enable input.

APPLICATION 13–4

Design a circuit and provide the input waveforms required to perform a parallel-to-serial conversion. Specifically, a hexadecimal B (1011) is to be parallel-loaded, then transmitted repeatedly to a serial device LSB first.

By controlling the mode control inputs (S_0, S_1) of a 74194 we can perform a parallel load and then shift right repeatedly. The serial output data are taken from Q_3 as shown in Figure 13–20. The 74194 universal

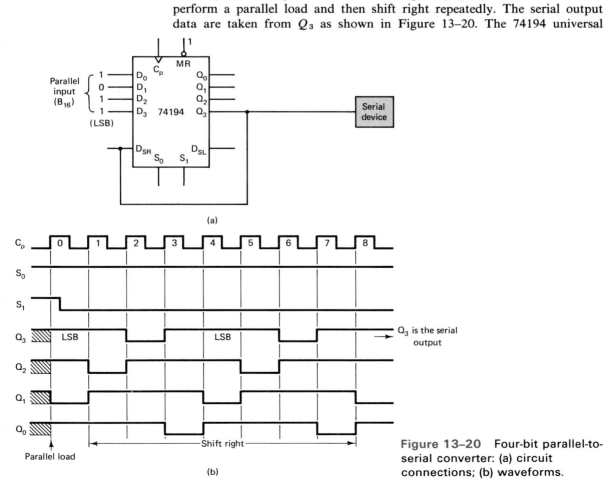

Figure 13–20 Four-bit parallel-to-serial converter: (a) circuit connections; (b) waveforms.

shift register is connected as a recirculating parallel-to-serial converter. Each time the Q_3 serial output level is sent to the serial device, it is also recirculated back into the left end of the shift register.

First, at the positive edge of clock pulse 0, the register is parallel-loaded with a 1011 (B_{16}) because the mode controls ($S_0 S_1$) are HIGH–HIGH. (D_3 is loaded with the LSB because it will be the first bit out when we shift right.)

Next, the mode controls ($S_0 S_1$) are changed to HIGH–LOW for a shift-right operation. Now, each successive positive clock edge will shift the data bit one position to the right. The Q_3 output will continuously have the levels 1101–1101–1101–etc., which is a backwards hexadecimal B (LSB first).

APPLICATION 13–5

Design an interface to an 8-bit serial printer. Sketch the waveforms required to transmit the single ASCII code for an asterisk (*). *Note*: ASCII is the 7-bit code that was given in Chapter 1. The ASCII code for an asterisk is 010 1010. Let's make the unused eighth bit (MSB) a zero.

Solution: The circuit design and waveforms are shown in Figure 13–21. The 74165 is chosen for the job because it is an 8-bit register that can be parallel loaded, then shifted synchronously by the clock input to provide the serial output to the printer.

During pulse 0 the register is loaded with the ASCII code for an asterisk (the LSB is put into D_7 because we want it to come out first). The clock input is then enabled by a LOW on $\overline{CE}$. Each positive pulse on C_p from then on will shift the data bits one position to the right. After the eighth clock pulse (0 to 7) the printer will have received all 8 serial data bits.

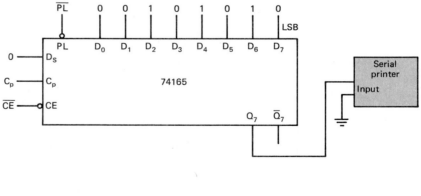

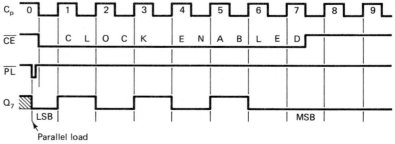

Figure 13–21   Circuit design and waveforms for the transmission of an ASCII character to a serial printer.

Then the $\overline{CE}$ line is brought HIGH to disable the synchronous clock input. To avoid any racing problems, the printer will read the Q_7 line at each negative edge of C_p so that the level will definitely be a stable HIGH or LOW, as shown in Figure 13–21.

At this point you may be wondering how we are practically going to electronically provide the necessary signals on the $\overline{CE}$ and $\overline{PL}$ lines. An exact degree of timing must be provided on these lines to ensure that the register–printer interface communicates properly. These signals will be provided by a microprocessor and are called the *handshaking* signals.

Microprocessor theory and programming is an advanced digital topic and is not discussed in this book. For now, it is important for us to realize that these signals are required and be able to sketch their timing diagrams.

13–8 THREE-STATE BUFFERS, LATCHES AND TRANSCEIVERS

When we start studying microprocessor hardware, we'll see a need for transmitting a number of bits simultaneously as a group. A single flip-flop will not suffice. What we need is a group of flip-flops, called a *register* to facilitate the movement and temporary storage of binary information. The most commonly-used registers are 8-bits wide and function as either a buffer, latch, or transceiver.

Three-State Buffers

In microprocessor systems, several input and output devices must share the same data lines going into the microprocessor IC. (These "shared" data lines are called the *data bus*). For example, if an 8-bit microprocessor interfaces with four separate 8-bit input devices, we must provide a way to enable just one of the devices to place its data on the data bus and disable the other three. One way this procedure can be accomplished is to use three-state octal buffers.

In Figure 13–22, the second buffer is enabled, which allows the 8 data bits from Input Device 2 to reach the data bus. The other three buffers are disabled, thus keeping their outputs in a "float" condition.

A buffer is simply a device that, when enabled, passes a digital level from its input, to its output, unchanged. It provides isolation, or a "buffer" between the input device and the data bus. A buffer also provides the sink or source current required by any devices connected to its output without loading down the input device. An octal buffer IC has eight individual buffers within a single package.

A popular three-state octal buffer is the 74LS244 shown in Figure 13–23. Notice that the buffers are configured in two groups of four. The first group (group a) is controlled by $\overline{OE}_a$ and the second group (group b) is controlled by $\overline{OE}_b$. OE is an abbreviation for Output Enable and is active-LOW, meaning that it takes a LOW to allow data to pass from the inputs (I) to the outputs (Y). Other features of the 74LS244 are that it has Schmitt trigger hysteresis, and very high sink and source current capabilities (24 mA and 15 mA respectively).

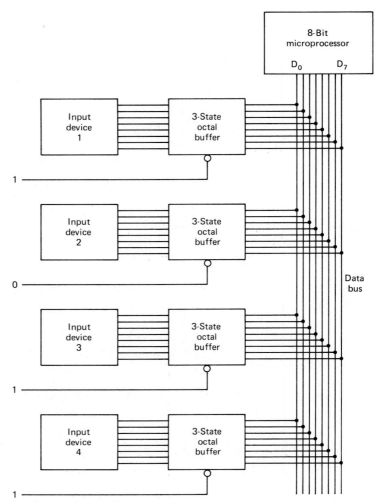

Figure 13–22 Using a three-state octal buffer to pass 8 data bits from Input Device 2 to the Data Bus.

Figure 13–23 Pin configuration for the 74LS244 three-state octal buffer.

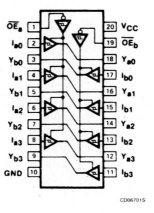

Octal Latches/Flip-Flops

In microprocessor systems we need latches and flip-flops to "remember" digital states that a microprocessor issues before it goes on to other tasks. Take, for example, a microprocessor system that drives two separate 8-bit output devices as shown in Figure 13–24.

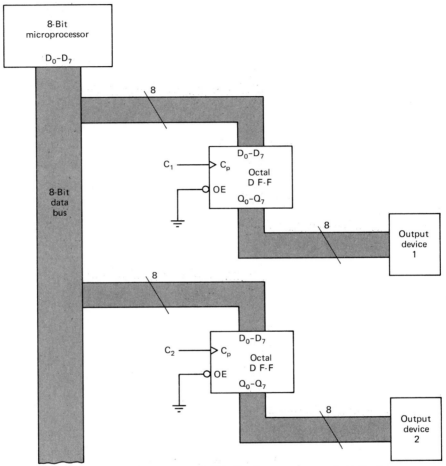

Figure 13–24 Using octal D flip-flops to capture data that appear momentarily on a microprocessor data bus.

To send information to Output Device 1, the microprocessor first sets up the Data Bus (D_0-D_7) with the appropriate data, then issues a LOW-to-HIGH pulse on Line C_1. The positive edge of the pulse causes the data at D_0-D_7 of the flip-flop to be stored at Q_0-Q_7. Because $\overline{OE}$ is tied LOW, its data are sent on to Output Device 1. (The diagonal line with the number 8 above it is a shorthand method used to indicate eight separate lines or conductors).

Next, the microprocessor sets up the data bus with data for Output Device 2 and issues a LOW-to-HIGH pulse on C_2. Now the second octal D flip-flop is loaded with valid data. The outputs of the D flip-flops will remain at those digital levels, thus allowing the microprocessor to go on to perform other tasks.

Earlier in this text we studied the 7475 transparent latch and the 7474 D flip-flop. The 74LS373 and 74LS374 shown in Figure 13–25 operate similarly except they were developed to handle 8-bit data operations.

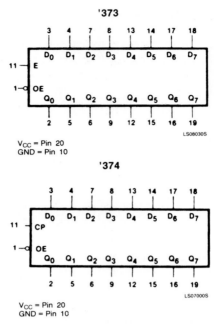

Figure 13–25 Logic symbol for the 74LS373 octal latch and the 74LS374 octal D flip-flop.

Transceivers

Another way to connect devices to a shared data bus is to use a transceiver (transmitter/receiver). The transceiver differs from a buffer or latch because it is *bi-directional*. This capability is necessary for interfacing devices that are used for *both input and output* to a microprocessor. Figure 13–26 shows a common way to connect an I/O device to a data bus via a transceiver.

To make Input/Output Device 1 the active interface, the $\overline{CE}$ (Chip Enable) line must first be made LOW. If $\overline{CE}$ is HIGH, the transceiver disconnects the I/O device from the bus by making the connection float.

Figure 13–26 Using an octal transceiver to interface an input/output device to an 8-bit data bus.

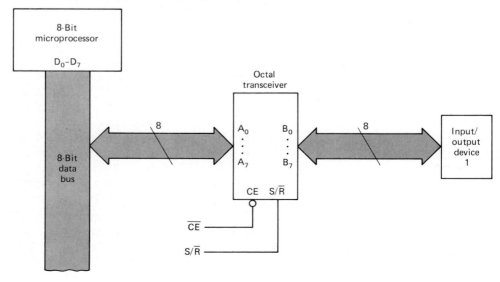

After making $\overline{CE}$ LOW, the microprocessor then issues the appropriate level on the S/$\overline{R}$ line depending on whether it wants to *send data to* the I/O device or *receive data from* the I/O device. If S/$\overline{R}$ is made HIGH, the transceiver allows data to pass to the I/O device (from A to B). If S/$\overline{R}$ is made LOW, the transceiver allows data to pass to the microprocessor data bus (from B to A).

To see how a transceiver is able to both send and receive data, study the internal logic of the 74LS245 shown in Figure 13–27.

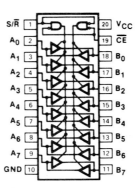

Figure 13–27 Pin configuration and internal logic of the 74LS245 octal 3-state transceiver.

GLOSSARY

Bi-directional: Allowing data to flow in either direction.

Bit string: Two or more binary numbers (bits) that together are used as data bits (a "string" of binary numbers).

Buffer: A logic device connected between two digital circuits, providing isolation, high sink and source current, and usually three-state control.

Clock enable: A separate input pin included on some ICs, used to enable or disable the clock input signal.

Data bit: A single binary representation (0 or 1) of digital information.

Data Bus: A group of eight lines or electrical conductors usually connected to a microprocessor and shared by a number of other devices connected to it.

Data conversion: Transformation of digital information from one format to another (e.g., serial-to-parallel conversion).

Data transmission: The movement of digital information from one location to another.

Digital sequencer: A system (like a shift counter) that can produce a specific series of digital waveforms to drive another device in a specific sequence.

Float: A digital output level which is neither HIGH nor LOW but instead is in a *high-impedance state.* In this state, the output acts like a high impedance with respect to ground and will float to any voltage level that happens to be connected to it.

High-impedance State: *See* float

Mode control: Input pins available on some ICs used to control the operating functions of that IC.

Octal: When referring to an IC, octal means that a single package contains *eight* logic devices.

Output enable: An input pin on an IC that can be used to enable or disable the outputs. When disabled, the outputs are in the "float condition."

Parallel enable: An IC input pin used to enable or disable a synchronous parallel load of data bits.

Recirculating: In a shift register, instead of letting the shifting data bits "drop" out of the end of the register, a recirculating connection can be made to pass the bits back into the front end of the register.

Register: Two or more flip-flops (or storage units) connected as a group and operated simultaneously.

Shift counter: A special-purpose shift register with modifications to its connections and preloaded with a specific value to enable it to output a special sequence of digital waveforms. It does not count in true binary, but instead is used for special sequential waveform generation.

Shift register: A storage device containing two or more data bits, capable of moving the data to the left or right and perform conversions between serial and parallel.

Strobe: A connection used in digital circuits to enable or disable a particular function.

Three-state output: A feature on some ICs that allows you to connect several outputs to a common point. When one of the outputs is HIGH or LOW, all others will be in the float condition (the three output levels are HIGH, LOW, and float).

Transceiver: A data transmission device that is bi-directional, allowing data to flow through it in either direction.

Transparent latch: An asynchronous device whose outputs "hold" onto the most recent digital state of the inputs. The outputs immediately follow the state of the inputs (transparent) while the trigger input is active, then latch onto that information when the trigger is removed.

REVIEW QUESTIONS

Sections 13–1 through 13–3

13–1.   All flip-flops within a shift register are driven by the same clock input (true or false)?

13–2.   What connections allow data to pass from one flip-flop to the next in a shift register?

13–3.   How is data parallel-loaded into a shift register constructed from J-K flip-flops?

13–4.   If a hexadecimal C is parallel-loaded into the shift register of Figure 13–3 and four clock pulses are applied, what is the state of the Q outputs? If recirculating lines are connected and the same operation occurs, what is the state of the Q outputs?

Sections 13–4 and 13–5

13–5.   What happens to the initial parallel-loaded data in the shift register of Figure 13–4 if the *Strobe* line is never disabled?

13–6.   To operate properly, a ring shift counter must be parallel-loaded with _____ and a Johnson shift counter must be parallel-loaded with _____ .

Section 13–6

13–7.   To input serial data into the 74164 shift register, one DS input must be held _____ (HIGH, LOW) while the other receives the serial data.

13–8.   What is the function of the $\overline{CE}$ input to the 74165 shift register?

13–9.   Why is the 74194 IC sometimes called a "universal" shift register?

13–10.   List the steps that you would follow to parallel-load a hexadecimal B into a 74194 shift register.

13–11. To make the 74194 act as a shift-left *recirculating* register, a connection must be made from _____ *DsL* _____ to _____ *Q₃* _____ and S_0 and S_1 must be _____ *0* _____ .

13–12. How does the operation of the Parallel Enable (PE) on the 74395A shift register differ from the Parallel Load (PL) of the 74165? *PE enable data to be load synchronously with neg-clock edge, and PL load data asynchronously.*

13–13. The outputs of the 74395A shift register are disabled by making OE _____ (HIGH, LOW), which makes Q_0-Q_3 _____ (HIGH, LOW, Float).

Section 13–7

13–14. The traffic light controller of Figure 13–16 flashes the yellow light at night because the level at the collector of the phototransistor is _____ (LOW, HIGH), which _____ (enables, disables) the AND gate.

13–15. What circuitry is responsible for parallel-loading a 1 into the first flip-flop of Figure 13–16 at the beginning of each day? *R c circuitry and the schmitt trigger*

Section 13–8

13–16. The 74LS244 provides buffering for a total of _____ *8* _____ signals. The outputs are all forced to their *float* state by making _____ *OEₐ* _____ and _____ *OE_b* _____ HIGH.

13–17. The 74LS374 octal D flip-flop is a _____ *sy* _____ device whereas the 74LS244 octal buffer is a _____ *asy* _____ device (synchronous, asynchronous).

13–18. A transceiver like the 74LS245 is *bidirectional* allowing data to flow in either direction through it (true or false)?

PROBLEMS

13–1. In Figure P13–1, will the data bits be shifted right or left with each clock pulse? Will they be shifted on the positive or negative clock edge?

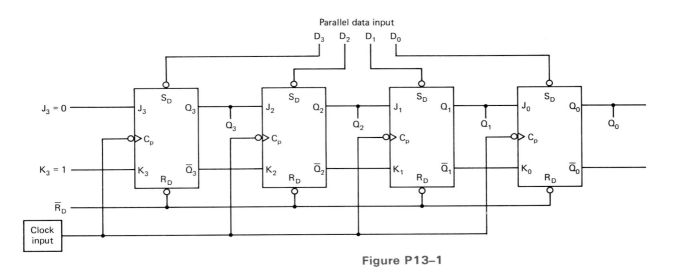

Figure P13–1

13–2. If the register of Figure P13–1 is initially parallel-loaded with $D_3 = 0$, $D_2 = 1$, $D_1 = 0$ and $D_0 = 0$, what will the output at Q_3 to Q_0 be after two clock pulses? After four clock pulses?

13–3. Repeat Problem 13–2 for $J_3 = 1$, $K_3 = 0$.

13–4. Change Figure P13–1 to a recirculating shift register by connecting Q_0 back to J_3 and $\overline{Q_0}$ back to K_3. If the register is initially loaded with a 0110, what is the output at Q_3 to Q_0:

(a) After two clock pulses?

(b) After four clock pulses?

13–5. Outline the steps that you would take to parallel-load the binary equivalent of a hex B into the register of Figure P13–1.

13–6. To use Figure P13–1 as a parallel-to-serial converter, where are the data input line(s) and data output line(s)?

13–7. Repeat Problem 13–6 for a serial-to-parallel converter.

13–8. What changes have to be made to the circuit of Figure P13–1 to make it a Johnson shift counter?

13–9. How many flip-flops are required to produce the waveform shown in Figure P13–9 at the Q_0 output of a ring shift counter?

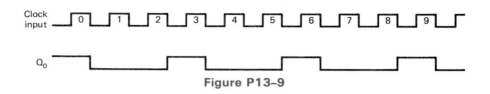

Figure P13–9

13–10. Repeat Problem 13–9 for the waveforms shown in Figure P13–10.

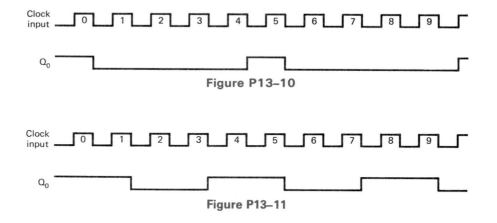

Figure P13–10

Figure P13–11

13–11. Which flip-flop(s) of a 4-bit ring shift counter must be initially Set to produce the waveform shown in Figure P13–11 at Q_0?

13–12. Sketch the waveforms at Q_2 for the first seven clock pulses generated by the circuit shown in Figure P13–12.

13–13. In Figure P13–12 connect the automatic Reset line to the three $\overline{S_D}$ inputs instead of the three $\overline{R_D}$ inputs and sketch the waveforms at Q_2 for the first seven clock pulses.

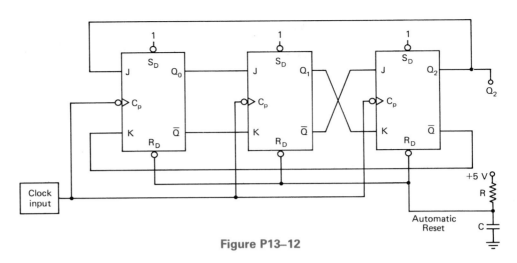

Figure P13–12

13–14. Sketch the waveforms at $\overline{C}_p$, Q_0, Q_1, and Q_2 for seven clock pulses for the ring shift counter shown in Figure P13–14.

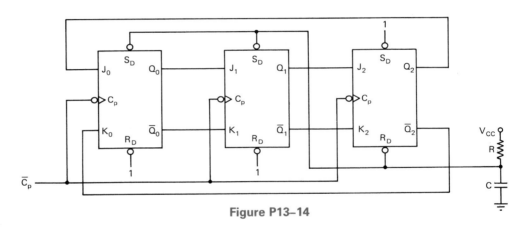

Figure P13–14

13–15. Using the Johnson shift counter output waveforms in Figure 13–6, add some logic gates to produce the waveforms at X, Y, and Z shown in Figure P13–15.

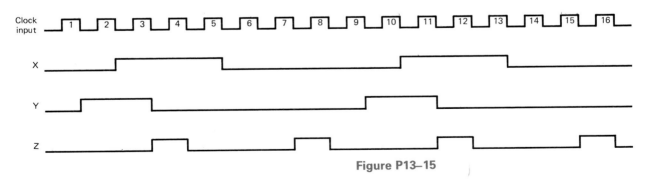

Figure P13–15

13–16. What modification could be made to the circuit in Figure 13–16 to cause the yellow light to flash all day on Sundays (assume that someone will throw a switch at the beginning and end of each Sunday).

13–17. Sketch the output waveforms at Q_0 to Q_3 for the 74194 circuit shown in Figure P13–17. Also, list the operating mode at each positive clock edge.

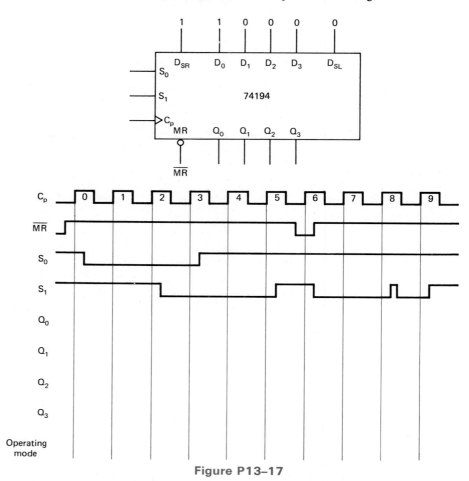

Figure P13–17

13–18. Repeat Problem 13–17 for the input waveforms shown in Figure P13–18.

Figure P13–18

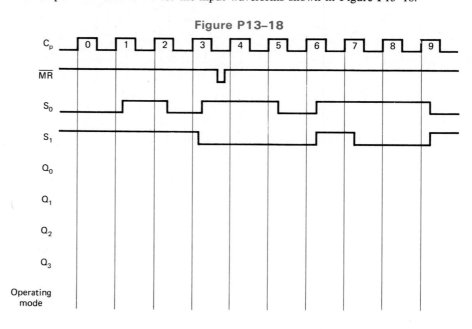

13–19. Sketch the output waveforms at Q_0 to Q_3 for the 74194 circuit shown in Figure P13–19. Also, list the operating mode at each positive clock edge.

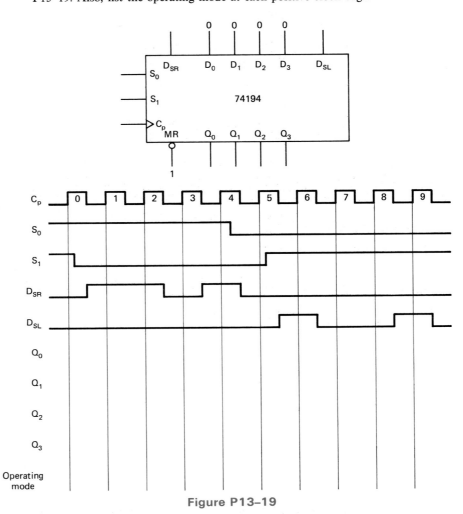

Figure P13–19

13–20. Repeat Problem 13–19 for the waveforms shown in Figure P13–20.

Figure P13–20

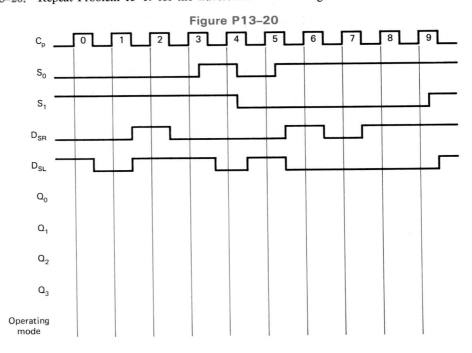

13–21. Draw the timing waveforms (similar to Figure 13–8) for a 74164 used to convert the serial binary number 10010110 into parallel.

13–22. Draw the circuit connections and timing waveforms for a 74165 used to convert the parallel binary number 1001 0110 into serial, MSB first.

13–23. Using your TTL data manual, describe the differences between the 74195 and the 74395A.

13–24. Using your TTL data manual, describe the differences between the 74164 and the 74165.

13–25. Describe how the procedure for parallel loading the 74165 differs from parallel loading a 74166.

13–26. Design a system that can be used to convert an 8-bit serial number LSB first into an 8-bit serial number MSB first. Show the timing waveforms for 16 clock pulses and any control pulses that may be required for the binary number 10110100.

13–27. Describe the difference between: a buffer and a latch, a buffer and a transceiver.

13–28. Why is it important to use devices with three-state outputs when interfacing to a microprocessor data bus?

14

Multivibrators
and the 555 Timer

OBJECTIVES

Upon completion of this chapter, you should be able to:

- Calculate capacitor charging and discharging rates in series RC timing circuits.
- Sketch the waveforms and calculate voltage and time values for astable and monostable multivibrators.
- Connect integrated-circuit monostable multivibrators to output a waveform with a specific pulse width.
- Explain the operation of the internal components of the 555 IC timer.
- Connect a 555 IC timer as an astable multivibrator and as a monostable multivibrator.
- Discuss the operation and application of crystal oscillator circuits.

INTRODUCTION

We have seen that timing is very important in digital electronics. Clock oscillators, used to drive counters and shift registers, must be designed to oscillate at a specific frequency. Specially designed pulse-stretching and time-delay circuits are also required to produce specific pulse widths and delay periods.

14–1 MULTIVIBRATORS

Multivibrator circuits have been around for years, designed from various technologies, to fulfill electronic circuit timing requirements. A multivibrator is a circuit that changes between the two digital levels on a continuous, "free-running" basis or on demand from some external trigger source. Basically there are three types of multivibrators: bistable, astable, and monostable.

The *bistable* multivibrator is triggered into one of the two digital states by an external source, and stays in that state until it is triggered into the opposite state. The *S-R* flip-flop is a bistable multivibrator; it is in either the Set or Reset state.

The *astable* multivibrator is a free-running oscillator that alternates between the two digital levels at a specific frequency and duty cycle.

The *monostable* multivibrator, also known as a *one-shot*, provides a single output pulse of a specific time length when it is triggered from an external source.

The bistable multivibrator (*S-R* flip-flop) was discussed in detail in Chapter 10. The astable and monostable multivibrators discussed in this chapter can be built from basic logic gates, or from special ICs designed specifically for timing applications. In either case, the charging and discharging rate of a capacitor is used to provide the specific time durations required for the circuits to operate.

14–2 CAPACITOR CHARGE AND DISCHARGE RATES

Since the capacitor is so critical in determining the time durations, let's briefly discuss the capacitor charge and discharge formulas. We will use Figure 14–1 to determine the voltages on the capacitor at various periods of time after the switch is closed. In Figure 14–1, with the switch in position 1, conventional current will flow clockwise from the *E* source through the *RC* circuit. The capacitor will charge at an exponential rate, toward the valve of the *E* source. The rate that the capacitor charges is dependent on the product of *R* times *C*:

$$\Delta v = E(1 - e^{-t/RC}) \tag{14–1}$$

where $\Delta v \equiv$ change in capacitor voltage over a period of time t
   $E \equiv$ voltage difference between the initial voltage on the capacitor and the total voltage that it is trying to reach
   $e \equiv$ natural logarithm
   $t \equiv$ time that the capacitor is allowed to charge
   $R \equiv$ resistance, ohms
   $C \equiv$ capacitance, farads

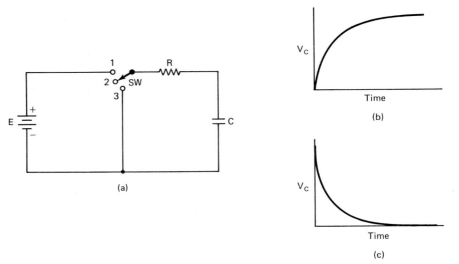

Figure 14–1 Basic *RC* charging/discharging circuit: (a) *RC* circuit; (b) charging curve; (c) discharging curve.

In some cases the capacitor is initially discharged, and Δv is equal to the final voltage on the capacitor. But with astable multivibrator circuits, the capacitor usually is not fully discharged and Δv is equal to the final voltage minus the starting voltage. If you think of the y-axis in the graph of Figure 14–1b as a distance that the capacitor voltage is traveling through, the variables in Equation 14–1 take on new meaning, as follows:

$$\Delta v \equiv \text{distance that the capacitor voltage travels}$$

$$E \equiv \text{total distance that the capacitor voltage is trying to travel}$$

Using these new definitions, Equation 14–1 can be used whether the capacitor is charging *or* discharging (a discharging capacitor can be thought of as *charging to a lower voltage*).

When the switch in Figure 14–1 is thrown to position 3, the capacitor discharges counterclockwise through the RC circuit. The values for the variables in Equation 14–1 are determined the same way as they were for the charging condition, except that the voltage on the capacitor is decreasing exponentially as shown in Figure 14–1c.

Transposing the Capacitor Charging Formula to Solve for t

Quite often in the design of timing circuits it is necessary to solve for t given Δv, E, R, and C. To make life easy for ourselves, let's develop a new equation by rearranging Equation 14–1 to solve for t instead of Δv.

$$\Delta v = E\,(1 - e^{-t/RC})$$

$$\frac{\Delta v}{E} = 1 - e^{-t/RC} \qquad\qquad \text{divide both sides by } E$$

$$\frac{\Delta v}{E} - 1 = -e^{-t/RC} \qquad\qquad \text{subtract 1 from both sides}$$

$$1 - \frac{\Delta v}{E} = e^{-t/RC} \qquad\qquad \text{multiply both sides by } (-1)$$

$$\frac{1}{1 - \Delta v/E} = \frac{1}{e^{-t/RC}} \qquad\qquad \text{take reciprocal of both sides}$$

$$\frac{1}{1 - \Delta v/E} = e^{t/RC} \qquad\qquad \frac{1}{e^{-x}} = e^{x}$$

$$\ln\left(\frac{1}{1 - \Delta v/E}\right) = \ln e^{t/RC} \qquad\qquad \text{take natural logarithm of both sides}$$

$$\ln\left(\frac{1}{1 - \Delta v/E}\right) = \frac{t}{RC} \qquad\qquad \ln e^{x} = x$$

$$t = RC \ln\left(\frac{1}{1 - \Delta v/E}\right) \qquad\qquad (14\text{–}2)$$

The following examples illustrate the use of Equations 14–1 and 14–2 for solving capacitor timing problems.

EXAMPLE 14–1

The capacitor in Figure 14–2 is initially discharged. Determine the voltage on the capacitor 0.5 ms after the switch is moved from position 2 to position 1.

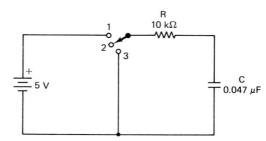

Figure 14–2   Circuit for Examples 14–1 through 14–4.

Solution: E, the total distance that the capacitor voltage is trying to charge to, is 5 V. Using Equation 14–1 yields

$$
\begin{aligned}
\Delta v &= E(1 - e^{-t/RC}) \\
&= 5.0 \text{ V}(1 - e^{-0.5\,\text{ms}/(10\text{k}\Omega \,\times\, 0.047\,\mu\text{F})}) \\
&= 5.0(1 - e^{-1.06}) \\
&= 5.0(1 - 0.345) \\
&= 5.0(0.655) \\
&= 3.27 \text{ V} \quad answer
\end{aligned}
$$

Thus the distance the capacitor voltage traveled in 0.5 ms is 3.27 V. Since it started at 0 V, $V_{\text{cap}} = 3.27$ V.

EXAMPLE 14–2

The capacitor in Figure 14–2 is initially discharged. How long after the switch is moved from position 2 to position 1 will it take for the capacitor to reach 3 V?

Solution: Δv, the distance that the capacitor voltage travels through, is 3 V. E, the total distance that the capacitor voltage is trying to travel, is 5 V. Using Equation 14–2, we obtain

$$
\begin{aligned}
t &= RC \ln\left(\frac{1}{1 - \Delta v/E}\right) \\
&= (10 \text{ k}\Omega)(0.047 \,\mu\text{F}) \ln\left(\frac{1}{1 - 3/5}\right) \\
&= 0.00047 \ln\left(\frac{1}{0.4}\right) \\
&= 0.00047 \ln(2.5) \\
&= 0.00047(0.916) \\
&= 0.431 \text{ ms} \quad answer
\end{aligned}
$$

EXAMPLE 14–3

For this example let's assume that the capacitor in Figure 14–2 is initially charged to 1 V. How long after the switch is thrown from position 2 to position 1 will it take for the capacitor to reach 3 V?

Solution: Δv, the distance that the capacitor voltage travels through, is 2 V (3 V − 1 V). E, the total distance that the capacitor voltage is trying to travel, is 4 V (5 V − 1 V). Using Equation 14–2 gives us

$$t = RC \ln \left(\frac{1}{1 - \Delta v/E} \right)$$

$$= (10 \text{ k}\Omega)(0.047 \text{ }\mu\text{F}) \ln \left(\frac{1}{1 - 2/4} \right)$$

$$= 0.326 \text{ ms} \quad answer$$

The graph of the capacitor voltage is shown in Figure 14–3.

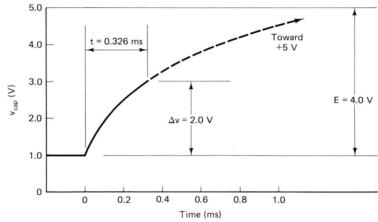

Figure 14–3 Graphical illustration of the capacitor voltage for Example 14–3.

EXAMPLE 14–4

The capacitor in Figure 14–2 is initially charged to 4.2 V. How long after the switch is thrown from position 2 to position 3 will it take to drop to 1.5 V?

Solution: Equation 14–2 can be used to solve for t by thinking of the capacitor as *charging to a lower voltage*. Δv, the distance that the capacitor voltage travels through, is 2.7 V (4.2 V − 1.5 V). E, the total distance that the capacitor voltage is trying to travel, is 4.2 V (4.2 V − 0 V). Using equation 14–2 yields

$$t = RC \ln \left(\frac{1}{1 - \Delta v/E} \right)$$

$$= (10 \text{ k}\Omega)(0.047 \text{ }\mu\text{F}) \ln \left(\frac{1}{1 - 2.7 \text{ V}/4.2 \text{ V}} \right)$$

$$= 0.484 \text{ ms} \quad answer$$

The graph of the capacitor voltage is shown in Figure 14–4.

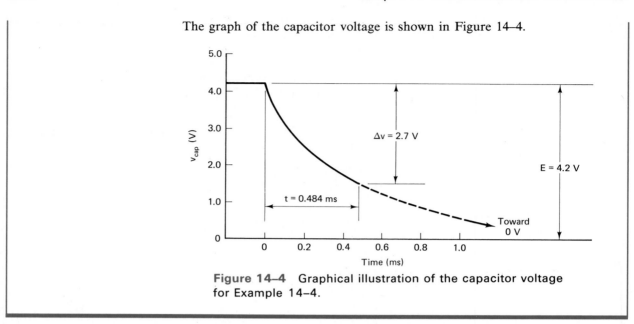

Figure 14–4 Graphical illustration of the capacitor voltage for Example 14–4.

14–3 ASTABLE MULTIVIBRATORS

A very simple astable multivibrator (free-running oscillator) can be built from a single Schmitt trigger inverter and an *RC* circuit as shown in Figure 14–5. The oscillator of Figure 14–5 operates as follows:

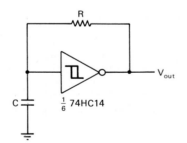

Figure 14–5 Schmitt trigger astable multivibrator.

1. When the IC supply power is first turned on, V_{cap} is 0 V, so V_{out} will be HIGH ($\approx$ 5.0 V for high-speed CMOS).
2. The capacitor will start charging toward the 5 V at V_{out}.
3. When V_{cap} reaches the positive-going threshold (V_{T+}) of the Schmitt trigger, the output of the Schmitt will change to a LOW ($\approx$ 0 V).
4. Now with $V_{out} \approx 0$ V, the capacitor will start discharging toward 0 V.
5. When V_{cap} drops below the negative-going threshold (V_{T-}), the output of the Schmitt will change back to a HIGH.
6. The cycle repeats now with the capacitor charging back up to V_{T+}, then down to V_{T-}, then up to V_{T+}, and so on. (The waveform at V_{out} will be a square wave oscillating between V_{OH} and V_{OL} as shown in Figure 14–6.)

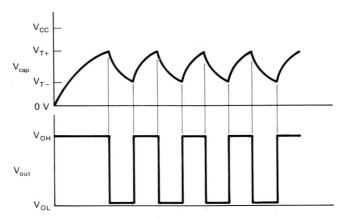

Figure 14–6   Waveforms from the oscillator circuit of Figure 14–5.

EXAMPLE 14–5

(a) Sketch and label the waveforms for the Schmitt RC oscillator of Figure 14–5 given the following specifications for a 74HC14 high-speed CMOS Schmitt inverter ($V_{CC} = 5.0$ V).

$$V_{OH} = 5.0 \text{ V} \qquad V_{OL} = 0.0 \text{ V}$$
$$V_{T+} = 2.75 \text{ V} \qquad V_{T-} = 1.67 \text{ V}$$

(b) Calculate the time HIGH (t_{HI}), time LOW (t_{LO}), duty cycle, and frequency if $R = 10$ kΩ and $C = 0.022$ μF.

Solution: (a) The waveforms for the oscillator are shown in Figure 14–7.

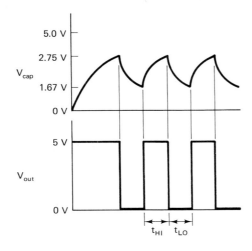

Figure 14–7   Solution to Example 14–5.

(b) To solve for t_{HI}:

$$\Delta V = 2.75 - 1.67 = 1.08 \text{ V}$$
$$E = 5.00 - 1.67 = 3.33 \text{ V}$$

$$t_{HI} = RC \ln \left(\frac{1}{1 - \Delta v/E} \right)$$

$$= (10 \text{ k}\Omega)(0.022 \text{ } \mu\text{F}) \ln \left(\frac{1}{1 - 1.08 \text{ V}/3.33 \text{ V}} \right)$$

$$= 86.2 \text{ } \mu\text{s}$$

To solve for t_{LO}:

$$\Delta v = 2.75 - 1.67 = 1.08 \text{ V}$$
$$E = 2.75 - 0 = 2.75 \text{ V}$$

$$t_{\text{LO}} = RC \ln\left(\frac{1}{1 - \Delta v / E}\right)$$

$$= (10 \text{ k}\Omega)(0.022 \text{ }\mu\text{F}) \ln\left(\frac{1}{1 - 1.08 \text{ V}/2.75 \text{ V}}\right)$$

$$= 110 \text{ }\mu\text{s}$$

To solve for duty cycle: Duty cycle is a ratio of the length of time a square wave is HIGH, versus the total period:

$$D = \frac{t_{\text{HI}}}{t_{\text{HI}} + t_{\text{LO}}}$$

$$= \frac{86.2 \text{ }\mu\text{s}}{86.2 \text{ }\mu\text{s} + 110 \text{ }\mu\text{s}}$$

$$= 0.439 = 43.9\%$$

To solve for frequency:

$$f = \frac{1}{t_{\text{HI}} + t_{\text{LO}}}$$

$$= \frac{1}{86.2 \text{ }\mu\text{s} + 110 \text{ }\mu\text{s}}$$

$$= 5.10 \text{ kHz}$$

14–4   MONOSTABLE MULTIVIBRATORS

The block diagram and I/O waveforms for a monostable multivibrator (commonly called a one-shot) are shown in Figure 14–8. The one-shot has one *stable state* which is $Q = $ LOW and $\overline{Q} = $ HIGH. The outputs switch to their opposite state for a length of time t_w only when a trigger is applied to the $\overline{A}$ input. $\overline{A}$ is a negative edge trigger in this case (other one-shots use a positive edge trigger or both). The input/output waveforms in Figure 14–8 show the effect that $\overline{A}$ has on the Q output. Q is LOW until the HIGH-to-LOW edge of $\overline{A}$ causes Q to go HIGH for the length of time t_w.

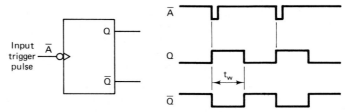

Figure 14–8   Block diagram and input/output waveforms for a monostable multivibrator.

The output pulse width (t_w) is determined by the discharge rate of a capacitor in an *RC* circuit. A simple monostable multivibrator can be built from NAND gates and an *RC* circuit as shown in Figure 14–9. The operation of Figure 14–9 is as follows:

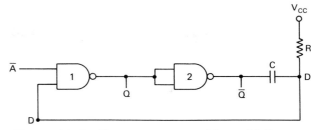

Figure 14–9 Two-gate monostable multivibrator.

1. When power is first applied, make the following assumptions: $\overline{A}$ is HIGH, Q is LOW, $\overline{Q}$ is HIGH, C is discharged. Therefore, point D is HIGH.

2. When a negative-going pulse is applied at $\overline{A}$, Q is forced HIGH, which forces $\overline{Q}$ LOW.

3. Since the capacitor voltage cannot change instantaneously, point D will drop to 0 V.

4. The 0 V at point D will hold one input to gate 1 LOW, even if the $\overline{A}$ trigger goes back HIGH. Therefore, Q stays HIGH, $\overline{Q}$ stays LOW.

5. Meanwhile, the capacitor is charging toward V_{CC}. When the capacitor voltage at point D reaches the HIGH-level input voltage rating (V_{IH}) of gate 1, Q will switch to a LOW, making $\overline{Q}$ HIGH.

6. The circuit is back in its stable state, awaiting another trigger signal from $\overline{A}$. The capacitor will discharge back to ≈ 0 V ($\approx V_{CC}$ on each side).

The waveforms in Figure 14–10 show the input/output characteristics of the circuit and will enable us to develop an equation to determine t_w. In the stable state ($\overline{Q} =$ HIGH), the voltage at point D will sit at V_{CC} ① because the capacitor is discharged (it has V_{CC} on both sides of it). When $\overline{Q}$ goes LOW due to an input trigger at $\overline{A}$, point D will follow $\overline{Q}$ LOW ② because the capacitor is still discharged. Now, the capacitor will start charging toward V_{CC}. When point D reaches V_{IH} ③, $\overline{Q}$ will switch back HIGH. The capacitor still has V_{IH} volts across it $\left(\dfrac{- \ | | \ +}{V_{IH}} \right)$. The capacitor voltage is added to the HIGH-level output of $\overline{Q}$, which causes point D to shoot up to $V_{CC} + V_{IH}$ ④. As the capacitor voltage discharges back to 0 V, point D drops back to the V_{CC} level ⑤ and awaits the next trigger.

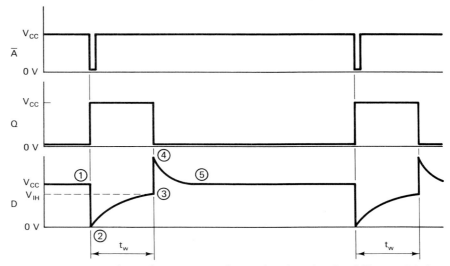

Figure 14–10 Input/output waveforms for the circuit of Figure 14–9.

EXAMPLE 14–6

(a) Sketch and label the waveforms for the monostable multivibrator of Figure 14–9 given the input waveform at $\overline{A}$ and the following specifications for a 74HC00 high-speed CMOS NAND gate ($V_{CC} = 5.0$ V).

$$V_{OH} = 5.0 \text{ V} \qquad V_{OL} = 0.0 \text{ V}$$
$$V_{IH} = 3.5 \text{ V} \qquad V_{IL} = 1.0 \text{ V}$$

(b) Calculate the output pulse width (t_w) for $R = 4.7$ kΩ and $C = 0.0047$ μF.

Solution: (a) The waveforms for the multivibrator are shown in Figure 14–11.

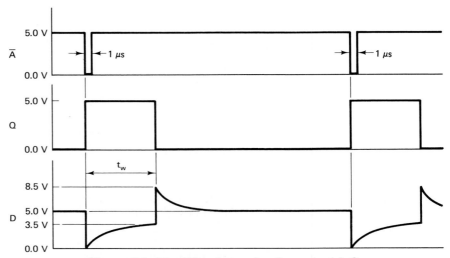

Figure 14–11 Waveforms for Example 14–6.

(b) To solve for t_w using Equation 14–2:

$$\Delta v = 3.5 \text{ V} - 0 \text{ V} = 3.5 \text{ V}$$
$$E = 5.0 \text{ V} - 0 \text{ V} = 5.0 \text{ V}$$

$$t_w = RC \ln\left(\frac{1}{1 - \Delta v/E}\right)$$

$$= (4.7 \text{ kΩ})(0.0047 \text{ μF}) \ln\left(\frac{1}{1 - 3.5 \text{ v}/5.0 \text{ v}}\right)$$

$$= 26.6 \text{ μs} \quad answer$$

14–5 IC MONOSTABLE MULTIVIBRATORS

Monostable multivibrators are available in an integrated-circuit package. Two popular ICs are the 74121 and the 74123 (retriggerable) monostable multivibrators. To use these ICs, you need to connect the RC timing components to achieve the proper pulse width. The 74121 provides for two active-LOW and one active-HIGH trigger inputs ($\overline{A}_1$, $\overline{A}_2$, B) and true and complemented outputs (Q, $\overline{Q}$). Figure 14–12 shows the 74121 block diagram and function table that we can use to figure out its operation.

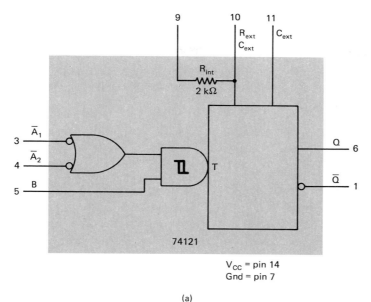

INPUTS			OUTPUTS	
$\overline{A}_1$	$\overline{A}_2$	B	Q	$\overline{Q}$
L	X	H	L	H
X	L	H	L	H
X	X	L	L	H
H	H	X	L	H
H	↓	H	⊓	⊔
↓	H	H	⊓	⊔
↓	↓	H	⊓	⊔
L	X	↑	⊓	⊔
X	L	↑	⊓	⊔

H = HIGH voltage level
L = LOW voltage level
X = Don't care
↑ = LOW-to-HIGH transition
↓ = HIGH-to-LOW transition

V_{CC} = pin 14
Gnd = pin 7

(a)   (b)

Figure 14–12 The 74121 monostable multivibrator one-shot: (a) block diagram; (b) function table. (Courtesy of Signetics Corporation.)

To trigger the multivibrator at point T in Figure 14–12, the inputs to the Schmitt AND gate must both be HIGH. To do that, you need B with ($\overline{A}_1$ or $\overline{A}_2$). Holding $\overline{A}_1$ or $\overline{A}_2$ LOW and bringing the input trigger in on B is useful if the trigger signal is slow-rising or if it has noise on it because the Schmitt input will provide a definite trigger point.

The *RC* timing components are set up on pins 9, 10, and 11. If you can use the 2kΩ *internal* resistor, just connect pin 9 to V_{CC} and put a timing capacitor between pins 10 and 11. An *external* timing resistor can be used instead by placing it between pin 11 and V_{CC}, and putting the timing capacitor between pins 10 and 11. If the external timing resistor is used, pin 9 must be left open. The allowable range of R_{ext} is 1.4 to 40 kΩ and C_{ext} is 0 to 1000 μF. If an electrolytic capacitor is used, its positive side must be connected to pin 11.

The formula that the IC manufacturer gives for determining the output pulse width is

$$t_w = R_{ext} C_{ext} \ln 2 \tag{14-3}$$

(Substitute 2 kΩ for R_{ext} if the internal timing resistor is used.)

For example, if the external timing *RC* components are 10 kΩ and 0.047 μF, then t_w will equal 10 kΩ × 0.047 μF × ln 2, which works out to be 326 μs. Using the maximum allowed values of $R_{ext}C_{ext}$, the maximum pulse width is almost 28 s (40 kΩ × 1000 μF × ln 2).

The function table in Figure 14–12 shows that the Q output is LOW and the $\overline{Q}$ output is HIGH as long as the $\overline{A}_1$, $\overline{A}_2$, B inputs do not provide a HIGH–HIGH to the Schmitt-AND inputs. But by holding B HIGH and applying a HIGH-to-LOW edge to $\overline{A}_1$ or $\overline{A}_2$, the outputs will produce a pulse. Also, the function table shows, in its last two entries, that a LOW-to-HIGH edge at input B will produce an output pulse as long as either $\overline{A}_1$ or $\overline{A}_2$ is held LOW.

The following examples illustrate the use of the 74121 for one-shot operation.

EXAMPLE 14–7

Design a circuit using a 74121 to convert a 50-kHz, 80% duty cycle square wave to a 50-kHz, 50% duty cycle square wave. (In other words, "stretch" the negative-going pulse to cover 50% of the total period.)

Solution: First, let's draw the original square wave (Figure 14–13a) to see what we have to work with ($t = \dfrac{1}{50 \text{ kHz}} = 20$ μs, $t_{\text{HI}} = 80\% \times 20$ μs $= 16$ μs).

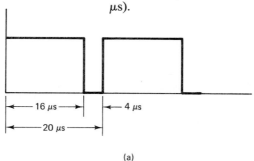

(a)

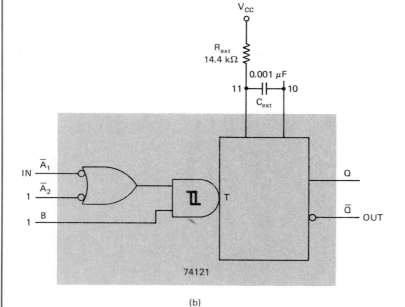

(b)

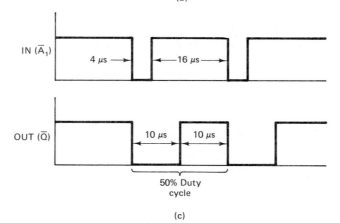

(c)

Figure 14–13 (a) Original square wave for Example 14–7; (b) monostable multivibrator circuit connections; (c) input/output waveforms.

Now, we want to stretch the 4-μs negative pulse out to 10 μs to make the duty cycle 50%. If we use the HIGH-to-LOW edge on the negative pulse to trigger the $\overline{A}_1$ input to a 74121 and set the output pulse width (t_w) to 10 μs, we should have the solution. The output will be taken from $\overline{Q}$ because it provides a negative pulse when triggered.

Using the formula given in the IC specifications, we can calculate an appropriate R_{ext}, C_{ext} to yield 10 μs.

$$t_w = R_{ext}C_{ext} \ln (2)$$
$$10 \ \mu s = R_{ext}C_{ext} (0.693)$$
$$R_{ext}C_{ext} = 14.4 \ \mu s$$

Pick $C_{ext} = 0.001 \ \mu F$ (1000 pF); then

$$R_{ext} = \frac{14.4 \ \mu s}{0.001 \ \mu F}$$

$$= 14.4 \ k\Omega \qquad \text{(use a 10-k}\Omega \text{ fixed resistor with a 5-k}\Omega \text{ potentiometer)}$$

The value 0.001 μF is a good choice for C_{ext} because it is much larger than any stray capacitance that might be encountered in a typical circuit. Values of capacitance less than 100 pF (0.0001 μF) may be unsuitable because it is not uncommon for there to be 50 pF of stray capacitance between traces in a printed-circuit board. Also, resistances in the kilohm range are a good choice because they are big enough to limit current flow but not so big to be susceptible to electrostatic noise. The final circuit design and waveforms are given in Figure 14–13b and c.

EXAMPLE 14–8

In microprocessor systems, most control signals are active-LOW and quite often one-shots are required to introduce delays for certain devices to wait for other, slower devices to respond. For example, to read from a memory device, a line called $\overline{READ}$ goes LOW to enable the memory device. Most systems have to introduce a delay after the memory device is enabled (to allow for internal propagation delays), before the microprocessor actually reads the data. Design a system using two 74121s to output a 200-ns LOW pulse (called $\overline{\text{Data-Ready}}$) 500 ns after the $\overline{READ}$ line goes LOW.

Solution: The first 74121 will be used to produce the 500-ns delay pulse as soon as the $\overline{READ}$ line goes LOW (see Figure 14–14). The second 74121 will be triggered by the end of the 500-ns delay pulse and will output its own 200-ns LOW pulse for the $\overline{\text{Data-Ready}}$ line. (The 74121s are edge-triggered, so they will trigger only on a HIGH-to-LOW or LOW-to-HIGH *edge*.)

For $t_w = 500$ ns (output for first 74121):

$$t_w = R_{ext}C_{ext} \ln (2)$$
$$500 \ ns = R_{ext}C_{ext}(0.693)$$
$$R_{ext}C_{ext} = 0.722 \ \mu s$$

Pick $C_{ext} = 100$ pF; then

$$R_{ext} = \frac{0.722 \ \mu s}{0.0001 \ \mu F} = 7.22 \ k\Omega$$

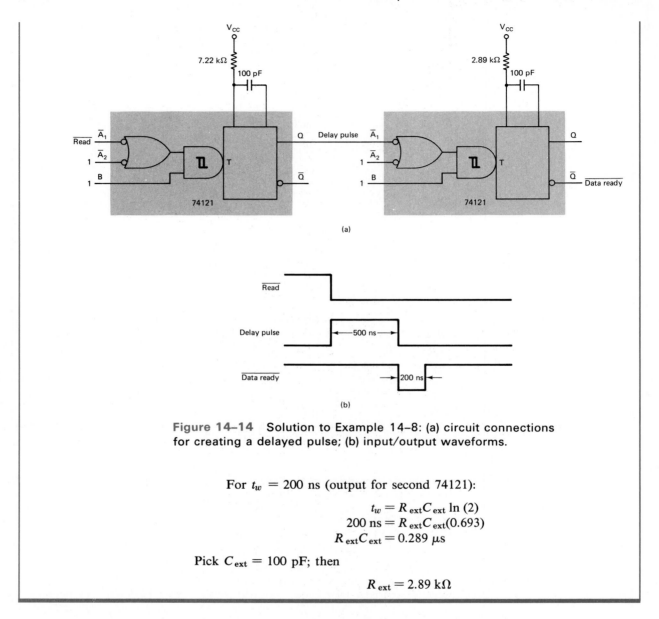

Figure 14–14 Solution to Example 14–8: (a) circuit connections for creating a delayed pulse; (b) input/output waveforms.

For $t_w = 200$ ns (output for second 74121):

$$t_w = R_{ext}C_{ext} \ln (2)$$
$$200 \text{ ns} = R_{ext}C_{ext}(0.693)$$
$$R_{ext}C_{ext} = 0.289 \ \mu\text{s}$$

Pick $C_{ext} = 100$ pF; then

$$R_{ext} = 2.89 \text{ k}\Omega$$

14–6 RETRIGGERABLE MONOSTABLE MULTIVIBRATORS

Have you wondered what might happen if a second input trigger came in before the end of the multivibrator's timing cycle? With the 74121 (which is nonretriggerable), any triggers that come in before the end of the timing cycle are ignored.

Retriggerable monostable multivibrators (such as the 74123) are available, which will start a new timing cycle each time a new trigger is applied. Figure 14–15 illustrates the differences between the retriggerable and nonretriggerable types assuming that $t_w = 500$ ns and a negative edge-triggered input.

As you can see in Figure 14–15, the retriggerable device starts its timing cycle all over again when the second (or subsequent) input trigger is applied. The nonretriggerable device ignores any additional triggers until it has completed its 500-ns timing pulse.

The logic symbol and function table for the 74123 retriggerable monostable multivibrator are given in Figure 14–16.

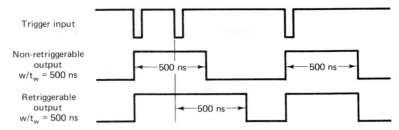

Figure 14–15 Comparison of retriggerable and nonretriggerable one-shot outputs.

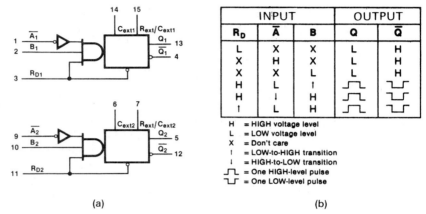

	INPUT			OUTPUT	
R_D	$\overline{A}$	B		Q	$\overline{Q}$
L	X	X		L	H
X	H	X		L	H
X	X	L		L	H
H	L	↑		⎍	⎍
H	↓	H		⎍	⎍
↑	L	H		⎍	⎍

H = HIGH voltage level
L = LOW voltage level
X = Don't care
↑ = LOW-to-HIGH transition
↓ = HIGH-to-LOW transition
⎍ = One HIGH-level pulse
⎍ = One LOW-level pulse

(a)   (b)

Figure 14–16 The 74123 retriggerable monostable multivibrator: (a) logic symbol; (b) function table. (Courtesy of Signetics Corporation.)

Besides being retriggerable, some of the other important differences of the 74123 are:

1. It is a *dual* multivibrator (two multivibrators in a single IC package).
2. It has an active-LOW Reset (R_D) which terminates all timing functions by forcing Q LOW, $\overline{Q}$ HIGH.
3. It has no internal timing resistor.
4. It uses a different method for determining the output pulse width, as explained below.

Output Pulse Width of the 74123

If $C_{ext} > 1000$ pF, the output pulse width is determined by the formula

$$t_w = 0.28 R_{ext} C_{ext} \left(1 + \frac{0.7}{R_{ext}} \right) \qquad (14\text{–}4)$$

If $C_{ext} \leq 1000$ pF, the timing chart shown in Figure 14–17 must be used to find t_w.

For example, let's say that we need an output pulse width of 200 ns. Using the chart in Figure 14–17, one choice for the timing components would be $R_{ext} = 10$ kΩ, $C_{ext} = 30$ pF, or a better choice might be $R_{ext} = 5$ kΩ, $C_{ext} = 90$ pf. (With such small capacitances, required for nanosecond delays, we must be careful to minimize stray capacitance by using proper printed-circuit layout and component placement techniques.)

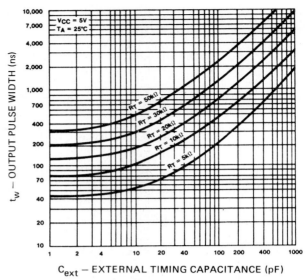

Figure 14–17   The 74123 timing chart for determining t_w when C_{ext} is $\leq$ 1000 pF.

EXAMPLE 14–9

The trigger input waveforms shown are applied to the multivibrator circuit of Figure 14–18. Determine the output at Q_1.

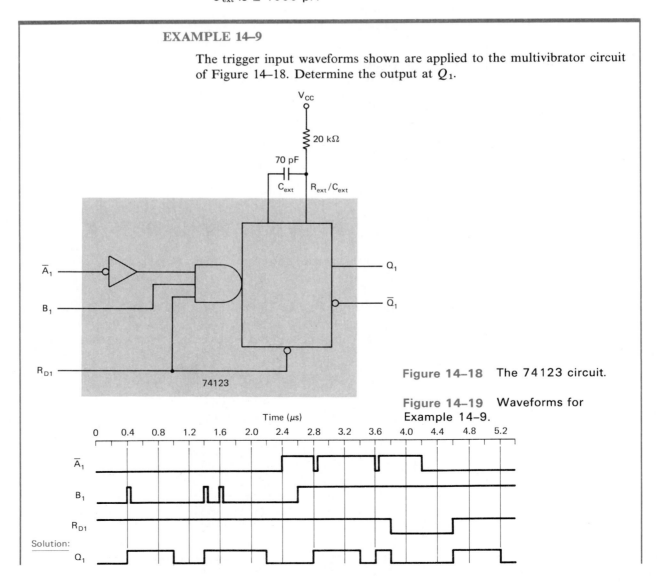

Figure 14–18   The 74123 circuit.

Figure 14–19   Waveforms for Example 14–9.

Solution:

t_w is determined from the timing chart for the 74123 (Figure 14–17). With $C_{ext} = 70$ pF and $R_{ext} = 20$ kΩ, $t_w = 0.6$ μs (600 ns).

0 to 0.4 μs.	Q is in its stable state (LOW); no trigger has been applied.
0.4 to 1.0 μs.	Q is triggered HIGH for 0.6 μs by the pulse on B_1.
1.0 to 1.4 μs.	Q returns to its stable state.
1.4 to 2.2 μs.	Q is triggered HIGH by B_1 at 1.4 μs; then Q is retriggered at 1.6 μs.
2.2 to 2.8 μs.	Q returns LOW; the conditions on $A_1 B_1 R_{D1}$ are not right to create a trigger.
2.8 to 3.4 μs.	Q is triggered HIGH by the LOW pulse on $\overline{A_1}$ while B_1 = HIGH and R_{D1} = HIGH.
3.4 to 3.6 μs.	Q returns LOW.
3.6 to 3.8 μs.	Q is triggered HIGH by $\overline{A_1}$ but the output pulse is terminated by a LOW on R_{D1}.
3.8 to 4.6 μs.	Q is held LOW by R_{D1} no matter what the other inputs are doing.
4.6 to 5.2 μs.	Q is triggered HIGH by the LOW-to-HIGH edge of R_{D1} while $\overline{A_1}$ = LOW, B_1 = HIGH.
5.2 to 5.4 μs.	Q returns LOW.

14–7 ASTABLE OPERATION OF THE 555 IC TIMER

The 555 is a very popular, general-purpose timer IC. It can be connected as a one-shot or an astable oscillator as well as being used for a multitude of custom designs. Figure 14–20 shows a block diagram of the chip with its internal components and the external components that are required to set it up as an astable oscillator.

The 555 got its name from the three 5-kΩ resistors. They are set up as a voltage divider from V_{CC} to ground. The top of the lower 5 kΩ is at $\frac{1}{3}V_{CC}$ and the top of the middle 5 kΩ is at $\frac{2}{3}V_{CC}$. For example, if V_{CC} is 6 V, each resistor will drop 2 V.

The triangle-shaped symbols represent *comparators*. A comparator simply outputs a HIGH or LOW based on a comparison of the analog voltage levels at its input. If the + input is *more positive* than the − input, it outputs a HIGH. If the + input is *less positive* than the − input, it outputs a LOW.

The *S-R flip-flop* is driven by the two comparators. It has an active-LOW Reset and its output is taken from the $\overline{Q}$.

The *discharge transistor* is an NPN which is used to short pins 7 to 1 when $\overline{Q}$ is HIGH.

The operation and function of the 555 pins are as follows:

Pin 1 (ground):	System ground.
Pin 2 (trigger):	Input to the lower comparator, which is used to Set the flip-flop. When the voltage at pin 2 crosses from above to below $\frac{1}{3}V_{CC}$, the comparator switches to a HIGH, setting the flip-flop.
Pin 3 (output):	The output of the 555 is driven by an inverting buffer capable of sinking or sourcing 200 mA. The output voltage levels are dependent on the output current but are approximately $V_{OH} = V_{CC} - 1.5$ V and $V_{OL} = 0.1$ V.

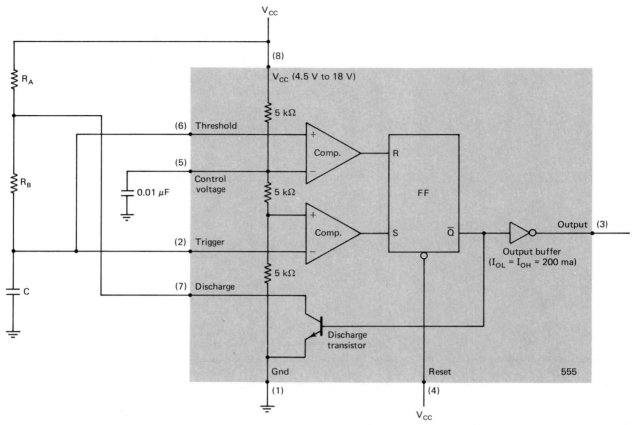

Figure 14–20 Simplified block diagram of a 555 timer with the external timing components to form an astable multivibrator.

Pin 4 (Reset): Active-LOW Reset, which forces $\overline{Q}$ HIGH and pin 3 (output) LOW.

Pin 5 (control): Used to override the $\frac{2}{3}V_{CC}$ level, if required. Usually, it is connected to a grounded 0.01-μF capacitor to bypass noise on the V_{CC} line.

Pin 6 (threshold): Input to the upper comparator, which is used to Reset the flip-flop. When the voltage at pin 6 crosses from below to above $\frac{2}{3}V_{CC}$, the comparator switches to a HIGH, resetting the flip-flop.

Pin 7 (discharge): Connected to the open collector of the *NPN* transistor. It is used to short pin 7 to ground when $\overline{Q}$ is HIGH (pin 3 LOW), which will discharge the external capacitor.

Pin 8 (V_{CC}): Supply voltage. V_{CC} can range from 4.5 to 18 V.

The operation of the 555 connected in the astable mode shown in Figure 14–20 is explained as follows.

1. When power is first turned on, the capacitor is discharged, which places 0 V at pin 2, forcing the lower comparator HIGH. This sets the flip-flop ($\overline{Q}$ = LOW, output = HIGH).
2. With the output HIGH ($\overline{Q}$ LOW) the discharge transistor is open, which allows the capacitor to charge toward V_{CC} via $R_A + R_B$.

3. When the capacitor voltage exceeds $\frac{1}{3}V_{CC}$, the lower comparitor goes LOW, which has no effect on the *S-R* flip-flop, but when the capacitor voltage exceeds $\frac{2}{3}V_{CC}$, the upper comparator goes HIGH, resetting the flip-flop, forcing $\overline{Q}$ HIGH and the output LOW.

4. With $\overline{Q}$ HIGH, the transistor shorts pin 7 to ground, which discharges the capacitor via R_B.

5. When the capacitor voltage drops below $\frac{1}{3}V_{CC}$, the lower comparator goes back HIGH again, setting the flip-flop and making $\overline{Q}$ LOW, output HIGH.

6. Now, with $\overline{Q}$ LOW, the transistor opens again, allowing the capacitor to start charging up again.

7. The cycle repeats with the capacitor charging up to $\frac{2}{3}V_{CC}$, then discharging down to $\frac{1}{3}V_{CC}$ continuously. While the capacitor is charging, the output is HIGH, and when the capacitor is discharging, the output is LOW.

The waveforms, depicting the operation of the 555 as an astable oscillator, are shown in Figure 14–21.

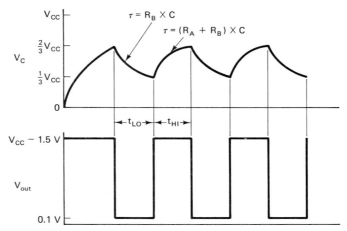

Figure 14–21 Waveforms for the 555 astable multivibrator circuit of Figure 14–20.

The formulas for the time durations t_{LO} and t_{HI} can be derived using the theory presented in Section 14–2 and Equation 14–2. The time duration t_{LO} is determined by realizing that the capacitor voltage (Δv) travels a distance of $\frac{1}{3}V_{CC}$ (from $\frac{2}{3}V_{CC}$ to $\frac{1}{3}V_{CC}$) and the total path that it is trying to travel (E) is equal to $\frac{2}{3}V_{CC}$ (from $\frac{2}{3}V_{CC}$ to 0 V). The path of the discharge current is through R_B and C, so the time constant, τ (tau), is $R_B \times C$. Therefore, the equation for t_{LO} is derived as follows:

$$t_W = RC \ln\left(\frac{1}{1 - \Delta v/E}\right) \tag{14–2}$$

$$t_{LO} = R_B C \ln\left(\frac{1}{1 - \frac{1}{3}V_{CC}/\frac{2}{3}V_{CC}}\right)$$

$$= R_B C \ln\left(\frac{1}{1 - 0.5}\right)$$

$$= R_B C \ln(2)$$

$$= 0.693 R_B C \tag{14–5}$$

To derive the equation for t_{HI}:

Δv = distance the capacitor voltage travels = $\frac{1}{3}V_{CC}$ $(\frac{2}{3}V_{CC} - \frac{1}{3}V_{CC})$

E = total distance that the capacitor voltage is trying to travel = $\frac{2}{3}V_{CC}$ $(V_{CC} - \frac{1}{3}V_{CC})$

τ = time constant, or the path that the charging current flows through, $(R_A + R_B) \times C$

$$t_{HI} = (R_A + R_B)C \ln\left(\frac{1}{1 - \frac{1}{3}V_{CC}/\frac{2}{3}V_{CC}}\right)$$

$$= (R_A + R_B)C \ln\left(\frac{1}{1 - 0.5}\right)$$

$$= (R_A + R_B)C \ln(2)$$

$$= 0.693(R_A + R_B)C \qquad\qquad (14\text{--}6)$$

EXAMPLE 14–10

Determine t_{HI}, t_{LO}, duty cycle, and frequency for the 555 astable multivibrator circuit of Figure 14–22.

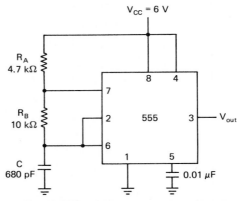

Figure 14–22   The 555 astable connections for Example 14–10.

Solution:

$$t_{LO} = 0.693 R_B C$$
$$= 0.693(10\ \text{k}\Omega)680\ \text{pF}$$
$$= 4.71\ \mu\text{s}$$

$$t_{HI} = 0.693(R_A + R_B)C$$
$$= 0.693(4.7\ \text{k}\Omega + 10\ \text{k}\Omega)680\ \text{pF}$$
$$= 6.93\ \mu\text{s}$$

$$\text{duty cycle} = \frac{t_{HI}}{t_{HI} + t_{LO}}$$

$$= \frac{6.93\ \mu\text{s}}{6.93\ \mu\text{s} + 4.71\ \mu\text{s}}$$

$$= 59.5\%$$

$$\text{frequency} = \frac{1}{t_{HI} + t_{LO}}$$

$$= \frac{1}{6.93 \ \mu s + 4.71 \ \mu s}$$

$$= 85.9 \ kHz$$

50% Duty Cycle Astable Oscillator

By studying Figure 14-21 you should realize that in order to get a 50% duty cycle, t_{LO} must equal t_{HI}. You should also realize that in order for that to occur, the capacitor charging time constant (τ) must equal the discharging time constant. But with the astable circuits that we have seen so far, this can never be true because the resistance in one case is just R_B but in the other case it is R_B *plus* R_A. You cannot just make R_A 0 Ω because that would put V_{CC} directly on pin 7.

However, if we make $R_A = R_B$ and short R_B with a diode during the capacitor charging cycle, we can achieve a 50% duty cycle. The circuit for a 50% duty cycle is shown in Figure 14-23.

The charging time constant in Figure 14-23 is $R_A \times C$ and the discharging time constant is $R_B \times C$. The formulas therefore become

$$t_{HI} = 0.693 R_A C \tag{14-7}$$

$$t_{LO} = 0.693 R_B C \tag{14-8}$$

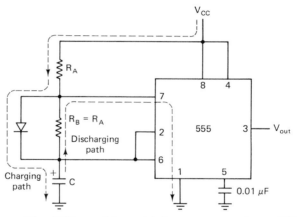

Figure 14-23 The 555 astable multivibrator set up for a 50% duty cycle.

If R_B is set equal to R_A, t_{HI} will equal t_{LO} and the duty cycle will be 50%. Also, duty cycles of *less than* 50% can be achieved by using the diode and making R_A less than R_B.

14-8 MONOSTABLE OPERATION OF THE 555 IC TIMER

Another common use for the 555 is as a monostable multivibrator, as shown in Figure 14-24. The one-shot of Figure 14-24, operates as follows:

1. Initially (before the trigger is applied), V_{out} is LOW, shorting pin 7 to ground and discharging C.

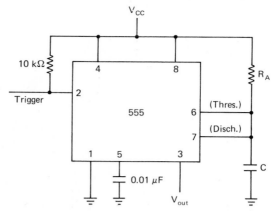

Figure 14–24 The 555 connections for one-shot operation.

2. Pin 2 is normally held HIGH by the 10-kΩ pull-up resistor. To trigger the one-shot, a negative-going pulse (less than $\frac{1}{3}V_{cc}$) is applied to pin 2.

3. The trigger forces the lower comparator HIGH (see Figure 14–20), which sets the flip-flop, making V_{out} HIGH and opening the discharge transistor (pin 7).

4. Now the capacitor is free to charge from 0 V up toward V_{cc} via R_A.

5. When V_c crosses the threshold of $\frac{2}{3}V_{cc}$, the upper comparator goes HIGH, resetting the flip-flop making V_{out} LOW and shorting the discharge transistor.

6. The capacitor discharges rapidly to 0 V and the one-shot is held in its stable state ($V_{out} = $ LOW) until another trigger is applied.

The waveforms that are generated for the one-shot operation are shown in Figure 14–25.

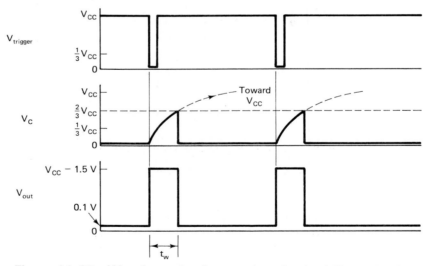

Figure 14–25 Waveforms for the one-shot circuit of Figure 14–24.

To derive the equation for t_w of the one-shot, we start with the same capacitor-charging formula (Equation 14–2):

$$t_w = RC \ln \left(\frac{1}{1 - \Delta v/E} \right) \qquad (14\text{–}2)$$

where $R = R_A$
        $\Delta v =$ distance that the capacitor voltage travels $= \frac{2}{3}V_{cc}$ (from 0 V up to $\frac{2}{3}V_{cc}$)
         $E =$ distance that the capacitor voltage is trying to travel $= V_{cc}$ (from 0 V up to V_{cc})
Substitution yields

$$t_w = R_A C \ln \left(\frac{1}{1 - \frac{2}{3}V_{cc}/V_{cc}} \right)$$

$$= R_A C \ln \left(\frac{1}{1 - 0.667} \right)$$

$$= R_A C \ln (3)$$

$$= 1.10 R_A C \qquad\qquad (14\text{--}9)$$

EXAMPLE 14-11

Design a circuit using a 555 one-shot that will stretch a 1-μs negative-going pulse that occurs every 60 μs into a 10-μs negative-going pulse.

Solution: To set the output pulse width to 10 μs:

$$t_w = 1.10 R_A C$$

$$10 \ \mu s = 1.10 R_A C$$

$$R_A C = 9.09 \ \mu s$$

Pick $C = 0.001 \ \mu$F; then

$$R_A = 9.09 \ k\Omega$$

Also, since the 555 outputs a positive-going pulse, an inverter must be added to change it to a negative-going pulse. (7404 inverter: $V_{OH} = 3.4$ V, $V_{OL} = 0.2$ V). The final circuit design and waveforms are shown in Figure 14-26.

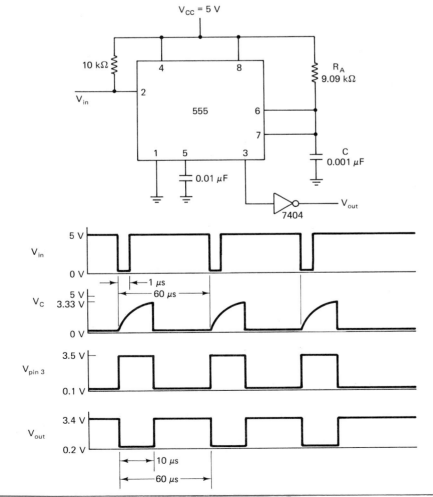

Figure 14-26 Solution to Example 14-11.

14–9 CRYSTAL OSCILLATORS

None of the *RC* oscillators or one-shots presented in the previous sections are extremely stable. In fact, the standard procedure for building those timing circuits is to prototype them based on the *R* and *C* values calculated using the formulas, then "tweak" (or make adjustments to) the resistor values while observing the time periods on an oscilloscope. Normally, standard values are chosen for the capacitors and potentiometers are used for the resistors.

However, even after a careful calibration of the time period, changes in the components and IC occur as the devices age and as the ambient temperature varies. To partially overcome this problem, some manufactures will allow their circuits to "burn in" or age for several weeks before the final calibration and shipment.

Instead of using *RC* components, another timing component is available to the design engineer when extremely critical timing is required. This highly stable and accurate timing component is the *quartz crystal*. A piece of quartz crystal is cut to a specific size and shape to vibrate at a specific frequency, similar to an *RLC* resonant circuit. Its frequency is typically in the range 10 kHz to 10 MHz. Accuracy of more than *five significant digits* can easily be achieved using this method.

Crystal oscillators are available as an integrated-circuit package or can be built using an external quartz crystal in circuits such as those shown in Figure 14–27. The circuits shown in the figure will oscillate at a frequency dictated by the crystal chosen. In Figure 14–27a the 100-kΩ pot may need adjustment to start oscillation.

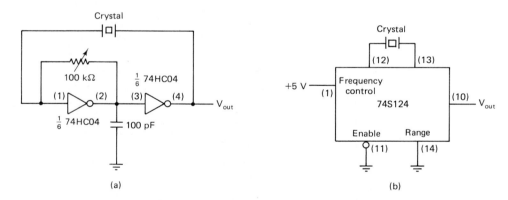

Figure 14–27 Crystal oscillator circuits: (a) high-speed CMOS oscillator; (b) Schottky-TTL oscillator.

The 74LS124 TTL chip in Figure 14–27b is a *voltage-controlled oscillator*, set up to generate a specific frequency at V_{out}. By changing the crystal to a capacitor, the output frequency will vary, depending on the voltage level at the frequency control (pin 1) and frequency range (pin 14) inputs. Using specifications presented in the manufacturer's data manual, you can determine the output frequency of the VCO, based on the voltage level applied to its inputs.

GLOSSARY

Burn-in: A step near the end of the production process in which a manufacturer "exercises" the functions of an electronic circuit and "ages" the components before the final calibration step.

Comparator: As used in a 555 timer, it compares the analog voltage level at its two inputs and outputs a HIGH or a LOW, depending on which input was higher.

(If the voltage level on the + input is higher than the voltage level on the − input, the output is HIGH; otherwise, it is LOW.)

Crystal: A material, usually made from quartz, that can be cut and shaped to oscillate at a very specific frequency. It is used in highly accurate clock and timing circuits.

Duty cycle: A ratio of the lengths of time that a digital signal is HIGH versus its total period:

$$\text{duty cycle} = \frac{t_{HI}}{t_{HI} + t_{LO}}$$

Exponential charge/discharge: An exponential rate of charge or discharge is nonlinear, meaning that the rate of change of capacitor voltage is greater in the beginning, then slows down toward the end.

Multivibrator: An electronic circuit or IC used in digital electronics to generate HIGH and LOW logic states. The *bistable* multivibrator is an *S-R* flip-flop triggered into its HIGH or LOW state. The *astable* multivibrator is a free-running oscillator that continuously alternates between its HIGH and LOW states. The *monostable* multivibrator is a one-shot that, when triggered, outputs a single pulse of a specific time duration.

Oscillator: An electronic circuit whose output continuously alternates between HIGH and LOW states at a specific frequency.

Pulse stretching: Increasing the time duration of a pulse width.

Retriggerable: A device that is capable of reacting to a second, or subsequent trigger before the action initiated by the first trigger is complete.

Time constant (tau, τ): τ is equal to the product of resistance times capacitance and is used to determine the *rate* of charge or discharge in a series *RC* circuit. (1τ is equal to the number of seconds that it takes for a capacitor's voltage to reach 63% of its final value.)

Voltage-controlled oscillator (VCO): An oscillator whose output frequency is dependent on the analog voltage level at its input.

REVIEW QUESTIONS

Sections 14–1 and 14–2

14–1. The *astable* multivibrator, also known as a "one-shot," produces a single output pulse after it is triggered (true or false)?

14–2. The voltage on a charging capacitor will increase _____ (faster, slower) if its series resistor is increased.

14–3. A 1 microfarad capacitor with a 10kΩ series resistor will have the same charging rate as a 10 microfarad capacitor with a 1 kΩ series resistor (true or false)?

Section 14–3

14–4. The capacitor voltage levels in a Schmitt trigger astable multivibrator are limited by _____ and the output voltage is limited by _____ .

14–5. One way to increase the frequency of a Schmitt trigger astable multivibrator is to _____ (increase, decrease) the resistor.

Sections 14–4 through 14–6

14–6. The output of a monostable multivibrator has a predictable pulse width based on the width of the input trigger pulse (true or false)?

14–7. To trigger a 74121 one-shot IC, A_1 _____ (and, or) A_2 must be made _____ (LOW, HIGH) _____ (and, or) B must be made _____ (HIGH, LOW).

14–8. Which of the three trigger inputs of the 74121 would you use to trigger from a falling edge of a pulse? What would you do with the other two inputs?

14–9. When the 74121 receives a trigger, the Q output goes _____ (HIGH, LOW) for a time duration t_w.

14–10. The 74123 one-shot IC is *retriggerable*, whereas the 74121 is not. What does this statement mean?

Sections 14–7 through 14–9

14–11. The comparators inside the 555 IC timer will output a LOW if their (−) input is more positive than their (+) input (true or false)?

14–12. The discharge transistor inside the 555 shorts Pin 7 to ground when the output at Pin 3 is _____ (LOW, HIGH).

14–13. When Pin 6 (Threshold) of the 555 IC exceeds _____ (1/3 Vcc, 2/3 Vcc), the flip-flop is _____ (Reset, Set), making the output at Pin 3 _____ (LOW, HIGH).

14–14. The 555 is connected as an astable multivibrator in Figure 14–20. V_{out} is HIGH while the capacitor charges through resistor(s) _____ and V_{out} is LOW while the capacitor discharges through resistor(s) _____ .

14–15. The 555 astable multivibrator in Figure 14–20 will always have a duty cycle _____ (greater than, less than) 50% because _____ .

14–16. When using the 555 as a monostable (one-shot) multivibrator, a _____ (LOW, HIGH) trigger is applied to Pin 2, which forces V_{out} _____ (LOW, HIGH) and initiates the capacitor to start _____ (charging, discharging).

14–17. What advantage does a quartz crystal have over an R-C circuit when used in timing applications?

PROBLEMS

14–1. Which type of multivibrator is also known as a:
 (a) One-shot?
 (b) *S-R* flip-flop?
 (c) Free-running oscillator?

14–2. (a) For the *RC* circuit of Figure P14–2, determine the voltage on the capacitor 50 μs after the switch is moved from position 2 to position 1. (Assume that V_c = 0 V initially.)
 (b) Repeat part (a) for 100 μs.
 (c) Repeat part (a) for 150 μs.
 (d) Sketch and label a graph of capacitor voltage versus time for the values that you found in parts (a), (b), and (c).

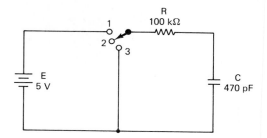

Figure P14–2

14–3. The capacitor in Figure P14–2 is initially discharged. How long after the switch is moved from position 2 to position 1 will it take for the capacitor to reach 4 V?

14–4. Assume that the capacitor in Figure P14–2 is initially charged to 2 V. How long after the switch is moved from position 2 to position 1 will it take for the capacitor voltage to reach 4 V?

14–5. Assume that the capacitor in Figure P14–2 is initially charged to 4 V. How long after the switch is moved from position 2 to position 3 will it take for the voltage to drop to 2 V?

14–6. If you were successful at solving for the time in Problems 14–4 and 14–5, you will notice that it takes longer for the capacitor voltage to go from 2 V to 4 V than it did to go from 4 V to 2 V. Why is that true?

14–7. Why is a Schmitt trigger inverter used for the astable multivibrator circuit of Figure 14–5 instead of a regular inverter like a 74HCO4?

14–8. In a Schmitt trigger astable multivibrator, if the hysteresis voltage (V_{T+} minus V_{T-}) decreases due to a temperature change, what happens to:
 (a) The output frequency?
 (b) The output voltage?

14–9. Specifications for the 74HC14 Schmitt inverter when powered from a 6-V supply are as follows: $V_{OH} = 6.0$ V, $V_{OL} = 0.0$ V, $V_{T+} = 3.3$ V, and $V_{T-} = 2.0$ V.
 (a) Sketch and label the waveforms for V_{cap} and V_{out} in the astable multivibrator circuit of Figure 14-5. (Use $R = 68$ k and $C = 0.0047$ μF).
 (b) Calculate t_{HI}, t_{LO}, duty cycle, and frequency.

Design

14–10. Design a monostable multivibrator using two 74HC00 NAND gates similar to Figure 14–9. Determine the values for R and C such that a negative-going, 2-μs input trigger will create a 50-μs positive-going output pulse.

14–11. Make the external connections to a 74121 monostable multivibrator to convert a 100-kHz, 30% duty cycle square wave to a 100-kHz, 50% duty cycle square wave.

14–12. Use two 74121s as a delay line to reproduce the waveforms shown in Figure P14–12. (The output pulse will look just like the input pulse but delayed by 30 μs.)

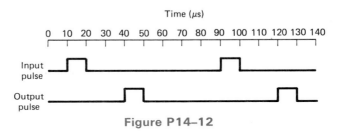

Figure P14–12

14–13. The NPRO microprocessor control line is suppose to issue a 10-μs LOW pulse every 150 μs as long as a certain process is running smoothly. Design a "missing pulse detector" using a 74123 that will normally output a HIGH, but will output a LOW if a single pulse on the NPRO line is skipped. (*Hint*: The 74123 will be retriggered by NPRO every 150 μs.)

14–14. Using the timing chart in Figure 14–17 for a 74123, determine a good value for R_{ext} and C_{ext} to give an output pulse width of 400 ns.

555

14–15. Sketch and label the waveforms at V_{out} for the 555 circuit of Figure P14–15 with the potentiometer set at 0 Ω.

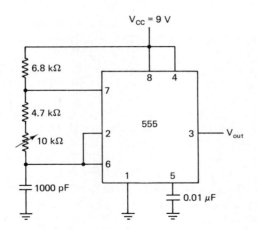

Figure P14–15

14–16. Determine the maximum and minimum frequency and the maximum and minimum duty cycle that can be achieved by adjusting the potentiometer in Figure P14–15.

14–17. Derive formulas for duty cycle and frequency in terms of R_A, R_B and C for a 555 astable multivibrator. (Test your formulas by resolving Problem 14–16.)

14–18. Using a 555, design an astable multivibrator that will oscillate at 50 kHz, 60% duty cycle. (So that we all get the same answer, let's pick $C = 0.0022 \, \mu F$.)

14–19. Design a circuit that will produce a 100-kHz square wave using:
  (a) A 74HC14
  (b) Two 74121s
  (c) A 74123
  (d) A 555

14–20. Sketch and label the waveforms at $V_{trigger}$, V_{cap}, and V_{out} for the 555 one-shot circuit of Figure 14–24. Assume that $V_{trigger}$ is a 5-μs negative-going pulse that occurs every 100 μs and $V_{CC} = 5$ V, $R_A = 47$ kΩ, $C = 1000$ pF.

15

Interfacing to the Analog World

OBJECTIVES

Upon completion of this chapter, you should be able to:

- Perform the basic calculations involved in the analysis of operational amplifier circuits.
- Explain the operation of binary-weighted and $R/2R$ digital-to-analog converters.
- Make the external connections to a digital-to-analog IC to convert a numeric binary string into a proportional analog voltage.
- Discuss the meaning of the specifications for converter ICs as given in a manufacturer's data manual.
- Explain the operation of parallel-encoded, counter-ramp, and successive-approximation analog-to-digital converters.
- Make the external connections to an analog-to-digital converter IC to convert an analog voltage to a corresponding binary string.
- Discuss the operation of a typical data acquisition system.

INTRODUCTION

Most physical quantities that we deal with in this world are *analog* in nature. For example, temperature, pressure, and speed are not simply 1's and 0's but instead take on an infinite number of possible values. To be understood by a digital system, these values must be converted into a binary string representing their value; thus we have the need for *analog-to-digital* conversion. Also, it is important when we need to use a computer to control analog devices to be able to convert from *digital to analog*.

413

Devices that convert physical quantities into electrical quantities are called *transducers*. Transducers are readily available to convert such quantities as temperature, pressure, velocity, position, and direction into a proportional analog voltage or current. For example, a common transducer for measuring temperature is a thermistor. A thermistor is simply a temperature-sensitive resistor. As its temperature changes, so does its resistance. If we send a constant current through the thermistor, then measure the voltage across it, we can determine its resistance *and* temperature.

15–1 DIGITAL AND ANALOG REPRESENTATIONS

For *analog-to-digital* (A/D) or *digital-to-analog* (D/A) converters to be useful there has to be a meaningful representation of the analog quantity as a digital representation and the digital quantity as an analog representation. If we choose a convenient range of analog levels such as 0 to 15 V, we could easily represent each 1-V step as a unique digital code, as shown in Figure 15–1.

Figure 15–1 shows that for each analog voltage we can determine an equivalent digital representation. Using four binary positions gives us 4-bit *resolution*, which allows us to develop 16 different representations, with the increment between each

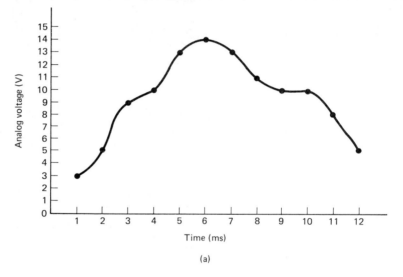

(a)

	Representation	
Time (ms)	Analog	Digital
1	3	0011
2	5	0101
3	9	1001
4	10	1010
5	13	1101
6	14	1110
7	13	1101
8	11	1011
9	10	1010
10	10	1010
11	8	1000
12	5	0101

(b)

Figure 15–1 Analog and digital representations: (a) voltage versus time; (b) representations at 1-ms intervals.

being 1 part in 16. If we need to represent more than just 16 different analog levels, we would have to use a digital code with more than four binary positions. For example, a D/A converter with 8-bit resolution will provide increments of 1 part in 256, which provides much more precise representations.

15-2 OPERATIONAL AMPLIFIER BASICS

Most A/D and D/A circuits require the use of an op amp for signal conditioning. There are three characteristics of op amps that make them an almost *ideal amplifier*: (1) very high input impedance, (2) very high voltage gain, and (3) very low output impedance. In this section we gain a basic understanding of how an op amp works, and in future sections we see how it is used in the conversion process. A basic op-amp circuit is shown in Figure 15-2.

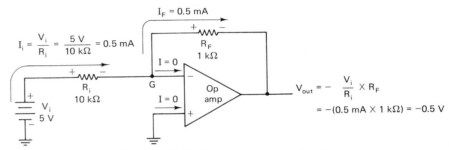

Figure 15-2 Basic op-amp operation.

The symbol for the op amp is the same as that for a comparator, but when it is connected as shown in Figure 15-2 it provides a much different function. The basic theory involved in the operation of the op-amp circuit in Figure 15-2 is as follows:

1. The impedance looking into the $+$ and $-$ input terminals is assumed to be infinite; therefore, I_{in} $(+)$, $(-) = 0$ A.

2. Point G is assumed to be at the same potential as the $+$ input; therefore, point G is at 0 V, called *virtual ground* (virtual means "in effect" but not actual. It is at 0 V, but it cannot sink current.)

3. With point G at 0 V, there will be 5 V across the 10-kΩ resistor, causing 0.5 mA to flow.

4. The 0.5 mA cannot flow into the op amp; therefore, it flows up through the 1-kΩ resistor.

5. Since point G is at virtual ground, and since V_{out} is measured with respect to ground, V_{out} is equal to the voltage across the 1-kΩ resistor, which is -0.5 V.

EXAMPLE 15-1

Find V_{out} in Figure 15-3.

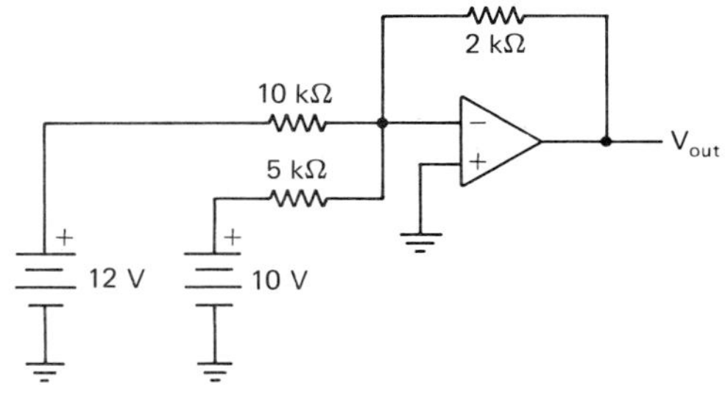

Figure 15-3 Op-amp circuit for Example 15-1.

Solution:

$$I_{10\,k\Omega} = \frac{12\text{ V}}{10\text{ k}\Omega} = 1.2\text{ mA}$$

$$I_{5\,k\Omega} = \frac{10\text{ V}}{5\text{ k}\Omega} = 2\text{ mA}$$

$$I_{2\,k\Omega} = 1.2\text{ mA} + 2\text{mA} = 3.2\text{ mA}$$

$$V_{\text{out}} = -(3.2\text{ mA} \times 2\text{ k}\Omega) = -6.4\text{ V}$$

15–3 BINARY-WEIGHTED DIGITAL-TO-ANALOG CONVERTERS

A basic D/A converter can be built by expanding on the information presented in Section 15–2. Example 15–1 showed us that the 2-kΩ resistor receives the *sum* of the currents heading toward the op amp from the two input resistors. If we scale the input resistors with a binary weighting factor, each input can be made to provide a binary-weighted amount of current and the output voltage will represent a sum of all the binary-weighted input currents, as shown in Figure 15–4.

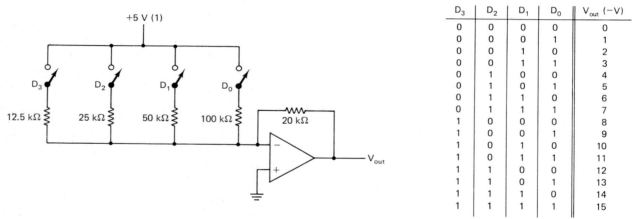

D_3	D_2	D_1	D_0	V_{out} (−V)
0	0	0	0	0
0	0	0	1	1
0	0	1	0	2
0	0	1	1	3
0	1	0	0	4
0	1	0	1	5
0	1	1	0	6
0	1	1	1	7
1	0	0	0	8
1	0	0	1	9
1	0	1	0	10
1	0	1	1	11
1	1	0	0	12
1	1	0	1	13
1	1	1	0	14
1	1	1	1	15

Figure 15–4 Binary-weighted D/A converter.

In Figure 15–4 the 20-kΩ resistor *sums* the currents that are provided by closing any of switches D_0 to D_3. The resistors are scaled in such a way as to provide a binary-weighted amount of current to be summed by the 20-kΩ resistor. Closing D_0 causes 50 μA to flow through the 20 kΩ, creating −1.0 V at V_{out}. Closing each successive switch creates *double* the amount of current of the previous switch. Work through several of the switch combinations presented in Figure 15–4 to prove its operation.

If we were to expand Figure 15–4 to an 8-bit D/A converter, the resistor for D_4 would be one-half of 12.5 kΩ, which is 6.25 kΩ. Each successive resistor is one-half of the previous one. Using this procedure, the resistor for D_7 would be 0.78125 kΩ!

Coming up with accurate resistances over such a large range of values is very difficult. This limits the practical use of this type of D/A converter for any more than 4-bit conversions.

15–4 R/2R *LADDER DIGITAL-TO-ANALOG CONVERTERS*

The method for D/A conversion that is most often used in integrated circuit D/A converters is known as the $R/2R$ ladder circuit. In this circuit, only two resistor values are required, which lends itself nicely to the fabrication of ICs with a resolution of 8, 10, or 12 bits, and higher. Figure 15–5 shows a 4-bit D/A $R/2R$ converter.

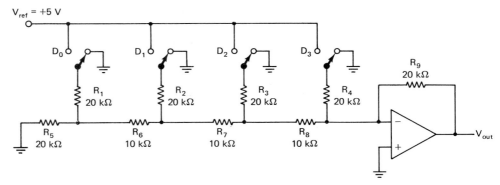

Figure 15–5 The $R/2R$ ladder D/A converter.

In Figure 15–5, the 4-bit digital information to be converted to analog is entered on the D_0 to D_3 switches. (In an actual IC those switches will be transistor switches.) The arrangement of the circuit is such that as the switches are moved to +5 V or 0 V (1 or 0), they cause a current to flow through R_9 that is proportional to their binary equivalent value. (Each successive switch is worth double the previous one.)

The analog output voltage from each of the 16 possible switch combinations is shown in Figure 15–6. Let's work through the calculation of V_{out} for three different switch combinations to see how the $R/2R$ method works.

1. For $D_0 = 0$, $D_1 = 0$, $D_2 = 0$, and $D_3 = 1$: R_1 is in parallel with R_5 to equal 10 kΩ, 10 kΩ is in series with R_6 to equal 20 kΩ, 20 kΩ is in

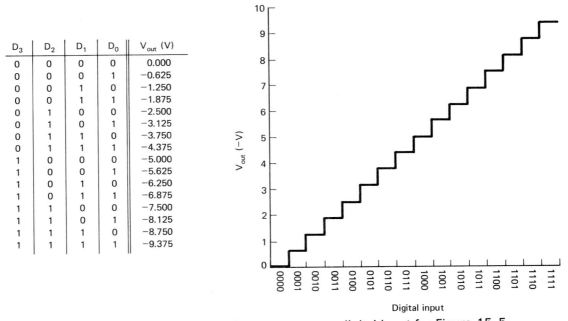

D_3	D_2	D_1	D_0	V_{out} (V)
0	0	0	0	0.000
0	0	0	1	−0.625
0	0	1	0	−1.250
0	0	1	1	−1.875
0	1	0	0	−2.500
0	1	0	1	−3.125
0	1	1	0	−3.750
0	1	1	1	−4.375
1	0	0	0	−5.000
1	0	0	1	−5.625
1	0	1	0	−6.250
1	0	1	1	−6.875
1	1	0	0	−7.500
1	1	0	1	−8.125
1	1	1	0	−8.750
1	1	1	1	−9.375

Figure 15–6 Analog output versus digital input for Figure 15–5.

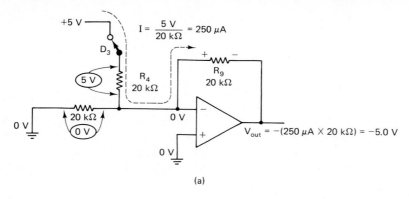

(a)

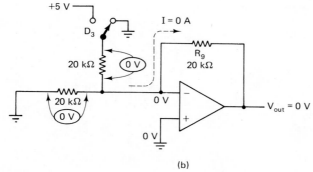

(b)

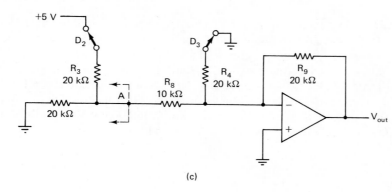

Figure 15–7 (a) The equivalent
R/2R circuit for $D_0 = 0$, $D_1 = 0$,
$D_2 = 0$, $D_3 = 1$; (b) the equivalent
R/2R circuit for $D_0 = 0$, $D_1 = 0$,
$D_2 = 0$, $D_3 = 0$; (c) the equivalent
R/2R circuit for $D_0 = 0$, $D_1 = 0$,
$D_2 = 1$, $D_3 = 0$; (d) the Thévenin
equivalent R/2R circuit for
$D_0 = 0$, $D_1 = 0$, $D_2 = 1$, $D_3 = 0$.

(c)

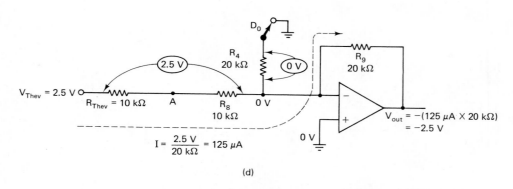

(d)

parallel with R_2 to equal 10 kΩ, and so on through R_7, R_3, and R_8. The
equivalent circuit becomes as shown in Figure 15–7a.

2. For $D_0 = 0$, $D_1 = 0$, $D_2 = 0$, $D_3 = 0$: The equivalent circuit (Figure 15–7b) will be similar to Figure 15–7a except that switch $D_3 = 0$.

3. For $D_0 = 0$, $D_1 = 0$, $D_2 = 1$, $D_3 = 0$: All switches are grounded except D_2, so the equivalent circuit becomes as shown in Figure 15–7c. The circuit in Figure 15–7c is still not simplified far enough to determine V_{out}. The Thevenin equivalent circuit at point A will reduce the circuit to that shown in Figure 15–7d.

As it turns out, no matter which combination of switch positions is used, the magnitude of voltage contributed by closing switch D_3 to 1 is equal to $2V_{ref}/2$; D_2 contributes $2V_{ref}/4$, D_1 contributes $2V_{ref}/8$, and D_0 contributes $2V_{ref}/16$.

15–5 INTEGRATED-CIRCUIT DIGITAL-TO-ANALOG CONVERTERS

One very popular and inexpensive 8-bit D/A converter (DAC) is the DAC0808 and its equivalent, the MC1408. A block diagram, pin configuration, and typical application are shown in Figure 15–8. The circuit in Figure 15–8c is set up to accept an 8-bit

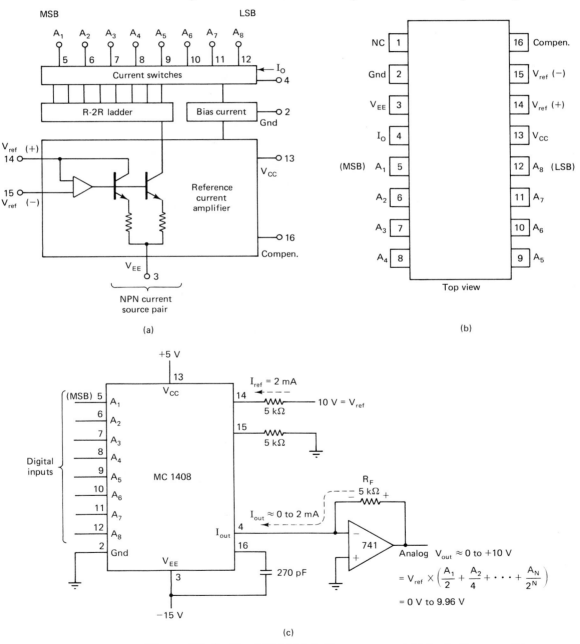

Figure 15–8 The MC1408 D/A converter: (a) block diagram; (b) pin configuration; (c) typical application.

digital input and provide a 0- to +10-V analog output. A reference current (I_{ref}) is required for the D/A and is provided by the 10-V, 5-kΩ combination shown. The negative reference (pin 15) is then tied to ground via an equal-size (5-kΩ) resistor.

That 2-mA reference current dictates the full-scale output current (I_{out}) also to be approximately 2 mA. To calculate the *actual* output current, use the formula

$$I_{out} = I_{ref}\left(\frac{A_1}{2} + \frac{A_2}{4} + \cdots + \frac{A_8}{256}\right) \tag{15-1}$$

[e.g., with all inputs (A_1 to A_8) HIGH, $I_{out} = I_{ref} \times (0.996)$]. To convert an output current to an output voltage, a series resistor could be connected from pin 4 to ground and the output taken across the resistor. That method is simple, but it may cause inaccuracies as various-size loads are connected to it.

A more accurate method uses an op amp such as the 741 shown in Figure 15–8c. The output current flows through R_F, which develops an output voltage equal to $I_{out} \times R_F$. The range of output voltage can be changed by changing R_F and is limited only by the specifications of the op amp used.

To test the circuit, an oscillator and an 8-bit counter can be used to drive the digital inputs and the analog output can be observed on an oscilloscope, as shown in Figure 15–9. In Figure 15–9, as the counters count from 0000 0000 up to 1111 1111, the analog output will go from 0 V up to almost +10 V in 256 steps. The time per step will be equal to the reciprocal of the input clock frequency.

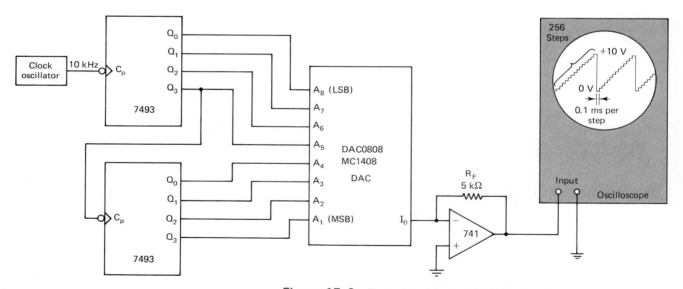

Figure 15–9 Test circuit for a DAC application.

15–6 IC *DATA CONVERTER SPECIFICATIONS*

Besides resolution, there are several other specifications that are important in the selection of D/A and A/D converters (DAC and ADC). It is important that the specifications and their definitions given in the manufacturer's data book be studied and understood before selecting a particular DAC or ADC. Figure 15–10 lists some of the more important specifications as presented in the Signetics Linear LSI Data Manual.

Absolute Accuracy Error

Absolute Accuracy Error is the difference between the theoretical analog input required to produce a given output code and the actual analog input required to produce the same code. The actual input is a range and the error is the midpoint of the measured band and the theoretical band.

Conversion Speed

Conversion Speed is the speed at which a converter can make repetitive conversions.

Conversion Time

Conversion time is the time required for a complete conversion cycle of an ADC. Conversion time is a function of the number of bits and the clock frequency.

Differential Non-Linearity (DNL) (a)

Differential Non-Linearity of a DAC is the deviation of the measured output step size from the ideal step size. In an ADC it is the deviation in the range of inputs from 1 LSB that causes the output to change from one given code to the next code. Excessive DNL gives rise to non-monotonic behavior in a DAC and missing codes in an ADC.

Gain Error (b)

Gain Error is the error of the slope of the line drawn through the midpoints of the steps of the transfer function as compared to the ideal slope. It is usually measured by determining the error of the analog input voltage to cause a full scale output word with the ideal value that should cause this full scale output. This gain error is usually expressed in LSB or in percent of full scale range.

Missing Code (c)

A Missing Code is a code combination that does not appear in the ADC's output range.

Monotonicity (d)

A DAC is monotonic if its output either increases or remains the same when the input code is incremented from any code to the next higher code.

Offset Error (e)

Offset error is the constant error or shift from the ideal transfer characteristic of a converter. In a DAC it is the output obtained when that output should be zero. In an ADC it is the difference between the input level that causes the first code transition and what that input level should be.

Output Voltage Compliance

Output Voltage Compliance of a current output DAC is the range of acceptable voltages at the DAC output for the DAC output current to remain within its specified limits.

Quantizing Error

In an A/D converter there is an infinite number of possible input levels, but only 2^n output codes (n = number of bits). There will, therefore, be an error in the output code that could be as great as $\frac{1}{2}$ LSB because of this quantizing effect. The greatest error occurs at the transition point where the output state changes.

Relative Accuracy (f)

Relative Accuracy is a measure of the difference of the theoretical output value with a given input after any offset and gain errors have been nulled out.

Resolution

Resolution is the number of bits at the input or output of an ADC or DAC. It is the number of discrete steps or states at the output and is equal to 2^n where n is the resolution of the converter. However, n bits of resolution does not guarantee n bits of accuracy.

Setting Time (g)

Setting Time is the delay in a DAC from the 50 percent point on the change in the input digital code to the effected change in the output signal. It is expressed in terms of how long it takes the output to settle to and remain within a certain error band around the final value and is usually specific for full scale range changes.

Transfer Characteristic (h)

The Transfer Characteristic is the relationship of the output to the input, D_{in} vs. A_{in} (ADC) or A_{out} vs. D_{in} (DAC).

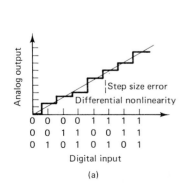

(a)

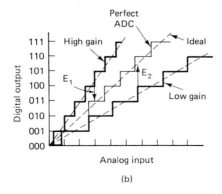

(b)

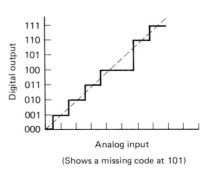

(Shows a missing code at 101)

(c)

Figure 15-10 DAC and ADC specification definitions: (a) differential nonlinearity; (b) gain error; (c) missing codes;

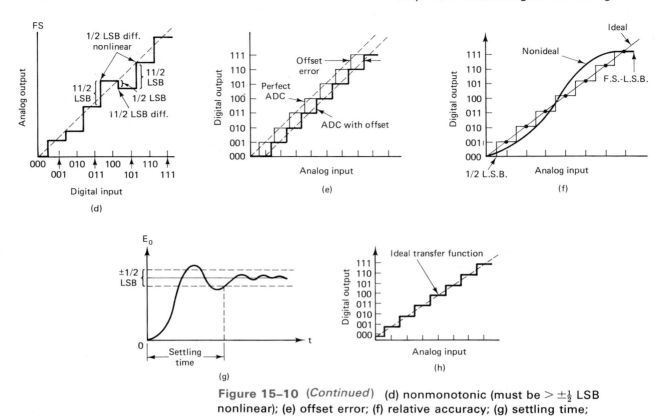

Figure 15–10 (*Continued*) (d) nonmonotonic (must be $> \pm\frac{1}{2}$ LSB nonlinear); (e) offset error; (f) relative accuracy; (g) settling time; (h) 3-bit ADC transfer characteristic. (Courtesy of Signetics Corporation.)

15–7 PARALLEL-ENCODED ANALOG-TO-DIGITAL CONVERTERS

The process of taking an analog voltage and converting it to a digital signal can be done in several ways. One simple way that is easy to visualize is by means of parallel encoding (also known as "simultaneous," "multiple comparator," or "flash" converting). In this method, several comparators are set up, each at a different voltage reference level with their outputs driving a priority encoder as shown in Figure 15–11. The voltage-divider network in Figure 15–11 is designed to drop 1 V across each resistor. This sets up a voltage reference at each comparator input in 1-V steps.

When V_{in} is 0 V, the + input on all seven comparators will be higher than the − input, so they will all output a HIGH. In that case, $\bar{I}_0$ is the only active-LOW input that is enabled, so the 74148 will output an active-LOW binary 0 (111).

When V_{in} exceeds 1.0 V, comparator 1 will output a LOW. Now $\bar{I}_0$ and $\bar{I}_1$ are both enabled, but since it is a *priority* encoder, the output will be a binary 1 (110). As V_{in} increases further, each successive comparator outputs a LOW. The highest input that receives a LOW is encoded into its binary equivalent output.

This particular A/D converter (Figure 15–11) is set up to convert analog voltages in the range 0 to 7 V. The range can be scaled higher or lower, depending on the input voltage levels that are expected. The resolution of this converter is only 3 bits, so it can only distinguish between eight different analog input levels. To expand to 4-bit resolution, eight more comparators are required to differentiate the 16 different voltage levels. To expand to 8-bit resolution, 256 comparators would be required! As you can see, circuit complexity becomes a real problem when using parallel encoding

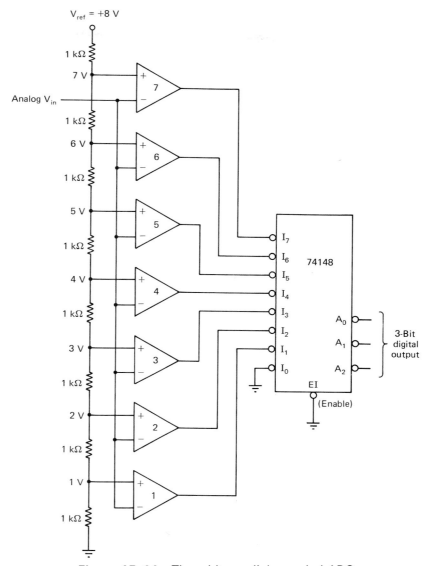

Figure 15–11 Three-bit parallel-encoded ADC.

for high-resolution conversion. However, a big advantage of using parallel encoding is its high speed. The conversion speed is limited only by the propagation delays of the comparators and encoder (less than 20 ns total).

15–8 COUNTER-RAMP ANALOG-TO-DIGITAL CONVERTERS

The counter-ramp method of A/D conversion (ADC) uses a counter in conjunction with a D/A converter (DAC) to determine a digital output that is equivalent to the unknown analog input voltage. In Figure 15–12, depressing the "start conversion" pushbutton clears the counter outputs to 0, which sets the DAC output to 0 V. The (−) input to the comparator is now 0 V, which is less than the positive analog input voltage at the (+) input. Therefore, the comparator outputs a HIGH which enables the AND gate, allowing the counter to start counting. As the counter's binary output increases, so does the DAC output voltage in the form of a staircase.

When the staircase voltage reaches, then exceeds the analog input voltage, the

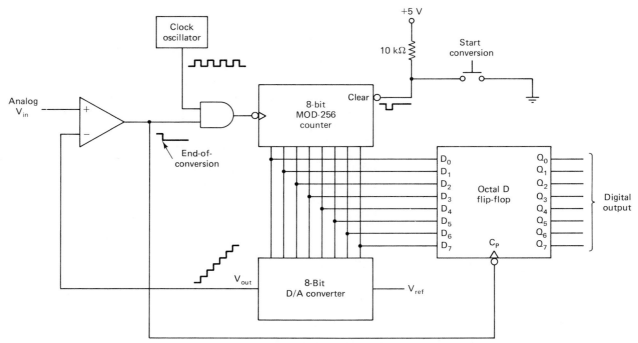

Figure 15–12   Counter-ramp A/D converter.

comparator output goes LOW, disabling the clock and stopping the counter. The counter output at that point is equal to the binary number that caused the DAC to output a voltage slightly greater than the analog input voltage. Thus we have the binary equivalent of the analog voltage!

The HIGH-to-LOW transition of the comparator is also used to trigger the *D* flip-flop to "latch" on to the binary number at that instant. To perform another conversion, the start pushbutton is depressed again and the process repeats. The result from the previous conversion remains in the D flip-flop until the next "end-of-conversion" HIGH-to-LOW edge comes along.

To change the circuit to perform *continuous conversions*, the end-of-conversion line could be tied back to the $\overline{\text{clear}}$ input of the counter. A short delay needs to be inserted into this new line, however, to allow the D flip-flop to read the binary number before the counter is Reset. Two inverters placed end to end in the line will produce a sufficient delay.

The main *disadvantage* of the counter-ramp method of conversion is its slow conversion speed. The worst-case maximum conversion time will occur when the counter has to count all 255 steps before the DAC output voltage matches the analog input voltage.

15–9   SUCCESSIVE-APPROXIMATION ANALOG-TO-DIGITAL CONVERSION

Other methods of A/D conversion employ *up/down-counters* and *integrating slope converters* to "track" the analog input, but the method used in most modern integrated-circuit ADCs is called *successive approximation*. This converter circuit is similar to the counter-ramp ADC circuit except that the method of narrowing in on the unknown analog input voltage is much improved. Instead of counting up from 0 and comparing the DAC output each step of the way, a successive-approximation register (SAR) is used in place of the counter (see Figure 15–13).

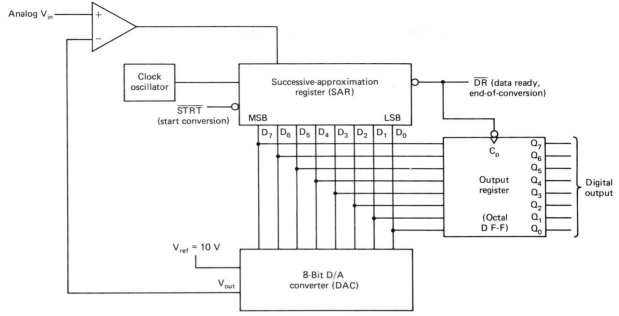

Figure 15–13 Simplified SAR A/D converter.

In Figure 15–13 the conversion is started by dropping the $\overline{\text{STRT}}$ line LOW. Then the SAR first tries a HIGH on the MSB (D_7) line to the DAC. (Remember, D_7 will cause the DAC to output half of its full-scale output.) If the DAC output is then *higher* than the unknown analog input voltage, the SAR returns the MSB LOW. If the DAC output was still *lower* than the unknown analog input voltage, the SAR leaves the MSB HIGH.

Now, the next lower bit (D_6) is tried. If a HIGH on D_6 causes the DAC output to be higher than the analog V_{in}, it is returned LOW. If not, it is left HIGH. The process continues until all 8 bits, down to the LSB, have been tried. At the end of this eight-step conversion process, the SAR contains a valid 8-bit binary output code that represents the unknown analog input. The $\overline{\text{DR}}$ output now goes LOW, indicating that the *conversion is complete* and the data are ready. That HIGH-to-LOW edge on $\overline{\text{DR}}$ "clocks" the D_0 to D_7 data into the octal D flip-flop to make the digital output results available at the Q_0 to Q_7 lines.

The main advantage of the SAR ADC method is its high speed. The ADC in Figure 15–13 takes only eight clock periods to complete a conversion, which is a vast improvement over the counter-ramp method.

EXAMPLE 15–2

Show the timing waveforms that would occur in the successive approximation ADC of Figure 15–13 when converting the analog voltage 6.84 V to 8-bit binary, assuming that the full-scale input voltage to the DAC is 10 V ($V_{\text{ref}} = 10$ V).

Solution: Each successive bit, starting with the MSB, will cause the DAC part of the system to output a voltage to be compared. If the full-scale output is 10 V, D_7 will be worth 5 V, D_6 will be worth 2.5 V, D_5 will be worth 1.25 V, and so on, as shown in Table 15–1.

TABLE 15–1

Voltage-Level
Contributions by Each
Successive Approximation
Register Bit

DAC input	DAC V_{out}
D_7	5.0000
D_6	2.5000
D_5	1.2500
D_4	0.6250
D_3	0.3125
D_2	0.15625
D_1	0.078125
D_0	0.0390625

Now, when $\overline{STRT}$ goes LOW, successive bits starting with D_7 will be tried, creating the waveforms shown in Figure 15–14. The HIGH-to-LOW edge on $\overline{DR}$ "clocks" the final binary number 1010 1111 into the D flip-flop and Q_0 to Q_7 outputs.

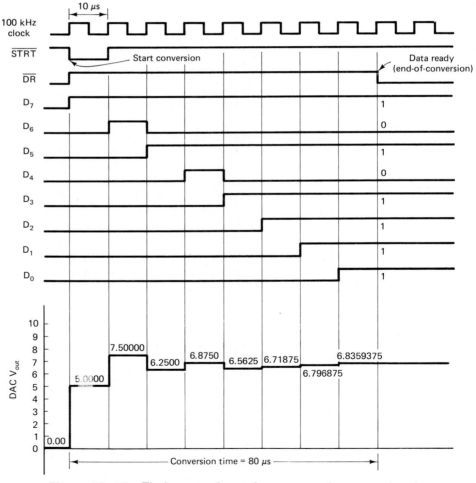

Figure 15–14 Timing waveforms for a successive approximation A/D conversion.

Now the Q_0 to Q_7 lines contain the 8-bit binary representation of the analog number 6.8359375, which is an error of only 0.0594% from the target number of 6.84:

$$\% \text{ error} = \frac{\text{actual voltage} - \text{final DAC output}}{\text{actual voltage}} \times 100\%$$

To watch the conversion in progress, an eight-channel oscilloscope or logic analyzer can be connected to the D_0 to D_7 outputs of the SAR.

For *continuous conversions* the $\overline{DR}$ line can be connected back to the $\overline{STRT}$ line. That way, as soon as the conversion is complete, the HIGH-to-LOW on $\overline{DR}$ will issue another start conversion ($\overline{STRT}$), which forces the data ready ($\overline{DR}$) line back HIGH for eight clock periods while the new conversion is being made. The latched Q_0 to Q_7 digital outputs will always display the results of the *previous conversion*.

15–10 *INTEGRATED-CIRCUIT ANALOG-TO-DIGITAL CONVERTERS*

Examples of two popular, commercially available ADCs are the NE5034 and the ADC0801 manufactured by Signetics Corporation.

The NE5034

The block diagram and pin configuration for the NE5034 are given in Figure 15–15. Operation of the NE5034 is almost identical to that of the SAR ADC presented in Section 15–9. One difference is that the NE5034 uses a three-state output buffer instead of a D flip-flop. With three-state outputs, when $\overline{OE}$ (Output Enable) is LOW, the DB_7 to DB_0 outputs display the continuous status of the eight SAR lines, and when the $\overline{OE}$ line goes HIGH, the DB_7 to DB_0 outputs return to a float or high-impedance state. This way, if the ADC outputs go to a common *data bus* shared

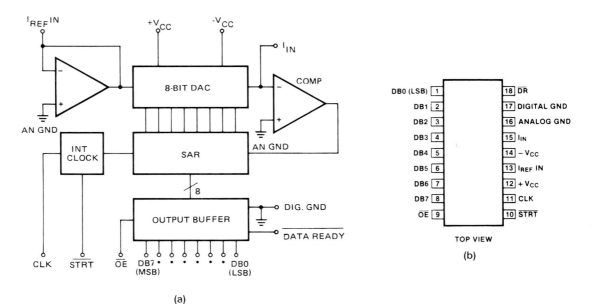

(a)

Figure 15–15 The NE5034 A/D converter: (a) block diagram; (b) pin configuration. (Courtesy of Signetics Corporation.)

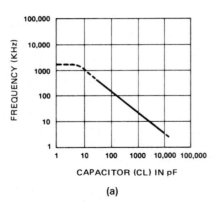
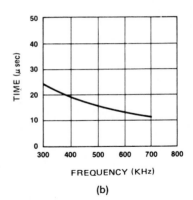

Figure 15-16 The NE5034 internal clock characteristics: (a) internal clock frequency versus external capacitor (CL); (b) conversion time versus clock frequency. (Courtesy of Signetics Corporation.)

by other devices, when DB_7 to DB_0 float, one of the other devices can output information to the data bus without interference.

The NE5034 can provide conversion speeds as high as one per 17 μs, and its three-state outputs make it compatible with bus-oriented microprocessor systems. It also has its own internal clock for providing timing pulses. The frequency is determined by an external capacitor placed between pins 11 and 17. Figure 15–16 shows the frequency and conversion time that can be achieved using the internal clock.

The ADC0801

The pin configuration and block diagram for the ADC0801 are given in Figure 15–17. The ADC0801 uses the successive-approximation method to convert an analog input to an 8-bit binary code. Two analog inputs are provided to allow differential measurements [analog $V_{in} = V_{in(+)} - V_{in(-)}$]. It has an internal clock that generates its own timing pulses at a frequency equal to $f = 1/(1.1RC)$ (Figure 15–18 shows the connections for the external R and C). It uses output D latches that are three-stated to facilitate easy bus interfacing.

The convention for naming the ADC0801 pins follows those used by microprocessors to ease interfacing. Basically, the operation of the ADC0801 is similar to that of the NE5034. The ADC0801 pins are defined as follows:

$\overline{CS}$—active-LOW *Chip Select*

$\overline{RD}$—active-LOW *Output Enable*

$\overline{WR}$—active-LOW *Start Conversion*

CLK IN—external clock input or capacitor connection point for the internal clock

$\overline{INTR}$—active-LOW *End-of-Conversion* (Data Ready)

$V_{in(+)}$, $V_{in(-)}$—differential analog inputs (ground one pin for single-ended measurements)

A. Gnd—analog ground

$V_{ref/2}$—optional reference voltage (used to override the reference voltage assumed at V_{CC})

D. Gnd—digital ground

V_{CC}—5-V power supply and assumed reference voltage

CLK R—resistor connection for the internal clock

D_0 to D_7—digital outputs

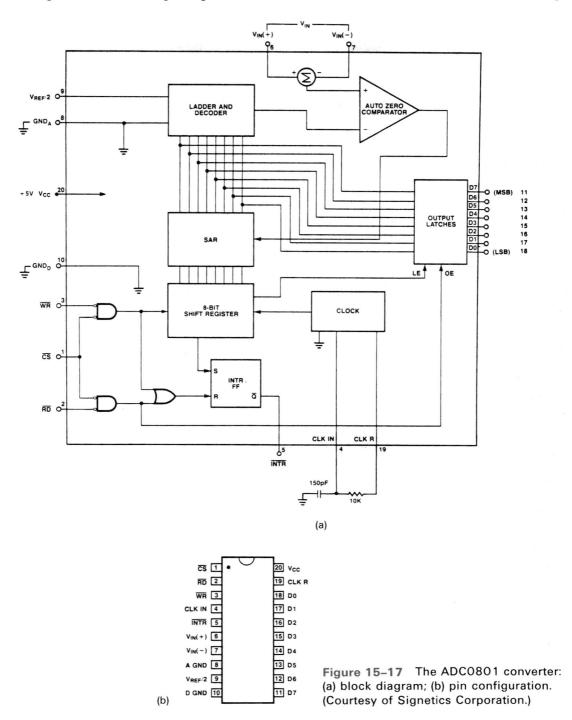

(a)

(b)

Figure 15–17 The ADC0801 converter:
(a) block diagram; (b) pin configuration.
(Courtesy of Signetics Corporation.)

To set the ADC0801 up for continuous A/D conversions, the connections shown in Figure 15–18 should be made. The external *RC* will set up a clock frequency of

$$f = \frac{1}{1.1RC} = \frac{1}{1.1(10\text{ k}\Omega)150\text{ pF}} = 606\text{ kHz}$$

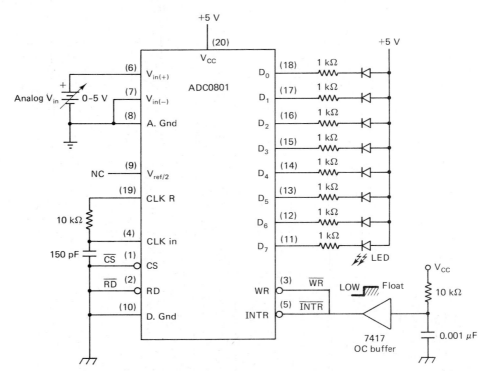

Figure 15–18   Connections for continuous conversions using the ADC0801.

The connection from $\overline{INTR}$ to $\overline{WR}$ will cause the ADC to start a new conversion each time the $\overline{INTR}$ (end-of-conversion) line goes LOW. The *RC* circuit with the 7417 open-collector buffer will issue a LOW-to-float pulse at power-up to ensure initial startup. An *open-collector* output gate is required instead of a totem-pole output because the $\overline{INTR}$ is forced LOW by the internal circuitry of the 0801 at the end of each conversion. That LOW would conflict with the HIGH output level if a totem-pole output were used. The $\overline{CS}$ is grounded to enable the ADC chip. $\overline{RD}$ is grounded to enable the D_0 to D_7 outputs. The analog input voltage is positive, 0 to 5 V, so it is connected to $V_{in(+)}$. If it were negative, $V_{in(+)}$ would be gounded and the input voltage would be connected to $V_{in(-)}$. Differential measurements (the difference between two analog voltages) can be made by using both $V_{in(+)}$ and $V_{in(-)}$. The LEDs connected to the digital output will monitor the operation of the ADC outputs. An LED ON indicates a LOW and an LED OFF indictes a HIGH. (In other words, they are displaying the *complement* of the binary output.) To test the circuit operation, you could watch the OFF LEDs count up in binary from 0 to 255 as the analog input voltage is slowly increased from 0 to +5 V.

The analog input voltage range can be changed to values other than 0 to 5 V by using the $V_{ref/2}$ input. This provides the means of encoding small analog voltages to the full 8 bits of resolution. The $V_{ref/2}$ pin is normally not connected and it sits at 2.500 V ($V_{CC}/2$). By connecting 2.00 V to $V_{ref/2}$ the analog input voltage range is changed to 0 to 4 V; 1.5 V would change it to 0 to 3.0 V; and so on. However, the accuracy of the ADC suffers as the input voltage range is decreased.

One final point on the ADC0801. An analog ground *and* a digital ground are both provided to enhance the accuracy of the system. The V_{CC}-to-digital ground lines are inherently noisy due to the switching transients of the digital signals. Using separate analog and digital grounds is not mandatory, but when used it ensures that the analog voltage comparator will not switch falsely due to digital noise and jitter.

15–11 DATA ACQUISITION SYSTEMS

The computerized acquisition of analog quantities is becoming more important than ever in today's automated world. Computer systems are capable of scanning several analog inputs on a particular schedule and sequence to monitor critical quantities and acquire data for future recall. A typical eight-channel computerized data acquisition system (DAS) is shown in Figure 15–19.

The entire system in Figure 15–19 communicates via two common buses, the *data bus* and the *control bus*. The data bus is simply a common set of eight electrical conductors shared by as many devices as necessary to send and receive 8 bits of parallel data to and from anywhere in the system. In this case there are three devices on the data bus: the ADC, the microprocessor, and memory. The control bus passes control signals to and from the various devices for such things as chip select ($\overline{CS}$), output enable ($\overline{RD}$), system clock, triggers, and selects.

Each of the eight transducers is set up to output a voltage that is proportional to the analog quantity being measured. The task of the microprocessor is to scan all the quantities at some precise interval and store the digital results in memory for future use.

To do this, the microprocessor must enable and send the proper control signals to each of the devices, in order, starting with the multiplexer and ending with the ADC. This is called *handshaking*, or *polling*, and is all done with software statements. If you are fortunate enough to take a course in microprocessor programming, you will learn how to perform some of these tasks.

All of the hardware interfacing and handshaking that takes place between the microprocessor and the transducers can be explained by taking a closer look at each of the devices in the system.

Analog Multiplexer Switch (AM3705)

The multiplexer reduces circuit complexity and eliminates duplication of circuitry by allowing each of the eight transducer outputs to take turns traveling through the other devices. The microprocessor selects each of the transducers at the appropriate time by setting up the appropriate binary select code on the A, B, C inputs via the control bus. That allows the selected transducer signal to pass through to the next device.

Sample-and Hold Circuit (LF198)

Since analog quantities can be constantly varying, it is important to be able to select a precise time to take the measurement. The sample-and-hold circuit, with its external *Hold capacitor*, allows the system to take (Sample) *and Hold* an analog value at the precise instant that the microprocessor issues the *acquisition trigger*.

Programmable-Gain Instrumentation Amplifier (LH0084)

Each of the eight transducers have different full-scale output ratings. For instance, the temperature transducer may output in the range 0 to 5 V while the pressure transducer may only output 0 to 500 mV. The LH0084 is capable of being programmed, via the gain select inputs, for gains of 1, 2, 5, or 10. When it is time to read the pressure transducer, the microprocessor will program the gain for 10 so that the range will be 0 to 5 V, to match that of the other transducers. That way the ADC can always operate in its most accurate range, 0 to 5 V.

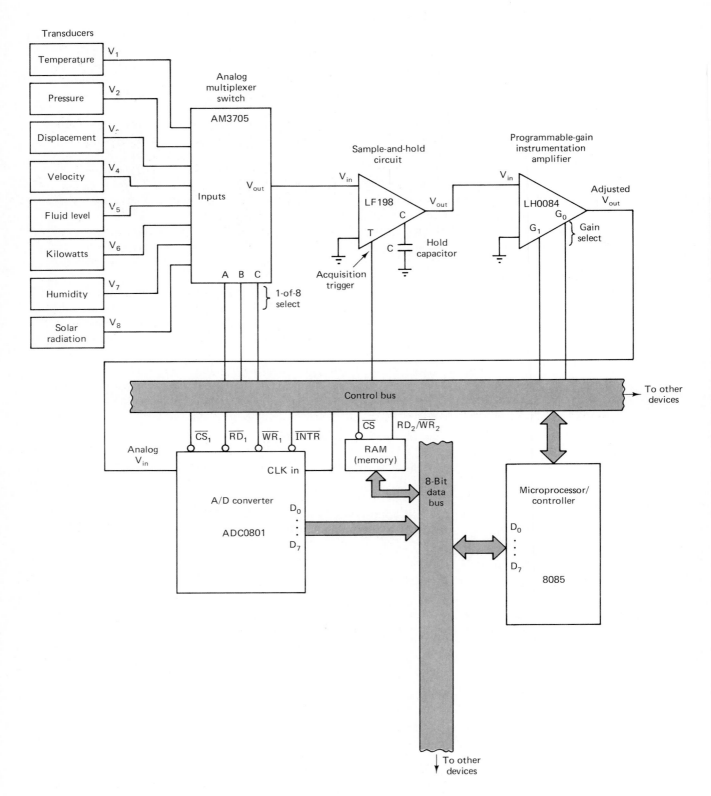

Figure 15–19 Data acquisition system.

Analog-to-Digital Converter (ADC0801)

The ADC receives the adjusted analog voltage and converts it to an equivalent 8-bit binary string. To do that, the microprocessor issues chip select ($\overline{CS_1}$) and start conversion ($\overline{WR_1}$) pulses. When the end-of-conversion ($\overline{INTR}$) line goes LOW, the microprocessor issues an output enable ($\overline{RD_1}$) to read the data (D_0 to D_7) that pass, via the data bus, into the microprocessor and then into the random-access-memory (RAM) chip (more on memory in Chapter 16).

This cycle repeats for all eight transducers whenever the microprocessor determines that it is time for the next scan. Other software routines executed by the microprocessor will act on the data that have been gathered. Some possible responses to the measured results might be to sound an alarm, speed up a fan, reduce energy consumption, increase a fluid level, or simply produce a tabular report of the measured quantities.

15–12 TRANSDUCERS AND SIGNAL CONDITIONING

Hundreds of *transducers* are available today that convert physical quantities such as heat, light, or force, into electrical quantities. The *electrical quantities* (or signal levels) must then be "conditioned" (or modified) before they can be interpreted by a digital computer.

Signal conditioning is required because transducers each output different ranges and types of electrical signals. For example, transducers can produce output voltages, output currents, or act like variable resistances. A transducer may have a non-linear response to input quantities, be inversely proportional, and may output signals in the microvolt range.

A transducer's response specifications are given by the manufacturer and must be studied carefully to determine the appropriate analog signal conditioning circuitry required to interface it to an analog-to-digital converter. After the information is read into a digital computer, software instructions convert the binary input into a meaningful output that can be used for further processing. Let's take a closer look at three commonly used transducers: a thermistor, an IC temperature sensor, and a strain gage.

Thermistors

A thermistor is an electronic component whose resistance is highly dependent on temperature. Its resistance changes by several percent with each degree change in temperature. It is a very sensitive temperature-measuring device. One problem however, is that its response is non-linear, meaning that one degree step changes in temperature will not create equal step changes in resistance. This fact is illustrated in the characteristic curve of the 10k ohm (at 25°C) thermistor shown in Figure 15–20.

From the characteristic curve you can see that not only is the thermistor non-linear, but it also has a negative temperature coefficient (i.e., Its resistance decreases with increasing temperatures).

To use a thermistor with an analog-to-digital converter like the ADC0801, we need to convert the thermistor resistance to a voltage in the range of 0-to-5 volts. One way to accomplish this task is with the circuit shown in Figure 15–21.

This circuit operates similarly to the op-amp circuit explained in Section 15–2. The output of the circuit is found using the formula:

$$V_{out} = -V_{in} \times R_f/R_i$$

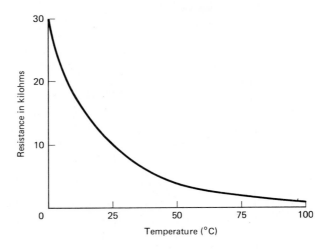

Figure 15–20 Thermistor characteristic curve of resistance versus temperature.

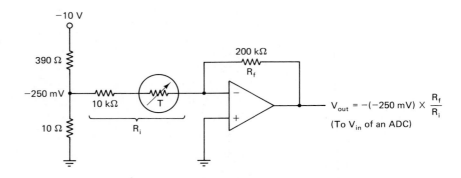

Figure 15–21 Circuit used to convert thermistor ohms to a DC voltage.

where V_{in} is a fixed reference voltage of -250mV and R_i is the sum of the thermistor's resistance, R_T, plus 10k ohms. Using specific values for R_T found in the manufacturer's data manual, we can create Table 15–2, which shows V_{out} as a function of temperature.

TABLE 15–2

Tabulation of Output Voltage Levels for a Temperature Range of 0 to 100°C in Figure 15–21

Temperature (in °C)	R_T (in kΩ)	R_i (in kΩ)	V_{out} (in volts)
0	29.490	39.490	1.27
25	10.000	20.000	2.50
50	3.893	13.893	3.60
75	1.700	11.700	4.27
100	0.817	10.817	4.62

The output voltage, V_{out}, is fed into an ADC that converts it into an 8-bit binary number. The binary number is then read by a microprocessor that converts it into the corresponding degrees celsius using software program instructions.

Linear IC Temperature Sensors

The computer software required to convert the output voltages of the previous thermistor circuit is fairly complicated because of the nonlinear characteristics of the device. *Linear temperature sensors* were developed to simplify the procedure. One such device is the LM35 integrated circuit temperature sensor. It is fabricated in a 3-terminal transistor package and is designed to output 10 millivolts for each degree celsius above zero. (Another temperature sensor, the LM34 is calibrated in degrees fahrenheit). For example, at 25°C the sensor outputs 250 mV, at 50°C it outputs 500 mV, and so on, in linear steps for its entire range. Figure 15–22 shows how we can interface the LM35 to an ADC and microprocessor.

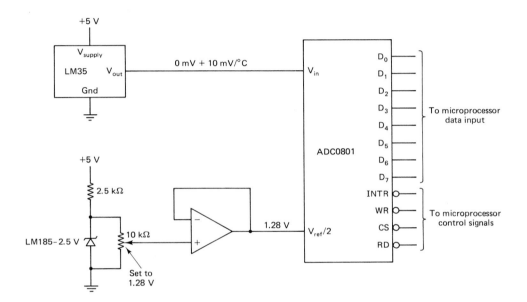

Figure 15–22 Interfacing the LM35 linear temperature sensor to an ADC.

The 1.28 volt reference level used in Figure 15–22 is the key to keeping the conversion software programming simple. With 1.28 volts at $V_{ref}/2$, the maximum full-scale analog V_{in} is defined as 2.56 volts (2560mV). This value corresponds one-for-one with the 256 binary output steps provided by an 8-bit ADC. A one degree rise in temperature increases V_{in} by 10mV, which increases the binary output by 1. Therefore, if V_{in} equals 0 volts, D_7-D_0 equals 0000 0000; if V_{in} equals 2.55 volts, D_7-D_0 equals 1111 1111; and, if V_{in} equals 1.00 volt, D_7-D_0 equals the binary equivalent of 100, which is 0110 0100. Table 15–3 lists some representative values of temperature versus binary output.

In Figure 15–22, the LM185 is a 2.5 volt precision voltage reference diode. This diode maintains a steady 2.5 volts across the 10kΩ potentiometer even if the 5 volt power supply line fluctuates. The 10kΩ potentiometer must be set to output exactly 1.280 volts. The op-amp is used as a unity-gain buffer between the potentiometer and ADC and will maintain a steady 1.280 volts for the $V_{ref}/2$ pin.

The Strain Gage

The strain gage is a device whose resistance changes when it is stretched. The

TABLE 15–3

Tabulation of Temperature versus Binary
Output for a Linear Temperature Sensor and
an ADC Set Up for 2560 mV Full Scale

Temperature (in °C)	V_{in} (in mV)	Binary Output (D_7-D_0)
0	0	0000 0000
1	10	0000 0001
2	20	0000 0010
25	250	0001 1001
50	500	0011 0010
75	750	0100 1011
100	1000	0110 0100

gage is stretched, or elongated when it is "strained" by a physical force. This property makes it useful for measuring weight, pressure, flow, and acceleration.

Several types of strain gages exist, the most common being the foil type illustrated in Figure 15–23.

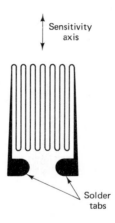

Figure 15–23   A foil type strain gage.

The gage is simply a thin electrical conductor that is looped back and forth and bonded securely to the piece of material to be strained (see Figure 15–24). Applying a force to the metal beam bends the beam slightly, which stretches the strain gage in the direction of its sensitivity axis.

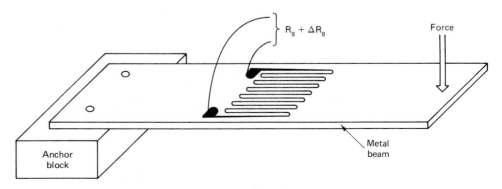

Figure 15–24   Using a strain gage to measure force.

As the strain gage conductor is stretched, its cross-sectional area decreases and its length increases, thus increasing the resistance measured at the solder tabs. The change in resistance is linear with respect to changes in length of the strain gage. However, the change in resistance is very slight, usually milliohms, and it must be converted to a voltage and amplified before it is input to an ADC. Figure 15–25 shows the signal conditioning circuitry for a 120 ohm strain gage. [R_g (unstrained) = 120Ω]

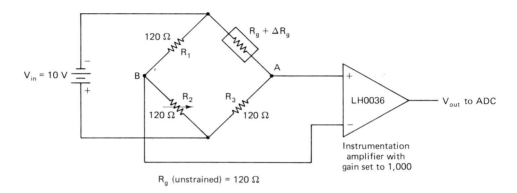

Figure 15–25 Signal conditioning for a strain gage.

The instrumentation amplifier is a special-purpose IC used to amplify small-signal differential voltages such as those at points A and B in the bridge circuit in Figure 15–25.

With the metal beam unstrained (no force applied) the 120Ω potentiometer is adjusted so that V_{out} equals 0 volts. Next, force is applied to the metal beam, elongating the strain gage, and increasing its resistance slightly from its unstrained value of 120 ohms. This increase causes the bridge circuit to become unbalanced, thus creating a voltage at Points A and B. From basic circuit theory, the voltage is calculated by the formula:

$$V_{AB} = V_{in} \left[\frac{R_3}{R_3 + (R_g + \Delta R_g)} - \frac{R_2}{R_1 + R_2} \right]$$

For example, if R_2 is set at 120Ω and ΔR_g is 150 milliohms, the voltage is:

$$V_{AB} = -10 \left[\frac{120}{120 + (120.150)} - \frac{120}{120 + 120} \right] = 3.12 \text{ mV}$$

Because the instrumentation amplifier gain is set at 1000, the output voltage sent to the ADC will be 3.12 volts.

Through experimentation with several known weights, the relationship of force versus V_{out} can be established and can be programmed into the microprocessor reading the ADC output.

GLOSSARY

ADC: Analog-to-digital converter.

Binary weighting: Each binary position in a string is worth double the amount of the bit to its right. By choosing resistors in that same proportion, binary-weighted current levels will flow.

Bus: A common set of electrical conductors shared by several devices and ICs.

Continuous conversions: An ADC that is connected to repeatedly perform analog-to-digital conversions by using the end-of-conversion signal to trigger the start-conversion input.

Conversion time: The length of time between the start of conversion and end of conversion of an ADC.

DAC: Digital-to-analog converter.

Data acquisition: A term generally used to refer to computer-controlled acquisition and conversion of analog values.

Differential measurement: The measurement of the difference between two values.

Handshaking: Devices and ICs that are interfaced together must follow a specific protocol, or sequence of control operations, in order to be understood by each other.

Interfacing: The device control and interconnection schemes required for electronic devices and ICs to communicate with each other.

Linearity: Linearity error describes how far the actual transfer function of an ADC or DAC varies from the ideal straight line drawn from zero up to the full-scale values.

Memory: A storage device capable of holding data that can be read by some other device.

Microprocessor: A large-scale IC capable of performing several functions, including the interpretation and execution of programmed software instructions.

Monotonicity: A monotonic DAC is one in which for every increase in the input digital code, the output level either remains the same or increases.

Op amp: An amplifier that exhibits almost ideal features (i.e., infinite input impedance, infinite gain, and zero output impedance).

Programmable-gain amplifier: An amplifier that has a variable voltage gain that is set by inputting the appropriate digital levels at the gain select inputs.

Reference voltage: In DAC and ADC circuits, a reference voltage or current is provided to the circuit to set the relative scale of the input and output values.

Resolution: The number of bits in an ADC or DAC. The higher the number, the closer the final representation can be to the actual input quantity.

Sample and hold: A procedure of taking a reading of a varying analog value at a precise instant and holding that reading.

Successive approximation: A method of arriving at a digital equivalent of an analog value by successively trying each of the individual digital bits, starting with the MSB.

Thermistor: An electronic component whose resistance changes with a change in temperature.

Transducer: A device that converts a physical quantity such as heat or light into an electrical quantity such as amperes or volts.

Virtual ground: In certain op-amp circuit configurations, with one input at actual ground potential the other input will be held at a 0-V potential but will not be able to sink or source current.

REVIEW QUESTIONS

Sections 15–1 and 15–2

15–1.   Transducers are devices that convert physical quantities like pressure and temperature into electrical quantities (true or false)?

15–2.   An 8-bit A/D converter is capable of producing how many unique digital output codes?

15–3. The input impedance to an operational amplifier is assumed to be _____. The voltage difference between the $(+)$ input and $(-)$ input is approximately _____ volts.

Sections 15–3 and 15–4
15–4. If the first three resistors in a binary-weighted D/A converter are 30kΩ, 60kΩ, and 120kΩ, the fourth resistor, used for the D_0 input, must be _____ ohms.

15–5. Why is it difficult to build an accurate *8-bit* binary-weighted D/A converter?

15–6. To build an 8-bit R/2R ladder D/A converter, you would need at least eight different resistor sizes (true or false)?

Sections 15–5 and 15–6
15–7. The analog output of the MC1408 DAC IC is represented by current or voltage?

15–8. Which digital input to the MC1408 DAC IC has the most significant effect on the analog output: A_1 or A_8?

15–9. The *resolution* of a DAC or ADC specifies the _____.

15–10. A DAC is *nonmonotonic* if its analog output *drops* after a one-bit increase in digital input (true or false)?

15–11. Which error affects the rate-of-change, or slope, of the ideal transfer function of an ADC, the gain error or the offset error?

Sections 15–7 and 15–8
15–12. In the parallel-encoded ADC of Figure 15–11, *only one* of the comparators will output a LOW for each analog input value (true or false)?

15–13. One difficulty in building a high-resolution, 10-bit parallel-encoded ADC is that it would take _____ comparators to complete the design.

15–14. The counter-ramp ADC of Figure 15–12 signifies an ''End-of-Conversion'' when the $(-)$ input voltage to the comparator drops below the $(+)$ input voltage (true or false)?

15–15. The digital output of the octal D flip-flop in Figure 15–12 is continuously changing at the same rate as the MOD-16 counter (true or false)?

Sections 15–9 and 15–10
15–16. The SAR ADC in Figure 15–13 starts making a conversion when _____ goes LOW, and signifies that the conversion is complete when _____ goes LOW.

15–17. The SAR method of A-to-D conversion is faster than the counter/ramp method because the SAR clock oscillator operates at a higher speed (true or false)?

15–18. Decide if the following pins on the ADC 0801 are for input or output signals.
   (a) $\overline{CS}$
   (b) $\overline{RD}$
   (c) $\overline{WR}$
   (d) $\overline{INTR}$

15–19. List the order in which the signals listed in Question 18 become active to perform an A-to-D conversion.

Sections 15–11 and 15–12
15–20. The AM7305 multiplexer in Figure 15–19 is used to apply the appropriate voltage gain to each of the transducers connected to it (true or false)?

15–21. The 8-bit data out from the ADC in Figure 15–19 passes to the microprocessor via the data bus (true or false)?

15–22. Signal conditioning is required to make transducer output levels compatible with ADC input requirements (true or false)?

15–23. What is the advantage of using the LM35 linear temperature sensor over a thermistor for measuring temperature?

PROBLEMS

15–1. Describe the function of a transducer.

15–2. How many different digital representations are allowed with:
(a) A 4-bit converter?
(b) A 6-bit converter?
(c) An 8-bit converter?
(d) A 12-bit converter?

15–3. List three characteristics of op amps that make them an almost ideal amplifier.

15–4. Determine V_{out} for the op-amp circuits of Figure P15–4.

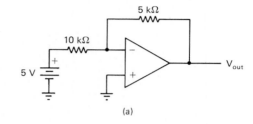

(a)

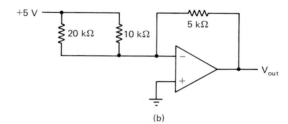

(b)

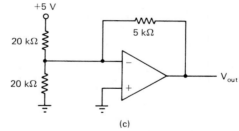

(c)

Figure P15–4

15–5. The "virtual ground" concept simplifies the analysis of op-amp circuits by allowing us to assume what?

15–6. (a) Change the resistor that is connected to the D_3 switch in Figure 15–4 to 10 kΩ. What values must be used for the other three resistors to ensure the correct binary weighting factors?
(b) Reconstruct the data table in Figure 15–4 with new values for V_{out} using the resistor values found in part (a).

15–7. What effect would doubling the 20-kΩ resistor have on the values for V_{out} in Figure 15–4?

15–8. What effect would changing the reference voltage (V_{ref}) in Figure 15–5 from +5 V to −5 V have on V_{out}?

15–9. Change V_{ref} in Figure 15–5 to +2 V and calculate V_{out} for $D_0 = 0$, $D_1 = 0$, $D_2 = 0$, $D_3 = 1$.

15–10. Reconstruct the data table in Figure 15–6 for a V_{ref} of +2 V instead of +5 V.

15–11. Does the MC1408 DAC use a binary-weighted or an $R/2R$ method of conversion?

15–12. What is the purpose of the op amp in the DAC application circuit of Figure 15–8c?

15–13. What is the resolution of the DAC0808/MC1408 DAC shown in Figure 15–8?

15–14. Sketch a partial transfer function of analog output versus digital input in Figure 15–8c for digital input values of 0000 0000 through 0000 0111.

15–15. How could the reference current (I_{ref}) in Figure 15–8 be changed to 1.5 mA? What effect would that have on the range of I_{out} and V_{out}?

15–16. In Figure 15–8c, if V_{ref} is changed to 5 V, find V_{out} full-scale (A_1 to $A_8 =$ HIGH).

15–17. Draw a graph of the transfer function (digital output versus analog input) for the parallel encoded ADC of Figure 15–11.

15–18. What is one advantage and one disadvantage of using the multiple-comparator parallel encoding method of A/D conversion?

15–19. Refer to the counter-ramp ADC of Figure 15–12.
  (a) What is the level at the DAC output the *instant after* the "start conversion" pushbutton is pressed?
  (b) What is the relationship between the $V(+)$ and $V(-)$ comparator inputs the *instant before* the HIGH-to-LOW edge of "end of conversion"?

15–20. In Figure 15–12, what is the worst-case (longest) conversion time that might be encountered if the clock frequency is 100 kHz?

15–21. Determine the conversion time for an 8-bit ADC that uses a successive-approximation circuit similar to Figure 15–13 if its clock frequency is 50 kHz.

15–22. What connections could be made in the ADC shown in Figure 15–13 to enable it to make continuous conversions?

15–23. Use the SAR ADC of Figure 15–13 to convert the analog voltage 7.28 to 8-bit binary. If $V_{ref} = 10$ V, determine the final binary answer and the percent error.

15–24. Why is the three-state buffer at the output of the NE5034 ADC an important feature?

15–25. Referring to the block diagram of the ADC0801 (Figure 15–17), which inputs are used to enable the three-state output latches? Are they active-LOW or active-HIGH inputs?

15–26. What type of application might require the use of the differential inputs [$V_{in(+)}$, $V_{in(-)}$] on the ADC0801?

15–27. Refer to Figures 15–17 and 15–18.
  (a) How would the operation change if $\overline{RD}$ were connected to +5 V instead of ground?
  (b) How would the operation change if $\overline{CS}$ were connected to +5 V instead of ground?
  (c) What is the purpose of the 10kΩ–0.001 μF RC circuit?
  (d) What is the maximum range of the analog V_{in} if $V_{ref/2}$ is changed to 0.5 V?

15–28. Briefly describe the flow of the signal from the temperature transducer as it travels through the circuit to the RAM memory in the data acquisition system of Figure 15–19.

16 Semiconductor Memory and Programmable Arrays

OBJECTIVES

Upon completion of this chapter, you should be able to:

- Explain the basic concepts involved in memory addressing and data storage.
- Interpret the specific timing requirements given in a manufacturer's data manual for reading or writing to a memory IC.
- Discuss the operation and application for the various types of semiconductor memory ICs.
- Design circuitry to facilitate memory expansion.
- Explain the "refresh" procedure for dynamic RAMs.
- Explain the programming procedure and applications for programmable array ICs.

INTRODUCTION

In digital systems, memory circuits provide the means of storing information (data) on a temporary or permanent basis for future recall. The storage medium can be either a semiconductor integrated circuit or a magnetic device such as magnetic tape or disk. Magnetic media generally are capable of storing larger quantities of data than semiconductor memories, but the access time (time it takes to locate, then read or write data) is usually much more for magnetic devices. With magnetic tape or disk it takes time to physically move the read/write mechanism to the exact location to be written to or read from.

With semiconductor memory ICs, electrical signals are used to identify a particular memory location within the integrated circuit and data can be stored in or read from that location in a matter of nanoseconds.

The technology used in the fabrication of memory ICs can be based on either bipolar or MOS transistors. In general, bipolar memories are faster than MOS memories, but MOS can be integrated more densely, providing much more memory locations in the same amount of area.

16-1 MEMORY CONCEPTS

Let's say that you have an application where you must store the digital states of eight binary switches once every hour for 16 hours. This would require 16 *memory locations*, each having a *unique 4-bit address* (0000 to 1111) and each location being capable of containing 8 bits of data. A group of 8 bits is also known as one *byte*, so what we would have is a 16-byte memory, as shown in Figure 16-1.

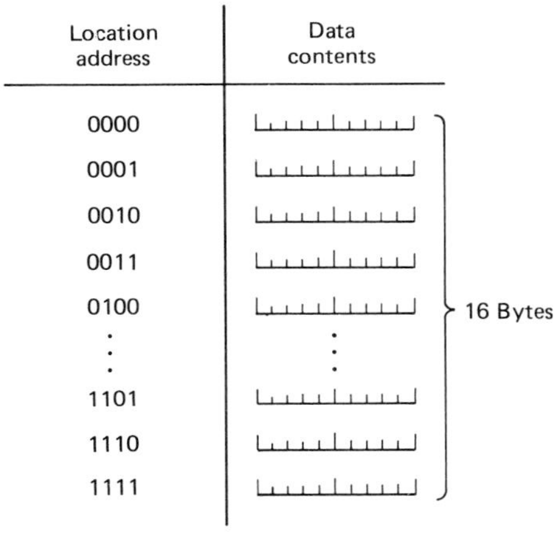

Figure 16-1   Layout for sixteen 8-bit memory locations.

To set up this memory system using actual ICs we could use sixteen 8-bit flip-flop registers to contain the 16 bytes of data. To identify the correct address a 4-line-to-16-line decoder can be used to decode the 4-bit location address into an active-LOW chip select to select the appropriate (1-of-16) data register for input/output. Figure 16-2 shows the circuit used to implement this memory application.

The 74LS374s are octal (eight) D flip-flops with three-state outputs. To store data in them, 8 bits of data are put on the D_0 to D_7 data inputs via the data bus. Then a LOW-to-HIGH edge on the C_p clock input will cause the data at D_0 to D_7 to be latched into each flip-flop. The value stored in the D flip-flops is observed at the Q_0 to Q_7 outputs by making the Output Enable ($\overline{OE}$) pin LOW.

To select the appropriate (1-of-16) memory location, a 4-bit address is input to the 74LS154 (4-line-to-16-line decoder), which outputs a LOW pulse on one of the output lines when the $\overline{\text{WRITE}}$ enable input is pulsed LOW.

As you can see, the timing of setting up the address bus, data bus, and pulsing the $\overline{\text{WRITE}}$ line is critical. Timing diagrams are necessary for understanding the operation of memory ICs, especially when you are using larger-scale memory ICs. The timing diagram for our 16-byte memory design of Figure 16-2 is given in Figure 16-3.

Figure 16-3 begins to show us some of the standard ways that manufacturers illustrate timing parameters for bus-driven devices. Rather than showing all four address lines and all eight data lines, they group them together and use an X (crossover) to show where any or all of the lines are allowed to change digital levels.

In Figure 16-3 the address and data lines must be set up some time (t_s) before the LOW-to-HIGH edge of $\overline{\text{WRITE}}$. In other words, the address and data lines must *be valid* (be at the appropriate levels) some period of time (t_s) *before* the LOW-

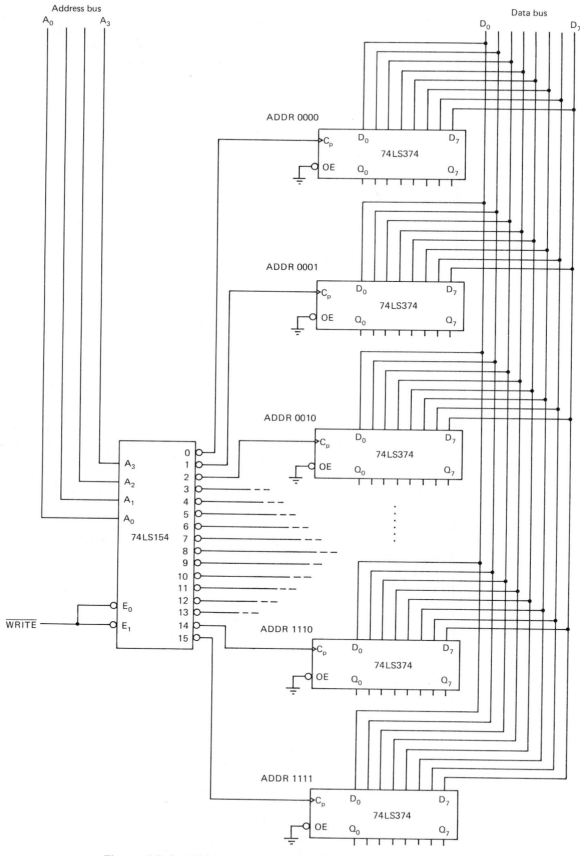

Figure 16–2 Writing to a 16-byte memory constructed from 16 octal *D* flip-flops and a 1-of-16 decoder.

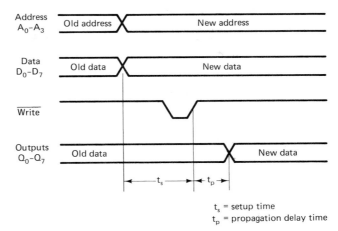

Figure 16–3 Timing requirements for writing data to the 16-byte memory circuit of Figure 16–2.

to-HIGH edge of $\overline{\text{WRITE}}$ in order for the 74LS374 D flip-flop to interpret the input correctly.

When the $\overline{\text{WRITE}}$ line is pulsed, the 74LS154 decoder outputs a LOW pulse on one of its 16 outputs, which clocks the appropriate memory location to receive data from the data bus. After the propagation delay (t_p), the data output at Q_0 to Q_7 will be the new data just entered into the D flip-flop. t_p will include the propagation delay of the decoder *and* the C_p-to-Q of the D flip-flop.

In Figure 16–2 all of the three-state outputs are continuously enabled so that their Q outputs are always active. To connect the Q_0 to Q_7 outputs of all 16 memory locations back to the data bus, the $\overline{OE}$ enables would have to be individually selected, at the appropriate time to avoid a conflict on the data bus, called *bus contention*. Bus contention occurs when two or more devices are trying to send their own digital levels to the shared data bus at the same time. To individually select each group of Q outputs in Figure 16–2, the grounds on the $\overline{OE}$ enables would be removed, and instead be connected to the output of another 74LS154 1-of-16 decoder, as shown in Figure 16–4.

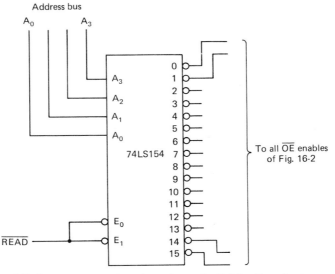

Figure 16–4 Using another decoder to individually select memory locations for Read operations.

We have designed in Figures 16–2, 16–3, and 16–4 a small 16-byte (16 $\times$ 8) random-access memory (RAM). Commercially available RAM ICs combine all the decoding and storage elements in a single package.

16–2   STATIC RAMs

Large-scale *random-access memory* (RAM), also known as *read/write memory*, is used for temporary storage of data and program instructions in microprocessor-based systems. The term "random access" means that the user can access (read or write) data at any location within the entire memory device randomly, without having to sequentially read through several data values until positioned at the desired memory location. [An example of a sequential (nonrandom) memory device is magnetic tape.]

A better term for RAM is *read/write memory* (RWM) because all semiconductor and disk memories have random access. RWM is more specific in that it tells us that data can be *read or written* to any memory location.

RAM is classified as either static or dynamic. *Static* RAMs (SRAMs) use flip-flops as basic storage elements, whereas *dynamic* RAMs (DRAMs) use internal capacitors as basic storage elements. Additional *refresh* circuitry is needed to maintain the charge on the internal capacitors of a dynamic RAM, which makes it more difficult to use. Dynamic RAMs can be packed very densely, however, yielding much more storage capacity per unit area than a static RAM. The cost per bit of dynamic RAMs is also much less than that of the static RAM.

The 2147H Static MOS RAM

The 2147H is a very popular static RAM that uses MOS technology. The 2147H is set up with 4096 (abbreviated 4K, where 1K = 1024) memory locations, with each location containing 1 bit of data. This configuration is called 4096 $\times$ 1.

To develop a unique address for each of the 4096 locations, 12 address lines must be input ($2^{12} = 4096$). The storage locations are set up as a 64 $\times$ 64 array with A_0 to A_5 identifying the row and A_6 to A_{11} identifying the column to pinpoint the specific location to be used. The data sheet for the 2147H is given in Figure 16–5. This figure shows the row and column circuitry used to pinpoint the memory cell within the 64 $\times$ 64 array. The box labeled "Row Select" is actually a 6-to-64 decoder for identifying the appropriate 1-of-64 row. The box labeled "Column Select" is also a 6-to-64 decoder for identifying the appropriate 1-of-64 column. Once the location is selected, the AND gates at the bottom of the block diagram allow the data bit to either pass into (D_{in}) or come out of (D_{out}) the memory location selected. Each memory location, or cell, is actually a configuration of transistors that function like a flip-flop that can be Set (1) or Reset (0).

During *write operations*, in order for D_{in} to pass through its three-state buffer, the Chip Select ($\overline{CS}$) must be LOW *and* the Write Enable ($\overline{WE}$) must also be LOW. During *read operations*, in order for D_{out} to receive data from its three-state buffer, the Chip Select ($\overline{CS}$) must be LOW *and* the Write Enable ($\overline{WE}$) must be HIGH, signifying a *Read operation*.

Read Operation.   The circuit connections and waveforms for reading data from a location in a 2147H are given in Figure 16–6 (page 424). The 12 address lines are brought in from the address bus for address selection. The $\overline{WE}$ input is held HIGH to enable the Read operation.

Referring to the timing diagram, when the new address is entered on the A_0 to A_{11} inputs and the $\overline{CS}$ lines goes LOW, it takes a short period of time, called the *access time*, before the data output is valid. The access time is the length of time from the beginning of the read cycle to the end of t_{ACS}, or t_{AA}, whichever

2147H
HIGH SPEED 4096 × 1 BIT STATIC RAM

	2147H-1	2147H-2	2147H-3	2147HL-3	2147H	2147HL
Max. Access Time (ns)	35	45	55	55	70	70
Max. Active Current (mA)	180	180	180	125	160	140
Max. Standby Current (mA)	30	30	30	15	20	10

- Pinout, Function, and Power Compatible to Industry Standard 2147
- HMOS II Technology
- Completely Static Memory—No Clock or Timing Strobe Required
- Equal Access and Cycle Times
- Single +5V Supply
- 0.8–2.0V Output Timing Reference Levels

- Direct Performance Upgrade for 2147
- Automatic Power-Down
- High Density 18-Pin Package
- Directly TTL Compatible—All Inputs and Output
- Separate Data Input and Output
- Three-State Output

The Intel® 2147H is a 4096-bit static Random Access Memory organized as 4096 words by 1-bit using HMOS-II, Intel's next generation high-performance MOS technology. It uses a uniquely innovative design approach which provides the ease-of-use features associated with non-clocked static memories and the reduced standby power dissipation associated with clocked static memories. To the user this means low standby power dissipation without the need for clocks, address setup and hold times, nor reduced data rates due to cycle times that are longer than access times.

$\overline{CS}$ controls the power-down feature. In less than a cycle time after $\overline{CS}$ goes high—deselecting the 2147H —the part automatically reduces its power requirements and remains in this low power standby mode as long as $\overline{CS}$ remains high. This device feature results in system power savings as great as 85% in larger systems, where the majority of devices are deselected.

The 2147H is placed in an 18-pin package configured with the industry standard 2147 pinout. It is directly TTL compatible in all respects: inputs, output, and a single +5V supply. The data is read out nondestructively and has the same polarity as the input data. A data input and a separate three-state output are used.

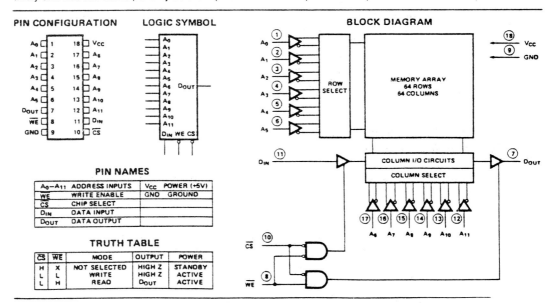

Figure 16–5 The 2147H 4K × 1 static RAM. (Courtesy of Intel Corporation.)

intel   **2147H**

ABSOLUTE MAXIMUM RATINGS*

Temperature Under Bias . . . . − 10°C to 85°C
Storage Temperature . . . . − 65°C to + 150°C
Voltage on Any Pin
  With Respect to Ground . . . . − 3.5V to + 7V
Power Dissipation 1.2W
D.C. Output Current . . . . 20 mA

COMMENT: Stresses above those listed under "Absolute Maximum Ratings" may cause permanent damage to the device. This is a stress rating only and functional operation of the device at these or any other conditions above those indicated in the operational sections of this specification is not implied. Exposure to absolute maximum rating conditions for extended periods may affect device reliability.

D.C. AND OPERATING CHARACTERISTICS[1]

(T_A = 0°C to 70°C, V_{CC} = + 5V ± 10%, unless otherwise noted.)

Symbol	Parameter	2147H-1, 2, 3			2147HL-3			2147H			2147HL			Unit	Test Conditions
		Min.	Typ.	Max.	Min.	Typ.	Max.	Min.	Typ.[2]	Max.	Min.	Typ.[2]	Max.		
I_{LI}	Input Load Current (All Input Pins)		0.01	10		0.01	10		0.01	10		0.01	10	μA	V_{CC} = Max., V_{IN} = GND to V_{CC}
$|I_{LO}|$	Output Leakage Current		0.1	50		0.1	50		0.1	50		0.1	50	μA	$\overline{CS}$ = V_{IH}, V_{CC} = Max., V_{OUT} = GND to 4.5V
I_{CC}	Operating Current		120	170			115		100	150		100	135	mA	T_A = 25°C, V_{CC} = Max., $\overline{CS}$ = V_{IL}, Outputs Open
				180			125			160			140	mA	T_A = 0°C
I_{SB}	Standby Current		18	30		8	15		12	20		7	10	mA	V_{CC} = Min. to Max., $\overline{CS}$ = V_{IH}
I_{PO}[3]	Peak Power-On Current		35	70		25	50		25	50		15	30	mA	V_{CC} = GND to V_{CC} Min., $\overline{CS}$ = Lower of V_{CC} or V_{IH} Min.
V_{IL}	Input Low Voltage	−3.0		0.8	−3.0		0.8	−3.0		0.8	−3.0		0.8	V	
V_{IH}	Input High Voltage	2.0		6.0	2.0		6.0	2.0		6.0	2.0		6.0	V	
V_{OL}	Output Low Voltage			0.4			0.4			0.4			0.4	V	I_{OL} = 8 mA
V_{OH}	Output High Voltage	2.4			2.4			2.4			2.4			V	I_{OH} = − 4.0 mA

NOTES:
1. The operating ambient temperature range is guaranteed with transverse air flow exceeding 400 linear feet per minute.
2. Typical limits are at V_{CC} = 5V, T_A = + 25°C, and specified loading.
3. A pull-up resistor to V_{CC} on the CS input is required to keep the device deselected; otherwise, power-on current approaches I_{CC} active.

A.C. TEST CONDITIONS

Input Pulse Levels	GND to 3.0V
Input Rise and Fall Times	5 ns
Input Timing Reference Levels	1.5V
Output Timing Reference Level (2147H-1)	1.5V
Output Timing Reference Levels (2147H, H-2, H-3, HL, HL-3)	0.8–2.0V
Output Load	See Figure 1

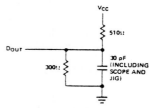

Figure 1. Output Load

CAPACITANCE[4]   (T_A = 25°C, f = 1.0 MHz)

Symbol	Parameter	Max.	Unit	Conditions
C_{IN}	Input Capacitance	5	pF	V_{IN} = 0V
C_{OUT}	Output Capacitance	6	pF	V_{OUT} = 0V

NOTE:
4. This parameter is sampled and not 100% tested.

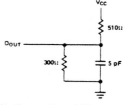

Figure 2. Output Load for t_{HZ}, t_{LZ}, t_{WZ}, t_{OW}

Figure 16–5   (*Continued*)

ends last. Before the $\overline{CS}$ is brought LOW, D_{out} is in a high-impedance (float) state. The $\overline{CS}$ *and* A_0 to A_{11} inputs must both be held stable for a minimum length of time, t_{RC}, before another Read cycle can be initiated.

After $\overline{CS}$ goes back HIGH, the data out is still valid for a short period of time, t_{HZ}, before returning to its high-impedance state.

intel

2147H

A.C. CHARACTERISTICS (T_A = 0°C to 70°C, V_CC = +5V ± 10%, unless otherwise noted.)

Read Cycle

Symbol	Parameter	2147H-1 Min.	2147H-1 Max.	2147H-2 Min.	2147H-2 Max.	2147H-3, HL-3 Min.	2147H-3, HL-3 Max.	2147H, 2147HL Min.	2147H, 2147HL Max.	Unit
t_{RC}[1]	Read Cycle Time	35		45		55		70		ns
t_{AA}	Address Access Time		35		45		55		70	ns
t_{ACS1}[8]	Chip Select Access Time		35		45		55		70	ns
t_{ACS2}[9]	Chip Select Access Time		35		45		65		80	ns
t_{OH}	Output Hold from Address Change	5		5		5		5		ns
t_{LZ}[2,3,7]	Chip Selection to Output in Low Z	5		5		10		10		ns
t_{HZ}[2,3,7]	Chip Deselection to Output in High Z	0	30	0	30	0	30	0	40	ns
t_{PU}	Chip Selection to Power Up Time	0		0		0		0		ns
t_{PD}	Chip Deselection to Power Down Time		20		20		20		30	ns

WAVEFORMS

Read Cycle No. 1[4,5]

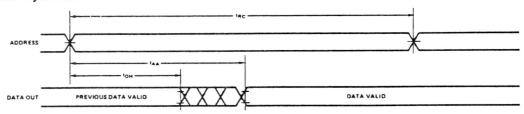

Read Cycle No. 2[4,6]

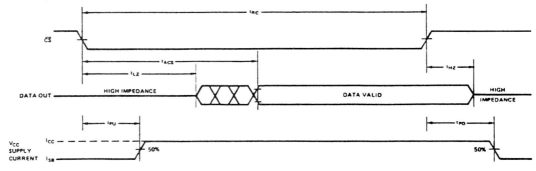

NOTES:
1. All Read Cycle timings are referenced from the last valid address to the first transitioning address.
2. At any given temperature and voltage condition, t_{HZ} max. is less than t_{LZ} min. both for a given device and from device to device.
3. Transition is measured ± 500 mV from steady state voltage with specified loading in Figure 2.
4. $\overline{WE}$ is high for Read Cycles.
5. Device is continuously selected, $\overline{CS} = V_{IL}$.
6. Addresses valid prior to or coincident with $\overline{CS}$ transition low.
7. This parameter is sampled and not 100% tested.
8. Chip deselected for greater than 55 ns prior to selection.
9. Chip deselected for a finite time that is less than 55 ns prior to selection. If the deselect time is 0 ns, the chip is by definition selected and access occurs according to Read Cycle No. 1. Applies to 2147H, 2147HL, 2147H-3, and 2147HL-3.

Figure 16–5 (*Continued*)

intel　　　　　　　　　　　　　　2147H

A.C. CHARACTERISTICS (Continued)
Write Cycle

Symbol	Parameter	2147H-1 Min.	2147H-1 Max.	2147H-2 Min.	2147H-2 Max.	2147H-3, HL-3 Min.	2147H-3, HL-3 Max.	2147H, 2147HL Min.	2147H, 2147HL Max.	Unit
t_{WC}[2]	Write Cycle Time	35		45		55		70		ns
t_{CW}	Chip Selection to End of Write	35		45		45		55		ns
t_{AW}	Address Valid to End of Write	35		45		45		55		ns
t_{AS}	Address Setup Time	0		0		0		0		ns
t_{WP}	Write Pulse Width	20		25		25		40		ns
t_{WR}	Write Recovery Time	0		0		10		15		ns
t_{DW}	Data Valid to End of Write	20		25		25		30		ns
t_{DH}	Data Hold Time	10		10		10		10		ns
t_{WZ}[3]	Write Enabled to Output in High Z	0	20	0	25	0	25	0	35	ns
t_{OW}[3]	Output Active from End of Write	0		0		0		0		ns

WAVEFORMS
Write Cycle No. 1
($\overline{WE}$ CONTROLLED)[4]

Write Cycle No. 2
($\overline{CS}$ CONTROLLED)[4]

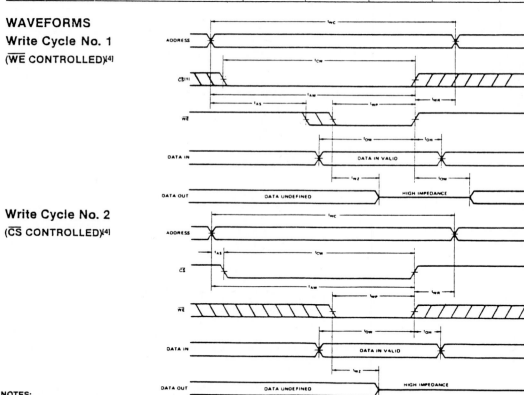

NOTES:
1. If $\overline{CS}$ goes high simultaneously with $\overline{WE}$ high, the output remains in a high impedance state.
2. All Write Cycle timings are referenced from the last valid address to the first transitioning address.
3. Transition is measured ±500 mV from steady state voltage with specified loading in Figure 2.
4. $\overline{CS}$ or $\overline{WE}$ must be high during address transitions.

Figure 16–5　*(Continued)*

Write Operation.　A similar set of waveforms are given in the data sheets (Figure 16–5) for the write operation. In this case the D_{in} is written into memory while the $\overline{CS}$ and $\overline{WE}$ are both LOW. The D_{in} must be set up for a length of time *before* either $\overline{CS}$ or $\overline{WE}$ go back HIGH, and it must also be held for a length of time *after* either $\overline{CS}$ or $\overline{WE}$ go back HIGH.

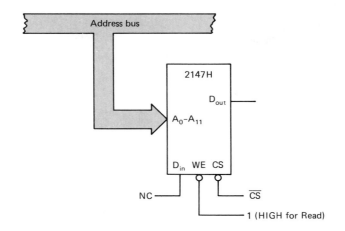

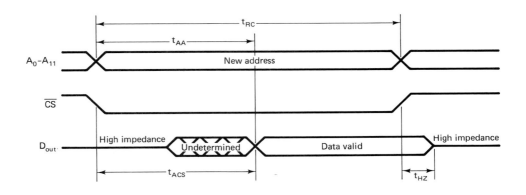

Symbol	Parameter	Min.	Max.	Unit
t_{RC}	Read cycle time	35		ns
t_{AA}	Address access time		35	ns
t_{ACS}	Chip select access time		35	ns
t_{HZ}	Chip deselection to high-Z out	0	30	ns

Figure 16–6 The 2147H Read cycle.

Memory Expansion. Since the contents of each memory location in the 2147H is only 1 bit, to be used in an 8-bit computer system, eight 2147Hs must be set up in such a way that when an address is specified, 8 bits of data will be read or written. With eight 2147s we have a 4096 by 8 (4K × 8) memory system, as shown in Figure 16–7.

The address selection for each 2147H in Figure 16–7 is identical because they are all connected to the same address bus lines. This way, when reading or writing from a specific address, 8 bits, each at the same address, will be sent to, or received from, the data bus simultaneously. The $\overline{WE}$ input determines which internal three-state buffer is enabled, connecting *either* D_{in} or D_{out} to the data bus. The $\overline{WE}$ input is sometimes labeled READ/$\overline{WRITE}$, meaning that it is HIGH for a Read operation, which puts data out to the data bus, via D_{out}, and it is LOW for a Write operation, which writes data into the memory via D_{in}.

There are several other configurations of RAM memory available. For example, the 2148H is configured as a 1024 × 4-bit (1K × 4) RAM, instead of the 4096 × 1 used by the 2147H. A 1024 × 4-bit RAM will input/output 4 bits at a time for each address specified. This way, interfacing to an 8-bit data bus is simplified by

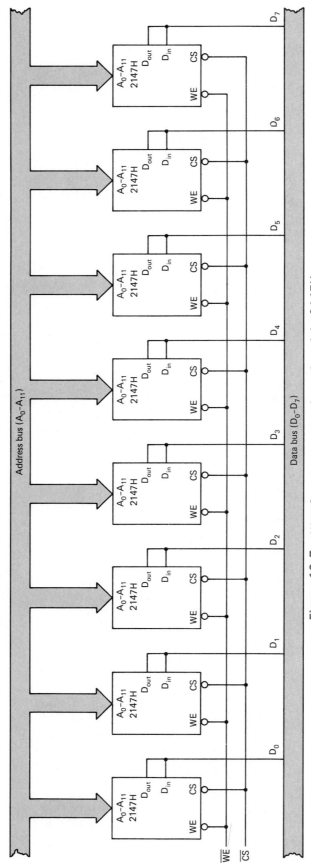

Figure 16–7 4K × 8 memory expansion using eight 2147Hs.

having to use only two 2148Hs, one for the LOW-order data bits (D_0 to D_3) and the other for the HIGH-order data bits (D_4 to D_7).

16–3 DYNAMIC RAMs

Although dynamic RAMs require more support circuitry and are more difficult to use than static RAMs, they are less expensive per bit and have a much higher density, minimizing circuit-board area. Most applications requiring large amounts of read/write memory will use dynamic RAMs instead of static.

Dynamic MOS RAMs store information on a small internal capacitor instead of a flip-flop. All the internal capacitors require recharging, or refreshing, every 2 ms or less to maintain the stored information. An example of a 16K × 1-bit dynamic RAM is the Intel 2118, whose data sheet is shown in Figure 16–8a.

To uniquely address 16,384 locations, 14 address lines are required ($2^{14} = 16,384$). However, Figure 16–8a shows only seven address lines (A_0 to A_6). This is because with larger memories such as this, in order to keep the IC pin count to a minimum, the address lines are *multiplexed* into two groups of seven. An external 14-line-to-7-line multiplexer is required in conjunction with the control signals, $\overline{RAS}$ and $\overline{CAS}$, in order to access a complete 14-line address.

The controlling device must put the valid 7-bit address of the desired memory array *row* on the A_0 to A_6 inputs, then send the Row Address Strobe ($\overline{RAS}$) LOW. Next, the controlling device must put the valid 7-bit address of the desired memory array *column* on the *same* A_0 to A_6 inputs, then send the Column Address Strobe ($\overline{CAS}$) LOW. Each of these 7-bit addresses is latched and will pinpoint the desired 1-bit memory location by its row–column coordinates.

Once the memory location is identified, the $\overline{WE}$ input is used to direct either a Read or Write cycle similar to the static RAM operation covered in Section 16–2. When $\overline{WE}$ is LOW, data are written to the RAM via D_{in}; when $\overline{WE}$ is HIGH, data are read from the RAM via D_{out}.

Read Cycle Timing   (Figure 16–8b)

1. $\overline{WE}$ is HIGH.
2. A_0 to A_6 are set up with the row address and $\overline{RAS}$ is sent LOW.
3. A_0 to A_6 are set up with the column address and $\overline{CAS}$ is sent LOW.
4. After the access time from $\overline{RAS}$ or $\overline{CAS}$ (whichever is longer), the D_{out} line will contain valid data.

Write Cycle Timing   (Figure 16–8c)

1. $\overline{WE}$ is LOW.
2. A_0 to A_6 are set up with the row address and $\overline{RAS}$ is sent LOW.
3. A_0 to A_6 are set up with the column address and $\overline{CAS}$ is sent LOW.
4. At the HIGH-to-LOW edge of $\overline{CAS}$, the level at D_{in} is stored at the specified row–column memory address. D_{in} must be set up prior to, and held after, the HIGH-to-LOW edge of $\overline{CAS}$ to be interpreted correctly. (There are other setup, hold, and delay times which are not shown. Refer to a memory data book for more complete specifications.)

Refresh Cycle Timing.   Each of the 128 rows of the 2118 must be *refreshed* every 2 ms or sooner to replenish the charge on the internal capacitors. There are three ways to refresh the memory cells:

2118 FAMILY
16,384 x 1 BIT DYNAMIC RAM

	2118-10	2118-12	2118-15
Maximum Access Time (ns)	100	120	150
Read, Write Cycle (ns)	235	270	320
Read–Modify–Write Cycle (ns)	285	320	410

- **Single +5V Supply, ±10% Tolerance**
- **HMOS Technology**
- **Low Power: 150 mW Max. Operating 11 mW Max. Standby**
- **Low V_{DD} Current Transients**
- **All Inputs, Including Clocks, TTL Compatible**

- **$\overline{CAS}$ Controlled Output is Three-State, TTL Compatible**
- **$\overline{RAS}$ Only Refresh**
- **128 Refresh Cycles Required Every 2ms**
- **Page Mode and Hidden Refresh Capability**
- **Allows Negative Overshoot V_{IL} min = -2V**

The Intel® 2118 is a 16,384 word by 1-bit Dynamic MOS RAM designed to operate from a single +5V power supply. The 2118 is fabricated using HMOS — a production proven process for high performance, high reliability, and high storage density.

The 2118 uses a single transistor dynamic storage cell and advanced dynamic circuitry to achieve high speed with low power dissipation. The circuit design minimizes the current transients typical of dynamic RAM operation. These low current transients contribute to the high noise immunity of the 2118 in a system environment.

Multiplexing the 14 address bits into the 7 address input pins allows the 2118 to be packaged in the industry standard 16-pin DIP. The two 7-bit address words are latched into the 2118 by the two TTL clocks, Row Address Strobe ($\overline{RAS}$) and Column Address Strobe ($\overline{CAS}$). Non-critical timing requirements for $\overline{RAS}$ and $\overline{CAS}$ allow use of the address multiplexing technique while maintaining high performance.

The 2118 three-state output is controlled by $\overline{CAS}$, independent of $\overline{RAS}$. After a valid read or read-modify-write cycle, data is latched on the output by holding $\overline{CAS}$ low. The data out pin is returned to the high impedance state by returning $\overline{CAS}$ to a high state. The 2118 hidden refresh feature allows $\overline{CAS}$ to be held low to maintain latched data while $\overline{RAS}$ is used to execute $\overline{RAS}$-only refresh cycles.

The single transistor storage cell requires refreshing for data retention. Refreshing is accomplished by performing $\overline{RAS}$-only refresh cycles, hidden refresh cycles, or normal read or write cycles on the 128 address combinations of A_0 through A_6 during a 2ms period. A write cycle will refresh stored data on all bits of the selected row except the bit which is addressed.

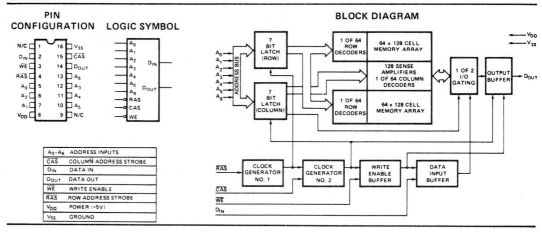

(a)

Figure 16–8 (a) The 2118 16K × 1 dynamic RAM;

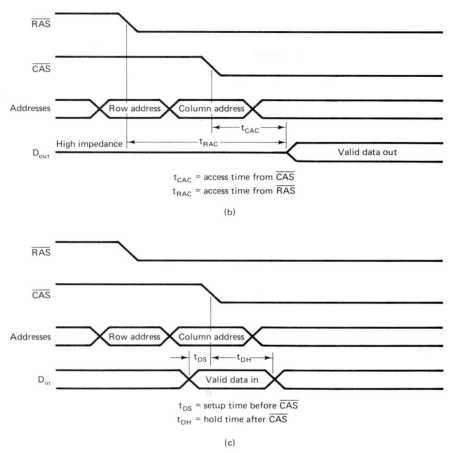

t_{CAC} = access time from $\overline{CAS}$
t_{RAC} = access time from $\overline{RAS}$

(b)

t_{DS} = setup time before $\overline{CAS}$
t_{DH} = hold time after $\overline{CAS}$

(c)

Figure 16–8 *(Continued)* (b) dynamic RAM Read cycle timing ($\overline{WE}$ = HIGH); (c) dynamic RAM Write cycle timing ($\overline{WE}$ = LOW). [(a) Courtesy of Intel Corporation.]

1. Read cycle
2. Write cycle
3. $\overline{RAS}$-only cycle

Unless you are reading or writing from all 128 rows every 2 ms, the $\overline{RAS}$-only cycle is the preferred technique to provide data retention. To perform a $\overline{RAS}$-only cycle, the following procedure is used:

1. $\overline{CAS}$ is HIGH.
2. A_0 to A_6 are set up with the row address 000 0000.
3. $\overline{RAS}$ is pulsed LOW.
4. Increment the A_0 to A_6 row address by 1.
5. Repeat steps 3 and 4 until all 128 rows have been accessed.

Dynamic RAM Controllers

It seems like a lot of work demultiplexing the addresses and refreshing the memory cells, doesn't it? Well, most manufacturers of dynamic RAMs (DRAMs) have developed controller ICs to simplify the task. Some of the newer dynamic RAMs have refresh and error detection/correction circuitry built right in, which makes the DRAM look *static* to the user.

A popular controller IC is the Intel 3242 address multiplexer and refresh counter for 16K dynamic RAMs. Figure 16–9 shows how this controller IC is used in conjunction with four 2118 DRAMs.

The 3242 in Figure 16–9 is used to multiplex the 14 input addresses A_0 to A_{13} to seven active-LOW output addresses $\overline{Q}_0$ to $\overline{Q}_6$. When the Row Enable input is HIGH, A_0 to A_6 are output inverted to $\overline{Q}_0$ to $\overline{Q}_6$ as the row addresses. When the Row Enable input is LOW, A_7 to A_{13} are output inverted to $\overline{Q}_0$ to $\overline{Q}_6$ as the column address. Of course, the timing of the $\overline{RAS}$ and $\overline{CAS}$ on the 2118s must be synchronized with the Row Enable signal.

To provide a "burst" refresh to all 128 rows of the 2118s, the Refresh Enable input in Figure 16–9 is made HIGH. That causes the $\overline{Q}_0$ to $\overline{Q}_6$ outputs to count

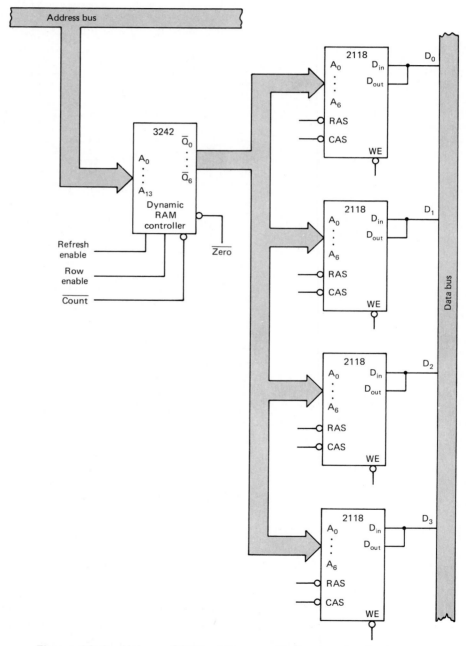

Figure 16–9 Using a 3242 address multiplexer and refresh counter in a 16K × 4 dynamic RAM memory system.

from 0 to 127 at a rate determined by the $\overline{\text{count}}$ input clock signal. When the first 6 significant bits of the counter sequence to all zeros, the $\overline{\text{zero}}$ output goes LOW, signifying the completion of the first 64 refresh cycles.

One commonly used method of setting up the timing for $\overline{\text{RAS}}$, $\overline{\text{CAS}}$, and Row Enable is with a multitap *delay line*, as shown in Figure 16–10. Basically, the four-tap delay line IC of Figure 16–10a is made up of four inverters with precision RCs to develop a 50-ns delay between each inverter. The pulses out of each tap have the same width, but each successive tap is inverted and delayed by 50 ns. (In Figure 16–10b every other tap was used to arrive at noninverted, 100-ns delay pulses.) Delay lines are very useful for circuits requiring sequencing, as dynamic RAM memory systems do.

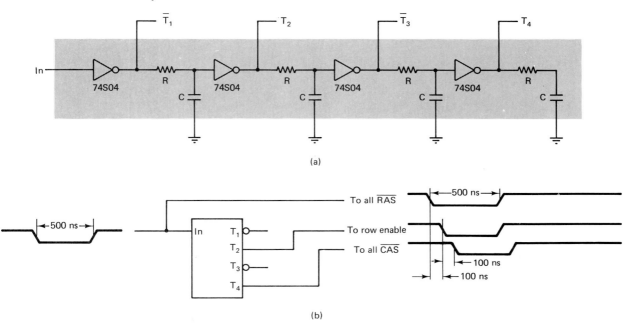

(a)

(b)

Figure 16–10 Four-tap 50-ns delay line used for dynamic RAM timing: (a) logic diagram; (b) logic symbol and timing.

The waveforms produced by the delay line of Figure 16–10b can be used to drive the control inputs to the 16K × 4 dynamic RAM memory system of Figure 16–9 (a LOW $\overline{\text{RAS}}$ pulse, then a LOW Row Enable pulse, then a LOW $\overline{\text{CAS}}$ pulse). Careful inspection of the data sheets for the 3242 and 2118 is required to determine the maximum and minimum allowable values for pulse widths and delay times. To design the absolute fastest possible memory circuit, all the times would be kept at their minimum value. But it is a good practice to design in a 10 to 20% margin to be safe.

16-4   READ-ONLY MEMORIES

ROMs are memory ICs used to store data on a permanent basis. They are capable of random access and are *nonvolatile*, meaning that they do not lose their memory contents when power is removed. This makes them very useful for the storage of computer operating systems, software language compilers, table look-ups, specialized code conversion routines, and programs for dedicated microprocessor applications.

ROMs are generally used for read-only operations and are not written to after they are initially programmed. However, there is an erasable variety of ROM called an EPROM (erasable-programmable-read-only-memory) that is very useful because it can be erased and then reprogrammed if desired.

To use a ROM the user simply specifies the correct address to be read and then enables the chip select ($\overline{CS}$). The data contents at that address (usually 8 bits) will then appear at the outputs of the ROM (some ROM outputs will be three-stated, so you will have to enable the output with a LOW on $\overline{OE}$).

Mask ROMs

Manufacturers will make a custom mask ROM for users who are absolutely sure of the desired contents of the ROM and have a need for at least 1000 or more chips. To fabricate a custom IC like the mask ROM, the manufacturer charges a one-time fee of about $1000 for the design of a unique mask that is required in the fabrication of the integrated circuit. After that, each identical ROM that is produced is very inexpensive. In basic terms, a mask is a cover placed over the silicon chip during fabrication that determines the permanent logic state to be formed at each memory location. Of course, before the mass production of a quantity of mask ROMs, the user should have throughly tested the program or data that will be used as the model for the mask. Most desktop computers use mask ROMs to contain their operating system and for executing procedures that do not change, such as decoding the keyboard and the generation of characters for the CRT.

Fusible-Link PROMs

To avoid the high one-time cost of producing a custom mask, IC manufacturers provide user-programmable ROMs (PROMs). They are available in standard configurations such as 4K × 4, 4K × 8, 8K × 4, and so on.

Initially, every memory cell has a fusible link, keeping its output at 0. A 0 is changed to a 1 by sending a high-enough current through the fuse to permanently open it, making the output of that cell a 1. The programming procedure involves addressing each memory location, in turn, and placing the 4-bit or 8-bit data to be programmed at the PROM outputs and then applying a programming pulse (either a HIGH voltage or a constant current to the programming pin). Details for programming are given in the next section.

Once the fusible link is burned open, the data are permanently stored in the PROM and can be read over and over again just by accessing the correct memory address. The process of programming such a large number of locations is best done by a PROM programmer or microprocessor development system (MDS). These systems can copy a good PROM or the data can be input via a computer keyboard or from a magnetic disk.

EPROMs and EEPROMs

When using mask ROMs or PROMs, if you need to make a change in the memory contents or if you make a mistake in the initial programming, you are out of luck! One solution to that problem is to use an erasable PROM (EPROM). These PROMs are erased by exposing an open "window" in the IC to an ultraviolet (UV) light source for a specified length of time. Another type of EPROM is also available, called an electrically erasable PROM (EEPROM or E²PROM) or electrically alterable PROM (EAROM). By applying a high voltage (about 21 V), a single byte, or the entire chip, can be erased in 10 ms. This is a lot faster than UV erasing and can be done easily while the chip is still in the circuit. One application of the EEPROM is in the tuner of a modern TV set. The EEPROM "remembers" (1) the channel you were watching when you turned off the set, and (2) the volume setting of the audio amplifier.

Examples of two erasable PROMs are the 2716 EPROM and 2816 EEPROM, both manufactured by Intel.

The 2716 EPROM.   The data sheet for the 2716 EPROM is given in Appendix B. Referring to the data sheet, notice that the 2716 has 16K bits of memory, organized as $2K \times 8$. 2K locations require 11 address inputs ($2^{11} = 2048$), which are labeled A_0 to A_{10}.

To read a byte (8 bits) of data from the chip, the 11 address lines are set up, then $\overline{CE}$ and $\overline{OE}$ are brought LOW to enable the chip and to enable the output. The AC waveforms for the chip show that the data outputs (O_0 to O_7) become valid after a time delay for setting up the addresses (t_{ACC}), or enabling the chip (t_{CE}), or enabling the output (t_{OE}), whichever is completed last. Figure 16–11 shows the circuit connections and waveforms for reading the 2716 EPROM.

In Figure 16–11 the X in the address waveform signifies the point where the address lines must change (1 to 0 or 0 to 1), if they are going to change. The $\overline{CE}/PGM$ line is LOW for Chip Enable and HIGH for programming mode. Outputs O_0 to O_7 are in the high-impedance state (float) until $\overline{OE}$ goes LOW. The outputs are then undetermined until the delay time t_{OE} has expired, at which time they become the valid levels from the addressed memory contents.

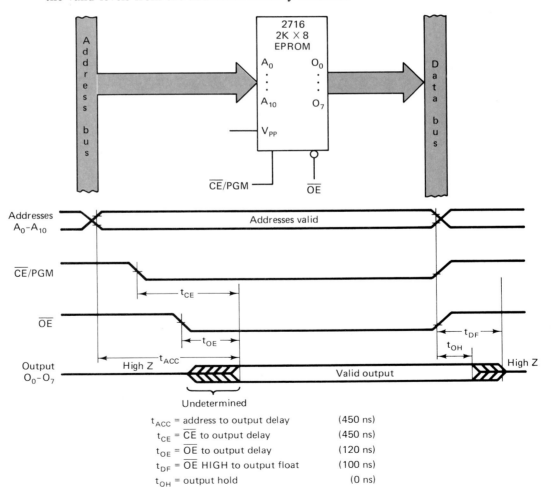

t_{ACC} = address to output delay   (450 ns)
t_{CE} = $\overline{CE}$ to output delay   (450 ns)
t_{OE} = $\overline{OE}$ to output delay   (120 ns)
t_{DF} = $\overline{OE}$ HIGH to output float   (100 ns)
t_{OH} = output hold   (0 ns)

Figure 16–11   The 2716 EPROM Read cycle.

Programming the 2716.   Initially, and after an erasure, all bits in the 2716 are 1's. To program the 2716, the following procedure is used:

1.   Set V_{pp} to 25 V and $\overline{OE}$ = HIGH (5 V).
2.   Set up the address of the byte location to be programmed.
3.   Set up the 8-bit data to be programmed on the O_0 to O_7 outputs.
4.   Apply a 50-ms positive TTL pulse to the $\overline{CE}/PGM$ input.
5.   Repeat steps 2, 3, and 4 until all the desired locations have been programmed.

Figure 16–12 shows the circuit connections and waveforms for programming a 2716.

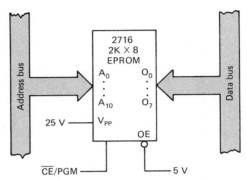

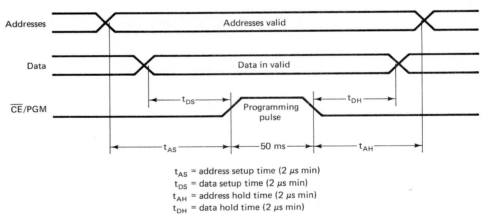

t_{AS} = address setup time (2 μs min)
t_{DS} = data setup time (2 μs min)
t_{AH} = address hold time (2 μs min)
t_{DH} = data hold time (2 μs min)

Figure 16–12   The 2716 program cycle.

16–5   MEMORY EXPANSION AND ADDRESS DECODING

When more than one memory IC is used in a circuit, a decoding technique (called *address decoding*) must be used to identify *which IC* is to be read or written to. Most 8-bit microprocessors use 16 separate address lines to identify unique addresses within the computer system. Some of those 16 lines will be used to identify the chip to be accessed, while the others pinpoint the exact memory location. For instance, the 2732 is a 4K $\times$ 8 EPROM that requires 12 of those address lines (A_0 to A_{11}) just to locate specific contents within its memory. This leaves four address lines (A_{12} to A_{15}) free for chip address decoding. A_{12} to A_{15} can be used to identify which IC within the system is to be accessed.

With 16 total address lines there will be 64K or 65,536 (2^{16} = 65,536) unique address locations. One 2732 will use up 4K of those. To design a large EPROM memory system, let's say 16K bytes, four 2732s would be required. The address decoding scheme shown in Figure 16–13 could be used to set up the four EPROMS consecutively in the first 16K addresses of a computer system.

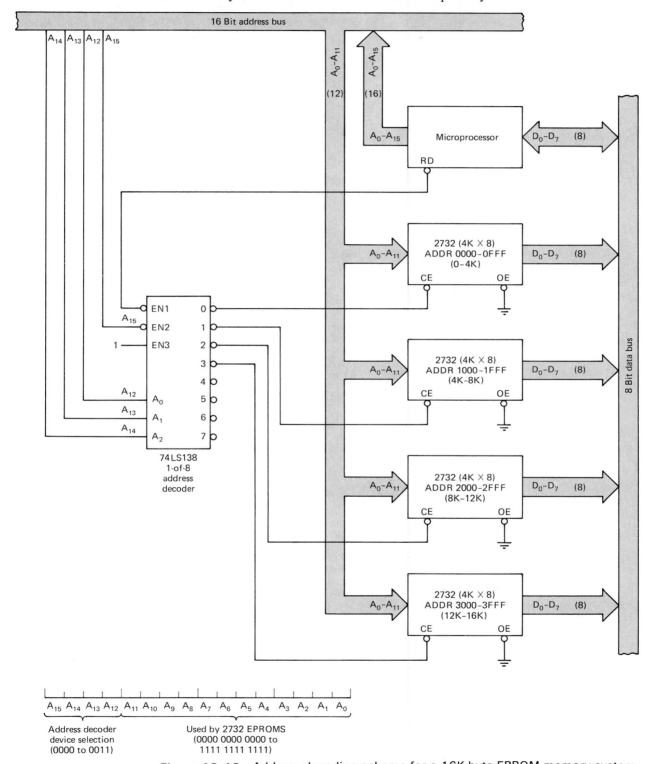

Figure 16–13 Address decoding scheme for a 16K-byte EPROM memory system.

The four EPROMS In Figure 16–13 are set up in consecutive memory locations between 0 to 16K and are individually enabled by the 74LS138 address decoder. The 4K × 8 EPROMS each require 12 address lines for internal memory selection, leaving the four HIGH-order address lines (A_{12} to A_{15}) free for chip selection by the 74LS138.

To read from the EPROMS, the microprocessor first sets up on the address bus the unique 16-bit address that it wants to read from. Then it issues a LOW level on its $\overline{RD}$ output. This satisfies the three enable inputs for the 74LS138, which then uses A_{12}, A_{13}, and A_{14} to determine which of its outputs is to go LOW, selecting one of the four EPROMs. Once an EPROM has been selected, it outputs its addressed 8-bit contents to the data bus. The outputs of the other EPROMs will float because their $\overline{CE}$s are HIGH. The microprocessor gives all the chips time to respond, then reads the data that it requested from the data bus.

The address decoding scheme shown in Figure 16–13 is a very common technique used for "mapping" out the memory allocations in microprocessor-based systems (called *memory mapping*). RAM (or RWM) is added to the memory system the same way.

For example, if we wanted to add four 4K × 8 RAMs, their chip enables would be connected to the 4–5–6–7 outputs of the 74LS138 and they would occupy locations 4XXX, 5XXX, 6XXX, and 7XXX. Then, when the microprocessor issues a Read or Write command for, let's say, address 4007, the first RAM would be accessed.

EXAMPLE 16–1

Determine which EPROM and which EPROM address is accessed when the microprocessor of Figure 16–13 issues a Read command for the following hex addresses: (a) READ 0007; (b) READ 26C4; (c) READ 3FFF; (d) READ 5007.

Solution: (a) The HIGH-order hex digit (0) will select the first EPROM. Address 007 (0000 0000 0111) in the first EPROM will be accessed. (Address 007 is actually the *eighth* location in that EPROM.)

(b) The HIGH-order hex digit (2) will select the third EPROM (A_{15} = 0, A_{14} = 0, A_{13} = 1, A_{12} = 0). Address 6C4 in the third EPROM will be accessed.

(c) The HIGH-order hex digit (3) will select the fourth EPROM (A_{15} = 0, A_{14} = 0, A_{13} = 1, A_{12} = 1). Address FFF (the last location) in the fourth EPROM will be accessed.

(d) The HIGH-order hex digit (5) will cause the output 5 of the 74LS138 to go LOW. Since no EPROM is connected to it, nothing will be read.

Expansion to 64K

The memory system of Figure 16–13 can be expanded to 64K bytes by utilizing two 74LS138 decoders as shown in Figure 16–14. Address lines A_0 to A_{12} are not shown in Figure 16–14, but they would go to each 2732 EPROM, just as they did in Figure 16–13. The HIGH-order addresses (A_{12} to A_{15}) are used to select the individual EPROMS. When A_{15} is LOW, the upper decoder in Figure 16–14 is enabled and EPROMs 1 to 8 can be selected. When A_{15} is HIGH, the lower decoder is enabled and EPROMs 9 to 16 can be selected. Using the circuit in Figure 16–14 will allow us to "map-in" sixteen 4K × 8 EPROMs, which will *completely* fill the memory map in a 16-bit address system. Actually, this would not be practical because some room must be set aside for RAM and input/output devices.

One final point on memory and bus operation: microprocessors and MOS mem-

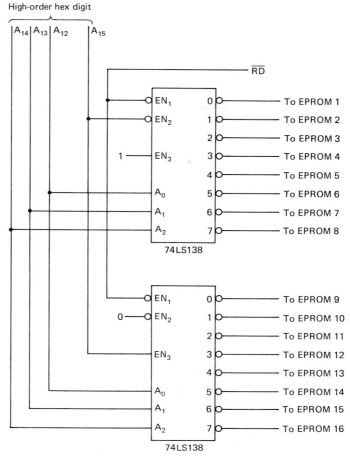

Figure 16–14 Expanding the memory of Figure 16–13 to 64K bytes.

ory ICs are generally designed to drive only a single TTL load. Therefore, when several inputs are being fed from the same bus, a MOS device driving the bus must be buffered. An octal buffer IC such as the 74241 connected between a MOS IC output and the data bus will provide the current capability to drive a heavily loaded data bus. Bidirectional bus drivers (or transceivers) such as the 74LS640 provide buffering in both directions for use by read/write memories (RAM or RWM).

APPLICATION 16–1: *A PROM Look-up Table*

Besides being used strictly for memory, ROMs, PROMs, and EPROMS can also be programmed to provide special-purpose functions. One common use is as a look-up table. A simple example is to use a PROM as a 4-bit binary-to-Gray code converter, as shown in Figure 16–15.

Binary				Gray code			
0	0	0	0	0	0	0	0
0	0	0	1	0	0	0	1
0	0	1	0	0	0	1	1
0	0	1	1	0	0	1	0
0	1	0	0	0	1	1	0
0	1	0	1	0	1	1	1
0	1	1	0	0	1	0	1
0	1	1	1	0	1	0	0
1	0	0	0	1	1	0	0
1	0	0	1	1	1	0	1
1	0	1	0	1	1	1	1
1	0	1	1	1	1	1	0
1	1	0	0	1	0	1	0
1	1	0	1	1	0	1	1
1	1	1	0	1	0	0	1
1	1	1	1	1	0	0	0

Figure 16–15 Using a PROM look-up table to convert binary to Gray code.

463

The PROM chosen for Figure 16–15 must have 16 memory locations, each location containing a 4-bit Gray code. The 4-bit binary string to be converted is used as the address inputs to the PROM. The PROM must be programmed such that each memory contains the equivalent Gray code to be output. For example, address location 0010 will contain 0011, 0100 will contain 0110, and so on, for the complete binary-to-Gray code data table. A more practical application would be to use a PROM to convert 7-bit binary to two BCD digits, which is a very complicated procedure using ordinary logic gates.

APPLICATION 16–2: *A Digital LCD Thermometer*

Another application, one that covers several topics from within this text, is a digital centigrade thermometer. In this application, using a PROM look-up table simplifies the task of converting meaningless digital strings into decimal digits. Figure 16–16 shows a block diagram of a two-digit centigrade thermometer.

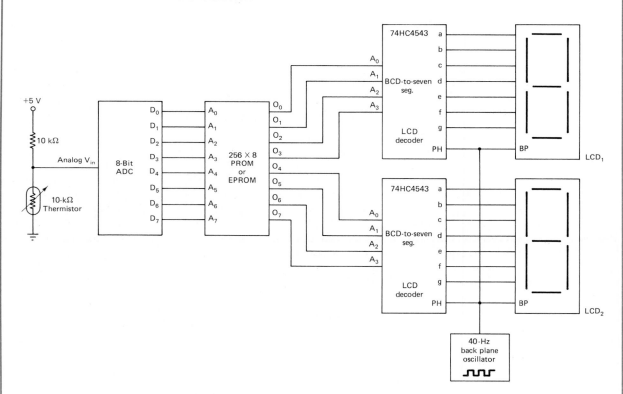

Figure 16–16   Using a PROM as a look-up table for binary-to-BCD conversion for an LCD thermometer.

For the circuit of Figure 16–16 to work, a binary-to-two-digit BCD look-up table has to be programmed into the PROM. Since a standard thermistor is a nonlinear device, as the temperature varies the binary output of the ADC will not change in proportional steps. Programming the PROM with the appropriate codes can compensate for that and can also assure that the output being fed to the two decoders is in the form of two BCD codes, each within the range 0 to 9. The appropriate codes for the PROM contents are best determined through experimentation.

> The 74HC4543 will convert its BCD input into a seven-segment code for the liquid-crystal displays (LCDs). Liquid-crystal displays consume significantly less power than LED displays but require a separate square-wave oscillator to drive their backplane. As shown in Figure 16–16, a 40-Hz oscillator is connected to the phase input (PH) of each decoder and the backplane (BP) of each LCD.

16–6 PROGRAMMABLE LOGIC DEVICES

In Chapter 5 we saw that complex combinational logic circuits could be reduced to their simplest sum-of-products (SOP) form using DeMorgan's theorem and Karnaugh mapping. An example of an SOP expression is

$$X = A\overline{B}\overline{C} + \overline{A}\overline{B}C + \overline{A}B\overline{C}$$

To implement that expression using conventional logic would require three different ICs: a hex inverter, a triple 3-input AND gate, and a 3-input OR gate. As SOP logic complexity increases, the number of SSI or MSI ICs becomes excessive.

An increasingly popular solution being used today is to implement the logic function using programmable logic devices (PLDs). PLD ICs can be selected from the TTL, CMOS, or ECL families, depending on your requirements for high speed, low power, and logic function availability. The three basic forms of PLDs are Programmable Read-Only Memory (PROM), Programmable Array Logic (PAL), and Programmable Logic Array (PLA). PROM, which was discussed earlier in this chapter, is most commonly used as a memory device and is not well suited for implementing complex logic equations.

Standard PAL has several multi-input AND gates connected to the input of an OR gate and inverter. The inputs are set up as a fusible-link programmable multi-variable array. The user, by burning specific fuses in an array, can program an IC to solve a multitude of various combinational logic problems. Hard array logic (HAL), which requires custom mask design by the manufacturer, is also available (a HAL is to a PAL as a ROM is to a PROM).

Standard PLA (or Field-Programmable Logic Array, FPLA) has multi-input programmable AND gates as well; but, it has the additional flexibility of having its AND gates connected to several *programmable OR gates*. Because of this additional flexibility, PLA is slightly more difficult to program than PAL and the additional level of logic gates increases the overall propagation delay times.

To keep logic diagrams for PLDs easy to read, a one-line convention has been adopted as illustrated in Figure 16–17.

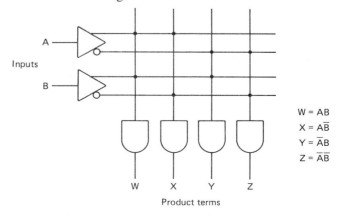

Figure 16–17 One-line convention for PLDs.

Each intersection of the straight lines has a fused link. The programmer selects which fuses are to be left intact and which fuses will be blown. A dot signifies the fuses that are left intact. All other fuses are blown, thus breaking their connection. Figure 16–17 shows four *product terms*; W, X, Y, and Z.

To form an SOP expression we need to feed the product terms into an OR gate. This difference distinguishes PALs from PLAs. PALs have *fixed* (hard wired) OR gates as shown in Figure 16–18, whereas PLAs have *programmable* OR gates, as shown in Figure 16–19.

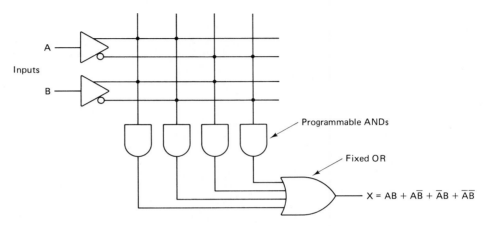

Figure 16–18   PAL architecture.

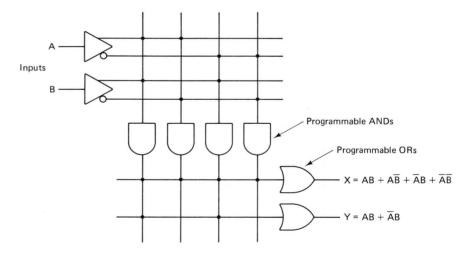

Figure 16–19   PLA (FPLA) architecture.

Improvements in standard PALs and PLAs have led to the introduction of *sequential logic* (*D* and *S-R* flip-flops) within the IC. Field-Programmable Logic Sequencers (FPLS) and sequential PALs provide the additional capability to allow the user to program *sequential operations* such as those required for counter and shift register operations. Electrically-Erasable PLDs (EEPLDs) are also available. They allow the user to erase a previous design and program a new one, thus saving the cost of buying a new PLD.

Programmable arrays are sometimes called *semicustom logic*. They are provided as a standard IC part with programmable links that allow users to develop their own custom parts. These programmable arrays bridge the gap between random combinational logic gates and expensive manufacturer-designed, mask-type custom ICs. Programmable arrays reduce the chip count on a typical PC board and allow a design engineer to create a desired logic circuit from a family of blank programmable ICs, instead of stocking a full line of TTL and CMOS chips.

FPLA Operation

Now let's look at an actual FPLA, the PLS100 manufactured by Signetics Corporation. The PLS100 is configured as a $16 \times 48 \times 8$ array and implements SOP expressions

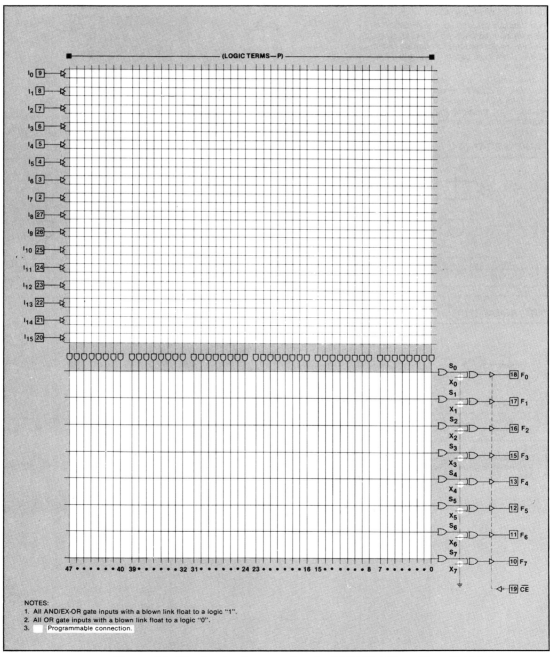

Figure 16–20   Logic diagram for the PLS100 ($16 \times 48 \times 8$) FPLA. (Courtesy of Signetics Corporation.)

that have a maximum of 16 inputs, 48 product terms, and eight sum outputs. The logic diagram for the PLS100 is given in Figure 16–20. In the figure the variables to be input to the circuit are connected to I_0 to I_{15}, which provide both true and complemented levels. Each intersection in the matrix is actually a fused connection that is left intact or blown by the user. There are 48 AND gates, providing for 48 product terms in a SOP expression. Each AND gate actually has 32 inputs intersecting its input line. The actual number of inputs to an AND gate is determined by the number of fuses that are left intact at each intersection.

The AND-OR matrix in the lower part of Figure 16–20 provides each of the eight OR gates with 48 product-term inputs. The OR gate inputs are programmable to determine which product terms (AND gates) are to be ORed together. An active-HIGH, active-LOW output function is provided by the programmable X_0 to X_7 fusible-link connections to the exclusive-OR gates. If the X_0 to X_7 fuses are left intact, the input to the Ex-OR is 0, providing true output. Any fuse blown at X_0 to X_7 places a 1 at the input to that Ex-OR, providing the complement output.

To summarize, all matrix intersections are initially intact. The AND input matrix provides 32 true and complemented inputs to 48 product-term AND gates. The AND-OR matrix allows the user to program the connections of any or all of the 48 AND gates to any of the eight output OR gates. The eight outputs can be programmed as either true or complement. The PLS100 also has an active-LOW Chip Enable ($\overline{CE}$) to provide three-state output capability.

The chip is programmed by blowing all the intersecting fusible links except those which must be left intact to complete the required functions. A special programming table is filled out first, and the data from it are entered into a special PROM programming system that interprets the data and blows the appropriate fuses. Free software is provided by the IC manufacturer to aid in the construction of the data table and to execute the data translation (interpretation) and blowing of fuses.

A data programming table for a PLS100 FPLA set up to implement the two SOP equations, $X_0 = AB + \overline{CD} + B\overline{D}$ and $\overline{X}_1 = \overline{AB} + \overline{CD} + EFG$, is shown in Figure 16–21.

Figure 16–21 Completed PLS100 FPLA program table; steps for completing the table. (Courtesy of Signetics Corporation.)

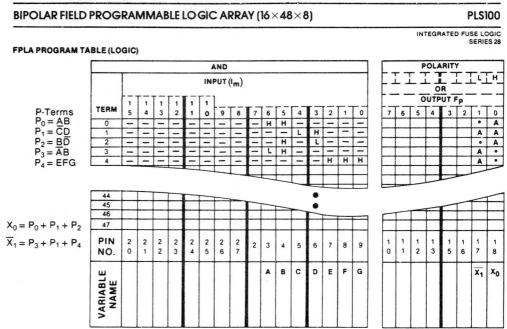

Step 1

Select which input pins I_0–I_{15} will correspond to the input variables. In this case A-G are the input variable names. I_6 through I_0 were selected to accept inputs A-G respectively.

Step 2

Transfer the Boolean Terms to the FPLA Program Table. This is done simply by defining each term and entering it on the Program Table.

$$e.g., P_0 = AB$$

This P-term translates to the Program Table by selecting $A = I_6 = H$ and $B = I_5 = H$ and entering the information in the appropriate column.

$$P_1 = \bar{C}D$$

This term is defined by selecting $C = I_4 = L$ and $D = I_3 = H$, and entering the data into the Program Table. Continue this operation until all P-terms are entered into the Program Table.

Step 3

Select which output pins correspond to each output function. In this case $F_0 = Pin 18 = X_0$, and $F_1 = Pin 17 = X_1$.

Step 4

Select the Output Active Level desired for each Output Function. For X_0 the active level is high for a positive logic expression of this equation. Therefore it is only necessary to place an (H) in the Active Level box above Output Function 0, (F_0). Conversely, X_1 can be expressed as $\bar{X}_1$ by palcing an (L) in the Active Level box above Output Function 1, (F_1).

Step 5

Select the P-Terms you wish to make active for each Output Function. In this case $X_0 = P_0 + P_1 + P_2$, so an A has been placed in the intersection box for P_0 and X_0, P_1 and X_0 and P_2 and X_0.
Terms which are not active for a given output are made inactive by placing a (●) in the box under that P-term. Leave all unused P-terms unprogrammed.
Continue this operation until all outputs have been defined in the Program Table.

Step 6

Enter the data into a Signetics approved programmer. The input format is identical to the Signetics Program Table. You specify the P-Terms, Output Active Level, and which P-Terms are active for each output exactly the way it appears on the Program Table.

APPLICATION 16–3: FPLA Design and Programming

Use a PLS100 to function as an active-LOW output BCD-to-seven segment decoder. Show the connection points that are to be left intact by placing a dot at the correct intersection points in the FPLA logic diagram of Figure 16–22a. Also, fill in the program table in Figure 16–22b with the data to be entered in the FPLA programmer computer.

Solution: First, complete the table in Figure 16–23, showing the input/output characteristics of a BCD-to-seven segment decoder. Figure 16–23 illustrates the input conditions that make each segment LOW. For example, you can see that the $\bar{a}$ segment is LOW for the numbers 0, 2, 3, 5, 7, 8, 9 ($\bar{A}_0\bar{A}_1\bar{A}_2\bar{A}_3$, $\bar{A}_0A_1\bar{A}_2\bar{A}_3$, $A_0A_1\bar{A}_2\bar{A}_3$, etc). Figure 16–22a shows a dot at each array intersection that is to be *left intact*. In Figure 16–22a a four-variable product term is set up for each of the 10 decimal digits and is shown by the connection dots in the upper matrix. The SOP expression for each of the seven segments is then set up by connecting the appropriate product terms to each OR gate. For example, the S_0 OR gate ($\bar{a}$ segment) is connected to seven product term AND gates (0, 2, 3, 5, 7, 8, 9). The S_4 OR gate ($\bar{e}$ segment) is connected to four product term AND gates (0, 2, 6, 8), making the equation for a LOW at $\bar{e}$ equal to $\bar{A}_0\bar{A}_1\bar{A}_2\bar{A}_3 + \bar{A}_0A_1\bar{A}_2\bar{A}_3 + \bar{A}_0A_1A_2\bar{A}_3 + \bar{A}_0\bar{A}_1A_2A_3$.

The outputs are all made active-LOW by blowing the fuses at X_0 to X_6 (no connection dot shown). A blown link at the input to the Ex-OR gates floats to a logic 1, causing its other input to be complemented.

The final solution to this application is to fill in data in Figure 16–22b as shown. (Notice the similarities between Figure 16–22b and 16–23.) The entries in the data table in Figure 16–22b are then used as input records to the software programs supplied by the IC manufacturer to execute the programming of the FPLA.

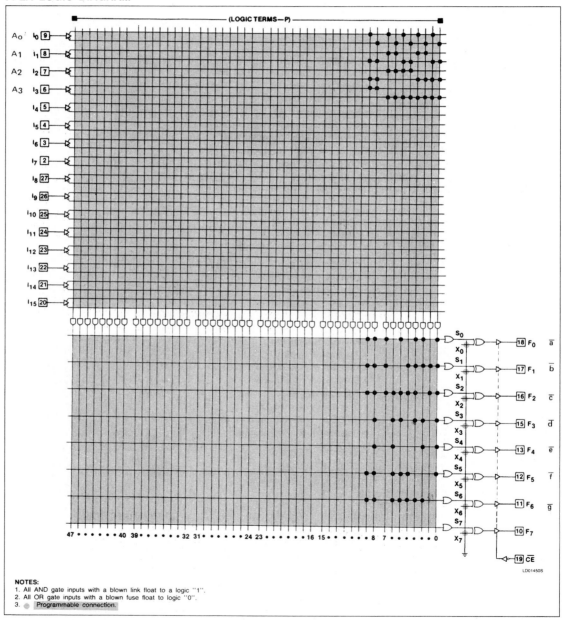

(a)

Figure 16–22 (a) The PLS100 FPLA logic diagram showing intersections left intact to form a BCD-to-seven segment decoder;

Field Programmable Array (16 x 48 x 8)   PLS100/PLS101

FPLA LOGIC DIAGRAM

NOTES:
1. All AND gate inputs with a blown link float to a logic "1".
2. All OR gate inputs with a blown fuse float to logic "0".
3. ● Programmable connection.

Field Programmable Array (16 x 48 x 8)   PLS100/PLS101

FPLA PROGRAM TABLE

TERM	\multicolumn{16}{c}{AND — INPUT (I_m)}																\multicolumn{8}{c}{OR — OUTPUT (F_P)}							
	15	14	13	12	11	10	9	8	7	6	5	4	3	2	1	0	7	6	5	4	3	2	1	0
0	–	–	–	–	–	–	–	–	–	–	–	–	L	L	L	L	•	A	A	A	A	A	A	A
1	–	–	–	–	–	–	–	–	–	–	–	–	L	L	L	H	•	•	•	•	A	A	•	
2	–	–	–	–	–	–	–	–	–	–	–	–	L	L	H	L	A	A	A	A	•	A	A	
3	–	–	–	–	–	–	–	–	–	–	–	–	L	L	H	H	A	•	A	A	A	A	A	
4	–	–	–	–	–	–	–	–	–	–	–	–	L	H	L	L	A	A	•	•	A	A	•	
5	–	–	–	–	–	–	–	–	–	–	–	–	L	H	L	H	A	A	•	A	A	•	A	
6	–	–	–	–	–	–	–	–	–	–	–	–	L	H	H	L	A	A	A	A	A	•	•	
7	–	–	–	–	–	–	–	–	–	–	–	–	L	H	H	H	•	•	•	•	A	A	A	
8	–	–	–	–	–	–	–	–	–	–	–	–	H	L	L	L	A	A	A	A	A	A	A	
9	–	–	–	–	–	–	–	–	–	–	–	–	H	L	L	H	A	A	•	•	A	A	A	

(Terms 10 through 47: blank)

POLARITY — Polarity programmed once only.

PROGRAM TABLE ENTRIES

OUTPUT ACTIVE LEVEL: Active High = H, Active Low = L
NOTES: 1. Polarity programmed once only. 2. Enter (H) for all unused outputs.

OUTPUT FUNCTION: Prod. Term Present in F_P = A, Prod. Term Not Present in F_P = • (period)
NOTES: 1. Entries independent of output polarity. 2. Enter (A) for unused outputs of used P-terms.

INPUT VARIABLE: I_m = H, $\bar{I}_m$ = L, Don't Care = – (dash)
NOTE: Enter (–) for unused inputs of used P-terms.

CUSTOMER NAME _____
PURCHASE ORDER # _____
SIGNETICS DEVICE # _____ CF (XXXX) _____
CUSTOMER SYMBOLIZED PART # _____
TOTAL NUMBER OF PARTS _____
PROGRAM TABLE # _____ REV _____ DATE _____

PIN NO.	20	21	22	23	24	25	26	27	2	3	4	5	6	7	8	9	10	11	12	13	15	16	17	18
VARIABLE NAME													A_3	A_2	A_1	A_0	$\bar{g}$	$\bar{f}$	$\bar{e}$	$\bar{d}$	$\bar{c}$	$\bar{b}$	$\bar{a}$	

(b)

Figure 16–22 (*Continued*) (b) the PLS100 FPLA program table solution for Application 16–3.

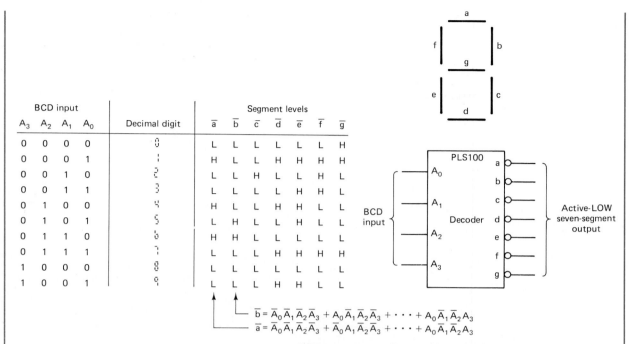

Figure 16–23   BCD-to-seven segment decoder input/output characteristics.

$\overline{A}_0 A_1 \overline{A}_2 \overline{A}_3, A_0 A_1 \overline{A}_2 \overline{A}_3$, etc). Figure 16–22a shows a dot at each array intersection that is to be *left intact*. In Figure 16–22a a four-variable product term is set up for each of the 10 decimal digits and is shown by the connection dots in the upper matrix. The SOP expression for each of the seven segments is then set up by connecting the appropriate product terms to each OR gate. For example, the S_0 OR gate ($\overline{a}$ segment) is connected to seven product term AND gates (0, 2, 3, 5, 7, 8, 9). The S_4 OR gate ($\overline{e}$ segment) is connected to four product term AND gates (0, 2, 6, 8), making the equation for a LOW at $\overline{e}$ equal to $\overline{A}_0\overline{A}_1\overline{A}_2\overline{A}_3 + \overline{A}_0 A_1\overline{A}_2\overline{A}_3 + \overline{A}_0 A_1 A_2\overline{A}_3 + \overline{A}_0\overline{A}_1\overline{A}_2 A_3$.

The outputs are all made active-LOW by blowing the fuses at X_0 to X_6 (no connection dot shown). A blown link at the input to the Ex-OR gates floats to a logic 1, causing its other input to be complemented.

The final solution to this application is to fill in data in Figure 16–22b as shown. (Notice the similarities between Figures 16–22b and 16–23.) The entries in the data table in Figure 16–22b are then used as input records to the software programs supplied by the IC manufacturer to execute the programming of the FPLA.

GLOSSARY

Address decoding: A scheme used to locate and enable the correct IC in a system with several addressable ICs.

Buffer: An IC placed between two other ICs to boost the load-handling capability of the source IC and to provide electrical isolation.

Bus contention: Bus contention arises when two or more devices are outputting to a common bus at the same time.

Byte: A group of 8 bits.

CAS: Column Address Strobe. An active-LOW signal provided when the address lines contain a valid column address.

Delay line: An integrated circuit that has a single pulse input and provides a sequence of true and complemented output pulses, with each output delayed from the preceding one by some predetermined time period.

Dynamic: A term used to describe a class of semiconductor memory that uses the charge on an internal capacitor as its basic storage element.

EEPROM: Electrically-erasable-programmable-read-only memory.

EPROM: Erasable-programmable-read-only memory.

FPLA (or PLA): Field-programmable logic array. Programmable arrays of AOI logic.

FPLS: Field-programmable logic sequencer. Programmable arrays of AOI and sequential logic.

Fusible link: Used in programmable ICs to determine the logic level at that particular location. Initially, all fuses are intact. Programming the IC either blows the fuse to change the logic state, or leaves it intact.

HAL: Hard array logic. Mask programmable arrays of AOI and sequential logic.

LCD: Liquid-crystal display. A multisegmented display similar to LED displays except that it uses liquid-crystal technology instead of light-emitting diodes.

Look-up table: A table of values that is sometimes programmed into an IC to provide a translation between two quantities.

Magnetic memory: A storage medium such as tape or disk that holds a magnetic image of large amounts of binary data.

Mask: A material covering the silicon of a masked ROM during the fabrication process. It determines the permanent logic state to be formed at each memory location.

Memory address: The location of the stored data to be accessed.

Memory cell: The smallest division of a memory circuit or IC. It contains a single bit of data (1 or 0).

Memory Contents: The binary data quantity stored at a particular memory address.

PAL: Programmable array logic. Programmable arrays of AOI and sequential logic.

Programmable array: A user-programmable array of AND-OR-INVERT logic on a single IC, capable of replacing the combinational logic requirements of several SSI and MSI ICs.

PROM: Programmable-read-only memory.

RAM: Random-access memory (Read/write memory).

RAS: Row Address Strobe. An active-LOW signal provided when the address lines contain a valid row address.

ROM: Read-only memory.

Semiconductor memory: Digital integrated circuits used for the storage of large amounts of binary data. The binary data at each memory cell is stored as the state of a flip-flop, or charge on a capacitor.

Static: A term used to describe a class of semiconductor memory that uses the state on an internal flip-flop as its basic storage element.

REVIEW QUESTIONS

Section 16–1

16–1. The ___address___ bus is used to specify the location of the data stored in a memory circuit.

16–2. Once a memory location is selected, data travels via the ___data___ bus.

16–3. In Figure 16–2, how is the correct octal D flip-flop chosen to receive data?

16–4. What is the significance of the X (crossover) on the address and data waveforms in Figure 16–3?

16–5. Why would a second 74LS154 decoder be required in Figure 16–2 to read the data from the D flip-flops if all Q-outputs were connected back to the data bus? (Hint: See Figure 16–4). *To avoid a bus conflict*

Section 16–2

16–6. The 2114 memory IC is a 1K × 4 static RAM, which means that it has __1024__ memory locations with __4__ data bits at each location.

16–7. To perform a *read operation* with a 2147H RAM, $\overline{CS}$ must be __Low__ (LOW, HIGH) and $\overline{WE}$ must be __HIGH__ (LOW, HIGH).

16–8. In the 2147H memory array, address lines __A_0__ through __A_5__ are used to select the *row* and __A_6__ through __A_{11}__ are used to select the column.

16–9. According to the Read cycle timing waveforms for the 2147H, how long must you wait after a chip select ($\overline{CS}$) before valid data is available at D_{out}? *35 ns max*

Section 16–3

16–10. Why are address lines on larger memory ICs multiplexed?

16–11. What is meant by "refreshing" a dynamic RAM?

Section 16–4

16–12. What is meant by the term "volatile"?

16–13. Describe a situation where you would want to convert your EPROM memory design over the Mask-ROMs.

16–14. According to the 2716 EPROM Read cycle timing waveforms, you must wait __120__ nanoseconds after $\overline{OE}$ goes LOW before the data at O_0-O_7 is valid. (Assuming $\overline{CE}$ has already been LOW for at least __330__ nanosecond.)

16–15. The time for the outputs to return to a float state for the 2716 is: $t_{DF} = 100nS$. Under what circumstances would that time be important to know? *when the other device has to use the bus.*

Section 16–5

16–16. Determine which EPROM and which EPROM address is accessed when the microprocessor of Figure 16–13 issues a Read command for the following hexadecimal addresses:
(a) READ 2002
(b) READ 0AF7

16–17. In Figure 16–13, connect A_{15} to EN_3 and ground EN_2. What is the new range of addresses that will access the second EPROM that was formerly accessed at 1000 through 1FFF? *9600 – 9FFF*

16–18. In Figure 16–16 assume that the thermistor resistance is 10 kΩ at 25 degrees celsius, thus making D_7-D_0 equal to 1000 0000 (one-half of full scale). Determine what data value should be programmed into the EPROM at address 1000 0000. *0010 0101*

Section 16–6

16–19. Using the one-line convention for PLDs, a dot signifies fuses that are _____ (blown, left intact).

16–20. A single PLD can be used to implement several _____ (POS, SOP) expressions.

16–21. An advantage that basic PLA architecture has over basic PAL architecture is that PLA has _____ (fixed, programmable) OR gates at its outputs.

16–22. The PLS100 PLA is capable of implementing up to __8__ unique SOP expressions, each expression having up to __48__ product terms. The number of input variables in each product term can be as high as __16__.

PROBLEMS

16–1. (a) In general, which type of memory technology is faster, bipolar or MOS?
 (b) Which is more dense, bipolar or MOS?

16–2. Design and sketch an eight-byte memory system similar to Figure 16–2, using eight 74LS374s and one 74LS138.

16–3. Briefly describe the difference between static and dynamic RAMs. What are the advantages and disadvantages of each?

16–4. How many address lines are required to select a specific memory location within a RAM having:
 (a) 1024 locations?
 (b) 4096 locations?
 (c) 8192 locations?

16–5. How many memory *locations* do the following RAM configurations have?
 (a) 2048 × 1
 (b) 2K × 4
 (c) 8192 × 8
 (d) 1024 × 4
 (e) 4K × 8
 (f) 16K × 1

16–6. What is the total number of *bits* that can be stored in the following RAM configurations?
 (a) 1K × 8
 (b) 4K × 4
 (c) 8K × 8
 (d) 16K × 1

16–7. Design and sketch a 1K × 8 RAM memory system using 2–2148Hs.

16–8. Which lines are multiplexed on dynamic RAMs, and why?

16–9. What is the purpose of $\overline{RAS}$ and $\overline{CAS}$ on dynamic RAMs?

16–10. (a) Draw the timing diagrams for a Read cycle and a Write cycle of a dynamic RAM similar to Figure 16–8b and c. Assume that CAS is delayed from RAS by 100 ns. Also assume that t_{CAC} = 120 ns (max.), t_{RAC} = 180 ns (max.), t_{DS} = 40 ns (min.), and t_{DH} = 30 ns (min.).
 (b) How long after the falling edge of $\overline{RAS}$ will the *data out* be valid?
 (c) How soon after the falling edge of RAS must the *data in* be set up?

16–11. How often does a 2118 dynamic RAM have to be *refreshed*, and why?

16–12. What functions does the 3242 dynamic RAM controller take care of?

16–13. Are the following memory ICs volatile or nonvolatile?
 (a) Mask ROM
 (b) Static RAM
 (c) Dynamic RAM
 (d) EPROM

16–14. Design and sketch an address decoding scheme similar to Figure 16–13 for an 8K × 8 EPROM memory system using 2716 EPROMs. (The 2716 is a 2K × 8 EPROM.)

16–15. What single decoder chip could be used in Figure 16–14 in place of the two 74LS138s?

16–16. Describe how a PAL or FPLA is different from a AOI gate such as the 74LS54.

APPENDICES

A Bibliography

BIGNELL, JAMES, AND ROBERT DONOVAN, *Digital Electronics*. Albany, N.Y.: Delmar Publishers, Inc., 1985.

COUGHLIN, ROBERT F., AND FREDERICK F. DRISCOLL, *Operational Amplifiers and Linear Integrated Circuits*, 2nd ed. Englewood Cliffs, N.J.: Prentice-Hall, Inc., 1982.

FLOYD, THOMAS L. *Digital Fundamentals*, 2nd ed. Columbus, Ohio: Charles E. Merrill Publishing Company, 1982.

FORBES, MARK, AND BARRY B. BREY. *Digital Electronics*. Indianapolis, Ind.: Bobbs-Merrill Company, Inc., 1985.

GREENFIELD, JOSEPH D. *Practical Digital Design Using ICs*, 2nd ed. New York: John Wiley & Sons, Inc., 1983.

HALL, DOUGLAS V. *Microprocessors and Digital Systems*, 2nd ed. New York: McGraw-Hill Book Company, 1983.

HOROWITZ, PAUL, AND WINFIELD HILL. *The Art of Electronics*. Cambridge: Cambridge University Press, 1981.

KERSHAW, JOHN D. *Digital Electronics: Logic and Systems*, 2nd ed. North Scituate, Mass.: Brenton Publishers, 1983.

MALVINO, ALBERT PAUL. *Digital Computer Electronics: An Introduction to Microcomputers*, 2nd ed. New York: McGraw-Hill Book Company, 1983.

McWHORTER, GENE. *Understanding Digital Electronics*, 2nd ed. Dallas, Tex.: Texas Instruments Information Publishing Center, 1984.

NASHELSKY, LOUIS. *Introduction to Digital Technology*, 3rd ed. New York: John Wiley & Sons, Inc., 1983.

PASAHOW, EDWARD J. *Microcomputer Interfacing for Electronics Technicians*. New York: McGraw-Hill Book Company, 1981.

TECHNICAL STAFF OF MONOLITHIC MEMORIES, INC. *Designing with Programmable Array Logic*, 2nd ed. New York: McGraw-Hill Book Company, 1981.

TOCCI, RONALD J. *Digital Systems: Principles and Applications*. Englewood Cliffs, N.J.: Prentice-Hall, Inc., 1980.

WARD, DENNIS M. *Applied Digital Electronics*. Columbus, Ohio: Charles E. Merrill Publishing Company, 1982.

Reference Books

Analog Data Manual. Sunnyvale, Calif.: Signetics Corporation, 1983.

Bipolar Memory Data Manual. Sunnyvale, Calif.: Signetics Corporation, 1984.

CMOS Databook. Santa Clara, Calif.: National Semiconductor Corporation, 1981.

CMOS HE4000B I.C. Family. Sunnyvale, Calif.: Signetics Corporation, 1983.

Component Data Catalog. Santa Clara, Calif.: Intel Corporation, 1981.

COS/MOS Integrated Circuits. Summerville, N.J.: RCA Corporation, 1980.

Data Conversion/Acquisition Databook. Santa Clara, Calif.: National Semiconductor Corporation, 1980.

Fast Data Manual. Sunnyvale, Calif.: Signetics Corporation, 1984.

High-Speed CMOS Logic Data Book. Dallas: Texas Instruments, Inc., 1984.

Integrated Fuse Logic Data Manual. Sunnyvale, Calif.: Signetics Corporation, 1984.

Linear LSI Data and Applications Manual. Sunnyvale, Calif.: Signetics Corporation, 1985.

MCS-80/85 Family User's Manual. Santa Clara, Calif.: Intel Corporation, 1983.

Memory Databook. Santa Clara, Calif.: National Semiconductor Corporation, 1980.

The TTL Data Book for Design Engineers. 2nd ed. Dallas: Texas Instruments, Inc., 1976.

TTL Data Manual. Sunnyvale, Calif.: Signetics Corporation, 1984.

TTL Data Manual. Sunnyvale, Calif.: Signetics Corporation, 1986.

B

Manufacturers' Data Sheets[1]

IC NUMBERS:

74HC00
7400
7414
74121
74192/193
74194
2716
ADC0801
MC1508/1408

[1] Courtesy of Signetics Corporation and Intel Corporation.

GATES

54/74HC00, 54/74HCT00

DESCRIPTION

The 54/74HC00 and 54/74HCT00 are high-speed Si-gate CMOS devices and are pin compatible with low power Schottky TTL (LSTTL). They are specified in compliance with JEDEC standard no. 7.

The 54/74HC00 and 54/74HCT00 provide the positive 2-input NAND function.

SYMBOL AND PARAMETER		CONDITIONS	TYPICAL		UNIT
			HC	HCT	
t_{PHL} t_{PLH}	Propagation delay nA, nB to nY	C_L = 15pF	8	8	ns
C_I	Input capacitance		3.5	3.5	pF
C_{PD}^1	Power dissipation capacitance per gate	See note 2	22	22	pF

NOTES:
1. C_{PD} is used to determine the dynamic power consumption -
$$P_D = C_{PD} \cdot V_{CC}^2 \cdot f_i + \Sigma\, C_L \cdot V_{CC}^2 \cdot f_o \text{ where:}$$
f_i = input frequency; f_o = output frequency
C_L = output load capacitance; V_{CC} = supply voltage
2. For HC, condition is V_I = GND to V_{CC}
For HCT, condtion is V_I = GND to V_{CC} − 1.5V

ORDERING CODE

PACKAGES	COMMERCIAL RANGES T_A = −40°C to +85°C	MILITARY RANGES T_A = −55°C to +125°C
Plastic DIP	N74HC00N, N74HCT00N	
Ceramic DIP		
Plastic SO	N74HC00D, N74HCT00D	

PIN DESCRIPTION

PIN NO.	SYMBOL	NAME AND FUNCTION
1,4,9,12	1A to 4A	Data inputs
2,5,10,13	1B to 4B	Data inputs
3,6,8,11	1Y to 4Y	Data outputs
7	GND	Ground (OV)
14	V_{CC}	Positive supply voltage

PIN CONFIGURATION

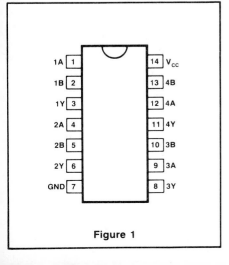

Figure 1

LOGIC SYMBOL

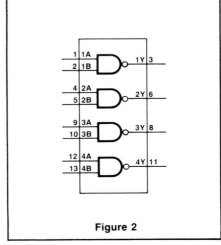

Figure 2

LOGIC SYMBOL (IEEE/IEC)

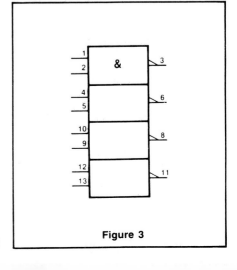

Figure 3

GATES

54/74HC00, 54/74HCT00

ABSOLUTE MAXIMUM RATINGS

Limiting values in accordance with the Absolute Maximum System (IEC134)

SYMBOL AND PARAMETER		RATING	UNIT
V_{CC}	Supply voltage	-0.5 to $+7.0$	V
$\pm I_{IK}$	Input diode current $V_I \leq -0.5V$ or $V_I \geq V_{CC} + 0.5V$	20	mA
$+I_{DK}$	Output diode current $V_O \leq -0.5V$ or $V_O \geq V_{CC} + 0.5V$	20	mA
$\pm I_{OH}$, $\pm I_{OL}$	Output source or sink current $-0.5V \leq V_O \leq V_{CC} + 0.5V$ Standard output	25	mA
$\pm I_{CC}$, $\pm I_{GND}$	V_{CC} or GND current Standard outputs	50	mA
T_{stg}	Storage temperature range	-65 to $+150$	°C
P_{tot}	Power dissipation per package Plastic and Ceramic (Cerdip) DIL (above $+60°C$; derate linearly with 8mW/K) Standard temp -40 to $+85°C$	500	mW
	Power dissipation per package Plastic minipack (SO) (above $+70°C$; derate linearly with 5mW/K) Standard temp -40 to $+85°C$	200	mW
	Power dissipation per package Ceramic (Cerdip) DIL (above $+100°C$; derate linearly with 8mW/K) Extended temp -55 to $+125°C$	500	mW

Voltages are referenced to GND (ground = OV)

RECOMMENDED OPERATION CONDITIONS

SYMBOL AND PARAMETER		54/74 HC			54/74 HCT			UNIT
		Min	Typ	Max	Min	Typ	Max	
V_{CC}	Supply voltage	2.0	5.0	6.0	4.5	5.0	5.5	V
V_I	Input voltage range	0		V_{CC}	0		V_{CC}	V
V_O	Output voltage range	0		V_{CC}	0		V_{CC}	V
T_{amb}	Operating ambient temperature range 54	-55		$+125$	-55		$+125$	°C
	74	-40		$+85$	-40		$+85$	
t_r t_f	Input rise and fall times $V_{CC} = 2.0V$			1000				ns
	$V_{CC} = 4.5V$		6.0	500		6.0	500	
	$V_{CC} = 6.0V$			400				

GATES

54/74HC00, 54/74HCT00

DC ELECTRICAL CHARACTERISTICS: 54/74HC

SYMBOL AND PARAMETER		T_{amb} (°C)						UNIT	TEST CONDITIONS[1]		
		54/74HC +25			74HC −40 to 85		54HC −55 to 125					
		Min	Typ	Max	Min	Max	Min	Max		V_{CC}	V_{IN}	OTHER
V_{IH}	HIGH-level input voltage	1.5 3.15 4.2			1.5 3.15 4.2		1.5 3.15 4.2		V	2V 4.5V 6V		
V_{IL}	LOW-level input voltage			0.3 0.9 1.2		0.3 0.9 1.2		0.3 0.9 1.2	V	2V 4.5V 6V		
V_{OH}	HIGH-level output voltage	1.9 4.4 5.9			1.9 4.4 5.9		1.9 4.4 5.9		V	2V 4.5V 6V	V_{IH} or V_{IL} V_{IH} or V_{IL} V_{IH} or V_{IL}	−I_O = 20µA −I_O = 20µA −I_O = 20µA
		3.98 5.48			3.84 5.84		3.7 5.2		V	4.5V 6V	V_{IH} or V_{IL} V_{IH} or V_{IL}	−I_O = 4mA −I_O = 5.2mA
V_{OL}	LOW-level output voltage			0.1 0.1 0.1		0.1 0.1 0.1		0.1 0.1 0.1	V	2V 4.5V 6V	V_{IH} or V_{IL} V_{IH} or V_{IL} V_{IH} or V_{IL}	I_O = 20µA I_O = 20µA I_O = 20µA
				0.26 0.26		0.33 0.33		0.4 0.4	V	4.5V 6V	V_{IH} or V_{IL} V_{IH} or V_{IL}	I_O = 4mA I_O = 5.2mA
±I_I	Input leakage current			0.1		1.0		1.0	µA	6V	V_{CC} or GND	
I_{CC}	Quiescent supply current SSI			2.0		20.0		40.0	µA	6V	V_{CC} or GND	I_O = 0

NOTE:
1. Voltages are referenced to GND (ground = OV).

AC ELECTRICAL CHARACTERISTICS: 54/74HC
GND = OV; t_r = t_f = 6ns; C_L = 50pF

SYMBOL AND PARAMETER		T_{amb}(°C)							UNIT	TEST CONDITIONS	
		54/74HC +25			74HC −40 to +85		54HC −55 to +125				
		Min	Typ	Max	Min	Max	Min	Max		V_{CC}	Figure
t_{PHL} t_{PLH}	Propagation delay nA, nB, to nY			100 20 17		125 25 21		150 30 26	ns	2V 4.5V 6V	4
t_{THL} t_{TLH}	Output transition time			75 15 13		95 19 16		112 22 19	ns	2V 4.5V 6V	4

GATES   **54/74HC00, 54/74HCT00**

DC ELECTRICAL CHARACTERISTICS: 54/74HCT

SYMBOL AND PARAMETER		54/74HCT +25			74HCT −40 to 85		54HCT −55 to 125		UNIT	TEST CONDITIONS[1]		
		Min	Typ	Max	Min	Max	Min	Max		V_{CC}	V_{IN}	OTHER
V_{IH}	HIGH-level input voltage	2.0			2.0		2.0		V	4.5 to 5.5V		
V_{IL}	LOW-level input voltage			0.8		0.8		0.8	V	4.5 to 5.5V		
V_{OH}	HIGH-level output voltage	4.4			4.4		4.4		V	4.5	V_{IH} or V_{IL}	$-I_O = 20\mu A$
		3.98			3.84		3.7		V	4.5	V_{IH} or V_{IL}	$-I_O = 4mA$
V_{OL}	LOW-level output voltage			0.1		0.1		0.1	V	4.5	V_{IH} or V_{IL}	$I_O = 20\mu A$
				0.26		0.33		0.4	V	4.5	V_{IH} or V_{IL}	$I_O = 4mA$
$\pm I_I$	Input leakage current			0.1		0.1		0.1	μA	5.5V	V_{IH} or V_{IL}	
I_{CC}	Quiescent supply current SSI			2.0		20.0		40.0	μA	5.5V	V_{CC} or GND	$I_O = 0$
I_C	Supply current								μA	5.5V	2.4V or 0.5V	$I_O = 0^2$

NOTES:
1. Voltages are referenced to GND (ground = OV).
2. Per input-pin, other inputs at V_{CC} or GND.

AC ELECTRICAL CHARACTERISTICS: 54/74HCT
GND = OV; $t_r = t_f$ = 6ns; C_L = 50pF

SYMBOL AND PARAMETER		54/74HCT +25			74HCT −40 to +85		54HCT −55 to +125		UNIT	TEST CONDITIONS	
		Min	Typ	Max	Min	Max	Min	Max		V_{CC}	Figure
t_{PHL} t_{PLH}	Propagation delay nA, nB to nY			20		25		30	ns	4.5V	4
t_{THL} t_{TLH}	Output transition time			15		19		22	ns	4.5V	4

AC WAVEFORM

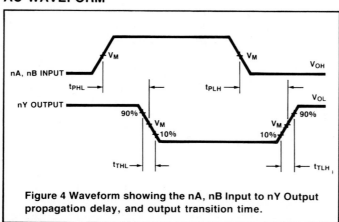

Figure 4 Waveform showing the nA, nB Input to nY Output propagation delay, and output transition time.

NOTE:
HC: V_I = GND to V_{CC}
    V_M = ½ V_{CC}
HCT: V_I = GND to 3.0V
    V_M = 1.3V

GATES

54/7400, LS00, S00

Quad Two-Input NAND Gate

TYPE	TYPICAL PROPAGATION DELAY	TYPICAL SUPPLY CURRENT (Total)
7400	9ns	8mA
74LS00	9.5ns	1.6mA
74S00	3ns	15mA

ORDERING CODE

PACKAGES	COMMERCIAL RANGES Vcc=5V ±5%; TA=0°C to +70°C	MILITARY RANGES Vcc=5V ±10%; TA=−55°C to +125°C
Plastic DIP	N7400N • N74LS00N / N74S00N	
Plastic SO	N74LS00D / N74S00D	
Ceramic DIP	S5400F • S54LS00F	
Flatpack	S5400W • S54LS00W / S54S00W	
LLCC	S54LS00G	

INPUT AND OUTPUT LOADING AND FAN-OUT TABLE

PINS	DESCRIPTION	54/74	54/74S	54/74LS
A, B	Inputs	1ul	1Sul	1LSul
Y	Output	10ul	10Sul	10LSul

NOTE
Where a 54/74 unit load (ul) is understood to be 40µA I_{IH} and −1.6mA I_{IL}, a 54/74S unit load (Sul) is 50µA I_{IH} and −2.0mA I_{IL}, and 54/74LS unit load (LSul) is 20µA I_{IH} and −0.4mA I_{IL}.

FUNCTION TABLE

INPUTS		OUTPUT
A	B	Y
L	L	H
L	H	H
H	L	H
H	H	L

H = HIGH voltage level
L = LOW voltage level

GATES

54/7400, LS00, S00

DC ELECTRICAL CHARACTERISTICS (Over recommended operating free-air temperature range unless otherwise noted.)

PARAMETER	TEST CONDITIONS		54/7400 Min	Typ[2]	Max	54/74LS00 Min	Typ[2]	Max	54/74S00 Min	Typ[2]	Max	UNIT
V_{OH} HIGH-level output voltage	Vcc=MIN, VIH=MIN, VIL=MAX, IOH=MAX	Mil	2.4	3.4		2.5	3.4		2.5	3.4		V
		Com'l	2.4	3.4		2.7	3.4		2.7	3.4		V
V_{OL} LOW-level output voltage	IOL=MAX			0.2	0.4		0.25	0.4			0.5[4]	V
	IOL=MAX			0.2	0.4		0.35	0.5			0.5	V
	IOL=4mA (74LS)						0.25	0.4				V
V_{IK} Input clamp voltage	Vcc=MIN, $I_I=I_{IK}$				−1.5			−1.5			−1.2	V
I_I Input current at maximum input voltage	Vcc=MAX, VI=5.5V (VI=7.0V, LS)				1.0			0.1			1.0	mA
I_{IH} HIGH-level input current	Vcc=MAX, VI=2.4V (VI=2.7V, S)				40			20			50	µA
I_{IL} LOW-level input current	Vcc=MAX, VI=0.4V (VI=0.5V)				−1.6			−0.4			−2.0	mA
I_{OS} Short-circuit output current[3]	Vcc=MAX	Mil	−20		−55	−20		−100	−40		−100	mA
		Com'l	−18		−55	−20		−100	−40		−100	mA
I_{CC} Supply current (total)	Vcc=MAX, I_{CCH} Outputs HIGH			4	8			1.6		10	16	mA
	Vcc=MAX, I_{CCL} Outputs LOW			12	22			4.4		20	36	mA

NOTES
1. For conditions shown as MIN or MAX, use the appropriate value specified under recommended operating conditions for the applicable type.
2. All typical values are at Vcc = +5V, TA = +25°C.
3. IOS is tested with VOUT = +0.5V and Vcc = Vcc MAX +0.5V. Not more than one output should be shorted at a time and duration of the short circuit should not exceed one second.
4. VOL = +0.45V MAX for 54S at TA = +125°C only.

AC WAVEFORM

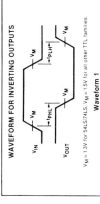

WAVEFORM FOR INVERTING OUTPUTS

VM = 1.3V for 54LS/74LS, VM = 1.5V for all other TTL families.
Waveform 1

AC CHARACTERISTICS TA=25°C, Vcc=5.0V

PARAMETER	TEST CONDITIONS	54/74 CL=15pF, RL=400Ω Min	Max	54/74LS CL=15pF, RL=2kΩ Min	Max	54/74S CL=15pF, RL=280Ω Min	Max	UNIT
t_{PLH} Propagation delay	Waveform 1		22		15		4.5	ns
t_{PHL}			15		15		5.0	

PIN CONFIGURATION

LOGIC SYMBOL

LOGIC SYMBOL (IEEE/IEC)

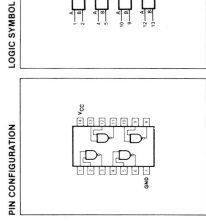

SCHMITT TRIGGERS

54/7414, LS14
Hex Inverter Schmitt Trigger

TYPE	TYPICAL PROPAGATION DELAY	TYPICAL SUPPLY CURRENT (Total)
7414	15ns	31mA
74LS14	15ns	10mA

DESCRIPTION

The '14 contains six logic inverters which accept standard TTL input signals and provide standard TTL output levels. They are capable of transforming slowly changing input signals into sharply defined, jitter-free output signals. In addition, they have greater noise margin than conventional inverters.

Each circuit contains a Schmitt trigger followed by a Darlington level shifter and a phase splitter driving a TTL totem-pole output. The Schmitt trigger uses positive feedback to effectively speed-up slow input transition, and provide different input threshold voltages for positive and negative-going transitions. This hysteresis between the positive-going and negative-going input thresholds (typically 800mV) is determined internally by resistor ratios and is essentially insensitive to temperature and supply voltage variations.

ORDERING CODE

PACKAGES	COMMERCIAL RANGES $V_{CC} = 5V \pm 5\%; T_A = 0°C$ to $+70°C$		MILITARY RANGES $V_{CC} = 5V \pm 10\%; T_A = -55°C$ to $+125°C$	
Plastic DIP	N7414N	N74LS14N	S5414F	S54LS14F
Plastic SO		N74LS14D		
Ceramic DIP	S5414F			
Flatpack	S5414W		S5414W	S54LS14W

FUNCTION TABLE

INPUT	OUTPUT
A	Y
0	1
1	0

INPUT AND OUTPUT LOADING AND FAN-OUT TABLE

PINS	DESCRIPTION	54/74	54/74LS
A	Inputs	1ul	1LSul
Y	Output	10ul	10LSul

NOTE
Where a 54/74 unit load (ul) is understood to be 40µA I_{IH} and -1.6mA I_{IL}, and a 54/74LS unit load (LSul) is 20µA I_{IH} and -0.4mA I_{IL}.

PIN CONFIGURATION

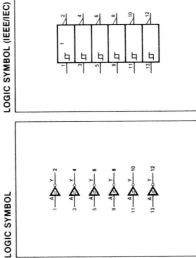

LOGIC SYMBOL

LOGIC SYMBOL (IEEE/IEC)

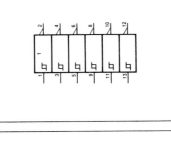

GATES

54/7400, LS00, S00

ABSOLUTE MAXIMUM RATINGS (Over operating free-air temperature range unless otherwise noted.)

	PARAMETER	54	54LS	54S	74	74LS	74S	UNIT
V_{CC}	Supply voltage	7.0	7.0	7.0	7.0	7.0	7.0	V
V_{IN}	Input voltage	-0.5 to $+5.5$	-0.5 to $+7.0$	-0.5 to $+5.5$	-0.5 to $+5.5$	-0.5 to $+7.0$	-0.5 to $+5.5$	V
I_{IN}	Input current	-30 to $+5$	-30 to $+1$	-30 to $+5$	-30 to $+5$	-30 to $+1$	-30 to $+5$	mA
V_{OUT}	Voltage applied to output in HIGH output state	-0.5 to $+V_{CC}$	-0.5 to $+V_{CC}$	-0.5 to $+V_{CC}$	-0.5 to $+V_{CC}$	-0.5 to $+V_{CC}$	-0.5 to $+V_{CC}$	V
T_A	Operating free-air temperature range		-55 to $+125$			0 to 70		°C

RECOMMENDED OPERATING CONDITIONS

	PARAMETER		54/74 Min	54/74 Nom	54/74 Max	54/74LS Min	54/74LS Nom	54/74LS Max	54/74S Min	54/74S Nom	54/74S Max	UNIT
V_{CC}	Supply voltage	Mil	4.5	5.0	5.5	4.5	5.0	5.5	4.5	5.0	5.5	V
		Com'l	4.75	5.0	5.25	4.75	5.0	5.25	4.75	5.0	5.25	V
V_{IH}	HIGH-level input voltage		2.0			2.0			2.0			V
V_{IL}	LOW-level input voltage	Mil			+0.8			+0.7			+0.8	V
		Com'l			+0.8			+0.8			+0.8	V
I_{IK}	Input clamp current				-12			-18			-18	mA
I_{OH}	HIGH-level output current	Mil			-400			-400			-1000	µA
I_{OL}	LOW-level output current	Mil			16			4			20	mA
		Com'l			16			8			20	mA
T_A	Operating free-air temperature	Mil	-55		$+125$	-55		$+125$	-55		$+125$	°C
		Com'l	0		70	0		70	0		70	°C

NOTE
$V_{IL} = +0.7$V MAX for 54S at $T_A = +125°C$ only.

TEST CIRCUITS AND WAVEFORMS

TEST CIRCUIT FOR 54/74 TOTEM-POLE OUTPUTS

DEFINITIONS
R_L = Load resistor to V_{CC}: see AC CHARACTERISTICS for value.
C_L = Load capacitance includes jig and probe capacitance; see AC CHARACTERISTICS for value.
R_T = Termination resistance should be equal to Z_{OUT} of Pulse Generators.
D = Diodes are 1N916, 1N3064, or equivalent.
t_{TLH}, t_{THL} Values should be less than or equal to the table entries.

INPUT PULSE DEFINITIONS

$V_M = 1.3V$ for 54LS/74LS; $V_M = 1.5V$ for all other TTL families.

INPUT PULSE REQUIREMENTS

FAMILY	Amplitude	Rep. Rate	Pulse Width	t_{TLH}	t_{THL}
54/74	3.0V	1MHz	500ns	7ns	7ns
54LS/74LS	3.0V	1MHz	500ns	15ns	6ns
54S/74S	3.0V	1MHz	500ns	2.5ns	2.5ns

SCHMITT TRIGGERS

ABSOLUTE MAXIMUM RATINGS (Over operating free-air temperature range unless otherwise noted.)

PARAMETER		54	74	54LS	74LS	UNIT
V_{CC}	Supply voltage	7.0	7.0	7.0	7.0	V
V_{IN}	Input voltage	-0.5 to +5.5	-0.5 to +5.5	-0.5 to +7.0	-0.5 to +7.0	V
I_{IN}	Input current	-30 to +5	-30 to +5	-30 to +1	-30 to +1	mA
V_{OUT}	Voltage applied to output in HIGH output state	-0.5 to +V_{CC}	-0.5 to +V_{CC}	-0.5 to +V_{CC}	-0.5 to +V_{CC}	V
T_A	Operating free-air temperature range	-55 to +125	0 to 70	-55 to +125	0 to 70	°C

RECOMMENDED OPERATING CONDITIONS

PARAMETER			54/74 Min	54/74 Nom	54/74 Max	54/74LS Min	54/74LS Nom	54/74LS Max	UNIT
V_{CC}	Supply voltage	Mil	4.5	5.0	5.5	4.5	5.0	5.5	V
		Com'l	4.75	5.0	5.25	4.75	5.0	5.25	V
I_{IK}	Input clamp current				-12			-18	mA
I_{OH}	HIGH-level output current				-800			-400	µA
I_{OL}	LOW-level output current	Mil			16			4	mA
		Com'l			16			8	mA
T_A	Operating free-air temperature	Mil	-55		+125	-55		+125	°C
		Com'l	0		70	0		70	°C

TEST CIRCUITS AND WAVEFORMS

TEST CIRCUIT FOR 54/74 TOTEM-POLE OUTPUTS

INPUT PULSE DEFINITIONS

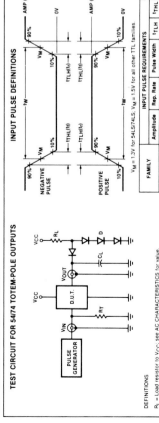

FAMILY	Amplitude	Rep. Rate	Pulse Width	t_{TLH}	t_{THL}
54/74	3.0V	1MHz	500ns	7ns	7ns
54LS/74LS	3.0V	1MHz	500ns	15ns	6ns
54S/74S	3.0V	1MHz	500ns	2.5ns	2.5ns

V_M = 1.3V for 54LS/74LS; V_M = 1.5V for all other TTL families

DEFINITIONS
R_L = Load resistor to V_{CC}; see AC CHARACTERISTICS for value.
C_L = Load capacitance includes jig and probe capacitance; see AC CHARACTERISTICS for value.
R_T = Termination resistance should be equal to Z_{OUT} of Pulse Generators.
D = Diodes are 1N916, 1N3064, or equivalent.
t_{TLH}, t_{THL} Values should be less than or equal to the table entries.

SCHMITT TRIGGERS

DC ELECTRICAL CHARACTERISTICS (Over recommended operating free-air temperature range unless otherwise noted.)

PARAMETER		TEST CONDITIONS[1]		54/7414 Min	54/7414 Typ[2]	54/7414 Max	54/74LS14 Min	54/74LS14 Typ[2]	54/74LS14 Max	UNIT
V_{T+}	Positive-going threshold	V_{CC} = 5.0V		1.5	1.7	2.0	1.4	1.6	1.9	V
V_{T-}	Negative-going threshold	V_{CC} = 5.0V		0.6	0.9	1.1	0.5	0.8	1.0	V
ΔV_T	Hysteresis ($V_{T+} - V_{T-}$)	V_{CC} = 5.0V		0.4	0.8		0.4	0.8		V
V_{OH}	HIGH-level output voltage	V_{CC} = MIN, V_I = V_{T-MIN}, I_{OH} = MAX	Mil	2.4	3.4		2.5	3.4		V
			Com'l	2.4	3.4		2.7	3.4		V
V_{OL}	LOW-level output voltage	I_{OL} = MAX	Mil		0.2	0.4		0.25	0.4	V
		V_{CC} = MIN, V_I = V_{T+MAX}	Com'l		0.2	0.4		0.35	0.5	V
		I_{OL} = 4mA	74LS					0.25	0.4	V
V_{IK}	Input clamp voltage	V_{CC} = MIN, I_I = I_{IK}				-1.5			-1.5	V
I_{T+}	Input current at positive-going threshold	V_{CC} = 5.0V, V_I = V_{T+}			-0.43			-0.14		mA
I_{T-}	Input current at negative-going threshold	V_{CC} = 5.0V, V_I = V_{T-}			-0.56			-0.18		mA
I_I	Input current at maximum input voltage	V_I = 5.5V				1.0				mA
		V_I = 7.0V							0.1	mA
I_{IH}	HIGH-level input current	V_I = 2.4V				40				µA
		V_I = 2.7V							20	µA
I_{IL}	LOW-level input current	V_{CC} = MAX, V_I = 0.4V				-1.2			-0.4	mA
I_{OS}	Short-circuit output current[3]	V_{CC} = MAX	Mil	-20		-55	-20		-100	mA
			Com'l	-18		-55	-20		-100	mA
I_{CC}	Supply current (total)	V_{CC} = MAX	Outputs HIGH I_{CCH}		22	36		8.6	16	mA
			Outputs LOW I_{CCL}		39	60		12	21	mA

NOTES
1. For conditions shown as MIN or MAX, use the appropriate value specified under recommended operating conditions for the applicable type.
2. All typical values are at V_{CC} = 5V, T_A = 25°C.
3. I_{OS} is tested with V_{OUT} = +0.5V and V_{CC} = V_{CC} MAX + 0.5V. Not more than one output should be shorted at a time and duration of the short circuit should not exceed one second.

AC WAVEFORMS

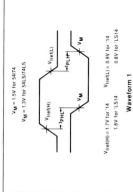

V_M = 1.5V for 54/74
V_M = 1.3V for 54LS/74LS

$V_{ref(H)}$ = 1.7V for '14 $V_{ref(H)}$ = 0.9V for '14
1.6V for LS14   0.8V for LS14

Waveform 1

AC CHARACTERISTICS T_A = 25°C, V_{CC} = 5.0V

PARAMETER		TEST CONDITIONS	54/74 (C_L = 15pF, R_L = 400Ω) Min	54/74 Max	54LS/74LS (C_L = 15pF, R_L = 2kΩ) Min	54LS/74LS Max	UNIT
t_{PLH} t_{PHL}	Propagation delay	Waveform 1		22		22	ns

MULTIVIBRATOR

Monostable Multivibrator

TYPE	TYPICAL PROPAGATION DELAY	TYPICAL SUPPLY CURRENT (Total)
74121	43ns	18mA

ORDERING CODE

PACKAGES	COMMERCIAL RANGES V_CC = 5V ±5%; T_A = 0°C to +70°C	MILITARY RANGES V_CC = 5V ±10%; T_A = -55°C to +125°C
Plastic DIP	N74121N	
Plastic SO	N74121D	
Ceramic DIP		S54121F
Flatpack		S54121W

- Very good pulse width stability
- Virtually immune to temperature and voltage variations
- Schmitt trigger input for slow input transitions
- Internal timing resistor provided

DESCRIPTION

These multivibrators feature dual active LOW going edge inputs and a single active HIGH going edge input which can be used as an active HIGH enable input. Complementary output pulses are provided.

Pulse triggering occurs at a particular voltage level and is not directly related to the transition time of the input pulse. Schmitt-trigger input circuitry (TTL hysteresis) for the B input allows jitter-free triggering from inputs with transition rates as slow as 1 volt/second, providing the circuit with an excellent noise immunity of typically 1.2 volts. A high immunity to V_CC noise of typically 1.5 volts is also provided by internal latching circuitry. Once fired, the outputs are independent of further transitions of the inputs and are a function only of the timing components. Input pulses may be of any duration relative to the output pulse. Output pulse length may be varied from 20 nanoseconds to 28 seconds by choosing appropriate timing components. With no external timing components (i.e., R_int connected to V_CC, C_ext and R_ext/C_ext open), an output pulse of typically 30 or 35 nanoseconds is achieved which may be used as a dc triggered reset signal. Output rise and fall times are TTL compatible and independent of pulse length.

FUNCTION TABLE

INPUTS			OUTPUTS	
Ā₁	Ā₂	B	Q	Q̄
L	X	H	⎍	⍾
X	L	H	⎍	⍾
X	X	L	⎍	⍾
H	↓	H	⎍	⍾
↓	H	H	⎍	⍾
↓	↓	H	⎍	⍾
L	X	↑	⎍	⍾
X	L	↑	⎍	⍾

H = HIGH voltage level
L = LOW voltage level
X = Don't care
↑ = LOW-to-HIGH transition
↓ = HIGH-to-LOW transition

INPUT AND OUTPUT LOADING AND FAN-OUT TABLE

PINS	DESCRIPTION	54/74
Ā₁, Ā₂	Inputs	1ul
B	Input	2ul
Q, Q̄	Outputs	10ul

NOTE
A 54/74 unit load (ul) is understood to be 40μA I_IH and -1.6mA I_IL.

Pulse width stability is achieved through internal compensation and is virtually independent of V_CC and temperature. In most applications, pulse stability will only be limited by the accuracy of external timing components.

Jitter-free operation is maintained over the full temperature and V_CC ranges for more than six decades of timing capacitance (10pF to 10μF) and more than one decade of timing resistance (2kΩ to 30kΩ)

for the 54121 and 2kΩ to 40kΩ for the 74121). Throughout these ranges, pulse width is defined by the relationship: (see Figure 1)

$$t_W(out) = C_{ext}R_{ext}ln2$$
$$t_W(out) \approx 0.7C_{ext}R_{ext}$$

In circuits where pulse cutoff is not critical, timing capacitance up to 1000μF and timing resistance as low as 1.4kΩ may be used.

LOGIC SYMBOL

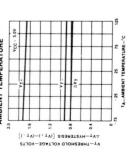

LOGIC SYMBOL (IEEE/IEC)

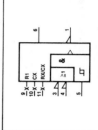

PIN CONFIGURATION

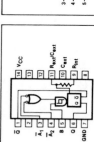

SCHMITT TRIGGERS

TYPICAL CHARACTERISTICS

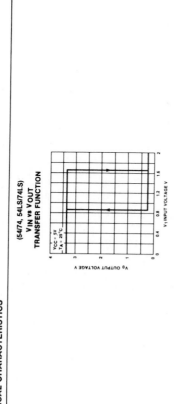

(54/74, 54LS/74LS)
V_IN vs V_OUT
TRANSFER FUNCTION

V_CC = 5V
T_A = 25°C

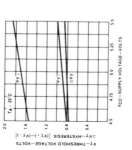

(54/74)
THRESHOLD VOLTAGE AND HYSTERESIS vs POWER SUPPLY VOLTAGE

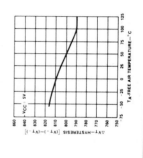

(54LS/74LS)
THRESHOLD VOLTAGE AND HYSTERESIS vs POWER SUPPLY VOLTAGE

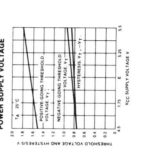

(54/74)
HYSTERESIS vs TEMPERATURE

(54LS/74LS)
THRESHOLD VOLTAGE AND HYSTERESIS vs AMBIENT TEMPERATURE

AC CHARACTERISTICS $T_A = 25°C$, $V_{CC} = 5.0V$

	PARAMETER	TEST CONDITIONS	54/74 $C_L = 15pF$, $R_L = 400\Omega$ Min	Max	UNIT
t_{PLH}	Propagation delay $\bar{A}$ input to Q & $\bar{Q}$ output	Waveform 1 $C_{ext} = 80pF$, R_{int} to V_{CC}		70	ns
t_{PHL}				80	
t_{PLH}	Propagation delay B input to Q & $\bar{Q}$ output	Waveform 2 $C_{ext} = 80pF$, R_{int} to V_{CC}		55	ns
t_{PHL}				65	
t_W	Minimum output pulse width	$C_{ext} = 0pF$, R_{int} to V_{CC}	20	50	ns
t_W	Output pulse width	$C_{ext} = 80pF$, R_{int} to V_{CC}	70	150	ns
		$C_{ext} = 100pF$, R_{int} to V_{CC}, $R_{ext} = 10k\Omega$	600	800	ns
		$C_{ext} = 1\mu F$, $R_{ext} = 10k\Omega$	6.0	8.0	ms

AC SETUP REQUIREMENTS $T_A = 25°C$, $V_{CC} = 5.0V$

PARAMETER	TEST CONDITIONS		54/74 Min	Max	UNIT
t_W Minimum input pulse width to trigger	Waveforms 1 & 2		50		ns
R_{ext} External timing resistor range		Mil	1.4	30	kΩ
		Com'l	1.4	40	kΩ
C_{ext} External timing capacitance range			0	1000	μF
Output duty cycle	$R_{ext} = 2k\Omega$			67	%
	$R_{ext} = R_{ext}(Max)$			90	%

AC WAVEFORMS

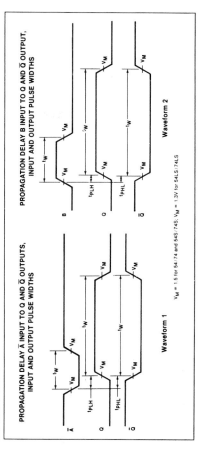

PROPAGATION DELAY $\bar{A}$ INPUT TO Q AND $\bar{Q}$ OUTPUTS, INPUT AND OUTPUT PULSE WIDTHS

Waveform 1

PROPAGATION DELAY B INPUT TO Q AND $\bar{Q}$ OUTPUT, INPUT AND OUTPUT PULSE WIDTHS

Waveform 2

$V_M = 1.5$ for 54/74 and 54S/74S. $V_M = 1.3V$ for 54LS/74LS

ABSOLUTE MAXIMUM RATINGS (Over operating free-air temperature range unless otherwise noted.)

	PARAMETER	54	74	UNIT
V_{CC}	Supply voltage	7.0	7.0	V
V_{IN}	Input voltage	-0.5 to $+5.5$	-0.5 to $+5.5$	V
I_{IN}	Input current	-30 to $+5$	-30 to $+5$	mA
V_{OUT}	Voltage applied to output in HIGH output state	-0.5 to $+V_{CC}$	-0.5 to $+V_{CC}$	V
T_A	Operating free-air temperature range	-55 to $+125$	0 to 70	°C

RECOMMENDED OPERATING CONDITIONS

	PARAMETER		54/74 Min	Nom	Max	UNIT
V_{CC}	Supply voltage	Mil	4.5	5.0	5.5	V
		Com'l	4.75	5.0	5.25	V
I_{IK}	Input clamp current				-12	mA
I_{OH}	HIGH-level output current				-400	μA
I_{OL}	LOW-level output current	Mil			16	mA
		Com'l			16	mA
dv/dt	Rate of rise or fall of input pulse	B input	1			V/s
		$\bar{A}_1, \bar{A}_2$ inputs	1			V/μs
T_A	Operating free-air temperature	Mil	-55			°C
		Com'l	0			°C

DC ELECTRICAL CHARACTERISTICS (Over recommended operating free-air temperature range unless otherwise noted.)

	PARAMETER	TEST CONDITIONS[1]		54/74121 Min	Typ[2]	Max	UNIT
V_{T+}	Positive-going threshold at $\bar{A}$ and B	$V_{CC} = $ MIN				2.0	V
V_{T-}	Negative-going threshold at $\bar{A}$ and B	$V_{CC} = $ MIN		0.8			V
V_{OH}	HIGH-level output voltage	$V_{CC} = $ MIN, $V_{IH} = $ MIN, $V_{IL} = $ MAX, $I_{OH} = $ MAX	Mil	2.4	3.4		V
			Com'l	2.4	3.4		V
V_{OL}	LOW-level output voltage	$V_{CC} = $ MIN, $V_{IH} = $ MIN, $V_{IL} = $ MAX, $I_{OL} = $ MAX	Mil		0.2	0.4	V
			Com'l		0.2	0.4	V
V_{IK}	Input clamp voltage	$V_{CC} = $ MIN, $I_I = I_{IK}$				-1.5	V
I_I	Input current at maximum input voltage	$V_{CC} = $ MAX, $V_I = 5.5V$				1.0	mA
I_{IH}	HIGH-level input current	$V_{CC} = $ MAX, $V_I = 2.4V$	$\bar{A}_1, \bar{A}_2$ inputs			40	μA
			B input			80	μA
I_{IL}	LOW-level input current	$V_{CC} = $ MAX, $V_I = 0.4V$	$\bar{A}_1, \bar{A}_2$ inputs			-1.6	mA
			B input			-3.2	mA
I_{OS}	Short-circuit output current[3]	$V_{CC} = $ MAX	Mil	-20		-55	mA
			Com'l	-18		-55	mA
I_{CC}	Supply current (total)	$V_{CC} = $ MAX	Quiescent		13	25	mA
			Triggered		23	40	mA

NOTES
1. For conditions shown as MIN or MAX, use the appropriate value specified under recommended operating conditions for the applicable type.
2. All typical values are at $V_{CC} = 5V$, $T_A = +25°C$.
3. I_{OS} is tested with $V_{OUT} = +0.5V$ and $V_{CC} = V_{CC}$ MAX $+0.5V$. Not more than one output should be shorted at a time and duration of the short circuit should not exceed one second.

'192 Presettable BCD Decade Up/Down Counter
'193 Presettable 4-Bit Binary Up/Down Counter

TYPE	TYPICAL f_{MAX}	TYPICAL SUPPLY CURRENT
74192	32MHz	65mA
74LS192	32MHz	19mA
74193	32MHz	65mA
74LS193	32MHz	19mA

ORDERING CODE

PACKAGES	COMMERCIAL RANGES $V_{CC} = 5V \pm 5\%; T_A = 0°C$ to $+70°C$		MILITARY RANGES $V_{CC} = 5V \pm 10\%; T_A = -55°C$ to $+125°C$
Plastic DIP	N74192N • N74193N	N74LS192N N74LS193N	
Plastic SO	N74LS193D		
Ceramic DIP			S54L S192F • S54LS193F
Flatpack			S54LS192W • S54LS193W
LLCC			S54LS193G

INPUT AND OUTPUT LOADING AND FAN-OUT TABLE

PINS	DESCRIPTION	54/74	54/74LS
All	Inputs	1ul	1LSul
All	Outputs	10ul	10LSul

NOTE
Where a 54/74 unit load (ul) is understood to be 40μA I_{IH} and -1.6mA I_{IL}, and a 54/74LS unit load (LSul) is 20μA I_{IH} and -0.4mA I_{IL}.

Features

- **Synchronous reversible 4-bit binary counting**
- **Asynchronous parallel load**
- **Asynchronous reset (clear)**
- **Expandable without external logic**

DESCRIPTION

The '192 and '193 are 4-bit synchronous up/down counters — the '192 counts in BCD mode and the '193 counts in the binary mode. Separate up/down clocks, CP_U and CP_D respectively, simplify operation. The outputs change state synchronously with the LOW-to-HIGH transition of either Clock input. If the CP_U clock is pulsed while CP_D is held HIGH, the device will count up... if CP_D is pulsed while CP_U is held HIGH, the device will count down. Only one Clock input can be held HIGH at any time, or erroneous operation will result. The device can be cleared at any time by the asynchronous reset pin — it may also be loaded in parallel by activating the asynchronous parallel load pin.

Inside the device are four master-slave JK flip-flops with the necessary steering logic to provide the asynchronous reset, load, and synchronous count up and count down functions.

Each flip-flop contains JK feedback from slave to master, such that a LOW-to-HIGH

transition on the CP_D input will decrease the count by one, while a similar transition on the CP_U input will advance the count by one.

One clock should be held HIGH while counting with the other, because the circuit will either count by two's or not at all, depending on the state of the first flip-flop, which cannot toggle as long as either Clock input is LOW. Applications requiring reversible operation must make the reversing decision while the activating clock is HIGH to avoid erroneous counts.

LOGIC SYMBOL

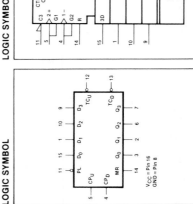

LOGIC SYMBOL (IEEE/IEC)

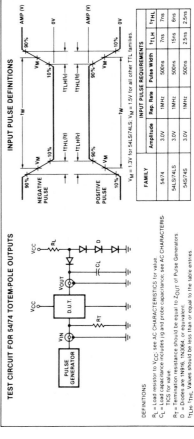

PIN CONFIGURATION

MULTIVIBRATOR

OUTPUT PULSE WIDTH vs. TIMING RESISTOR VALUE

$V_{CC} = 5V$
$T_A = 25°C$

R_{ext} — Timing Resistor Value—kΩ

Figure 1

TEST CIRCUITS AND WAVEFORMS

TEST CIRCUIT FOR 54/74 TOTEM-POLE OUTPUTS

DEFINITIONS
R_L = Load resistor to V_{CC}; see AC CHARACTERISTICS for value.
C_L = Load capacitance includes jig and probe capacitance; see AC CHARACTERISTICS.
TICS for value.
R_T = Termination resistance should be equal to Z_{OUT} of Pulse Generators.
D = Diodes are 1N916, 1N3064, or equivalent.
t_{TLH}, t_{THL} Values should be less than or equal to the table entries.

INPUT PULSE DEFINITIONS

$V_M = 1.3V$ for 54LS/74LS; $V_M = 1.5V$ for all other TTL families.

FAMILY	INPUT PULSE REQUIREMENTS				
	Amplitude	Rep. Rate	Pulse Width	t_{TLH}	t_{THL}
54/74	3.0V	1MHz	500ns	7ns	7ns
54LS/74LS	3.0V	1MHz	500ns	15ns	6ns
54S/74S	3.0V	1MHz	500ns	2.5ns	2.5ns

LOGIC DIAGRAM, '193

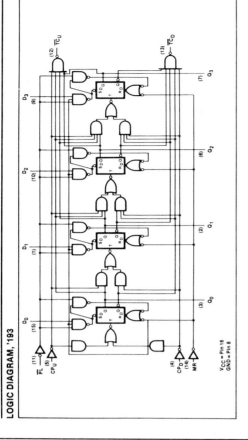

V_{CC} = Pin 16
GND = Pin 8

MODE SELECT—FUNCTION TABLE, '193

OPERATING MODE	INPUTS								OUTPUTS					
	MR	$\overline{PL}$	CP_U	CP_D	D_0	D_1	D_2	D_3	Q_0	Q_1	Q_2	Q_3	$\overline{TC}_U$	$\overline{TC}_D$
Reset (clear)	H	X	X	X	X	X	X	X	L	L	L	L	H	H
	H	X	X	⊓	X	X	X	X	L	L	L	L	H	⊔
Parallel load	L	L	X	L	L	X	X	X	L	L	L	L	H	⊔
	L	L	⊓	X	H	X	X	X	H	L	L	L	H	H
	L	L	X	L	X	X	X	L	L	L	L	L	⊔	H
	L	L	X	⊓	X	X	X	H	L	L	L	H	H	H
Count up	L	H	↑	H	X	X	X	X	Count up				H[(c)]	H
Count down	L	H	H	↑	X	X	X	X	Count down				H	H[(d)]

H = HIGH voltage level
L = LOW voltage level
X = Don't care
↑ = LOW-to-HIGH clock transition

NOTES
c. $\overline{TC}_U = CP_U$ at terminal count up (HHHH).
d. $\overline{TC}_D = CP_D$ at terminal count down (LLLL).

STATE DIAGRAM, '193

LOGIC EQUATIONS FOR TERMINAL COUNT

$\overline{TC}_U = Q_0 \cdot Q_1 \cdot Q_2 \cdot Q_3 \cdot \overline{CP}_U$
$\overline{TC}_D = \overline{Q}_0 \cdot \overline{Q}_1 \cdot \overline{Q}_2 \cdot \overline{Q}_3 \cdot \overline{CP}_D$

COUNT UP ———
COUNT DOWN - - - -

The Terminal Count Up ($\overline{TC}_U$) and Terminal Count down ($\overline{TC}_D$) outputs are normally HIGH. When the circuit has reached the maximum count state of 9 (for the '192 and 15 for the '193), the next HIGH-to-LOW transition of CP_U will cause $\overline{TC}_U$ to go LOW. $\overline{TC}_U$ will stay LOW until CP_U goes HIGH again, duplicating the count up clock, although delayed by two gate delays. Likewise, the $\overline{TC}_D$ output will go LOW when the circuit is in the zero state and the CP_D goes LOW. The $\overline{TC}$ outputs can be

used as the Clock input signals to the next higher order circuit in a multistage counter, since they duplicate the clock waveforms. Multistage counters will not be fully synchronous, since there is a two-gate delay time difference added for each stage that is added.

The counter may be preset by the asynchronous parallel load capability of the circuit. Information present on the parallel Data inputs (D_0–D_3) is loaded into the

counter and appears on the outputs regardless of the conditions of the Clock inputs when the Parallel Load ($\overline{PL}$) input is LOW. A HIGH level on the Master Reset (MR) input will disable the parallel load gates, override both Clock inputs, and set all Q outputs LOW. If one of the Clock inputs is LOW during and after a reset or load operation, the next LOW-to-HIGH transition of that clock will be interpreted as a legitimate signal and will be counted.

LOGIC DIAGRAM, '192

V_{CC} = Pin 16
GND = Pin 8

MODE SELECT—FUNCTION TABLE, '192

OPERATING MODE	INPUTS								OUTPUTS					
	MR	$\overline{PL}$	CP_U	CP_D	D_0	D_1	D_2	D_3	Q_0	Q_1	Q_2	Q_3	$\overline{TC}_U$	$\overline{TC}_D$
Reset (clear)	H	X	X	X	X	X	X	X	L	L	L	L	H	H
	H	X	X	⊓	X	X	X	X	L	L	L	L	H	⊔
Parallel load	L	L	X	L	L	X	X	X	L	L	L	L	H	⊔
	L	L	⊓	X	H	X	X	X	H	⊔	$Q_n = D_n$		H	H
	L	L	X	L	X	X	X	L	⊔	H	$Q_n = D_n$		⊔	H
	L	L	X	⊓	X	X	X	H	H	H	H	H	H	H
Count up	L	H	↑	H	X	X	X	X	Count up				H[(a)]	H
Count down	L	H	H	↑	X	X	X	X	Count down				H	H[(b)]

H = HIGH voltage level
L = LOW voltage level
X = Don't care
↑ = LOW-to-HIGH clock transition

NOTES
a. $\overline{TC}_U = CP_U$ at terminal count up (HLLH).
b. $\overline{TC}_D = CP_D$ at terminal count down (LLLL).

STATE DIAGRAM, '192

LOGIC EQUATIONS FOR TERMINAL COUNT

$\overline{TC}_U = Q_0 \cdot Q_3 \cdot \overline{CP}_U$
$\overline{TC}_D = \overline{Q}_0 \cdot \overline{Q}_1 \cdot \overline{Q}_2 \cdot \overline{Q}_3 \cdot \overline{CP}_D$

COUNT UP ———
COUNT DOWN - - - -

ABSOLUTE MAXIMUM RATINGS (Over operating free-air temperature range unless otherwise noted)

PARAMETER	54	54LS	74	74LS	UNIT
V_{CC} Supply voltage	7.0	7.0	7.0	7.0	V
V_{IN} Input voltage	-0.5 to +5.5	-0.5 to +7.0	-0.5 to +5.5	-0.5 to +7.0	V
I_{IN} Input current	-30 to +5	-30 to +1	-30 to +5	-30 to +1	mA
V_{OUT} Voltage applied to output in HIGH output state	-0.5 to +V_{CC}	-0.5 to +V_{CC}	-0.5 to +V_{CC}	-0.5 to +V_{CC}	V
T_A Operating free-air temperature range	-55 to +125		0 to 70		°C

RECOMMENDED OPERATING CONDITIONS

PARAMETER		54/74 Min	54/74 Nom	54/74 Max	54LS Min	54LS Nom	54LS Max	UNIT
V_{CC} Supply voltage	Mil	4.5	5.0	5.5	4.5	5.0	5.5	V
	Com'l	4.75	5.0	5.25	4.75	5.0	5.25	V
V_{IH} HIGH-level input voltage		2.0			2.0			V
V_{IL} LOW-level input voltage	Mil			+0.8			+0.7	V
	Com'l			+0.8			+0.8	V
I_{IK} Input clamp current				-12			-18	mA
I_{OH} HIGH-level output current				-800			-400	μA
I_{OL} LOW-level output current	Mil			16			4	mA
	Com'l			16			8	mA
T_A Operating free-air temperature	Mil	-55		+125	-55		+125	°C
	Com'l	0		70	0		70	°C

DC ELECTRICAL CHARACTERISTICS (Over recommended operating free-air temperature range unless otherwise noted.)

PARAMETER	TEST CONDITIONS[1]		54/74192,'193 Min	Typ[2]	Max	54/74LS192,'193 Min	Typ[2]	Max	UNIT
V_{OH} HIGH-level output voltage	V_{CC}=MIN, V_{IH}=MIN, V_{IL}=MAX, I_{OH}=MAX	Mil	2.4	3.4		2.5	3.4		V
		Com'l	2.4	3.4		2.7	3.4		V
V_{OL} LOW-level output voltage	V_{CC}=MIN, V_{IH}=MIN, V_{IL}=MAX, I_{OL}=MAX	Mil		0.2	0.4		0.25	0.4	V
		Com'l		0.2	0.4		0.35	0.5	V
	I_{OL}=4mA	74LS					0.25	0.4	V
V_{IK} Input clamp voltage	V_{CC}=MIN, I_I=I_{IK}				-1.5			-1.5	V
I_I Input current at maximum input voltage	V_{CC}=MAX, V_I=5.5V				1.0				mA
	V_I=7.0V							0.1	mA
I_{IH} HIGH-level input current	V_I=2.4V				40				μA
	V_I=2.7V							20	μA
I_{IL} LOW-level input current	V_{CC}=MAX, V_I=0.4V				-1.6			-0.4	mA
I_{OS} Short-circuit output current[3]	V_{CC}=MAX	Mil	-20		-65	-20		-100	mA
		Com'l	-18		-65	-20		-100	mA
I_{CC} Supply current[4] (total)	V_{CC}=MAX	Mil		65	89		19	34	mA
		Com'l		65	102		19	34	mA

NOTES
1. For conditions shown as MIN or MAX, use the appropriate value specified under recommended operating conditions for the applicable type.
2. All typical values are at V_{CC} = 5V, T_A = 25°C.
3. I_{OS} is tested with V_{OUT} = +0.5V and V_{CC} = V_{CC} MAX +0.5V. Not more than one output should be shorted at a time and duration of the short circuit should not exceed one second.
4. Measure I_{CC} with Parallel Load and Master Reset inputs grounded, all other outputs at 4.5V and all outputs open.

FUNCTIONAL WAVEFORMS (Typical clear, load, and count sequences)

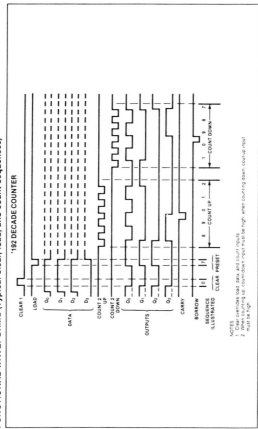

'192 DECADE COUNTER

NOTES
1. Clear overrides load, data and count inputs.
2. When counting up, count-down input must be high; when counting down, count-up input must be high.

FUNCTIONAL WAVEFORMS (Typical clear, load, and count sequences)

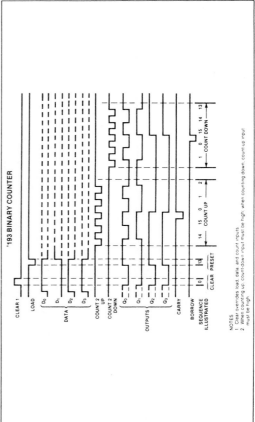

'193 BINARY COUNTER

NOTES
1. Clear overrides load, data and count inputs.
2. When counting up, count-down input must be high; when counting down, count-up input must be high.

AC WAVEFORMS

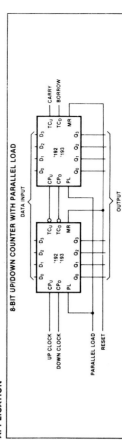

CLOCK TO OUTPUT DELAYS AND CLOCK PULSE WIDTH

Waveform 1

PARALLEL LOAD PULSE WIDTH, PARALLEL LOAD TO OUTPUT DELAYS, AND PARALLEL LOAD TO CLOCK RECOVERY TIME

Waveform 3

CLOCK TO TERMINAL COUNT DELAYS

Waveform 2

MASTER RESET PULSE WIDTH, MASTER RESET TO OUTPUT DELAY & MASTER RESET TO CLOCK RECOVERY TIME

Waveform 4

SETUP AND HOLD TIMES DATA TO PARALLEL LOAD (PL)

Waveform 5

$V_M = 1.5V$ for 54/74 and 54S/74S, $V_M = 1.3V$ for 54LS. The shaded areas indicate when the input is permitted to change for predictable output performance.

APPLICATION

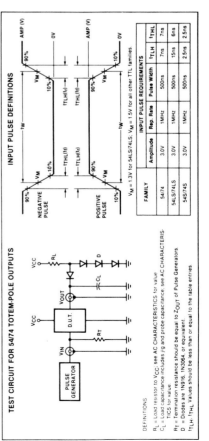

8-BIT UP/DOWN COUNTER WITH PARALLEL LOAD

AC CHARACTERISTICS $T_A = 25°C$, $V_{CC} = 5.0V$

			54/74 $C_L = 15pF$, $R_L = 400\Omega$		54LS/74LS $C_L = 15pF$, $R_L = 2k\Omega$		UNIT
	PARAMETER	TEST CONDITIONS	Min	Max	Min	Max	
t_{MAX}	Maximum input count frequency	Waveform 1	25		25		MHz
t_{PLH} t_{PHL}	Propagation delay CP_U input to $\overline{TC}_U$ output	Waveform 2		26 24		26 24	ns
t_{PLH} t_{PHL}	Propagation delay CP_D input to $\overline{TC}_D$ output	Waveform 2		24 24		24 24	ns
t_{PLH} t_{PHL}	Propagation delay CP_U or CP_D to Q_n outputs	Waveform 1		38 47		38 47	ns
t_{PLH} t_{PHL}	Propagation delay $\overline{PL}$ input to Q_n output	Waveform 3		40 40		40 40	ns
t_{PHL}	Propagation delay, MR to output	Waveform 4		35		35	ns

NOTE
Per industry convention, t_{MAX} is the worst case value of the maximum device operating frequency with no constraints on t_r, t_f, pulse width or duty cycle

AC SETUP REQUIREMENTS $T_A = 25°C$, $V_{CC} = 5.0V$

			54/74		54LS/74LS		UNIT
	PARAMETER	TEST CONDITIONS	Min	Max	Min	Max	
t_W	CP_U pulse width	Waveform 1	20		20		ns
t_W	CP_D pulse width	Waveform 2	20		20		ns
t_W	$\overline{PL}$ pulse width	Waveform 3	20		20		ns
t_W	MR pulse width	Waveform 4	20		20		ns
t_S	Setup time, Data to $\overline{PL}$	Waveform 5	20		20		ns
t_h	Hold time, Data to $\overline{PL}$	Waveform 5	0		5		ns
t_{rec}	Recovery time, $\overline{PL}$ to CP	Waveform 3	40		40		ns
t_{rec}	Recovery time, MR to CP	Waveform 4	40		40		ns

TEST CIRCUITS AND WAVEFORMS

TEST CIRCUIT FOR 54/74 TOTEM-POLE OUTPUTS

INPUT PULSE DEFINITIONS

INPUT PULSE REQUIREMENTS

FAMILY	Amplitude	Rep. Rate	Pulse Width	t_{TLH}	t_{THL}
54/74	3.0V	1MHz	500ns	7ns	7ns
54LS/74LS	3.0V	1MHz	500ns	15ns	6ns
54S/74S	3.0V	1MHz	500ns	2.5ns	2.5ns

$V_M = 1.3V$ for 54LS/74LS; $V_M = 1.5V$ for all other TTL families

DEFINITIONS
R_L = Load resistor to V_{CC}; see AC CHARACTERISTICS for value
C_L = Load capacitance includes jig and probe capacitance; see AC CHARACTERIS-TICS for value.
R_T = Termination resistance should be equal to Z_{OUT} of Pulse Generators
D = Diodes are 1N916, 1N3064, or equivalent.
t_{TLH}, t_{THL} Values should be less than or equal to the table entries

SHIFT REGISTERS

54/74194, LS194A, S194

4-Bit Bidirectional Universal Shift Register

- **Buffered clock and control inputs**
- **Shift left and shift right capability**
- **Synchronous parallel and serial data transfers**
- **Easily expanded for both serial and parallel operation**
- **Asynchronous Master Reset**
- **Hold (do nothing) mode**

DESCRIPTION

The functional characteristics of the '194 4-Bit Bidirectional Shift Register are indicated in the Logic Diagram and Function Table. The register is fully synchronous, with all operations taking place in less than 20ns (typical) for the 54/74 and 54LS/ 74LS, and 12ns (typical) for the 54S/74S, making the device especially useful for implementing very high speed CPUs, or for memory buffer registers.

The '194 design has special logic features which increase the range of application. The synchronous operation of the device is determined by two Mode Select inputs, S_0 and S_1. As shown in the Mode Select Table, data can be entered and shifted from left to right (shift right, $Q_0 \rightarrow Q_1$, etc.) or, right to left (shift left, $Q_1 \rightarrow Q_0$, etc.), or parallel data can be entered, loading all 4 bits of the register simultaneously. When both S_0 and S_1 are LOW, existing data is retained in a hold (do nothing) mode. The first and last stages provide D-type Serial Data inputs (D_{SR}, D_{SL}) to allow multistage shift right or shift left data transfers without interfering with parallel load operation.

The Mode Select and Data inputs on the 54S/ 74S194 and 54LS/74LS194A are edge-triggered, responding only to the LOW-to-HIGH transition of the Clock (CP). Therefore, the only timing restriction is that the Mode Control and selected Data inputs must be stable one setup time prior to the positive transition of the clock pulse. The Mode Select inputs of the 54/74194 are

gated with the clock and should be changed from HIGH-to-LOW only while the Clock input is HIGH.

The four parallel data inputs (D_0–D_3) are D-type inputs. Data appearing on D_0–D_3 inputs when S_0 and S_1 are HIGH is transferred to the Q_0–Q_3 outputs respectively, following the next LOW-to-HIGH transition of the clock. When LOW, the asynchronous Master Reset ($\overline{MR}$) overrides all other input conditions and forces the Q outputs LOW.

TYPICAL SUPPLY CURRENT

TYPE	TYPICAL f_{MAX}	TYPICAL SUPPLY CURRENT (Total)
74194	36MHz	39mA
74LS194A	36MHz	15mA
74S194	105MHz	85mA

ORDERING CODE

PACKAGES	COMMERCIAL RANGES $V_{CC}=5V \pm 5\%; T_A=0°C$ to $+70°C$	MILITARY RANGES $V_{CC}=5V \pm 10\%; T_A=-55°C$ to $+125°C$
Plastic DIP	N74194N • N74LS194AN N74S194N	
Plastic SO	N74LS194AD • N74S194D	
Ceramic DIP		S54194F • S54LS194AF S54S194F
Flatpack		S54194W • S54LS194AW S54S194W
LLCC		S54194G

INPUT AND OUTPUT LOADING AND FAN-OUT TABLE

PINS	DESCRIPTION	54/74	54/74S	54/74LS
All	Inputs	1ul	1Sul	1LSul
Q_0–Q_3	Outputs	10ul	10Sul	10LSul

NOTE
Where a 54/74 unit load (ul) is understood to be 40µA I_{IH} and −1.6mA I_{IL}, a 54/74S unit load (Sul) is 50µA I_{IH} and −2.0mA I_{IL}, and a 54/74LS unit load (LSul) is 20µA I_{IH} and −0.4mA I_{IL}.

PIN CONFIGURATION

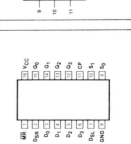

LOGIC SYMBOL

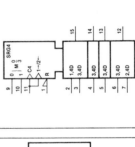

V_{CC} = Pin 16
GND = Pin 8

LOGIC SYMBOL (IEEE/IEC)

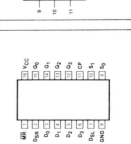

SHIFT REGISTERS

54/74194, LS194A, S194

MODE SELECT—FUNCTION TABLE

OPERATING MODE	CP	$\overline{MR}$	S_1	S	D_{SR}	D_{SL}	D_n	Q_0	Q_1	Q_2	Q_3
Reset (clear)	X	L	X	X	X	X	X	L	L	L	L
Hold (do nothing)	X	H	l(a)	l(a)	X	X	X	q_0	q_1	q_2	q_3
Shift Left	↑	H	h	l(a)	X	l	X	q_1	q_2	q_3	L
	↑	H	h	l(a)	X	h	X	q_1	q_2	q_3	H
Shift Right	↑	H	l(a)	h	l	X	X	L	q_0	q_1	q_2
	↑	H	l(a)	h	h	X	X	H	q_0	q_1	q_2
Parallel Load	↑	H	h	h	X	X	d_n	d_0	d_1	d_2	d_3

H = HIGH voltage level
h = HIGH voltage level one setup time prior to the LOW-to-HIGH clock transition
L = LOW voltage level
l = LOW voltage level one setup time prior to the LOW-to-HIGH clock transition
$d_n(q_n)$ = Lower case letters indicate the state of the referenced input (or output) one setup time prior to the LOW-to-HIGH clock transition.
X = Don't care
↑ = LOW-to-HIGH clock transition.

NOTES
a. The HIGH-to-LOW transition of the S_0 and S_1 inputs on the 54/74194 should only take place while CP is HIGH for conventional operation.

TYPICAL CLEAR, LOAD, RIGHT-SHIFT, LEFT-SHIFT, INHIBIT AND CLEAR SEQUENCES

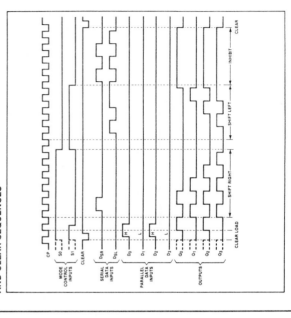

ABSOLUTE MAXIMUM RATINGS (Over operating free-air temperature range unless otherwise noted.)

	PARAMETER	54	54LS	54S	74	74LS	74S	UNIT
V_{CC}	Supply voltage	7.0	7.0	7.0	7.0	7.0	7.0	V
V_{IN}	Input voltage	−0.5 to +5.5	−0.5 to +7.0	−0.5 to +5.5	−0.5 to +5.5	−0.5 to +7.0	−0.5 to +5.5	V
I_{IN}	Input current	−30 to +5	−30 to +1	−30 to +5	−30 to +5	−30 to +1	−30 to +5	mA
V_{OUT}	Voltage applied to output in HIGH output state	−0.5 to +V_{CC}	−0.5 to +V_{CC}	−0.5 to +V_{CC}	−0.5 to +V_{CC}	−0.5 to +V_{CC}	−0.5 to +V_{CC}	V
T_A	Operating free-air temperature range	−55 to +125			0 to 70			°C

RECOMMENDED OPERATING CONDITIONS

	PARAMETER		54/74 Min	Nom	Max	54/74LS Min	Nom	Max	54/74S Min	Nom	Max	UNIT
V_{CC}	Supply voltage	Mil	4.5	5.0	5.5	4.5	5.0	5.5	4.5	5.0	5.5	V
		Com'l	4.75	5.0	5.25	4.75	5.0	5.25	4.75	5.0	5.25	V
V_{IH}	HIGH-level input voltage	Mil	2.0			2.0			2.0			V
		Com'l										V
V_{IL}	LOW-level input voltage	Mil			+0.8			+0.7			+0.8	V
		Com'l			+0.8			+0.8			+0.8	V
I_{IK}	Input clamp current				−12			−18			−18	mA
I_{OH}	HIGH-level output current				−800			−400			−1000	μA
I_{OL}	LOW-level output current	Mil			16			4			20	mA
		Com'l			16			8			20	mA
T_A	Operating free-air temperature	Mil	−55		+125	−55		+125	−55		+125	°C
		Com'l	0		70	0		70	0		70	°C

NOTE
V_{IL} = +0.7V MAX for 54S at T_A = +125°C only.

LOGIC DIAGRAM

54/74194

V_{CC} = Pin 16
GND = Pin 8

LOGIC DIAGRAM

54S/74S194, 54LS/74LS194A

V_{CC} = Pin 16
GND = Pin 8

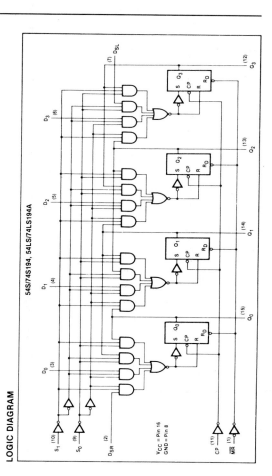

AC WAVEFORMS

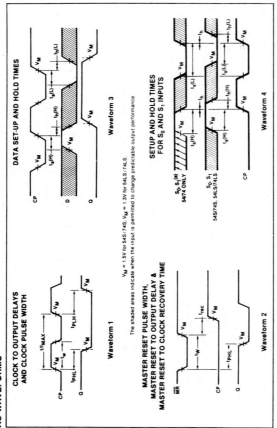

CLOCK TO OUTPUT DELAYS AND CLOCK PULSE WIDTH

Waveform 1

MASTER RESET PULSE WIDTH, MASTER RESET TO OUTPUT DELAY & MASTER RESET TO CLOCK RECOVERY TIME

Waveform 2

DATA SET-UP AND HOLD TIMES

Waveform 3

$V_M = 1.5V$ for 54S/74S; $V_M = 1.3V$ for 54LS/74LS

The shaded areas indicate when the input is permitted to change predictable output performance

SETUP AND HOLD TIMES FOR S_0 AND S_1 INPUTS

$S_0 S_1$
74/74 ONLY

$S_0 S_1$
54S/74S, 54LS/74LS

Waveform 4

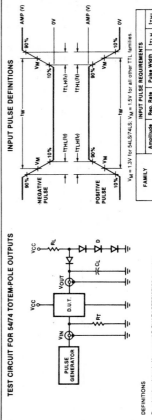

INPUT PULSE DEFINITIONS

NEGATIVE PULSE

POSITIVE PULSE

$V_M = 1.3V$ for 54LS/74LS; $V_M = 1.5V$ for all other TTL families

INPUT PULSE REQUIREMENTS

FAMILY	Amplitude	Rep. Rate	Pulse Width	t_{TLH}	t_{THL}
54/74	3.0V	1MHz	500ns	7ns	7ns
54LS/74LS	3.0V	1MHz	500ns	15ns	6ns
54S/74S	3.0V	1MHz	500ns	2.5ns	2.5ns

TEST CIRCUITS AND WAVEFORMS

TEST CIRCUIT FOR 54/74 TOTEM-POLE OUTPUTS

DEFINITIONS
R_L = Load resistor to V_{CC}; see AC CHARACTERISTICS for value.
C_L = Load capacitance includes jig and probe capacitance; see AC CHARACTERIS-TICS for value.
R_T = Termination resistance should be equal to Z_{OUT} of Pulse Generators.
D = Diodes are 1N916, 1N3064, or equivalent.
t_{TLH}, t_{THL}: Values should be less than or equal to the table entries.

DC ELECTRICAL CHARACTERISTICS (Over recommended operating free-air temperature range unless otherwise noted.)

PARAMETER		TEST CONDITIONS[1]		54/74194 Min	54/74194 Typ[2]	54/74194 Max	54/74LS194A Min	54/74LS194A Typ[2]	54/74LS194A Max	54/74S194 Min	54/74S194 Typ[2]	54/74S194 Max	UNIT
V_{OH} HIGH-level output voltage	Mil	V_{CC} = MIN, V_{IH} = MIN, V_{IL} = MAX, I_{OH} = MAX		2.4	3.4		2.5	3.5		2.5	3.4		V
	Com'l			2.4	3.4		2.7	3.5		2.7	3.4		V
V_{OL} LOW-level output voltage	Mil	V_{CC} = MIN, V_{IH} = MIN, I_{OL} = MAX			0.2	0.4		0.25	0.4			0.5[5]	V
	Com'l				0.2	0.4		0.35	0.5			0.5	V
	74LS	I_{OL} = 4mA						0.25	0.4				V
V_{IK} Input clamp voltage		V_{CC} = MIN, I_I = I_{IK}				−1.5			−1.5			−1.2	V
I_I Input current at maximum input voltage		V_{CC} = 5.5V	V_I = 5.5V			1.0			0.1			1.0	mA
		V_{CC} = 7.0V	V_I = 7.0V										mA
I_{IH} HIGH-level input current		V_{CC} = MAX	V_I = 2.4V			40			20			50	µA
			V_I = 2.7V										µA
I_{IL} LOW-level input current		V_{CC} = MAX	V_I = 0.4V			−1.6			−0.4			−2.0	mA
			V_I = 0.5V										mA
I_{OS} Short-circuit output current[3]	Mil	V_{CC} = MAX		−20		−57	−20		−100	−40		−100	mA
	Com'l			−18		−57	−20		−100	−40		−100	mA
I_{CC} Supply current (total)		V_{CC} = MAX			39	63		15	23		85	135	mA

NOTES
1. For conditions shown as MIN or MAX, use the appropriate value specified under recommended operating conditions for the applicable type.
2. All typical values are at V_{CC} = 5V, T_A = 25°C.
3. I_{OS} is tested with V_{OUT} = +0.5V and V_{CC} = V_{CC} MAX +0.5V. Not more than one output should be shorted at a time and duration of the short circuit should not exceed one second.
4. With all outputs open, D_I inputs grounded and 4.5V applied to S_0, S_1, $\overline{MR}$ and the serial inputs, I_{CC} is tested with a momentary ground, then 4.5V applied to CP.
5. V_{OL} = +0.45V MAX for 54S at T_A = +125°C only.

AC CHARACTERISTICS T_A = 25°C, V_{CC} = 5.0V

	PARAMETER	TEST CONDITIONS	54/74 C_L = 15pF, R_L = 400Ω Min	54/74 Max	54LS/74LS C_L = 15pF, R_L = 2kΩ Min	54LS/74LS Max	54S/74S C_L = 15pF, R_L = 280Ω Min	54S/74S Max	UNIT
f_{MAX}	Maximum clock frequency	Waveform 1	25		25		70		MHz
t_{PLH}	Propagation delay Clock to output	Waveform 1		22		22		12	ns
t_{PHL}				26		26		16.5	ns
t_{PHL}	Propagation delay $\overline{MR}$ to output	Waveform 2		37		30		18.5	ns

NOTE
Per industry convention, f_{MAX} is the worst case value of the maximum device operating frequency with no constraints on t_r, t_f, pulse width or duty cycle.

AC SETUP REQUIREMENTS T_A = 25°C, V_{CC} = 5.0V

	PARAMETER	TEST CONDITIONS	54/74 Min	54/74 Max	54LS/74LS Min	54LS/74LS Max	54S/74S Min	54S/74S Max	UNIT
$t_W(H)$	Clock pulse width, HIGH	Waveform 1	20		20		7		ns
$t_W(L)$	$\overline{MR}$ pulse width, LOW	Waveform 2	20		20		12		ns
t_s	Setup time, Data to Clock	Waveform 3	20		20		5.0		ns
t_h	Hold time, Data to Clock	Waveform 3	0		0		3.0		ns
$t_s(L)$	Setup time LOW, S_n to CP[a]	Waveform 4	30		30		11		ns
$t_s(H)$	Setup time HIGH, S_n to CP	Waveform 4	30		30		11		ns
t_h	Hold time, S_n to CP	Waveform 4	0		0		3.0		ns
t_{rec}	Recovery time, $\overline{MR}$ to CP	Waveform 2	25		25		9.0		ns

intel®

2716*
16K (2K × 8) UV ERASABLE PROM

- **Fast Access Time**
  - 350 ns Max. 2716-1
  - 390 ns Max. 2716-2
  - 450 ns Max. 2716
  - 490 ns Max. 2716-5
  - 650 ns Max. 2716-6

- **Single +5V Power Supply**

- **Low Power Dissipation**
  - 525 mW Max. Active Power
  - 132 mW Max. Standby Power

- **Pin Compatible to Intel® 2732 EPROM**

- **Simple Programming Requirements**
  - Single Location Programming
  - Programs with One 50 ms Pulse

- **Inputs and Outputs TTL Compatible during Read and Program**

- **Completely Static**

The Intel® 2716 is a 16,384-bit ultraviolet erasable and electrically programmable read-only memory (EPROM). The 2716 operates from a single 5-volt power supply, has a static standby mode, and features fast single address location programming. It makes designing with EPROMs faster, easier and more economical.

The 2716, with its single 5-volt supply and with an access time up to 350 ns, is ideal for use with the newer high performance +5V microprocessors such as Intel's 8085 and 8086. A selected 2716-5 and 2716-6 is available for slower speed applications. The 2716 is also the first EPROM with a static standby mode which reduces the power dissipation without increasing access time. The maximum active power dissipation is 525 mW while the maximum standby power dissipation is only 132 mW, a 75% savings.

The 2716 has the simplest and fastest method yet devised for programming EPROMs – single pulse TTL level programming. No need for high voltage pulsing because all programming controls are handled by TTL signals. Program any location at any time—either individually, sequentially or at random, with the 2716's single address location programming. Total programming time for all 16,384 bits is only 100 seconds.

PIN CONFIGURATION

2716

```
A7   1      24  VCC
A6   2      23  A8
A5   3      22  A9
A4   4      21  Vpp
A3   5  16K 20  OE
A2   6      19  A10
A1   7      18  CE
A0   8      17  O7
O0   9      16  O6
O1  10      15  O5
O2  11      14  O4
GND 12      13  O3
```

2732†

```
A7   1      24  VCC
A6   2      23  A8
A5   3      22  A9
A4   4      21  A11
A3   5  32K 20  OE/Vpp
A2   6      19  A10
A1   7      18  CE
A0   8      17  O7
O0   9      16  O6
O1  10      15  O5
O2  11      14  O4
GND 12      13  O3
```

†Refer to 2732 data sheet for specifications

MODE SELECTION

PINS / MODE	CE/PGM (18)	OE (20)	Vpp (21)	Vcc (24)	OUTPUTS (9-11, 13-17)
Read	VIL	VIL	+5	+5	DOUT
Standby	VIH	Don't Care	+5	+5	High Z
Program	Pulsed VIL to VIH	VIH	+25	+5	DIN
Program Verify	VIL	VIL	+25	+5	DOUT
Program Inhibit	VIL	VIH	+25	+5	High Z

BLOCK DIAGRAM

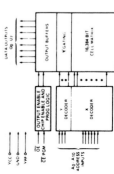

PIN NAMES

A0-A10	ADDRESSES
CE/PGM	CHIP ENABLE/PROGRAM
OE	OUTPUT ENABLE
O0-O7	OUTPUTS

PROGRAMMING

The programming specifications are described in the Data Catalog PROM/ROM Programming Instructions Section.

Absolute Maximum Ratings*

Temperature Under Bias .... -10°C to +80°C
Storage Temperature .... -65°C to +125°C
All Input or Output Voltages with Respect to Ground .... +6V to -0.3V
Vpp Supply Voltage with Respect to Ground During Program ...... +26.5V to -0.3V

*COMMENT: Stresses above those listed under "Absolute Maximum Ratings" may cause permanent damage to the device. This is a stress rating only and functional operation of the device at these or any other conditions above those indicated in the operational sections of this specification is not implied. Exposure to absolute maximum rating conditions for extended periods may affect device reliability.

DC and AC Operating Conditions During Read

	2716	2716-1	2716-2	2716-5	2716-6
Temperature Range	0°C – 70°C	0°C – 70°C	0°C – 70°C	0°C – 70°C	0°C – 70°C
V_{CC} Power Supply[1,2]	5V ±5%	5V ±10%	5V ±5%	5V ±5%	5V ±5%
V_{PP} Power Supply[2]	V_{CC}	V_{CC}	V_{CC}	V_{CC}	V_{CC}

READ OPERATION

D.C. and Operating Characteristics

Symbol	Parameter	Min.	Typ.[3]	Max.	Unit	Conditions
I_{LI}	Input Load Current			10	µA	V_{IN} = 5.25V
I_{LO}	Output Leakage Current			10	µA	V_{OUT} = 5.25V
I_{PP1}[2]	Vpp Current			5	mA	V_{PP} = 5.25V
I_{CC1}[2]	V_{CC} Current (Standby)		10	25	mA	$\overline{CE}$ = V_{IH}, $\overline{OE}$ = V_{IL}
I_{CC2}[2]	V_{CC} Current (Active)		57	100	mA	$\overline{OE}$ = $\overline{CE}$ = V_{IL}
V_{IL}	Input Low Voltage	-0.1		0.8	V	
V_{IH}	Input High Voltage	2.0		V_{CC}+1	V	
V_{OL}	Output Low Voltage			0.45	V	I_{OL} = 2.1 mA
V_{OH}	Output High Voltage	2.4			V	I_{OH} = -400 µA

NOTES:
1. V_{CC} must be applied simultaneously or before Vpp and removed simultaneously or after Vpp.
2. Vpp may be connected directly to V_{CC} except during programming. The supply current would then be the sum of I_{CC} and I_{PP1}.
3. Typical values are for T_A = 25°C and nominal supply voltages.
4. This parameter is only sampled and is not 100% tested.

Typical Characteristics

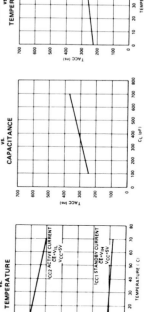

ACCESS TIME vs. TEMPERATURE

ACCESS TIME vs. CAPACITANCE

Icc CURRENT vs. TEMPERATURE

ERASURE CHARACTERISTICS

The erasure characteristics of the 2716 are such that erasure begins to occur when exposed to light with wavelengths shorter than approximately 4000 Angstroms (Å). It should be noted that sunlight and certain types of fluorescent lamps have wavelengths in the 3000–4000Å range. Data show that constant exposure to room level fluorescent lighting could erase the typical 2716 in approximately 3 years, while it would take approximatley 1 week to cause erasure when exposed to direct sunlight. If the 2716 is to be exposed to these types of lighting conditions for extended periods of time, opaque labels are available from Intel which should be placed over the 2716 window to prevent unintentional erasure.

The recommended erasure procedure (see Data Catalog PROM/ROM Programming Instruction Section) for the 2716 is exposure to shortwave ultraviolet light which has a wavelength of 2537 Angstroms (Å). The integrated dose (i.e., UV intensity X exposure time) for erasure should be a minimum of 15 W-sec/cm². The erasure time with this dosage is approximately 15 to 20 minutes using an ultraviolet lamp with a 12000 μW/cm² power rating. The 2716 should be placed within 1 inch of the lamp tubes during erasure. Some lamps have a filter on their tubes which should be removed before erasure.

DEVICE OPERATION

The five modes of operation of the 2716 are listed in Table I. It should be noted that all inputs for the five modesare at TTL levels. The power supplies required are a +5V V_{CC} and a V_{PP}. The V_{PP} power supply must be at 25V during the three programming modes, and must be at 5V in the other two modes.

OUTPUT OR-TIEING

Because 2716's are usually used in larger memory arrays, Intel has provided a 2 line control function that accomodates this use of multiple memory connections. The two line control function allows for:

a) the lowest possible memory power dissipation, and

b) complete assurance that output bus contention will not occur.

To most efficiently use these two control lines, it is recommended that $\overline{CE}$ (pin 18) be decoded and used as the primary device selecting function, while $\overline{OE}$ (pin 20) be made a common connection to all devices in the array and connected to the READ line from the system control bus. This assures that all deselected memory devices are in their low power standby mode and that the output pins are only active when data is desired from a particular memory device.

PROGRAMMING (See Programming Instruction Section for Waveforms.)

Initially, and after each erasure, all bits of the 2716 are in the "1" state. Data is introduced by selectively programming "0's" into the desired bit locations. Although only "0's" will be programmed, both "1's" and "0's" can be presented in the data word. The only way to change a "0" to a "1" is by ultraviolet light erasure.

The 2716 is in the programming mode when the V_{PP} power supply is at 25V and $\overline{OE}$ is at V_{IH}. The data to be programmed is applied 8 bits in parallel to the data output pins. The levels required for the address and data inputs are TTL.

When the address and data are stable, a 50 msec, active high, TTL program pulse is applied to the $\overline{CE}/PGM$ input. A program pulse must be applied at each address location to be programmed. You can program any location at any time – either individually, sequentially, or at random. The program pulse has a maximum width of 55 msec. The 2716 must not be programmed with a DC signal applied to the $\overline{CE}/PGM$ input.

Programming of multiple 2716s in parallel with the same data can be easily accomplished due to the simplicity of the programming requirements. Like inputs of the paralleled 2716s may be connected together when they are programmed with the same data. A high level TTL pulse applied to the $\overline{CE}/PGM$ input programs the paralleled 2716s.

PROGRAM INHIBIT

Programming of multiple 2716s in parallel with different data is also easily accomplished. Except for $\overline{CE}/PGM$, all like inputs (including $\overline{OE}$) of the parallel 2716s may be common. A TTL level program pulse applied to a 2716's $\overline{CE}/PGM$ input with V_{PP} at 25V will program that 2716. A low level $\overline{CE}/PGM$ input inhibits the other 2716 from being programmed.

PROGRAM VERIFY

A verify should be performed on the programmed bits to determine that they were correctly programmed. The verify may be performed with V_{PP} at 25V. Except during programming and program verify, V_{PP} must be at 5V.

READ MODE

The 2716 has two control functions, both of which must be logically satisfied in order to obtain data at the outputs. Chip Enable (CE) is the power control and should be used for device selection. Output Enable (OE) is the output control and should be used to gate data to the output pins, independent of device selection. Assuming that addresses are stable, address access time (t_{ACC}) is equal to the delay from $\overline{CE}$ to output (t_{CE}). Data is available at the outputs 120 ns (t_{OE}) after the falling edge of $\overline{OE}$, assuming that $\overline{CE}$ has been low and addresses have been stable for at least $t_{ACC} - t_{OE}$.

STANDBY MODE

The 2716 has a standby mode which reduces the active power dissipation by 75%, from 525 mW to 132 mW. The 2716 is placed in the standby mode by applying a TTL high signal to the $\overline{CE}$ input. When in standby mode, the outputs are in a high impedence state, independent of the $\overline{OE}$ input.

TABLE I. MODE SELECTION

PINS / MODE	$\overline{CE}/PGM$ (18)	$\overline{OE}$ (20)	V_{PP} (21)	V_{CC} (24)	OUTPUTS (9-11, 13-17)
Read	V_{IL}	V_{IL}	+5	+5	D_{OUT}
Standby	V_{IH}	Don't Care	+5	+5	High Z
Program	Pulsed V_{IL} to V_{IH}	V_{IH}	+25	+5	D_{IN}
Program Verify	V_{IL}	V_{IL}	+25	+5	D_{OUT}
Program Inhibit	V_{IL}	V_{IH}	+25	+5	High Z

A.C. Characteristics

Symbol	Parameter	2716 Min.	2716 Max.	2716-1 Min.	2716-1 Max.	2716-2 Min.	2716-2 Max.	2716-5 Min.	2716-5 Max.	2716-6 Min.	2716-6 Max.	Test Conditions
t_{ACC}	Address to Output Delay		450		350		390		450		450	$\overline{CE} = \overline{OE} = V_{IL}$
t_{CE}	$\overline{CE}$ to Output Delay		450		350		390		490		650	$\overline{OE} = V_{IL}$
t_{OE}	Output Enable to Output Delay		120		120		120		160		200	$\overline{CE} = V_{IL}$
t_{DF}	Output Enable High to Output Float	0	100	0	100	0	100	0	100	0	100	$\overline{CE} = V_{IL}$
t_{OH}	Output Hold from Addresses, $\overline{CE}$ or $\overline{OE}$ Whichever Occurred First	0		0		0		0		0		$\overline{CE} = \overline{OE} = V_{IL}$

Capacitance [4] $T_A = 25°C$, f = 1 MHz

Symbol	Parameter	Typ.	Max.	Unit	Conditions
C_{IN}	Input Capacitance	4	6	pF	$V_{IN} = 0V$
C_{OUT}	Output Capacitance	8	12	pF	$V_{OUT} = 0V$

A.C. Test Conditions:

Output Load: 1 TTL gate and C_L = 100 pF
Input Rise and Fall Times: ≤20 ns
Input Pulse Levels: 0.8V to 2.2V
Timing Measurement Reference Level:
   Inputs   1V and 2V
   Outputs 0.8V and 2V

A. C. Waveforms [1]

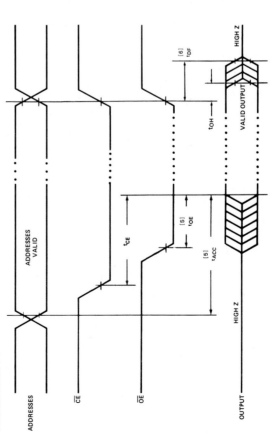

NOTE:
1. V_{CC} must be applied simultaneously or before V_{PP} and removed simultaneously or after V_{PP}.
2. V_{PP} may be connected directly to V_{CC} except during programming. The supply current would then be the sum of I_{CC} and I_{PP1}.
3. Typical values are for $T_A = 25°C$ and nominal supply voltages.
4. This parameter is only sampled and is not 100% tested.
5. This parameter is only sampled and is not 100% tested.
6. $\overline{OE}$ may be delayed up to $t_{ACC} - t_{OE}$ after the falling edge of $\overline{CE}$ without impact on t_{ACC}.
7. t_{DF} is specified from $\overline{OE}$ or $\overline{CE}$, whichever occurs first.

CMOS 8-BIT A/D CONVERTERS

ADC0801/2/3/4/5-1

Preliminary

DESCRIPTION

The ADC0801 family is a series of five CMOS 8-bit successive approximation A/D converters using a resistive ladder and capacitive array together with an auto-zero comparator. These converters are designed to operate with microprocessor controlled buses using a minimum of external circuitry. The three-state output data lines can be connected directly to the data bus.

The differential analog voltage input allows for increased common-mode rejection and provides a means to adjust the zero scale offset. Additionally, the voltage reference input provides a means of encoding small analog voltages to the full 8 bits of resolution.

FEATURES

- Compatible with most microprocessors
- Differential inputs
- Three-state outputs
- Logic levels TTL and MOS compatible
- Can be used with internal or external clock
- Analog input range 0V to V_{CC}
- Single 5V supply
- Guaranteed specification with 1MHz clock

APPLICATIONS

- Transducer to microprocessor interface
- Digital thermometer
- Digitally-controlled thermostat
- Microprocessor-based monitoring and control systems

PIN CONFIGURATION

F,N PACKAGE

CS	1	20	V_{CC}
RD	2	19	CLK R
WR	3	18	D0
CLK IN	4	17	D1
INTR	5	16	D2
$V_{IN}(+)$	6	15	D3
$V_{IN}(-)$	7	14	D4
A GND	8	13	D5
$V_{REF}/2$	9	12	D6
D GND	10	11	D7

TOP VIEW

ORDER NUMBERS
ADC0801/02-1F
ADC0801/02/03-1 LCF
ADC0801/02/03/04/05-1 LCN
ADC0804-1 CN

Preliminary

BLOCK DIAGRAMS

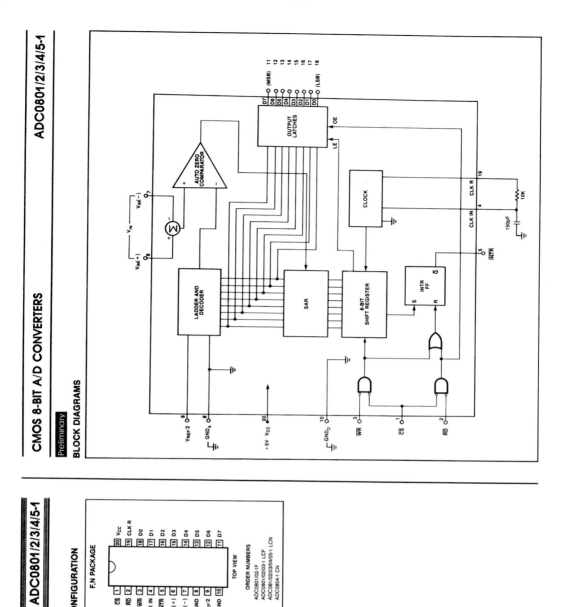

ABSOLUTE MAXIMUM RATINGS

	SYMBOL & PARAMETER	RATING	UNIT
V_{CC}	Supply Voltage	6.5	V
	Logic Control Input Voltages	−0.3 to + 16	V
	All Other Input Voltages	−0.3 to (V_{CC} +0.3)	V
T_A	Operating Temperature Range		
	ADC0801/02-1 F	−55 to +125	°C
	ADC0801/02/03-1 LCF	−40 to +85	°C
	ADC0801/02/03/04/05-1 LCN	−40 to +85	°C
	ADC0804-1 CN	0 to +70	°C
T_{STG}	Storage Temperature	−65 to +150	°C
T_{SOLD}	Lead Soldering Temperature (10 seconds)	300	°C
P_D	Package Power Dissipation at T_A = 25°C	875	mW

CMOS 8-BIT A/D CONVERTERS

ADC0801/2/3/4/5-1

DC ELECTRICAL CHARACTERISTICS

$V_{CC} = 5.0V$, $f_{CLK} = 1MHz$, $T_{MIN} \leq T_A \leq T_{MAX}$, unless otherwise specified.

SYMBOL & PARAMETER	TEST CONDITIONS	ADC0801/2/3/4/5			UNIT
		Min	Typ	Max	
ADC0801 Relative Accuracy Error (Adjusted)	Full Scale Adjusted			0.25	LSB
ADC0802 Relative Accuracy Error (Unadjusted)	$\frac{V_{REF}}{2} = 2.500\ V_{DC}$			0.50	LSB
ADC0803 Relative Accuracy Error (Adjusted)	Full Scale Adjusted			0.50	LSB
ADC0804 Relative Accuracy Error (Unadjusted)	$\frac{V_{REF}}{2} = 2.500\ V_{DC}$			1	LSB
ADC0805 Relative Accuracy Error (Unadjusted)	$\frac{V_{REF}}{2}$ = has no connection			1	LSB
$\frac{V_{REF}}{2}$ Input Resistance		400	640		Ω
Analog Input Voltage Range	Over Analog Input Voltage Range	−0.05		V_{CC} +0.05	V
DC Common Mode Error			1/16	1/8	LSB
Power Supply Sensitivity	$V_{CC} = 5V \pm 10\%$[1]				
CONTROL INPUTS					
V_{IH} Logical "1" Input Voltage	$V_{CC} = 5.25\,V_{DC}$	2.0		15	V_{DC}
V_{IL} Logical "0" Input Voltage	$V_{CC} = 4.75\,V_{DC}$			0.8	V_{DC}
I_{IH} Logical "1" Input Current	$V_{IN} = 5V_{DC}$		0.005	1	μA_{DC}
I_{IL} Logical "0" Input Current	$V_{IN} = 0V_{DC}$	−1	−0.005		μA_{DC}
CLOCK IN AND CLOCK R					
V_{T+} Clk In Positive-Going Threshold Voltage		2.7	3.1	3.5	V_{DC}
V_{T-} Clk In Negative-Going Threshold Voltage		1.5	1.8	2.1	V_{DC}
V_H Clk In Hysteresis $(V_{T+}) - (V_{T-})$		0.6	1.3	2.0	V_{DC}
V_{OL} Logical "0" Clk R Output Voltage	$I_{OL} = 360\mu A$, $V_{CC} = 4.75\ V_{DC}$			0.4	V_{DC}
V_{OH} Logical "1" Clk R Output Voltage	$I_{OH} = -360\mu A$, $V_{CC} = 4.75\ V_{DC}$	2.4			V_{DC}
DATA OUTPUT AND INTR					
V_{OL} Logical "0" Output Voltage					
Data Outputs	$I_{OL} = 1.6mA$, $V_{CC} = 4.75\ V_{DC}$			0.4	V_{DC}
INTR Outputs	$I_{OL} = 1.0mA$, $V_{CC} = 4.75\ V_{DC}$			0.4	V_{DC}
V_{OH} Logical "1" Output Voltage	$I_{OH} = -360\mu A$, $V_{CC} = 4.75\ V_{DC}$	2.4			V_{DC}
	$I_{OH} = -10\mu A$, $V_{CC} = 4.75\ V_{DC}$	4.5			V_{DC}
I_{OZL} 3-State Output Leakage	$V_{OUT} = 0V_{DC}$, $\overline{CS}$= Logical "1"	−3			μA_{DC}
I_{OZH} 3-State Output Leakage	$V_{OUT} = 5V_{DC}$, $\overline{CS}$= Logical "1"			3	μA_{DC}
I_{SC} + Output Short Circuit Current	$V_{OUT} = 0V$, $T_A = 25°C$	4.5	6		mA_{DC}
I_{SC} − Output Short Circuit Current	$V_{OUT} = V_{CC}$, $T_A = 25°C$	9.0	16		mA_{DC}
I_{CC} Power Supply Current	$f_{CLK} = 1MHz$, $V_{REF2} =$ Open, $\overline{CS}$ = Logical "1", $T_A = 25°C$		3.0	3.5	mA

NOTE:
1. Analog inputs must remain within the range: $-0.05 \leq V_{IN} \leq V_{CC} + 0.05V$.

CMOS 8-BIT A/D CONVERTERS

ADC0801/2/3/4/5-1

AC ELECTRICAL CHARACTERISTICS

SYMBOL & PARAMETER	TO	FROM	TEST CONDITIONS	ADC0801/2/3/4/5			UNIT
				Min	Typ	Max	
Conversion Time			$f_{CLK} = 1MHz$[1]	66		73	μS
f_{CLK} Clock Frequency			See Note 1.	0.1	1.0	3.0	MHz
Clock Duty Cycle			See Note 1.	40		60	%
CR Free-Running Conversion Rate			$\overline{CS} = 0$, $f_{CLK} = 1MHz$ $\overline{INTR}$ Tied To $\overline{WR}$			13690	conv/s
$t_{W(\overline{WR})L}$ Start Pulse Width			$\overline{CS} = 0$	30			ns
t_{ACC} Access Time	Output	$\overline{RD}$			75	100	ns
t_{1H}, t_{0H} Three-State Control	Output	$\overline{RD}$	$C_L = 10\ pF$, $C_L = 100\ pF$ See Three-State Test Circuit		70	100	ns
t_{WI}, t_{RI} $\overline{INTR}$ Delay	$\overline{INTR}$	$\overline{WD}$ or $\overline{RD}$					ns
C_{IN} Logic Input =Capacitance					5	7.5	pF
C_{OUT} Three-State Output Capacitance					5	7.5	pF

NOTE:
1. Accuracy is guaranteed at $f_{CLK} = 1MHz$. Accuracy may degrade at higher clock frequencies.

CMOS 8-BIT A/D CONVERTERS

CMOS 8-BIT A/D CONVERTERS

Preliminary

FUNCTIONAL DESCRIPTION

The ADC0801 through ADC0805 series of A/D converters are successive approximation devices with 8-bit resolution and no missing codes. The most significant bit is tested first and after 64 clock cycles a digital 8-bit binary word is transferred to an output latch and the INTR pin goes low, indicating that conversion is complete. A conversion in progress can be interrupted by issuing another start command. The device may be operated in a continuous conversion mode by connecting the INTR and WR pins together and holding the CS pin low. To insure start-up when connected this way, an external WR pulse is required at power-up.

As the WR input goes low, when CS is low, the SAR is cleared and remains so as long as these two inputs are low. Conversion begins between 1 and 8 clock periods after at least one of these inputs goes high. As the conversion begins, the INTR line goes high. Note that the INTR line will remain low until 1 to 8 clock cycles after either the WR or the CS input (or both) goes high.

When the CS and RD inputs are both brought low to read the data, the INTR line will go low and the three-state output latches are enabled.

The digital control lines (CS, RD, and WR) operate with standard TTL levels and have been renamed when compared with standard A/D Start and Output Enable labels. For non-microprocessor based applications, the CS pin can be grounded, the WR pin can be interpreted as a START pulse pin, and the RD pin performs the OE (Output Enable) function.

The $V_{IN}(-)$ input can be used to subtract a fixed voltage from the input voltage. Because there is a time interval between sampling the $V_{IN}(+)$ and the $V_I(-)$ inputs, it is important that these inputs remain constant, during the entire conversion cycle.

THREE-STATE TEST CIRCUITS AND WAVEFORMS

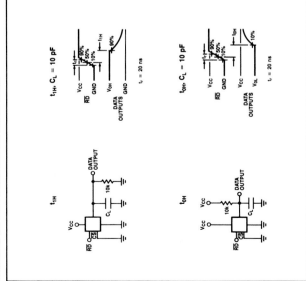

TIMING DIAGRAMS (All timing is measured from the 50% voltage points)

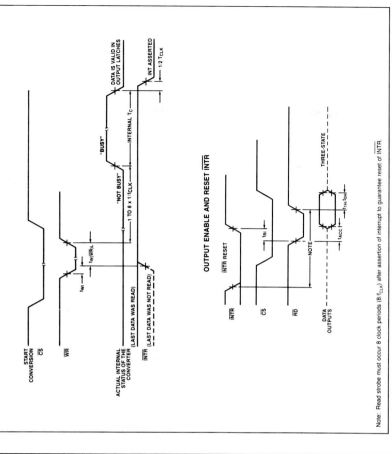

Note: Read strobe must occur 8 clock periods ($8/f_{CLK}$) after assertion of interrupt to guarantee reset of INTR.

DESCRIPTION

The MC1508/MC1408 series of 8-bit monolithic digital-to-analog converters provide high speed performance with low cost. They are designed for use where the output current is a linear product of an 8-bit digital word and an analog reference voltage.

FEATURES

- Fast settling time—70ns (typ)
- Relative accuracy ±0.19% (max error)
- Non-inverting digital inputs are TTL and CMOS compatible
- High speed multiplying rate 4.0mA/µs (input slew)
- Output voltage swing +5V to -5.0V
- Standard supply voltages +5.0V and -5.0V to -15V
- Military qualifications pending

APPLICATIONS

- Tracking A-to-D converters
- 2½-digit panel meters and DVM's
- Waveform synthesis
- Sample and hold
- Peak detector
- Programmable gain and attenuation
- CRT character generation
- Audio digitizing and decoding
- Programmable power supplies
- Analog-digital multiplication
- Digital-digital multiplication
- Analog-digital division
- Digital addition and subtraction
- Speech compression and expansion
- Stepping motor drive
- Modems
- Servo motor and pen drivers

CIRCUIT DESCRIPTION

The MC1508/MC1408 consists of a reference current amplifier, an R-2R ladder, and 8 high speed current switches. For many applications, only a reference resistor and reference voltage need be added.

The switches are non-inverting in operation; therefore, a high state on the input turns on the specified output current component.

The switch uses current steering for high speed, and a termination amplifier consisting of an active load gain stage with unity gain feedback. The termination amplifier holds the parasitic capacitance of the ladder at a constant voltage during switching, and provides a low impedance termination of equal voltage for all legs of the ladder.

The R-2R ladder divides the reference amplifier current into binarily-related components, which are fed to the switches. Note that there is always a remainder current which is equal to the least significant bit. This current is shunted to ground, and the maximum output current is 255/256 of the reference amplifier current, or 1.992mA for a 2.0mA reference amplifier current if the NPN current source pair is perfectly matched.

DC ELECTRICAL CHARACTERISTICS[1]

Pin 3 must be 3V more negative than the potential to which R_{15} is returned. $V_{CC} = +5.0Vdc$, $V_{EE} = -15Vdc$, $\frac{V_{ref}}{R_{14}} = 2.0mA$ unless otherwise specified. MC1508: $T_A = -55°C$ to $125°C$. MC1408: $T_A = 0°C$ to $75°C$ unless otherwise noted.

PARAMETER		TEST CONDITIONS	MC1508-8 Min	Typ	Max	MC1408-8 Min	Typ	Max	MC1408-7 Min	Typ	Max	UNIT
E_r	Relative accuracy	Error relative to full scale Io, Figure 3			±0.19			±0.19			±0.39	%
t_s	Setting time[1]	To within ½ LSB, includes t_{PLH}, $T_A = +25°C$, Figure 4		70			70			70		ns
	Propagation delay time											ns
t_{PLH}	Low-to-high	$T_A = +25°C$, Figure 4		35	100		35	100		35	100	
t_{PHL}	High-to-low											
$TCIo$	Output full scale current drift			-20			-20			-20		PPM/°C
	Digital input logic level											Vdc
V_{IH}	High	Figure 5	2.0			2.0			2.0			
V_{IL}	Low	Figure 5			0.8			0.8			0.8	
	Digital input current (MSB)											mA
I_{IH}	High	$V_{IH} = 5.0V$		0	0.04		0	0.04		0	0.04	
I_{IL}	Low	$V_{IL} = 0.8V$		-0.4	-0.8		-0.4	-0.8		-0.4	-0.8	
I_{15}	Reference input bias current	Pin 15, Figure 5		-1.0	-5.0		-1.0	-5.0		-1.0	-5.0	µA
I_{OR}	Output current range	$V_{EE} = -5.0V$	0	2.0	2.1	0	2.0	2.1	0	2.0	2.1	mA
		$V_{EE} = -7.0V$ to -15V	0	2.0	4.2	0	2.0	4.2	0	2.0	4.2	
I_o	Output current	$V_{ref} = 2.000V$, $R14 = 1000Ω$	1.9	1.99	2.1	1.9	1.99	2.1	1.9	1.99	2.1	mA
$I_{o(min)}$	Off-state	All bits low		0	4.0		0	4.0		0	4.0	µA
V_o	Output voltage compliance	$E_r \leq 0.19\%$ at $T_A = +25°C$, Figure 5, $V_{EE} = -5V$		-0.6, +10	-0.55, +0.5		-0.6, +10	-0.55, +0.5		-0.6, +10	-0.55, +0.5	Vdc
		V_{EE} below -10V		-5.5, +10	-5.0, +0.5		-5.5, +10	-5.0, +0.5		-5.5, +10	-5.0, +0.5	
SRI_{ref}	Reference current slew rate	Figure 6		8.0			8.0			8.0		mA/µs
$PSRR_{(-)}$	Output current power supply sensitivity	$I_{ref} = 1mA$		0.5	2.7		0.5	2.7		0.5	2.7	µA/V
	Power supply current											mA
I_{CC} Positive		All bits low, Figure 5		+2.5	+22		+2.5	+22		+2.5	+22	
I_{EE} Negative				-6.5	-13		-6.5	-13		-6.5	-13	
	Power supply voltage range											Vdc
V_{CCR} Positive		$T_A = +25°C$, Figure 5	+4.5	+5.0	+5.5	+4.5	+5.0	+5.5	+4.5	+5.0	+5.5	
V_{EER} Negative			-4.5	-15	-16.5	-4.5	-15	-16.5	-4.5	-15	-16.5	
P_D	Power dissipation	All bits low, $V_{EE} = -5.0Vdc$		34	170		34	170		34	170	mW
		$V_{EE} = -15Vdc$		110	305		110	305		110	305	

NOTES:
1. All bits switched.

PIN CONFIGURATION

F,N PACKAGE
TOP VIEW

```
NC        1    16  COMPEN
GND       2    15  VREF(-)
VEE       3    14  VREF(+)
Io        4    13  VCC
(MSB) A1  5    12  A8 (LSB)
A2        6    11  A7
A3        7    10  A6
A4        8     9  A5
```

ORDER NUMBERS
MC1508-8F   MC1408-7N
MC1408-7F

D³ PACKAGE
TOP VIEW

```
V+        1    16  A8 (LSB)
VREF(+)   2    15  A7
VREF(-)   3    14  A6
COMPEN    4    13  A5
NC        5    12  A4
GND       6    11  A3
V-        7    10  A2
Io        8     9  A1 (MSB)
```

ORDER NUMBER
MC1408-8D

NOTES:
1. SOL. Released in Large SO package only.
2. SOL and non-standard pinout.
3. SO and non-standard pinouts.

BLOCK DIAGRAM

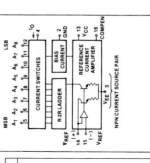

ABSOLUTE MAXIMUM RATINGS $T_A = +25°C$ unless otherwise specified

	PARAMETER	RATING	UNIT
	Power Supply Voltage		
V_{CC}	Positive	+5.5	V
V_{EE}	Negative	-16.5	V
V_5-V_{12}	Digital Input Voltage	0 to V_{CC}	V
V_o	Applied Output Voltage	-5.2 to +18	V
I_{14}	Reference Current	5.0	mA
V_{14}, V_{15}	Reference Amplifier Inputs	V_{EE} to V_{CC}	V
P_D	Power Dissipation (Package Limitation)		
	Ceramic Package	1000	mW
	Plastic Package	800	mW
	Lead Soldering Temperature (60 sec)	300	mW
T_A	Operating Temperature Range		
	MC1508	-55 to +125	°C
	MC1408	0 to +75	°C
T_{STG}	Storage Temperature Range	-65 to +150	°C

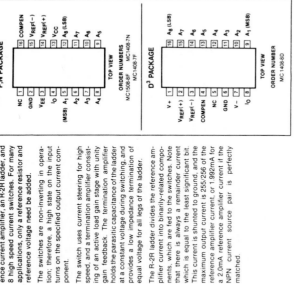

8-BIT MULTIPLYING D/A CONVERTER

TEST CIRCUITS

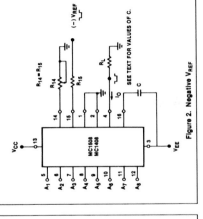

Figure 1. Positive V_{REF}

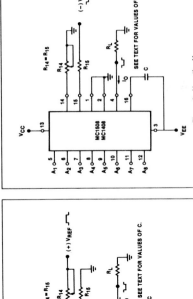

Figure 2. Negative V_{REF}

TYPICAL PERFORMANCE CHARACTERISTICS

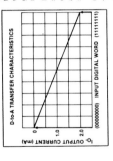

D-to-A TRANSFER CHARACTERISTICS

FUNCTIONAL DESCRIPTION

Reference Amplifier Drive and Compensation

The reference amplifier input current must always flow into pin 14 regardless of the setup method or reference supply voltage polarity.

Connections for a positive reference voltage are shown in Figure 1. The reference voltage source supplies the full reference current. For bipolar reference signals, as in the multiplying mode, R_{15} can be tied to a negative voltage corresponding to the minimum input level. R_{15} may be eliminated and pin 15 grounded, with only a small sacrifice in accuracy and temperature drift.

The compensation capacitor value must be increased with increasing values of R_{14} to maintain proper phase margin. For R_{14} values of 1.0, 2.5, and 5.0K ohms, minimum capacitor values are 15, 37, and 75pF. The capacitor may be tied to either V_{EE} or ground, but using V_{EE} increases negative supply rejection. (Fluctuations in the negative supply have more effect on accuracy than do any changes in the positive supply).

A negative reference voltage may be used if R_{14} is grounded and the reference voltage is applied to R_{15}, as shown in Figure 2. A high input impedance is the main advantage of this method. The negative reference voltage must be at least 3.0V above the V_{EE} supply. Bipolar input signals may be handled by connecting R_{14} to a positive reference voltage equal to the peak positive input level at pin 15.

Capacitive bypass to ground is recommended when a DC reference voltage is used. The 5.0V logic supply is not recommended as a reference voltage, but if a

well regulated 5.0V supply which drives logic is to be used as the reference, R_{14} should be formed of two series resistors and the junction of the two resistors bypassed with 0.1μF to ground. For reference voltages greater than 5.0V, a clamp diode is recommended between pin 14 and ground.

If pin 14 is driven by a high impedance such as a transistor current source, none of the above compensation methods apply since the amplifier must be heavily compensated, decreasing the overall bandwidth.

Output Voltage Range

The voltage at pin 4 must always be at least 4.5 volts more positive than the voltage of the negative supply (pin 3) when the reference current is 2mA or less, and at least 8 volts more positive than the negative supply when the reference current is between 2mA and 4mA. This is necessary to avoid saturation of the output transistors, which would cause serious degradation of accuracy.

Signetics' MC1508/MC1408 does not need a range control because the design extends the compliance range down to 4.5 volts (or 8 volts—see above) above the negative supply voltage without significant degradation of accuracy. Signetics' MC1508/MC1408 can be used in sockets designed for other manufacturers' MC1508/MC1408 without circuit modification.

The MC1508/MC1408 series is guaranteed accurate to within ±1/2 LSB at +25°C at a full scale output current of 1.99mA. The relative accuracy test circuit is shown in Figure 3. The 12-bit converter is calibrated to a full scale output current of 1.99219mA; then the MC1508/MC1408's full scale current is trimmed to the same value with R_{14} so that a zero value appears at the error amplifier output. The counter is activated and the error band may be displayed on the oscilloscope, detected by comparators, or stored in a peak detector.

Two 8-bit D-to-A converters may not be used to construct a 16-bit accurate D-to-A converter. Sixteen-bit accuracy implies a total of ±1/2 part in 65,536, or ±0.00076%, which is much more accurate than the ±0.19% specification of the MC1508/MC1408.

Monotonicity

A monotonic converter is one which always provides an analog output greater than or equal to the preceding value for a corresponding increment in the digital input code. The MC1508/MC1408 is monotonic for all values of reference current above 0.5mA. The recommended range for operation is a DC reference current between 0.5mA and 4.0mA.

Output Current Range

Any time the full scale output current exceeds 2mA, the negative supply must be at least 8 volts more negative than the output voltage. This is due to the increased internal voltage drops between the negative supply and the outputs with higher reference currents.

Accuracy

Absolute accuracy is the measure of each output current level with respect to its intended value, and is dependent upon relative accuracy, full scale accuracy and full scale current drift. Relative accuracy is the measure of each output current level as a fraction of the full scale current after zero scale current has been nulled out. The relative accuracy of the MC1508/MC1408 is essentially constant over the operating temperature range because of the excellent temperature tracking of the monolithic resistor ladder. The reference current may drift with temperature, causing a change in the absolute accuracy of output current; however, the MC1508/MC1408 has a very low full scale current drift over the operating temperature range.

Settling Time

The worst case switching condition occurs when all bits are switched on, which corresponds to a low-to-high transition for all input bits. This time is typically 70ns for settling to within 1/2 LSB for 8-bit accuracy. This time applies when R_L <500 ohms and C_O <25pF. The slowest single switch is the least significant bit, which typically turns on and settles in 65ns. In applications where the D-to-A converter functions in a positive going ramp mode, the worst case condition does not occur and settling times less than 70ns may be realized.

Extra care must be taken in board layout since this usually is the dominant factor in satisfactory test results when measuring settling time. Short leads, 100μF supply bypassing for low frequencies, minimum scope lead length, good ground planes, and avoidance of ground loops are all mandatory.

TEST CIRCUITS (Cont'd)

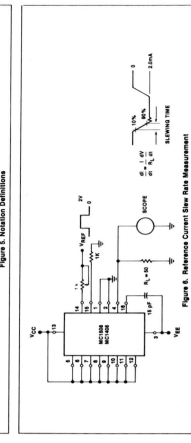

TYPICAL VALUES $R_{14} = R_{15} = 1K$
$V_{REF} = + 2.0V$
$C = 15pF$

(SEE TEXT FOR VALUES OF C.)

$$I_O = K \left\{ \frac{A_1}{2} + \frac{A_2}{4} + \frac{A_3}{8} + \frac{A_4}{16} + \frac{A_5}{32} + \frac{A_6}{64} + \frac{A_7}{128} + \frac{A_8}{256} \right\}$$

where $K = \dfrac{V_{REF}}{R_{14}}$

and A_N = "1" IF A_N IS AT HIGH LEVEL
A_N = "0" IF A_N IS AT LOW LEVEL

V_I AND I_I APPLY TO INPUTS A_1 THROUGH A_8

THE RESISTOR TIED TO PIN 15 IS TO TEMPERATURE COMPENSATE THE BIAS CURRENT AND MAY NOT BE NECESSARY FOR ALL APPLICATIONS.

Figure 5. Notation Definitions

$$\frac{dI}{dt} = \frac{1}{R_L} \frac{dV}{dt}$$

Figure 8. Reference Current Slew Rate Measurement

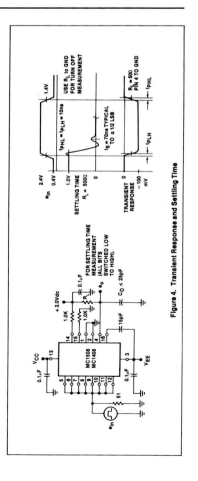

TEST CIRCUITS (Cont'd)

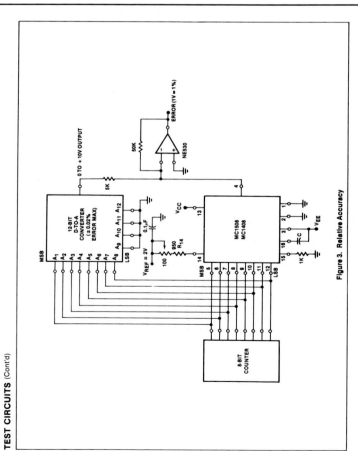

Figure 3. Relative Accuracy

Figure 4. Transient Response and Settling Time

C

Explanation of the IEEE/IEC Standard for Logic Symbols (Dependency Notation)[1]

The IEEE/IEC standard for logic symbols introduces a method of determining the complete logical operation of a given device just by interpreting the notations on the symbol for the device. At the heart of the standard is *dependency notation* which provides a means of denoting the relationship between inputs and outputs without actually showing all of the internal elements and interconnections involved. The information that follows briefly explains the standards publication IEEE Std. 91–1984 and is intended to help in the understanding of these new symbols.

[1] Courtesy of Texas Instruments, Inc.

Explanation of Logic Symbols

F. A. Mann

Contents

If you have questions on this Explanation of Logic Symbols, please contact:

Texas Instruments Incorporated
F.A. Mann, MS 49
P.O. Box 225012
Dallas, Texas 75265
Telephone (214) 995-2867

IEEE Standards may be purchased from:
Institute of Electrical and Electronics Engineers, Inc.
IEEE Standards Office
345 East 47th Street
New York, N.Y. 10017

International Electrotechnical Commission (IEC) publications may be purchased from:
American National Standards Institute, Inc.
1430 Broadway
New York, N.Y. 10018

List of Tables

List of Illustrations

1.0 INTRODUCTION

The International Electrotechnical Commission (IEC) has been developing a very powerful symbolic language that can show the relationship of each input of a digital logic circuit to each output without showing explicitly the internal logic. At the heart of the system is dependency notation, which will be explained in Section 4.

The system was introduced in the USA in a rudimentary form in IEEE/ANSI Standard Y32.14-1973. Lacking at that time a complete development of dependency notation, it offered little more than a substitution of rectangular shapes for the familiar distinctive shapes for representing the basic functions of AND, OR, negation, etc. This is no longer the case.

Internationally, Working Group 2 of IEC Technical Committee TC-3 has prepared a new document (Publication 617-12) that consolidates the original work started in the mid 1960's and published in 1972 (Publication 117-15) and the amendments and supplements that have followed. Similarly for the USA, IEEE Committee SCC 11.9 has revised the publication IEEE Std 91/ANSI Y32.14. Now numbered simply IEEE Std 91-1984, the IEEE standard contains all of the IEC work that has been approved, and also a small amount of material still under international consideration. Texas Instruments is participating in the work of both organizations and this document introduces new logic symbols in accordance with the new standards. When changes are made as the standards develop, future editions will take those changes into account.

The following explanation of the new symbolic language is necessarily brief and greatly condensed from what the standards publications will contain. This is not intended to be sufficient for those people who will be developing symbols for new devices. It is primarily intended to make possible the understanding of the symbols used in various data books and the comparison of the symbols with logic diagrams, functional block diagrams, and/or function tables will further help that understanding.

2.0 SYMBOL COMPOSITION

A symbol comprises an outline or a combination of outlines together with one or more qualifying symbols. The shape of the symbols is not significant. As shown in Figure 1, general qualifying symbols are used to tell exactly what logical operation is performed by the elements. Table I shows general qualifying symbols defined in the new standards. Input lines are placed on the left and output lines are placed on the right. When an exception is made to that convention, the direction of signal flow is indicated by an arrow as shown in Figure 11.

All outputs of a single, unsubdivided element always have identical internal logic states determined by the function of the element except when otherwise indicated by an associated qualifying symbol or label inside the element.

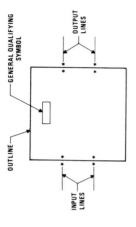

Figure 1. Symbol Composition

*Possible positions for qualifying symbols relating to inputs and outputs

The outlines of elements may be abutted or embedded in which case the following conventions apply. There is no logic connection between the elements when the line common to their outlines is in the direction of signal flow. There is at least one logic connection between the elements when the line common to their outlines is perpendicular to the direction of signal flow. The number of logic connections between elements will be clarified by the use of qualifying symbols and this is discussed further under that topic. If no indications are shown on either side of the common line, it is assumed there is only one connection.

When a circuit has one or more inputs that are common to more than one element of the circuit, the common-control block may be used. This is the only distinctively shaped outline used in the IEC system. Figure 2 shows that unless otherwise qualified by dependency notation, an input to the common-control block is an input to each of the elements below the common-control block.

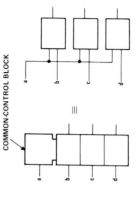

Figure 2. Common-Control Block

505

A common output depending on all elements of the array can be shown as the output of a common-output element. Its distinctive visual feature is the double line at its top. In addition the common-output element may have other inputs as shown in Figure 3. The function of the common-output element must be shown by use of a general qualifying symbol.

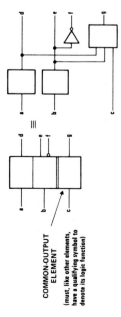

COMMON-OUTPUT ELEMENT

(must, like other elements, have a qualifying symbol to denote its logic function)

Figure 3. Common-Output Element

3.0 QUALIFYING SYMBOLS

3.1 General Qualifying Symbols

Table I shows general qualifying symbols defined by IEEE Standard 91. These characters are placed near the top center or the geometric center of a symbol or symbol element to define the basic function of the device represented by the symbol or of the element.

3.2 Qualifying Symbols for Inputs and Outputs

Qualifying symbols for inputs and outputs are shown in Table II and will be familiar to most users with the possible exception of the logic polarity and analog signal indicators. The older logic negation indicator means that the external 0 state produces the internal 1 state. The internal 1 state means the active state. Logic negation may be used in pure logic diagrams; in order to tie the external 1 and 0 logic states to the levels H (high) and L (low), a statement of whether positive logic (1 = H, 0 = L) or negative logic (1 = L, 0 = H) is being used is required or must be assumed. Logic polarity indicators eliminate the need for calling out the logic convention and are used in various data books in the symbology for actual devices. The presence of the triangular polarity indicator indicates that the L logic level will produce the internal 1 state (the active state) or that, in the case of an output, the internal 1 state will produce the external L level. Note how the active direction of transition for a dynamic input is indicated in positive logic, negative logic, and with polarity indication.

The internal connections between logic elements abutted together in a symbol may be indicated by the symbols shown in Table II. Each logic connection may be shown by the presence of qualifying symbols at one or both sides of the common line and if confusion can arise about the numbers of connections, use can be made of one of the internal connection symbols.

Table I. General Qualifying Symbols

SYMBOL	DESCRIPTION	CMOS EXAMPLE	TTL EXAMPLE
&	AND gate or function.	'HC00	SN7400
≥1	OR gate or function. The symbol was chosen to indicate that at least one active input is needed to activate the output.	'HC02	SN7402
=1	Exclusive OR. One and only one input must be active to activate the output.	'HC86	SN7486
=	Logic identity. All inputs must stand at the same state.	'HC86	SN74180
2k	An even number of inputs must be active.	'HC280	SN74180
2k+1	An odd number of inputs must be active.	'HC86	SN74ALS86
1	The one input must be active.	'HC04	SN7404
▷ or ▽	A buffer or element with more than usual output capability (symbol is oriented in the direction of signal flow).	'HC240	SN74S436
⎍	Schmitt trigger; element with hysteresis.	'HC132	SN74LS18
X/Y	Coder, code converter (DEC/BCD, BIN/OUT, BIN/7-SEG, etc.).	'HC42	SN74LS347
MUX	Multiplexer/data selector.	'HC151	SN74150
DMUX or DX	Demultiplexer.	'HC138	SN74138
Σ	Adder.	'HC283	SN74LS385
P−Q	Subtracter.	*	SN74LS385
CPG	Look-ahead carry generator.	'HC182	SN74182
π	Multiplier.	*	SN74LS384
COMP	Magnitude comparator.	'HC85	SN74LS682
ALU	Arithmetic logic unit.	'HC181	SN74LS381
⎍⎍	Retriggerable monostable.	'HC123	SN74LS422
1⎍	Nonretriggerable monostable (one-shot).	'HC221	SN74121
G	Astable element. Showing waveform is optional.	*	SN74LS320
!G	Synchronously starting astable.	*	SN74LS624
G!	Astable element that stops with a completed pulse.	*	*
SRGm	Shift register. m = number of bits.	'HC164	SN74LS595
CTRm	Counter. m = number of bits; cycle length = 2^m.	'HC590	SN54LS590
CTR DIVm	Counter with cycle length = m.	'HC160	SN74LS668
RCTRm	Asynchronous (ripple-carry) counter; cycle length = 2^m.	'HC4020	
ROM	Read-only memory.	'HC187	SN74187
RAM	Random-access read/write memory.	'HC189	SN74170
FIFO	First-in, first-out memory.	*	SN74LS222
I=0	Element powers up cleared to 0 state.	'HC7022	SN74AS877
I=1	Element powers up set to 1 state.	*	SN74AS877
Φ	Highly complex function; "gray box" symbol with limited detail shown under special rules.	*	SN74LS608

*Not all of the general qualifying symbols have been used in TI's CMOS and TTL data books, but they are included here for the sake of completeness.

Table II. Qualifying Symbols for Inputs and Outputs

Logic negation at input. External 0 produces internal 1.

Logic negation at output. Internal 1 produces external 0.

Active-low input. Equivalent to —◦| in positive logic.

Active-low output. Equivalent to |◦— in positive logic.

Active-low input in the case of right-to-left signal flow.

Active-low output in the case of right-to-left signal flow.

Signal flow from right to left. If not otherwise indicated, signal flow is from left to right.

Bidirectional signal flow.

	POSITIVE LOGIC	NEGATIVE LOGIC	POLARITY INDICATION
Dynamic inputs active on indicated transition	1 0	0 1	H L
	not used	not used	not used
	1 0	0 1	L H

Nonlogic connection. A label inside the symbol will usually define the nature of this pin.

Input for analog signals (on a digital symbol) (see Figure 14).

Input for digital signals (on an analog symbol) (see Figure 14).

Internal connection. 1 state on left produces 1 state on right.

Negated internal connection. 1 state on left produces 0 state on right.

Dynamic internal connection. Transition from 0 to 1 on left produces transitory 1 state on right.

Internal input (virtual input). It always stands at its internal 1 state unless affected by an overriding dependency relationship.

Internal output (virtual output). Its effect on an internal input to which it is connected is indicated by dependency notation.

The internal (virtual) input is an input originating somewhere else in the circuit and is not connected directly to a terminal. The internal (virtual) output is likewise not connected directly to a terminal. The application of internal inputs and outputs requires an understanding of dependency notation, which is explained in Section 4.

Table III. Symbols Inside the Outline

Postponed output (of a pulse-triggered flip-flop). The output changes when input initiating change (e.g., a C input) returns to its initial external state or level. See § 5.

Bi-threshold input (input with hysteresis).

N-P-N open-collector or similar output that can supply a relatively low-impedance L level when not turned off. Requires external pull-up. Capable of positive-logic wired-AND connection.

Passive-pull-up output is similar to N-P-N open-collector output but is supplemented with a built-in passive pull-up.

N-P-N open-emitter or similar output that can supply a relatively low-impedance H level when not turned off. Requires external pull-down. Capable of positive-logic wired-OR connection.

Passive-pull-down output is similar to N-P-N open-emitter output but is supplemented with a built-in passive pull-down.

3-state output.

Output with more than usual output capability (symbol is oriented in the direction of signal flow).

Enable input
When at its internal 1-state, all outputs are enabled.
When at its internal 0-state, open-collector and open-emitter outputs are off, three-state outputs are in the high-impedance state, and all other outputs (e.g., totem-poles) are at the internal 0-state.

Usual meanings associated with flip-flops (e.g., R = reset, T = toggle)

Data input to a storage element equivalent to:

Shift right (left) inputs, m = 1, 2, 3, etc. If m = 1, it is usually not shown.

Counting up (down) inputs, m = 1, 2, 3, etc. If m = 1, it is usually not shown.

Binary grouping. m is highest power of 2.

The contents-setting input, when active, causes the content of a register to take on the indicated value.

The content output is active if the content of the register is as indicated.

Input line grouping . . . indicates two or more terminals used to implement a single logic input.
e.g., The paired expander inputs of SN7450.

Fixed-state output always stands at its internal 1 state. For example, see SN74185.

In an array of elements, if the same general qualifying symbol and the same qualifying symbols associated with inputs and outputs would appear inside each of the elements of the array, these qualifying symbols are usually shown only in the first element. This is done to reduce clutter and to save time in recognition. Similarly, large identical elements that are subdivided into smaller elements may each be represented by an unsubdivided outline. The SN54HC242 or SN54LS440 symbol illustrates this principle.

3.3 Symbols Inside the Outline

Table III shows some symbols used inside the outline. Note particularly that open-collector (open-drain), open-emitter (open-source), and three-state outputs have distinctive symbols. An EN input affects all the external outputs of the element in which it is placed, plus the external outputs of any elements shown to be influenced by that element. It has no effect on inputs. When an enable input affects only certain outputs, affects outputs located outside the indicated influence of the element in which the enable input is placed, and/or affects one or more inputs, a form of dependency notation will indicate this (see 4.10). The effects of the EN input on the various types of outputs are shown.

It is particularly important to note that a D input is always the data input of a storage element. At its internal 1 state, the D input sets the storage element to its 1 state, and at its internal 0 state it resets the storage element to its 0 state.

The binary grouping symbol will be explained more fully in Section 8. Binary-weighted inputs are arranged in order and the binary weights of the least-significant and the most-significant lines are indicated by numbers. In this document weights of input and output lines will be represented by powers of two usually only when the binary grouping symbol is used, otherwise decimal numbers will be used. The grouped inputs generate an internal number on which a mathematical function can be performed or that can be an identifying number for dependency notation (Figure 28). A frequent use is in addresses for memories.

Reversed in direction, the binary grouping symbol can be used with outputs. The concept is analogous to that for the inputs and the weighted outputs will indicate the internal number assumed to be developed within the circuit.

Other symbols are used inside the outlines in accordance with the IEC/IEEE standards but are not shown here. Generally these are associated with arithmetic operations and are self-explanatory.

When nonstandardized information is shown inside an outline, it is usually enclosed in square brackets [like these].

4.0 DEPENDENCY NOTATION

4.1 General Explanation

Dependency notation is the powerful tool that sets the IEC symbols apart from previous systems and makes compact, meaningful, symbols possible. It provides the means of denoting the relationship between inputs, outputs, or inputs and outputs without actually showing all the elements and interconnections involved. The information provided by dependency notation supplements that provided by the qualifying symbols for an element's function.

In the convention for the dependency notation, use will be made of the terms ''affecting'' and ''affected.'' In cases where it is not evident which inputs must be considered as being the affecting or the affected ones (e.g., if they stand in an AND relationship), the choice may be made in any convenient way.

So far, eleven types of dependency have been defined and all of these are used in various TI data books. X dependency is used mainly with CMOS circuits. They are listed below in the order in which they are presented and are summarized in Table IV following 4.12.

Section	Dependency Type or Other Subject
4.2	G, AND
4.3	General Rules for Dependency Notation
4.4	V, OR
4.5	N, Negate (Exclusive-OR)
4.6	Z, Interconnection
4.7	X, Transmission
4.8	C, Control
4.9	S, Set and R, Reset
4.10	EN, Enable
4.11	M, Mode
4.12	A, Address

4.2 G (AND) Dependency

A common relationship between two signals is to have them ANDed together. This has traditionally been shown by explicitly drawing an AND gate with the signals connected to the inputs of the gate. The 1972 IEC publication and the 1973 IEEE/ANSI standard showed several ways to show this AND relationship using dependency notation. While ten other forms of dependency have since been defined, the ways to invoke AND dependency are now reduced to one.

In Figure 4 input **b** is ANDed with input **a** and the complement of **b** is ANDed with **c**. The letter G has been chosen to indicate AND relationships and is placed at input **b**, inside the symbol. A number considered appropriate by the symbol designer (1 has been used here) is placed after the letter G and also at each affected input. Note the bar over the 1 at input **c**.

Figure 4. G Dependency Between Inputs

In Figure 5, output **b** affects input **a** with an AND relationship. The lower example shows that it is the internal logic state of **b**, unaffected by the negation sign, that is ANDed. Figure 6 shows input **a** to be ANDed with a dynamic input **b**.

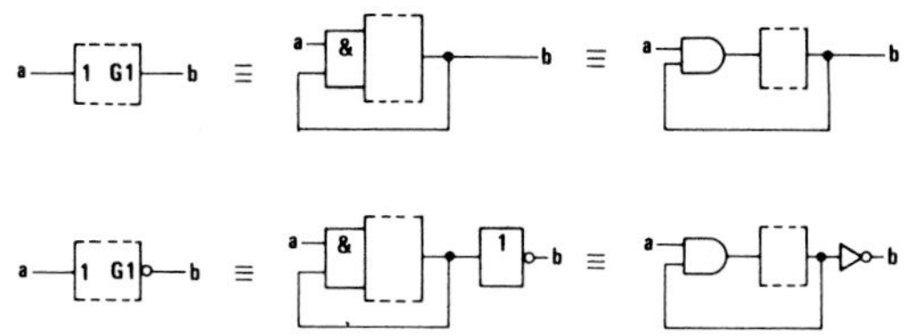

If the affected input or output requires a label to denote its function (e.g., "D"), this label will be *prefixed* by the identifying number of the affecting input (Figure 15).

If an input or output is affected by more than one affecting input, the identifying numbers of each of the affecting inputs will appear in the label of the affected one, separated by commas. The normal reading order of these numbers is the same as the sequence of the affecting relationships (Figure 15).

If the labels denoting the functions of affected inputs or outputs must be numbers (e.g., outputs of a coder), the identifying numbers to be associated with both affecting inputs and affected inputs or outputs will be replaced by another character selected to avoid ambiguity, e.g., Greek letters (Figure 8).

Figure 8. Substitution for Numbers

4.4 V (OR) Dependency

The symbol denoting OR dependency is the letter V (Figure 9).

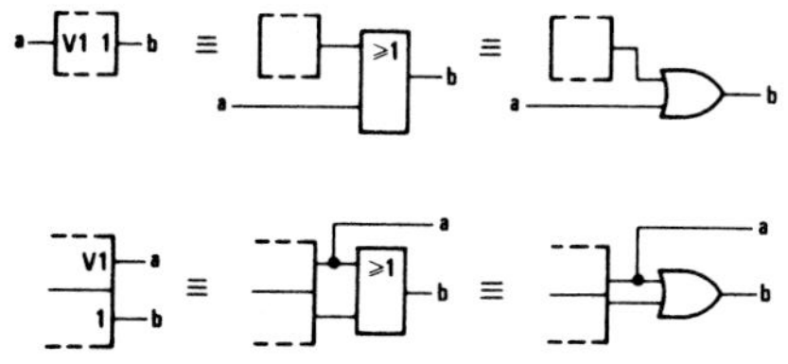

Figure 9. V (OR) Dependency

When a Vm input or output stands at its internal 1 state, all inputs and outputs affected by Vm stand at their internal 1 states. When the Vm input or output stands at its internal 0 state, all inputs and outputs affected by Vm stand at their normally defined internal logic states.

4.5 N (Negate) (Exclusive-OR) Dependency

The symbol denoting negate dependency is the letter N (Figure 10). Each input or output affected by an Nm input or output stands in an Exclusive-OR relationship with the Nm input or output.

Figure 5. G Dependency Between Outputs and INputs

Figure 6. G Dependency with a Dynamic Input

The rules for G dependency can be summarized thus:

When a Gm input or output (m is a number) stands at its internal 1 state, all inputs and outputs affected by Gm stand at their normally defined internal logic states. When the Gm input or output stands at its 0 state, all inputs and outputs affected by Gm stand at their internal 0 states.

4.3 Conventions for the Application of Dependency Notation in General

The rules for applying dependency relationships in general follow the same pattern as was illustrated for G dependency.

Application of dependency notation is accomplished by:

1) labeling the input (or output) *affecting* other inputs or outputs with the letter symbol indicating the relationship involved (e.g., G for AND) followed by an identifying number, appropriately chosen, and

2) labeling each input or output *affected* by that affecting input (or output) with that same number.

If it is the complement of the internal logic state of the affecting input or output that does the affecting, then a bar is placed over the identifying numbers at the affected inputs or outputs (Figure 4).

If two affecting inputs or outputs have the same letter and same identifying number, they stand in an OR relationship to each other (Figure 7).

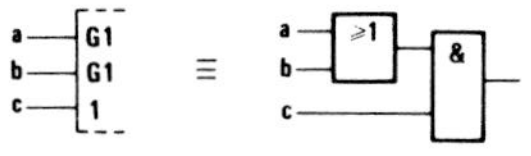

Figure 7. ORed Affecting Inputs

$$a \quad \boxed{N1} \quad {}^b_c \quad \equiv \quad a \quad \boxed{=1}^{N=1} \quad {}^b_c \quad \equiv$$

If a = 0, then c = b
If a = 1, then c = $\bar{b}$

Figure 10. N (Negate) (Exclusive-OR) Dependency

When an Nm input or output stands at its internal 1 state, the internal logic state of each input and each output affected by Nm is the complement of what it would otherwise be. When an Nm input or output stands at its internal 0 state, all inputs and outputs affected by Nm stand at their normally defined internal logic states.

4.6 Z (Interconnection) Dependency

The symbol denoting interconnection dependency is the letter Z.

Interconnection dependency is used to indicate the existence of internal logic connections between inputs, outputs, internal inputs, and/or internal outputs.

The internal logic state of an input or output affected by a Zm input or output will be the same as the internal logic state of the Zm input or output, unless modified by additional dependency notation (Figure 11).

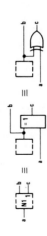

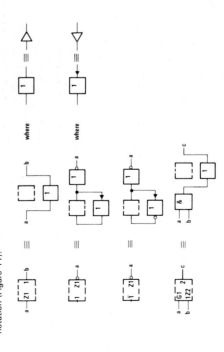

Figure 11. Z (Interconnection) Dependency

4.7 X (Transmission) Dependency

The symbol denoting transmission dependency is the letter X.

Transmission dependency is used to indicate controlled bidirectional connections between affected input/output ports (Figure 12).

If a = 1, there is a bidirectional connection between b and c.

If a = 0, there is a bidirectional connection between c and d.

Figure 12. X (Transmission) Dependency

When an Xm input or output stands at its internal 1 state, all input-output ports affected by this Xm input or output are bidirectionally connected together and stand at the same internal logic state or analog signal level. When an Xm input or output stands at its internal 0 state, the connection associated with this set of dependency notation does not exist.

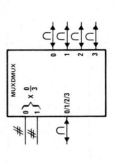

Figure 13. CMOS Transmission Gate Symbol and Schematic

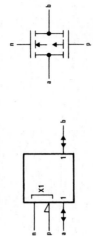

Figure 14. Analog Data Selector (Multiplexer/Demultiplexer)

Although the transmission paths represented by X dependency are inherently bidirectional, use is not always made of this property. This is analogous to a piece of wire, which may be constrained to carry current in only one direction. If this is the case in a particular application, then the directional arrows shown in Figures 12, 13, and 14 would be omitted.

510

4.8 C (Control) Dependency

The symbol denoting control dependency is the letter C.

Control inputs are usually used to enable or disable the data (D, J, K, R, or S) inputs of storage elements. They may take on their internal 1 states (be active) either statically or dynamically. In the latter case the dynamic input symbol is used as shown in the third example of Figure 15.

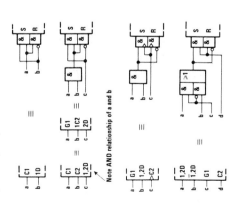

Note AND relationship of a and b

Input c selects which of a or b is stored when d goes low.

Figure 15. C (Control) Dependency

When a Cm input or output stands at its internal 1 state, the inputs affected by Cm have their normally defined effect on the function of the element, i.e., these inputs are enabled. When a Cm input or output stands at its internal 0 state, the inputs affected by Cm are disabled and have no effect on the function of the element.

4.9 S (Set) and R (Reset) Dependencies

The symbol denoting set dependency is the letter S. The symbol denoting reset dependency is the letter R.

Set and reset dependencies are used if it is necessary to specify the effect of the combination $R = S = 1$ on a bistable element. Case 1 in Figure 16 does not use S or R dependency.

When an Sm input is at its internal 1 state, outputs affected by the Sm input will react, regardless of the state of an R input, as they normally would react to the combination $S = 1$, $R = 0$. See cases 2, 4, and 5 in Figure 16.

When an Rm input is at its internal 1 state, outputs affected by the Rm input will react, regardless of the state of an S input, as they normally would react to the combination $S = 0$, $R = 1$. See cases 3, 4, and 5 in Figure 16.

When an Sm or Rm input is at its internal 0 state, it has no effect.

Note that the noncomplementary output patterns in cases 4 and 5 are only pseudo stable. The simultaneous return of the inputs to $S = R = 0$ produces an unforeseeable stable and complementary output pattern.

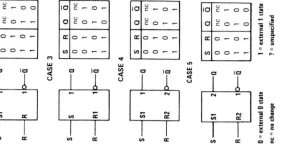

CASE 1

S	R	Q	Q̄
0	0	nc	nc
0	1	0	1
1	0	1	0
1	1	?	?

CASE 2

S	R	Q	Q̄
0	0	nc	nc
0	1	0	1
1	0	1	0
1	1	1	1

CASE 3

S	R	Q	Q̄
0	0	nc	nc
0	1	0	1
1	0	1	0
1	1	1	0

CASE 4

S	R	Q	Q̄
0	0	nc	nc
0	1	0	1
1	0	1	0
1	1	1	0

CASE 5

S	R	Q	Q̄
0	0	nc	nc
0	1	0	1
1	0	1	0
1	1	1	0

1 = external 1 state
0 = external 0 state
nc = no change
? = unspecified

Figure 16. S (Set) and R (Reset) Dependencies

4.10 EN (Enable) Dependency

The symbol denoting enable dependency is the combination of letters EN.

An ENm input has the same effect on outputs as an EN input, see 3.3, but it affects only those outputs labeled with the identifying number m. It also affects those inputs labeled with the identifying number m. By contrast, an EN input affects all outputs and no inputs. The effect of an ENm input on an affected input is identical to that of a Cm input (Figure 17).

When an ENm input stands at its internal 1 state, the inputs affected by ENm have their normally defined effect on the function of the element and the outputs affected by this input stand at their normally defined internal logic states, i.e., these inputs and outputs are enabled.

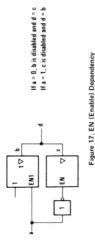

If a = 0, b is disabled and d = c
If a = 1, c is disabled and d = b

Figure 17. EN (Enable) Dependency

When an ENm input stands at its internal 0 state, the inputs affected by ENm are disabled and have no effect on the function of the element, and the outputs affected by ENm are also disabled. Open-collector outputs are turned off, three-state outputs stand at their normally defined internal logic states but externally exhibit high impedance, and all other outputs (e.g., totem-pole outputs) stand at their internal 0 states.

4.11 M (MODE) Dependency

The symbol denoting mode dependency is the letter M.

Mode dependency is used to indicate that the effects of particular inputs and outputs of an element depend on the mode in which the element is operating.

If an input or output has the same effect in different modes of operation, the identifying numbers of the relevant affecting Mm inputs will appear in the label of that affected input or output between parentheses and separated by solidi (Figure 22).

4.11.1 M Dependency Affecting Inputs

M dependency affects inputs the same as C dependency. When an Mm input or Mm output stands at its internal 1 state, the inputs affected by this Mm input or Mm output have their normally defined effect on the function of the element, i.e., the inputs are enabled.

When an Mm input or Mm output stands at its internal 0 state, the inputs affected by this Mm input or Mm output have no effect on the function of the element. When an affected input has several sets of labels separated by solidi (e.g., C4/2−/3+), any set in which the identifying number of the Mm input or Mm output appears has no effect and is to be ignored. This represents disabling of some of the functions of a multifunction input.

The circuit in Figure 18 has two inputs, b and c, that control which one of four modes (0, 1, 2, or 3) will exist at any time. Inputs d, e, and f are D inputs subject to dynamic control (clocking) by the a input. The numbers 1 and 2 are in the series chosen to indicate the modes so inputs e and f are only enabled in mode 1 (for parallel loading) and input d is only enabled in mode 2 (for serial loading). Note that input a has three functions. It is the clock for entering data. In mode 2, it causes right shifting of data, which means a shift away from the control block. In mode 3, it causes the contents of the register to be incremented by one count.

Note that all operations are synchronous.

In MODE 0 (b = 0, c = 0), the outputs remain at their existing states as none of the inputs has an effect.

In MODE 1 (b = 1, c = 0), parallel loading takes place thru inputs e and f.

In MODE 2 (b = 0, c = 1), shifting down and serial loading thru input d take place.

In MODE 3 (b = c = 1), counting up by increment of 1 per clock pulse takes place.

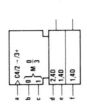

Figure 18. M (Mode) Dependency Affecting Inputs

4.11.2 M Dependency Affecting Outputs

When an Mm input or Mm output stands at its internal 1 state, the affected outputs stand at their normally defined internal logic states, i.e., the outputs are enabled.

When an Mm input or Mm output stands at its internal 0 state, at each affected output any set of labels containing the identifying number of that Mm input or Mm output has no effect and is to be ignored. When an output has several different sets of labels separated by solidi (e.g., 2.4/3.5), only those sets in which the identifying number of this Mm input or Mm output appears are to be ignored.

Figure 19 shows a symbol for a device whose output can behave like either a 3-state output or an open-collector output depending on the signal applied to input a. Mode 1 exists when input a stands at its internal 1 state and, in that case, the three-state symbol applies and the open-element symbol has no effect. When a = 0, mode 1 does not exist so the three-state symbol has no effect and the open-element symbol applies.

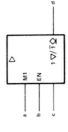

Figure 19. Type of Output Determined by Mode

In Figure 20, if input **a** stands at its internal 1 state establishing mode 1, output **b** will stand at its internal 1 state only when the content of the register equals 9. Since output **b** is located in the common-control block with no defined function outside of mode 1, the state of this output outside of mode 1 is not defined by the symbol.

In Figure 21, if input **a** stands at its internal 1 state establishing mode 1, output **b** will stand at its internal 1 state only when the content of the register equals 15. If input **a** stands at its internal 0 state, output **b** will stand at its internal 1 state only when the content of the register equals 0.

In Figure 22 inputs **a** and **b** are binary weighted to generate the numbers 0, 1, 2, or 3. This determines which one of the four modes exists.

At output **e** the label set causing negation (if **c** = 1) is effective only in modes 2 and 3. In modes 0 and 1 this output stands at its normally defined state as if it had no labels. At output **f** the label set has no effect when the mode is not 0 so output **e** is negated (if **c** = 1) in modes 1, 2, and 3. In mode 0 the label set has no effect so the output stands at its normally defined state. In this example 0,4 is equivalent to (1/2/3)4. At output **g** there are two label sets. The first set, causing negation (if **c** = 1), is effective only in mode 2. The second set, subjecting **g** to AND dependency on **d**, has effect only in mode 3.

Note that in mode 0 none of the dependency relationships has any effect on the outputs, so **e**, **f**, and **g** will all stand at the same state.

4.12 A (Address) Dependency

The symbol denoting address dependency is the letter A.

Address dependency provides a clear representation of those elements, particularly memories, that use address control inputs to select specified sections of a multidimensional arrays. Such a section of a memory array is usually called a word. The purpose of address dependency is to allow a symbolic presentation of the entire array. An input of the array shown at a particular

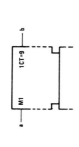

Figure 20. An Output of the Common-Control Block

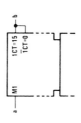

Figure 21. Determining an Output's Function

Figure 22. Dependent Relationships Affected by Mode

element of this general section is common to the corresponding elements of all selected sections of the array. An output of the array shown at a particular element of this general section is the result of the OR function of the outputs of the corresponding elements of selected sections.

Inputs that are not affected by any affecting address input have their normally defined effect on all sections of the array, whereas inputs affected by an address input have their normally defined effect only on the section selected by that address input.

An affecting address input is labeled with the letter A followed by an identifying number that corresponds with the address of the particular section of the array selected by this input. Within the general section presented by the symbol, inputs and outputs affected by an Am input are labeled with the letter A, which stands for the identifying numbers, i.e., the addresses, of the particular sections.

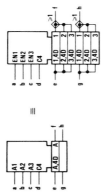

Figure 23. A (Address) Dependency

Figure 23 shows a 3-word by 2-bit memory having a separate address line for each word and uses EN dependency to explain the operation. To select word 1, input **a** is taken to its 1 state, which establishes mode 1. Data can now be clocked into the inputs marked "1,4D." Unless words 2 and 3 are also selected, data cannot be clocked in at the inputs marked "2,4D" and "3,4D." The outputs will be the OR functions of the selected outputs, i.e., only those enabled by the active EN functions.

The identifying numbers of affecting address inputs correspond with the addresses of the sections selected by these inputs. They need not necessarily differ from those of other affecting dependency-inputs (e.g., G, V, N, . . .), because in the general section presented by the symbol they are replaced by the letter A.

If there are several sets of affecting Am inputs for the purpose of independent and possibly simultaneous access to sections of the array, then the letter A is modified to 1A, 2A, ... Because they have access to the same sections of the array, these sets of A inputs may have the same identifying numbers. The symbols for 'HC170 or SN74LS170 make use of this.

Figure 24 is another illustration of the concept.

require the setup of data before the start of the control pulse; the C input is considered static since the data must be maintained as long as C is at its 1 state. The output is postponed until C returns to its 0 state. The data-lock-out element is similar to the pulse-triggered version except that the C input is considered dynamic in that shortly after C goes through its active transition, the data inputs are disabled and data does not have to be held. However, the output is still postponed until the C input returns to its initial external level.

Notice that synchronous inputs can be readily recognized by their dependency labels (1D, 1J, 1K, 1S, 1R) compared to the asynchronous inputs (S, R), which are not dependent on the C inputs.

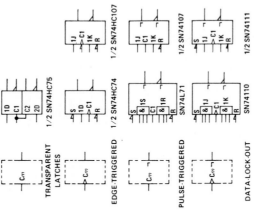

Figure 25. Four Types of Bistable Circuits

6.0 CODERS

The general symbol for a coder or code converter is shown in Figure 26. X and Y may be replaced by appropriate indications of the code used to represent the information at the inputs and at the outputs, respectively.

Figure 26. Coder General Symbol

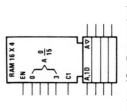

Figure 24. Array of 16 Sections of Four Transparent Latches with 3-State Outputs Comprising a 16-Word × 4-Bit Random-Access Memory

Table IV. Summary of Dependency Notation

TYPE OF DEPENDENCY	LETTER SYMBOL*	AFFECTING INPUT AT ITS 1-STATE	AFFECTING INPUT AT ITS 0-STATE
Address	A	Permits action (address selected)	Prevents action (address not selected)
Control	C	Permits action	Prevents action
Enable	EN	Permits action	Prevents action of inputs; ◊outputs off ◊outputs at external high impedance, no change in internal logic state. Other outputs at internal 0 state
AND	G	Permits action	Imposes 0 state
Mode	M	Permits action (mode selected)	Prevents action (mode not selected)
Negate (Ex-OR)	N	Complements state	No effect
Reset	R	Affected output reacts as it would to S = 0, R = 1	No effect
Set	S	Affected output reacts as it would to S = 1, R = 0	No effect
OR	V	Imposes 1 state	Permits action
Transmission	X	Bidirectional connection exists	Bidirectional connection does not exist
Interconnection	Z	Imposes 1 state	Imposes 0 state

*These letter symbols appear at the AFFECTING input (or output) and are followed by a number. Each input (or output) AFFECTED by that input is labeled with that same number. When the labels EN, R, and S appear at inputs without the following numbers, the descriptions above do not apply. The action of these inputs is described under "Symbols inside the Outline," see 3.3.

5.0 BISTABLE ELEMENTS

The dynamic input symbol, the postponed output symbol, and dependency notation provide the tools to differentiate four main types of bistable elements and make synchronous and asynchronous inputs easily recognizable (Figure 25). The first column shows the essential distinguishing features; the other columns show examples.

Transparent latches have a level-operated control input. The D input is active as long as the C input is at its internal 1 state. The outputs respond immediately. Edge-triggered elements accept data from D, J, K, R, or S inputs on the active transition of C. Pulse-triggered elements

Indication of code conversion is based on the following rule:

Depending on the input code, the internal logic states of the inputs determine an internal value. This value is reproduced by the internal logic states of the outputs, depending on the output code.

The indication of the relationships between the internal logic states of the inputs and the internal value is accomplished by:

1) labeling the inputs with numbers. In this case the internal value equals the sum of the weights associated with those inputs that stand at their internal 1-state, or by

2) replacing X by an appropriate indication of the input code and labeling the inputs with characters that refer to this code.

The relationships between the internal value and the internal logic states of the outputs are indicated by:

1) labeling each output with a list of numbers representing those internal values that lead to the internal 1-state of that output. These numbers shall be separated by solidi as in Figure 27. This labeling may also be applied when Y is replaced by a letter denoting a type of dependency (see Section 7). If a continuous range of internal values produces the internal 1 state of an output, this can be indicated by two numbers that are inclusively the beginning and the end of the range, with these two numbers separated by three dots (e.g., 4 . . . 9 = 4/5/6/7/8/9) or by

2) replacing Y by an appropriate indication of the output code and labeling the outputs with characters that refer to this code as in Figure 28.

Alternatively, the general symbol may be used together with an appropriate reference to a table in which the relationship between the inputs and outputs is indicated. This is a recommended way to symbolize a PROM after it has been programmed.

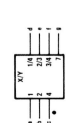

FUNCTION TABLE

INPUTS			OUTPUTS			
c	b	a	g	f	e	d
0	0	0	0	0	0	0
0	0	1	0	0	1	0
0	1	0	0	1	0	0
0	1	1	0	1	1	0
1	0	0	0	0	1	1
1	0	1	1	0	0	1
1	1	0	0	0	1	0
1	1	1	1	0	0	0

Figure 27. An X/Y Code Converter

FUNCTION TABLE

INPUTS			OUTPUTS						
c	b	a	j	i	h	g	f	e	d
0	0	0	0	0	0	0	0	0	0
0	0	1	0	0	0	0	0	0	1
0	1	0	0	0	0	0	0	1	0
0	1	1	0	0	0	0	1	0	0
1	0	0	0	0	0	1	0	0	0
1	0	1	0	0	1	0	0	0	0
1	1	0	0	1	0	0	0	0	0
1	1	1	1	0	0	0	0	0	0

Figure 28. An X/Octal Code Converter

7.0 USE OF A CODER TO PRODUCE AFFECTING INPUTS

It often occurs that a set of affecting inputs for dependency notation is produced by decoding the signals on certain inputs to an element. In such a case use can be made of the symbol for a coder as an embedded symbol (Figure 29).

If all affecting inputs produced by a coder are of the same type and their identifying numbers shown at the outputs of the coder, Y (in the qualifying symbol X/Y) may be replaced by the letter denoting the type of dependency. The indications of the affecting inputs should then be omitted (Figure 30).

Figure 29. Producing Various Types of Dependencies

Figure 30. Producing One Type of Dependency

8.0 USE OF BINARY GROUPING TO PRODUCE AFFECTING INPUTS

If all affecting inputs produced by a coder are of the same type and have consecutive identifying numbers not necessarily corresponding with the numbers that would have been shown at the outputs of the coder, use can be made of the binary grouping symbol. k external lines effectively generate 2^k internal inputs. The bracket is followed by the letter denoting the type of dependency followed by m1/m2. The m1 is to be replaced by the smallest identifying number and the m2 by the largest one, as shown in Figure 31.

515

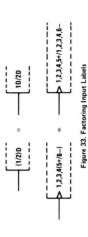

Figure 31. Use of the Binary Grouping Symbol

9.0 SEQUENCE OF INPUT LABELS

If an input having a single functional effect is affected by other inputs, the qualifying symbol (if there is any) for that functional effect is preceded by the labels corresponding to the affecting inputs. The left-to-right order of these preceding labels is the order in which the effects or modifications must be applied. The affected input has no functional effect on the element if the logic state of any one of the affecting inputs, considered separately, would cause the affected input to have no effect, regardless of the logic states of other affecting inputs.

If an input has several different functional effects or has several different sets of affecting inputs, depending on the mode of action, the input may be shown as often as required. However, there are cases in which this method of presentation is not advantageous. In those cases the input may be shown once with the different sets of labels separated by solidi (Figure 32). No meaning is attached to the order of these sets of labels. If one of the functional effects of an input is that of an unlabeled input to the element, a solidus will precede the first set of labels shown.

If all inputs of a combinational element are disabled (caused to have no effect on the function of the element), the internal logic states of the outputs of the element are not specified by the symbol. If all inputs of a sequential element are disabled, the content of this element is not changed and the outputs remain at their existing internal logic states.

Labels may be factored using algebraic techniques (Figure 33).

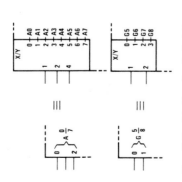

Figure 32. Input Labels

Figure 33. Factoring Input Labels

10.0 SEQUENCE OF OUTPUT LABELS

If an output has a number of different labels, regardless of whether they are identifying numbers of affecting inputs or outputs or not, these labels are shown in the following order:

1) If the postponed output symbol has to be shown, this comes first, if necessary preceded by the indications of the inputs to which it must be applied

2) Followed by the labels indicating modifications of the internal logic state of the output, such that the left-to-right order of these labels corresponds with the order in which their effects must be applied

3) Followed by the label indicating the effect of the output on inputs and other outputs of the element.

Symbols for open-circuit or three-state outputs, where applicable, are placed just inside the outside boundary of the symbol adjacent to the output line (Figure 34).

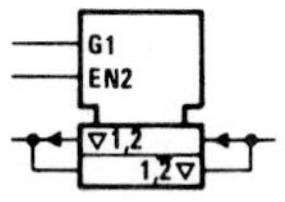

If an output needs several different sets of labels that represent alternative functions (e.g., depending on the mode of action), these sets may be shown on different output lines that must be connected outside the outline. However, there are cases in which this method of presentation is not advantageous. In those cases the output may be shown once with the different sets of labels separated by solidi (Figure 35).

Two adjacent identifying numbers of affecting inputs in a set of labels that are not already separated by a nonnumeric character should be separated by a comma.

If a set of labels of an output not containing a solidus contains the identifying number of an affecting Mm input standing at its internal 0 state, this set of labels has no effect on that output.

Labels may be factored using algebraic techniques (Figure 36).

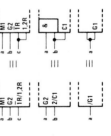

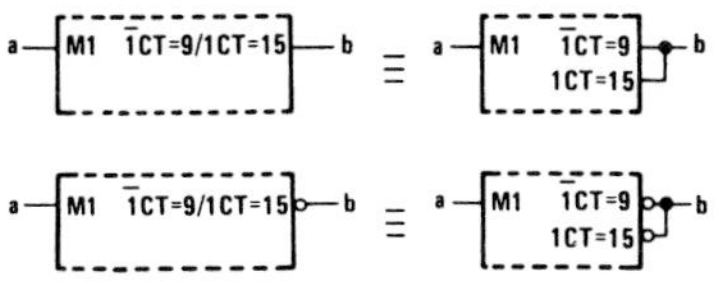

Figure 34. Placement of 3-State Symbols

Figure 35. Output Labels

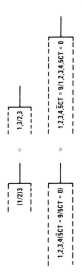

Figure 36. Factoring Output Labels

If you have questions on this Explanation of Logic Symbols, please contact:

Texas Instruments Incorporated
F.A. Mann, MS 49
P.O. Box 225012
Dallas, Texas 75265
Telephone (214) 995-2867

IEEE Standards may be purchased from:

Institute of Electrical and Electronics Engineers, Inc.
IEEE Standards Office
345 East 47th Street
New York, N.Y. 10017

International Electrotechnical Commission (IEC) publications may be purchased from:

American National Standards Institute, Inc.
1430 Broadway
New York, N.Y. 10018

D
Answers to Selected Problems

CHAPTER ONE

1–1. (a) 6_{10} (b) 11_{10} (c) 9_{10} (d) 7_{10} (e) 12_{10} (f) 75_{10} (g) 55_{10} (h) 181_{10} (i) 167_{10} (j) 118_{10}

1–3. (a) 31_8 (b) 35_8 (c) 134_8 (d) 131_8 (e) 155_8

1–5. (a) 23_{10} (b) 31_{10} (c) 12_{10} (d) 58_{10} (e) 41_{10}

1–7. (a) $B9_{16}$ (b) DC_{16} (c) 74_{16} (d) FB_{16} (e) $C6_{16}$

1–9. (a) 134_{10} (b) 244_{10} (c) 146_{10} (d) 171_{10} (e) 965_{10}

1–11. (a) 98_{10} (b) 69_{10} (c) 74_{10} (d) 36_{10} (e) 81_{10}

1–13. (a) 010 0101
(b) 0100100 0110001 0110100
(c) 1001110 0101101 0110110
(d) 1000011 1010000 1010101
(e) 1010000 1100111

CHAPTER TWO

2–1. (a) 0.5 μs (b) 2 μs (c) 0.234 μs (d) 58.8 ns (e) 500 kHz (f) 10 kHz (g) 1.33 kHz (h) 0.667 MHz

2–3. 2.16 μs

2–4. 0.375 μs

2–7. $V_1 = 0$ V, $V_2 = 4.3$ V, $V_3 = 4.3$ V, $V_4 = 0$ V, $V_5 = 4.3$ V, $V_6 = 5.0$ V, $V_7 = 0$ V

2–9. That diode will conduct, raising V_7 to 4.3 V, ("OR").

2–13. $V_{\text{out}} = 4.998$ V

2–14. $V_{\text{out}} = 2.94$ V

2–16. 50 mA

CHAPTER THREE

3–1.

A	B	C	X
0	0	0	0
0	0	1	0
0	1	0	0
0	1	1	0
1	0	0	0
1	0	1	0
1	1	0	0
1	1	1	1

3–3. 256

3–6. $X = ABC$
$X = ABCD$
$X = A + B + C$

3–11. A

(a)

3.11 (*cont.*) A

(b)

3–16. Four

3–17. Two

3–18. HIGH, LOW, and FLOAT

3–20. LOW, to enable the output to change with pulser (if gate is good)

3–21. HIGH, to enable the output to change with pulser (if gate is good)

3–23. The enable switch is bad.

3–24. There is a bad ground connection to pin 7.

CHAPTER FOUR

4–1. $X = \overline{A}, X = 0$

4–2. $X = \overline{A}, Z = A, X = 1, Z = 0$

4–4. $X = \overline{AB}, Y = \overline{CD}$

4–5.

A	B	X	C	D	Y
0	0	1	0	0	1
0	1	1	0	1	1
1	0	1	1	0	1
1	1	0	1	1	0

4–8. It disables the other two inputs when it is DOWN for the NAND and UP for the NOR.

4–13.

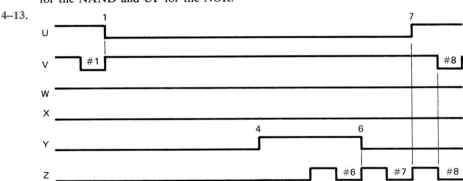

4–14. (a) $\overline{A}C$ (b) CD (c) $\overline{A}CD$ (d) $C_p\overline{A}\,\overline{B}$ (e) AC (f) C_pAB

4–15. $U = C_pAB$, $V = \overline{CD}$, $W = BC$, $X = C_pCD$

4–18. LOW

4–19. HIGH

4–21. There is no problem.

4–22. The inverter is not working.

4–24. Pins 8 and 12 should be LOW; the NORs connected to those pins are bad.

CHAPTER FIVE

5–1. (a) $W = (A + B)(C + D)$ (b) $X = AB + BC$ (c) $Y = (AB + B)C$ (d) $Z = (AB + B + (B + C))D$

5–3.

A	B	C	D	M	N	Q	R	S	A	B	C	P
0	0	0	0	0	0	0	0	0	0	0	0	0
0	0	0	1	1	0	0	1	1	0	0	1	0
0	0	1	0	1	0	0	0	0	0	1	0	0
0	0	1	1	1	1	0	1	1	0	1	1	1
0	1	0	0	0	0	0	0	0	1	0	0	0
0	1	0	1	1	1	0	1	1	1	0	1	1
0	1	1	0	1	0	0	1	1	1	1	0	0
0	1	1	1	1	1	1	1	1	1	1	1	1
1	0	0	0	0	0	0	0	0				
1	0	0	1	1	1	0	1	1				
1	0	1	0	1	0	0	0	1				
1	0	1	1	1	1	0	1	1				
1	1	0	0	1	0	0	0	1				
1	1	0	1	1	1	0	1	1				
1	1	1	0	1	0	0	1	1				
1	1	1	1	1	1	1	1	1				

5–5. (a) Commutative law (b) associative law (c) distributive law

5–6. (a) $M = 0$ (b) $N = 1$ (c) $P = AB$ (d) $Q = C + D$ (e) $R = A$ (f) $S = 0$ (g) $T = A$ (h) $U = 1$ (i) $V = A$ (j) $W = A$

5–7. (a) $W = BC$ (b) $X = B + AC$ (c) $Y = A + BC$ $Z = B$

5–9. (a) $V = C(A + D)$ (b) $W = CD$ (c) $X = (A + C)(B + D)$ (d) $Y = (A + C)B$ $Z = ABC + CD$

5–11. $X = (A + B)(D + C)$

5–13. Break the long bar and change the AND to an OR, or the OR to an AND.

5–15. Y and Z are both ORs.

5–17. (a) $W = \overline{A} + \overline{B}$ (b) $X = \overline{B} + \overline{C}$ (c) $Y = \overline{C}$ $Z = A\overline{B}C$

5–19. $W = \overline{A} + B + \overline{C} + D$ $X = 1$ $Y = \overline{D}A + \overline{D}B + \overline{D}C + \overline{A}B + \overline{A}C + BC$ $Z = \overline{C} + AD$

5–21. $X = AB(C + D)$

5–23. $X = \overline{(A + B)(\overline{C} + \overline{D})}$

5–33. (a) $X = \overline{A} + B\overline{C}$ (b) $Y = B + \overline{A}C$ (c) $Z = A\overline{C} + AB + \overline{A}\overline{B}C$

5–34. (a) $W = \overline{B}\overline{C} + \overline{B}\overline{D} + \overline{A}\overline{B}$ (b) $X = \overline{C}\overline{D} + \overline{B}\overline{D} + ABCD$ (c) $Y = A\overline{B} + A\overline{D} + \overline{B}C\overline{D}$ (d) $Z = \overline{C} + B\overline{D} + \overline{A}D$

5–35. (a) $X = \overline{C}D + AC + B$ (b) $Y = 1$

5–37. $X = \overline{A}C\overline{D} + \overline{B}C\overline{D}$ (A = MSB, D = LSB)

5–39. The IC checks out OK; the problem is that pin 9 should be connected to pin 10 (not 9 to gnd).

CHAPTER SIX

6–1. (a) Exclusive-OR produces a HIGH output for one or the other input HIGH but not both. (b) Exclusive-NOR produces a HIGH output for both inputs HIGH or both inputs LOW.

6–4. (a) $W =$ (ex-NOR) (b) $X =$ (ex-NOR) (c) $Y =$ (ex-OR) (d) $Z =$ (neither)

6–7. (a) $X = A\overline{B}$ (b) $Y = 1$

6–8. (a) $X = \overline{A}BC + AB\overline{C}$ (b) $Y = \overline{C} + AB$

6–9. A7 = 1010 0111 0, 4C = 0100 1100 0, 79 = 0111 1001 0, F3 = 1111 0011 1, 00 = 0000 0000 1, FF = 1111 1111 1

6–12. Odd

6–15. Yes, LOW

CHAPTER SEVEN

7–1. (a) 1001 (b) 1111 (c) 11100 (d) 1000010 (e) 1100 1000 (f) 10010 0010 (g) 10100 1111 (h) 10110 0000

7–3. (a) 10101 (b) 101010 (c) 111100 (d) 100010001 (e) 11110 1100 0011 (f) 111 0111 0001 (g) 1 1001 0011 (h) 1111110 1000 0001

7–5.

+15	0000 1111	−1	1111 1111
+14	0000 1110	−2	1111 1110
+13	0000 1101	−3	1111 1101
+12	0000 1100	−4	1111 1100
+11	0000 1011	−5	1111 1011
+10	0000 1010	−6	1111 1010
+9	0000 1001	−7	1111 1001
+8	0000 1000	−8	1111 1000
+7	0000 0111	−9	1111 0111
+6	0000 0110	−10	1111 0110
+5	0000 0101	−11	1111 0101
+4	0000 0100	−12	1111 0100
+3	0000 0011	−13	1111 0011
+2	0000 0010	−14	1111 0010
+1	0000 0001	−15	1111 0001
0	0000 0000		

7–7. (a) $+22$ (b) $+15$ (c) $+92$ (d) -122 (e) -18 (f) -127 (g) $+127$ (h) -1

7–9. (a) 0000 1100 (b) 0000 0110 (c) 0011 0010 (d) 0000 1110 (e) 0000 1010 (f) 0011 1011 (g) 1111 0100 (h) 1010 1100

7–11. (a) E (b) D (c) 21 (d) CA (e) 10C (f) 162 (g) AB45 (h) A000

7–13. b, c, e

7–15. For the LSB addition of two binary numbers

7–17. $\Sigma_0 =$ Yes, $C_0 =$ No

7–19. There is no carry-in to the LSB of the low-order adder, so C_{in} must be grounded to ensure that it is zero; the carry-out of the low-order adder must be connected to the carry-in of the high-order adder to pass any carry from the 2^3 addition over to the 2^4 addition.

7–21. When using more than one adder IC to add long binary strings, the fast-lookahead-carry speeds up the addition by providing the carry-in to the higher-order ICs almost simultaneously with the binary inputs to be added.

7–23. Reverse the switch (up to add, down to subtract); also, put an inverter on the input line to C_{in} of the LSB.

7–25. The B inputs should be $B_3 = 0$, $B_2 = 0$, $B_1 = 1$, $B_0 = 0$; also, the function-select inputs should be $S_3 = 1$, $S_2 = 0$, $S_1 = 0$, $S_0 = 1$.

CHAPTER EIGHT

8–5.

2^3	2^2	2^1	2^0	$\bar{0}$	$\bar{1}$	$\bar{2}$	$\bar{3}$	$\bar{4}$	$\bar{5}$	$\bar{6}$	$\bar{7}$	$\bar{8}$	$\bar{9}$
0	0	0	0	0	1	1	1	1	1	1	1	1	1
0	0	0	1	1	0	1	1	1	1	1	1	1	1
0	0	1	0	1	1	0	1	1	1	1	1	1	1
0	0	1	1	1	1	1	0	1	1	1	1	1	1
0	1	0	0	1	1	1	1	0	1	1	1	1	1
0	1	0	1	1	1	1	1	1	0	1	1	1	1
0	1	1	0	1	1	1	1	1	1	0	1	1	1
0	1	1	1	1	1	1	1	1	1	1	0	1	1
1	0	0	0	1	1	1	1	1	1	1	1	0	1
1	0	0	1	1	1	1	1	1	1	1	1	1	0

8–7. That input is a "Don't Care" and will have no effect on the output for that particular table entry.

8–9.

Time interval	Low output pulse at:
t_0–t_1	None (E_3 disabled)
t_1–t_2	None (E_3 disabled)
t_2–t_3	$\bar{5}$
t_3–t_4	$\bar{4}$
t_4–t_5	$\bar{3}$
t_5–t_6	$\bar{2}$
t_6–t_7	$\bar{1}$
t_7–t_8	$\bar{0}$
t_8–t_9	$\bar{7}$
t_9–t_{10}	$\bar{6}$
t_{10}–t_{11}	$\bar{5}$
t_{11}–t_{12}	None (E_3 disabled)
t_{12}–t_{13}	None (E_3 disabled)

8–10.

Time interval	Low output pulse at:
t_0–t_1	$\bar{0}$
t_1–t_2	$\bar{1}$
t_2–t_3	None ($\bar{E}_2$ disabled)
t_3–t_4	None ($\bar{E}_2$ disabled)
t_4–t_5	$\bar{4}$
t_5–t_6	$\bar{5}$
t_6–t_7	None ($\bar{E}_1$, E_3 disabled)
t_7–t_8	None ($\bar{E}_1$, E_3 disabled)
t_8–t_9	$\bar{0}$
t_9–t_{10}	$\bar{1}$

8–11. All HIGH

8–13. The higher number

8–15.

	t_0–t_1	t_1–t_2	t_2–t_3	t_3–t_4	t_4–t_5	t_5–t_6
$\overline{EI}$	0	0	0	1	0	0
$\bar{I}_3$	0	1	0	0	0	1
$\bar{I}_4$	1	0	0	0	1	1
$\bar{A}_0$	0	1	1	1	0	1
$\bar{A}_1$	0	1	1	1	0	1
$\bar{A}_2$	1	0	0	1	1	1
$\overline{EO}$	1	1	1	1	1	0
$\overline{GS}$	0	0	0	1	0	1

8–22. (a) 1000_2 (b) 0110_2 (c) 1011_2 (d) 0101_2

8–23. (a) 1111 (b) 1000 (c) 0010 (d) 0001

8–28.

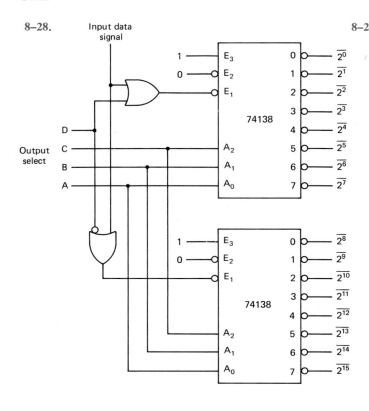

8–29. (a) The 74150 is not working; the data select is set for input D_7, which is 0; therefore, $\overline{Y}$ should be 1, but it is not. (b) The 74151 is OK; the data select is set for input I_o, which is 1; Y should equal 1 and $\overline{Y} = 0$, which they do. (c) The 74139 has two bad decoders; decoder A is enabled and should output 1011 but does not; decoder B is disabled and should output 1111 but does not. (d) The 74154 is OK; the chip is disabled, so all outputs should be HIGH, which they are.

CHAPTER NINE

9–1. D_1 and D_2 provide some protection against negative input voltages.

9–3. From Figure 9–2(a) there is approximately 0.2 V dropped across the 1.6 kΩ, 0.7 V across $V_{BE\,3}$, and 0.7 V across $D3$, leaving approximately 3.4 V at the output terminal.

9–5. Negative sign signifies current *leaving* the input or output of the gate.

9–7. (a) (a) $V_a = 3.4$ V (typ.), $I_a = 120$ μA; (b) $V_a = 4.6$ V, at $V_{in} =$ LOW, $I_a = 0.0$ A, at $V_{in} =$ HIGH, $I_a = 340$ μA; (c) $V_a = 0.2$ V (typ.), $I_a = 3.2$ mA; (d) $V_a = 3.4$ V (typ.), $I_a = 380$ μA (b) (a) $V_a = 3.4$ V (typ.), $I_a = 60$ μA; (b) $V_a = 4.8$ V, at $V_{in} =$ LOW, $I_a = 0.0$ A, at $V_{in} =$ HIGH, $I_a = 340$ μA; (c) $V_a = 0.35$ V (typ.), $I_a = 0.8$ mA; (d) $V_a = 3.4$ V (typ.), $I_a = 360$ μA.

9–8. (a) $f = 4.55$ kHz (b) $t_r = 2$ μs, $t_f = 3$ μs (c) $t_{PLH} = 8$ μs, $t_{PHL} = 6$ μs

9–11. 7400: $P_D = 75$ mW (max.), 74LS00: $P_D = 15$ mW (max.)

9–13. (a) 7400 HIGH-state (min. levels) = 0.4 V, LOW-state (max. levels) = 0.4 V; 74LS00 HIGH-state (min. levels) = 0.7 V, LOW-state (max. levels) = 0.3 V (b) The 74LS00 has a wider margin for the HIGH-state; the 7400 has a wider margin for the LOW-state.

9–15. The open-collector FLOAT level is made a HIGH-level by using a pull-up resistor.

9–17. The 7400 series is faster than the 4000B series but dissipates more power.

9–19. Because MOS ICs are prone to electrostatic burn-out.

9–21. Where speed is most important, ECL is faster but uses more power.

9–23. The 74HC family

9–25. Interfacing (c) and (e) will require a pull-up resistor to "pull up" the TTL HIGH-level output to meet the minimum HIGH-level input specifications of the CMOS gates.

9–27. (a) Ten (b) four hundred

Chapter Ten

10–6. Two, a quad NOR and a quad AND.

10–12. It is called "transparent" because the Q-output follows the level of the D input as long as E is HIGH; when E goes LOW, Q "latches," or holds on to, the level of D before the HIGH-to-LOW edge of E.

10–13. HIGH, LOW

10–14. (a) $\overline{S_D}$, $\overline{R_D}$ (b) C_p, D

10–15.

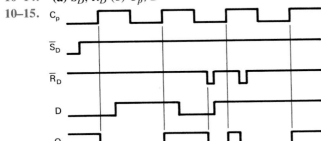

Chapter Eleven

11–3. $t_a = 20$ ns, $t_b = 30$ ns, $t_c = 20$ ns, $t_d = 30$ ns, $t_e = 20$ ns, $t_f = 30$ ns

11–4. $t_a = 20$ ns, $t_b = 30$ ns, $t_c = 20$ ns, $t_d = 30$ ns, $t_e = 20$ ns, $t_f = 30$ ns

11–5. Proper circuit operation is dependent on t_p of the 7432 being ≥ 10 ns; the worst-case t_p is specified as 15 ns but the actual t_p may be less; if it is actually less than 10 ns, the circuit will not operate properly.

Chapter Twelve

12–1. Sequential circuits follow a predetermined sequence of digital states triggered by a timing pulse or clock; combination logic circuits operate almost instantaneously based on the levels placed at their inputs.

12–2.

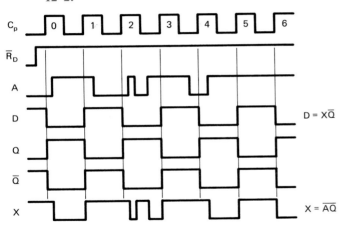

$D = X\overline{Q}$

$X = \overline{AQ}$

10–17. The 7474 is edge-triggered, the 7475 is pulse-triggered; the 7474 has asynchronous inputs at $\overline{S_D}$ and $\overline{R_D}$.

10–18. The synchronous input at D is only read at the positive edge of C_p; the active-LOW asynchronous inputs at $\overline{S_D}$ and $\overline{R_D}$ override any operations at C_p and D.

10–19. The triangle indicates that it is an edge-triggered device as opposed to being pulse-triggered.

10–20. HIGH

10–21. The TOGGLE mode

10–22. $\overline{S_D}$ and $\overline{R_D}$; active-LOW

10–23. The 7476 accepts J and K data during the entire positive level of C_p, whereas the 74LS76 only looks at J and K at the negative edge of C_p.

11–6.

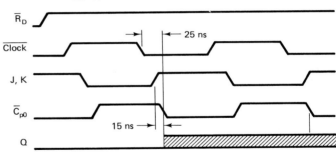

12–6. (a) 8 (b) 19 (c) 6 (d) 11 (e) 14 (f) 5

12–7. (a) 3 (b) 3 (c) 1 (d) 5 (e) 6 (f) 4

12–8. (a) 5 MHz (b) 2.5 MHz (c) 1.25 MHz (d) 0.625 MHz (e) 0.3125 MHz (f) 0.15625 MHz

12–11. (a) 3 (b) 15 (c) 127 (d) 1

12–12. (a) $\frac{1}{2}$ (b) $\frac{1}{4}$ (c) $\frac{1}{8}$ (d) $\frac{1}{16}$ (e) $\frac{1}{32}$

12–13. (a) 2 (b) 4 (c) 4 (d) 5

12–14. The time period (t_p) of the input clock is less and less at higher frequencies; if it becomes less than the total propagation delay of all flip-flops, the input will be switching before the last flip-flop has a chance to switch states.

12–23. The 7490 is a divide-by-10 counter, the 7492 is a divide-by-12 counter, and the 7493 is a divide-by-16 counter; the 7490 has master Set and master Reset inputs; the 7492 and 7493 have master Reset inputs.

12–30. Connect a Reset push button across the 0.001 μF capacitor; when momentarily pressed, it will Reset the circuit to its initial condition.

12–31. $R = 220 \ \Omega$

12–32. With all the current going through the same resistor, as more segments are turned ON, the voltage that reaches the segments is reduced, making them dimmer; the displayed #8 is much dimmer than the #1.

12–33. All flip-flops are driven from the same clock in synchronous counters. This eliminates the problem of accumulated propagation delay that occurs with ripple counters.

12–35. $DC = 20\%$

12–36.

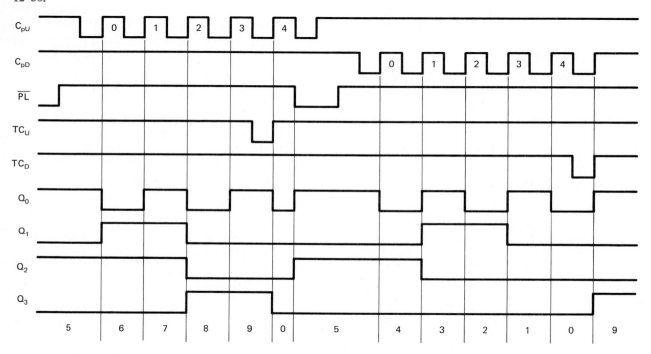

CHAPTER THIRTEEN

13–1. Right, negative

13–3. 1110, 1111

13–5. Apply a LOW pulse to $\overline{R_D}$ to Reset all Q outputs to zero; next, apply a LOW pulse to the active-LOW D_3, D_1, D_0 inputs.

13–7. J_3, K_3 are the data input lines; Q_3, Q_2, Q_1, Q_0 are the data output lines (D_3, D_2, D_1, D_0 are held HIGH).

13–9. Five

13–11. The Q_0 flip-flop and the Q_3 flip-flop

13–16. Put a switch in series with the phototransistor's collector; with the switch open, the input to inverter 1 will be HIGH, simulating nighttime conditions, causing the yellow light to flash; day or night.

13-17.

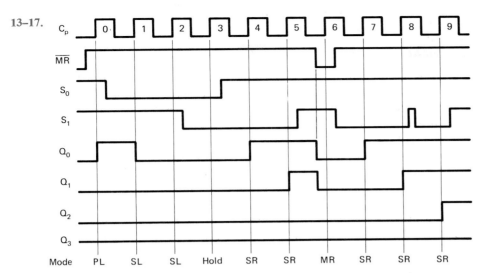

13-23. The parallel-load and clock inputs are $\overline{PE}$, C_p on the 74195 and PE, $\overline{C_p}$ on the 74395A; The 74195 provides J-K type functions on its first flip-flop via the J-$\overline{K}$ inputs. The outputs of the 74395A are three-stated, made active by a LOW on $\overline{OE}$.

13-24. The 74164 is a serial-in, parallel-out, whereas the 74165 is a serial or parallel-in, serial-out shift regis-ter; the 74165 provides a clock-enable input, $\overline{CE}$; The serial input to the 74164 is the logical AND of two data inputs ($D_{sa} \cdot D_{sb}$).

13-25. Data is parallel-loaded *asynchronously* with the 74165 by applying a LOW to $\overline{PL}$; data are parallel-loaded *synchronously* with the 74166 at the positive edge of C_p while $\overline{PE}$ is held LOW.

CHAPTER FOURTEEN

14-1. (a) Monostable (b) bistable (c) astable

14-3. $t = 75.6$ μs

14-5. $t = 32.6$ μs

14-7. Because a Schmitt device has two distinct switching thresholds, V_{T+} and V_{T-}, a regular inverter does not; the capacitor voltage charges and discharges between those two levels.

14-9. (b) $t_{HI} = 126$ μs, $t_{LO} = 160$ μs, DC = 44.1%, $f = 3.5$ kHz

14-10. $R = 8.84$ kΩ, $C = 0.0047$ μF

14-11. $R_X = 7.21$ kΩ, $C_X = 0.001$ μF

14-14. $R_{ext} = 10$ kΩ, $C_{ext} = 80$ pF

14-15. (b) $t_{LO} = 3.26$ μs, $t_{HI} = 7.97$ μs

14-16. At 0 Ω, $f = 89.0$ kHz, DC = 71.0%; at 10 kΩ, $f = 39.8$ kHz, DC = 59.4%

14-17. DC $= \dfrac{R_A + R_B}{R_A + 2R_B}$, $F = \dfrac{1.44}{(R_A + 2R_B)C}$

14-18. $R_A = 2618$ Ω, $R_B = 5236$ Ω

14-20. $t_w = 51.7$ μs

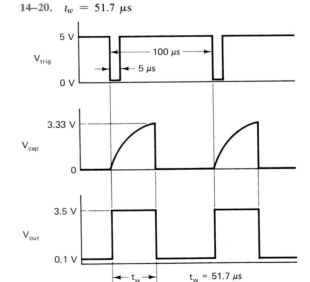

CHAPTER FIFTEEN

15-1. Converts physical quantities into electrical quantities

15-3. Very high input impedance, very high voltage gain, and very low output impedance

15-5. The (−) input is at 0 V potential.

15-7. The output voltages (V_{out}) would all double (V_{out} would be limited, however, by the size of the supply powering the op-amp).

15–9. $V_{out} = -2.0$ V

15–11. $R/2R$ method

15–13. 8-bit resolution

15–15. By making $V_{ref} = 7.5$ V; the range of I_{out} would then be 0 to 1.5 mA; the range of V_{out} would be 0 to 7.47 V.

15–16. $V_{out} = 4.98$ V

15–19. (a) 0 V   (b) They are equal.

15–21. $t_{tot} = 0.16$ ms

15–23. 1011 1010, % error $= -0.197\%$

15–25. $\overline{CS}$ (Chip Select) and $\overline{RD}$ (Read); active-LOW

15–27. (a) The three-state output latches ($D_0–D_7$) would be in the float condition. (b) The outputs would float and $\overline{WR}$ (start conversion) would be disabled. (c) It issues a LOW at power-up to start the first conversion. (d) 1.0 V

CHAPTER SIXTEEN

16–1. (a) Bipolar faster (b) MOS more dense

16–3. Static RAMs use flip-flops as their basic storage elements and dynamic RAMs store a charge on an internal capacitor; dynamic RAMs require refresh circuitry but are more dense and less expensive per bit.

16–5. (a) 2048 (b) 2048 (c) 8192 (d) 1024 (e) 4096 (f) 16,384

16–7.

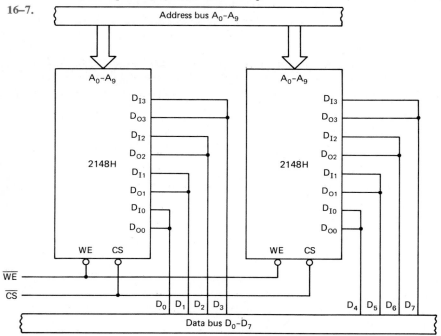

16–9. The Row Address Strobe ($\overline{RAS}$) signifies that a row address is present on the address lines; then $\overline{CAS}$ is used to signify the column address is present.

16–11. The charge on the internal capacitors must be refreshed every 2 ms or sooner to prevent loss of data.

16–13. (a) Nonvolatile (b) volative (c) volatile (d) nonvolatile

16–15. The 74154 1-of-16 decoder.

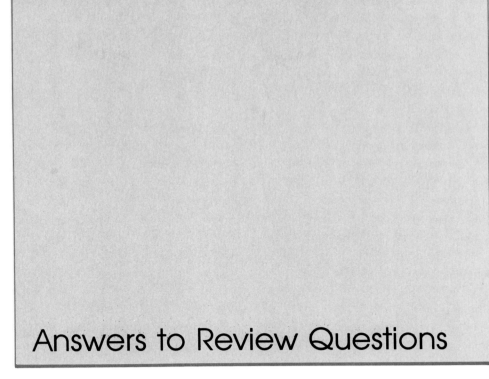

E Answers to Review Questions

CHAPTER ONE

1–1. Temperature, pressure, velocity
1–2. Because digital quantities are easier for a computer system to store and interpret.
1–3. Because it uses only two digits 0 and 1, which can be used to represent two distinct voltages levels.
1–4. By powers of 2.
1–5. False
1–6. Because hexadecimal uses 4-bit groupings.
1–7. True
1–8. BCD is used only to represent decimal digits 0–9 in 4-bit groupings.
1–9. To get alphanumeric data into and out of a computer.

CHAPTER TWO

2–1. X-axis, time; Y-axis, voltage
2–2. Clock frequency is the reciprocal of the clock period.
2–3. It is faster.
2–4. Parallel
2–5. The relay coil is energized by placing a voltage at its terminals. The contacts will either make a connection (NO relay) or break a connection (NC relay) when the coil is energized.
2–6. A NO relay makes connection when energized. A NC relay breaks connection when energized.
2–7. Positive
2–8. Approximately 0.7 V.

2–9. Emitter, base, collector
2–10. Positive
2–11. Short
2–12. Large, small
2–13. Q4

CHAPTER THREE

3–1. True
3–2. To illustrate how the output level of a gate responds to all possible input level combinations.
3–3. To depict algebraically the operation of a logic gate.
3–4. All inputs must be LOW.
3–5. To illustrate graphically how the output levels change in response to input level changes.
3–6. When the level of a signal will have no effect on the output.
3–7. High
3–8. Pin 14, positive power supply; pin 7, ground.
3–9. It uses an indicator lamp to tell you the digital level whenever it is placed in a circuit.
3–10. It provides digital pulses to the circuit being tested, which can be observed using a logic probe.

CHAPTER FOUR

4–1. An inverter is used to complement or invert a digital signal.
4–2. A NAND gate is an AND gate with an inverter on its output.

527

4–3. HIGH

4–4. $X = \overline{A + B + C}$

4–5. It is used as a repetitive waveform generator.

4–6. 7404; 4001

4–7. 3, 3-input NAND gates; 3, 3-input NOR gates

CHAPTER FIVE

5–1. (a) 2 (b) 3 (c) 4

5–2. (a) associative law of addition (b) commutative law of multiplication (c) distributive law

5–3. True

5–4. False

5–5. False

5–6. Because it enables you to convert an expression having an inversion bar into an expression with inversion bars over only single variables.

5–7. AND

5–8. NOR

5–9. Because by utilizing a combination of these gates all other gates can be formed.

5–10. Because in designing a circuit you may have extra NAND gates available.

5–11. 4

5–12. SOP

5–13. SOP

5–14. They must be connected to a 1.

5–15. True

5–16. False

5–17. False

5–18. One group of eight.

CHAPTER SIX

6–1. False

6–2. True

6–3. $X = AB + \overline{A}\overline{B}$

6–4. False

6–5. False

6–6. Σ_E (sum even)

CHAPTER SEVEN

7–1. 2 inputs, 2 outputs

7–2. True

7–3. True

7–4. D_7

7–5. (a) negative (b) positive (c) negative

7–6. b, d

7–7. True

7–8. Because it simplifies the documentation and use of the equipment.

7–9. Add 6 (0110)

7–10. Inputs: A_0, B_0; outputs, Σ_0, C_{out}

7–11. Because it needs a C_{in} from the previous adder.

7–12. Odd

7–13. When any two of the inputs are HIGH.

7–14. Connect it to zero.

7–15. To speed up the arithmetic process.

7–16. It provides a C_{in} and it puts a 1 on the inputs of the X-OR gates which inverts B.

7–17. They check for a sum greater than 9 and provide a C_{out}.

7–18. It sets the mode of operation for either logic or arithmetic.

7–19. True

7–20. "+" means logical OR, "plus" means arithmetic sum

CHAPTER EIGHT

8–1. False

8–2. $A < B = 1$

8–3. 4 inputs, 10 outputs

8–4. False

8–5. False

8–6. False

8–7. HIGH, LOW

8–8. An encoder is the opposite of a decoder. It generates a coded output from a numeric input.

8–9. The highest numeric input.

8–10. (a) all HIGH (b) $A_3 = L$, $A_2 = H$, $A_1 = H$, $A_0 = L$

8–11. A_0, A_1, A_2: binary outputs, $\overline{EO}$: enable output, $\overline{GS}$: group signal output. All outputs are active LOW.

8–12. 80

8–13. 6

8–14. Because it varies by only 1 bit when the shaft is rotated from one position to the next.

8–15. Because it selects which data input is to be sent to the data output.

8–16. Because it takes a single input data line and routes it to one of several outputs.

8–17. They select which one of the input lines is sent to the output.

8–18. They select which one of the output lines the input data is sent to.

CHAPTER NINE

9–1. False

9–2. Totem-pole output

9–3. 0.7, 0.3

9–4. Because of the voltage drops across the internal transistors of the gate.

9–5. It is the number of gates of the same subfamily that can be connected to a single output without exceeding the current rating of the gate.

9–6. Input current HIGH condition (I_{IH}), input current LOW condition (I_{IL}), output current HIGH condition (I_{OH}), output current LOW condition (I_{OL})

9–7. Sink current flows into the gate and goes to ground. Source current is the current the gate supplies to other gates.

9–8. (a) HIGH (b) HIGH (c) undetermined (d) LOW

9–9. False

9–10. Output
9–11. It pulls the output of the gate up to 5V when the output transistor is off (float).
9–12. It reduced the propagation delay to achieve faster speeds.
9–13. Lower power dissipation, slower speeds.
9–14. False
9–15. 74ALS
9–16. 74LS
9–17. To raise the output level of the TTL gate so it is recognized as a HIGH by the CMOS gate.
9–18. The CMOS gate has severe output current limitations.
9–19. 74HCTMOS, because its voltage is almost perfect at 4.9 V HIGH and 0.1 V LOW.
9–20. Input current requirements (I_{IL}, I_{IH}) and output current capability (I_{OL}, I_{OH}).

CHAPTER TEN

10–1. True
10–2. S = 1, R = 0
10–3. None
10–4. An S-R flip-flop is asynchronous because the output responds immediately to input changes. The gated S-R flip-flop is synchronous because it operates sequentially with the control input at the gate.
10–5. False
10–6. D = 0, G = 1
10–7. 4
10–8. High
10–9. True
10–10. Because the master will latch on to any HIGH inputs while the input clock pulse is HIGH and transfers them to the slave when the clock goes LOW.
10–11. J, K
10–12. True
10–13. It switches the Q and $\overline{Q}$ outputs to their opposite state.
10–14. Apply a LOW on the $\overline{R_D}$ input.
10–15. False
10–16. HIGH
10–17. The upper-case letters mean steady state. The lower-case letters are used for levels one setup time prior to the negative clock edge.

CHAPTER ELEVEN

11–1. False
11–2. False
11–3. It means that the input levels don't have to be held beyond the active clock edge.
11–4. Propagation delay, output
11–5. To enable proper set-up and hold times.
11–6. Capacitor
11–7. Positive-going threshold, negative-going threshold, hysteresis

11–8. The switching threshold on a positive-going input signal is at a higher level than the switching threshold on a negative-going input signal. This is called hysteresis. The output is steady as long as the input noise does not exceed the hysteresis voltage.
11–9. Input, output
11–10. It is caused by the springing action of the contacts, and it can cause false triggering of a digital circuit.
11–11. 10kΩ
11–12. 7812
11–13. It cuts off the negative cycle of the sine wave and limits the positive cycle to 4.3 V.
11–14. Because the ICs they're connected to can sink more current than they can source.

CHAPTER TWELVE

12–1. True
12–2. HIGH, HIGH
12–3. It places limitations in the maximum frequency allowed by the input trigger clock because each output is delayed from the previous one.
12–4. By taking the binary output from the $\overline{Q}$ outputs.
12–5. 2^3
12–6. 12
12–7. When the pushbutton is pressed, 5V is applied to the NOR gate driving its output LOW. The 100Ω pull-down resistor will keep the input LOW when the pushbutton is in the open position.
12–8. MOD-10, MOD-12, MOD-16
12–9. One is for the divide-by-2 section, and the other is for the divide-by-8 section.
12–10. $Q_0 = 1$ $Q_1 = 0$ $Q_2 = 0$ $Q_3 = 1$
12–11. By cascading a divide-by-10 with a divide-by-6.
12–12. The Q associated with the most significant bit.
12–13. This means that all the anodes or cathodes of all the LED segments are connected together.
12–14. a c d f g, a b c d e f
12–15. To limit the current flowing through the LED segments.
12–16. They don't have the problem of accumulated propagation delay.
12–17. J and K inputs are tied together and are controlled through the use of an AND gate.
12–18. They are the terminal count pins, which are used to indicate when the terminal count is reached and the count is about to recycle.
12–19. $\overline{U}/D = 1$
12–20. False

CHAPTER THIRTEEN

13–1. True
13–2. The output of a flip-flop connected to the input of the next flip-flop (Q to J, $\overline{Q}$ to K).

13–3. By using the active-LOW asynchronous set ($\overline{S_D}$).

13–4. $Q_3 = 0\ Q_2 = 0\ Q_1 = 0\ Q_0 = 0$, $Q_3 = 1\ Q_2 = 1\ Q_1 = 0\ Q_0 = 0$

13–5. The data would continue shifting out of the register and would be lost.

13–6. 1000, 0000

13–7. HIGH

13–8. It's an active-LOW clock enable for starting/stopping the shift operation.

13–9. Because data can be input or output, serial or parallel, shifted left or right, held, and reset.

13–10. $\overline{MR} = 1\ S_1 = 1\ S_0 = 1\ D_0 = 1\ D_1 = 1\ D_2 = 0\ D_3 = 1$, Data is loaded on the rising edge of Cp.

13–11. $D_{SL}\ Q_3$, 0 1

13–12. Parallel enable (PE) enables the data to be loaded synchronously on the negative clock edge, and parallel load (PL) loads the data asynchronously.

13–13. HIGH, float

13–14. HIGH, enables

13–15. RC circuit and the Schmitt trigger

13–16. 8, $\overline{OE_a}\ \overline{OE_b}$

13–17. Synchronous, asynchronous

13–18. True

CHAPTER FOURTEEN

14–1. False

14–2. Slower

14–3. True

14–4. V_{T+} and V_{T-}, V_{OH} and V_{OL}

14–5. Decrease

14–6. False

14–7. Or, LOW, and, HIGH

14–8. $\overline{A_1}$ or $\overline{A_2}$, HIGH-HIGH

14–9. HIGH

14–10. It means that input triggers are ignored during the timing cycle of a 74121, but not for the 74123. A new timing cycle is started each time a trigger is applied to a 74123.

14–11. True

14–12. LOW

14–13. 2/3 Vcc, Reset, LOW

14–14. $R_A + R_B$, R_B

14–15. Greater than, the charging path consists of $R_A + R_B$, while the discharge path consists of only R_B.

14–16. LOW, HIGH, charging

14–17. It has greater stability and accuracy than an RC circuit.

CHAPTER FIFTEEN

15–1. True

15–2. 256

15–3. Infinite, 0

15–4. 240kΩ

15–5. Because finding accurate resistances over such a large range of values would be very difficult.

15–6. False

15–7. Current

15–8. A_1

15–9. Number of bits at the input or output

15–10. True

15–11. Gain error

15–12. False

15–13. 1023

15–14. False

15–15. False

15–16. $\overline{STRT}$, $\overline{DR}$

15–17. False

15–18. (a) input (b) input (c) input (d) output

15–19. $\overline{CS}$, $\overline{WR}$, $\overline{INTR}$, $\overline{RD}$

15–20. False

15–21. True

15–22. True

15–23. It is a linear device, whereas the thermistor is nonlinear.

CHAPTER SIXTEEN

16–1. Address

16–2. Data

16–3. By inputting the 4-bit address to the 74LS154, which outputs a LOW pulse on one of the output lines when $\overline{WRITE}$ is pulsed LOW.

16–4. It shows when any or all of the lines are allowed to change digital levels.

16–5. To avoid a bus conflict.

16–6. 1024, 4

16–7. LOW, HIGH

16–8. $A_0\ A_5$, $A_6\ A_{11}$

16–9. 35ns max.

16–10. To keep IC pin count to a minimum. They are demultiplexed by using control signals $\overline{RAS}$ and $\overline{CAS}$.

16–11. The charge on the internal capacitors in the RAM is replenished.

16–12. It means when the power is removed the memory contents are lost.

16–13. After the EPROM program has been thoroughly tested.

16–14. 120, 330 (450 total)

16–15. When another device has to use the bus.

16–16. (a) third EPROM, address 002 (b) first EPROM, address AF7

16–17. 9000–9FFF

16–18. 0010 0101

16–19. Left intact

16–20. SOP

16–21. Programmable

16–22. 8, 48, 16

Index

NOTE: Page number in **boldface** type indicates end-of-chapter glossary definition for the term.

Supplementary Index of ICs

This is an index of the integrated circuits (ICs) discussed in this book. The page numbers indicate where the IC is first discussed. Page numbers in **boldface** type indicate pages containing a data sheet for the device.